Abnormal Child and Adolescent Psychology

Jean E. Dumas

Purdue University

Wendy J. Nilsen

University of Rochester

Allyn and Bacon

Boston • New York • San Francisco • Mexico City
Montreal • Toronto • London • Madrid • Munich • Paris
Hong Kong • Singapore • Tokyo • Cape Town • Sydney

To Yvonne, Patrick, Ryan, and Anne-Marie (JED)
To Ed and Christopher (WJN)

Series Editor: *Kelly May*
Series Editorial Assistant: *Marlana M. Voerster*
Marketing Manager: *Wendy Gordon*
Production Administrator: *Annette Pagliaro*
Editorial Production: *Trinity Publishers Services*
Composition Buyer: *Linda Cox*
Manufacturing Buyer: *JoAnne Sweeney*
Cover Administrator: *Linda Knowles*
Photo Research: *Katharine S. Cook*
Text Design and Composition: *Omegatype Typography, Inc.*

For related titles and support materials, visit our online catalog at www.ablongman.com

Between the time Website information is gathered and then published, it is not unusual for some sites to have closed. Also, the transcription of URLs can result in unintended typographical errors. The publisher would appreciate notification where these errors occur so that they may be corrected in subsequent editions.

Library of Congress Cataloging-in-Publication Data

Dumas, Jean E.
   Abnormal child and adolescent psychology / Jean E. Dumas, Wendy J. Nilsen.
      p. cm.
   Includes bibliographical references and index.
   ISBN 0-205-32205-0
   1. Child psychiatry. 2. Adolescent psychiatry. I. Nilsen, Wendy J. II. Title.

RJ499 .D846 2003
618.92'89—dc21   2002027659

Printed in the United States of America

Contents

Preface

The many psychological disorders of childhood and adolescence have long been a source of considerable interest among clinical psychologists, psychiatrists, and other mental health professionals. However, only in recent years have these disorders become the focus of careful, systematic scientific research. In professional circles and in the public at large, rapid advances in research have been accompanied by increasing awareness of the often crippling, lifelong consequences of psychological disorders, not only for those who suffer from them, but also for their families and, in many cases, their schools and communities.

Growing interest in abnormal child and adolescent psychology was fueled in large part by the publication of comprehensive diagnostic manuals in the late 1970s and early 1980s. For the first time, these manuals provided researchers with a common language to describe and classify the different behavioral and emotional disorders of childhood and adolescence. Coupled with a growing interest in normal child development, this led to an explosion of empirical studies and to a considerable growth in knowledge in what is today called developmental psychopathology. Developmental psychopathology is the study of how some young people's development differs from that of their average peers and leads to psychological problems that result in pain and suffering for all involved.

Growing interest in abnormal child and adolescent psychology can also be seen in the academic and career interests of large numbers of psychology students. In informal discussions with our students and colleagues, we are pleased to see that our undergraduates seek more and more courses that focus on child and adolescent disorders (as opposed to the traditional abnormal psychology courses that usually place little emphasis on childhood and adolescence). We are also pleased to see that these students often volunteer for research or practical experience in this area. The same is true at the graduate level, where large numbers of highly qualified applicants seek to be admitted to doctoral programs in clinical child psychology.

Contents, Organization, and Style

This textbook was written to respond to this growing interest in abnormal child and adolescent psychology, and to provide students with comprehensive, up-to-date coverage of this rapidly changing area. Throughout the book, you will note that we adopt a perspective that is descriptive, developmental, and transactional:

Descriptive because a scientific approach to any phenomenon requires a detailed understanding of its major, observable characteristics.

Developmental because disorders of childhood and adolescence are not static: They represent an ongoing process in which the developmental trajectory—the child's growing emotional, social, and academic competence—is less than optimal.

Transactional because at any age the importance of the familial, social, cultural, and historical contexts can never be ignored. These contexts play a major role in defining emotional and behavioral difficulties and explaining their origin and development over time.

This broad perspective is reflected in the organization of the text. In each chapter, we present a particular disorder (or several related disorders) on the basis of the diagnostic criteria used to define it and the empirical data available to describe its key characteristics. We then focus on the epidemiology of each disorder—that is, on how often and to whom it occurs—as well as the developmental progression of the disorder over time. We also establish the factors most likely to account for its etiology. Finally, we consider treatment and prevention issues.

Each chapter also presents a number of case studies drawn mainly from our clinical experience. These cases are included to help the reader understand and appreciate difficulties of the youth suffering from these disorders and to illustrate how these problems cause devastating consequences at home, at school, and beyond. More important, we hope that these case studies will show clearly that young people with psychological disorders can never be reduced to a set of diagnostic criteria. Rather, like everyone else, they are highly complex human beings who play active roles in their development and shape their destiny as much as they are shaped by it.

The text references many scientific studies. We strongly encourage students to explore these references on their own to gain a deeper understanding of the issues that interest them most. At the end of each chapter, students will also find Web links that present additional information about each disorder, both from a scientific and a personal perspective. We invite students to go on the Internet for the latest research findings about the disorders covered and for links to children and families, resources, discussion groups, and more. Although the Internet provides a convenient source of information, students should evaluate what they read critically and check it against sources outside of the Internet to guard against unfounded claims.

Acknowledgments

We were very fortunate to benefit from the help and insight of many talented individuals in writing this book, and it is a real pleasure to acknowledge them here. We thank our colleagues Scott Vrana (Virginia Commonwealth University), Nancy Robinson (University of Washington), Lyman and Adele Wynne (University of Rochester, Wynne Center for Family Research), and Alicia Nordstrom and Jenelle Nissley (Pennsylvania State University) for their critical advice and support in what proved to be a long and, at times, arduous task. In addition, we would like to thank the following reviewers: Eric Cooley, Western Oregon University; Joseph Durlak, Loyola University, Chicago; Laura Freberg, California Polytechnic State University; Martin Murphy, University of Akron; and Wendy Silverman, Florida International University.

We are also grateful to a small group of students for taking on the task of reading one or more chapters to tell us frankly if what we wrote made sense. Our stars in this major effort were Jessica Gockley and Meghan Miller, but we also benefited from the help of Magan Bezy, Megan Carlson, Kate Child, Kristen Dobyns, Amanda Fisher, Victoria Rodriguez, Corinne Stoner, and Kristen Sweat. We thank all of them for their candor and determination to make sure that the text was interesting and easy to follow for undergraduate students.

A task as complex as writing a textbook would not have been possible without the expert help of our secretaries Nancy Mowat, Tracey Kennedy, and Peggy Treece. To all three of them, a big thank you! And thank you also for the many able people at Allyn and Bacon, our publisher, for all their work in bringing this work to completion.

Finally, we come to our most important supporters and emotional helpers—our families. Jean E. Dumas thanks his wife and soul mate of many years, Yvonne, for her steadfast love and acceptance, even when the going gets tough. He is also most grateful to his children, Patrick, Ryan, and Anne-Marie, for putting things in perspective when all he can see is work. Wendy J. Nilsen is very grateful and thankful for Ed Schelb, the most wonderful person a researcher/author (or partner) could ask for. She would also like to thank Christopher Schelb for his love and support and constant reminder of how wonderful it is to be a parent.

Introduction to Abnormal Child and Adolescent Psychology

Children are a wonderful gift. . . . They have an extraordinary capacity to see into the heart of things and to expose sham and humbug for what they are.

—Desmond Tutu

What is abnormal child or adolescent behavior? As you can easily imagine, there are several answers to this question. Before we consider them, read Rachel's story and ask yourself in what ways her behavior might be said to be abnormal. Rachel is 9. She was referred to our clinic by her grandmother, who is a schoolteacher. In our initial contact with the family, her mother described her daughter's challenging conduct in considerable detail.

Rachel has been throwing tantrums for quite some time now—violent, screaming tantrums that cause her to hyperventilate, perspire, and just be completely out of control and sometimes inconsolable. We can't even speak and get anywhere when she has one of her fits. . . . I have actually written some of them down to tell you. The most recent one was last week. She and I took a trip to North Carolina. It was just mother and daughter. We went down to visit my parents. We were all getting ready to go for a walk on the beach and hunt shells and she begins agonizing over what to wear and how to fix her hair. Like, "Oh, my God, what do I

wear? My hair looks terrible!" Now I had told her the night before and totally prepped her that we were simply going to be getting up early, putting something on, and go hunting shells. We weren't going to shower, we weren't going to worry about what we looked like. But she got upset anyway. . . . I found a hat and I told her if she didn't like her hair we could stuff it under the hat and nobody would ever know. She just couldn't seem to make a decision about this, but finally she asked me to put her hat on. I put it on for her, pulled her pony tail through, and got it all fixed nicely; but she wasn't happy. Then she wanted me to comb it, and everybody else was waiting for us—not just my parents but my cousin and her boyfriend. . . . I mean, it was getting embarrassing. So I began to comb her pony tail and I hit a tangle. And she just screamed and took the hat off and threw it across the room and screamed and yelled and just threw a horrible fit. All because of that! So I had to walk out of the room and shut the door to keep myself from losing my patience because everyone was waiting on us. And of course I was mortified that my daughter was making this kind of impression on my family. Now I have to admit that she got out of it quite quickly; [in] seven or eight minutes she had finished screaming and she came out without the hat on, and she walked past us like nothing had ever happened. . . .

This has been going on since she was 2. Even when she was a tiny infant, she didn't just cry, she screamed. My son cried, had colic, and I knew what that was like. Now she never had colic or any of those problems, but when she cried it sounded like somebody was murdering her. I'm not joking. It was such a loud, high-pitched scream. Even as a tiny newborn. And I thought that was kind of unusual. And she has always been very hypersensitive to things, to all kinds of things—emotions, animals, situations, even the weather. She is very emotional and very caught up in things, and often sad actually . . . but not hateful. Now and again, in a middle of her fits, she'll say, "I hate you" or "I hate my hair," but only because she is upset. Normally she's just screaming and hitting things and she's pretty wild. And the thing is she gets herself all caught up in her own anger and if it's real bad she hyperventilates. Like she'll say, "I can't get my breath," and she'll try to breathe and she'll perspire and her face turns beet red and her eyes water, and then finally she calms down exhausted. . . . She carries on like that sometimes more than once a day. Sometimes just once a day, but definitely on average four to five times a week. . . . And later she's not mad or hateful, but just in a huff. She refuses to talk about it and she makes you feel like it's all your fault that she got upset in the first place. I mean, you wouldn't believe it but she's a real artist, and she'll turn things around and blame you for her bad behavior in no time!

When she was going through this in the beginning, [my husband and I] never thought anything of it. We thought typical twos, typical whatever, this is just a phase with her. And then when she was 5 and 6, I just thought, "Well, this is taking a little longer than most children." And then when she turned 7 and then 8 last year and she started second grade and it was still happening, I really started to become concerned. And that is when we saw [a counselor] for the first time. But that didn't help. I mean, the woman was nice enough but all she kept saying was that it was normal growing up, that Rachel was trying to become independent, and that I shouldn't really force the issue and [should] allow the

tantrums to occur. But [the tantrums] have only gotten worse. . . . It's ridiculous now. It's just unacceptable. And I'm no counselor but I know that's not normal.

[Rachel has problems at school also.] She didn't use to have problems at all in school. I mean, she is still doing very well with learning, but this year her teacher has noticed that when she asks Rachel to do things over again, she is belligerent about it. She doesn't like to be corrected. She doesn't want to have to do her work over and she'll give her teacher this turn-her-head-and-look-up-out-of-the-top-of-her-eyes kinda look. She's never gotten what I would call out of control at school but she can be quite a handful. . . . I spoke with her teacher a couple of weeks ago, and she was really concerned that [Rachel] seems to have few good friends because she argues with the other kids all of the time, usually over small things like, you know, wanting to be first and things like that. My mother is a teacher and she is concerned that this is often a sign of trouble with kids at that age. . . . I am concerned too, because I don't want her to start having problems at school also.

Rachel has oppositional defiant disorder—a relatively common disorder in children, which we will consider in detail in Chapter 8. Her longstanding problems at home and more recent difficulties at school illustrate the many facets of what is generally considered "abnormal behavior," at least by Western cultural standards.

Defining Abnormal Behavior

All social groups—from small nuclear families to entire societies—have norms for appropriate conduct; that is, rules that tell group members, directly or indirectly, how they are expected to behave. A child or an adolescent's behavior is described as abnormal when it consistently violates some of these rules and begins to interfere with essential developmental tasks, such as forming positive relationships with family members and peers, succeeding in school, and acquiring an increasing level of personal autonomy. Specifically, abnormal child or adolescent behavior is usually defined by one or more of the following, often overlapping, criteria:

1. *Excess or insufficiency.* Behavior is often said to be abnormal when it clearly differs from what most people do under similar circumstances (i.e., when it deviates substantially from the average or statistical mean). Even though all children will occasionally have temper tantrums, Rachel's frequent screaming tantrums and hyperventilation were clearly excessive.
2. *Norm violation.* Rachel's mother had tolerated her daughter's excessive angry outbursts for years. However, when she brought Rachel to our clinic, she was no longer willing to put up with these outbursts. Rachel had finally violated parental norms: "It's ridiculous now. It's just unacceptable."
3. *Developmental inappropriateness.* Rachel's behavior was not only socially inappropriate. It was developmentally inappropriate as well. Temper tantrums, at times severe, are relatively frequent in young preschoolers. However, older children are expected to manage their emotions in more socially acceptable ways. Rachel's mother was aware of this developmental inappropriateness when she said, "[At first, my husband and I] thought typical twos, typical whatever, this is just a phase with her. . . . [But later] I really started to become concerned."
4. *Maladaptiveness.* Finally and most important, a child or adolescent's behavior is typically considered abnormal when it interferes with the usual course of development and brings undue suffering to the affected person and those around them. Before her mother decided to seek help, Rachel's oppositional conduct had interfered for years with her family life. In addition, her behavior was beginning to interfere with her progress at school, because of frequent conflicts with her teacher and peers.

Each of the disorders we present in this book illustrates these different criteria, as do the case studies describing real children and adolescents with these disorders. But these criteria are never clear-cut—so that, at an individual level, it is often difficult to determine who behaves abnormally and who does not. In Rachel's case, her mother initially sought advice from a counselor who "kept saying . . . that it was normal growing up, that Rachel was trying to become independent." In other words, abnormal behavior in young people can be difficult to define; and researchers, clinicians, and members of the general public often disagree.

Significance of the Problem

How Many Children and Adolescents Have a Psychological Disorder?

By all accounts, the number of children and adolescents who have a psychological disorder is high and the challenges they face significant. As **longitudinal studies** (studies that follow a group of children for an extended amount of time) have shown, approximately 10% of all youth have a psychological disorder, and another 10% have behavioral and emotional problems that are not severe enough to be defined as a disorder but that interfere with their development (Bird et al., 1988; Costello & Angold, 1995b). These percentages are even higher among disadvantaged children and adolescents—especially youth with a history of maltreatment, victimization, discrimination, racism, or other social injustices. In a majority of cases, youth with psychological disorders receive little or no professional help to improve their condition (Costello, Burns, Angold, & Leaf, 1993).

To get a sense of the extent of the problem, picture a typical school with one thousand students. The **prevalence** estimates (the number of affected youth in the population) we have just mentioned indicate that approximately one hundred can be expected to have one or more of the psychological disorders we will cover in this book; and another one hundred are likely to have significant behavioral and emotional problems, although not an actual disorder. Some of these students will have been formally diagnosed and will be receiving services, but most will not. Whether they are diagnosed or not, some of these troubled youth will be known to teachers and peers as having psychological difficulties, because the way they behave sets them apart from others. Others, whose challenges are not as obvious, will attempt to cope as best as they

Psychological problems and disorders are common in childhood and adolescence. Imagine any large group of young people. Statistics show that, in industrial countries, approximately one person in ten has one or more psychological disorders, and that another one in ten exhibits significant psychological problems. On average, then, two out of every ten youth face important behavioral and emotional challenges.

can in silence, most often because they are ashamed of their problems and don't want anybody to know about them.

Beyond Numbers: Human Suffering and Social and Economic Costs

The significance of psychological difficulties in childhood and adolescence is not only a matter of numbers. These difficulties are also of considerable importance because of the suffering they entail. Typically, behavioral and emotional problems interfere in many ways with the course of normal development. Contrary to a widely held belief, most psychological disorders do not go away with time. Rather, a large proportion of youth continue to face major difficulties as they grow up, even though the nature and severity of their difficulties may change over time. As you will see throughout this book, the adaptive functioning of affected children often remains compromised well into adolescence and adulthood.

In a majority of cases, the suffering brought about by psychological disorders not only lasts for many years but also extends beyond the affected youth—to families, schools, and communities. Because most parents love their children, they suffer with them in their psychological struggles, wanting to help them but often not knowing how (Catalano, 1998). In addition, entire schools and neighborhoods are frequently disrupted by the conduct of young "bullies" and older youth who are aggressive and violent (Richters & Martinez, 1993). These social costs are high; and evidence suggests that they are probably rising, especially in poor communities, where young people often face multiple challenges in addition to their own psychological difficulties (Farrington, Lambert, & West, 1998).

Finally, psychological disorders entail major economic costs—namely, the cost of medical, psychological, educational, and legal services for children and their families. In addition, because many of these disorders are chronic, long-term costs—incurred by extended use of a variety of social services and losses in productivity—are borne by society as a whole (Loeber & Farrington, 1998). In other words, youth who have severe psychological problems may continue to need social and financial support throughout adulthood.

Five Key Questions

Researchers and clinicians working in this area continue to face a number of major questions. That is, although they have a broad understanding of the social, emotional, and cognitive difficulties many youth face, they still know relatively little about the **comorbidity, epidemiology, developmental trajectories,** and **etiology** of these difficulties, or about effective means of treatment or **prevention.**

1. *Comorbidity. What psychological problems or disorders typically co-occur with each major disorder?* For example, what is the likelihood that an adolescent with a severe eating disorder such as anorexia nervosa (see Chapter 11) will also be depressed, possibly to the point of attempting suicide?
2. *Epidemiology. What is the prevalence of each major disorder in the population and what factors influence this prevalence?* How many young people suffer from anxiety disorders (Chapter 10); and what role, if any, do factors such as gender, socioeconomic status, ethnicity, and culture play in determining who is most likely to be affected?
3. *Developmental trajectories. How does each disorder develop over time, and what are its consequences for immediate and long-term development and adaptation?* What are the first signs of autism (Chapter 4)? How does the disorder progress and how does it affect social, emotional, and cognitive functioning in childhood, adolescence, and beyond?

4. *Etiology. What are the origins or causes of each disorder?* What are the factors that explain the appearance of attention deficit hyperactivity disorder (Chapter 7), and how do these factors operate together to produce the characteristic manifestations of the disorder?
5. *Treatment and prevention. What can researchers and clinicians do to treat each disorder or to prevent it from occurring in the first place?* What treatments are available to help adolescents with conduct disorder (Chapter 8), and how successful are these treatments likely to be? Can effective steps be taken to prevent the disorder or limit its devastating effects?

Answers to these five questions are obviously important to those who work with affected children and adolescents. Clinicians must know how a disorder develops and what problems often co-occur with it, so that these matters can be explored in therapy. They must also know which treatments have been found to be most effective. Similarly, public health officials cannot plan mental health services, or prevention campaigns, without knowing the extent of the problem they want to ameliorate, some of its likely causes, and the social groups most often affected.

Fundamental knowledge in abnormal child and adolescent psychology remains incomplete, in large part because systematic studies involving large samples of young people are relatively recent, as are concerted efforts to develop and test effective interventions. We will briefly retrace key historical advances that have contributed to the progress of knowledge to date, leaving more detailed historical coverage about each disorder to the chapter in which it is presented.

Historical Advances

The Discovery of Childhood

Until the nineteenth century, Western societies regarded children as small adults and treated them as such. The belief that young people have specific social, emotional, and cognitive needs—needs that develop over time and must be carefully nurtured—is very

Childhood as we know it did not exist until fairly recently. Young people were given many adult responsibilities and often worked long hours instead of playing or going to school, as illustrated in this early-1900s photograph of the Woodward Coal Mines in Kingston, Pennsylvania.

modern. So is the considerable emotional and economic investment that most Western parents make in their children today. For centuries, large numbers of children died very young. And those who did not were seldom educated, because they were given important responsibilities in the social organization and economic survival of their family and community as soon as they were able to work. Children who were unable to fulfill these responsibilities, or who did not do so satisfactorily, were frequently abandoned, severely punished and maltreated, locked up, or even killed. "In Colonial America, as many as two-thirds of all children died prior to the age of 5 years, and those who survived

continued to be subjected to harsh treatment by adults. For example, the Stubborn Child Act of 1654 permitted a parent to put 'stubborn' children to death for noncompliance, and insane children were kept in cages and cellars into the mid-1800s" (Mash & Dozois, 1996, p. 7).

Under the influence of philosophers such as John Locke (1632–1704) and Jean-Jacques Rousseau (1712–1778), the nineteenth century ushered in a new era in the care and treatment of children in general, and of persons with psychological disorders in particular. For example, Benjamin Rush, a signer of the Declaration of Independence, was among the first in America to advocate for the humane treatment of persons with psychological disorders. He argued that, like physical illnesses, behavioral and emotional problems often have biological causes and, therefore, should be treated with medical interventions. This was a radical departure from the widely accepted belief at the time that people with psychological disorders were "lunatics" or "imbeciles" who acted the way they did because they were possessed by evil forces or suffered from deep personal, intellectual or moral failings. As you will see in Chapter 3, this attitude of acceptance took considerable time to gain ground and was repeatedly challenged by opposing attitudes of rejection and condemnation. However, from the outset, this humanitarian perspective put psychological disorders in a new light and encouraged scientific research into their origins and cure.

More generally, the economic prosperity and social reforms of the nineteenth century greatly improved the outlook for children in Western societies. For example, laws passed in Europe and America regulated child labor and limited the most extreme forms of child exploitation. These reforms were paralleled by new discoveries in medicine and by rapid progress in the treatment and prevention of many diseases (e.g., through vaccination). In addition, compulsory education was introduced in many countries during the second half of the nineteenth century and played a major role in the "discovery" of childhood. Specifically, formal schooling and the challenges it represented for many students demonstrated the importance of individual differences in education and achievement, and highlighted the need to see each child less as a small adult than as a work in progress.

All these changes were undoubtedly significant. However, they did not immediately translate into a detailed understanding of the strengths, vulnerabilities, and needs of children with behavioral and emotional problems, or into the development of effective interventions to help them. Indeed, it took considerable time—almost another century—for people to appreciate fully that certain psychological disorders typically begin in childhood and adolescence, and that these disorders have characteristics that are not simply mirror images of their adult manifestations.

The Slow Progress of Abnormal Child and Adolescent Psychology

Focus on Adults. One reason for the slow progress of abnormal child and adolescent psychology has to do with the emergence of psychology and psychiatry as distinct disciplines from biology, medicine, and philosophy in the second half of the nineteenth century. From the outset, these new disciplines did not concern themselves with human development and functioning throughout a person's life. Rather, they focused almost entirely on adults with psychological disorders. Consequently, most

of the early theoretical models put forth to explain the origins, development, and course of childhood and adolescent disorders were generalizations or extensions of work initially conducted with adults (or conducted with animals and later applied to human beings). In most cases, these generalizations ignored important developmental issues and proved inadequate.

Theoretical Conflicts. Progress was also slowed for much of the twentieth century by major disputes among theorists of different orientations. Lively theoretical debates and, in some cases, open conflicts are common in science, especially as new fields of inquiry become established. However, in psychology and psychiatry, debates were often conducted in lieu of careful, empirical research. In other words, for decades professionals, instead of conducting systematic studies of young people with and without psychological problems, engaged mainly in theoretical debates on the origins and treatments of those problems. These debates regularly occurred among theoreticians from different persuasions, in particular the proponents of a **psychoanalytic approach** (see Box 1.1) and the proponents of a **behavioral approach** (see Box 1.2, p. 9).

BOX 1.1 • *The Psychoanalytic Approach*

Sigmund Freud (1856–1939), an Austrian neurologist, is the father of one of the most influential schools of thought in the history of psychology: the psychoanalytic approach. Freud's theory is complex, and it changed in important ways over the course of his career. At its core, however, traditional psychoanalytic theory assumes that human behavior—whether normal or abnormal—is largely determined by unconscious emotional processes (processes that people are unaware of). The theory has both *structural* and *developmental* aspects.

Freud believed that our behavior results from interaction and conflict among three personality structures: the id, ego, and superego. The **id,** which is the first structure to emerge in the course of development, is totally unconscious and driven by instincts. It provides psychological energy or drive but is entirely selfish; that is, it operates on the *pleasure principle,* seeking its own immediate gratification, without regard for practical or moral considerations. Infants are controlled by the id. However, as children grow, they soon have to adjust to the demands and constraints of living with others. They do so through the development of the **ego,** a personality structure that operates on the *reality principle.* The ego acts as a broker between the instinctual urges of the id and the limits imposed by the environment, especially parents. Although the ego is able to draw on reason and on other cognitive and social skills in its mediating role, it is similar to the id in that it does not abide by moral principles. Its sole purpose is to fulfill the id's wishes without getting into trouble. A third personality structure, the **superego,** enables people to distinguish right from wrong and to behave in a socially responsible and ethical manner. This structure emerges last in the course of development. It reflects the values and rules that children acquire from their

(continued)

BOX 1.1 • Continued

family and social environment. As they grow up, children internalize these values and rules, which act as their moral guide or conscience in their attempts to channel and restrain the selfish priorities of the id and ego.

Freud also theorized that all human beings go through distinctive stages of development as they strive to satisfy their instinctual needs.

Freud believed that youth who do not adequately negotiate the usual developmental progression become either fixated (stuck) at a particular stage or regress (move back) to an earlier stage, and that fixation or regression leads to psychological disorders. More generally, he assumed that each stage of development brings important psychological conflicts as children and later adolescents attempt to satisfy their instinctual urges and the many demands that the adult world places on them. If these conflicts are not resolved satisfactorily, they will provoke anxiety and contribute to psychological disorders. The ego has essentially two ways of dealing with anxiety: consciously and rationally or unconsciously and irrationally, through **defense mechanisms.** Defense mechanisms are psychological processes that distort reality and thus protect the ego from overwhelming anxiety. The most important defense mechanism is *repression.* It works by keeping unacceptable thoughts or urges from the id out of conscious awareness. However, repression requires considerable psychological energy and is rarely entirely successful. In some cases, energy levels break down, or repressed thoughts or urges reappear in different, at times pathological, ways. For example, Freud believed that adolescents who develop obsessive-compulsive disorder (see Chapter 10) engage in elaborate rituals in which they clean or do something else almost endlessly because of repressed sexual urges.

Freud was a keen observer of human behavior and a prolific writer. He has undoubtedly had a major influence on Western psychology and on Western culture as a whole. However, his theory lacks scientific support, for two reasons. First, it was based almost exclusively on clinical work and was never subjected to scientific analysis. Second, many of its concepts are not open to observation and are very difficult to measure. Recall the story of Rachel, who opened this chapter. In psychoanalytic terms, one could say that her severe temper tantrums and her frequent conflicts with her mother indicate that she remained fixated at an anal stage of development, presumably because of unresolved struggles with her mother around toilet training. However, testing such an explanation scientifically is extremely difficult, since Freudian theory offers no reliable methods of measuring the unconscious processes that are supposedly at work in all psychological problems.

A number of theorists of psychoanalytic persuasion—including Freud's daughter, Anna Freud (1895–1982)—have carried on Freud's tradition. These theorists continue to emphasize the central role of unconscious processes in the determination of human behavior, but they put more importance than Freud did on developmental, social, and cultural influences, and less on psychosexual urges. Anna Freud was the founder of child psychoanalysis and played a particularly important role in the growth of interest in abnormal child and adolescent psychology as a discipline in its own right, rather than as a downward extension of abnormal adult psychology.

Examples of the way in which theoretical disputes slowed the advancement of knowledge abound. One such example concerns mood disorders in childhood and adolescence. Until the 1970s, when systematic studies of these disorders began to be conducted, a majority of psychoanalytic theorists claimed that mood disorders were rare, or even impossible, before adulthood (see Chapter 9). Similarly, most behavioral theorists showed little interest in the largely private and subjective nature of depressive feelings, which did not lend themselves to direct observation—their traditional method of investigation. It is relatively easy to observe a disruptive boy in a classroom and to count the number of times he gets out of his chair in an hour. It is much more difficult to quantify the behavior of a boy who is alone and withdrawn, and is likely to sit quietly at his desk for the entire hour and go almost unnoticed.

Psychological Problems as Passing Phases of Development.   For much of the twentieth century, professionals regarded many difficulties reported by parents and teachers as normal or passing "phases" of development. Researchers and practitioners often ignored such symptoms as severe or chronic language

BOX 1.2 • *The Behavioral Approach*

As Freud was developing his theory, behavioral psychologists—such as Ivan Pavlov (1849–1936) in Russia and John Watson (1878–1958) and B. F. Skinner (1904–1990) in the United States—conducted research with people and animals to discover the general principles of behavior and behavior change. Although their work did not focus directly on psychopathology, it helped other researchers understand the etiology of behavior disorders, so that they could create effective interventions for affected children and adolescents.

As the name of this perspective—the behavioral approach—indicates, behavioral psychologists assume that the proper subject matter for psychology is directly observable behavior and the environmental conditions under which it occurs. They assume further that, whether normal or abnormal, most behavior is learned and that psychological theories must account for how this learning takes place. There are two major behavioral approaches: operant conditioning and classical conditioning.

From an **operant conditioning** perspective, Rachel's extreme temper tantrums and struggles with her mother would be attributed to the fact that she has learned to behave that way, just as hers peers have learned to behave in a more socially acceptable manner. More generally, this perspective assumes that behavior is largely determined by its **antecedents** and **consequences**; that is, by the environmental conditions that precede and follow the behavior. For example, if the consequence of a young girl's whining and complaining is that she does not have to do her homework, she is likely to learn to whine and complain to avoid doing it. Or if a young boy finds that he can make other children do as he says by threatening to hit them, he may learn to become a bully.

Reinforcement and **punishment** are key concepts in operant conditioning. Reinforcement refers to environmental conditions that tend to increase the likelihood of a particular behavior, whereas punishment refers to environmental conditions that tend to decrease that likelihood. A behavioral psychologist would thus assume that Rachel has learned to "throw fits" and to be generally disagreeable at home because, over the course of her development, she has been repeatedly reinforced for behaving that way. Her tantrums may have prompted considerable attention from family members and may have enabled her to avoid doing what she was told. Also, her parents may have failed to punish her effectively for her unacceptable conduct. For example, her mother reported that she often sent Rachel to her room when she misbehaved. Although many children find such a behavioral consequence unpleasant, Rachel may have had toys, games, and other pleasurable things to do in her room, so that what her mother intended as a punishment was actually reinforcing her.

Adaptive and maladaptive learning can also take place through processes of **classical conditioning.** In his famous experiments with dogs, Pavlov showed that a response such as salivation could be elicited when an unconditioned stimulus (food) was paired with a conditioned stimulus (such as the sound of a bell). Pavlov repeatedly sounded a bell just before feeding his laboratory dogs and found that after a few trials the sound of the bell was enough to get the animals to salivate. They had learned that the bell was a reliable predictor of food and responded to it as they would to chow. Classical conditioning principles have long played an important role in abnormal psychology, especially in our understanding of disorders in which strong negative emotions, such as fear and anxiety, are prominent. Children who have experienced overwhelming fear in situations beyond their control—for example, as the result of being bitten by a dog or witnessing violence against a loved one—may develop an anxiety disorder. Behavioral psychologists believe that these children may later avoid situations that remind them of such incidents, because these situations have become associated with negative emotions through classical conditioning (see Chapter 10).

The behavioral approach has been used to explain the origins of many psychological disorders of childhood and adolescence and continues to exercise a strong influence on contemporary views of abnormal behavior. However, most researchers and clinicians who are sympathetic to this approach today believe that children and adolescents do not simply react to external events; instead, they play an active role in determining their own behavior, mainly through cognitive processes that mediate the link between environment and behavior. Thus, a young boy who has often witnessed people behaving aggressively, and who has been the victim of aggressive acts himself, may learn to behave in similar ways—not simply because he has been exposed to socially inappropriate models and personal victimization but also because he has learned to *think* of the world as a hostile place and to interpret even neutral actions on the part of others as threatening (see Chapter 8). We will discuss this *cognitive-behavioral* approach in greater detail in the next chapter.

delays, angry outbursts, fearfulness, and bedwetting because these symptoms were expected to disappear spontaneously as children grew older. However, this notion was based largely on theoretical or clinical opinions rather than on scientific data. Longitudinal studies have since shown that when such problems interfere with a child's daily functioning, they tend to persist and may actually worsen over time. Persistent problems occur because the child's difficulties evolve in a complex manner and, over the years, define a pathological developmental trajectory. For example, there are obvious differences between repeated angry outbursts at age 3 or 4, fighting at age 7, lying and stealing at age 10, vandalism and cruelty at age 12, rape at age 16, and armed robbery or even murder at age 19. However, as shown in Chapter 8, all these actions are indicative of an early-onset conduct disorder that has evolved from preschool to late adolescence.

Ethical, Social, and Political Considerations. Most studies conducted with young people require that they *and* their caregivers give consent before they can participate. When the topic of a particular research project is sensitive, as it often is in abnormal psychology, consent can be difficult to obtain. For example, suppose that you want to conduct a survey on family violence and that you plan to interview parents and children separately. To ensure the protection of human subjects, your research institution will require you to obtain written informed consent from all participants before you can ask them any questions. You also will have to inform the children's caregivers that you might have to report them to local authorities if you uncover evidence of child maltreatment in the course of your interview (see Chapter 12). Caregivers of youth who live in violent homes may obviously be reluctant to participate in your study. In other words, the ethical protection of research participants is always paramount and takes precedence over the quest for scientific knowledge—thus at times slowing progress, especially of research with minors.

More fundamentally, less is known about disorders in youth than in adults because children and adolescents are very limited in their ability to influence the way they are perceived and treated by society. Their social "voice" and their political power are almost non-

This 1938 poster by Erik H. Krause was part of a public campaign to promote proper childcare in the United States. It illustrates the fact that, unlike adults, children and adolescents largely depend on others to ensure that they are treated fairly and cared for adequately.

existent. News headlines about child maltreatment regularly provide tragic reminders of the powerlessness of children and adolescents, as do the case studies presented in Chapter 12. All Western countries have laws against child abuse and neglect. However, legislation is effective only when the adults who are in a position to protect young people can identify likely victims and take effective steps to intervene on their behalf.

In situations far less extreme than those in which abuse or neglect is suspected, a child or an adolescent's behavior is evaluated mainly by adults in the family, at school, or in the community, who decide whether that behavior is normal or abnormal. But determining abnormality is by no means simple. Adult expectations can vary considerably across settings. A teacher may argue that a child has a serious behavior problem, whereas the child's parents insist that their son or daughter is doing fine. Even when adults agree in their assessment, it is often difficult to distinguish what is abnormal from what is not—both because of important individual differences and because knowledge of normal development remains limited. In other words, "normal" and "abnormal" are relative notions that are largely established by adults, often on the basis of insufficient knowledge about child and adolescent development.

Current Focus of Abnormal Child and Adolescent Psychology

Current research explores the potential roles of biological, psychological, or social and cultural factors in abnormal functioning. Researchers now tend to emphasize the major contributions of each of these perspectives (which are described in Chapter 2), rather than pitting them against each other. Longitudinal research also is contributing to a better understanding of child development and helping the field distinguish between behaviors that are passing "phases" of development and psychological disorders. Finally, the voice of children continues to grow in America, thanks to the willingness of many people—researchers and clinicians included—to advocate for their welfare. All these factors are contributing to rapid progress in the field of abnormal child and adolescent psychology.

Recent Advances in Classification and Diagnosis

In recent decades, important changes have contributed to a better balance between theoretical debates and empirical research in abnormal child and adolescent psychology. These changes began in the 1970s, with systematic efforts to:

- Establish clear criteria to define, classify, and diagnose disorders.
- Develop assessment tools that consistently and accurately measure behavioral and emotional problems.

- Set up and conduct large-scale, longitudinal studies of children.

We will discuss the first of these changes here, leaving the other two for consideration in Chapter 2.

To make significant progress, all sciences require detailed descriptions of the phenomena they are investigating, as well as consistent means of classifying these phenomena. The first widely used system of classification for psychological disorders—the *Diagnostic and Statistical Manual of Mental Disorders* of the American Psychiatric Association (DSM)—appeared in 1952. Initially, this system (and its second edition, DSM-II, published in 1968) had little impact on the study of abnormal behavior in children or adolescents. The reason is twofold. First, both of these editions focused almost entirely on adult disorders, providing only brief and incomplete descriptions of a few conditions specific to childhood and adolescence. Second, these two editions were heavily influenced by the psychoanalytic approach, which did not easily lend itself to *valid* and *reliable* diagnoses of either childhood or adult disorders because it was based almost exclusively on clinical judgments rather than on detailed observations of individuals as they interacted with parents, teachers, and peers (Mash & Dozois, 1996). **Validity** refers to the extent to which a scientific instrument adequately measures what it is designed to measure. **Reliability** refers to the extent to which that same instrument yields the same results when it is used by different professionals or administered on different occasions. Scientifically oriented researchers and clinicians rejected or ignored the first two editions of the DSM in large part because (1) there was little evidence that the disorders they described corresponded well to the way in which people with psychological problems actually behaved, and (2) professionals using the DSM often disagreed about how to classify people with such problems.

Things changed rapidly at the beginning of the 1980s with the publication of the DSM-III (APA, 1980). This edition marked a radical shift in the classification of all psychological disorders in both adults and children. Based on careful clinical observations and growing empirical research, the DSM-III described several disorders that had their beginning or onset in childhood or adolescence. In addition, it "introduced a number of important methodological innovations, including explicit diagnostic criteria, a multiaxial system [see below], and a descriptive approach that attempted to be neutral with respect to theories of etiology" (APA, 1994, pp. xvii–xviii). In other words, the editors of the DSM-III dropped the psychoanalytic approach of earlier versions. They replaced it with fairly detailed descriptions of how youth with specific disorders can be expected to behave, and they left out all theoretical interpretations of the behavior of young people with these disorders. For the first time, the DSM-III provided researchers and clinicians in the field of abnormal child and adolescent psychology with a *common descriptive language* of major disorders and observable diagnostic criteria.

The DSM-III was revised in 1987, and then, a few years later, in 1994, it was replaced by an entirely new edition, the DSM-IV. Each new publication included significant changes reflecting the rapidly growing state of knowledge in abnormal psychology and responding to critics who alleged that the descriptions of several disorders were vague and that numerous diagnostic criteria were unclear or inconsistent. Finally, in 2000, the text of the DSM-IV was revised, yielding the DSM-IV-TR (for *Text Revision*) (APA, 2000a). This revision updates the text of the DSM-IV, corrects factual errors, and improves the text's clarity and overall presentation. It does not introduce new disorders, nor does it modify the diagnostic criteria of the DSM-IV.

The DSM-IV-TR Multiaxial Approach

The DSM-IV-TR is a **multiaxial system.** That is, it requires diagnosticians to specify the psychological disorder(s) a child or adolescent may have, and also to describe the broader context in which the difficulties occur. With the help of five axes or dimensions of functioning, the diagnostician is able to provide a comprehensive summary of the child or adolescent's personal circumstances, and to plan a treatment regimen.

Axis I	Clinical Disorders
	Other Conditions That May
	Be a Focus of Clinical Attention

Axis II	Personality Disorders
	Mental Retardation
Axis III	General Medical Conditions
Axis IV	Psychosocial and Environmental Problems
Axis V	Global Assessment of Functioning

Axis I is used to specify the disorder that the child or adolescent has (except for disorders reported on Axis II). In the case presented at the beginning of the chapter, Rachel's noncompliance, tantrums, and irritability led to an Axis I diagnosis of oppositional defiant disorder. Her mother also described her as "often sad." If her sadness had reached the level of a mood disorder, that disorder would also have been listed on this axis.

Axis II covers disorders not reported on Axis I. These are chronic, often lifelong disorders. In children and adolescents, mental retardation is the disorder most often listed on Axis II. For example, this axis is used to specify when a child with autism or schizophrenia (see Chapters 4 and 5) also has mental retardation. **Personality disorders** also are reported on this axis. These disorders are thought to reflect entrenched, maladaptive personality characteristics and are rarely diagnosed before late adolescence or early adulthood, essentially because childhood and adolescence are periods of rapid changes in which young people are still developing their personalities. However, when children present enduring personality traits that are pathological in nature, this information is reported on Axis II. Because Rachel's intellectual functioning was within the average range and she showed no signs of entrenched maladaptive personality traits, she was not given any diagnosis on Axis II.

Axis III is used to specify the presence of medical conditions that might be related to the youth's psychological difficulties. For example, a malfunctioning thyroid gland (a small organ that regulates body metabolism) may aggravate a child's symptoms of hyperactivity and distractibility. When this medical condition is listed as part of the diagnostic picture, professionals on the youth's treatment team are made aware that medical changes may have a significant impact on behavior. When Rachel's mother was questioned about her daughter's health, she reported no concerns or problems. Thus, Rachel was not given any diagnosis on Axis III.

Axis IV is used to specify any psychosocial or environmental problems that may be relevant to a comprehensive understanding of the disorders reported on the first two axes and to their proper treatment. As Box 1.3 shows, many factors can be included on this axis. Rachel's mother reported significant problems that probably aggravated her daughter's condition. Specifically, she noted that Rachel had few friends, that the family had little social support, and that there were frequent conflicts between the parents about how to manage her behavior. Identifying and recording such issues is essential to developing an individualized treatment plan likely to meet each child's particular needs.

Axis V provides an overall rating of the child or adolescent's current level of functioning (see Figure 1.1, p. 14). This rating, which ranges from 1 to 100, evaluates the extent to which the disorders reported on Axis I or II interfere with the young person's ability to function from day to day and to meet important responsibilities (e.g., attend school, be aware of danger, take care of personal hygiene). For example, an adolescent boy with major depressive disorder (see Chapter 9) would obtain a higher rating on the Global Assessment of Functioning Scale (GAF) if he continued to attend school and look after his personal hygiene than if he often refused to leave the house and paid little attention to his physical appearance or to his cleanliness. Rachel was diagnosed with a GAF score of 55 because her behavior impaired both her social and her academic functioning.

A multiaxial approach is important for several reasons. First, it provides a detailed picture of psychological disorders. Second, it points to different factors of direct relevance to intervention. Third, it promotes a **biopsychosocial model** within which to describe, understand, and treat these disorders (APA, 2000a). As its name implies, this model takes into account the

---

BOX 1.3 • *The DSM-IV-TR Axis IV: Psychosocial and Environmental Problems*

Axis IV of the DSM-IV-TR multiaxial system is used to specify the presence of psychosocial or environmental stressors that may interfere with normal functioning and that need to be taken into account as part of a complete treatment plan. Youth with psychological disorders or their families may have additional problems in one or more of the following areas:

1. Primary support group: Includes problems with parents, siblings, and extended family members (e.g., parental alcoholism).
2. Social environment: Includes conflicts with peers or social isolation because of inappropriate behaviors or skills; or participation in a deviant peer group, such as a gang, that encourages maladaptive behavior.
3. Educational problems: Include learning problems (but not learning disorders, which are listed on Axis I), conflicts with teachers, or academic difficulties with the program (e.g., completing homework).
4. Occupational problems: Include employment difficulties affecting the youth or the youth's caregiver;

with older adolescents, unemployment may be listed here.
5. Housing problems: Include homelessness and unsafe or inadequate housing.
6. Economic problems: Include family financial hardship and other economic problems affecting the family.
7. Access to health care: This is often tied to occupational and economic problems. Low-income youth may not be covered by insurance and may only be eligible to receive limited medical or psychological services.
8. Legal system/crime: Includes legal problems faced by the child or other family members. Probation for a juvenile offense, incarceration of a caregiver, and child maltreatment may be listed here.
9. Other psychosocial and environmental problems: Stressors not listed in any of the other categories are listed here. For example, the fact that the youth had a friend who recently committed suicide may be listed here as an important consideration in treatment planning.

Score	Description
100–91	Superior functioning—Child has no major problems and good coping skills; is unlikely to be found in a clinical setting.
90–81	Minimal problems—Child has an average level of functioning and copes well in a majority of circumstances.
80–71	Temporary and expectable reactions to stress—Child exhibits passing and expected reactions to stressful life events, such as sadness in response to the death of a loved one; impairment in functioning is temporary and not accompanied by significant psychological problems.
70–61	Mild symptoms—Child has adequate interpersonal relationships but experiences some difficulties at home or school, such as depressed mood or arguments with family or friends.
60–51	Moderate symptoms—Child has limited interpersonal relationships and experiences symptoms such as significant learning or communication problems or moderate difficulties in academic, vocational, or social settings. Problems at home or school are frequent.
50–41	Serious symptoms—Child has very limited and often conflictual interpersonal relationships, and experiences serious symptoms, such as suicidal thoughts or severe (but not life-threatening) weight loss due to anorexia. Problems at home or school are frequent and often severe.
40–31	Impairments in reality testing, communication, judgment, thinking, mood, or family or school relationships—Difficulties in many areas interfere significantly with everyday functioning. Or child's behavior and speech are at times illogical or unclear, or not in touch with reality.
30–21	Serious impairments in reality testing, communication, judgment, thinking, mood, or family or school relationships—Important difficulties in many areas interfere significantly with everyday functioning. Or child's behavior and speech are illogical or unclear, or not in touch with reality.
20–11	Some dangerousness (to self or others)—Child may frequently be violent toward self or others. Or child has severe difficulties in all areas of functioning and may be unable to communicate or maintain personal grooming at an age-appropriate level.
10–1	Persistent danger (to self or others)—Child requires almost constant supervision because of serious threats to self or others (e.g., recurrent violence, repeated suicidal threats). Or child has severe difficulties in all areas of functioning and may be unable to communicate or maintain personal grooming at an age-appropriate level.

FIGURE 1.1   *The DSM-IV-TR Global Assessment of Functioning Scale.* This scale is part of the DSM-IV-TR multiaxial system. It is used to assess the extent to which the disorders reported on Axis I or II interfere with the child or adolescent's ability to lead a normal life. Scores, which range from 0 to 100, are described here in general terms.

Source: American Psychiatric Association, *Diagnostic and Statistical Manual of Mental Disorders, Fourth Edition, Text Revision* (Washington, DC: American Psychiatric Association, 2000a). Copyright 2000 American Psychiatric Association. Reprinted with permission.

biological, psychological, and social and cultural factors that may be associated with a child's specific difficulties, and it integrates these factors into a comprehensive treatment approach. Unfortunately, the DSM-IV-TR has been rightly criticized for listing these factors but failing to account for the complex ways in which they operate (Jensen & Hoagwood, 1997). Nevertheless, the biopsychosocial model embedded in its multiaxial approach highlights the complex nature of all psychological disorders. Take the example of an adolescent boy who is very sad and depressed, has few friends, is significantly overweight, and lives in a home where his parents fight regularly. By focusing attention not only on his depressed mood but also on other important factors in this boy's life, a biopsychosocial model points to a variety of treatment options. Thus, the boy may benefit not only from individual therapy but also from a social skills group to develop new friendships. He may also be referred to a nutritionist to help control his weight through diet and exercise; and his parents may be referred to a marital therapist in an attempt to improve their relationship.

Limitations of a Diagnostic Approach

Like all complex endeavors, diagnostic classification systems can be criticized on a number of accounts. We cannot review all the criticism leveled at the DSM-IV-TR here. However, we must consider some of the limitations of a diagnostic approach and caution against the potential abuse of diagnostic labels to describe a child or adolescent's behavioral or emotional difficulties.

Category or Dimension? Classification systems are categorical in nature. They make it possible to determine the presence or absence of specific disorders on the basis of explicitly stated diagnostic criteria. In a **categorical approach,** a child or adolescent does or does not have a disorder; there is no in-between state. This approach is essentially medical, in that it assumes that each psychological disorder consists of a distinctive set of symptoms, or **syndrome,** which allows for its identification and proper classification. A categorical approach is very useful for organizing data from different sources and for facilitating communication among researchers and clinicians. For example, it enables researchers to estimate the number of youth who have a specific disorder and to make recommendations to officials in charge of planning treatment and prevention services for mental health problems. However, practitioners often need to know much more than whether a particular condition is present or absent, and

the either/or nature of a categorical approach limits their understanding of individual differences in the appearance and severity of these disorders.

An example illustrates this important point. As shown in Chapter 6, learning disorders have their origins in an array of cognitive and neurological deficits. These deficits result in difficulties in letter and number identification, decoding and phonetics, attention and visual memory, and comprehension. Problems in these skill areas form a developmental continuum. That is, any of the deficits just listed can range from very mild to severe, and a child who has moderate or severe difficulties identifying letters, paying attention, and remembering is much more likely to have a reading disorder than a child who has mild problems in only one of these areas. Professionals who look at psychological difficulties in this way adopt a **dimensional approach** and put much less emphasis on determining whether a child has a specific disorder than on describing the child's particular strengths and weaknesses. This approach has the advantage of considering individual differences in adaptation and of emphasizing that most psychological problems lie on a continuum. However, it is also limited because it does not specify where the threshold of dysfunction is along this continuum—that is, at what point a weakness becomes a disorder. For example, how are slow readers differentiated from children with a reading disorder? The answer is important, not only for the definition of reading disorder but also for the development of educational and psychological services. Obviously, a relatively low threshold of dysfunction will identify too many children and label some of them inaccurately; at the same time, a relatively high threshold will not identify enough children, possibly depriving some of them of beneficial services.

Today most researchers and clinicians use a combination of the categorical and dimensional approaches. That is, they may conclude that a child or an adolescent has a particular disorder (or disorders), but they also rely on various dimensional measures to describe specific behavior patterns. For example, many professionals include not only a diagnostic interview in their assessment, but also checklists and rating scales completed by different persons (e.g., child, parent, and teacher) to describe important facets of the child's behavior (see Chapter 2). This book adopts a primarily categorical approach: it presents each major disorder in terms similar to those of the DSM-IV-TR. This choice does not imply that this approach is preferable to a dimensional one, only that it is very commonly used in the field of abnormal child and adolescent psychology.

Labeling.   All classification systems run the risk of being inadvertently or deliberately misused, and of harming rather than helping children and their families. A real danger is that a diagnostic label applied in haste and with little evidence for its appropriateness may become a self-fulfilling prophesy. For example, a third-grade teacher who describes students who are very active and do not immediately follow her instructions as "hyperactive" may be encouraging the very behaviors she objects to by failing to set clear limits because she is convinced that they have a disorder requiring professional treatment. Similarly, diagnostic labels can be very harmful when they are applied in a selective manner to discriminate against particular groups of children or adolescents—for example, on the basis of race, ethnicity, or socioeconomic status (Dupree, Beale-Spencer, & Bell, 1997).

Although the dangers of labeling are real, it still would exist even if classification systems were never used. Human beings of all ages are quick to compare themselves to others and to conclude that people who behave differently may have problems. Children often ignore or reject peers who are different from them, and will refer to these peers in negative terms (Dodge, Coie, Pettit, & Price, 1990). When diagnostic labels are used for the purpose of helping people, however, classification systems can actually prevent arbitrary or discriminatory labeling, because these systems clearly specify the conditions that must be met before a particular diagnosis can be made. For example, even though elementary school teachers may describe students as "hyperactive," you will see in Chapter 7 that a diagnosis of attention deficit hyperactivity disorder (or ADHD) can be made only when a child has six or more specific symptoms that have lasted at least six months and began before age 7. These strict criteria are designed to ensure that the diagnosis is reserved for children with significant problems, rather than given hastily to children whom adults find challenging at home or at school.

In any event, diagnostic labels should always be used with considerable care and consideration, and with an awareness that *labels are designed to describe disorders, not people.* When children or adolescents receive a diagnosis, it does not tell us all there is to know about them. It only identifies the condition that is limiting their functioning and development. Consequently, we refer throughout this book to youth *with* particular disorders, rather than to disordered youth. It may seem strange or sound unfamiliar to you to read about "children with autism" rather than autistic children. However, this wording conveys the message that *psychological disorders are not something that some children are, only something that they have.* Our focus must always be on children as complete human beings who, like everyone else, negotiate their environment with all of their abilities, rather than with their limitations only.

Orientation of This Book

This book provides a detailed and critical summary of scientific knowledge about abnormal child and adolescent psychology. You will learn about disorders that are relatively well known and understood and that tend to occur quite frequently. You will also be introduced to some rare and unfamiliar disorders that nevertheless are important because of their devastating effects on children and their families. Finally, you will learn about programs and methods designed to treat youth with psychological disorders or to help prevent some disorders before they have had a chance to disrupt the normal course of development.

The in-depth coverage we provide is up to date. Most of the studies we review have been published in the last ten years. We have also attempted to report findings from different countries, and to compare studies of the same disorder carried out in different cultures and with people of more than one ethnic group. Nevertheless, much of what we know about abnormal child and adolescent psychology comes from studies conducted in the United States and other Western countries. Furthermore, many studies have relied on school-age, white children (often boys) as participants, because they are most likely to be seen at child and adolescent mental health clinics. Whenever possible, we point to the fact that findings obtained in one country or with one ethnic group do not necessarily apply to youth who live in a different country or who come from another ethnic background (see Box 1.4).

In line with recent advances in abnormal child and adolescent psychology, the approach we adopt here reflects the key assumptions of **developmental psychopathology** (Achenbach, 1990). As Figure 1.2 (p. 18) illustrates, developmental psychopathology is an approach to research and intervention that emphasizes the importance of normal development for a comprehensive understanding of psychological disorders. In this approach, knowledge about the ways that children and adolescents cope with developmental tasks and challenges is used to throw light on these disorders and on the services that need to be provided to treat or prevent them. Researchers and clinicians who adopt a developmental psychopathology approach do not see disorders as separate entities that are distinct from normal

---

BOX 1.4 • *Gender and Ethnic Diversity in Abnormal Child and Adolescent Psychology*

It may be tempting to think of psychological disorders as conditions that affect children and adolescents in much the same way, irrespective of their characteristics or background. However, as a growing body of research attests, results obtained with a particular sample of youth cannot automatically be applied to other youth as well. A couple of examples regarding gender and ethnicity illustrate this important point.

As you will discover in Chapter 7, ADHD (attention deficit hyperactivity disorder) can manifest itself quite differently in boys and girls. For example, researchers recently examined the symptom patterns of almost 300 school-age children with the disorder (Biederman et al., 2002). Their results showed that girls had more symptoms of inattention than boys; were only half as likely as boys to have additional behavior problems (such as noncompliant or aggressive conduct; see Chapter 8); and were more likely than boys to abuse drugs or alcohol as they grew up. Obviously, these results caution against broad generalizations about gender by showing that boys and girls with ADHD may not have the same kinds of difficulties or may develop different problems as they become older.

A similar note of caution comes from research conducted with youth from different ethnic groups. In the United States, for example, severe and overreactive discipline in early childhood predicts the appearance of disruptive and antisocial behaviors in European American children but not in African American children. In other words, a particular form of parenting does not invariably lead to the same developmental outcome. Rather, outcome in this case reflects both familial and cultural factors, and discipline that may be detrimental in one cultural context may not have the same effects in another (Deater-Deckard, Dodge, Bates, & Pettit, 1996).

In some instances, ethnic group differences are more subtle than would appear at first glance. For example, European American adolescent girls are more likely to suffer from eating disorders than their African American peers are; but European American teenagers are also more likely than African American teenagers to identify with the cultural ideals of beauty—including excessive thinness—conveyed in the majority American culture. Thus, the processes underlying eating disorders may not necessarily be different in the two groups. Support for this point comes from the finding that African American girls who identify with mainstream ideals of beauty face as great a risk of having eating disorders as their European American counterparts (Peterson & Mitchell, 1999).

Finally, there is considerable evidence that many psychological disorders are more frequent in socially disadvantaged or rejected groups. For example, although little is known about the relation between sexual orientation and general adaptation in young people, gay and lesbian youth are more likely to suffer from depression, anxiety, and alcohol or substance abuse than their heterosexual peers; they are also more likely to be diagnosed with multiple psychological disorders and to report thinking about suicide or attempting to commit suicide (Fergusson, Horwood, & Beautrais, 1999).

Taken together, the examples briefly summarized here illustrate the importance of gaining a better understanding of how psychological disorders manifest themselves and evolve in different groups of children and adolescents.

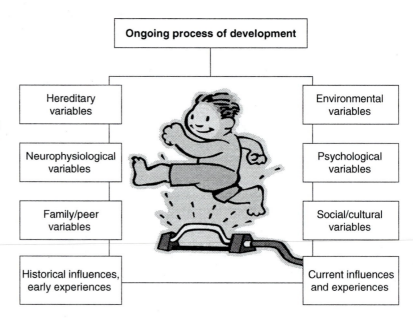

FIGURE 1.2 *Schematic Illustration of the Developmental Psychopathology Perspective.* Developmental psychopathology assumes that (1) one cannot know what is abnormal and clearly pathological in childhood and adolescence without knowing what is normal and healthy; and (2) one cannot distinguish between what is normal and what is not without studying the multiple sources of influence affecting the process of development. This figure illustrates these multiple sources, which we will explore more fully in Chapter 2.

ways of coping. Rather, they see them as *deviations from optimal patterns of development.* Over time, these deviations define specific developmental trajectories that, in spite of significant variability among children, tend to be characteristic of different disorders. However, these trajectories overlap regularly with normal ways of coping, at times blurring the distinction between normal and abnormal development and making clear-cut definitions of disorders difficult.

A Descriptive Orientation

As mentioned earlier, our descriptions of the major characteristics of the disorders we present are based on the DSM-IV-TR, not because it provides the "best" descriptions available but because it is used as a common reference by a large number of researchers and clinicians. For each disorder, we provide a detailed description of its major symptoms, and specify the set or "mix" of symptoms required before a diagnosis can be made. Because childhood and adolescence are periods of rapid developmental changes, we also pay careful attention to the duration of symptoms and to the age that children must have reached before certain diagnoses can be made. For example, as mentioned earlier,

ADHD cannot be diagnosed unless symptoms begin before age 7 and have been present for at least six months. Finally, our descriptions include a discussion of each disorder's associated characteristics—psychological, educational, or medical problems that are not necessary for a diagnosis, but that often accompany and complicate the disorder.

The common language provided by the DSM-IV-TR is a social construction rather than a formal description of an objective reality. Simply because a disorder has been given a name and a list of symptoms, one cannot assume that it necessarily exists as described. Similarly, just because another disorder is not found in the DSM-IV-TR, one cannot assume that that disorder does not exist (Achenbach, 1993). In other words, we view the DSM-IV-TR as a working tool that must be criticized and corrected whenever its descriptions are contradicted by scientific evidence. As you will see, in each chapter—under the heading **empirical validity**—we discuss the extent to which research supports the existence of the disorders we present. Our purpose is to point to limitations in current understanding and to the need for continued research.

The descriptions found in the DSM-IV-TR can never escape value judgments or the different theoretical or personal interpretations of those who use them. Thoughtful researchers and clinicians know that the distinction between what is normal and what is not is very difficult and, at times, almost impossible to make. In his short novel *Billy Budd,* Herman Melville pointed to this issue when he asked: "Who in the rainbow can draw the line where the violet tint ends and the orange tint begins? Distinctly we see the difference of the color, but where exactly does the one first visibly enter into the other? So with sanity and insanity. In pronounced cases there is no question about them. But in some supposed cases, in various degrees supposedly less pronounced, to draw the exact line of demarcation few will undertake though for a fee some professional experts will. . . . In other words there are instances when it is next to impossible to determine whether a man is in his mind or beginning to be otherwise" (1891/1948, p. 233).

Even when there is no doubt that a child or adolescent has psychological problems, a diagnosis is not always obvious. A well-known example of this point comes from research on ADHD. The symptoms of the disorder are relatively well established and not a topic of much controversy. However, until recently, ADHD was diagnosed much more often in North America than in Europe, although children did not behave very differently on one side of the Atlantic than on the other. The differences in diagnosis apparently were attributable to differences in perceptions. European clinicians tended to emphasize the disruptive nature of these children's difficulties and to diagnose conduct disorder (see Chapter 8), whereas their North American colleagues focused on the children's inattentiveness and hyperactivity and therefore determined that they had ADHD (Prendergast et al., 1988).

More fundamentally, to say that a child has ADHD or any other disorder *always* implies a value judgment; it is equivalent to saying that the child is not "on par" with other children. No matter what extenuating circumstances or euphemisms people use to cushion the negative impact of such a judgment, they are in effect saying that the child is not meeting expectations—and often, by extension, that neither is the child's family, school, or community. Psychological disorders have always been a source of considerable fear and misunderstanding; and they still are, in spite of

important advances in research and education. Consequently, it is essential to remember that the descriptions we offer here can never be purely objective or neutral.

A Developmental Orientation

Detailed descriptions enable clinicians and researchers to identify and classify psychological disorders correctly, and therefore to conduct basic research studies or effective interventions. However, descriptions cannot capture the complexity of these disorders, because descriptions generally ignore the developmental, social, and cultural context in which psychological disorders emerge and evolve. These disorders always occur in a broad context that affects their expression. In particular, the effects of development on individual differences are often as significant within a disorder as they are across disorders. We will illustrate this important point with two common variables: the age and gender of the child.

Age and Gender. The DSM-IV-TR frequently mentions that psychological disorders manifest themselves quite differently depending on the age and/or gender of the child. But these two variables are rarely reflected in the DSM's own diagnostic criteria. For example, nocturnal **enuresis,** or bedwetting, is more frequent in boys than girls, probably because girls achieve bladder control earlier, on average, than boys. For example, a Dutch epidemiological study shows that approximately 90% of girls are dry at night by age 5, but only by age 8 are 90% of boys dry at night (Verhulst et al., 1985). Because the DSM-IV-TR ignores these developmental differences, boys meet the age criterion necessary for a diagnosis more often than girls do. However, the overrepresentation of boys with the disorder may reflect a genuine gender difference or the fact that the diagnostic criteria used today ignore normal developmental differences in the acquisition of bladder control (see Chapter 13).

Comorbidity. Descriptions of psychological disorders are further complicated when a child or adolescent has more than one disorder at the same time, or when comorbid symptoms or disorders interact with the primary disorder. For example, children who are oppositional and prone to verbal and physical aggression when they begin elementary school are quickly rejected by peers and in frequent conflict with teachers. As we saw in Rachel's case, their behavior problems frequently result in academic failure as well. When these multiple difficulties persist, a child may soon develop not only a comorbid learning disorder but also poor self-concept and depressed feelings, which may eventually result in a comorbid mood disorder (see Chapter 9).

High rates of comorbidity also indicate that the definitions of psychological disorders overlap and that their diagnostic criteria are not mutually exclusive. For example, a third-grade girl who refuses to go to school for fear that something terrible will happen to her family in her absence will often have trouble falling asleep and may refuse to eat breakfast the next morning. If these difficulties persist, they may become associated with feelings of helplessness and despair. Taken together, these symptoms, if they are severe enough, may indicate that the girl has both an anxiety disorder and a mood disorder. However, because these disorders share overlapping diagnostic features, she may not actually have two comorbid conditions (see Chapter 10).

Developmental Challenges and Adaptation. More fundamentally, diagnostic descriptions are limited because they are essentially static: they present psychological disorders as relatively stable clinical entities—like diseases such as measles or strep throat—that affect children and adolescents in distinct and predictable ways. However, most disorders of childhood and adolescence are not the expression of an underlying medical condition that follows an expected course. Rather, they are *the outcome of a developmental process in which the child's coping skills are not optimal* (Sroufe, 1997). They indicate that the child is unable to cope effectively with a variety of developmental tasks and challenges—such as getting up in the morning, going to school, following adult directions, learning to read, cooperating with peers, facing normal fears—to the point where adaptation and learning are compromised. Although challenges overlap, they generally fall into one of three domains (Dumas, Prinz, Smith, & Laughlin, 1999):

- *Social,* for challenges involving primarily interpersonal and social situations and demands.
- *Affective,* for challenges requiring solutions to predominantly emotional problems.
- *Achievement,* for challenges pertaining primarily to goal-directed activities, such as self-care tasks or academic and work-related demands and responsibilities.

In a developmental perspective, disorders are evolving deviations from an optimal course of development. That is, over time, some children acquire a mode of functioning in which the symptoms of one or more disorders become increasingly apparent in their daily behavior. This developmental process depends on individual, family, social, and cultural factors—all acting together as they shape and are shaped by each other. This process depends also on *timing;* that is, on the period of development during which these factors are most influential. In other words, the same factors can have different effects according to the timing and duration of their action. For example, injuries to the brain can affect behavioral and emotional development very differently depending on whether they occurred before or after birth, in infancy, or later in childhood or adolescence (Schore, 1996).

In short, abnormal behavior is always the expression of a process of unfinished development. Thus, a diagnosis is at best a snapshot that accurately captures a child's condition at a specific point in time. It can be very useful, but only when it is regarded as a frame in the ongoing movie of the child's life.

From Normal to Pathological. In many cases, psychological disorders actually evolve from developmental processes that were initially normal and healthy. Consider some examples. Between 6 and 12 months of age, a majority of infants are distressed and fearful when separated from their loved ones and frequently cry to bring about a rapid return of their caregiver. This strong reaction is adaptive because it protects the young child from the potential danger of being left alone and helpless. Separation anxiety disorder develops when these feelings of distress and fearfulness persist or intensify in the course of childhood, and begin to seriously interfere with normative developmental experiences such as attending school. Likewise, all human beings lack bladder control during the first two or three years of life. Elimination disorders appear when this incontinence interferes with normative development by continuing past the time when children are expected to gain control over their biological functions.

As these examples show, a thorough appreciation of normative developmental processes is essential to a comprehensive understanding of child and adolescent disorders. However, researchers in this area face a double challenge: (1) they must demonstrate that multiple factors work together to lead to abnormal development; and (2) they must distinguish that development from the many individual differences that are characteristic of normal functioning in childhood and adolescence. In this undertaking, researchers often call upon the concept of developmental trajectory. This concept enables them to show that psychological disorders are dynamic and ever changing, and that, within each disorder, there are often considerable differences in the way affected youth actually behave.

A Transactional Orientation

Narrowly understood, the descriptive and developmental orientations we adopt could give the impression that most psychological disorders are primarily individual disorders and lead us to ignore the interpersonal, social, and cultural aspects of all psychological difficulties. As we have emphasized several times already, however, we realize that psychological disorders are not stable and predictable entities that somehow "clothe" all the people they affect in the same "garments." They arise in a particular context and at a specific point in time, within a familial, social, cultural, historical, and individual context (Dumas, Rollock, Prinz, Hops, & Blechman, 1999; Jensen & Hoagwood, 1997).

Anorexia nervosa provides an extreme but clear example of the multiple influences on child and adolescent adaptation. This complex disorder undoubtedly reflects various biological, psychological, family, and social influences acting in concert to produce its devastating effects. However, anorexia also takes place in a historical and cultural context that has changed considerably in the last decades. Today, in most Western

countries, a substantial number of adolescents worry about eating too much and about maintaining their weight at a culturally prescribed level that is unrealistic and unhealthy (see Chapter 11).

"Shared" Diagnoses. Irrespective of theoretical orientation, researchers and clinicians interested in abnormal psychology recognize that many behavioral and emotional difficulties have their origins in a complex interplay of factors—including biological dysfunctions or vulnerabilities, disturbed family relationships, unfavorable social conditions, and/or cultural expectations that are in conflict with the well-being of children and adolescents. In other words, with the exception of conditions that are clearly attributable to specific causes, such as some forms of mental retardation (see Chapter 3), a diagnosis is always "shared": it reflects abnormal processes taking place less "inside" a particular child than in the child's relationships with the immediate environment, as well as with the historical and cultural background (Emde, 1994).

An emphasis on the shared or relational aspects of most diagnoses reflects a **transactional approach** to human development—a focus on what happens when young people come in contact with others and with their environment (Dewey & Bentley, 1949; Kantor & Smith, 1975). The transactional approach points to the fact that the same circumstances in a child's early development can lead to different long-term outcomes. Thus, children who are irritable and resistant to control around age 2 may develop normally under favorable circumstances in the family and beyond. Over time, such children are likely to show a continued need for consistent discipline and clear limits to function well, and may often be described as "strong-willed" or as "having a lot of personality." However, they are unlikely to be described as "disordered" or "disturbed." In contrast, other children with the same early characteristics may develop a disorder in which their difficulties at home increase and generalize to school. Still others may become very anxious and fearful, not because of their own characteristics but primarily because of their relationships.

Equifinality and Multifinality. It is rare to find a characteristic or life circumstance that always has the same effect on developing children. Rather, different causes may have the same consequence for development—a principle known as **equifinality.** Likewise, the same cause may have different consequences for development—a principle known as **multifinality.** These two principles, which are illustrated in Figure 1.3, underscore the fact that developmental processes are transactional rather than mechanical. For example, brain injuries caused by chromosomal abnormalities, severe abuse in infancy, or maternal drug abuse during pregnancy can all result in mental retardation. Likewise, adolescents may develop a major depressive disorder for a variety of reasons, including an inherited predisposition to mood disorders, a disturbed pattern of attachment to one or both parents in the early years, or repeated experiences of helplessness in middle childhood.

Transactions and Timing.   A host of factors that might negatively affect a child's development—brain injuries, diseases, family conflict and divorce, peer problems—can also have very different consequences, depending on the person's age. For example, divorce generally affects the well-being of children most when it happens in the school years; it tends to have fewer harmful consequences when it occurs in the preschool or college years (Amato & Keith, 1991).

By themselves, most circumstances that affect the development of a psychological disorder (with the exception of disorders known to be caused by specific factors, such as genetic abnormalities) have only limited influence. Such adverse circumstances are powerful *only* when they act together to affect important relationships and when their timing is taken into account. Again, parental conflict and divorce will have very different consequences for different children, depending on when they occur in the child's life, for how long they occur, and what other circumstances put the child at risk for (or protect the child from) behavioral or emotional problems (Katz & Gottman, 1993).

Transactions and their timing define the unique developmental trajectory of every human being. *This trajectory is probabilistic in nature.* It does not have force of destiny. Biology or society cannot alone determine what a person will become. Developmental trajectories predict probable, but not certain, outcomes.

To sum up, the disorders you will learn about in this book are more than individual deficits or dysfunctions. Rather, they are the observable manifestations, at a given point in time, of a child or adolescent's "best" adaptation to biological or environmental conditions or circumstances that are less than optimal. In other words, *we believe that all children and adolescents strive to adapt and function to the best of their abilities, but that in certain circumstances some of these attempts fall short of what is required.* These circumstances can be primarily biological, as in many forms of mental retardation, in pervasive developmental disorders such as autism, and in childhood-onset schizophrenia (see Chapters 3, 4, and 5). Or they can be primarily environmental, as is the case, for example, in oppositional defiant disorder, conduct disorder, and

FIGURE 1.3   *Schematic Illustration of the Principles of Equifinality and Multifinality.* The same individual characteristics or life circumstances rarely have the same effects on developing children. Different causes may have the same consequence for development, and the same cause may have different consequences. Therefore, children may have acquired the same psychological disorder for a variety of reasons, and the same set of circumstances may lead to different disorders or to no disorder at all.

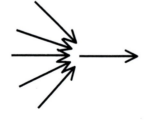

Equifinality:
Different causes can have the same consequence

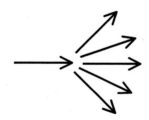

Multifinality:
The same cause can have different consequences

eating disorders (see Chapters 8 and 11). However, in all cases, biological and environmental circumstances are so closely intertwined that it makes little sense to try to separate them—a point to which we will return in Chapter 2 (see Box 2.1).

Organization of Each Chapter

To facilitate learning, and to make the information we provide easy to locate and follow, we have organized each chapter in the same way. Specifically, each chapter presents a particular disorder (or several related disorders) on the basis of the diagnostic criteria used to define it and of the empirical data available to describe its key characteristics. For each disorder, the DSM-IV-TR diagnostic criteria are presented and critically evaluated. The comorbidity, epidemiology, and development of the disorder are then described, as well as the factors most likely to account for its etiology. Finally, we discuss how the disorder is treated and how it may be prevented. When critical information about a particular condition is lacking or contradictory, we point to the challenges that researchers and clinicians face when they attempt to understand the disorder or help young people and their families on the basis of incomplete knowledge.

Table 1.1 outlines the organization of each chapter. This organization is designed to help answer the five fundamental questions we presented earlier in light of what is known today, as well as to make it easy for you to locate the same type of information across chapters. Each chapter also contains a number of case studies illustrating the complexity of each disorder. These studies—many of them drawn from our own clinical experience—are designed to make the descriptive material come alive, by showing that children and adolescents with major disorders are real, and by illustrating the devastating consequences that their problems often have at home, school, and beyond. More important, we hope that these studies will show you that young people who suffer from a psychological disorder can never be reduced to a set of diagnostic criteria, but are highly complex human beings.

At the end of each chapter, you will find Web sites that provide additional information about each disorder, both from a scientific and a personal perspective. For more information, we strongly encourage you to visit your library to obtain other references we cite in the text. We also invite you to go on the Internet for the latest research findings about the disorders we cover, and for links to children and families, resources, discussion groups, and more. We have listed major sites only, such as those of research universities and of national and international associations offering information or advocating for the rights of children and adolescents with psychological disorders. However,

TABLE 1.1   *Organization of Chapters in This Book*

Key Questions in Child Psychopathology	*Organization of Each Chapter*
What is the disorder, and what psychological problems co-occur with it?	Introduction
	Historical overview
	Definitions, diagnostic criteria, and major characteristics
	Diagnostic and developmental considerations (when appropriate)
	Empirical validity
	Associated characteristics; comorbidity
How many children/adolescents have the disorder?	Epidemiology
How does the disorder develop?	Developmental trajectories and prognosis
Where does the disorder come from?	Etiology
What can be done to treat or prevent the disorder?	Treatment and prevention

because the Internet changes at a rapid pace, we cannot guarantee that all the addresses we provide will be available when you attempt to connect. The Web is not monitored for its contents; so evaluate what you read and check it against other sources, to guard against unfounded claims.

Web Links

www.nimh.nih.gov (U.S. National Institute
    of Mental Health)
www.nichd.nih.gov (U.S. National Institute
    of Child Health and Human Development)
www.apa.org (American Psychological Association)

www.psychologicalscience.org (American
    Psychological Society)
www.srcd.org (Society for Research in Child
    Development)
www.s-r-a.org (Society for Research on Adolescence)

2

Theoretical Perspectives and Research Methods

Before I got married, I had six theories about bringing up children; now, I have six children and no theories.

—John Wilmot

Researchers and clinicians who study abnormal child and adolescent behavior share a twofold purpose: they want to understand it and, if possible, to modify or prevent it. Parents, teachers, and other adults who live and work with youth with psychological problems also share this purpose. Just like researchers, these adults often develop their own explanations for the behaviors they observe and often make multiple attempts to change them before seeking professional help. You will remember Rachel, the 9-year-old with violent tantrums whose case we presented at the beginning of Chapter 1. Here is what her mother had to say about how she explained and dealt with her daughter's tantrums:

Normally what I do, if the tantrum begins when she is downstairs with the family, is say, "Rachel, you're out of control. Go to your room please and shut the door until you get back in control." I hate to use her room as the bad place, but there is really no place else in the house that's appropriate. . . . And she cannot come down and re-engage until she is under control. And then when she comes back down, we usually don't talk

about the tantrum right away because she is still very emotional. So I will wait for a while until she is engaged in something else and then I'll say, "Rachel, we need to talk about what's just happened. You really got upset. Do you know why you were mad?" Like, I try to reason out why she threw it and kinda where we're at. . . .

One time I just got so upset with her and I said, "Rachel, you are such a problem to this family. You cause nothing but problems. The rest of us seem to be able to handle situations and you can't." . . . And I went too far with it. And I think that has probably stuck with her. Because I know if my mom, well my mom did say those things to me, so I am probably just doing what was done to me without even thinking about it. And then after it was all over, I just broke down and cried and I told my husband I should never have said that to her, because I heard those same words. I was always called a difficult child and now I am starting to put the same label on her. [Starts to cry softly.] Well, it's not easy. Because I realize now as a child I was not handled appropriately and I've talked about this at length in counseling. . . . I come from an alcoholic, abusive family. I still say some of the things [my parents] said to me and I still get stuck in that sometimes. It just makes me feel horrible. But at least I am doing something more constructive about it than they were able to do at that time. . . . I just want her to be happy.

Like Rachel's mother, most parents want their children to be happy and are deeply disturbed when their son or daughter struggles with significant psychological difficulties. For years, Rachel's mother had attempted to deal with her daughter's tantrums in different ways: by losing her own temper and becoming angry; by sending her to her room; or by giving her long, emotional lectures on family harmony—harmony missing in her own family as she grew up. However, these tactics rarely worked. Rachel liked her room and did not find it a punishment to spend time there alone. She had also learned to ignore her mother's lectures and to tune out her angry outbursts.

When she came to our clinic, Rachel's mother was largely blaming herself for her daughter's difficulties. She believed that, in spite of her best efforts, she was raising Rachel as poorly as her own mother had raised her. In short, parents have different explanations for their children's psychological problems, and they use these explanations to help them make sense of their children's behavior.

Like Rachel's mother, scientists attempting to understand abnormal child and adolescent behavior face an exceedingly difficult task. The field of abnormal child and adolescent psychology is littered with theories that once seemed to hold promise but have since been abandoned because they were not supported by scientific research and did not help children and families. Today, this field is no longer dominated by relatively narrow sets of explanatory principles. Instead, broad research perspectives that extend beyond a single theoretical viewpoint characterize the field. Dominant perspectives range from biological to psychological, social, and cultural ones, and are too broad to be integrated into a single theory. In other words, depending on their research training and interests, individual scientists tend to prefer one type of explanation over another. However, the field as a whole works to integrate these perspectives, because most researchers

and clinicians recognize that the problems they face are too complex to be explained by a single theory.

The Bioecological Model

Imagine that each child is at the center of interconnected circles of influence (see Figure 2.1). Urie Bronfenbrenner's **bioecological model** is similar to the biopsychosocial model and the multiaxial system of the DSM-IV-TR described in Chapter 1 (Bronfenbrenner, 1979, 1999). Both models emphasize the importance of recognizing multiple sources of influence on children's development and adaptation. The bioecological model provides a useful way of thinking about developmental psychopathology and the multiple sources of influence affecting human development, and about the different perspectives guiding research in abnormal psychology.

The *microsystem* includes the people and objects the child encounters in everyday life. At first, the child's main microsystem is the family, but with age this system expands to include the child's school, peers, and other activities outside the home.

The *mesosystem* is composed of the various interconnections within the microsystem. For example, a child who is exposed to adult conflict at home often has problems at school. Similarly, a child who is struggling academically or rejected by peers is often challenging at home.

The *exosystem* refers to the many social settings that influence the child, often indirectly. For example, children are influenced by their caregivers' relationships with extended family members, friends, and co-workers. Thus, Dumas (1986) found that, irrespective of how their children behaved, mothers of aggressive children were more likely to be harsh with them when they themselves had had a bad day outside the home than when they had had a good day. Children are also influenced by multiple aspects of their environment, such as neighborhood safety, access to health services, policing, and social and racial discrimination.

The attitudes, beliefs, and practices that are shared by the culture in which the child grows up make up the *macrosystem*. In Western societies, for example, the problems of children with learning disabilities

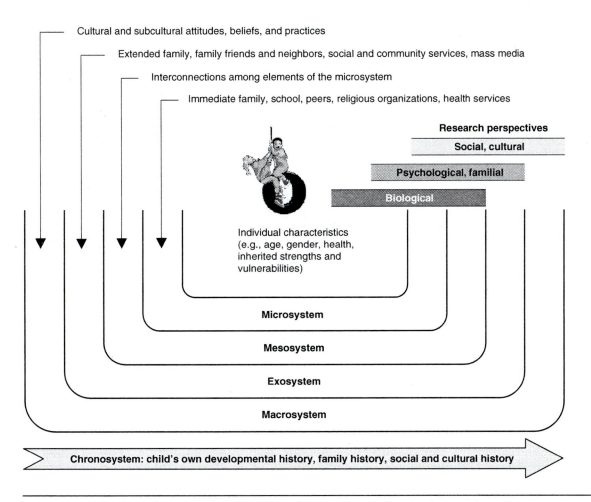

Cultural and subcultural attitudes, beliefs, and practices

Extended family, family friends and neighbors, social and community services, mass media

Interconnections among elements of the microsystem

Immediate family, school, peers, religious organizations, health services

Research perspectives

Social, cultural

Psychological, familial

Biological

Individual characteristics
(e.g., age, gender, health,
inherited strengths and
vulnerabilities)

Microsystem

Mesosystem

Exosystem

Macrosystem

Chronosystem: child's own developmental history, family history, social and cultural history

FIGURE 2.1 *The Bioecological Model of Child Development.* Proposed by developmental psychologist Urie Bronfenbrenner (1979, 1999), the bioecological model puts the child at the center of a set of nested transactional systems that shape all aspects of development—whether normal or dysfunctional.

often are compounded because the culture puts considerable emphasis on school success (see Chapter 6). Likewise, cultural pressures on adolescent girls to be thin have been implicated in the etiology of eating disorders (see Chapter 11).

All these nested systems are not static. They are part of a *chronosystem* and evolve with time. As a result, factors that are particularly influential at one point in development may no longer be important later. For example, as noted in Chapter 1, the impact of divorce is not the same at all phases of development. Similarly, major

historical events, such as wars and periods of economic depression or prosperity, can affect entire generations in lasting ways (Conger, Elder, Lorenz, Simons, & Whitbeck, 1994). There is little doubt that the tragedies of September 11, 2001, will have a profound impact on one or more generations of American youth, although the nature of that impact remains to be discovered.

This brief description of the bioecological model may inadvertently give the impression that the child at its center is a puppet, with external forces mostly beyond his or her control pulling the strings. This is certainly not the case. As Bronfenbrenner (1999) writes: "Human development takes place through processes of progressively more complex reciprocal interaction between an active, evolving biopsychological human organism and the persons, objects, and symbols in its immediate external environment" (p. 5). These processes are bioecological: they reflect individual as well as environmental factors. For example, a child's age, gender, physical appearance, temperament, and inherited strengths and vulnerabilities all play a role in development. Being male is a significant risk factor for conduct disorder, including serious and violent offending, whereas being female is an important risk factor for depressive disorder. And children who have a natural tendency to be fearful and shy are more likely to develop an anxiety disorder than boisterous children who always seek out stimulation and thrive on novelty. Furthermore, at any point in time, these characteristics are both a consequence of the child's development to date and a cause of development still to come.

The different research perspectives that scientists adopt today in their attempts to make sense of abnormal behavior overlap considerably with the systems of influence described in the bioecological model. We discuss these perspectives in the following sections.

The Biological Perspective

The **biological perspective** has its roots in biology and medicine. In its extreme form, it states that psychological disorders are diseases of the brain and the central nervous system. These diseases have distinct behavioral and emotional symptoms, just as physical diseases have physiological and biochemical symptoms. Few researchers adopt such a position, primarily because evidence shows that multiple factors are implicated in the etiology of most psychological conditions. However, many researchers take a less extreme stance by focusing on the genetic, neurochemical, and hormonal influences on brain development and behavior—without denying the existence of other etiological factors.

Brain Development

Contrary to widespread belief, the brain is not a sophisticated computing device in which countless physical and psychological characteristics are hard-wired at birth. Rather, the brain is a work in progress, thanks in large part to a unique feature known as **neural plasticity.** From its early embryonic beginnings, the brain relies heavily on an overabundance of nerve cells or neurons as it grows from a few undifferentiated cells to a highly complex organ with distinct structures and functions. In the first months of pregnancy, most neurons are "generic." They are not yet associated with specific structures or functions, and are highly malleable. Very rapidly, however, neurons become more and more specialized. This specialization is the outcome not only of the growth of myriads of interconnections among them, but also of considerable trimming or pruning of their overabundance. These processes are well advanced but by no means complete by the time of birth. The brain remains highly malleable or plastic throughout the life course, but especially in the early years. Nelson (1999) describes neural plasticity as a "subtle but orchestrated dance that occurs between the brain and the environment; specifically, it is the ability of the brain to be shaped by experience and, in turn, for this newly remodeled brain to facilitate the embrace of new experiences, which leads to further neural changes, *ad infinitum. . . .* Alas, this malleability is a two-edged sword, in that such changes can be both adaptive and maladaptive for the organism" (p. 42).

Evidence points to the role of experience in brain development, both before and after birth. Much of this evidence is based on animal studies, since it would be unethical to conduct brain experiments on humans. For example, rats taught to perform complex motor coordination tasks develop rich neural pathways in the area of the brain that controls motor movement. Similarly, rats or monkeys exposed to stressful circumstances before or after birth suffer from abnormal brain development (Nelson, 1999).

There are comparable findings in humans. For example, the brain region that controls the sense of touch is much more developed in musicians who play string instruments than in nonmusicians (Elbert, Pantev, Wienbruch, Rockstroh, & Taub, 1995; cited in Nelson, 1999). Likewise, smoking and drug abuse during pregnancy can severely disturb fetal development and have multiple, harmful consequences for brain functioning (Nordentoft et al., 1996). Causal links are more difficult to establish in other areas of development. However, evidence is growing that children who lack healthy relationships with trusted adults in early life suffer lasting harmful behavioral and emotional consequences, in part because of the effects of this uncontrollable stress on brain development (Schore, 1996). For example, child abuse is linked to elevated risk for major depression, probably because of the adverse effects of early trauma on brain structure and function (Kaufman, Plotsky, Nemeroff, & Charney, 2000). Similarly, adults who developed posttraumatic stress disorder (PTSD) as a result of severe physical and/or sexual abuse in childhood have a smaller **hippocampus,** on average, than adults who were not abused (Bremner et al., 1997). (The hippocampus is a brain structure that plays a central role in learning, memory, and emotion regulation.) These findings do not establish causality. Nevertheless, it is more likely that chronic stress, fear, and helplessness associated with abuse lead to abnormal brain development than the other way around. It is indeed difficult to imagine how children with a small hippocampus would be more likely to be abused than their peers.

Neural plasticity does not imply that brain changes are possible at any developmental period and in all areas of functioning, but it demonstrates that brain development is much more flexible than commonly thought. More fundamentally, it shows that, from conception, biological or inherited characteristics are closely tied to experiences in the environment. In fact, they are so closely connected that any attempt to separate and oppose them—in terms of nature versus nurture or heredity versus environment—is futile. We will return to this essential point shortly.

Genetic Influences

> *Organisms do not simply adapt to . . . [their] environment; they create, destroy, modify, and internally transform aspects of the external world by their own life activities to make this environment. Just as there is no organism without an environment, so there is no environment without an organism.*
>
> —R. C. Lewontin, Steven Rose, and Leon Kamin

Genes are segments of DNA that produce proteins. These proteins control a host of biochemical processes responsible for the development and proper function-

ing of the entire organism. As you will see, genes are implicated in the etiology of many of the disorders we cover in this book. However, contrary to widespread belief, *genes do not determine any behavior directly.*

In December of 1994, the *International Herald Tribune* carried a front-page article reporting the discovery of a "renegade gene" said to be responsible for some forms of obesity. In the first paragraph, the journalist wrote: "Lending mighty support to the theory that fat people are not made but, rather, born that way, scientists have discovered a genetic mutation that is thought to be responsible for at least some types of obesity." The article went on to explain that, because of this mutation, the "body doesn't cry 'Enough!' at meals" (Dec. 2, 1994, pp. 3–4). This conception of genetic influences is not just naïve; it is wrong. None of your genes has ever made you think or feel in a particular way, or made you eat that second brownie you could have done without, because our genes do not control our behavior directly. Rather, they influence the development and functioning of our nervous system. In turn, this system affects the way we interact with and respond to our environment and the extent to which our behavior can be modified by environmental circumstances.

The influence of genes, therefore, is probabilistic. If genes could talk, their favorite word would be *maybe.* Genes establish ranges within which behavior can vary. However, within those ranges, they do not dictate how a person behaves. No one is destined to become overweight. However, some individuals are more likely to be overweight than others, in part because of the genes they have inherited. Their genes make them *vulnerable* to gain weight easily and, in some cases, to develop an eating disorder. But their genes do not dictate when, what, or how much they eat, or whether they will actually develop an eating disorder (see Chapter 11). Similarly, some children and adolescents are more likely to be hyperactive and impulsive because of their inherited disposition. But the way they behave at home and at school, and their chances of developing a psychological disorder, depend on a host of factors in addition to their genetic vulnerability (see Chapter 7).

Most genetic influences are **polygenic**—the result of multiple genes acting in concert. The subtle processes of polygenic inheritance are complex, in large part because their actions depend on the environment

BOX 2.1 • *Intelligence: The Futile Opposition of Nature and Nurture, Heredity and Environment*

In the long history of research on intelligence, countless scientists have sought to oppose nature and nurture, or heredity and environment, with the goal of establishing the relative importance of each in determining an individual's intelligence. Many of them find data that appear to fit nicely into an either-or approach to reality in the relatively new field of *human behavioral genetics*. Behavioral genetics research relies heavily on the concept of **heritability** to quantify how much observed differences between people—in intelligence, aggressiveness, fearfulness, and other such characteristics—can be attributed to genetic influences.

Large-scale longitudinal studies, some of which are still in progress, seek to establish the extent to which intelligence is an inherited characteristic (e.g., Plomin, Fulker, Corley, & DeFries, 1997). These studies show that approximately 50% to 70% of variations in human intelligence can be attributed to hereditary differences among people. From these figures, some researchers and countless consumers of research findings conclude that the remaining 30% to 50% can be attributed to environmental differences. At first glance, this conclusion seems logical. But it is wrong, for at least three reasons.

The first comes from the manner in which measures of heritability are commonly interpreted. When people hear that human intelligence has a heritability value ranging from 50% to 70%, most of them jump to the conclusion that human beings in general—and they in particular—owe half or more of their intelligence to the genes they inherited from their parents. This conclusion is wrong because *all measures of heritability are group, not individ-*

ual, measures: they specify the extent to which variations in a particular characteristic of a group of people can be explained by genetic differences among these people. Heritability measures are only relevant to differences *between* people. They say nothing about the extent to which an individual's intelligence or other personality characteristics reflect the contribution of his or her genes.

It would be foolish to deny that important personality characteristics have a strong genetic predisposition. But whether and in what way a genetic predisposition manifests itself depends to a large extent on the environment. A potential for intelligence, musical talent, or any other ability can become a reality only in a historical and social context.

In many respects, children construct their intelligence and other abilities; they do not simply inherit them as one might inherit a family fortune. The same is true of mental retardation (see Chapter 3). The intelligence of children with Down syndrome is limited for genetic reasons. However, the way in which children with the disorder develop and actualize their intellectual potential depends largely on the means placed at their disposal in the environment.

The second problem with either-or interpretations of heritability figures centers on the assumption of additivity. It is wrong to assume that the genetic and environmental variations that characterize a particular group can be summed to account for all group variations. Because of *statistical interaction effects,* genes and environments cannot be considered as two pieces of pie which, when put together, account for the entire pie, crumbs and all.

in which the child with specific inherited strengths and vulnerabilities grows up. We explore this important issue in Box 2.1, taking the development of intelligence as an example.

Genetic research has made considerable progress in recent decades, but it remains a very young science, especially when it comes to understanding behavioral and emotional problems in young people. Consequently, much current knowledge about genetic influences in abnormal child and adolescent psychology is indirect. It comes less from research on specific genes

than from studies of the families of affected youth. Twin, family aggregation, and adoption studies are common in this area.

Twin studies are designed to establish the extent to which the *monozygotic* or *identical* twins of children with a particular disorder have the disorder themselves. Because identical twins share the same genetic makeup, one would expect their **concordance rate** to be 100% if that disorder was caused exclusively by genetic factors. (Concordance rates are estimates of how often a disorder co-occurs in relatives such as parents

That is, genes and environments do not make separate, additive contributions to our development: they influence each other in complex—and poorly understood—ways that cannot be readily added.

Statistical interaction effects are common in the intelligence domain. On the one hand, intelligent parents pass on genes likely to favor intelligence to their children—a genetic effect. On the other, the same parents are likely to provide their children with stimulating environments in which they are exposed to materials and ideas that favor the development of their intelligence—an environmental effect. But *these two effects are never independent of each other.* They overlap because, from the vast array of stimulation they experience, intelligent children *actively* create for themselves environments that challenge and stimulate their abilities. For example, they ask endless questions, read, develop unusual hobbies or interests, and generally look for new experiences and for problems to solve. Two sisters may both be *exposed to* comparable environmental stimulation at home and school. However, the one who is genetically predisposed to be more intelligent will actually *experience* a different environment, because she will, among other things, ask more questions or choose to read more often than her sister will.

The third misunderstanding surrounding the concept of heritability is even more fundamental than the first two. It stems from the fact that *all* measures of heritability are relevant only to the specific environmental conditions in which they are taken and to the particular population on which they are calculated. If a measure of heritability is to have any meaning, there must be environmental variations (or else heritability equals 100%). Therefore, when you hear that variations in intelligence have a heritability value of approximately 50–70%, you are not learning a fact that is a defining feature of the human race and that will remain true forever. You are hearing figures that are inseparably bound to the context in which they were obtained. These figures are correct for a particular time, place, population, and method of measurement. They are correct as long as studies keep measuring intelligence in environments that vary to the same extent and with populations that are comparable, and that they use similar methods of measurement. If these conditions change—if, for example, one study is conducted on an upper-middle-class, professional, urban sample and another on a sample representative of people from a wide variety of backgrounds—measures of heritability may become higher or lower.

There is a paradox here: A measure meant to reflect heredity reflects also the environment in which it is taken! *Just when we thought we were inside (in nature), we're outside (in nurture), and the simplistic safety of either-or thinking is slipping away.* Like the two sides of a coin, nature and nurture have no separate existence, so that one cannot talk meaningfully about either of them by isolating it from the other. The key question in the field of human development in general, and of intelligence in particular, is not how much our characteristics owe to heredity and environment, but how these two sources of influence act in concert to contribute to the complex and ongoing development of each person.

---

or siblings.) Perfect concordance rates are almost nonexistent in psychology, since factors other than genetic ones also play important etiological roles. However, concordance rates for identical twins are often relatively high—higher than for *dizygotic* or *fraternal twins,* who are no more similar genetically than brothers or sisters. For example, concordance rates for schizophrenia are approximately two and a half to three times higher in identical than in fraternal twins, averaging 45–50% in the former and 15–20% in the latter (see Chapter 5).

Genetic influences can also be assessed by *family aggregation studies,* which compare prevalence rates of a disorder among relatives of affected children or adolescents (see Box 2.2, p. 32). Many such studies show that relatives are more likely than people in the general population to have the disorder or some of its symptoms; they also show that concordance rates are highest for relatives who are most closely related genetically. For example, first-degree relatives of persons with schizophrenia, such as the child of an affected parent, run a higher risk of developing the disorder and of developing

BOX 2.2 • *Studying Genetic Influences with Family Aggregation Methods: Asperger's Disorder in One Family*

Swedish researcher Christopher Gillberg (1991a) has explored the family trees of children with Asperger's disorder, a condition we will consider in Chapter 4. This disorder begins in early childhood and is characterized by serious disturbances in social interactions and by restricted patterns of interest or behavior that resemble autism. Unlike autism, however, the disorder does not involve language delays, mental retardation, or major problems in cognitive development and adaptive functioning.

In this family tree of a 6-year-old boy, you can see that Asperger's disorder, autism, and depression are clearly present in the child's immediate family. Therefore, as Gillberg notes, there may well be a genetic link among these conditions. Gillberg writes:

The boy's father has typical Asperger syndrome as manifested in the following features. He has a monotonous voice, a circumscribed interest in electronics (runs an electronics firm), and a sincere wish to understand other people but a total lack of intuition in this respect. He has no friends and adheres to a set of daily rituals. The failure to perform one of these rituals (for instance, while traveling) makes him extremely tense and he cannot sleep. . . . He always takes notes when he is listening to other people "in case something is missed." The father's brother also has many traits reminiscent of Asperger syndrome. . . . The boy's eleven-year-old brother is normal but has suffered from recurrent depression since the age of seven. Both parental grandparents suffered from severe recurrent depressions.

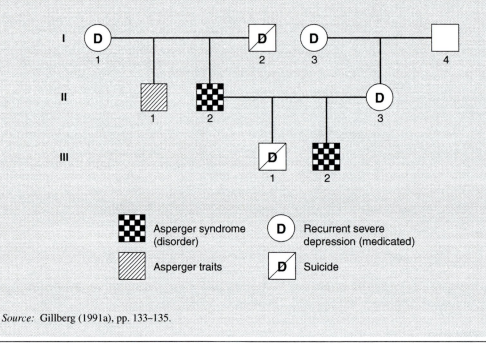

Source: Gillberg (1991a), pp. 133–135.

it at an earlier age than second- or third-degree relatives such as grandchildren or cousins (see Chapter 5).

Adoption studies provide a third set of methods to study genetic factors in abnormal psychology. In this

approach, researchers focus either on children with a particular disorder who have been adopted (and on their biological and adoptive siblings) or on their biological and adoptive parents. In both cases, if higher concordance rates for specific disorders are found in biological rather than adoptive relatives, those results can be interpreted as evidence of genetic influences. For example, adopted children who develop schizophrenia tend to have large percentages of biological, but not adoptive, relatives with the disorder (see Chapter 5). This approach, like the first two, has limitations that we will point out when we discuss specific disorders. However, when all these methods agree, they provide strong evidence for the importance of genetic factors in the etiology of a disorder.

Neurochemical Influences

The nervous system has been repeatedly implicated in the etiology of behavioral and emotional problems, in part because **neurotransmitters** in this system play a major role in the way that people feel and act. Neurotransmitters are naturally occurring chemicals in the body that are responsible for the transmission of neural impulses along the nerve axon and across the synapse to the next neuron (see Figure 2.2, p. 34). Evidence indicates that many disorders may be brought about or maintained by neurochemical imbalances. This evidence is strongest for adult disorders but is growing rapidly for many disorders of childhood and adolescence. Neurochemical imbalances can occur at the level of the presynaptic neuron, the synapse, or the postsynaptic neuron. For example, some neurons may produce too much or too little of a particular neurotransmitter, or have oversensitive or insensitive postsynaptic receptors. Alternatively, the manner in which neurotransmitters are processed in the synapse, and reabsorbed in part into the axon endings (a process known as reuptake), may be abnormal. In addition, neurons can change over time, often in a natural attempt to compensate for such dysfunctions. Thus, adapting to experience, postsynaptic receptors may become more or less sensitive to a particular neurotransmitter when too little or too much of it is being produced and released in the synapse.

Much remains to be learned about the role that neurotransmitters play in behavioral and emotional regulation. However, we know already that some of them are implicated in the etiology of several disorders or at least in their maintenance. These include:

- *Acetylcholine.* Besides its involvement in the control of many body systems and functions, acetylcholine plays an important role in learning, attention, and memory.
- *Dopamine.* This neurotransmitter inhibits the transmission of nerve impulses in several regions of the brain and plays an important function in reward-seeking behaviors. It has been studied in disorders such as schizophrenia, major depression, and attention deficit hyperactivity disorder. Dopamine is a chemical precursor of epinephrine and norepinephrine.
- *Gamma-amino-butyric acid (GABA).* GABA contributes to neural functioning by preventing neurons from firing. It is involved in the control of fear and other emotions and has a role in anxiety disorders.
- *Norepinephrine.* This chemical is a hormone produced in the adrenal glands and in some nerve cells, where it acts as a neurotransmitter. In the brain, it plays a central role in the processing of environmental information, especially by alerting the organism to danger and focusing attention. In the autonomic nervous system, it prepares the organism for "fight or flight" to cope with stressful demands or danger.
- *Serotonin.* This neurotransmitter acts to control behavioral and emotional expression. Along with norepinephrine, it probably plays a key role in several disorders, including mood, anxiety, and eating disorders.

The influence of these and other neurotransmitters is not invariably unidirectional; that is, although chemical imbalances can cause or help maintain behavioral and emotional problems, the reverse may also apply, since these processes are bidirectional. Psychologically stressful or traumatic circumstances can provoke lasting imbalances in neurochemical regulation and adversely influence brain development and functioning.

Hormonal Influences

Closely related to neurochemical influences are a host of hormonal influences. **Hormones,** which are

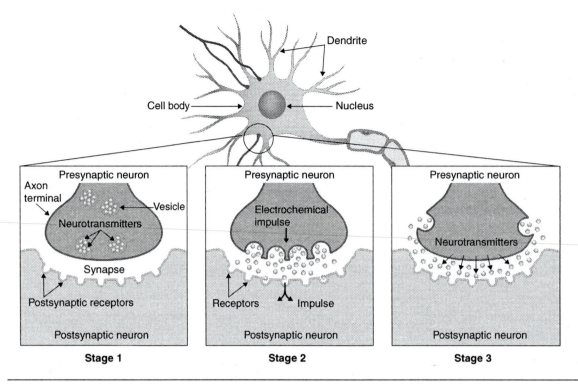

FIGURE 2.2 *Schematic Representation of the Process of Neural Transmission.* The process of neural transmission is both electrical and chemical. A neuron consists of a cell body and an axon. Nerve impulses, which are essentially electrical, travel from the cell body along the axon. The end of each axon branches out like a tree to connect the *presynaptic* neurons to other, *postsynaptic* neurons. Neural transmission between neurons takes place at the level of the *synapse,* a small gap separating the axon endings of one neuron from the dendrites or cell body of other neurons. Neurotransmitters, the biochemical compounds responsible for this transmission, are stored in small vesicles at the end of the axon (stage 1). Nerve impulses release these neurotransmitters into the synapse, causing the next neurons to fire or inhibit their firing (stage 2). Once released in the synapse, neurotransmitters are either destroyed or reabsorbed in part into the axon endings. This reabsorption is known as reuptake (stage 3).

produced by endocrine glands, travel in the bloodstream and influence the development and functioning of the entire organism. Not surprisingly, hormonal imbalances play a role in some psychological disorders. For example, **testosterone** controls the development of male sex organs, facial hair, deepening of the voice, and other masculine characteristics; and **cortisol** enables the organism to manage stress effectively. High levels of testosterone and low levels of cortisol have been associated with aggression, dominance, and violence in adults and children

(Bernhardt, 1997; McBurnett, Lahey, Rathouz, & Loeber, 2000).

Of particular interest in abnormal child and adolescent psychology are hormones produced by the pituitary gland, which lies within the brain, and by the adrenal glands, which sit on top of the kidneys. The pituitary gland provides an essential bridge between the brain and the endocrine system, because this gland is controlled by the hypothalamus in the brain, and in turn controls the activity of the other endocrine glands. The adrenal glands produce norepinephrine and cortisol, which alert the organism to danger and prepare it for "fight or flight." Together, these structures—hypothalamus, pituitary gland, and adrenal glands—form the **hypothalamic-pituitary-adrenal axis,** or HPA axis. This hormonal system plays a major role in behavioral and emotional regulation and, by implication, in many psychological disorders.

The Psychological Perspective

Children are likely to live up to what you believe in them.

—Lady Bird Johnson

Few of the biological factors have a direct, readily observable impact on normal or abnormal functioning. Rather, they influence the manner in which children and adolescents act, feel, and think; in turn, biological factors are influenced by these psychological processes. The **psychological perspective** focuses on the influences of behavioral, emotional, and cognitive factors on the development and maintenance of specific disorders; the influences of psychological processes within the family and the peer group; and the possibility of changing these processes in order to treat youths with psychological disorders or to prevent some of these disorders from developing in the first place.

Temperamental Differences

Studies of **constitutional factors** provide an important bridge between the biological and the psychological perspectives. Constitutional factors are characteristics that are inherited or that develop very early, often in the course of pregnancy. For example, not all children are born with the physical constitution necessary to be Olympic athletes; they are born with varying degrees of physical ability, and some face major physical challenges such as a physical disability or a chronic disease (Belfer & Munir, 1997; see Chapter 13). Early on, children also exhibit temperamental dispositions or early personality characteristics. **Temperament** reflects "constitutionally based individual differences in reactivity and self-regulation" (Rothbart & Bates,

1998, p. 109). Temperamental dispositions, unlike the normal phases of development, remain fairly consistent across situations and are stable over time. Thus, although preschoolers often are afraid of dogs or of imaginary creatures lurking in the dark, some children tend to be fearful in many situations and remain fearful as they grow up. Their fearfulness is assumed to be a major temperamental characteristic, rather than reflecting normal—and passing—phases of development.

The methods used to measure temperament differ, as do the samples of children studied. The various questionnaires and direct observations do not always yield the same dimensions; even when they do, they cannot summarize all the temperamental characteristics of infants, preschoolers, older children, and adolescents (Rothbart & Bates, 1998). A review of infant studies, however, identified six dimensions of temperament, which overlap with those found in studies of older samples (Rothbart & Mauro, 1990):

- *Fearful distress:* the infant's adaptability and tendency to approach or withdraw in novel situations.
- *Irritable distress:* the infant's tendency to be fussy, irritable, or demanding, and to react angrily when restrained or frustrated.
- *Positive affect:* the infant's cooperativeness and readiness to smile and laugh.
- *Activity level:* the infant's tendency to be active and to take the initiative in different situations or to remain passive.
- *Attention span/persistence:* the infant's ability to show interest, to remain attentive, and to persist in different activities.
- *Rhythmicity:* the extent to which the infant is predictable and has a predictable schedule for activities such as eating and sleeping.

Temperamental differences are of considerable interest for at least three reasons. First, they are reflected in the way in which children and adolescents learn to control their behavior and to express their emotions. Second, these differences predict the appearance of a variety of psychological disorders. Third, research findings show that these differences can be related to

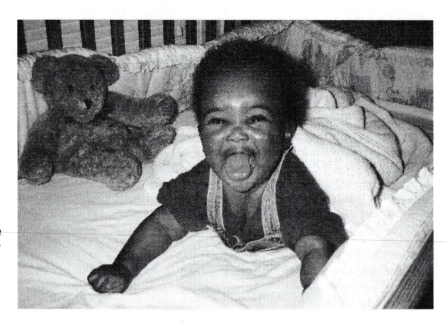

From a very young age, children display differences in their temperamental characteristics. Some have a happy disposition that may shield them to some extent from stressful life events, whereas others have a more difficult disposition that may make them vulnerable to psychological disorders.

some of the biological processes discussed earlier. We consider each of these issues next.

Behavioral and Emotional Regulation

The influence of temperamental characteristics is in many ways similar to that of genes: it is probabilistic rather than deterministic. In other words, temperamental characteristics make children more or less *susceptible* to displaying specific behavioral and emotional reactions, but they do not cause these reactions directly. This susceptibility has at least two facets. First, children differ in the *threshold* needed to elicit a particular behavioral or emotional reaction. Second, once that threshold has been exceeded, they differ in the *intensity and duration* of their reaction. For example, temperamentally fearful children show signs of fear and anxiety in situations where their peers do not show these signs. In addition, these children express their fearfulness in different ways. Some have relatively mild reactions of short duration, whereas others become extremely disturbed and remain agitated for a long time.

How can we account for such important differences? Several theories have been proposed. One of the most influential is that of British researcher Jef-

frey Gray (e.g., 1987). Originally developed to account for the role of emotions in anxiety disorders, Gray's theory assumes that children's reactions in social, emotional, and instrumental situations reflect the activity of three fundamental emotion systems: a **behavioral approach or activation system,** a **behavioral inhibition system,** and a nonspecific arousal or fight/flight system. Gray has shown that these systems have neurobiological bases that overlap with the HPA axis described earlier. The first two are of greatest importance here, because they contribute to the development of various disorders.

The behavioral approach or activation system is a reward system that plays a major role in purposeful activity—the tendency to approach and interact with the environment, especially to seek and respond to positive stimuli and situations. Impelled by this activation system, some children will seek immediate reinforcement in spite of possible negative consequences such as failure, punishment, or social disapproval. This system is associated with brain structures such as the hypothalamus and with neurotransmitters such as dopamine and norepinephrine.

The behavioral inhibition system is a threat or punishment system. It enables people to stop what they are doing, to pay attention to their surroundings, and to plan their behavior in light of what is happening around them. It allows children to control what they say and do in familiar circumstances, and thus to avoid acting in ways that they may later regret. It also allows them to avoid novel or unfamiliar situations or to approach them with considerable care and necessary caution. Behavioral inhibition is associated with brain structures such as the reticular activating system and the hippocampus, and with neurotransmitters such as serotonin and norepinephrine.

The way in which children behave in the presence of possible rewards or punishments is assumed to reflect the functioning of the activation and inhibition systems (Gray, 1994). Because of individual differences in these two systems, the same rewards will be more attractive to some children than to others, and the same punishments or threats will inhibit some children more readily than others (Gray, 1994). Generally, children with a relatively strong behavioral activation system are likely to be outgoing and, at times, impulsive, as they seek rewards and readily respond to them. In extreme cases, some of these children may display high levels of motor activity and irritability, lack of tolerance for frustration, and difficulties in regulating their emotions. With time, they may become disobedient and aggressive, and develop one or more disruptive behavior disorders, such as attention deficit hyperactivity disorder (ADHD), oppositional defiant disorder, or conduct disorder. Such disorders are most likely to occur when other developmental and environmental risk factors in the family and beyond are present. The following case illustrates some of the behavioral and emotional difficulties of children with ADHD in the presence of attractive rewards.

Kathy is 10. Her mother complains that Kathy never stops talking, even when talking gets her in trouble. For example, on their way to a therapy session, mother and daughter stopped at a mall to pick up a gift for an upcoming birthday party. While they were shopping, Kathy asked her mother for a new CD. Her mother refused, explaining to Kathy that she would have to wait for her own birthday. When they arrived at our clinic almost two hours later, Kathy was still talking about the CD, alternatively asking, begging, and demanding *that her mother buy it. Visibly upset, her mother told her in front of the therapist that she would not watch her favorite TV show that evening. As Kathy kept insisting, her mother finally lost her temper and told her rudely to "shut up!"*

Like Kathy, children with ADHD talk at times almost incessantly, even when they have lost or angered their audience; or they move or walk around, even when they have been asked repeatedly to sit still. As you will see in Chapter 7, several theorists attribute the development of ADHD in part to an overactive behavioral activation system.

In contrast to children with a very active activation system, children with a strong behavioral inhibition system have a tendency to be cautious. They work hard to minimize the likelihood of negative events and become easily tense and anxious. Some are particularly fearful and react very negatively to novel, unfamiliar, or unpredictable situations, thus running the risk of developing symptoms of anxiety or an anxiety disorder. Again, such symptoms are especially likely to develop when other risk factors are present—for example, when a child's parents become overprotective and try to shield her against potentially stressful situations. In Chapter 10, we describe Joelle, an 8-year-old child who was pathologically afraid of thunder and lightning. Retrospective accounts of her behavior in infancy and early childhood suggest that she was very cautious and inhibited from an early age, and that her parents frequently reinforced her fearfulness by trying to protect her instead of teaching her to overcome her fears. Over time, temperamental dispositions and parenting practices probably contributed to the development of her anxiety disorder.

Cognitive Influences

Children and adolescents also differ in their efforts to make sense of the world they live in. Within the psychological perspective, the **cognitive-behavioral approach** focuses on the ways that people interpret information about themselves, others, and their environment. Proponents of this approach assume that behavior is largely determined by cognitive processes. Assume, for example, that you learn that you performed poorly on an important exam. Your reaction to this information will probably determine how you approach the rest of the course. If you say to yourself, "Well, a little more studying and a little less partying is all I need to pull my grade up," you are much more likely to set yourself up for success than if you ruminate angrily on how stupid or unfair your professor is, or if you feel sorry for yourself and take your poor grade as evidence that you are dumb and will never get a good grade in the class. In either case, your thoughts will influence your behavior in that class, as well as your grade.

The cognitive-behavioral approach is influential in abnormal child and adolescent psychology for at least two reasons. First, research shows that youth with behavior and emotional problems often engage in dysfunctional forms of thinking that maintain or worsen their difficulties. Second, practitioners have used this approach successfully in treating various disorders, essentially by challenging problematic ways of processing information and replacing them with more adaptive thoughts. Several concepts have been developed to account for cognitive influences on behavior. Three of the most important ones are **attributions, negative automatic thoughts,** and **cognitive errors.** We will introduce them here briefly and return to them at greater length in specific chapters.

Attributions.   Attributions refer to the process of explaining events in causal terms. Human beings make countless attributions every day to make sense of their world. Causal attributions vary on a number of dimensions. For example, they can be:

- *External or internal:* "I failed the exam because it was hard" or "I failed the exam because I'm stupid."
- *Specific or global:* "The accident happened because she was driving too fast" or "The accident happened because all teenagers drive like maniacs."
- *Neutral or hostile:* "He pushed me because he wasn't looking" or "He pushed me because he was mad at me."

Attributions can have a significant impact on how a person feels and acts, and therefore can facilitate or hinder adaptive functioning. For example, a 10-year-old boy with conduct disorder (see Chapter 8) who came to our clinic made frequent hostile attributions about peers. He was particularly aggressive and hateful toward another boy and justified his attacks against him through hostile statements such as "All he gets he deserves, because all he does is just to p—— me off." Such attributions led to behavior that directly contributed to numerous fights between this boy and his peers.

Negative Automatic Thoughts.   The last time you lost your keys or locked yourself out of your car, you probably mumbled a few words that we cannot print here, or you blamed yourself for your misfortune by saying, "Am I stupid or what?" Cognitive-behavioral theorists believe that when negative thoughts such as these become habitual, they can lead to a psychological disorder. Aaron Beck (1967, 1999), one of the most influential cognitive theorists today, explains depression, anxiety, and aggression in such terms. For example, he believes that depression results from a cycle of negative automatic thoughts about *the self, the world,* and *the future.* These thoughts form what Beck calls a negative **cognitive triad.** This triad predisposes some people to depression and, once the disorder occurs, helps to maintain it because, whatever these people look at, all they see is grim and negative.

Negative automatic thoughts are often indicative of cognitive distortions, biases, or dysfunctions, and are regularly challenged in cognitive-behavioral treatments. Some therapists actually have lists of common cognitive distortions to help depressed people learn to identify their automatic thoughts. You will find examples from such a list in Box 2.3. Look at them. You are likely to find that you resort to some of these distortions at times, essentially because they affect all human beings to some extent—but usually not to the point of being associated with a psychological disorder.

Cognitive Errors.   Cognitive errors are mistaken beliefs that promote continued psychological problems because they are based on false, but unchallenged, negative predictions about potential threats and about one's ability to cope with them. Cognitive errors are frequent in youth with psychological disorders. We il-

BOX 2.3 • *Negative Automatic Thoughts*

Depressed youth are quick to engage in negative automatic thinking; that is, to make pessimistic or negative judgments about themselves and others. The following are examples of common cognitive distortions and of the negative thoughts that often accompany them. It is likely that most readers will recognize themselves here to some extent.

Cognitive distortions	Descriptions	Examples
All-or-nothing thinking	You look at everything as a total success or failure. You can see no middle ground.	"I got an 85 on my history test. I failed because I didn't get 100."
Overgeneralization	You view one bad situation or event as indicative of a pattern of failure.	"He didn't want to go out with me so no one ever will. I will die without ever having had a boyfriend."
Mental filter	The opposite of rose-colored glasses. You see the world through a negative mental filter and focus almost entirely on what is negative.	"What does it matter that I get good grades, have lots of friends, and have a great family. I am ugly and fat."
Jumping to conclusions (mind reading)	You think you know what others are thinking and assume that it is negative.	"I could just tell by the way she looked at me that she thought I was the biggest jerk she had ever met!"
"Should" statements	You have a list of things that "should be" and criticize yourself when they are not as they should be.	"I should always get 100% on tests because that is what smart people get."

Source: Table adapted from Burns (1989).

lustrate some of them here with research conducted with highly anxious children.

Children who worry a lot often see danger where average children see fun, excitement, or a challenge to be overcome. That is what investigators showed in an ingenious study that compared school-age children with high levels of social anxiety to nonanxious peers (Muris, Merckelbach, & Damsma, 2000). Working with the children individually, the researchers read them short stories and asked them to rate how scary each story was and how they would feel if they were in the same situation. All children heard seven stories. One was clearly threatening, but the others were ambiguous enough to leave considerable room for interpretation and reaction. Here are two of these stories:

Ambiguous story: Next week is your birthday and you want to organize a birthday party. You have made a list of children you want to invite. You plan to ask the children during break. The break starts. You walk toward the children you want to invite.

Threatening story: There is a new boy in your class. You know him from nursery school and you don't like him. In the past, he has bullied you once or twice. In class, he whispers: "You just wait! I'll get you later!" After school, he comes to you and pushes you (p. 358).

Not surprisingly, children in the high-anxiety group rated all the stories as more scary or threatening than their peers in the comparison group. For example, 54% of anxious children described the threatening story as scary, compared to 31% of nonanxious children. In addition, anxious children had a lower threshold for threat perception: they needed to hear fewer sentences from each story before rating it as scary.

Finally, compared to their average peers, anxious children saw themselves as more scared, more shy, more unaware of what to do, and more sure that the situation would end up badly in all the stories.

This study is one of a growing body of literature showing that highly anxious children have a strong tendency to *catastrophize*—that is, to make cognitive errors in which doom and gloom predominate and their odds of being able to cope are low (Bögels & Zigterman, 2000). These errors maintain and often aggravate their anxiety because they are based on mistaken predictions that the children never test—simply because they are too frightened to do so. Cognitive-behavioral treatments for anxious children usually challenge their cognitive errors, both directly and by placing these children in real or imaginary situations that are threatening—thereby showing them that their fears have no basis in reality and encouraging them to revise their mistaken predictions.

Family and Peer Influences

> *Call it a clan, call it a network, call it a tribe,*
> *call it a family. Whatever you call it, whoever*
> *you are, you need one.*
>
> —Jane Howard

Children and adolescents are also exposed to important psychological influences from family and peers. Nurturing families can often protect children who are at risk of developing psychological disorders because of temperamental characteristics or adverse life circumstances. In contrast, youth who grow up in families where they receive inadequate care or where adults struggle with depression, alcoholism, or other problems are at increased risk of developing one or more psychological disorders. The same is true of youth who are isolated or rejected by peers at school or in the community, or who have only a few friends who are themselves facing significant difficulties. We will discuss these sources of influence repeatedly throughout this text and will only illustrate some key concepts here.

Attachment.   **Attachment** refers to the close relationship or bond between a young child and his or her caregiver. **Attachment theory** was first proposed by

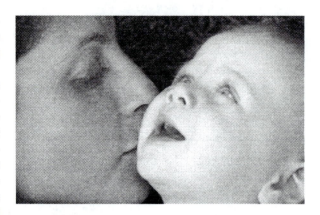

The attachment or bond between a young child and his or her primary caregiver plays an important role in how the child develops emotionally and adapts to the environment. It may also be a factor in how older children and adolescents think about their relationships with other people to whom they are close, and in the development of some psychological disorders.

the English psychiatrist John Bowlby (e.g., 1973). According to the theory, the quality of the relationship that young children develop with their mother or mother substitute plays a major role in determining their behavioral and emotional development. It serves also as a model or guide for other close relationships they will forge later in life.

Following Bowlby's work, Mary Ainsworth developed an observational procedure to assess the quality of attachment between children and their caregivers (Ainsworth, Blehar, Waters, & Wall, 1978). In this procedure, called the *Strange Situation,* toddlers are brought into a playroom with their mother and encouraged to play. Stressors are then added to the situation. First, a stranger—a female assistant—enters the room. Shortly afterward, the mother is called out of the room, leaving the child alone with the assistant. Finally, mother and child are reunited. The major behaviors of interest to attachment theorists are the child's ability to explore and play when the mother is in the room, the child's reaction to the mother's departure, and the child's reaction upon her return.

Numerous studies have shown that most young children can be classified into one of three main attachment patterns on the basis of the Strange Situation:

- *Secure attachment:* Securely attached children use their mother as a trusted base from which to explore their environment. They react cautiously when they first meet the stranger and show moderate anxiety when their mother leaves. However, they are easily comforted and calm down rapidly when she returns.

- *Insecure-ambivalent/resistant attachment:* Children in this group appear to be wary even when their mother is present. They are unlikely to explore their environment willingly, presumably because their anxiety level is high enough for them to feel that venturing away from their mother may be unsafe. They are usually upset by the presence of the stranger and react negatively to their mother's departure. However, these children are not immediately comforted when she returns and temporarily resist, rather than welcome, her affection.

- *Insecure-avoidant attachment:* Children in this last group often act as if they had no relationship with their mother; they actively ignore or avoid her. They do not react strongly to the arrival of the stranger and show little distress when they are separated from their mother. When the mother returns, these children usually deliberately avoid her by turning away or looking in another direction.

Attachment quality has been implicated in the etiology of a number of psychological disorders. Insecurely attached children, particularly ambivalent/resistant ones, may be vulnerable to anxiety disorder because their relationship with their primary caregiver gave them only limited opportunities to develop a sense of predictability and control over their environment (see Chapter 10). Conversely, securely attached children are likely to believe that they can predict and control what happens to them, because time and again their caregivers have been responsive to their needs. In particular, they have been comforted whenever they were scared, instead of being left alone to deal with overwhelming feelings of anxiety and distress.

In sum, attachment theory illustrates the role that early family influences may play in the development of psychological disorders. First, it suggests that an insecure attachment in early life may have adverse consequences that only become obvious later in childhood or adolescence. Second, it brings together family and cognitive influences by suggesting that an insecure attachment may contribute to psychological disorders by facilitating the development of cognitive errors; that is, by leading some children to believe that they have little or no control over their environment.

Parenting. The quality of a child's early attachments reflects to an important extent the quality of the **parenting** the child receives—that is, the attitudes, beliefs, and skills that parents bring to the childrearing task.

Diane Baumrind's (1967) pioneering work in this area has led to a useful distinction between *authoritative, authoritarian,* and *permissive* parenting practices. Authoritative parents are very accepting of their children and grant them increasing levels of autonomy as they grow up. However, they set clear and firm standards, expect their children to behave in mature ways, and impose consequences when their expectations are violated. In contrast, authoritarian parents impose their will in a strict, at times arbitrary, manner, and leave their children little freedom to question rules or negotiate around discipline issues. And permissive parents impose few clear limits and often leave their children wondering how they ought to behave in different situations.

In an ambitious program of research involving adolescents from multiple ethnic groups in the United States, Steinberg and colleagues have shown that the *prevalence* of authoritative parenting varies across groups. Specifically, it is most often found in European American, middle-class, two-parent families. However, the *effect* of authoritative parenting varies little across groups. Irrespective of ethnicity, class, or family composition, parents who are authoritative have adolescents who are better adjusted and more competent than their peers with authoritarian or permissive parents. They are confident in their abilities, competent in many different areas, and unlikely to have psychological difficulties or to get in trouble for school or conduct problems (Steinberg & Darling, 1994). Comparable findings have been reported in studies of younger children.

I take a very practical view of raising children. I put a sign in each of their rooms: "Checkout Time Is 18 years."

—Erma Bombeck

The beneficial effects of authoritative parenting may best be understood in transactional terms (see Chapter 1). Authoritative parents help their children become competent in many areas primarily because this form of parenting promotes effective communication in the entire family: parents communicate their rules and expectations clearly but encourage their children to voice their own opinions and preferences, and allow them at times to modify a parental decision through dialogue and negotiation (Lewis, 1981). Not surprisingly, parents who do not promote open communication in the family are often in conflict with their children. Ineffective parenting has been linked to a number of psychological disorders, especially oppositional defiant and conduct disorders (see Chapter 8). Gerald Patterson's **coercion theory** features prominently in this area (Patterson, 1982; Patterson, Reid, & Dishion, 1992). This theory states that, in some families, parents and children learn to influence each other mainly through the use of negative and coercive behaviors—such as provocation, disobedience, yelling, and criticism—rather than through dialogue. Over time, coercive exchanges teach children to become increasingly defiant and aggressive, and teach parents to be easily angered and to rely on more and more forceful but ineffective attempts at discipline (in extreme cases, to the point of physical abuse). Unfortunately, *when they continue, coercive exchanges end up trapping parents and children in a situation where everyone loses; parents have little or no authority and children develop serious behavior problems that often*

BOX 2.4 • *Coercion Theory and the Negative Reinforcement Trap*

According to coercion theory, parents and children *negatively reinforce* each other's undesirable behaviors, so that, over time, they will use such behaviors when they interact. To illustrate this negative reinforcement trap, imagine the following scene, which we borrow from Patterson and colleagues (1992):

Act 1. Timmy, age 9, is failing in school. It is 4 p.m. and, instead of doing his homework, Timmy is watching television, even though his parents have repeatedly told him that he had to do his homework before he could play or watch television.

Act 2. Mother enters and immediately criticizes Timmy for watching television. "How many times do I have to tell you to do your homework as soon as you get back from school? Turn off that TV right now!"

Act 3. Timmy punishes mother by counterattacking swiftly . . . and lying: "Be quiet, I want to watch the end of this show, it's funny. I don't have any homework anyway."

Act 4. Mother stops scolding but continues talking to Timmy. She repeats the homework rule but does not enforce it, either by turning the television off or by checking that Timmy does not have any homework. As soon as she stops scolding, Timmy stops arguing also and watches the end of his show quietly.

The learning process underlying this encounter is one of negative reinforcement: Timmy is negatively reinforced for talking back and lying, since his mother drops her command and allows him to continue doing what he is doing as soon as he argues. Likewise, his mother is negatively reinforced for dropping her command because Timmy becomes much more pleasant as soon as he gets his own way. When similar encounters take place repeatedly in a family, parents and children learn to control each other with increasing levels of arguing, criticism, and rudeness. Furthermore, the issues that lead to family conflict are not addressed and, consequently, worsen over time. In this example, not only did Timmy and his mother reinforce each other's negative behavior, but the issue that led to their confrontation—homework—was left unresolved, thus contributing further to Timmy's school problems.

have detrimental repercussions beyond the family (see Box 2.4).

There is considerable support for coercion theory and, more generally, for the role that ineffective parenting plays in escalating child behavior problems. For example, parents of children referred for treatment because of oppositional and aggressive conduct are more critical, less positive in their interactions with their children, less involved in monitoring their children's behavior, and, paradoxically, more permissive than parents of average children (Patterson et al., 1992). Similarly, children raised with ineffective, inconsistent discipline are more likely to develop serious behavior problems than their peers who grow up exposed to effective discipline (Bates, Pettit, Dodge, & Ridge, 1998). Therefore, treatment programs for children who are oppositional and aggressive (see Chapter 8) are most effective when they also train parents to use firm but noncoercive discipline.

> *Experts say you should never hit your children in anger. When is a good time? When you're feeling festive?*
>
> —Roseanne Barr

Although parents exercise considerable influence on their children, especially when they are young, influence is not a one-way street, going only from parent to child. Rather, parenting largely reflects the quality of the parent-child relationship. In this perspective, many of the behavioral and emotional problems that put children at risk of developing a psychological disorder are best conceived of in terms of **relationship stress** (Dumas & LaFreniere, 1993). This concept reflects the fact that many of the disorders we present in

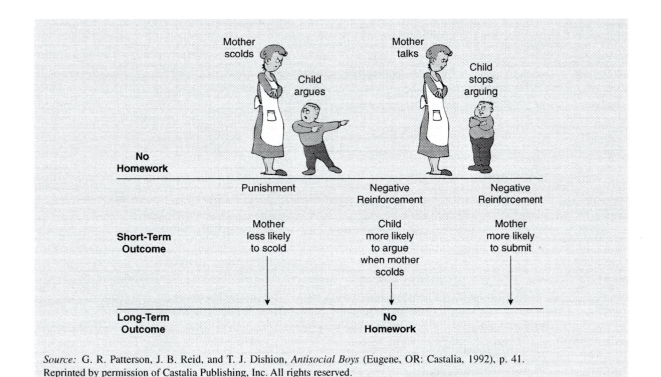

this text are not limited solely to the children and adolescents they affect. Rather, they occur in families in which adults and children often have chronic relationship problems.

Relationship stress was aptly illustrated in a study in which researchers invited mothers and their preschool children to complete a game-like task and observed their interactions as they played (Dumas & LaFreniere, 1993). Some of the children had been rated as socially competent or average by their preschool teachers, whereas others had been rated as highly aggressive or highly anxious. Results showed that mothers of aggressive children were relatively positive but inconsistent with their children. In particular, they often ignored their children when they behaved well, but responded in positive ways to their inappropriate and coercive behaviors. However, this inconsistency appeared to be an attribute of the mother–child relationship more than of the mothers themselves, for *it was observed only when mothers played with their own children.* When they played the same game with a child they did not know (another aggressive child of the same age and gender), mothers of aggressive children were as positive and consistent as mothers of socially competent or average children.

In comparison, mothers of anxious children were often excessively controlling. They granted little autonomy to their preschoolers, expressed little affection toward them, and were quick to criticize rather than to praise them. However, here again, excessive control and lack of affection were characteristic of the mother–child relationship, for it was observed only when these mothers interacted with their own children. When they played with an anxious child they did not know, the same mothers behaved similarly to mothers of socially competent and average children. They were not overcontrolling and were very affectionate.

Peers.   From early childhood on, parents and other family members selectively encourage their children's friendships. They do so in two ways: directly, by facilitating some relationships and limiting others; and indirectly, by sharing beliefs and teaching values that steer their children toward peers who come from similar homes.

Friendship is the hardest thing in the world to explain. It's not something you learn in school. But if you haven't learned the meaning of friendship, you really haven't learned anything.

—Muhammad Ali

Peers exercise a major influence on developing children and adolescents. As with parents and other family members, this influence is a two-way street. In other words, young people are not passive recipients of peer modeling or pressure. Rather, they often resemble their peers, not only because they are influenced by them but also because they actively choose to associate with friends who have similar interests, values, and upbringing (Berndt, 1999). Such associations can promote social competence and adaptive functioning—for instance, when children who are interested in sports or the arts get together with like-minded friends. It can also contribute to the development of psychological disorders, as in the friendships that arise among antisocial youth (see Chapter 8).

The importance of considering family and peers as interrelated sources of influence is also evident when it comes to school success. Research shows that the family is most influential when it comes to young people's long-term educational goals, whereas peers exercise the strongest influence on their day-to-day behaviors in school. Not surprisingly, youth who are encouraged to succeed academically by both family and peers do better than those who receive encouragement from only one source. However, in the United States, peers have a stronger influence on African American and Hispanic American students than on European American students; and European American students are more likely than minority youth to receive academic encouragement from both family and peers. Specifically, although African American parents are as supportive of academic success as European American parents, their children are less likely to have peers who support the same goal. As a result, many African American youth "are caught in a bind between performing well in school and being popular among their peers" (Steinberg & Darling, 1994). This bind may, in turn, contribute to the development of disorders in some minority youth, although not enough research is available to support that conclusion.

Sociocultural Influences

Cross-cultural studies show that most child and adolescent disorders cannot be understood apart from the social, economic, and cultural context in which they are observed. For example, as Chapter 8 will show, neighborhoods have measurable effects on the way that caregivers raise their children, and on the nature and extent of peer influences. Briefly stated here, disruptive behavior problems—such as severe aggression and delinquency—are more frequent in urban than in rural environments, and tend to be concentrated in under-privileged neighborhoods where chronic social problems regularly disrupt the lives of children and families. Neighborhood characteristics also influence school achievement over and above the influence of family and peers (Steinberg & Darling, 1994).

Likewise, beliefs and expectations shared by members of different ethnic groups are influential throughout child and adolescent development, as are the cultural values of different ethnic groups. An awareness of cultural similarities and differences is therefore essential to a comprehensive understanding of psychological disorders in childhood and adolescence and to the development of effective treatment and prevention programs. For example, in a pioneering clinical research program, José Szapocznik and colleagues developed a brief family therapy approach to treat adolescents with severe disruptive behavior problems and their families. This program was developed and tested by Hispanic researchers working with Hispanic families living in Hispanic neighborhoods. It integrates cultural values and traditions, such as storytelling, with clinical principles of family therapy to promote positive change in ways that are consistent with the cultural background of the families served. Findings from this program are not only important to the development of effective services for Hispanic families. They are also informing professionals who work with families from other cultural backgrounds; and they are setting this approach on firm empirical ground while embracing rather than ignoring cultural diversity (Szapocznik & Williams, 2000).

Much remains to be learned in this area, since researchers and clinicians have been slow to integrate sociocultural factors at all stages of their work—from the description and diagnosis of specific disorders to their treatment and prevention. However, there is a growing awareness that the social, economic, and cultural context plays a major role in psychological disorders because it guides the experience and adaptation of all children who grow up in that context (Dumas, Rollock, Prinz, Hops, & Blechman, 1999).

Historical Influences

Most psychological disorders in youth cannot be fully understood without reference to the historical context in which they are observed. A good example of historical influences is found in research on antisocial behavior in young people, which has increased dramatically since the 1960s in most industrialized countries. Simply put, young people are, on average, more antisocial now than they were a few decades ago. Consequently, epidemiological data collected today are unlikely to correspond to similar data collected earlier, because of **cohort effects**—namely, effects that depend less on the nature of the disorder being studied than on the historical period in which a particular sample was recruited to study it (see Figure 2.3, p. 46). Cohort effects have been found in many other disorders. For example, eating disorders have increased dramatically in Western societies in the last decades also (see Chapter 11), as have some mood disorders (see Chapter 9).

Research Methods: Observation and Instrumentation

Observation

Human beings are keen observers of their surroundings. If you see a teenager with bright green hair, you are likely to take notice because her hair color is *abnormal*; that is, it is unexpected or surprising and outside the norm. The same is true if you walk into a kindergarten classroom and see a child sitting alone, looking withdrawn and unhappy. From what you know about young children and your culture's expectations about childhood, you probably believe that children should be happy. In both cases, you are likely to ask yourself why the child and the adolescent behave the

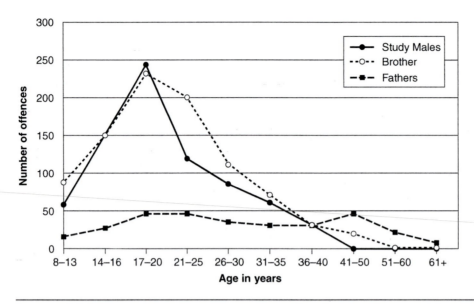

FIGURE 2.3 *Illustrating Cohort Effects by Comparing Trends in Criminal Behavior in Two Generations of Relatives.* In a study conducted in England, Farrington, Lambert, and West (1998) kept track of the criminal records of four hundred men from childhood to age 40, as well as of the records of their immediate family members. As this figure shows, offending peaked sharply in adolescence, but only in the youngest generation—namely, that of the study subjects and of their brothers. In their parents' generation, offending increased in adolescence also but tended to remain more constant overall. These intergenerational findings illustrate the importance of considering cohort effects when studying psychological disorders, because what is true of the developmental trajectories of disorders at one period of time may not be at another.

Source: Farrington et al. (1998), p. 93. Reprinted by permission.

way they do and to come up with different possible explanations.

The foundation of child and adolescent psychology—and all sciences—rests on careful observation. For example, in the 1950s Nathaniel Kleitman noticed that his infant daughter's eyelids moved rapidly when she was sleeping. On the basis of this observation, Kleitman and his research team began to conduct systematic observations to see whether all infants' eyelids moved when they slept (Kleitman, 1963). They found that the eyelids did move, but only during specific phases of sleep. This observation led to the formulation of precise **hypotheses** about the timing and role of eye movements in sleep. And testing of these hypotheses led to the development of considerable knowledge about brain activity during sleep and dreaming.

Hypothesis Testing. Hypotheses arise from observations. As in Kleitman's case, researchers often begin their work with a set of interesting or puzzling observations, and then generate hypotheses and design studies to test these observations. Hypothesis testing requires the systematic collection and analysis of data. Data analysis makes it possible to determine the extent to which the initial hypotheses are correct and to develop a theory, or modify an existing theory, to account for the findings. Invariably, this process continues with new observations and further hypothesis testing, as the work of science progresses.

Hypotheses do not come only from interesting observations. They also arise from existing theories. For example, on the basis of revictimization theory, Conner and Nilsen (2001) predicted that women who were abused as children and then revictimized as adults would think more often about suicide than women who had experienced only child abuse or adult victimization, but not both. To test this hypothesis, they collected data on women's histories of abuse and victimization, and on their thoughts about suicide. The data did not support the hypothesis; that is, thoughts about suicide were as common in women who had experienced either abuse or victimization as they were in women who were victimized as children and later revictimized as adults. These findings are being used to revise revictimization theory and to develop new hypotheses that will be subjected to further testing.

Replicability. Observation is too important to science to be left to chance. To yield scientifically useful data, observations must be conducted carefully and systematically, and they must be replicable. Scientists cannot attach much importance to findings that were observed only once or twice. For example, you may know two or three children who are doing well at home and school even though their parents are divorced; but that observation is not enough to establish that divorce has no impact on child development. Similarly, some caregivers might report that their children's behavioral and emotional problems improved dramatically after they began taking large doses of vitamins, but that observation also is not enough to make vitamins the treatment of choice for such problems. In these, as in all situations of relevance to abnormal psychology, one must observe children and adolescents in a variety of circumstances and compare their development with that of children who differ from them in systematic ways. For example, to study the effects of divorce on development, one would have to compare children from intact and divorced families and to systematically consider important variables—such as the children's gender, age, and ethnicity, as well as a host of individual and family characteristics—that might play a role in this area.

Instrumentation

The instruments available to researchers and clinicians in abnormal psychology include questionnaires, structured interviews, direct observation systems, and physiological measures, among others. These instruments are designed to yield detailed and accurate descriptions of the behavioral and emotional strengths and vulnerabilities of children and adolescents, or to assess the nature of their interactions with adults or peers. Researchers can then use these descriptions—for instance, those provided in the DSM classification system—to study specific disorders and to develop programs to treat or prevent them.

Proper instrumentation increases the validity and reliability of observations in research and clinical work. As we mentioned earlier, valid instruments adequately measure what they are designed to measure. For example, the aggression subscale of the *Child Behavior Checklist* (see Box 2.5, p. 48) is said to be valid because children scoring high on this measure are also identified as aggressive by other means, such as parental interviews, school observations, and police reports. Instruments must also be reliable—that is, lead to the same conclusion when they are used by different people or administered on different occasions. When administered correctly, the *Diagnostic Interview Schedule for Children* (see Box 2.6, p. 49) is reliable because trained interviewers who assess the same child usually arrive at the same diagnosis.

To increase the confidence one can place in a clinical assessment, professionals often use more than one instrument in a youth's evaluation. They also mix instruments that cover multiple areas of functioning (such as the *Child Behavior Checklist* or the *Diagnostic Interview Schedule for Children*) with instruments that focus more specifically on areas in which the child or adolescent appears to have problems (such as the *Children's Depression Inventory* or the *Anxiety Disorders Interview Schedule for Children*). Whenever possible, researchers and clinicians also like to observe the youth's behavior in different settings and to ask other persons to offer complementary perspectives on the youth's functioning. Instruments are often developed for that purpose. For example, the *Child Behavior Checklist* has parallel forms that can be completed by parents, teachers, and youth. Likewise, there are parental and child versions of the *Diagnostic Interview Schedule for Children*. Such instruments enable professionals to obtain information from different perspectives and to evaluate adjustment in different contexts—something that is often crucial, since children

BOX 2.5 • *Using Behavior Checklists: The* Child Behavior Checklist

Behavior checklists are rating scales used by researchers and clinicians to assess the frequency of naturally occurring clusters of behavior problems within a dimensional approach. The instrument most commonly used with children and adolescents is the *Child Behavior Checklist* or CBCL (Achenbach & Edelbrock, 1991). The CBCL consists of over 110 short, behavior-specific items that are rated as "not at all true," "somewhat true," or "always true" of a particular child or adolescent. Ratings can be provided—on separate forms—by parents, teachers, or the youth themselves (if they are 11 or older). By summing the responses of each informant and comparing them with the responses obtained from a large national sample of children and adolescents (or standardization sample), psychologists can identify youth whose behavior warrants clinical attention. Scores that are higher than those attained by 95% or 98% of youth in the standardization sample are generally considered to be indicative of the presence of significant behavioral or emotional problems.

The CBCL provides information on two broad dimensions of behavior: *externalizing* problems, which include symptoms of hyperactivity, opposition, aggression, and antisocial conduct; and *internalizing* problems, which include symptoms of depression, withdrawal, and anxiety. These scales, which were created by statistical analysis, summarize items that cluster together closely. For example, the *aggression* and *delinquency* scales include items such as:

Aggression	Disobedient at home
	Cruelty, bullying, or meanness to others
	Temper tantrums or hot temper
Delinquency	Lying or cheating
	Doesn't seem to feel guilty after misbehaving
	Steals outside the home
	Vandalism

The CBCL's dimensional approach allows clinicians and researchers to determine the overall nature and severity of a child or adolescent's symptoms in comparison to other youth of the same age and gender. Also, when information is gathered from multiple informants, such as child, teacher, and parents, the data collected can provide a rich perspective on the child's level of functioning and pattern of strengths and vulnerabilities in different contexts.

and adolescents who have difficulties in one setting, such as home or school, may function adequately elsewhere.

Research Methods: Descriptive and Experimental Studies

Descriptive Studies

As their name implies, **descriptive studies** are designed to provide careful, detailed descriptions of the characteristics of a phenomenon. In abnormal child and adolescent psychology, the most common forms of descriptive studies are surveys, case studies, and comparative studies.

Surveys. Surveys are one of the foundations of modern psychological research. Survey studies use questionnaires or interviews to collect information of relevance to a range of scientific questions. Some of the most common are epidemiological questions. For example, in Chapter 13 you will read about the work of Campo and colleagues, who surveyed parents of over 21,000 youth to study the frequency of unexplained physical symptoms in the general population (Campo, Jansen-McWilliams, Comer, & Kelleher, 1999). This study showed, among other things, that occasional aches and pains are very common in average children, as are doctors' visits for physical symptoms that have no obvious medical cause.

Case Studies. Case studies provide detailed, in-depth descriptions about an individual, family, or community. Case studies are best suited to gather information that cannot be collected with large groups. For example, much of the available information about children with early-onset schizophrenia comes from

BOX 2.6 • *Using Structured Interviews: The* Diagnostic Interview Schedule for Children

The growing use of developmentally sensitive, structured standardized interview schedules has greatly improved the quality of diagnostic work with children and adolescents in the past twenty years. Structured interviews such as the *Diagnostic Interview Schedule for Children* (DISC) provide researchers and clinicians with a set of standardized questions to arrive at a diagnosis. For each major disorder classified in the DSM-IV-TR, the DISC includes a series of questions that make it possible to determine whether a particular child has symptoms that are characteristic of that disorder. Questions are asked of the parent(s) in one interview and the child in a separate interview (if the child is 9 or older). Answers are scored according to specific coding rules and then compared with other available data to reach a diagnosis. This systematic form of interviewing requires specialized training on the part of researchers and clinicians but has been shown to improve greatly the validity and reliability of diagnostic work.

For example, to identify childhood-onset schizophrenia (see Chapter 5), the DISC has a series of questions that cover all the key symptoms of the disorder. Sample questions asked of parents include:

- In the last year . . . did [he/she] ever say that [he/she] saw something or someone that others who

were present could not see—that is, *had a vision when [he/she] was completely awake?*
- In the last year . . . did [he/she] ever say that [he/she] *heard things that other people couldn't hear,* such as a voice?
- In the last year . . . did [he/she] ever say that [he/she] *believed* that *someone was* plotting against [him/her] or *trying to hurt* [him/her] or poison [him/her]?
- In the last year . . . has [he/she] ever said that *[he/she] was being sent special messages* through television or the radio, or that the program had been arranged just for [him/her] alone?
- In the last year . . . has [he/she] ever said that *[he/she] was under the control of some power or force,* so that [his/her] actions and thoughts were not [his/her] own?
- In the last year . . . did [he/she] ever say that [he/she] was *bothered* by *strange smells around [him/her] that nobody else seemed* to be able *to smell,* perhaps even odors coming from [his/her] own body?

Source: National Institute of Mental Health, DISC Editorial Board (1998).

case studies (see Chapter 5). Because the disorder is rare, large samples of affected children are not readily available. Thus, researchers and clinicians working with youth with schizophrenia often write detailed descriptive narratives about their symptoms, behavior, and treatment, so that other professionals and families can learn from these examples. Unfortunately, case studies are limited because the data collected might not be representative of the general population. For instance, case studies may show that some children with schizophrenia respond well to a particular pharmacological intervention (medication). This finding is informative; but one cannot conclude from it that a majority of children with the disorder are likely to benefit from that intervention, because the children who received the medication were not compared with children who received a placebo or no medication at all. Nonetheless, information from case studies can reveal

patterns that can later be investigated in more costly and time-consuming experimental studies.

Comparative Studies. Researchers also can gather descriptive information by comparing groups of children and adolescents with different characteristics. Thus, youth who obtain elevated scores on measures of common problems—such as aggression, anxiety, depression, or impulsivity—are often compared with youth who obtain average or low scores on the same measures. Groups with known characteristics can also be compared on measures of child and adolescent functioning. Thus, researchers often ask whether findings that apply to one gender or to one ethnic group also apply to the other gender or to another ethnic group, or whether the characteristics of a particular disorder are the same at different ages or in different cultural contexts. For example, comparative research shows that the symptoms and prevalence of eating disorders differ in important ways across cultures (see Chapter 11).

Analyzing Descriptive Data.   Numerous methods have been developed to analyze descriptive data, several of which will be illustrated in later chapters. One of the most common is the correlational analysis. A **correlation** is a statistical estimate of the extent to which two variables are related or associated. Correlations can range from –1.0 to +1.0. The integer describes the degree of association, with 0 indicating no association and 1 a perfect association. The sign before the integer describes the direction of the association. *Positive correlations* indicate that both variables increase or decrease simultaneously. *Negative correlations* indicate that as one variable increases, the other decreases. Imagine a descriptive study in which researchers find a correlation of +0.25 between children's aggression and the amount of time they watch violent television programs. This number would mean that, on average, increases in the amount of time spent watching violent television tend to be associated with increases in aggressiveness. Conversely, a correlation of –0.25 would mean that, on average, increases in the amount of time spent watching television are associated with decreases in aggressiveness.

Correlational research is useful but limited by the fact that it cannot establish causation. Take the example of children's aggression and television-viewing habits. There is a high, positive correlation between these two variables (Huesmann, Eron, Lefkowitz, & Walder, 1992). However, that finding does not demonstrate that violent television shows cause children to become aggressive. The same correlation could also mean that children who tend to be aggressive seek out more violent shows. Alternatively, these two variables might be related because of a third variable not taken into account in the analysis. For example, ineffective parenting might allow some children to watch large amounts of television violence *and also* might contribute to aggression and other behavior problems. In other words, a significant correlation indicates simply that two variables are related. To determine causality, researchers would need to conduct experiments designed for that purpose, or they would

need to study variables repeatedly over time to see how they are related.

Experimental Studies

Experimental studies are designed to make causal interpretations of findings possible. Basically, experiments consist of manipulating one variable and measuring the effect of that manipulation on another variable. For instance, investigators have tried to determine whether parental involvement in therapy contributes to the effectiveness of a psychological intervention for adolescents with depression (Clarke, Rhode, Lewinsohn, Hops, & Seeley, 1999; see Chapter 9). They therefore set up an experiment in which they randomly assigned affected adolescents either to receive treatment with their parents or to receive treatment alone. These adolescents could choose to be part of the study, but they could not choose the experimental condition to which they would be assigned. That assignment was random. **Random assignment** is necessary in experimental studies to ensure as much as possible that the groups being compared are actually comparable. If the adolescents had been allowed to choose the condition in which they wanted to participate, the two groups might have differed in ways that could have significantly influenced the results. As we will discuss in greater detail in Chapter 9, the authors found that parental involvement did not improve or reduce the effectiveness of the intervention.

Although well-conducted experimental studies enable researchers to draw conclusions about the impact of one variable on another, the results of these studies are rarely final. Rather, a host of variables that could not be measured and controlled in the course of the study limit most experimental findings. For example, in the study of parental involvement in therapy, the researchers did not use a **representative sample** of the entire population of depressed adolescents. Rather, they used a sample of adolescents drawn from the geographical region where the study was conducted. They took care to ensure that their sample was as representative as possible, but other studies of the same kind will be necessary before one can safely conclude that parental involvement is not essential to the success of psychological interventions for adolescents with depression. In other words, because samples that are representative of an entire population are almost always impractical to obtain, researchers look for patterns of results across studies conducted in different geographical areas and with participants who vary in socioeconomic status, ethnicity, and other characteristics. When similar patterns emerge, increasing confidence can be placed in experimental results and, more broadly, in the scientific knowledge accumulated in a particular area of study.

Research Methods: Time Span of Inquiry

Whether descriptive or experimental in nature, studies are affected—and often limited—by the time span of inquiry selected by researchers. Because of cohort effects, findings obtained at one point in time do not necessarily apply at another. Similarly, in studies of children and adolescents, the timing and length of data collection can be crucial because each developmental stage brings its own demands and challenges. For example, to study the impact of divorce on child development, researchers must give careful consideration to the ages of the participants and to the length of time they will be evaluated. They can then decide whether to rely on longitudinal or cross-sectional designs.

Longitudinal Designs

Longitudinal studies follow and assess the same group of children repeatedly over time. For instance, in what are now classic studies, McCord and McCord (1959) followed a group of boys and their families to understand the development of crime and delinquency across generations; and Thomas and Chess (1977) studied the stability of temperamental characteristics during the developing years. Such studies make it possible to trace the developmental trajectories of participants as they grow up and to establish when, how, and for what reasons youth with problems begin to differ from their peers.

Although longitudinal research often results in important findings, it has two major drawbacks: cost and participant **attrition** (i.e., dropping out of the re-

search). Longitudinal studies can last for twenty years or more and are very costly. Significant costs arise from the need to keep track of youth and families year after year in order to follow their development over time. Careful tracking of participants in longitudinal research is designed to minimize attrition, since participants tend to drop out of any lengthy project over time, for various reasons: they move, become uninterested, or have significant changes in their lives that they do not wish to share with researchers. Any significant loss of participants can seriously undermine the most carefully conducted longitudinal study, because the participants who remain in the sample may be substantially different from those who cannot be located or who choose not to continue.

Cross-Sectional Designs

Child and adolescent researchers often rely on **cross-sectional studies** to avoid the drawbacks just mentioned. Cross-sectional studies compare two or more groups of youth who share similar characteristics but who are not of the same age. For example, a study may compare the social, emotional, and cognitive functioning of groups of children and adolescents with schizophrenia in order to sketch the developmental trajectory of the disorder and evaluate its impact on functioning over time. The obvious advantage of cross-sectional designs is that researchers do not have to wait for study participants to grow up to study their development. However, their major drawback is that any comparison of youth of different ages can be affected by the fact that they were not born at the same time and did not necessarily share the same developmental history. Thus, a cross-sectional study of children and adolescents with schizophrenia may yield results that are suggestive of important developmental changes in the disorder. However, competing explanations of the same results may need to be considered. For example, adolescents with schizophrenia may differ significantly from children with the disorder, less because of underlying developmental factors than because they have had the disorder and have taken medication to control their symptoms for a much longer period of time than younger participants (see Chapter 5).

Understanding Research Findings

There is nothing more deceptive than an obvious fact.

—Sir Arthur Conan Doyle

The ultimate purpose of studying abnormal child and adolescent psychology is to account for the origins of psychological disorders and to develop ways of treating or preventing them. Although considerable progress has been made in recent years, our understanding of psychological disorders remains limited, as does our ability to treat or prevent them, largely because the task is extremely challenging. Most of the disorders we will consider have multiple causes. Many of these causes are poorly understood and difficult to study, often because they are buried in the child's history or in the history of the child's family. In addition, the same causes do not always have the same effects on human behavior. For different reasons, some youth are better able to cope with adverse circumstances affecting their development than others, and treatment and prevention efforts work in some but not all cases.

Causality in Abnormal Child and Adolescent Psychology

To understand research findings in abnormal child and adolescent psychology, you must appreciate the nature of causality in this area. Researchers commonly distinguish between sufficient causes, necessary causes, and risk factors. *Sufficient causes* are biological or environmental factors that, when present, make the occurrence of a disorder unavoidable. Some chromosomal abnormalities invariably result in different forms of mental retardation, as do severe brain injuries brought about by physical abuse (see Chapter 3). *Necessary causes* are factors that must be present for a disorder to occur; however, necessary does not mean unavoidable. Alcohol consumption during pregnancy is a necessary cause of fetal alcohol syndrome but does not always cause it (see Chapter 3). Similarly, exposure to a traumatic event is necessary for posttraumatic stress disorder to develop but does not invariably lead to it (see Chapter 10). **Risk factors** are neither necessary nor sufficient for a disorder to occur but increase the probability that it will occur.

Sufficient and necessary causes are rare in abnormal psychology—largely because human behavior is complex and evolving, rather than the result of a limited number of causal factors, and also because biological and environmental variables do not all have the same effect on different individuals or at different points in development. Therefore, the field of abnormal child and adolescent psychology is characterized less by a small set of sufficient or necessary causes than by a large number of risk factors. Risk factors, which are found at all levels of the bioecological model, are events or circumstances that work in concert to hinder the child's development and result in dysfunction. Risk factors can be ongoing or historical. For example, parental divorce may contribute to a child's psychological difficulties immediately or several years after the event. Similarly, risk factors can act directly on the child or indirectly, such as through a caregiver, a community, or a culture. For example, family and peer pressures to be thin increase the risk of eating disorders in adolescence, as do other widely shared but unhealthy cultural ideals of beauty.

Researchers and clinicians seeking to understand and treat or prevent psychological disorders commonly account for the contribution of multiple risk factors within a **diathesis-stress model.** This model, which has many variants depending on the disorder and on the risk factors under consideration, assumes that a diathesis or vulnerability combines with stressful life circumstances to give rise to psychological dysfunction. For example, children who are fearful and easily startled from an early age run a greater risk than children without such a vulnerability of developing an anxiety disorder when faced with stressors over which they have little control (such as parental discord, school failure, or peer problems). Likewise, adolescents who are faced with normal developmental challenges are more likely to develop behavioral or emotional problems if they were abused or neglected as children than if they received adequate parenting. We will account for the etiology of many of the disorders we present in the following chapters within a diathesis-stress perspective.

Abnormal Child and Adolescent Psychology and the Nature of Scientific Inquiry

To understand research findings in abnormal child and adolescent psychology requires an appreciation of the nature of scientific inquiry. As in all fields of science, knowledge in abnormal psychology is gained through the cumulative efforts of numerous scientists conducting countless studies on similar topics. For at least three reasons, no single study provides definite or absolute knowledge about a disorder. First, psychological disorders have too many facets that cannot be studied in a single study. They can only become better known as the results of different studies are compared and accumulated, and as old theories are revised or discarded in light of new empirical findings. Second, disorders are evolving entities. What is known about them today may no longer be valid tomorrow, because the context in which they evolve is changing (see Figure 2.3). Third, all studies have limitations that must be taken into account when their findings are interpreted. For example, results obtained with children or adolescents from one ethnic or cultural group do not necessarily apply to children from another background. Likewise, results based on information provided by parents or teachers do not always correspond to results based on information gathered from peers or observers. We will come across these and other methodological limitations in our coverage of each disorder.

Cultural and Ethical Considerations

Because human behavior and welfare are at the heart of abnormal child and adolescent psychology, researchers and clinicians must be particularly sensitive to cultural and ethical issues—whether they work with young participants in a research study or with youth being treated for a psychological disorder. We will introduce these issues here and return to them at different points throughout the text.

Cultural Considerations

Researchers and clinicians generally recognize that most aspects of a child's behavior are significantly in-fluenced by the cultural context in which the child develops. However, surprisingly little is known about the role that cultural variables play in the epidemiology, development, and evolution of most psychological disorders. Studies of the same disorder in different countries are rare, as are comparative studies of different ethnic groups within the same country. Consequently, much of what can be said in this area remains general, and cultural comparisons should be made with great caution until more becomes known. Hasty statements do not advance knowledge or understanding. Rather, they promote stereotypical views of cultural groups and of child and adolescent members of these groups who have psychological disorders (Dumas, Rollock, Prinz, Hops, & Blechman, 1999).

Clinicians must keep cultural considerations in mind when they are assessing or treating youth from different backgrounds. For instance, a teacher may describe twin sisters who are refugees from a war-torn country as extremely shy and withdrawn because they rarely speak at school and avoid eye contact. Before the girls are labeled as anxious, however, information about their cultural background must be obtained from the family or members of the same culture and taken into account in the assessment. Perhaps what is regarded as shyness and withdrawal in a Western culture is seen as social competence and politeness in the girls' culture of origin. Alternatively, perhaps their behavior simply reflects the challenges associated with speaking a foreign language and adjusting to a new culture.

Ethical Considerations

As we noted earlier, there are ethical concerns—especially around the issue of consent for participation in research or intervention—that are particularly sensitive in child and adolescent research. For example, caregivers may be reluctant to have their child interviewed and may not consent to the process if they feel they have done something inappropriate or embarrassing as parents or, more simply, if they fear that their privacy will be threatened. Alternatively, adolescents may not want to report illegal activities or suicidal thoughts for fear that a researcher or clinician will see them as disruptive or dangerous and inform their caregivers.

More generally, even when children and families are willing to participate in research or intervention, professionals are under an ethical obligation to ensure that they are not coerced in any way to give their consent, that they are free to withdraw that consent at any time, and that they are always treated with respect. Furthermore, before they give their consent, children and families must be informed about the potential risks and benefits associated with the research or intervention in which they are asked to participate and about any payment they may receive. When children are too young to give their formal consent, a parent may do so on their behalf. It is common practice then to ask young children whether they are willing to perform the tasks associated with a particular research project, and to work with them only if they agree.

Ethical issues also arise in the design of research studies. As mentioned earlier, random assignment to conditions is an essential element of experiments set up to establish causality. However, to use extreme examples, a researcher cannot study the effects of poverty or maltreatment by randomly assigning one group of newborns to be raised in poverty and another in affluence, or one group of preschoolers to be physically or emotionally abused and another group to receive adequate parenting. Similar problems arise in some treatment studies. As you will see in Chapter 5, for example, the treatment of choice for youth with schizophrenia is medication. However, when someone is testing new drugs to reduce the symptoms of this devastating disorder, is it fair to give these drugs to one group of deeply disturbed youth but to withhold them from another in order to see whether decreases in symptoms are the result of the medication or simply of the passage of time? These are some of the questions researchers deal with every day as they try to untangle the complexity that is the hallmark of all psychological disorders and to develop effective ways of helping affected youth.

Web Links

www.mentalhealth.org (U.S. Department of Health and Human Services, Center for Mental Health Services Knowledge Exchange Network)

www.med.nyu.edu/psych/public.html (New York University's Department of Psychiatry, Psychiatry Information for the General Public)

www.aacap.org/web/aacap/info_families/index.htm (American Academy of Child and Adolescent Psychiatry, Facts for Families and Other Resources)

www.nami.org (National Alliance for the Mentally Ill)

www.aabt.org (Association for the Advancement of Behavior Therapy)

www.preventionresearch.org (Society for Prevention Research)

3

Mental Retardation

Our dignity is not in our ability but in our humanity.

Mental retardation is not a single condition with well-defined boundaries. Rather, it is a broad diagnostic category encompassing a wide variety of conditions that share three key features:

1. The child or adolescent's level of intellectual functioning is significantly below average.
2. The child or adolescent's adaptation across different life domains (e.g., social behavior, language, personal autonomy) and contexts (e.g., home and school) is impaired.
3. These deficits or impairments begin before age 18.

The first of these features is often considered the hallmark of mental retardation, but the second feature is equally important. Thus, before a child or adolescent is diagnosed as having mental retardation, he or she must not only function at an intellectual level significantly below that of average peers, but must also face significant difficulties in adjusting to the daily demands and expectations of home, school, or work. The third key feature—**age of onset** before 18—is included to distinguish mental retardation from other disorders, such as Alzheimer's disease, that lead to deficits in cognitive functioning and social adaptation but appear only in adulthood. In most cases, the difficulties of youth with mental retardation are obvious at birth, or in infancy or early childhood.

An Area Characterized by Diversity

Diversity is a key characteristic of mental retardation. It is most obvious in the area of adaptive functioning. Among other things, diversity is found in the ability of children and adolescents with mental retardation to function at home, school, or work; in the way that their difficulties develop over time; in the degree of autonomy they attain as they reach adulthood; and in the many physical and medical problems that can accompany their retardation. In none of these areas is there a standard outcome for individuals with mental retardation. As the famous Russian developmental psychologist L. S. Vygotsky (1931) remarked more than seventy years ago, to say that a child has mental retardation is equivalent to saying that the child is sick without specifying the nature of the disease.

The behaviors classified under the broad heading of mental retardation have multiple causes and different developmental trajectories. Broadly speaking, mental retardation implies that a child or adolescent's intellectual level and adaptive functioning are at the lower end of a wide-ranging continuum. At the lowest end are youth with severe or profound mental retardation. Typically, their condition is the result of abnormal brain development before birth or of a brain lesion following an infection or injury, and their development is limited in all areas of functioning. Specifically, their ability to learn is very limited, and they need constant, or almost constant, care and monitoring throughout their life.

In the middle of this continuum are children and adolescents with moderate mental retardation. They also need consistent care and monitoring. However, these youth are capable of acquiring a certain degree of personal autonomy and often play an active part in the social life of the people around them. They also are capable of learning to complete simple tasks and frequently work in a sheltered environment. Although some grow up to live relatively independent lives, most of them need considerable support. Genetic abnormalities (e.g., **Down syndrome, fragile X syndrome**) and prenatal damage (e.g., **fetal alcohol syndrome**) are common causes of this level of moderate retardation.

Finally, at the upper end of the continuum, a large number of children and adolescents with mild mental retardation can be found. These youth usually do not show alarming or even noticeable difficulties during the first years of life. Their mild mental retardation may become evident for the first time in elementary school, when their academic performance falls significantly below expectations. Their school years can also be accompanied by important behavioral problems. However, many of these youth grow up to function as independent adults and may no longer be considered to have mental retardation.

An Area Characterized by Controversy

Because mental retardation reflects a continuum of intellectual and adaptive functioning, in which the distinction between "average" and "below average" is not clear-cut, its scientific study has always been surrounded by heated social, political, and philosophical debates. What is intelligence? What is adaptation? What is normality? Who is well adapted and belongs to the group of people said to be intelligent and normal? And who is excluded? How should the excluded be treated? The lower end of the continuum that defines mental retardation is usually obvious in all social and cultural contexts. But the upper end, which is bounded by what a society considers "normal," is always much more difficult to establish. Some children have so many special needs that, irrespective of the context and the criteria used to define mental retardation, their condition is not a subject of controversy. More frequently, however, a child's functioning is limited only in specific contexts or when the child is expected to master certain skills, such as reading. To say, then, that the child has mental retardation is as much to pass a social judgment as to make a diagnosis of disorder. Consider the following example:

Tania did not appear to have any difficulties before she started school. Her preschool teachers did say that she was not as advanced as other children in identifying colors and numbers, but she participated fully in class and seemed happy. Tania began having problems in kindergarten. She did not learn to read or write the alphabet as quickly as her peers. In first grade, Tania's learning difficulties became more pronounced and her achievement fell rapidly behind that of her peers. A school psychologist evaluated her at the end of second grade and determined that she had mild mental retardation.

As this brief example shows, mental retardation is not exclusively a psychopathological phenomenon. It is also a social phenomenon that reflects, at the upper end of the continuum at least, the context in which a diagnosis is made and, more specifically:

- the criteria used to define intellectual and adaptive functioning in that context (e.g., school, professional, community, cultural);
- the services offered to children with mental retardation and their families;
- the acceptance of intellectual and behavioral differences;
- and the many social and economic inequalities that give some children more opportunities for help and encouragement, and thus for success, than others.

A child's difficulties are more likely to become a source of concern in a class where most children are making satisfactory progress than in one in which many are struggling. They are also more likely to be addressed adequately in a community that emphasizes the importance of educational achievement and offers services that the child's family can afford.

Well-validated and commonly used measures of intelligence include the *Wechsler Intelligence Scale for Children, Third Edition* (WISC-III; Wechsler, 1991), the *Stanford-Binet Intelligence Scale: Fourth Edition* (Stanford-Binet IV; Thorndike, Hagen, & Sattler, 1986), and the *Kaufman Assessment Battery for Children* (K-ABC; Kaufman & Kaufman, 1983). The criteria used to establish the threshold between low-average functioning and mental retardation on such measures have always been controversial (Scheerenberger, 1983). Most current definitions place the threshold at an **intelligence quotient** (IQ) of 70 or less on a measure where the average IQ is set at 100 and the standard deviation at 15. Statistically, if we assume that intelligence is normally distributed in the general population, a threshold score of 70 means that 2–3% of the population can be

expected to have mental retardation—when retardation is defined on the basis of IQ only (see Figure 3.1). As we will show later, large-scale community studies show that the actual figure is closer to 1–2% of the population (Kiely & Lubin, 1991; Zigler & Hodapp, 1986), highlighting the fact that IQ alone does not establish the presence of mental retardation (see Epidemiology).

Historical Overview

For centuries, people with mental retardation have been a source of considerable ambivalence. They often provoke fear and invite rejection simply because they are different. Their understanding is limited; their behavior is often considered inappropriate; and their physical appearance may be seen as repulsive. However, just as often, the very same differences invite concern, kindness, and care, if only to protect affected individuals from exploitation and abuse.

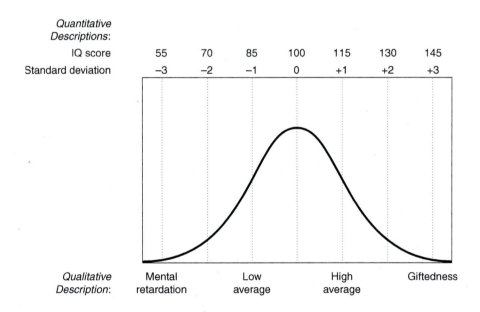

FIGURE 3.1 *Normal Curve Showing the Percentage of People in the General Population Who Would Be Expected to Have Mental Retardation on the Basis of IQ Alone.* When IQ scores are obtained for a large, random sample of the population in a given age group, scores can be expected to follow a normal, bell-shaped curve. This curve shows that approximately 2–3% of the sample will obtain IQ scores of 70 or below (on IQ tests in which the mean is set at 100 and the standard deviation at 15).

The first attempts to understand individual human differences from a scientific perspective came from the field of mental retardation. R. C. Scheerenberger has provided a detailed historical account of the origins and evolution of the different perspectives that have dominated this field (Scheerenberger, 1983; see also Hodapp & Zigler, 1995). The following overview is largely based on this work.

Mental Retardation as Divine Punishment

From the Middle Ages to the eighteenth century, mental retardation was generally viewed as a form of divine punishment. In that perspective, affected individuals were regarded as objects of God's wrath and were subjected to social condemnation, rejection, and mockery. Until almost the end of the eighteenth century, people with mental retardation were largely left to fend for themselves; or, in order to contain the risk of contamination (since mental retardation was regarded as morally and spiritually contagious), they were confined to prison-like asylums, where they were regularly exploited and abused. For example, in the 1700s, an anonymous visitor to such an asylum wrote:

> [People living in the hospital included the] foulest dregs of society . . . vicious persons of every kind, swindlers, defaulters, pickpockets, thieves, forgerers, pederasts, etc. It is distressing to see them side by side with the epileptics, imbeciles, lunatics, the aged, and infirm. . . . Five or six hundred inmates are packed together there (cited in Scheerenberger, 1983, p. 46).

This vocabulary is offensive today, but terms such as *feeble-minded, idiot, imbecile,* and *lunatic* were widespread at the time. The writings of that era make it clear that most authors used these terms descriptively, although it is hard to believe that even then terms such as these did not have a derogatory connotation.

People with mental retardation have not always been ridiculed and rejected. However, as we mentioned earlier, they have always been a source of considerable ambivalence. For centuries, many societies maintained courts where kings and queens had their jesters, and most villages had one or more idiots. These people of limited understanding were frequently cared for by others and generally treated humanely. Some of them were actually believed to have a clearness of vision that enabled them to understand and express major truths that people of greater intelligence were unable to see or did not have the courage to pronounce. This belief has survived to this day. For example, in the film *Forrest Gump,* Tom Hanks portrays a man of limited understanding who becomes a hero through his simple but clear vision of the world. Throughout the movie, his concrete view of the world and its problems is presumed to reflect a deep wisdom that those around him lack.

Mental Retardation as a Challenge to Educators and Reformers

The late eighteenth century brought about the American and French revolutions and, with them, a fundamental change in attitudes toward people with mental retardation. Based on the idea that all human beings are worthy of respect because they are human, these revolutions fostered a new social climate in which it was no longer acceptable to reject people just because they were different.

Examples of care and concern for people with mental retardation, especially children, abound in the first part of the nineteenth century. For instance, in Switzerland, Johann Jakob Guggenbühl opened the first facility dedicated to improving the general condition and education of children with mental retardation. A little later, Samuel Gridley Howe in Massachusetts and Hervey B. Wilbur in New York opened the first American institutions dedicated to improving the education and general condition of children with mental retardation (see Box 3.1). Although they advocated respect for people with mental retardation, as well as education and even social integration, many of these first undertakings failed. In the alternation between acceptance and rejection that mental retardation has always evoked, a very different perspective slowly replaced the idealism of many pioneers. By the middle of the nineteenth century, the focus of medical, social, and political thinkers had shifted from the care and education of persons with mental retardation to the perceived dangers they posed for society as a whole.

BOX 3.1 • *Two American Pioneers: Samuel Gridley Howe and Hervey B. Wilbur*

Samuel Gridley Howe was an American model of nineteenth-century progressive thought. The son of a successful businessman, Howe studied medicine at Harvard. On completing his degree, he became involved in the Greek civil war, as a soldier and a fund-raiser. After the war, he returned briefly to America, but was again drawn to Europe, this time to explore model schools for the blind. When he returned home, he petitioned the Massachusetts legislature to fund a residential school to educate the blind. He was very successful in teaching his students, even those who also had mental retardation. His success prompted him to petition the legislature once more to fund an additional school, this time wholly devoted to the care and education of children with mental retardation. In his 1848 message to the legislature, Howe wrote: "Not only would the idiots who should be received into it [the school] be improved in their bodily and mental condition . . . it would be demonstrated that no idiot need be confined or restrained by force, that the young can be trained for industry, order, and self-respect . . . and be made more of man and less of a brute by patience and kindness directed by energy and skill."

His success in this new endeavor equaled his earlier victories in educating the blind. Two years after the school began, he noted: "A great change has come over them [the children with mental retardation]. They have improved in health, strength, and activity of the body. . . . They can be governed without a blow or an unkind word. . . . They have learned their letters, and some of them, who were speechless . . . can read easy sentences and short stories."

Interestingly, neither Howe nor his contemporary Hervey Wilbur, another pioneer in the education of youth with below-average intellectual ability, believed that they could cure mental retardation. However, both men thought that children and adolescents could greatly profit from formal education and quality care. As Wilbur remarked in 1852: "We do not propose . . . to bring all forms of idiocy to the same standard of development . . . but rather to give to dormant faculties their greatest possible development, and to apply those awakened faculties to a useful purpose."

Source: Citations from Scheerenberger (1983), pp. 104, 120.

Mental Retardation and the Eugenics Movement

Scheerenberger (1983) reports that there were officially 9,334 persons with mental retardation in American institutions in 1890. By 1930, their number had risen to a staggering 68,305. Faced with the impossible challenge of helping so many people in meaningful ways, Western societies began looking on mental retardation as an incurable and dangerous condition. Specifically, around the 1850s it became commonly accepted that persons with mental retardation suffered from innate deficiencies and were for the most part uneducable. By the end of the nineteenth century, genetic theories in this area were often extreme. In many respectable scientific and political circles, mental retardation was commonly viewed as the outward expression of moral failure. This failure was attributed not to the children themselves but to their families. This position was based on the belief that moral shortcomings were transmitted in an inescap-

able fashion from one generation to the next and that society needed to take steps to protect itself against them. In 1912, Henry Goddard provided a classical example of this line of thought in his description of a family with mental retardation (see Box 3.2, pp. 60–61). A few years later, the famous psychologist Lewis Terman (1916) expressed similar feelings: "Not all criminals are feeble-minded, but all feeble-minded are at least potential criminals. . . . Moral judgment, . . . like any other higher thought process, is a function of intelligence. Morality cannot flower and fruit if intelligence remains infantile" (p. 11).

In its most benevolent form, this genetic perspective led to a strict, moralistic approach to mental retardation and justified the abusive treatment of many people in large institutions that resembled prisons more than schools or hospitals. In its most offensive form, this perspective encouraged systematic discrimination against individuals with mental retardation and their families, served as pseudo-scientific justification for

BOX 3.2 • *The Legend of the Kallikaks*

In 1912, Henry Goddard, psychologist and director of the prestigious Vineland Training School in New Jersey, published the story of a family he fictitiously named the Kallikaks. Goddard's work was presented as a "scientific study" of the transmission of what he called "feeble-mindedness" (what we now call mental retardation). He described the family line of one Martin Kallikak, a man who had fathered children by two different women. The first woman was a "feeble-minded girl" whom he had met in a tavern while he was a soldier; the second, a woman from a respectable family. In an accompanying genealogical chart, Goddard allegedly "proved" that the offspring

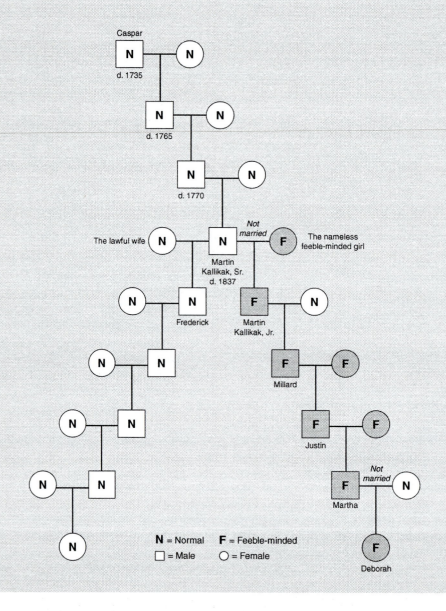

of the "nameless feeble-minded girl" tended to be feeble-minded, whereas the children of the "lawful wife" showed no such tendencies and were all upright citizens.

In the introduction to his book, Goddard acknowledged that his conclusions did "not seem scientifically warranted from the data." In fact, the data had been collected by a field worker who did not actually meet the majority of the descendents of the two women and had based many of her judgments on descriptions by third parties or on notes in "family bibles." These important facts did not prevent Goddard from concluding that "Feeble-mindedness is hereditary and transmitted as surely as any other character. . . . We cannot successfully cope with these conditions until we recognize feeble-mindedness

and its hereditary nature, recognize it early, and take care of it. In considering the question of care, segregation through colonization seems . . . to be a perfectly satisfactory method."

Though based on opinion rather than on scientific evidence, these conclusions were widely disseminated. In particular, they served as powerful arguments for the eugenics movement.

Source: Citations and figure from D. Kanner, *A History of the Care and Study of the Mentally Retarded* (Springfield, IL: Charles C. Thomas, 1964), pp. 132–133. Reprinted by courtesy of Charles C. Thomas, Publisher, Ltd.

---

blatant racism, and led to the excesses associated with the **eugenics** movement. The movement's stated goal was to improve the human race through selective breeding. Just as cows and other animals are bred for specific features, the movement claimed that humans with valued characteristics such as high intelligence must be encouraged to mate with "suitable" individuals to produce children endowed with similar characteristics. Members of the eugenics movement did not stop there, however. They wanted also to reduce, even prevent, breeding of individuals who had "undesirable" qualities; and they championed the systematic sterilization of persons with mental retardation and other "unsuitable" characteristics.

In many states, legislation requiring sterilization of persons with mental retardation was enacted and often zealously enforced (for instance, in California). Davies (1959) reports that, from 1907 to 1958, thirty states with such laws sterilized 31,038 persons— 10,990 men and 20,048 women—in most cases probably for mental retardation. Sterilization laws were repealed only a few decades ago.

Modern Perspectives

Obviously, not all people working in this field were so extreme, and careful research was conducted while debates and controversies about the nature of mental

retardation raged. The first thorough studies of the diverse manifestations of mental retardation were conducted in the latter part of the nineteenth century, just as education was becoming compulsory. Although school provides a place for many children to succeed academically and socially, an unintended consequence of compulsory education was the appearance of school failure. Much, if not all, of this failure was initially attributed to insufficient intellectual abilities on the part of some children. Consequently, schools began to search for a way to measure these abilities empirically.

This empirical approach got a major boost from a crisis in the Paris school system. At the beginning of the twentieth century, French educators decided to open special classes for children with limited intellectual abilities, in order to adapt the curriculum to their needs. However, they had no way of identifying these children objectively, aside from allowing them first to fail in a regular classroom. In 1905, Alfred Binet and his student Theodore Simon introduced the first quantitative method to measure intellectual functioning, the intelligence test. This test proved successful and rapidly became very popular. Since then, intelligence tests, along with measures of adaptive functioning, have become the major tools used to identify mental retardation and to define its various degrees of severity.

Definitions, Diagnostic Criteria, and Major Characteristics

Table 3.1 shows the DSM-IV-TR diagnostic criteria for mental retardation. As shown in Chapter 1, mental retardation is diagnosed on Axis II of the DSM. In contrast, most of the disorders covered in this book are diagnosed on Axis I. Mental retardation begins before the age of 18, so that mental retardation is excluded as a diagnosis for major intellectual and behavioral disturbances that may accompany specific injuries or diseases, such as traumatic head injuries and Alzheimer's disease, found during adulthood (Hodapp & Dykens, 1996).

Adaptive Functioning

A diagnosis of mental retardation is appropriate only in the presence of marked delays or deteriorations in adaptive functioning. In many Western cultures, this functioning is evaluated with scales created specifically for that purpose. For example, the *Vineland Adap-*

tive Behavior Scales directly assess different areas of adaptation outlined in the DSM-IV-TR (Sparrow, Balla, & Cicchetti, 1984; see Table 3.2). A person who knows the child or adolescent well must complete these scales, so that the examiner can determine how well the youth is able to fulfill different daily demands and tasks. Although the use of standardized scales is preferable to a diagnosis based only on a clinician's qualitative judgment, these scales are limited by the fact that adaptive functioning depends to a large extent on the environment in which the child is observed. For example, a child who, at age 5, is still spoon-fed may be considered well adjusted at home but poorly adjusted at school, where children of that age are expected to eat without help. Likewise, a low score on an adaptive scale may be truly characteristic of the child's abilities or indicative of too few opportunities to develop adaptive skills in the home, school, or social environment. For example, according to the *Vineland Adaptive Behavior Scales,* 5-year-old children are expected to be able to recite the alphabet (see Table 3.2).

TABLE 3.1   *Mental Retardation: DSM-IV-TR Diagnostic Criteria*

A. Significantly subaverage intellectual functioning: an IQ of approximately 70 or below on an individually administered IQ test (for infants, a clinical judgment of significantly subaverage intellectual functioning).

B. Concurrent deficits or impairments in present adaptive functioning (i.e., the person's effectiveness in meeting the standards expected for his or her age by his or her cultural group) in at least two of the following areas: communication, self-care, home living, social/interpersonal skills, use of community resources, self-direction, functional academic skills, work, leisure, health, and safety.

C. The onset is before age 18 years.

Code based on degree of severity reflecting level of intellectual impairment:

Mild Mental Retardation:	IQ level 50–55 to approximately 70
Moderate Mental Retardation:	IQ level 35–40 to 50–55
Severe Mental Retardation:	IQ level 20–25 to 35–40
Profound Mental Retardation:	IQ level below 20 or 25
Mental Retardation, Severity Unspecified:	when there is strong presumption of Mental Retardation but the person's intelligence is untestable by standard tests

Source: American Psychiatric Association, *Diagnostic and Statistical Manual of Mental Disorders, Fourth Edition, Text Revision* (Washington, DC: American Psychiatric Association, 2000a). Copyright 2000 American Psychiatric Association. Reprinted with permission.

TABLE 3.2 *Sample Items from the Vineland Adaptive Behavior Scales*

Age Level	Adaptive Behavior
2 Years	Delivers a simple message
	Drinks from cup or glass unassisted
5 years	Recites all letters of the alphabet from memory
	Dresses self completely, except for tying shoelaces
9 years	Reads book of at least fourth-grade level
	Controls anger or hurt feelings when denied own way
16 years	Has realistic long-range goals and describes in detail plans to achieve them
	Goes to evening school or facility events with friends, without adult supervision

Source: Sparrow et al. (1984). Reprinted by permission.

When they cannot, however, the test is unable to tell us whether they have major learning problems or whether nobody ever took the time to teach them the alphabet.

Intellectual Functioning

The DSM-IV-TR specifies an IQ of "approximately 70" as the upper limit at which mental retardation may be said to be present if the child also has significant limitations in adaptive functioning. This upper limit has some flexibility—approximately ± 5 points. Inclusion of a flexible diagnostic threshold for mental retardation is justified on both scientific and clinical grounds. Scientifically, there is a margin of error in any psychometric evaluation, which for most IQ tests is roughly five points. Clinically, these five IQ points may be associated with considerable differences in adaptive functioning. Thus, when IQ is close to that threshold, a flexible upper limit gives clinicians and researchers the possibility of determining the child's diagnosis by assessing the child's adaptive behavior, as well as the social and cultural environment in which the child lives.

However, this flexible threshold has major consequences for social policy. This is because, when the intelligence scores of the population are considered as a whole, there is a sizable difference between a threshold of 70 and 75. A cutoff of 70 indicates that approximately 2–3% of the population can be expected to have mental retardation (when retardation is defined solely on the basis of IQ). But a threshold of 75 doubles this figure! Assuming that there are approximately 8 million people with an IQ of 70 or less in the United States, some 16 million people would have an IQ of 75 or less. That difference would have a profound impact on the provision of services for affected children and adolescents and their families.

Although intellectual functioning must be significantly below average for a diagnosis of mental retardation to be made, a person's overall IQ can be difficult to determine. Intelligence is a multifaceted concept. A child or adolescent may show satisfactory intellectual abilities in some areas evaluated by an IQ test but important gaps in others. For example, children often obtain scores that place them within the average range of functioning on the nonverbal or performance sections of an intelligence test, but at a mild mental retardation level on the verbal sections of the same test. When discrepancies such as these are found, combining the child's verbal and nonverbal scores to obtain an overall IQ is often arbitrary. Unfortunately, discrepancies between different sections of an intelligence test are not unusual for youth whose intellectual functioning is limited but not severely delayed.

The DSM-IV-TR also recognizes that an intellectual assessment is not always possible and that it may be necessary—when the child is too young or too disabled to be tested—to base a diagnosis only on clinical observations, or on the evaluations of parents, teachers, or other people who know the child well. In such cases, a diagnosis depends even more heavily on the child's adaptive functioning. Finally, the DSM-IV-TR stresses the importance of taking into account issues that might contribute to a low IQ score. Before making a diagnosis of mental retardation, clinicians should consider factors such as the child's socioeconomic status, native language, physical limitations, or the presence of other psychological disorders (APA, 2000a).

Levels of Severity

Disability is natural. We must stop believing that disabilities keep a person from doing something. Because that's not true. . . . Having a disability doesn't stop me from doing anything.

—Benjamin Snow, Grade 8

The DSM-IV-TR defines four levels of severity of mental retardation—*mild, moderate, severe,* and *profound*—to describe the extent of a child or adolescent's difficulties. These difficulties, which are obviously more pronounced in severe and profound mental retardation, are generally evident in different areas of functioning. The most important involve social behavior, language, personal autonomy (e.g., self-care), and motor skills. The key behavioral characteristics of these levels and the approximate percentages of children found at each level are summarized in Table 3.3.

Mild Mental Retardation.   For the most part, children with mild mental retardation learn to speak without major difficulties, but often at a slower rate than their average peers. Although they learn to speak, their understanding and use of language are often limited and very concrete. Typically, these children acquire a level of personal autonomy (e.g., feeding, grooming, hygiene) and social behavior (e.g., learning of social rules and conventions, use of services such as post office or public transportation) comparable to that of children of average intelligence. But they require more time to learn or a greater level of support during the learning process. If their sensory and motor capacities are affected, these disturbances are usually minor and do not involve significant developmental delays. The case of

TABLE 3.3   *Key Behavioral Characteristics of the Four Levels of Mental Retardation Described in the DSM-IV-TR*

Qualitative Level of Retardation	Quantitative IQ Range	Percentages of All Children with Mental Retardation	Level of Functioning
Mild	50–55 to approx. 70	85	Outside of school, intellectual deficits may or may not be apparent. Children often grow up to live independently, although may need occasional support and assistance, especially during periods of stress.
Moderate	35–40 to 50–55	10	Capable of acquiring a certain degree of personal autonomy and of developing social relationships with those around them. Often acquire necessary skills to work in a sheltered workshop.
Severe	20–25 to 35–40	3–4	Generally require assistance and care from others throughout their lives, although work in a sheltered workshop is sometimes possible.
Profound	Below 25	1–2	Development is limited in all areas of functioning, as ability to learn is grossly impaired and most if not all physical needs must be met by constant care.

Source: American Psychiatric Association, *Diagnostic and Statistical Manual of Mental Disorders,* Fourth Edition, Text Revision (Washington, DC: American Psychiatric Association, 2000a). Copyright 2000 American Psychiatric Association. Reprinted with permission.

Maude illustrates some of the daily difficulties of children with mild mental retardation:

Maude was a little over 5 when her school principal referred her to us. Her kindergarten teacher reports that Maude appears to have important cognitive and developmental delays when compared to fellow students. She seems also very immature. "Her language is very delayed," her teacher explains. "She hardly ever speaks and when she does, it is only a word or two here and there. She is very hard to understand. It's sad, but a little boy asked me the other day if she spoke German. . . . She makes herself understood by pointing to things, crying, grunting, or stomping her feet when she is upset. But she is never aggressive. . . . She has a great deal of difficulty intellectually—in understanding what the other children pick up immediately, in following the rules of a game, for example, or in solving a simple puzzle or laughing at a joke. She laughs, but too late; or she laughs because everybody else is laughing, not because she understands. . . . Observations of the child during two class periods confirm the teacher's report.

Maude lives with her parents and her three siblings—an 8-year-old brother who is in a special class for children with behavioral difficulties and 3-year-old twin sisters. Her father does not work, but receives disability benefits for heart problems associated with severe, chronic obesity. He is bound to a wheelchair that Maude loves to push for him. Her mother, solely responsible for the household, does not work outside the home but watches a small girl during the week to contribute to the family income. Both parents are very affectionate toward their children and take good care of their daily needs. However, they are limited intellectually and therefore are unable to stimulate the children's development in an adequate fashion, especially academically, because her father cannot read fluently and her mother is illiterate.

Given her limited language, Maude's evaluation is based entirely on the nonverbal sections of the Kaufman Achievement Battery for Children. *Results indicate that her IQ is estimated at 64 points. Her ability to pay attention and to concentrate is relatively adequate. So are her motor skills. But her memory and her ability to understand and apply simple rules are below average. The evaluation of her adaptive behavior—based on the* Vineland Adaptive Behavior Scales *completed by her parents—reveals comparable delays, especially in the areas of communication and social relationships.*

Treatment is conducted at home and school with the cooperation of Maude's parents and teacher. It is designed (1) to challenge her to speak by responding to her needs only when she expresses them verbally, and encourage her to repeat the stories she hears or sing the songs she loves; and (2) to help her parents develop their parenting skills, and provide them with support to facilitate the social functioning of the family as a whole. Maude makes rapid progress, due in large part to the enthusiasm of her parents, who participate fully in the treatment, and to the dedication of her teacher who, with her assistant, works each day to facilitate her social integration at school.

Like Tania's story mentioned earlier, this case study illustrates that the delays of children with mild mental retardation usually do not cause major problems during the first years of life. They are often detected only when these children begin school, or even later when they are confronted with the challenge of learning to read and write. Unfortunately, for most persons with mild mental retardation, academic progress beyond elementary school concepts is limited, since these children find it difficult—often impossible—to think in abstract ways. However, they can benefit from schooling adapted to their needs—schooling that will help them acquire daily living skills rather than more advanced academic learning. Toward the end of adolescence and into adulthood, a significant number of people with mild mental retardation lead a relatively normal life. Many of them live independently, especially when their mental retardation is not accompanied by other psychological problems.

Moderate Mental Retardation. Most children with moderate mental retardation learn to speak, but they have major difficulties communicating beyond the simple and concrete exchange of information. They learn rules and social conventions with difficulty and usually require close monitoring and supervision. Their personal autonomy is generally limited, as are their motor skills. Irrespective of social and cultural background, their delay is obvious from early childhood, making schooling particularly challenging. Most of these children do not learn to read or write. However, they can benefit from structured educational programs in which they learn to complete specific tasks. Such knowledge contributes to their personal autonomy, although they generally need to remain in a structured environment throughout their lives. In adulthood, the majority of people with moderate mental retardation can share an active social life in a supportive family or group home, and work in a sheltered workshop or similar setting.

John was 21 when he was referred to us. John suffers from a neurological disorder, most likely of genetic origin, and has moderate mental retardation. He lives at home with his parents, but spends his days in a sheltered workshop. He has an older brother of average intelligence.

John is a tall, slender man of normal physical appearance. But he never passes unnoticed. He spends most of his time with both hands in front of his face in a very peculiar manner: right index behind his right ear, left index behind his left ear, thumbs touching under his chin and his remaining six fingers moving constantly around his mouth. John has spent the past fifteen years or so in this posture, except when he is asleep. As a result, he has almost completely lost the use of his arms and hands, which have become weak and clumsy. If he must carry something, he can hold it for only a short time before dropping it. And if he is made to feed himself, he spills his food and drink. At home, his parents do almost everything for him—except for his personal hygiene, which he has mastered. They explain that they have always done everything for him because he is clumsy and gets quickly angry when asked to feed or dress himself.

John understands simple English and loves to watch television—particularly soccer. He speaks in short phrases, but usually only to ask for something, not for conversation. People who do not know him well find him difficult to understand, because his words are "sluggish" and drawn out as if they were spoken in echo. Thanks to the one-on-one support of a dedicated teacher and a specially programmed computer, John has acquired some elementary school knowledge (e.g.,

vocabulary words, colors, numbers, and simple games). Finally, John loves to laugh and understands concrete jokes. At times, he will even take his hands off his face to tickle people he knows well, or give them a hug or a friendly slap. More generally, he is positive, smiles a lot, and is easygoing as long as he is allowed to keep his hands on his face.

The treatment that was designed to give John back the use of his hands is described elsewhere (Dumas, 1979). From the beginning, this treatment was established in collaboration with his teachers and parents, and took place simultaneously in the sheltered workshop and at home. Treatment followed three principles: (1) change John's daily routine as little as possible; (2) modify his behavior in all of his daily activities, rather than in special activities only; and (3) from the start, give full responsibility for the program to his teachers and parents. The program relied on a series of increasingly complex activities that John was required to do with his hands, and on a precise routine that teachers and parents followed whenever John placed his hands on his face. The successful treatment lasted nineteen days. It reduced the time John spent with his hands on his face from 92% to less than 17%. This reduction was not temporary, but continued during a four-month follow-up.

Severe Mental Retardation. Children with severe mental retardation exhibit difficulties similar to those that characterize moderate mental retardation. However, their impairment is more pronounced and significantly limits their autonomy. Their difficulties are evident in several domains—speech, comprehension, self-care, social behavior, motor skills—and affect their entire development. Children with severe mental retardation may acquire some elements of language and are usually able to learn to complete very simple tasks. However, they require close support and monitoring throughout their life. In addition, they frequently need specialized care because of reduced mobility and of multiple medical disorders that complicate their condition. Figure 3.2 presents the self-portrait of Larry, an 18-year-old with severe mental retardation. People like Larry may lack speech, but creative activities often give them a way of communicating with those around them.

FIGURE 3.2 *Larry's Self-Portrait.* The artist is 18 and has severe mental retardation. Art can be a powerful form of communication for children and adolescents with mental retardation.

Source: From B. Gorski, *Beyond Limitations: The Creative Art of the Mentally Retarded* (Springfield, IL: Charles C. Thomas, 1979), p. 25. Reprinted courtesy of Charles C. Thomas, Publisher, Ltd.

> *Not being able to speak is not the same as not having anything to say.*
>
> —Anonymous

Profound Mental Retardation. In a majority of cases, profound mental retardation is evident at birth or shortly thereafter, and affects all facets of development. Children with profound mental retardation require constant supervision and care, often in an institutional set-ting. Their language is extremely limited or nonexistent, although they can sometimes communicate through gestures or isolated words or sounds. Their personal autonomy is also very limited: most of them need help to eat, to dress, and to get around, and they lack bladder and bowel control. Like children and adolescents with severe mental retardation, they often have multiple physical disorders that necessitate regular medical care and limit their life expectancy.

Jimmy is almost 16 years old. He lives in a large institution for children and adults with mental retardation. Jimmy was born with microcephaly (a disease in which the infant has an unusually small head) and has always depended on his caregivers for all his needs. Unable to walk unaided, he spends long hours lying on his bed or sitting in an armchair that has padded supports on both sides to keep him upright and prevent him from falling. He is spoon-fed and dressed by a nurse or by his parents, who visit him regularly. He has no bladder or bowel control and wears diapers day and night. His health is fragile.

Jimmy does not speak. He does not seem aware of the people around him and does not communicate, except for a few helpless grunts when he is uncomfortable or in pain. He rarely reacts to noise and appears unable to look at people. When somebody looks at him and attempts to fix his gaze, he looks into infinity, beyond the eyes that stare at him. We attempt to make contact with him—by gently caressing his hands or by squeezing them hard, for example, or by speaking to him, tickling him, or singing to him—but always without success, to the point of being persuaded that Jimmy lives in another world.

The children of the ward where Jimmy lives are visited regularly by a talented musician, Vince, who comes to lead an hour or two of musical activity. Everyone at the hospital knows Vince and appreciates his visits, because he has the art of making the most depressed patients—and staff—smile, laugh, and even sing. Vince arrives on the ward one afternoon, carrying his guitar and a large, beat-up suitcase filled with small musical instruments. As soon as he walks in, several children greet him with smiles or grunts of joy, and those who can walk without help gather around him. Vince returns their warm welcome with obvious pleasure as he says hello to each of them by name. Even the staff, who are not a particularly cheerful bunch, seem genuinely pleased to see him.

Each child is eager to take part in an orchestra that Vince improvises by distributing the instruments that he has brought along. Each child except Jimmy, who does not react at all to the growing excitement filling the air. Children and staff sing, they make noise, they sing again, in joy and good spirits. After the celebration, Vince sings alone accompanied by his guitar and surrounded by several attentive young fans. Then he gets up and, still singing, walks slowly to Jimmy's bed, where Jimmy is lying immobile. He sits down. After a few songs, Vince moves closer to Jimmy and, leaning toward him, begins to sing again, but this time almost into his ear. And then something wonderful happens. Jimmy smiles! Not one time but twice, even three times—showing us that he lives in our world and teaching us, very personally, that all children, no matter how severe their mental retardation may be, belong to the great human family.

American Association on Mental Retardation (AAMR) Diagnostic Criteria

The DSM-IV-TR criteria are not the only ones developed to diagnose mental retardation. The American Association on Mental Retardation (AAMR) has developed its own set of criteria. They define the threshold for "subaverage intellectual functioning" as an IQ of "approximately 70 to 75 and below" (AAMR, 1992, p. 5), and require that children show deficits in adaptive behavior in two of ten skill areas before a diagnosis is made. These skill areas include "communication, self-care, home living, social skills, community use, self-direction, health and safety, functional academics, leisure, and work" (p. 1). Consequently, a child with multiple difficulties in adaptation and an IQ of 76 may be diagnosed with mental retardation according to these criteria, making them less stringent than those of the DSM-IV-TR.

The AAMR definition is controversial, mainly because of the major implications that an increase in the IQ criterion from 70 to 75 would have on services for persons with mental retardation and their families (Hodapp & Dykens, 1996). As we saw earlier, a shift of

five IQ points appears small in magnitude but potentially doubles the percentage of the population with mental retardation.

The AAMR definition differs from that of the DSM-IV-TR in another major way: it does not focus on the levels of functioning of persons with mental retardation (i.e., mild, moderate, severe, or profound) but rather on their need for supportive services (Hodapp & Dykens, 1996). The rationale for this fundamental shift in emphasis is that the level-of-functioning approach focuses too much on deficits and not on potential. That is, the AAMR believes that, with appropriate services, children with mental retardation can be helped to fully develop their abilities. As Table 3.4 shows, the AAMR defines four new levels of mental retardation—*intermittent, limited, extensive,* and *pervasive*—based on the amount of supportive services required in each of the ten skill areas listed above. For example, whereas the DSM-IV-TR criteria might suggest that a child has severe mental retardation, the AAMR might specify that the child requires limited support in the leisure area; extensive support in the areas of communication, self-care, home life, social skills, and health and safety; and pervasive support in the areas of

TABLE 3.4   *American Association on Mental Retardation (AAAR) Categories of Mental Retardation, as Defined by the Child's Needs for Supportive Services*

Level	Description
Intermittent	High or low intensity support only when needed and often during life transitions.
Limited	Consistent support on a time-limited basis. Includes support that lasts for longer periods, although the support is not required for the entire lifetime.
Extensive	Consistent support for long periods of time in one or more settings.
Pervasive	Consistent long-term support in all settings.

Source: Adapted from the American Association on Mental Retardation (1992).

community use, self-direction, academics, and work. Although the AAMR describes each of these areas of functioning, few assessment tools are available to measure the child's performance in each of them. Consequently, the validity of this new approach remains unknown.

Diagnostic and Developmental Considerations

Intelligence and IQ are not synonymous. However, for the past century or so, intelligence as measured by IQ tests has been central to the definition of mental retardation. Before we describe the epidemiological, developmental, and etiological dimensions of mental retardation, we will briefly discuss three important issues related to this important point.

IQ and Individual Differences

IQ tests make it possible to classify children and adolescents with retardation on a quantitative scale of intellectual functioning. However, the continuum that this scale represents provides very limited information, because it does not reveal major behavioral, developmental, and etiological differences among people who receive a diagnosis of mental retardation. Very simply, two children may have the same IQ, but not be at all comparable. A child with an IQ of 35 may have few social contacts, but may be able to walk, eat, and get dressed with little assistance, whereas another child with a comparable IQ may lack personal autonomy and require assistance to walk, eat, or get dressed, but be very friendly and sociable. The same applies to two children with mental retardation caused by different factors. IQ numbers do not tell us anything about their behavior; nor do they predict their development or explain the origins of their difficulties.

Furthermore, since a person's IQ is a measure taken at a particular time and place, an IQ test measures not only the child's performance but also the circumstances in which the test was taken. In other words, factors that have little or nothing to do with the intellectual abilities of the child being tested—factors such as tiredness or nervousness at the time of testing, or

encouragement from the examiner—can influence the test results (Sattler, 1992).

The Stability of IQ over Time

Intelligence is relatively stable but it is not fixed. The IQ score of a person with mental retardation, like that of an average person, can change in the course of development (Carr, 1990; see Developmental Trajectories and Prognosis). Nevertheless, in the general public and in certain scientific circles, intelligence still is widely regarded as a gift or talent: it can be put to good use but it cannot be modified significantly, except by extreme and generally traumatic circumstances, such as a serious illness or an accident. This belief is mistaken.

In studies designed to address this question, correlations among IQ measures taken at regular intervals from age 4 to adulthood are generally very high, in people with and without mental retardation (Ross, Begab, Dondis, Giampiccolo, & Meyers, 1985; Vernon, 1979). Actually, IQ measures are particularly stable among people having limited intellectual abilities (Bernheimer & Keogh, 1988). However, the correlations reported in such studies reflect *group measurements*. The same studies demonstrate that an individual's IQ does not always remain stable throughout development. In fact, the opposite is true. *Individual measurements* of IQ often change several points from one testing to another, especially among people whose intellectual performance is at the threshold between low-average intellectual functioning and mental retardation (Bernheimer & Keogh, 1988). An IQ test administered on one occasion may suggest that a child has mild mental retardation, but the same test administered on a later occasion may indicate that the child no longer qualifies for the diagnosis.

The same conclusion comes from studies of intensive intervention programs for children from underprivileged families, which are designed to foster intellectual development and to prevent mental retardation (Schweinhart & Weikart, 1997). Several programs have shown substantial increases—up to fifteen points—in the IQ scores of experimental as compared to control children. In other words, if intelligence (as measured by IQ tests) is a relatively stable entity, data caution against interpreting this stability as fixed.

Intelligence is not like eye color; a person's eye color will not change over a lifetime, but chances are that IQ will.

Intelligence and Heritability

Ever since intelligence became a major source of concern in the industrial world, a considerable amount of scientific research and countless social and political debates have centered on its nature and origins. As noted in Chapter 2, researchers in this area have often opposed nature and nurture, heredity and environment, with the goal of establishing the relative importance of each in determining an individual's IQ. Studies show that 50–70% of the variations in human intelligence can be attributed to hereditary differences among people (Rende & Plomin, 1995). However, these figures must be interpreted with caution. We will not return to the detailed discussion of this topic presented in the previous chapter, but only summarize its key points with respect to mental retardation. Specifically:

1. Measures of heritability are group measures, not measures of individual characteristics; therefore, they have little to say about how much of a person's intelligence depends on heredity and how much on the environment.
2. Heredity and environment are not independent, but interdependent, sources of influence on development that interact in complex ways that make it impossible to separate their effects in any simple fashion.
3. All measures of heritability depend on the specific environmental conditions in which they were taken. They are not figures that describe unchanging characteristics of the human race, but figures that are bound to the context in which they were obtained.

Empirical Validity

The validity of a diagnosis of mental retardation depends on the level of intellectual and adaptive functioning of the child or adolescent being evaluated, as well as on the methods of evaluation. In general, the validity of a diagnosis of moderate, severe, or profound mental retardation is rarely in doubt, because of the obvious, often pervasive, challenges that these children face daily. However, a precise diagnosis can sometimes be impossible to make (for instance, when the child cannot be tested because of physical limitations), and valid distinctions between these levels may be difficult to establish.

Empirical validity problems arise mainly with respect to mild mental retardation. As you know, there is no clear boundary between low-average functioning and mild mental retardation. In addition, it is not clear that all youth who receive a diagnosis of mild mental retardation have a psychological disorder, because their difficulties can vary considerably from one context and from one period of development to another—being most obvious in a school context and during the school years.

Associated Characteristics; Comorbidity

Medical Conditions

Children and adolescents with mental retardation—especially moderate, severe, or profound—often have serious, chronic medical problems. However, none of these are specific to mental retardation. Medical conditions such as epilepsy and sensory and motor disorders are common and vary greatly in severity. For example, in the case of motor disorders, symptoms can range from mild awkwardness to serious problems with muscle control and motion. Medical conditions are often tied to the etiology of the retardation and vary in severity as a function of numerous factors, such as age, early diagnosis, and access to professional services.

Psychological Symptoms and Disorders

Comorbid disorders are three to four times more frequent among people with mental retardation than in the population in general, and symptoms of such disorders are up to ten times more frequent. Thus, between 10% and 50% of people with mental retardation face additional psychological challenges. In this area, as in other areas of abnormal child and adolescent psychology, comorbidity estimates vary considerably (Frame & Matson, 1987). In general, comorbidity is higher in clinical than in community samples and increases with the severity of mental retardation. High levels of comorbidity are explained partly by the fact that some forms of mental retardation share a common etiology with other serious conditions, such as the pervasive developmental disorders we will consider in the next chapter.

Youth with mental retardation can suffer from all known psychological disorders of childhood and adolescence. When they do, their symptoms are usually similar to those of people without mental retardation. The DSM-IV-TR notes that attention deficit hyperactivity disorder (ADHD), mood disorders, and pervasive developmental disorders are commonly associated with mental retardation (APA, 2000a). The mechanisms responsible for these associations remain unknown for the most part. However, in some cases at least, the association probably reflects both the nature of the child's challenges and the manner in which the environment responds and adjusts to them. For example, a comorbid diagnosis of ADHD may reflect in part the limited tolerance of the environment for the disruptive behaviors that some children with mental retardation display, as well as the intellectual difficulties these children face when they have to attend to, understand, remember, and follow instructions.

Symptoms of immaturity, social insensitivity, passivity, or extreme agitation often accompany mental retardation also, but in many cases affected children do not meet criteria for the diagnosis of a comorbid disorder. In severe and profound mental retardation, these problems are often worsened by stereotypical, repetitive movements such as rocking, and by **self-injurious behaviors** such as scratching and head banging. Self-injurious behaviors, which affect some 10% of youth with mental retardation, can lead to serious injuries and considerably limit their ability to interact and learn new skills.

The majority of children and adolescents with mental retardation also have language and communication difficulties. Their problems in this area are usually closely connected to their intellectual difficulties and are evident in articulation, pronunciation, syntax, grammar, and/or comprehension difficulties, as well as in problems with the practical use of language in everyday communication. Difficulties of communication may explain some of the disruptive behaviors of youth with mental retardation. These behaviors often reflect their attempts to communicate when more effective modes of communication are unavailable to them (APA, 2000a).

Beyond Intellectual Limitations

We know much more about the cognitive and language limitations of youth with mental retardation than about other important personality characteristics that may be associated with limited intellectual and adaptive functioning. A narrow focus on intelligence and its correlates at times makes it seem as though affected children have no important personal or behavioral characteristic outside of their IQ score. Some research has focused on factors such as self-esteem, motivation, and the understanding that children with mental retardation have of their own condition, but the role played by personality variables in the development and daily manifestations of retardation remains for the most part to be discovered.

Many children and adolescents with mental retardation have low expectations of their abilities—intellectual and otherwise—and at times seem unmotivated to tackle new or familiar tasks, for fear of frustration and failure. Adults may inadvertently reinforce this helpless stance by expecting little of youth with mental retardation (Hodapp & Zigler, 1995). But helplessness and lack of motivation are by no means unavoidable. In *Count Us In: Growing Up with Down Syndrome,* Jason Kingsley and Mitchell Levitz (1994), two young adults with mental retardation, describe how they learned to overcome the many daily challenges they face with the love and support of family and friends. Here is a short dialogue between them:

> ***Mitchell:*** I think . . . that we should never call us Down syndrome. We should call each other Up syndrome because Up syndrome would help each other out, being involved in communities because it's part of being Up syndrome. . . . Up is positive, down is sad. There are two perspectives here. Down

syndrome meaning a disability. Up syndrome meaning positive with disability. . . .

Jason: I think Up syndrome is positive with a disability and Down syndrome is, well, you're feeling depressed a little bit, going down. This Down syndrome is the wrong name of our disability. . . . The positive side of Up syndrome is to be proud of you, learn about it, how you do it, and be happy. Put it into actions. Be motivated. (p. 44)

Epidemiology

Prevalence

The prevalence rates of mental retardation reported in epidemiological studies depend on the diagnostic criteria used and particularly on the upper limit of intellectual functioning adopted to define retardation. If intelligence follows a normal distribution, an IQ threshold of 70 on a majority of tests would result in an overall prevalence rate of 2% to 3%. However, community studies show that this rate is closer to 1% to 2% (Hodapp & Dykens, 1996; Kiely & Lubin, 1991). Several reasons explain why the actual prevalence rate of mental retardation is lower than what would be expected on the basis of statistical prediction alone:

1. Diagnostic criteria require that both intellectual and adaptive functioning be limited before a diagnosis can be made. Since the probability that both will be impaired is less than a deficit in either IQ or adaptive functioning the observed rate of mental retardation is often lower than the rate one would expect on the basis of the distribution of IQ alone. Practically, much of this difference is accounted for by the large group of people whose IQ score is around 70, because many of these people do not have significant difficulties in adaptation; therefore, a diagnosis of mental retardation would be inappropriate.
2. Childhood mortality rates for people with mental retardation are three to four times higher than in the general population—especially for those with severe or profound retardation. Unfortu-

nately, this means that a significant number of youth with mental retardation do not survive to be included in epidemiological statistics.
3. Mild mental retardation is a phenomenon closely linked to compulsory education. However, once students with mild mental retardation leave school, many of them go on to lead ordinary lives and are no longer counted in epidemiological surveys.
4. IQ and adaptive functioning are not fixed entities. Consequently, people who meet diagnostic criteria for mild mental retardation at a certain period of development do not necessarily do so at another period. This variation can also contribute to lower prevalence rates in epidemiological research.

Although the overall prevalence rate of mental retardation is lower than what would be expected on the basis of the distribution of intelligence in the population, the prevalence rate for moderate, severe, and profound retardation is actually *higher* than one would expect if the distribution of intelligence followed strictly a normal curve. Specifically, people with IQs of 50 or less form their own distribution at the lower limit of the normal distribution of intelligence (see Figure 3.3) (Zigler & Hodapp, 1986). In contrast to the tail end of the overall distribution of IQ, which represents mostly "cultural familial" retardation (i.e., retardation of familial, social, or cultural origins), this smaller, overlapping distribution represents mostly "organic" retardation (i.e., retardation of biological origin). Moderate, severe, and profound retardation affect approximately 4 people per 1,000 or 0.4% of the population (Abramowicz & Richardson, 1975). The most common biological causes of the more severe levels of retardation are Down syndrome (1 to 1.5 per 1,000), fragile X syndrome (0.7 to 0.9 per 1,000), and **Prader-Willi syndrome** (1 per 15,000) (Hodapp & Dykens, 1996).

Age and Gender Characteristics

When mental retardation is of biological origin, the child's difficulties usually begin at birth, in infancy, or in early childhood. When mental retardation is the result of a childhood disease, difficulties can appear rather

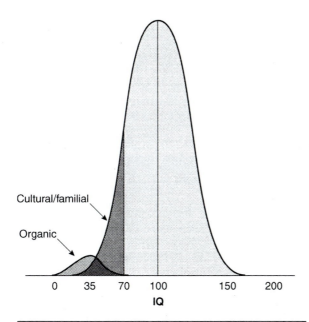

Cultural/familial

Organic

IQ

0   35   70   100   150   200

FIGURE 3.3 *Graph of Two Overlapping IQ Score Distributions.* The left-hand tail of the overall distribution of IQ represents people with mental retardation primarily of familial, social, or cultural origins. The smaller overlapping distribution represents mostly people with mental retardation of biological origins. This graph shows that the proportion of people with moderate, severe, and profound mental retardation is actually *higher* than one would predict if the distribution of intelligence followed strictly a normal curve.

Source: Adapted from E. Zigler and R. M. Hodapp, *Understanding Mental Retardation* (New York: Cambridge University Press, 1986). Copyright 1986 by Cambridge University Press. Adapted by permission.

abruptly, depending mainly on the nature of the disease and the care the child receives. When mental retardation is first identified in an educational setting, the onset of difficulties usually reflects specific aspects of the environment—such as the academic demands of the school system and availability of specialized services—as much as the child's own limitations.

Finally, mental retardation is more frequent in boys than girls. The sex ratio, which is approximately one-and-a-half boys per girl (1.6:1), tends to become more equal with age and severity of retardation. Sex differences appear mostly in people with mild or moderate mental retardation. There are few if any differences related to gender in people with more severe forms of retardation (Misès, Perron, & Salbreux, 1994). Some forms of mental retardation, such as fragile X syndrome, affect primarily boys. Others, such as Rett's disorder (see Chapter 4), are found almost exclusively in girls.

Social and Cultural Differences

Mental retardation is a universal phenomenon. However, it is not evenly distributed across different regions and groups. Cross-culturally, the prevalence of mild mental retardation varies considerably from one country to another, even during the school years, when rates are highest. For example, it is significantly higher in the United States than in Sweden, in part because of differences in the criteria used to define mental retardation and in the services offered to young children with learning or developmental difficulties in these two countries (Sonnander, Emanuelsson, & Kebbon, 1993).

In contrast, the prevalence rates of more severe forms of mental retardation are generally comparable around the world, although some conditions associated with limited intellectual and adaptive functioning are particularly frequent in certain regions (Abramowicz & Richardson, 1975; Salbreux & d'Anthenaise, 1982). For example, for reasons still unknown, **spina bifida** is much more frequent in Great Britain than in other industrialized countries. Spina bifida results from a malformation of the spinal cord and causes hydrocephalus, which is an accumulation of cerebrospinal fluid in the brain. This disease leads to mental retardation in 20% to 25% of affected children (Misès, Perron, & Salbreux, 1994).

Children whose mental retardation has a known biological etiology (e.g., Down syndrome) are found in comparable numbers in all social and ethnic groups. This is not the case for mental retardation for which a biological etiology has not been established (Hodapp & Dykens, 1996). Mild mental retardation, which rarely has any identifiable biological origin, is particularly frequent among children and adolescents from underprivileged families and, in societies such as the United States, from ethnic minority families. For example, in a study that compared the prevalence of mild mental retardation in African American and European American children from different socioeconomic backgrounds, the researchers found that, in high-income families, only 0.3% of European American children and 1.2% of African American children had mild mental retardation. However, in low-income families, the corresponding figures were 3.6% and 7.8%, respectively (Broman, Nichols, Shaughnessy, & Kennedy, 1987). Results such as these have sparked considerable debate in the United States over why mild mental retardation is so closely associated with socioeconomic status and ethnicity (see Box 3.3). Over the past few decades, this debate led to changes in American social policy. Some states, such as California, have made it illegal to use IQ tests in special education placement decisions, on the assumption that these tests are biased against minority children (Lambert, 1981). However, these changes have not had their intended effect: the prevalence of mild mental retardation remains particularly high in the United States among low-income, ethnic minority youth (Artiles & Trent, 1994).

Developmental Trajectories and Prognosis

Developmental trajectories and prognosis for children with mental retardation vary considerably according to the etiology and severity of their difficulties. Therefore,

BOX 3.3 • *Ethnicity and IQ: Untangling Science from Politics*

Do IQ scores provide objective, unbiased measures of intelligence? The answer to this question has social, educational, and political ramifications because, throughout the years, African Americans and other American minorities have scored significantly lower on average than European Americans on intelligence tests. Some researchers believe that intelligence, as measured by IQ tests, is highly stable because it is mainly heritable and, consequently, that differences in intelligence between ethnic groups reflect differences in natural ability. This is, for example, the conclusion of *The Bell Curve,* a controversial book whose title refers to the shape of the normal distribution of intelligence as measured by IQ (Herrnstein & Murray, 1994). The authors of *The Bell Curve* believe that European Americans are inherently superior in intelligence to members of many minority groups in America, and to African Americans in particular. They also believe that attempts to narrow group differences in IQ scores through educational or social policies are doomed to failure, because most inherited traits are highly resistant to change; therefore, programs designed to improve the academic performance of minority children represent a waste of resources.

Is this true? Can group differences in IQ scores be accounted for almost entirely in terms of genetic differences between groups? We hope you realize that this deceivingly simple position does not correspond to the scientific evidence available today. First, as we stressed in Chapter 2, there is no one-to-one relationship between genes and IQ scores. From the time of conception, human beings are products of both nature and nurture, and any attempt to oppose the two ignores the fact that their contributions to development cannot be meaningfully separated. In other words, any IQ score reflects not only the ability of the child being tested but also the social and cultural context of which the child is a part. *In all ethnic groups,* children who have had only limited opportunities to develop their intellectual skills—because of poverty, inadequate schooling, discrimination, and other negative influences—obtain lower IQ scores on average than children who have never had to face similar challenges (Serpell, 2000). Second, although IQ scores are very stable they are not unchangeable. A number of prevention programs have been very successful in raising these scores in young, mostly African American children—showing clearly that these children are not doomed to go through life with more limited intellectual skills than their European American peers (see Treatment and Prevention).

The study of group differences in IQ has always been fraught with controversy in America. Perhaps the furor soon will die down. There is indeed evidence that since the 1990s, IQ scores have been increasing for ethnic minorities in the United States, and that the gap in average IQ scores between minority and nonminority youth is narrowing (Neisser et al., 1996).

we will limit ourselves to an overview of important points on which scientific evidence converges.

Mental retardation is chronic and, in a majority of cases, affects a person's functioning throughout life. As we have shown, intellectual and adaptive functioning are relatively stable in children with moderate, severe, or profound retardation, and their developmental trajectories are fairly predictable. However, these trajectories are more variable in cases of mild retardation. Whatever their origins, the manner in which young people with mental retardation develop depends considerably on the care and support they receive. In a stimulating environment offering adequate educational and social opportunities, many of them make significant progress and acquire competencies that enable them to lead active lives.

Studies focusing on the development and organization of cognitive abilities in children with mental retardation have traditionally been conducted in one of two distinct theoretical perspectives. A **developmental perspective** assumes that children with mental retardation have the same abilities as average peers, but that these abilities develop at a different pace. In contrast, a **differential perspective** presupposes that children with mental retardation have abilities that are different from those of average children and that often reflect the specific nature of their retardation. Although researchers typically adopt one of these two positions when designing and conducting scientific studies in this area, there is evidence to support both perspectives. Specifically, research shows that cognitive abilities generally develop in a similar sequence in children with and without mental retardation, but that the rate and quality at which these abilities develop vary in large part according to the nature and etiology of the child's limitations (Hodapp & Zigler, 1995).

Down Syndrome

Down syndrome is usually caused by a genetic abnormality on chromosome 21; the abnormality is called *trisomy* because it involves partial duplication of chromosome 21, yielding three of these chromosomes. The probability of a child's being born with the disorder rises as a function of maternal age. When mothers are in their twenties, approximately 1 child in 1,000 live

births has the disorder. This rate increases rapidly to 4 children in 1,000 births for mothers in their thirties, to more than 30 children in 1,000 births for mothers in their forties (Hook, 1982). Affected children have moderate or severe mental retardation and a developmental trajectory in which their difficulties become increasingly pronounced over time. For example, in the cognitive area, their intellectual functioning tends to slow down over the course of the childhood years (Hodapp & Zigler, 1990). Children with Down syndrome are usually very sociable but can be stubborn and prone to temper tantrums. Most have significant language difficulties and comorbid medical conditions that limit their life expectancy. When these children live beyond the age of 30 or 40, which is increasingly the case, their intellectual and adaptive challenges are often compounded by the development of Alzheimer's disease (Hodapp & Dykens, 1996; Lambert, 1997).

Fragile X Syndrome

Fragile X is a syndrome caused by a genetic abnormality on the X chromosome. In youth affected with this abnormality, a slowdown in intellectual functioning is frequently observed, but it usually does not appear before adolescence (Hodapp, Dykens, Ort, Zelinsky, & Leckman, 1991). Although children with Down syndrome and fragile X syndrome both show a similar decline in intellectual functioning in the course of development, their cognitive limitations are not the same. Children and adolescents with fragile X syndrome are particularly weak on problems that require sequential or step-by-step solutions, whereas their peers with Down syndrome show significant language difficulties, especially in the use of grammar (Hodapp & Dykens, 1996). These differences highlight the validity of a differential perspective for understanding biologically based mental retardation.

Prader-Willi Syndrome

Children with Prader-Willi syndrome—a syndrome caused by a genetic abnormality on chromosome 15—usually have mild mental retardation. Their developmental trajectory has a typical pattern, although it is very different from that of children with Down syndrome.

During the first two or three years of life, they are sociable and affectionate but show delays in many areas. They have muscular problems and eating difficulties, and often fail to put on normal weight. By the age of 2 and 3, these same children become perpetually hungry and can grow to be obese if their food intake is not limited. In many cases, children with Prader-Willi syndrome become so preoccupied with food that they qualify for an additional diagnosis of obsessive-compulsive disorder (Hodapp & Dykens, 1996), a disorder we will consider in Chapter 9. Their social behavior tends to deteriorate also. More specifically, as they become older, these children show marked emotional immaturity and can become moody and easily upset.

Etiology

Because mental retardation is associated with a number of different conditions, it has several etiologies. To organize knowledge in this field, researchers and clinicians often make a distinction between "organic" and "cultural/familial" retardation. This distinction can easily lead to a simplistic opposition between heredity and environment. However, in practice, it usually does not, since it merely recognizes that certain forms of mental retardation have a known biological etiology, whereas others have not—either because such an etiology does not exist or because it remains to be discovered. In other words, when a biological origin cannot be established, mental retardation is presumed to be the result of inadequate opportunities and lack of stimulation at home and in the broader social and cultural environment. When a biological etiology can be specified, it usually precedes the time of birth. Table 3.5 lists some proximal (immediate) causes of mental retardation, distinguishing between causes that precede, surround, or follow the birth of the child.

Biological Factors

Biological factors that can lead to mental retardation are too numerous to be described in any detail. There are literally thousands of such factors, and ongoing research discovers new ones at increasingly faster rates (Luckasson et al., 1992). Biological research has taken major strides in recent years, thanks to the development of new investigative techniques in molecular genetics (e.g., DNA mapping) and neurophysiology (e.g., **magnetic resonance imaging,** or MRI).

On average, more than 75% of youth with moderate, severe, or profound mental retardation (IQ < 50) have documented biological reasons for their delays (Zigler & Hodapp, 1986). As Table 3.5 shows, the biological factors associated with mental retardation can be of hereditary or environmental origin, and can manifest themselves at various periods of development.

When its origin is hereditary, mental retardation can be caused by defective genes or by genetic mutations. The majority of these genetic aberrations are related to abnormalities in chromosome number (e.g., Down syndrome) or structure (e.g., Prader-Willi syndrome, fragile X syndrome). Many disorders of hereditary origin are transmitted on non-sex chromosomes. **Phenylketonuria** (or PKU) is an example of such a condition. Children with this syndrome cannot process a protein called phenylalanine. This protein accumulates in the body and creates toxins that cause brain damage, leading to mental retardation. More rarely, disorders are transmitted on sex chromosomes. An example of this type of disorder is **Lesch-Nyhan syndrome.** This syndrome, which affects boys only, is characterized by moderate mental retardation, marked cerebral palsy, digestive difficulties, and self-injurious behaviors.

The immediate causes of mental retardation listed in Table 3.5, and the periods of development with which they are usually associated, can be used to describe a child's condition but not to predict the child's development. Although these biological factors can determine the *probability* of mental retardation, its form and severity, as well as its developmental course, depend on ongoing transactions between the child and the environment. PKU offers a classical example of such transactions. A single gene located on chromosome 12 causes this disorder, which can lead to severe or profound mental retardation. However, children who carry the defective gene are born healthy, and the likelihood that they will suffer from brain damage depends on their diet. In most cases, a diet low in phenylalanine from birth makes it possible to avoid the development of mental retardation. Thus, when it appears, PKU has

TABLE 3.5 *Examples of Proximal Causes of Mental Retardation in the Pre-, Peri-, and Postnatal Periods of Development*

Prenatal Period	Perinatal Period (at birth)	Postnatal Period
Chromosome abnormalities	Complications during delivery	Encephalitis (inflammation of brain tissue)
Down syndrome (Trisomy 21: partial duplication of chromosome)		Meningitis (inflammation of membranes covering brain tissue)
Turner's syndrome (XO: missing second X chromosome in females)		Poisoning (e.g., lead)
Klinefelter's syndrome (XXY: extra Y chromosome in males)		Child abuse
Fragile X syndrome (weaker or "pinched" section of X chromosome)		Accidents
Prader-Willi syndrome (loss or dysfunction of some paternal genes on chromosome 15)		Malnutrition
Genetic metabolism disorders		
Lesch-Nyhan syndrome (error in the metabolism of purine; affects males only)		
Phenylketonuria (error in the metabolism of phenylalanine; affects males and females)		
Embryonic exposure or events		
Syphilis		
HIV virus		
Rubella (German measles)		
Toxoplasmosis (infection passed from mother to fetus)		
Fetal alcohol syndrome (maternal drug and alcohol use/abuse during pregnancy)		
Spina bifida (neural tube defect interfering with central nervous system development)		

hereditary (prenatal) and environmental (postnatal) origins. Box 3.4 (p. 78) describes other conditions in which the inseparability of nature and nurture is evident.

Family, Social, and Cultural Factors

Most researchers today believe that the majority of cases of mild mental retardation reflect a complex transaction between biological, psychosocial, and cultural forces. In this perspective, mild mental retardation is usually the observable manifestation of the lower limit of a normal distribution of human intelligence and adaptive skills, which interact throughout development with multiple adverse factors, such as poverty, parental psychopathology (e.g., alcoholism, abuse, or neglect), lack of adequate prenatal and infant care (e.g., medical care, vaccinations), and discrimination (e.g., racism, inadequate schooling).

These complex transactions are poorly understood. However, studies show that they probably play an important role in the etiology and development of mental retardation. For example, research on social support shows that the ability of parents to adapt to a child's challenging behaviors both influences *and* reflects the child's own adaptation. On average, parents and especially mothers of children with mental retardation report higher levels of personal stress than parents of average children (Dumas, Wolf,

BOX 3.4 • *The Complex Interplay Between Nature and Nurture in Mental Retardation*

As we show in the text, PKU provides a classical example of the interplay between genes and environment in shaping a child's intellectual and adaptive skills. Another notable example is provided by fetal alcohol syndrome (FAS), the result of widespread dysfunction in the central nervous system. In addition to mental retardation and severe behavior problems, such as inattentiveness, hyperactivity, and impulsivity, children with FAS have characteristic physical features: a small head circumference; small eye openings, with skin folds in the inner corners of the eyes; a short nose with a low nasal bridge; a small upper lip; and a receding chin. FAS is linked to alcohol consumption during pregnancy. Even moderate consumption is associated with sig-

nificant risk, because alcohol interferes with prenatal growth (Autti-Raemoe, 2000). This interference is the immediate cause of the child's mental retardation. However, the etiology of FAS is obviously as much in nurture (a mother's alcohol intake) as in nature (prenatal growth), as much in the child's environment as in the child's biology. The same is true in many cases of child abuse (see Chapter 12). For example, shaking infants violently to stop them from crying can lead to brain hemorrhage and result in mental retardation. If these injuries are the immediate cause of the retardation that can accompany **shaken baby syndrome,** its etiology is again as much in nurture (abuse) as in nature (brain hemorrhage).

Fisman, & Culligan, 1991). Feelings of depression, incompetence, and guilt are particularly frequent in mothers, although the severity of these feelings depends to a great extent on other factors, such as the availability of spousal and social support and the so-

cioeconomic status of the family. This line of research suggests that, in most cases, these feelings are a reaction to the multiple challenges related to raising a child with special needs, rather than a form of maternal psychopathology.

Special Olympics. Children and adolescents with mental retardation can live happy and productive lives given proper support and encouragement, and can excel in sports and other areas.

Family adaptation is not always negative; rather, it depends mainly on the child or adolescent's specific difficulties. For example, the presence of a Down syndrome child in the home may have a positive effect on family functioning (Mink, Nihira, & Meyers, 1983; Noh, Dumas, Wolf, & Fisman, 1989). Although parents of children with Down syndrome may face challenges in accepting their children's delays, they describe their children as being just as happy as children without problems, if not more so (Noh et al.). Many convincing examples of this positive outlook on mental retardation appear in Kingsley and Levitz's (1994) book, which we mentioned earlier. Also, anyone who is familiar with the Special Olympics—a sporting competition for individuals with disabilities—knows the positive impact that children with mental retardation can have on their families and beyond.

Treatment and Prevention

A lot of people with a disability say, "This is who I am. I don't come here hoping my disability will go away, but because I want to participate."

—Carolyn R. Thompson

Because youth with mental retardation face a range of psychological, educational, social, vocational, and medical challenges, treatment usually encompasses a variety of interventions. In early childhood, and even before birth, detection and thorough assessment are crucial. Appropriate treatment decisions require a proper understanding of (1) the child's intellectual and adaptive functioning, (2) any medical condition that may complicate matters, and (3) support services that are already in place or need to be provided.

Since youth with mental retardation have such diverse needs, there is no single psychological or educational treatment of choice in this area. A child with severe or profound mental retardation and significant physical challenges may need comprehensive services provided by a team of professionals. These services are likely to focus primarily on the child's physical health and daily needs, such as feeding, toileting, and mobility. In addition, if the child lives at home, the family may need support services in the form of visiting home health

care, therapeutic staff support, and respite care. In contrast, a child with mild mental retardation who does not have any comorbid medical or psychological disorder is likely to benefit most from educational and vocational help, with services provided mainly through the school system. In the United States, the 1975 Education for All Handicapped Children Act and the 1997 Individuals with Disabilities Education Act specify that all children with mental retardation have a right to free diagnostic, educational, and support services. These services have one goal: *normalization*—that is, "making available to the mentally retarded patterns and conditions of everyday life which are as close as possible to the norms and patterns of the mainstream of society" (Nirje, 1969, p. 181).

Early Childhood

As in many other areas of human functioning and health, early intervention is considered crucial in mental retardation. Early intervention is designed to help affected children reach and maintain their full potential, and to reduce the risk that untreated problems will worsen and add to the child's challenges. To be successful, it is generally agreed that early intervention should address most if not all of the areas of concern: physical, psychosocial, and needed supports. For example, it should foster the child's intellectual and adaptive skills through appropriate stimulation at home and early schooling; and it should tackle comorbid difficulties, such as motor, speech, and language delays or disorders. In the United States, such interventions usually are provided through an *individualized family service plan* (IFSP) for infants and toddlers, and through an *individualized education plan* (IEP) for preschoolers and school-age children. IFSPs and IEPs are federally mandated assessment and intervention programs that children with mental retardation are eligible to receive through publicly funded agencies such as schools. These individualized programs are implemented to varying degrees across states, and the extent and quality of available services vary considerably from state to state. IFSPs and IEPs must have the following features:

- They must involve the child's parents or caregivers, and be respectful of their cultural background and language.

- They must be based on a comprehensive evaluation of the child's needs, conducted by a multidisciplinary team of professionals.
- They must offer services in the least restrictive environment—that is, in a setting where the child has opportunities to interact with average peers and access to community resources.
- They must be reviewed and adjusted annually (or more frequently if necessary).

In the case of IEPs, the professional team usually includes a school psychologist, a special education teacher, other school personnel (e.g., teachers, principal, counselor, nurse), a physician, and a social worker or family counselor. In other words, IEPs are not based solely on an evaluation of the child's educational needs, as their name mistakenly implies. Instead, IEPs act ideally as blueprints for comprehensive, developmentally sensitive interventions or support services for the child and the family. The case of Casey illustrates the IEP process and the multiple services that can be provided for a child with mental retardation.

Casey is 5. She was referred to our clinic for intellectual testing by her school district. A review of her history shows that, at age 2, Casey had fallen and lost all of her front teeth. At the time of the accident, she had been talking in one- or two-word phrases, but after she lost her teeth her mother reported that her speech became so difficult to understand that "she just stopped talking." Her lack of speech persisted and, by age 3, she was identified by her pediatrician as having a significant speech delay. An IEP was set up, and Casey began receiving individualized speech therapy.

Casey continued to receive speech services until kindergarten, when her annual IEP review showed that her speech was now within normal limits. This review, which included Casey's mother, her teacher, the school psychologist, and the speech pathologist, focused on Casey's current difficulties in mastering the academic material of kindergarten. Specifically, the review showed that, in spite of her improved communication, she was having considerable difficulties learning letters, numbers, and colors. Since these difficulties could not be explained by lack of effort or emotional or behavior problems, it was decided that Casey would no *longer receive speech therapy, but that she would be tested to determine whether she had mental retardation or a learning disability, and that her IEP would be revised accordingly.*

Casey's IQ test shows that she is functioning in the mild mental retardation range. Her adaptive functioning is also significantly poorer than would be expected of a child of her age. With her mother's agreement, a decision is made to retain her in kindergarten for another year and to assign her a special education teacher to augment her regular classroom experiences.

Middle Childhood

The difficulties of many children with mild mental retardation are often diagnosed for the first time when they enter school. In the United States, most of these children attend regular schools, as do many of their peers with moderate and even severe mental retardation. When affected children are able to attend school, treatment usually focuses on ways to meet their educational needs and to help them benefit from regular exposure to average peers. Therefore, whenever possible, these children are taught in a regular classroom with support services to address their specific needs. Children with more severe mental retardation or comorbid psychological problems and/or physical disabilities are taught in special education classrooms. These classrooms are staffed by a special education teacher and one or more aides, and have a high teacher-to-student ratio. When children are placed in such classrooms, efforts are usually made to include them in any regular activities that are appropriate—such as music, lunch, recess, or school assemblies—because one of the goals of the education program is to give these children an opportunity to develop their peer relationship skills. To achieve this goal, schools also have to work with the peers, in order to foster their understanding of children with special needs, encourage the celebration of differences, and minimize the stigma associated with a diagnosis of mental retardation or with attendance in special education classes.

Residential placement is sometimes warranted for youth with more severe mental retardation or with comorbid problems that cannot be effectively managed at home or school. Placement can be in a long-term psychiatric facility, a group home where youth with mental retardation live with and are supervised by trained professionals, or a **treatment foster care** setting. Treatment foster care allows a child to live with a family that has been specially trained to receive children with emotional or behavioral problems and/or medical conditions. Services provided in such facilities vary considerably, both in focus and in quality. Treatment for one child may focus on decreasing aggressive behavior and improving social skills; for another, on reducing self-injurious behavior and increasing autonomy and self-care skills. Out-of-home placements for youth with mental retardation are relatively rare, at least in the United States, where it is estimated that no more than 10% of affected individuals live in residential care facilities (American Academy of Child and Adolescent Psychiatry, 1999b).

Applied behavior analysis methods have been found particularly useful for treating a variety of symptoms associated with mental retardation in children. These methods, which are part of a behavioral approach to understanding human behavior (see Box 1.2), assume that many of the challenging problems often displayed by children with mental retardation are learned and maintained by the settings in which these children live. Clinicians who use these methods to modify undesirable behaviors (such as aggression, temper tantrums, and self-injury) make a careful assessment of these **target behaviors** before any intervention takes place. By observing the child in the settings where the target behavior occurs, they try to determine which of the events that occur immediately before and after the behavior are associated with the target behavior. They can then use that knowledge to change the behavior in desirable ways by modifying these events (Pierce & Epling, 1999).

An example illustrates these assessment methods. Imagine that you have been trained to observe preschool children and that you are particularly skilled at defining target behaviors with precision and at counting how often they occur. You are sent to a special education classroom where you observe a 5-year-old boy with Down syndrome who regularly whines or stomps his feet when he has to move from a pleasurable activity to one that is less enjoyable (e.g., from playing to

eating). You also observe that, when he becomes disruptive, the boy's teacher usually attends to him immediately by talking to him or helping him. Whining and tantrums may be so effective in getting this child attention (which is very pleasurable) that they actually prevent him from learning more acceptable ways of communicating. You can then use the detailed information you have collected about what happens before (i.e., transition from one activity to another) and after the event (i.e., positive teacher attention) to set up a treatment program in which the teacher systematically ignores the boy when he whines, but praises him when he attempts to communicate with appropriate gestures and words. That program might also include steps to facilitate transitions, such as warning the child a few minutes ahead of time when an activity is about to end.

Adolescence

> *People make me feel important in life, especially my family with all their love and support. I got guidance from my parents being there when I needed them, plus my sisters were the same way. . . . Stephanie and Leah have been very helpful, very supportive to me, who gave me a lot of potential. They have shown me what is right and wrong and also let me know how supportive I have been to them.*
>
> —Mitchell Levitz, who has Down syndrome

Many intervention programs for adolescents with mental retardation target independent-living skills (autonomy, self-care skills, social skills, and job training) in order to facilitate the transition from school into the larger community. The programs also often focus on symptoms associated with comorbid disorders. For example, a teenage girl with mental retardation may develop a mood disorder because of her interpersonal and social difficulties. Treatment may then attempt to reduce her depressive symptoms (see Chapter 9) and increase her social skills. **Social skills training** is a common component of many treatment programs for children and adolescents with mental retardation. This approach aims at improving essential interpersonal skills—such as listening, following directions, smiling, and problem solving—that enable youth to function socially and to hold a job. Trained staff or peers model the desired skills; the youth then practice these skills, and staff or peers provide encouragement and reinforcement. Remember John, the young man with moderate mental retardation we described earlier. The treatment he received to teach him to use his hands appropriately instead of keeping them on his face was a form of social skills training. However, in his case as in many others, treatment was aimed not only at teaching him new skills, but also at facilitating his social integration. Obviously, an adolescent who uses his hands appropriately appears much more normal than one who does not, regardless of ability. And youth who smile appropriately are more likely to be accepted than youth who do not. They are also more likely to get on well with others and, with adequate support, to be able to hold a job and, in some cases, live independently.

Pharmacological Interventions

There is no pharmacological intervention for mental retardation. Instead, **psychotropic drugs**—drugs prescribed to alleviate symptoms of other disorders—are often used to control specific maladaptive behaviors in youth with mental retardation. In a ten-year review of the literature, medication was shown to be most often used to reduce self-injurious, aggressive, and repetitive behaviors (Matson et al., 2000). Drugs are also sometimes prescribed to alleviate symptoms of comorbid disorders, such as mood and anxiety disorders.

The scientific literature points to disturbing trends in this area (Madrid, State, & King, 2000; Matson et al., 2000). First, it appears that psychotropic drugs are increasingly used to control the behavior of youth with mental retardation, although there is little evidence that they improve these youths' overall functioning or help them learn more effectively. Second, medications are often prescribed with little or no scientific evidence that they are suitable for children and adolescents, or that their potential benefits clearly outweigh the risks of their often long-term use. Third, medications that are effective in controlling disruptive symptoms tend to suppress general activity level and adaptive functioning as well. In other words, many medicated youth stop engaging in maladaptive behav-

iors, such as aggression, hyperactivity, or self-injury, but at the expense of an overall decrease in *all* behaviors. It is understandable that parents, teachers, and caregivers who look after and work with youth with mental retardation want to control their maladaptive conduct. However, growing reliance on medication in this area runs the major risk of "chemically restraining" young people, instead of providing them with opportunities to function more adaptively (Matson et al., p. 263).

Alternative Treatments

Although some forms of mental retardation require careful control of the child's food intake (e.g., a diet low in phenylalanine for children with PKU), there is little evidence to support the effectiveness of alternative pharmacological, nutritional, or dietary treatments—such as the use of multivitamins and minerals in Down syndrome or folic acid in fragile X syndrome—in mental retardation. Contrary to countless case reports that attest to the benefits of such alternatives, controlled clinical trials are rare, and those that have been conducted generally show that these treatments are not better than placebos (Ellis, Singh, & Ruane, 1999). In addition, many of these treatments are not prescribed and supervised by trained professionals, and may actually be detrimental to the child's health because they are potentially toxic or deprive the child of the benefits of a balanced diet (Kozlowski, 1992).

Prevention

In mental retardation, as in many other areas, there is widespread agreement that prevention is better than remediation. Important prevention efforts rely on public health policies and public education campaigns. For example, to reduce birth defects and childhood injuries, federal and state agencies conduct large-scale education campaigns to inform women about the risks associated with drug and alcohol use during pregnancy, and to encourage parents to put infants in car seats and to make children wear safety helmets when they bike. Similarly, growing public awareness of the ill effects of lead on intellectual functioning has resulted in more attention being paid to cleaning up this health hazard.

Medicine plays an important role in prevention also. Medical efforts are evident in birth screenings for disorders that result in mental retardation, such as PKU, and in vaccination campaigns aimed at reducing the incidence of diseases such as rubella that are known to affect a fetus's brain development. Advances in medical technologies have also contributed to prevention in recent decades. For example, **amniocentesis,** a prenatal test of the amniotic fluid, makes it possible to determine the presence of diseases or genetic defects in the developing fetus. Amniocentesis also can be used to test mothers who already have a child with mental retardation; similarly, it can be used to test older mothers, who run a greater risk of giving birth to a child with Down syndrome than their younger counterparts. Results of the test can then be used to plan interventions during the pregnancy (e.g., surgery to remedy a potentially damaging abnormality) and to counsel mothers who carry an affected child to help them in their decision of whether to proceed with the pregnancy or not.

Finally, education has always played a major role in the prevention of mental retardation. We mentioned earlier that intensive intervention programs designed to foster intellectual development in children from underprivileged families have resulted in substantial increases in the average IQ score of participants. Most important, children who participate in these programs *early*—that is, in the preschool years—are less likely to develop mild mental retardation than children who do not (Schweinhart & Weikart, 1997). One such program is the Perry Preschool Project, which began in the 1960s in Michigan. The professionals in charge of this project have been observing a group of African American children of low socioeconomic status for twenty-seven years. These children, who participated in an intensive preschool program, had low IQ scores (between 70 and 85) and were at high risk of failing in school at the beginning of the study. However, over the years, these children performed better than control group children on many measures of academic and social achievement. Specifically, they had better grades,

higher standardized test scores, and higher high school graduation rates (71% vs. 54%). Most important, only 15% of program participants were placed in special education classrooms for children with mental retardation, compared to 34% of control group children (Parks, 2000).

Other preschool prevention programs have also demonstrated considerable improvements in student academic and social abilities. Programs such as the Abecedarian Project (Ramey et al., 2000) and the Infant Health and Development Project (Ramey & Ramey, 1998) also focus on children at high risk for academic failure—by virtue of the fact that they were born into poverty or were born prematurely. These programs typically include a specialized, enriched educational curriculum, a parenting component (e.g., teaching parenting skills to improve child functioning), and an opportunity for the family to work with social workers to make changes in their environment (e.g., educational opportunities to increase parental earning potential). Like the Perry Preschool Project, these programs have had a significant impact on the children and families they serve. For example, the Abecedarian Project has found that high-quality preschool education consistently improves cognitive development and academic achievements in young children; and that mothers of participating children, especially when they are teenage mothers, make greater strides in their own education and obtain higher levels of employment than mothers of comparison children. The Infant Health and Development Project has obtained comparable results with younger children (from birth to age 3). This program has also shown that, contrary to common expectations, children from the most disadvantaged families generally benefit most from early preventive intervention (see Figure 3.4, p. 84). These studies have major implications for social policy, because they show clearly that many cases of school failure and possible diagnoses of mild mental retardation can be avoided when at-risk children and their families are given access to quality services early in development. We consider this issue further in Box 3.5 (p. 84), where we discuss the factors that are believed to be key to successful prevention of mild mental retardation.

FIGURE 3.4 *Improvements in Children's IQ Scores through Early Preventive Intervention.* This figure illustrates the gains in IQ scores of children who participated in the Infant Health and Development Program, given the level of their mothers' education. Results show that infants of mothers with the lowest level of education (i.e., some high school) showed greater improvements than infants of better-educated mothers. Several reasons may explain why children from more disadvantaged families benefit most from early preventive intervention, although it may simply be that intervention offers them many stimulating experiences that their families cannot give them at home.

Source: From C. T. Ramey and S. L. Ramey (1998), "Prevention of Intellectual Disabilities," *Preventive Medicine 27,* pp. 224–232. Reprinted by permission.

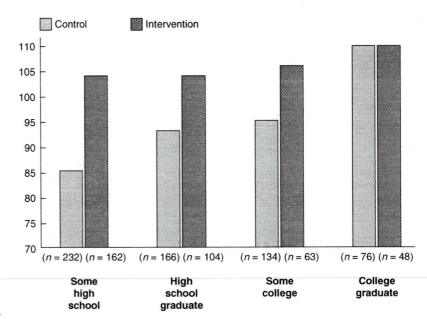

BOX 3.5 • *"Priming" Young Children to Succeed as a Means of Preventing Mild Mental Retardation*

Mental retardation is an area in which systematic prevention efforts have been most successful to date. As we emphasize in the text, prevention programs targeted at young children who are at risk of developing mild mental retardation—because they live in poverty, have teenage mothers who lack education, or were born prematurely—produce significant increases in IQ and academic achievement. Proponents of these programs have shown that intellectual skills typically flourish in environments where a child's cognitive, social, and affective development is "primed" (Ramey & Ramey, 1992). But what makes prevention in this area successful? Ramey and Ramey believe that there are six ingredients for success when it comes to "priming" the development of at-risk children:

- *Encouragement:* Success comes when children are encouraged by adults to explore and gather information about the environment.
- *Celebration:* Success comes when children's development is rewarded and celebrated.

- *Rehearsal:* Success comes when children are helped to practice new skills until they are mastered.
- *Safe environment:* Success comes when children are provided with an emotionally safe environment where trusted adults do not allow negative behavior, such as teasing, to discourage new learning.
- *Coaching:* Success comes when basic cognitive skills, such as naming and comparing, are coached and modeled by trusted adults.
- *Language exposure:* Success comes when children are exposed to a fertile language environment that encourages and rewards verbal communication.

As you can see, there is no magical ingredient in that list. Each of these features reflects well-established educational procedures that foster coping competence in young children. Many cases of mild mental retardation might be prevented if, as a society, we decide to provide all young children with safe learning environments where they can be primed to succeed.

Web Links

www.aamr.org (American Association on Mental Retardation)

www.ndss.org (National Down Syndrome Society)

www.spinabifida.org (Queensland Association for People with Spina Bifida or Hydrocephalus)

www.fraxa.org (Fragile X Syndrome Research Foundation)

www.aap.org (American Academy of Pediatrics; search for disorder of interest, such as fetal alcohol syndrome)

www.pwsausa.org (Prader-Willi Syndrome Association (USA))

4

Autism and Other Pervasive Developmental Disorders

He tests in the normal range for intelligence. But he can't tell me how his day was, or what hurts.

—Father of a child with autism

Children and adolescents with a pervasive developmental disorder exhibit an array of behavior disturbances. The DSM-IV-TR includes four pervasive developmental disorders: autistic disorder, Asperger's disorder, Rett's disorder, and childhood disintegrative disorder. The first two are described in detail, whereas the other two are covered only briefly. According to the DSM-IV-TR, these disorders are characterized by widespread "impairment in several areas of development: reciprocal social interaction skills, communication skills, or the presence of stereotyped behavior, interests, and activities" (APA, 2000a, p. 69). In a majority of cases, symptoms:

1. Appear early (in infancy or early childhood).
2. Are manifest across different areas of functioning.
3. Affect the child's entire development, seldom showing significant improvement with age.
4. Are accompanied by mental retardation and/or serious medical conditions.

The DSM-IV-TR terminology emphasizes also the primarily *developmental* nature of the disorders we

consider in this chapter. The term *developmental* highlights two features that are key here: these disorders develop in a characteristic fashion from an early age and are not simply scaled-down versions of adult conditions; and these disorders have a primarily biological, rather than psychological or social, origin.

Autism

Autism is the best known of the pervasive developmental disorders. Often accompanied by mental retardation, it is a disorder that develops early and involves major disturbances in social interactions, communication, and daily behavior patterns. Consider David's story, as told by his mother:

A child's kiss, a hug, saying "I love you." As parents, we expect this from our children. We take simple things for granted. My son David has taught me not to take anything for granted. Not even little things. However, I've learned that miracles do happen.

David is seven years old, tall for his age, with thick brown hair, a dark complexion, and beautiful eyes. David is exceptionally cute and adorable.

David is autistic.

When he was younger, he did not like to be held or touched. He didn't talk. He would just sit alone in his room spinning the wheels on his toy dump truck. No one else existed for him. When he was two, I tried to force him to let me hold and rock him. He screamed and began hitting and kicking me. I was devastated. We took him from professional to professional to try and find out what was wrong with him. They would all say the same thing: "He's fine, he's just behind developmentally." One doctor even told me, "There's nothing wrong with him, you're just overprotective." Well, when he was three, we finally found out what was wrong. "Your son is autistic."

I have learned so much from my son. To take things one day at a time and never give up hope. David has so much determination. I've watched him struggle just to make eye contact. He would know what he wanted but had great difficulty saying it. One of the happiest moments in my life was when he stood in front of me, reached his arms in the air, and said "hug."

David has shown me that there is more than one kind of miracle. He has so many miracles. He will always be autistic. He won't suddenly wake up one morning and be "normal." There are many things that David can't do and other children his age can. That doesn't matter to me. In his own way, David can communicate, and love. He hugs, he kisses, laughs, and smiles, and he is happy. We have had a different kind of miracle.

My son David is now nine. He continues to make progress. The most important thing that I've learned from him is to never give up and not to overlook the other miracles in life that are a little different than the one we may want (Autism Society, 1999, on line).

Historical Overview

Children and adolescents with autism have always attracted considerable attention, not only because of their puzzling behaviors but also because of the fundamental questions the disorder raises about human nature. The first cases of autism—or, at least, of autistic-like

behavior—were described approximately two centuries ago by Jean Marc Gaspard Itard in France and John Haslam in England. Itard, who was a physician, chronicled the story of Victor, the "wild boy of Aveyron." Victor was approximately 12 years old when he was found in a forest in the center of France. He was wild and had no language. Itard's descriptions of Victor seem to suggest that Victor may have suffered from autism (see Box 4.1).

Although descriptions of autistic behavior have been on record for centuries, autism was not recognized as a distinct psychological disorder until the 1940s, when Leo Kanner (1943) in the United States and Hans Asperger (1944) in Austria independently published detailed case studies describing the social, linguistic, and behavioral characteristics of the disorder. The terminology used today comes from their work: Kanner described the symptoms of eleven children suffering from what he called "extreme autistic loneliness," while Asperger reported on four children suffering from what he termed "autistic psychopathy." The term *autism* comes from the Latin word *auto*, which means "self." Affected children are suffering from "selfism" (not selfishness); that is, they appear to be living almost entirely in a world that they alone occupy. Even though Kanner and Asperger originally shared the same diagnostic terminology, many researchers and clinicians today distinguish between autism and Asperger's disorder.

Kanner's original paper described the physical, emotional, and intellectual development of the children he studied, as well as their level of functioning at the time of his assessment. He also provided detailed descriptions of their parents. In particular, he stressed that all eleven children came from "*highly intelligent families*" (1943, p. 248; italics in original). Their fathers were all distinguished professionals, and nine out of the eleven children's mothers had a university education, which was rare at the time. However, Kanner concluded his first report on the disorder by presuming that their difficulties had a biological, rather than a psychological or social, origin: "The children's aloneness from the beginning of life makes it difficult to attribute the whole picture exclusively to the type of the early parental relations with our patients. We must, then, assume that these children have come into the world with

BOX 4.1 • *Did Victor, the "Wild" Boy of Aveyron, Have Autism?*

Victor is one of the so-called "feral" children who, at some time in their development, were abandoned in the woods of nineteenth-century Europe. These children "grew up wild, outside human contact of any kind, had no language, and were so different from ordinary folk that they were classified . . . as a different species" (Frith, 1989, p. 16).

Victor's story began with his capture near Aveyron in the center of France. He was approximately 12 at the time, without speech, clothes, or any understanding of social behavior. His discovery captured the public's attention. Philosophers and social commentators surmised that his lack of language and social skills reflected the benefit or harm—depending on which position one adopted—of being raised without societal constraints.

Jean Marc Gaspard Itard, a prominent physician, decided that the way to answer these questions was to try to educate Victor. He welcomed the boy into his home; and for five years Itard, his friends, and his servants took on the daily task of intellectually and socially helping the adolescent become normal. The experiment essentially failed. Victor never learned to live on his own. He acquired some sign language and many manual skills, but he never developed the social skills and understanding that would have allowed him to live appropriately with others.

Did Victor have autism, or were his language and social skills deficits the result of severe isolation and deprivation? Harlan Lane (1977), an authority on this subject, finds many reasons to believe that Victor did not have autism. Specifically, Lane emphasizes that (1) he was not completely withdrawn from others and even showed affection to those he knew well; (2) he developed some communicative skills (through gestures) in the course of his education; (3) he showed mood changes in response to the behaviors of others; (4) he was not obsessed with order and sameness; and (5) he had the ability to learn practical skills and to complete simple tasks. Deficits in *all of these areas,* Lane believes, would be required to demonstrate that Victor had autism. Other experts disagree. For example, Uta Frith (1989) notes that Lane's analysis ignores the *developmental* nature of autism. She

believes that Victor manifested the symptoms of an adolescent with autism, rather than those of a young child with the disorder. More specifically, as they age, most children with autism become more social (although they remain often very limited in their social interaction), and exhibit changes in mood based on their interactions with others. They also acquire the ability to communicate (through a limited verbal or sign language if they do not speak) and to complete a variety of everyday tasks. Frith concludes that Victor's behavior was consistent with the clinical manifestations of autism in some adolescents and that his prolonged communication and social difficulties—even after his education with Itard—further support the idea that he had autism. Since we have no information on Victor's early years, we will probably never know.

innate inability to form the usual, biologically provided affective contact with people, just as other children come into the world with innate physical or intellectual handicaps" (p. 250).

In later writings, Kanner put less emphasis on the presumably biological origins of autism and began to focus more and more on psychological and family factors. In 1954, for example, he speculated that the autistic symptoms he was observing in many children were the result of what he considered to be the cold and often rejecting nature of their intellectual parents—especially the mothers. And he concluded that, in many if not all cases, the children's symptoms represented a primitive attempt to protect themselves from the extremely harmful effects of parental "emotional refrigeration" (quoted by Howlin & Yule, 1990). This psychological perspective is no longer accepted today, but it had a major influence on the first generation of researchers and clinicians in this area (e.g., Bettelheim, 1967; see Box 4.6, p. 111).

A large body of scientific data collected in different countries over the past thirty years contradicts this theoretical perspective, and the vast majority of researchers and clinicians who study the disorder today no longer believe that it is linked to a certain kind of parenting. In fact, the evidence we present in this chapter shows that blaming parents for their child's autistic disorder is tantamount to adding pain, injury, and guilt to the multiple challenges they face already. Moreover, as David's story shows, it disregards the loving concern that most of these parents have for their children, and the suffering they endure as they see their children struggle to make contact with the world around them.

Definitions, Diagnostic Criteria, and Major Characteristics

Autism is a pervasive developmental disorder that begins in early childhood, before age 3. It is characterized by serious disturbances in social interactions and communication, and by patterns of behavior that are considerably restricted, repetitive, or stereotyped. In a majority of cases, children with autism also have a moderate level of mental retardation.

Table 4.1 (p. 90) shows the DSM-IV-TR diagnostic criteria for autism. As the length of this table illustrates, multiple symptoms attest to the pervasive nature of the disorder. However, their number is less important than the fact that these symptoms represent distinct, *qualitative* differences in development more than excesses or deficiencies in otherwise appropriate behaviors. The case of Greg illustrates these developmental difficulties very clearly.

Greg was six years old when he was referred to our . . . program. He looked as if he had walked right out of a Norman Rockwell painting, with his blond hair, sparkling sky-blue eyes, pug nose, and the freckles sprinkled across his cheeks and nose. At first glance, Greg appeared to be a sweet, shy child, avoiding eye contact with others by continually staring at his feet. However, it did not take long for the extreme behaviors characteristic of autism to become quite evident.

While he was an infant, Greg's mother had not been concerned about him. Her pregnancy and delivery had been uneventful, and from the moment Greg was born . . . he was an "easy" child. He never demanded much attention and seldom cried. . . . As Greg grew, his developmental milestones appeared on time and, in some cases, earlier than normal. . . . As a result, Greg's mother was not worried about his "loner" attitude and his lack of interest in being hugged or cuddled. However, Greg began to appear so unresponsive to his environment that his mother suspected that he might be deaf. These suspicions were allayed when the pediatrician found Greg's hearing to be intact. . . .

As Greg got older, his lack of interest in his environment and in people became more obvious. Greg was unaffectionate with his parents and disinterested in playing with his older brother. Indeed, Greg was not interested in playing with toys. If he did approach a toy, he usually mouthed it or waved it in front of his face in a self-stimulatory manner. Greg began to speak, but his words did not make sense. At this time, at around the age of 4, Greg's autistic characteristics became most evident. . . .

Greg's speech, at one point, was almost completely echolalic and obsessional. Greg would not use words to communicate but would merely repeat what had just been said (immediate echolalia). This echolalia [i.e., the repetition of words or phrases] interfered greatly with Greg's learning as he tended to repeat the instructions for a task rather than follow them. . . . Greg would initiate spontaneous speech only if it was obsessional in nature. As an example of his obsessional desire for sameness in his environment, Greg would ask every time he left a setting, "Where are we gonna go next?" This question would be asked even if he merely walked from one room to another. . . . Greg

TABLE 4.1   *Autistic Disorder: DSM-IV-TR Diagnostic Criteria*

A. A total of six (or more) items from (1), (2), and (3), with at least two from (1), and one of each from (2) and (3):

  (1) qualitative impairment in social interaction, as manifested by at least two of the following:

   (a) marked impairment in the use of multiple nonverbal behaviors such as eye-to-eye gaze, facial expression, body postures, and gestures to regulate social interaction

   (b) failure to develop peer relationships appropriate to developmental level

   (c) a lack of spontaneous seeking to share enjoyment, interests, or achievements with other people (e.g., by a lack of showing, bringing, or pointing out objects of interest)

   (d) lack of social or emotional reciprocity

  (2) qualitative impairments in communication, as manifested by at least one of the following:

   (a) delay in, or total lack of, the development of spoken language (not accompanied by an attempt to compensate through alternative modes of communication such as gesture or mime)

   (b) in individuals with adequate speech, marked impairment in the ability to initiate or sustain a conversation with others

   (c) stereotyped and repetitive use of language or idiosyncratic language

   (d) lack of varied, spontaneous make-believe play or social imitative play appropriate to developmental level

  (3) restricted repetitive and stereotyped patterns of behavior, interests, and activities, as manifested by at least one of the following:

   (a) encompassing preoccupation with one or more stereotyped and restricted patterns of interest that is abnormal either in intensity or focus

   (b) apparently inflexible adherence to specific, nonfunctional routines or rituals

   (c) stereotyped and repetitive motor mannerisms (e.g., hand or finger flapping or twisting, or complex whole-body movements)

   (d) persistent preoccupation with parts of objects

B. Delays or abnormal functioning in at least one of the following areas, with onset prior to age 3 years: (1) social interaction, (2) language as used in social communication, or (3) symbolic or imaginative play.

C. The disturbance is not better accounted for by Rett's Disorder or Childhood Disintegrative Disorder.

Source: American Psychiatric Association, *Diagnostic and Statistical Manual of Mental Disorders, Fourth Edition, Text Revision* (Washington, DC: American Psychiatric Association, 2000a). Copyright 2000 American Psychiatric Association. Reprinted with permission.

also displays great confusion of pronouns and continues to have difficulty with I/you usage. He generally tries to avoid this problem by referring to himself and others by name only (e.g., "May Greg play with Trish?"). Greg also displays speech dysprosody (the timing and rhythm of the words is odd), his articulation being good but his intonation remaining quite poor.

As is characteristic of autistic children, Greg displays an intense desire for sameness and engages in ritualistic behavior. He must read his books in a cer-

tain order and in a certain way. He insists on reading books by complete rows first, even if the content is separated into columns. He must keep all doors closed. When the microwave oven is in use, he must have the egg beaters running. His parents can watch the news only on a certain television channel. If any of these orders or situations are changed, Greg gets extremely agitated and tantrums. . . .

Greg also maintains obsessions or bizarre and intense preoccupations with certain objects. He continually seeks out these objects or talks about them. In addition to marshmallow (with which he is obsessed), Greg is obsessed with toilets: his mother describes this obsession as a great "love." He has even hugged toilets. . . . Greg is also obsessed with lawn mowers and chain saws. He climbs up on his back fence and looks for his neighbors mowing the lawn. That obsession, compounded with his obsession with Honda cars (specifically 1977 Honda Civics), has led to the dangerous problem of his leaving his house in search of neighbors mowing their lawns or in search of chain saws and Hondas in his neighbor's garages. Greg can identify a Honda car key by even a casual, long-distance glance at someone's key chain.

Like so many autistic children, Greg engages in self-stimulatory behavior. Thus, he usually plays with toys in a repetitive and inappropriate manner, such as taking [a doll or truck] and running [it] through his hair. He plays with crayons and paper but will repetitively write EXXON (a gas station with which he is obsessed). . . . Greg has never displayed any self-injurious behavior.

Greg's only irrational fear is of microwave ovens. Rather, as is typical of autistic children, Greg is relatively fearless, even of situations in which he should demonstrate some fear or caution. Greg has no fear of climbing up on his backyard fence or of getting lost when he runs away in search of Hondas and lawn mowers. He has no fear of getting hit by a car and casually and frequently walks into the middle of a street. In addition, Greg's emotional behavior is inappropriate. He may start laughing for no apparent reason; sometimes, he has great difficulty controlling his giggling.

Finally, Greg displays isolated areas of good performance that are very striking in comparison to *the extreme deficits described above. . . . Greg is extremely good at certain tasks, such as block design and puzzles. Indeed, his IQ, derived from a nonverbal standardized test, is 76. . . . Also, Greg's mother describes his memory as "incredible." He remembers people's names after being told only once. Once he acquires a task or is told information, he will remember it for quite some time without any review.*

Because of Greg's communicative speech, his responsiveness to treatment, his high mental age, and his family's active participation in treatment, we are encouraged and optimistic about continued progress in the future (Schreibman & Charlop, 1989, pp. 122–123).

As this careful description shows, it is difficult to summarize the major characteristics of autism in a short paragraph. First, the disorder affects the child's entire functioning, leaving few if any areas of development untouched. Second, even though children with autism have many similarities, the disorder can manifest itself very differently from one child to another. Third, its symptoms often change in the same child from one developmental period to the next. Researchers and clinicians generally agree that, for a diagnosis of autism to be appropriate, impairments and limitations must be present in the three key areas that we describe next.

Qualitative Impairments in Reciprocal Social Interactions.

Children with autism have social and emotional deficits that severely limit their ability to participate in **reciprocal social interactions**—that is, social exchanges in which two or more partners actively share and contribute. Typically, these children do not seek out other people, except as means to an end—for example, to get something to eat or to obtain a toy out of reach. They may even appear unaware that people exist as people rather than as things. Their behavior makes for very one-sided exchanges. Over time, this one-sidedness limits their ability to develop and maintain social relationships based on mutual exchanges of affection, concern, and shared interests; thus, most children with autism lack one of the fundamental building blocks necessary for the growth of social competence (for an exception, see David's story above).

Reciprocal play and interest are integral parts of being human.

Although all children and adolescents with autism have numerous and, in many cases, severe social and emotional deficits, the precise nature of these deficits remains unclear. In line with clinical research often presented in the popular press, some authors believe that these young people are actually incapable of forming close, affectionate bonds with their parents or siblings, or even of differentiating between people they know and strangers. Yet, as David's story illustrates, children with autism can distinguish familiar from unfamiliar people and clearly prefer the company of their mothers to that of a stranger (Sigman & Mundy, 1989). At age 1, the proportion of children with autism who develop a secure bond with their mothers is almost as high as it is among children with mental retardation and average children (Dissanayake & Crossley, 1996).

As these findings indicate, youth with autism are not unable or unwilling to engage in meaningful social interactions; rather, it is more likely that these children have major difficulties in understanding and managing the complex, rapidly changing information necessary for developing and maintaining the "social dance" that is characteristic of human relationships. These difficulties are particularly obvious in studies that focus on social reciprocity and awareness.

Researchers use the term **social reciprocity** to describe a child's actions in response to someone else's behavior, and the term **social awareness** to refer to a child's awareness of the social elements of the environment (i.e., of people and their behavior). For example, in an experiment that compared a group of children with autism to a group of same-age control children, children with autism smiled as often and as long as average children in face-to-face interactions with their mothers (Dawson, Hill, Spencer, Galpert, & Watson, 1990). However, children with autism smiled much less often *in response to* their mothers' smiles and rarely combined a smile and a glance; that is, they smiled, but usually without glancing in their mothers' direction.

These results are not unique. Comparable disturbances have been reported in other studies. For example, one team of researchers asked children to sort photographs of people, some of whom were wearing hats and others not. Children with autism sorted the photographs on the basis of the hats the people wore, whereas same-age children of comparable intelligence based their sorting on the facial expressions of the people in the photographs (Weeks & Hobson, 1987). Similarly, children with the disorder find it more difficult than average children of comparable intelligence to recognize faces they have seen earlier (Klin et al., 1999). Taken together, these results indicate that children with autism are often unaware of important social elements in their environment, or when they are aware of these elements, they have considerable difficulty responding to them in a reciprocal manner.

The social awareness deficits of children with autism are also evident in their limited imitation skills. For example, they have difficulty imitating the gestures or actions of another person. Since imitation helps a young child understand, develop, and influence social relationships, the inability to imitate could at least partly explain why children with autism have such inadequate social relationships (Dawson & Adams, 1984).

Qualitative Impairments in Various Modes of Communication. Children and adolescents with autism face major disturbances in all forms of communication: verbal, nonverbal, and symbolic (Rutter, 1978). For example, a longitudinal study found that in

adulthood only 20% of persons with autism spoke without significant impairment, and that 43% spoke a few words only or did not speak at all (Aussilloux & Misès, 1997).

Verbal Communication. In a majority of cases, affected youth who learn to speak cannot sustain a normal conversation. These difficulties are particularly pronounced in the social and pragmatic aspects of language. Typically, although their syntax and grammar are adequate, as you can see in Ruth's conversation (see Box 4.2), they tend to have a flat, unemotional, and concrete way of speaking that is poorly suited to normal conversation. They may also express themselves in ways that are qualitatively different from those of average children and that further impair normal conversation—saying, for example, "The frog ate the bug and made his mouth sad" (Capps, Losh, & Thurber, 2000).

To add to their communication difficulties, the verbal exchanges of children with autism often lack

---

BOX 4.2 • *What Do You Do for Fun? A Conversation with an Adolescent with Autism*

To illustrate the unique conversational style that is characteristic of individuals with autism, even when their level of functioning is relatively high, Uta Frith (1991) recorded the following dialogue with 17-year-old Ruth.

> *Frith:* And what do you do for fun?
> *Ruth:* Nothing.
> *Frith:* Perhaps you do some knitting?
> *Ruth:* Yes-suh.
> *Frith:* Or watching television?
> *Ruth:* Yes-suh.
> *Frith:* And do you read?
> *Ruth:* Yes-suh.
> *Frith:* What sort of things? (no reply) Do you read magazines?
> *Ruth:* No, just look at them.
> . . .
> *Ruth:* Work time now.

Frith notes many oddities in this dialogue. She describes Ruth's conversational style as "wooden." Ruth does not modulate her tone to express interest in what she reads or to sustain the conversation. Also apparent is Ruth's literal interpretation of Frith's words and her apparent lack of interest in her conversational partner. She answers questions willingly, but does not talk spontaneously. Similarly, whereas most people would consider glancing through a magazine as reading, Ruth can only understand it as looking at pictures. Finally, note the abrupt ending that Ruth brings to the dialogue. Sudden breaks in conversation—and, by implication, in the social relationships that make them possible—are often observed in persons with autism.

Source: Frith (1991), pp. 118–119.

spontaneity, rhythm, and reciprocity. They may speak continuously on the same topic for long periods of time or jump from one topic to another without transition. Alternatively, they may introduce irrelevant details (such as figures, dates, or historical facts) into a conversation or totally disregard the rules of turn-taking that make it possible for each person to know when to speak and to listen. They pay no attention to the questions others ask them, and they rarely ask questions themselves; when they do, they may repeat the same question several times or ignore the answers they receive. These disruptive behaviors regularly give the impression that children and adolescents with autism do not understand the information and the emotions that are conveyed through language (Strain, Kohler, & Goldstein, 1996). Most affected youth also have difficulty following even simple instructions, probably because they do not understand what is being asked.

Besides their limited ability to use language to exchange information and manage social interactions, many children with autism have characteristic ways of speaking that further add to their impairments in communication. **Echolalia** affects more than half of the children who are able to speak: they often repeat one or two words or an entire sentence without regard to its relevance to the immediate context. Echolalia can be irritating and invariably disrupts any normal conversation. However, through careful observation of the situations in which echolalia typically occurs, many researchers believe that it represents a genuine attempt at communication and not simply a meaningless or disruptive behavior (Nadel & Pezé, 1993). For example, children with autism use echolalia far more often in unfamiliar settings and during novel tasks, perhaps as a way of mastering these situations (Schreibman & Charlop, 1989).

Pronoun reversal is another characteristic pattern of speech in autism. Children with the disorder who learn to speak are particularly likely to use "you" or their first name instead of "I" to refer to themselves. For example, they may say, "You are hungry" or "Peter is hungry," when what they actually mean is "I am hungry." Pronoun reversal suggests that these children have a specific difficulty in understanding that each person has a different perspective that must be taken into account in any conversation. The inability of chil-

dren with autism to consider alternative perspectives is the focus of a growing area of research on **theory of mind,** which we explore in Box 4.3.

Nonverbal Communication.   Communication deficits are also apparent in the nonverbal behavior of persons with autism. In one study, researchers observed the communicative gestures used during play by young children with the disorder or with Down syndrome, and compared these gestures with those used by average preschoolers (Attwood, Frith, & Hermelin, 1988). They grouped gestures into three categories: simple pointing; instrumental gestures (which included nonverbal hand signals used to convey specific commands, such as "quiet," "stop," or "come here"); and expressive gestures (which included gestures indicative of feelings and emotions, such as love, embarrassment, or friendship). Youth with autism made pointing and instrumental gestures as often as their peers in the other two groups, but failed to use any expressive gestures to communicate feelings. We saw earlier that, like Ruth, youth with the disorder generally speak in a very concrete manner; so it may be that they use few if any expressive gestures precisely because those gestures convey abstract information (i.e., feelings and emotions). Another important finding of the study was that almost all the instrumental gestures used by the preschoolers with autism were made for the purpose of reducing social interaction. Typically, their nonverbal commands to others were generally to "be quiet" or "go away," further emphasizing the qualitative impairments in social behavior that are characteristic of the disorder.

Symbolic Communication.   Children with autism often have difficulty thinking abstractly and engaging in symbolic activities. For example, Kanner (1943) noted that one child in his original sample "can set the table for numbers of people if the names are given her . . . but she cannot set the table for 'three.' If sent for a specific object in a certain place, she cannot bring it if it is somewhere else but still visible" (p. 240). In the same way, children with autism who are able to speak tend to interpret what is said literally. In answer to the question "What do you do when you cut yourself?" a child with autism might answer, "You bleed,"

BOX 4.3 • *Do Children with Autism Have a Theory of Mind?*

By the age of 3 or 4, most children have developed a *theory of mind*. That is, they know that other people have beliefs or feelings different from their own, which must be taken into account if one is to understand their behavior (Sabbagh & Taylor, 2000). Evidence suggests that children and adolescents with autism lack a normally developed theory of the mind—or a theory of another person's mind, to be more accurate (e.g., Baron-Cohen, Leslie, & Frith, 1985; Frith, 1989). Some researchers actually believe that the impairments in communication and in social awareness and empathy that are characteristic of the disorder stem in part from the fact that affected youth have a limited understanding of the mentalistic states of others and, consequently, are unable to predict and respond to their behavior appropriately.

The three cartoons below give examples of picture stories used in experiments designed to test this hypothesis. In each story, children must determine the logical sequence of the four pictures (which are presented scrambled to the child). The first story is mechanical: children must determine that the balloon escaped the child's hand, flew up high into the air, and burst when it hit a tree. The second story is behavioral: children must recognize the nature of the activity—buying candy—to determine the pictures' correct sequence. The last story is *mentalistic*. In

order to understand the correct sequence of events, children must be able to identify what the main character is anticipating and therefore thinking. Here, the boy hides his candy and goes out to play. A woman comes in, finds the candy, and eats it. The boy returns and is surprised to find his candy missing. To accomplish this task, children must understand that the boy has a belief that differs from their own, for they know that the woman took the candy but he does not.

Mentalistic stories regularly baffle children with autism. They perform similarly to same-age, average peers or peers with mental retardation on mechanical and behavioral stories. However, when they are asked to solve and describe what is happening in mentalistic stories, they have considerable difficulty: children with autism are typically unable to understand why the boy would expect to find his candy in the box.

This difficulty in understanding the mentalistic states of others—or lack of a theory of mind—may be central to the deficits observed in autism. Pause for a minute and try to imagine a world where you were unable to understand or even guess the thoughts behind other people's actions. This world probably would seem bizarre and unpredictable to you, and at times very scary. This may be the world in which many children and adolescents with autism live.

A mechanical story

A behavioral story

A mentalistic story

Source: Cartoons courtesy of Axel Scheffler (1989). Reprinted by permission.

instead of offering a practical solution to the question, as average children generally do. Limitations in symbolic thought also hamper these children's ability to play in the way that other children do. Unlike most children over age 2, children with autism rarely play make-believe and later are often unable to understand jokes or games (Ungerer, 1989). For example, they may be absorbed by the wheels of a toy car and spin them endlessly, but they never play with the car by pretending to drive it or imitating the sound of the engine. These difficulties prevent them from taking part in the normal imaginary play of childhood that is crucial to the practice and mastery of social rules and conventions.

Limitations in Behavioral Repertoire.   The behavioral repertoire of children with autism is also seriously limited. Most of their activities and interests are narrow, rigid, repetitive, or without an apparent functional goal. Kanner (1943) noted that children with autism often seem to be completely absorbed in a "world of objects." He wrote of a particular child he had studied: "The most striking feature in his behavior was the difference . . . in his reactions to objects and to people. Objects absorbed him easily and he showed good attention and perseverance in playing with them. He seemed to regard people as unwelcome intruders to whom he paid as little attention as they would permit" (p. 224). In most cases this observation is too extreme to be accurate. However, in early childhood, children with autism become fascinated and even obsessed by specific objects or details of objects: marshmallows, toilets, and Honda cars or car wheels. Their narrow interests do not generally focus on how *people* work, but rather on how *things* work (Baron-Cohen & Wheelwright, 1999). Later on, these children—if they do not suffer from severe mental retardation—frequently become preoccupied with dates, figures, or events that they memorize and repeat, often regardless of situation or context (Wing, 1988). An older child may have learned, for example, all the dates and scores of major football games, but have little or no appreciation for the sport itself or for the people behind the figures.

Many children with autism also develop specific routines in their daily activities (for instance, when getting up or going to bed, or at mealtime) and become extremely distressed by any changes in them. For example, each day before Don came down from his bedroom after naptime, he asked his mother to say, "Don, do you want to get down?" He would come downstairs only after his mother said the phrase exactly as instructed (Kanner, 1943, p. 219). Similarly, children with autism are often highly resistant to changes in their physical environment and can become very upset when familiar objects—like a piece of furniture or an ornament—are moved even slightly. Behaviors such as these are clearly inappropriate in most situations, and are a source of puzzlement and, at times, of conflict for family members. However, this "anxiously obsessive desire for the maintenance of sameness"—through rituals, routines, or an unchanging physical world—may provide children with autism with consistent temporal and physical reference points (Kanner, 1943, p. 245), which might help them manage their orientation in time and space, and somewhat alleviate the daily challenges they face in navigating through their social world (Bullinger, 1996).

Finally, a majority of children with autism have a high level of motor activity that is often accompanied by stereotyped, repetitive behaviors: they may rock back and forth, move or flap their arms and hands aimlessly, or walk on their toes (Klinger & Dawson, 1996). Mannerisms such as these are particularly frequent in affected children who suffer from mental retardation, and can become especially pronounced when they are trying to communicate (Koegel & Koegel, 1996).

Subtypes.   The DSM-IV-TR does not describe subtypes of autism. However, the very diverse manifestations of the disorder, and the fact that it can affect people with intellectual abilities ranging from superior intelligence to severe mental retardation, suggest that autism is not a single condition but rather a spectrum or group of disorders. Epidemiological, biological, and cognitive data support such a claim. For example, in a large study conducted in England, Wing and Gould (1979) identified three subtypes of children with autism on the basis of differences in their social behavior. The validity of these subtypes—which the authors labeled *aloof, passive,* and *actively social-but-odd*—has since been supported by others, who showed that there are neurological, cognitive, linguistic, and social differences between these groups (Bachevalier,

1994; Castelloe & Dawson, 1993). This research does not establish the existence of well-defined subtypes of autism. However, the consistency of findings to date may enable researchers to understand better the complexity of the disorder, and to determine if its various manifestations have different developmental trajectories and etiologies.

Empirical Validity

The empirical validity of autism is well established (Rutter & Schopler, 1992), even though researchers still do not know how best to classify its diverse manifestations. In short, there is no doubt that autism is a condition that is distinct from other psychological disorders of childhood and adolescence. Its symptomatology and development are unique (see Developmental Trajectories and Prognosis), and it has been observed in children from around the world.

Although the empirical validity of the disorder is not in doubt, autism and childhood-onset schizophrenia (see Chapter 5) have often been confused, especially when empirical research first began in this area. In 1949, Kanner stated that "early infantile autism may . . . be looked upon as the earliest possible manifestation of childhood schizophrenia" (p. 419). However, a clear distinction must be made between these two disorders.

Associated Characteristics; Comorbidity

Medical Conditions. Many medical conditions have been associated with autism, although the extent of this association depends on how strictly such conditions are defined (Barton & Volkmar, 1998). Epilepsy is the medical condition most often linked to autism, affecting 20–30% of children with the disorder. Epilepsy typically appears during early childhood or at the time of puberty, and is especially prevalent among children who have severe mental retardation also (Gillberg, 1991b). Although the association between autism and epilepsy was mentioned in the earliest writings on the disorder, its nature remains to be elucidated.

Psychological Symptoms and Disorders. Contrary to the popular view of autism portrayed in some movies, only a small number of affected children have average or superior intellectual abilities. In fact, more than 75% of youth with autism have an IQ lower than 70. Mental retardation, when it is present, is usually of moderate level (i.e., IQ from 35 to 50). You will recall from Chapter 3 that an IQ in that range would indicate moderate to severe disruptions in most areas of cognitive functioning (Pennington & Ozonoff, 1996). However, the cognitive difficulties that accompany autism are usually uneven and may often appear paradoxical. For example, a young girl with the disorder may show significant delays on an intelligence test but be able to read fluently years before her peers (APA, 2000a).

In general, children with autism succeed better on nonverbal than on verbal tests of intelligence (Bryson, Clark, & Smith, 1988). However, this broad generalization is not unique to autism. It applies to a number of other psychological conditions, such as mental retardation and learning disabilities. More specifically, test profiles of children with autism often reveal remarkable success in spatial organization and auditory memory, but failure in language comprehension and sequencing tasks, such as tracking the order of events in a story. This specific profile may reflect a cognitive disorder that is distinctive of autism, since it is found in affected children of varying intellectual abilities, but not in children who have mental retardation without autism (Fombonne, 1995).

In a majority of cases, children with autism have serious behavioral difficulties that present a major challenge for their caregivers. They may exhibit inattentive, hyperactive, or impulsive behaviors similar to those of children with attention deficit hyperactivity disorder (ADHD; see Chapter 7); or severe temper tantrums or aggressiveness that resemble the problems of youth with oppositional defiant disorder (ODD; see Chapter 8). They may also engage in self-injurious behaviors (such as banging their head against a hard surface until they bleed), but usually only when they have significant language delays and mental retardation. These disruptive behaviors may be, at least in part, a way of expressing frustration at the difficulties they have whenever they try to communicate (Koegel & Koegel, 1996). Finally, persons with autism may have a number of depressive symptoms or a mood disorder, particularly during adolescence or at the beginning of adulthood (Lainhart & Folstein, 1994).

Although empirical evidence is sparse, clinical descriptions of children with autism are filled with accounts of extreme and unexpected reactions to sensory stimuli. You will remember that Greg was terribly frightened by the noise of the microwave but loved raucous chain saws. Similarly, many children with autism show a total disregard for real dangers but an intense fear of harmless objects or situations. These findings suggest the presence of sensory or regulatory disruptions, but the processes responsible for these disruptions have yet to be identified.

Epidemiology

Prevalence; Age and Gender Characteristics. Autism is a relatively rare disorder, although not as rare as originally thought (Gillberg & Wing, 1999). The first epidemiological studies, which began in the 1960s, reported prevalence rates ranging from 2 to 5 persons per 10,000 (Lotter, 1966; Wing & Gould, 1979). More recent research from around the world puts that range closer to 5 to 10 persons per 10,000 (Fombonne, 1998; Tanguay, 2000). Most researchers agree that this change in prevalence does not represent an actual increase in affected individuals in recent years, but rather the fact that the disorder is now better known. This increase also reflects the fact that diagnostic criteria have evolved over the past decades and are now broader than they used to be, thus allowing more children to be diagnosed with autism than before.

By definition, autism begins before the age of 3. However, the disorder is often diagnosed later. In most cases, developmental difficulties appear in the first year of life, even though parents or caregivers do not always immediately realize their seriousness (Siegel, Pilner, Eschler, & Elliot, 1988). Regular pediatric visits and developmental screenings have become common in many industrial countries and may explain why autism is probably diagnosed earlier today than it was before, especially when it is accompanied by mental retardation. However, it probably remains underdiagnosed in children and adolescents of average or superior intelligence (Klinger & Dawson, 1996).

Overall, autism is approximately four to five times more frequent in boys than girls. However, these figures hide the fact that girls with autism generally have a lower level of intellectual functioning than boys. Specifically, the disorder's sex ratio shows a large overrepresentation of boys in the normal and superior ranges of intellectual functioning, but an approximately equal representation of both genders in children with severe mental retardation (Volkmar, Szatmari, & Sparrow, 1993).

Social and Cultural Differences. Autism is a universal phenomenon. The disorder has been described in similar ways in several countries, such as England (Wing, Yeates, Brierley, & Gould, 1976), Canada (Bryson, Clark, & Smith, 1988), France (Fombonne, 1998), Japan (Tanoue, Oda, Asano, & Kawashima, 1988), and Scandinavia (Steffenburg et al., 1989). These studies show that there are few—if any—social, cultural, or ethnic differences in the epidemiology and characteristics of autism. As noted earlier, initial research in this field was based primarily on clinical samples of middle- to upper-class children. This research led to the belief that autism occurs primarily in children from affluent families. In fact, the disorder affects all social groups in comparable ways. Children from middle- to upper-middle-class families were often overrepresented because these families were the ones most able to obtain and pay for the expensive diagnostic work and care their children required.

Developmental Trajectories and Prognosis

Autism is a chronic disorder that tends to develop in a fairly continuous and predictable manner. It may be present at birth but often is impossible to detect because there are no tests for autism, and the physical appearance of children with the disorder does not differ from that of children without difficulties (many children with autism are actually very attractive). The first signs of the disorder sometimes appear shortly after birth; others, only several months later.

Infancy and Early Childhood. Although autism develops differently from one child to another, the first signs of the disorder are often relatively minor and may not draw much concern. One child may respond to being carried by becoming limp and passive or rigid and tense. Another may not make eye contact or smile. Still another may react strongly to various noises but fail to respond to his or her own name. In a majority of cases, these early signs become more obvious and alarming as the child develops. By age 2, the child tends to avoid adults and peers alike, seldom seeks to be held and comforted, and shows little or no interest in what others are doing. These social problems often lead to an initial professional consultation (Siegel et al., 1988).

As the child develops, communication difficulties, stereotyped behaviors, and/or learning difficulties emerge also and are, in many cases, related to increasingly obvious mental retardation. Interestingly, in videotapes of infants between 9 months and 1 year of age, children later diagnosed with autism could be clearly distinguished by their behavior from children with other developmental disabilities and from average children (Baranek, 1999). Thus, it may be that symptoms of the disorder are usually present in mild form before age 1 but that unsuspecting parents do not detect them until they become more pronounced.

Later Childhood, Adolescence, and Adulthood.
Symptoms that are present by age 4 or 5 tend to persist throughout childhood. But specific behaviors change as a function of the child's development; the manner in which family members, teachers, and peers respond to the child; and the interventions the child may receive. For example, younger children with autism are rarely interested in their peers, whereas older children with the disorder often appear to want to develop reciprocal relationships but do not know how (APA, 2000a).

For reasons that remain poorly understood, the passage to adolescence is often a period of major change for youth with autism. Research from around the world shows that up to 30% of affected adolescents exhibit a temporary or permanent deterioration in functioning during the teenage years (Gillberg, 1991b; Kobayashi, Murata, & Yoshinaga, 1992). This deterioration, which seems to affect girls more often than boys, can be observed in all areas of behavior. However, it usually appears as increased hyperactivity, aggressiveness, and stereotyped mannerisms or interests, as well as in amplified language difficulties. Some-

times, however, the passage to adolescence is accompanied by an improvement in the difficulties of children with autism (Kanner, 1971). For example, a Japanese research team found that the symptoms of approximately 40% of the children they studied improved during the course of adolescence (Kobayashi et al., 1992). This figure is encouraging. However, the majority of adolescents with autism continue to have considerable problems in adult life, especially in social interactions. Follow-up studies show that only a very small number of adults with autism are able to live independently and to work in unstructured settings (Aussilloux & Misès, 1997; Gillberg, 1991b; Kobayashi et al., 1992; Venter, Lord, & Schopler, 1992).

Variables Associated with Prognosis.
Overall, follow-up studies show that long-term prognosis is most favorable when children (1) have only mild (IQ > 50) or no mental retardation (IQ > 70); (2) develop some— even limited—language skills before age 5; and (3) participate in intensive early educational intervention programs. Early intervention is a major factor in determining outcome for many children with autism (see Treatment and Prevention).

Etiology

Biological Factors

Genetic Factors. Genetic factors play an important but still poorly understood role in the etiology of autism. Studies of families of children with autism indicate that 3% to 5% of affected children have a brother or sister with the same disorder. This number increases to between 12% and 20% if one includes brothers and sisters who suffer from cognitive deficits, social deficits, or another pervasive developmental disorder (Rutter, 2000; Smalley, 1991). At first glance, a **concordance rate** of 3% to 5% may not seem particularly high. (This is the rate at which the same or similar disorders or personality traits are found among close relatives such as twins). However, this rate is as much as one hundred times higher than the overall prevalence rate of autism in the general population.

The use of twins to study genetic contributions to autism is difficult because autism is rare and twins with the disorder are even rarer. Despite these difficulties, a few twin studies have been conducted. Their results indicate that genetic factors play a part in the etiology of the disorder. For example, in a study of twenty-one children with autism and their twins, researchers found that four of the eleven identical or monozygotic twins (36%) also suffered from autism, but that none of the ten fraternal or dizygotic twins did (Folstein & Rutter, 1977). When these researchers checked to see whether the twins who did not have autism had other developmental disorders (such as another pervasive disorder or a cognitive disorder), they found that 82% of the monozygotic twins, but only 10% of the dizygotic twins, did have such a disorder. A Scandinavian study used more recent diagnostic criteria and found a much higher concordance rate among identical twins: ten of eleven identical twins (91%) had autism, whereas none of ten fraternal twins was affected (Steffenburg et al., 1989). The various twin studies, even though they do not all use the same diagnostic criteria or the same sampling methods, clearly show that concordance rates of autism are consistently higher among monozygotic twins (where they range from 36% to 96%, with an average rate of 64%) than among dizygotic twins (where they range from 0% to 24%, with an average rate of 9%) (Smalley, 1991).

Although genetic factors play a role in the etiology of autism, the genetic processes involved remain to be elucidated (Rutter, 2000; Tanguay, 2000). Studies that have looked at genetic abnormalities in children with autism show that these abnormalities vary considerably from one child to another (Konstantareas & Homatidis, 1999). Approximately 10% of children with autism have a genetic disorder of known origin, such as fragile X syndrome. However, since these children also have mental retardation, the genetic disorder may account for overall intellectual functioning more than for autism specifically (Lombroso, Pauls, & Leckman, 1994).

Neurological Factors.   A number of studies have focused on the neurological differences that may exist between persons with autism, persons with mental retardation, and average persons (see Klinger & Dawson, 1996). In general, youth with autism have more neurological abnormalities than other groups of children to whom they are compared. Likewise, many biochemical, radiological, and pathological studies—studies of neurotransmitters such as serotonin and dopamine, or of brain structures such as the cerebellum—have found important abnormalities in *some* individuals with autism. However, these findings do not allow us to draw any firm conclusions about the etiology—or, more likely, the etiologies—of the disorder, because their results usually apply only to a minority of affected individuals, and because several of the abnormalities they have found are also present in children with disorders such as mental retardation and childhood-onset schizophrenia (Ghaziuddin, Zaccagnini, Tsai, & Elardo, 1999). Finally, the interpretation of most neurological findings is complicated by the fact that the majority of participants in research studies have had autism for several years by the time they are studied. Consequently, their abnormalities could be the consequence of living with autism as much as the cause of the disorder—since the disorder itself may bring about neurological changes over time.

Factors Related to Pregnancy and Birth.   Some studies indicate that mothers of children with autism have a higher incidence of prenatal difficulties (e.g., intrauterine bleeding) and of birth complications (e.g., breech deliveries) than mothers of comparison children (Bolton et al., 1997). Such complications are present in only a small number of cases; thus, their etiological role—if any—would apply only to some children with the disorder.

Early embryonic exposure to certain chemicals might also contribute to the development of autism. For example, maternal exposure to diseases such as German measles (rubella) in the course of pregnancy has been related to increases in the probability that their children would develop autism. Likewise, the children of mothers who took thalidomide while pregnant were thirty times more likely to have autism than children in the general population (Rodier, 2000). (Thalidomide was a drug prescribed to reduce symptoms of morning sickness in pregnant women. It caused a spate of severe birth defects in the 1960s and was removed from the market.)

A growing body of research is helping to isolate specific areas of the brain that differ between persons with and without autism. Some researchers have focused on the brain stem—a part of the brain that develops within the first few weeks of embryonic life (see Figure 4.1). This work suggests that minor defects in the brain stem—especially in the facial nucleus (which controls movements of the face) and in the superior olive (which is part of the auditory relaying system)—may account for symptoms of the disorder in some youth. More generally, this work is consistent with the widely shared belief that there are different causes of autism—some genetic, others reflecting exposures to toxic agents in pregnancy—that affect brain development before and after birth, and that give rise to different manifestations of the disorder (Rodier, 2001).

Psychological and Family Factors. Most of the early researchers and clinicians who studied autism believed that it was caused by psychological and family factors (see Rimland, 1964, for an early opposing view). This perspective is no longer accepted today—largely because it assumes an incredible feat on the part of children with autism: it assumes, in effect, that within the first few years of life these children *learn not to*

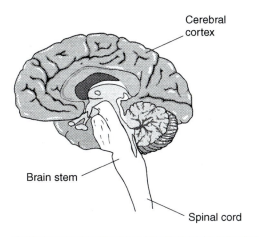

Cerebral cortex

Brain stem

Spinal cord

FIGURE 4.1 ***The Brain with the Brain Stem Highlighted.*** The brain stem is one of the oldest parts of the brain, and it controls the body's most basic functions. Research by Rodier (2000) suggests that subtle changes in the brain stem—especially in those areas that control facial movement and relay auditory information—may occur very early during pregnancy and result in the characteristic symptoms of autism.

communicate, and actively withdraw from the world. That is a most unlikely assumption, particularly since autism begins in infancy and is usually associated with mental retardation. It is easy to believe that rejected or abandoned children who have no opportunities to explore and control their environment may develop major problems of adaptation (as many maltreated children do; see Chapter 12). However, it is much more difficult to see how these harmful experiences could lead to the extreme behaviors that characterize autism, especially when the child with autism has brothers or sisters without psychological problems (as is the case in the large majority of families where there are siblings).

Empirical evidence against a psychological or familial etiology of autism abounds. Specifically, the disorder is not associated with a family's socioeconomic status or education, and parents of children with autism have personality characteristics similar to those of other parents. In particular, most parents of children with autism do not have more psychological disorders or marital or family problems than parents of average children (e.g., Koegel, Schreibman, O'Neill, & Burke, 1983). Nonetheless, psychological considerations are important in autism, since the pervasive nature of the disorder invariably affects family functioning. However, when personality differences are found between parents of children with autism and other parents, they are more likely to be a *consequence,* rather than a cause, of the disorder (Konstantareas, 1991). The challenges that children with autism and their caregivers face every day can lead to serious psychological and relational problems. Over time, these problems may perpetuate or even aggravate certain symptoms of autism. For example, parents of children with autism report comparable or higher levels of stress than parents of children with disruptive behaviors, and significantly higher levels of stress than parents of average children or of children with mental retardation (see Dumas, Wolf, Fisman, & Culligan, 1991). In the absence of longitudinal evidence, however, these correlational findings do not make it possible to establish cause and effect.

In conclusion, empirical data agree on four points:

1. The etiology of autism is complex and most probably heterogeneous (multifaceted).

2. Biological factors play a dominant role in this etiology, in spite of the emphasis that has traditionally been placed on psychological and family factors.

3. The processes through which biological factors exercise their effects on the child's symptoms remain poorly understood, although brain development in early pregnancy is now a prominent area of study.

4. The relationship between autism and family stress, as well as the role that stress may play in the child's difficulties, has not yet been elucidated.

More generally, it is probable that what we now call autism does not have a single cause or even a single group of causes—particularly since autism may not be a single disorder but, as noted earlier, a spectrum of disorders or a disorder with poorly understood subtypes.

Asperger's Disorder

Historical Overview

You will recall that, one year after the appearance of Kanner's first article on autism, Hans Asperger (1944) published a detailed description of the symptoms of four children with "autistic psychopathy." Although Kanner and Asperger both used the term *autistic* to describe the children they worked with, some researchers now believe that the two men were describing two overlapping but distinct disorders. Asperger's paper did not attract the same attention as Kanner's— probably because it was written in German—and Asperger syndrome was not immediately recognized as a pervasive developmental disorder distinct from autism. Actually, fifty years passed before the editors of the DSM-IV classified Asperger's disorder separately from autism. This decision is far from unanimous, as you will see below. Interestingly, the four children described by Asperger in 1944 would probably meet diagnostic criteria for autism today, and not for the disorder that bears his name (Miller & Ozonoff, 1997).

Definitions, Diagnostic Criteria, and Major Characteristics

Like autism, **Asperger's disorder** (or Asperger syndrome) appears in early childhood and is manifested by significant disturbances in social interactions, and restricted patterns of interest and behavior. However, unlike autism, the disorder does not involve language delays, mental retardation, or major problems in cognitive development and adaptive functioning.

Table 4.2 highlights the DSM-IV-TR diagnostic criteria for Asperger's disorder. Because this condition shares many characteristics with autism, diagnosis can be particularly difficult. Many clinicians even refer to Asperger's disorder as "high-functioning autism." Tom's story shows why.

Tom is a tall, stocky 15-year-old. [He has Asperger's disorder.] He is the older of two children; his father is a successful engineer and his mother is a secretary. . . . His medical history is unremarkable. Developmental milestones were within normal limits; Tom talked before he walked. He started nursery school at age 2½ years and already had unusual interests which were pursued to the exclusion of other activities. Over the years his interests have included stop signs, arrows, storm drains, and windmills, and, more recently, have changed to clocks, mathematics, and computers. Tom was a self-taught reader by age 3 and was reading adult-level books by age 4. In nursery school he had poor peer relations, talked about topics of interest only to himself, failed to listen to other children's comments, and was often oppositional and impulsive. At the same time he was aware of his social isolation. . . . A clumsy and poorly coordinated child, Tom often seemed markedly odd outside home or school settings. In his preoccupation with clocks he might approach a stranger and proceed to reset the person's watch without asking permission and often reset public clocks, e.g., at school.

[W]hen he was 9½ years old, Tom had no friends, very limited interpersonal skills, and signs of depression. . . . His fascination with clocks pervaded all conversation. . . . Nonverbal clues of social context, e.g., gestures, facial grimaces, emphasis of voice, and non-literal communications (e.g., abstract concepts),

TABLE 4.2   *Asperger's Disorder: DSM-IV-TR Diagnostic Criteria*

A. Qualitative impairment in social interaction, as manifested by at least two of the following:

  (1) marked impairment in the use of multiple nonverbal behaviors such as eye-to-eye gaze, facial expressions, body postures, and gestures to regulate social interaction

  (2) failure to develop peer relationships appropriate to developmental level

  (3) a lack of spontaneous seeking to share enjoyment, interests, or achievements with other people (e.g., by a lack of showing, bringing, or pointing out objects of interest to other people)

  (4) lack of social or emotional reciprocity

B. Restricted repetitive and stereotyped patterns of behavior, interests, and activities, as manifested by at least one of the following:

  (1) encompassing preoccupation with one or more stereotyped and restricted patterns of interest that is abnormal either in intensity or focus

  (2) apparently inflexible adherence to specific, nonfunctional routines or rituals

  (3) stereotyped and repetitive motor mannerisms (e.g., hand or finger flapping or twisting, or complex whole-body movements)

  (4) persistent preoccupation with parts of objects

C. The disturbance causes clinically significant impairment in social, occupational, or other important areas of functioning.

D. There is no clinically significant general delay in language (e.g., single words used by age 2 years, communicative phrases used by age 3 years).

E. There is no clinically significant delay in cognitive development or in the development of age-appropriate self-help skills, adaptive behavior (other than in social interaction), and curiosity about the environment in childhood.

F. Criteria are not met for another specific Pervasive Developmental Disorder or Schizophrenia.

Source: American Psychiatric Association, *Diagnostic and Statistical Manual of Mental Disorders, Fourth Edition, Text Revision* (Washington, DC: American Psychiatric Association, 2000a). Copyright 2000 American Psychiatric Association. Reprinted with permission.

were limited. A positive history for similar problems was noted in Tom's father....

Tom's second evaluation was conducted ... 2½ years later, when he was 12 years old. It followed a brief hospitalization following what school staff thought to be a suicidal gesture, but which seemed to us to more likely reflect his social and behavioral rigidity (he had frozen in a crosswalk when the signal changed to "Don't Walk").... He continued to have a markedly eccentric social style and engaged in one-sided conversations about computers and mathematical concepts in a loud, unmodulated voice. His very limited awareness of social conventions was illustrated by his one-sided conversational style, his tendency to belch and pass gas, and his use of graphic expletives with little apparent intention to shock his conversational partner....

    Psychometric Assessments. *... Tom has superior scores on verbal reasoning tasks, except for a task involving comprehension of social norms and conven-*

tions.... Tom had significant deficits in visual-motor skills, processing speed, and motor functioning....

    Speech-Communication Evaluation. *There was significant variability in Tom's speech-communication competence. His skills in the areas of single-word receptive [what he understood] and expressive [what he could say] vocabulary were excellent, but far weaker when he had to cope with non-literal and social language.... Thus, while Tom is reported to have had early language skills well within normal limits, his current skills are unusual in a host of ways (Volkmar et al., 1996, pp. 119–120).*

    As this case illustrates, the symptomatology of Asperger's disorder is similar to that of autism, but problems are more limited in scope. In fact, the disorder is characterized more by the *absence* of significant delays in language, cognitive development, and adaptive functioning (e.g., self-help skills) than by the presence of unique symptoms. Children with Asperger's disorder have normal intelligence and generally learn to speak at the same time as other children, using single words around 2 years of age and speaking in simple sentences around age 3. Likewise, the cognitive development of these children is normal or only slightly delayed; and they show age-appropriate levels of curiosity, interest in their environment, and autonomy (Frith, 1991).

The difficulties associated with Asperger's disorder are primarily evident in the social arena: all children and adolescents with the syndrome have severe and sustained impairments in reciprocal social interactions. These problems are very similar to those of children with autism, but usually less pronounced or made less obvious by their average or superior level of intelligence (Volkmar et al., 1996). Their language skills are intact, but their communication is limited to specific exchanges of factual information or to narrow topics in which they alone are interested. In addition, they often have a "bookish" way of speaking that is monotonous and conveys little or no emotion (Wing, 1991). In fact, they have great difficulty taking part in sustained reciprocal exchanges, and appear to be unable to take the perspective of others into account or to understand that others may have needs or preferences different from their own. Consequently, they regularly come across as "odd" or "eccentric" (see Box 4.4). Impairments in nonverbal communication also disturb their social relationships. For example, their facial expressions, gestures, and tone of voice are frequently limited, often inappropriate, and not "in tune" with what they are saying.

Young people with Asperger syndrome also have limited interests and activities. For example, they can become entirely absorbed by frogs, dinosaurs, or

---

BOX 4.4 • *Understanding the Social Interactions of People with Asperger's Disorder*

Margaret Dewey (1991) has done a considerable amount of research on the specific social deficits associated with autism and Asperger's disorder. To evaluate these deficits, Dewey created stories designed to test her subjects' "knowledge of human behavior" (p. 184). The following is one of Dewey's test stories. Read the paragraph and then rate each behavior in italics as you think that most people would rate it (from 1 = normal to 4 = shocking). Put your ratings in the brackets after each statement.

Roger, twenty-two, lived in a rented room alone. He was quite a nervous person, but it seemed to him he felt better if he ate every two hours and limited his diet to certain foods. One day a lady called and invited him to dinner explaining that she was a friend of his parents. Roger gladly accepted. *However, he warned his hostess that he ate no meat and would like his vegetables served unsalted []*. When Roger arrived at the appointed time he recalled that he had not eaten for two hours. *Without wasting any time, even before introductions, he asked the woman when dinner would be served []*. She replied that it would be about an hour before the meal would be ready. *Hearing this, Roger opened his briefcase, removed an apple and some nuts, and promptly ate them []* After that, he was introduced to the family and they sat around talking for an hour. Just before dinner, the hostess showed him an attractive platter of fruits and vegetables, asking whether it looked like enough. *"It looks fine, thank you,"* Roger said, *"but if you don't mind I will wait another hour to eat. I just had some food an hour ago."[]*

You might find this story funny, since you are very unlikely to act as Roger did. Dewey found that college students rated Roger's social manners as "very eccentric" or "shocking." In contrast, Dewey found that high-functioning young men with autism (more appropriately diagnosed with Asperger's disorder) did not think that Roger's behavior was abnormal. In fact, many of them found his actions to control his nervousness through dieting admirable. Most important, their responses showed that (1) they failed to take someone else's perspective into account, since they did not realize that Roger's behavior would be insulting to his hostess and her family; and (2) they ignored the importance of common social rules, such as waiting to ask about dinner until introductions are complete. The differences between your perceptions of Roger's behavior and those of Dewey's subjects highlight the difficulties facing children and adolescents with Asperger's disorder as they attempt to meet the ever-changing demands of human relationships.

Source: Dewey (1991), pp. 186–187.

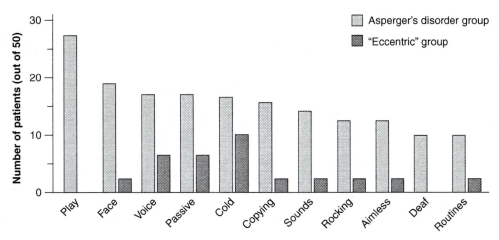

Play — play narrow, restricted
Face — facial expression difficult for parents to interpret
Voice — voice flat, monotonous, mechanical
Passive — no initiation of social contact
Cold — avoidance of cuddling, dislike of touch
Copying — difficulty in copying actions
Sounds — inexplicable aversion to certain sounds
Rocking — rocking in a stereotyped manner
Aimless — movements sometimes aimless or purposeless
Deaf — lack of sensitivity to sound, suspicion of deafness
Routines — strict routines and rituals for everyday life

FIGURE 4.2 *Childhood Symptoms Retrospectively Reported by Parents of Adults with Asperger's Disorder.* In a study comparing key characteristics of adults with Asperger's disorder and "eccentric" psychiatric patients without the disorder, Digby Tantam (1991) asked their parents to recall how they were as children. Results showed that, in childhood, patients with the disorder had a distinctive pattern of symptoms that set them apart from other "eccentric" patients. The most frequent developmental impairments that parents recalled were restricted play and lack of facial and vocal expression.

Source: D. Tantam, "Asperger Syndrome in Adulthood" in U. Frith (Ed.), *Autism and Asperger Syndrome* (Cambridge, England: Cambridge University Press, 1991), p. 165. Reprinted by permission.

recipes for gun powder—and devote all their time and energy to them, to the detriment of most other activities, including social interactions. Their interests or activities are not always inappropriate or lacking in a useful purpose; but the very narrow focus of these interests and/or the youth's abnormally intense and exclusive involvement in them become more and more obvious and alarming to parents and teachers. In contrast, the activities and interests of children with autism typically are

not only narrow but often without apparent functional goal. Figure 4.2 summarizes key developmental characteristics of children with Asperger's disorder.

Children and adolescents with Asperger's disorder do, at times, engage in repetitive and stereotyped behaviors that resemble those of young people with autism (e.g., hand or arm flapping, odd mannerisms). Their movements seem awkward, clumsy, or odd—probably because they are poorly coordinated or regulated, and the youth are unaware of how they appear to others (Wing, 1991).

Empirical Validity

To ask about the empirical validity of Asperger's disorder is to ask whether the syndrome is a less severe form or subtype of autism, or whether it is a similar but distinct condition (Rutter & Schopler, 1992). Two studies illustrate some of the difficulties this question poses. In comparing a group of children with Asperger's disorder with a group of children with autism who had similar intellectual abilities, one research team found that the children with Asperger's disorder had a better verbal memory and less difficulty completing a series of cognitive tasks (Ozonoff, Rogers, & Pennington, 1991). However, in a similar comparison, another team did not find cognitive differences between the two groups (Szatmari, Tuff, Finlayson, & Bartolucci, 1989). Furthermore, in a review of the literature comparing youth with autism and Asperger syndrome, investigators found that most children with Asperger's disorder had language delays and communication problems, contrary to what the DSM-IV-TR diagnostic criteria specify (Mayes, Calhoun, & Crites, 2001). Such findings call into question the empirical validity of Asperger's disorder. This validity is also questionable because:

1. Asperger's disorder and autism tend to be found in the same families (Gillberg, 1991a).
2. Much of the research in this area has not employed precise or comparable diagnostic criteria.
3. There is a lack of longitudinal studies to determine whether the developmental trajectories and long-term prognosis of Asperger's disorder and autism differ.

Future studies will need to clarify this situation. Currently, researchers and clinicians have the option to emphasize the symptoms that autism and Asperger's disorder have in common and to regard them as different manifestations of an "autistic continuum," or to focus on characteristics that may be distinctive and treat them as two separate conditions (Wing, 1988).

Ongoing research on what are called **nonverbal learning disabilities** (or NLD) complicates matters further, but may eventually help solve the question of the empirical validity of Asperger's disorder (Klin, Volkmar, Sparrow, Cicchetti, & Rourke, 1995). We discuss possible links between the disorder and NLD in Box 4.5. More generally, contradictory findings in this area highlight the fact that our current diagnostic categories are constantly evolving, descriptive groupings that will undoubtedly have to be modified in light of new research and clinical observations.

Associated Characteristics; Comorbidity

Medical Conditions. As many as 60% of children with Asperger's disorder have some kind of medical or neurological abnormality (Gillberg, 1989). Pregnancy or birth complications are also relatively frequent in the history of these children (Ghaziuddin, Shakal, & Tsai, 1995). However, as with autism, the importance of these factors is not clear, because these complications vary considerably from one child to another, and not all children with the disorder have a history of pre- or perinatal problems.

Many people with Asperger syndrome are either oversensitive or lacking in sensitivity to certain sensations (Frith, 1991). For example, a person with the disorder often can tolerate extremely high levels of pain, but is unable to wear certain types of clothing. As in autism, this characteristic suggests sensory disruptions that have yet to be fully explained.

Psychological Symptoms and Disorders. There may be an association between Asperger's disorder and mood disorders (see Chapter 9). In a genetic study, bipolar disorder was more frequent in families of persons with the disorder than in the population in general (DeLong & Dwyer, 1988). In addition, in a sample followed into adulthood, approximately one-third of participants suffered from depression and other psychological disturbances sometime during the course of the study (Tantam, 1991). Finally, some persons with Asperger syndrome may have some symptoms of schizophrenia (see Chapter 5) (Frith, 1991).

Epidemiology, Developmental Trajectories, and Prognosis

Precise figures on the prevalence of Asperger's disorder are not available. Published data indicate that it is less

BOX 4.5 • *Asperger's Disorder and Nonverbal Learning Disabilities*

Could Asperger's disorder be an example of a nonverbal learning disability (NLD)? Nonverbal disabilities are a group of deficits believed to occur in children and adolescents with significant impairments in the ability to identify, understand, and use nonverbal cues. Persons with such impairments have a fairly consistent psychological profile (Klin et al., 1995; Rourke, 1995):

1. They have excellent rote memory, as well as memory for verbal information.
2. They are very talkative, but the tone of their speech is poorly modulated and its content is often repetitive and of little interest to others.
3. They have difficulty adapting to new situations and, consequently, tend to rely on a selection of "stock behaviors" that may or may not be appropriate in these situations.
4. They have deficits in social perception and social interactions, and demonstrate poor social judgment.

All these behaviors should sound familiar to you by now, because they are also common characteristics of Asperger's disorder. But NLD has been shown to be associated with disruptions in functions under the control of the *right* hemisphere of the brain, whereas Asperger's disorder has traditionally been assumed to be associated with *left* hemisphere dysfunctions, because such dysfunctions are found in persons with autism. In an attempt to resolve this puzzle—and test whether Asperger's disorder and NLD are related disorders, distinct from autism—Klin and associates (1995) compared the psychological profiles of high-functioning adolescents with autism (i.e., with an IQ greater than 85) to those of groups of adolescents diagnosed with Asperger's disorder or NLD. Results showed that children with Asperger syndrome had deficits in fine and gross motor skills that were not found in children with autism. Specifically, their ability to integrate motor movements with visual information (such as the skill needed to hit a baseball) was impaired, as were their visual-spatial abilities (such as depth perception) and their memory for visually presented information (such as the recognition of people's faces). These deficits, which parallel those found in NLD, prompted Klin and associates to conclude that Asperger's disorder and autism are two distinct conditions and that future research should continue to focus on the relation between this disorder and NLD.

---

frequent than autism, affecting approximately one person per 10,000. The disorder generally begins or is recognized later than autism, and is more common in boys than girls (APA, 2000a). Thus far, there are no data on its social and cultural epidemiology, besides the fact that it has been described in similar ways in various countries (Frith, 1991).

Like autism, Asperger's disorder is a chronic condition that evolves as the child develops. However, there are not enough empirical studies to describe its developmental trajectory in any detail. Case studies suggest that social difficulties are often present before the child begins school, but that their intensity varies considerably from one child to the next and not all families perceive them as abnormal (Gillberg, 1991a). During the school years, the social difficulties of affected children, such as their narrow interests and "bookish" language, limit their contacts with peers. In fact, peers often regard them as odd and ignore them. In most cases, these problems persist unchanged through adolescence and into adulthood, and continue to distinguish persons with the disorder from most of their peers (Tantam, 1991). But even though they may be different from other adults, affected individuals are often able to lead a relatively normal life.

Etiology

The cause or causes of Asperger's disorder are not known. However, a growing number of family studies indicate that genetic or neurobiological factors play an important role in its etiology. For example, in families having a child with Asperger's disorder or autism, the rate at which another sibling is affected with one of these two disorders is far greater than in the general population (see Box 2.2, p. 32). This suggests that the disorder is partly of hereditary origin. As we mentioned earlier, the syndrome is also associated in many cases with medical conditions or neurological symptoms. These and other potentially etiological factors are the object of considerable attention today, but the role that they may play in causing or precipitating the disorder remains unknown.

Other Pervasive Developmental Disorders

Rett's Disorder

In 1966, Andreas Rett, an Austrian physician, described for the first time the pervasive developmental disorder that now bears his name: **Rett's disorder** (or Rett syndrome). Unfortunately, his description did not receive the attention it deserved, and the disorder remained almost unknown for many years. In fact, it was only classified as a distinct developmental disorder in the most recent edition of the DSM (APA, 1994). Consequently, Rett's disorder has not yet been the focus of much research attention.

Rett's disorder is a progressive debilitating condition that appears in early childhood *but only after a period of 5 to 48 months of normal development*. It is characterized by a host of serious problems, including:

- A deterioration in social interactions.
- A partial or complete loss of language (if the child has already begun to speak).
- A loss of purposeful hand use, which is replaced by stereotyped hand movements (often washing or wringing motions in front of the chest or below the chin).
- A slowing of normal head growth.
- The appearance of major motor problems, especially in walking.

Initial deterioration usually begins during the first or second year of life and is very rapid; it lasts less than a year and is usually complete before age 3. Rett syndrome is always accompanied by severe or profound mental retardation (Nandu, Murphy, Moser, & Rett, 1986). Unlike children with autism or Asperger syndrome, children with Rett's disorder still show interest in social relationships, even though they may be unable to initiate or maintain most social contacts.

A mother's account of the deterioration brought about by Rett's disorder describes the rapid and devastating changes brought about by the syndrome:

Meg walked at 12 months, the exact same age as her younger brother. Her regression was somewhat slow—first cognitive and then the physical regression happened rather quickly. She was a typically developing child until 15–18 months. She said fifteen words or so, including "mama" and "dada." I felt something was wrong, yet I couldn't articulate it. . . . Gross and fine motor skills were normal or somewhat advanced. By 18 months, she had lost most words and learned one new one, "bubbles." Doctors still didn't think anything was wrong. I believe the cognitive regression happened from 18 months to 30 months. She became autistic-like in that period and obsessed with coloring. . . . Right around 32–36 months she started to lose hand use and developed finger rolling. This is when she developed increased muscle tone [causing muscles to become tight and rigid] and lost the ability to squat. She lost all hand use and her gait became very stiff and jerky. She lost the ability to climb stairs, but has since regained it. She developed seizures at 4 years (Hunter, 1999, pp. 29–30).

Rett's disorder is rare. Current estimates place its prevalence rate at approximately one child in 12,000 to 15,000. The great majority—if not all of them—are girls (Hagberg, 1985; Kerr & Stephenson, 1986). Because the disorder remains poorly understood and detailed diagnostic criteria have only recently become available, these figures may underestimate the actual prevalence of the condition.

The characteristic symptomatology and rapid and dramatic progression of the disorder suggest that it has its roots in biological or neurological processes, very likely of genetic origin. In fact, the condition is frequently found among female relatives of affected children; and in one study the concordance rate for seven sets of identical twins was 100% (van Acker, 1991). Rett's disorder has also been linked to a defective gene on the X chromosome, known as MeCP2, although not all affected girls studied have this defective gene (Bienvenu et al., 2000).

Very few interventions to treat Rett's disorder have been evaluated. Evidence suggests that some ed-

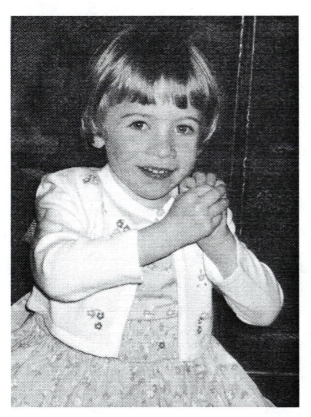

A young girl with Rett's disorder. Note the child's hand position. A parent describes the washing or wringing hand motions that are characteristic of many children with the disorder: "Jenn mouthed her hands constantly for a long time. She would insert one hand into her mouth and within two seconds replace it with the other, and then two seconds later she'd switch again. About age 4–5 it was not only periodic, but different in form. She would just pat her mouth with her right hand while her left patted her chest" (Hunter, 1999, p. 96).

ucational, clinical, and pharmacological approaches make it possible to slow down the child's physical deterioration or to improve specific symptoms, at least temporarily. These approaches include specialized education programs, intensive occupational and physical therapy, and anticonvulsive drugs, usually combined with family support. Unfortunately, these approaches cannot stop the progression of the disorder (van Acker, 1991).

Childhood Disintegrative Disorder

Childhood disintegrative disorder (or CDD) qualifies as the "oldest" of the pervasive developmental disorders, having been first described in 1908 (Hendry, 2000). However, it is also the least well known. Like Rett's disorder, it was described as a distinct psychological disorder for the first time in the DSM-IV (APA, 1994).

CDD, which is always accompanied by mental retardation, is characterized by a significant loss of skills in many areas of functioning *following two years or more of normal development.* Children who have learned to walk, drink from a cup, and speak in simple sentences, among other things, lose most of their skills after the onset of the disorder. This loss usually begins when the child is between 3 and 4 (although the DSM-IV-TR specifies a much wider age range, allowing a diagnosis when disintegration begins between ages 2 and 10). Disintegration is usually rapid and dramatic. It can occur in the course of a few weeks and always affects the child's adaptive functioning as a whole, including language, communication, social, and motor skills; play; and biological functions (in particular, bladder and bowel control). After this period of deterioration, the remaining skills reach a plateau and the child's symptoms resemble those of autism (APA, 2000a).

The mother of a boy with CDD writes about the pain, frustration, and distress this devastating disorder causes:

The doctors were basically saying he was all right—no brain tumors, no rare form of epilepsy, no infection, no anything. It made me want to scream. I had a perfectly normal, happy child only a few weeks ago, and now I had a child who pooped in his pants and stared at his hands. People did not empathize that I could accept Aaron's condition better if he had stepped onto the road and got hit by a car. At least then there would be a reason for the way he was (Day, 1998, p. 75).

The prevalence of CDD is unknown, but the epidemiological data reported to date indicate that the disorder is very rare. A Japanese study estimates that it affects approximately one child in 100,000 (Kurita, Kita, & Miyake, 1992). A review of the sparse literature on this disorder indicates that it begins, on average, around 3½ years of age (with onset ranging from 1½ to 9 years) and that it is more frequent in boys than girls (with an approximate sex ratio of 4 to 8 boys per girl) (Volkmar, 1992).

Prognosis is poor for all children with CDD, since their many difficulties persist throughout life. Research suggests that a distinction can be made between a stable form of the disorder, in which deterioration is rapid and dramatic, and a more progressive form, which is almost always associated with an identified neurological condition. Follow-up data are sparse but they suggest that approximately 75% of affected children have a stable form of the disorder, where loss is dramatic and reaches a plateau relatively quickly. The remaining 25% have a progressive form of the disorder, where symptoms gradually become more severe. Follow-up data show also that, of all children with CDD, only 20% regain some ability to speak, approximately 40% do not speak at all, and the remaining 40% can only express themselves with a few words (Volkmar, 1992).

No empirical evaluations of interventions for CDD have been published to date. However, as with Rett's disorder, the interventions available today do not make it possible to stop the tragic progression of the disorder. As we noted earlier, after the initial period of deterioration, children with CDD are not distinguishable from children with autism. Therefore, the American Academy of Child and Adolescent Psychiatry (1999a) considers that intervention programs designed for children with autism may contribute to the development of skills in children with CDD also. We turn now to a review of the treatment literature in that area.

Treatment and Prevention

> *A journey of a thousand miles begins with a single step.*
>
> —Chinese proverb

Early Psychological Treatment Approaches

Although the pervasive developmental disorders vary greatly in their presentation and course, intervention efforts to date have focused almost entirely on autism. Several early treatments for autism were developed within a psychoanalytic perspective and sought to help presumably rejecting parents, who were mostly mothers, to become better caregivers. Most of these treatments were never evaluated, although it is widely accepted that they were not successful in decreasing autistic behavior. (See Box 4.6 for an early empirical investigation of psychoanalytic theory and treatment.) Current treatment recommendations stress that psychodynamic therapies are ineffective for youth with autism and other pervasive developmental disorders (AACAP, 1999b). In addition, because these therapies may take the place of more effective interventions, many clinicians consider them harmful.

Current Treatment Approaches

According to the American Academy of Child and Adolescent Psychiatry (1999a), early, intensive behavioral interventions are the treatment of choice for youth with pervasive developmental disorders in general, and autism in particular. The common feature of behavioral interventions is that they work to increase appropriate behaviors and skills through reinforcement, and to decrease inappropriate conduct through punishment or extinction. (Extinction consists of ignoring an undesirable behavior to make it disappear.) Most intensive interventions focus on increasing or decreasing behaviors in five target areas: aberrant behaviors, social skills, language, daily living skills, and academic competencies (Matson, Benavidez, Compton, Paclawskyj, & Baglio, 1996).

Aberrant Behaviors.   Aberrant behaviors include an array of self-injurious, aggressive, and self-stimulating activities. These behaviors are problematic because they result in harm to the child (self-injury) or others (aggression), or because they shift attention away from the acquisition of more adaptive skills (self-stimulation). Behavioral interventions designed to reduce aberrant behaviors are often based on applied behavior analysis methods (see Chapter 1) and, specifically, on a functional analysis of behavior. This analysis examines the antecedents and consequences of the behavior one wants to change, in order to determine the *functions* it serves in the child's overall adjustment. Take the example of Kevin, a 12-year-old boy with autism who also refuses to eat anything but a few foods he

BOX 4.6 • *The Myth of the "Empty Fortress"*

As we note in the text, much of the early theorizing on autism pointed to abnormal or ineffective parenting as the cause of the disorder. When treatments had to be developed to help children with autism, it followed from Bruno Bettelheim's (1967) theory in particular that, if parenting practices could force a child to take refuge into an "empty fortress," positive changes in these practices should allow the child to escape from that self-imposed isolation. This belief led to the development of numerous psychoanalytic therapies for autism. Briefly stated, these therapies were mostly designed to help children with autism return to an earlier stage of development, in order to enable them to develop a healthier personality based on a warmer and more affectionate relationship with their mothers.

As we note in the text also, most psychoanalytic therapies were never evaluated. However, in a landmark study, Rutter and Bartak (1973) compared the effectiveness of three residential treatments for autism. In Unit A, emphasis was put on allowing children to regress to an earlier stage of development by providing them with a healthy, safe, and accepting environment where they would receive the type of nurturing and affection that is given to very young children. This unit included only children with autism and had a ratio of one staff person for each child. In Unit B, emphasis was also put on regression to an earlier stage of development, but in combination with education techniques aimed at teaching the children specific skills in a relatively unstructured setting. The techniques included pairing children with autism with average students, in order to increase communication and interest in normal play activity. This unit included children with autism and average children, and had a ratio of one staff person for approximately three and a half children. In Unit C, no attempt at psychological regression was made. Rather, the unit focused directly on reducing inappropriate behavior, increasing social behavior, and teaching specific academic skills in a very structured setting. In this unit, academic materials were employed that were designed to remedy the cognitive and perceptual deficits associated with autism. As in Unit B, this unit had a ratio of one staff person for approximately three and a half children. However, as in Unit A, Unit C included only children with autism.

Treatment outcome was judged on the basis of each child's improvement in developmentally appropriate skills, such as reading and mathematics. Not surprisingly, children in Unit C made larger improvements in both reading and mathematics than their peers in either Unit A or B (who actually became worse over time). These findings suggested that children with autism would be best served by treatments that focused on developing their skills in specific areas, rather than on helping them regress to an earlier stage of development, and provided a major impetus for much of the work done in this area ever since.

Source: Rutter & Bartak (1973), pp. 253–254.

---

likes. His parents report that he has aggressive outbursts at home whenever his mother attempts to expand his diet by introducing new foods. Careful home observations of this aberrant behavior show that it usually occurs not only when his mother gives him something unfamiliar to eat, but also when she does not present his food exactly as he wants it presented (for instance, peanut butter and jelly sandwiches have to be cut in four equal-sized triangles and served without anything else on the plate). As soon as an outburst begins, Kevin's mother gives him exactly what he wants or tries to distract him by allowing him to do something he enjoys more than eating, such as reading comic books. In other words, the functional analysis reveals that Kevin's mother is inadvertently training him to be aggressive when he is upset or frustrated, because his outbursts *function* to get him the foods he wants or to postpone eating. The results of such an analysis can later be used to design an intervention in which the child's aberrant behavior is no longer attended to positively, but is systematically ignored or punished.

Functional communication training also is often used to decrease aberrant behaviors. This training consists of teaching youth with autism socially appropriate responses that serve the same function as their self-injurious, aggressive, or self-stimulating behaviors. For example, a boy with autism may learn to ask for help or to take a short break when he feels frustrated with his homework or other tasks; and his parents may learn to respond to him with minimal attention, and not to allow him to use outbursts to shirk his responsibilities. Research shows that functional communication training is effective not only in decreasing such behaviors but also in evoking more positive consequences from caregivers (Matson et al., 1996). However, this approach requires considerable time and commitment on the part of family members or other dedicated caregivers.

Finally, in the past, researchers and clinicians commonly relied on punishment to decrease aberrant behaviors. For example, early behavior therapists often slapped children on the leg or yelled "No!" very loudly to decrease aggressive or self-injurious behaviors. Since children with autism tend to be hypersensitive to touch and sound, punishing consequences such as these can be highly effective in reducing aberrant behaviors. However, critics rightly point out that punishment can easily be misused and even abused. Because of this important ethical concern, most clinicians try to reduce aberrant behaviors through other means and, if they use punishment at all, to reserve it only for extreme behaviors, such as severe aggression and self-injury. Alternatives include using rewards for positive behaviors and ignoring less severe aberrant behaviors in order to bring about their extinction.

Social Skills.   Children with autism have an array of social skill deficits. Therefore, most behavioral treatment programs focus on increasing reciprocal social interactions, reciprocal play, conversation, and the appropriate display of affection and emotion (Matson et al., 1996). However, because proficiency in any of these areas requires complex social skills, treatment usually consists of teaching these skills one by one before *chaining* them together to approximate appropriate performance. For example, to have a conversation, a person must be able to attend, make eye contact, ask and respond to questions, and use an appropriate tone of voice. In many cases, children with autism have to be taught each of these skills separately before they are progressively put together to approximate a normal conversation. This training is very time-consuming. It is often done by adults, although it may be especially effective when administered by peers, as in the LEAP program described below (Strain, Kohler, & Goldstein, 1996).

Language.   Given that approximately half of all children with autism do not speak and that the other half often have significant communication problems, language is a central concern of most behavioral treatment programs (Rogers, 1998). Depending on the child's intelligence and existing skills, programs may target verbal or nonverbal behavior, or both, and focus on more or less complex skills (such as single words, two- or three-word sentences, and whole sentences). Language is usually taught by three methods: incidental teaching, natural language, and time delay (Matson et al., 1996).

- *Incidental teaching* relies on naturally occurring situations to teach language, as well as on situations deliberately set up for that purpose. For example, a clinician may place a desirable toy out of reach to get the child to ask for it—either verbally or by sign language. Similarly, a parent may give a child something to eat or drink if the child asks appropriately, and deliberately ignore all inappropriate requests, such as grunts or whining.
- *Natural language teaching* combines language modeling with incidental teaching. For example, the child may play ball with a clinician or parent who models the word or sign for "ball" and asks the child to repeat it. Appropriate responses or responses that come progressively closer to the word or sign are rewarded with praise and, in many cases, a small piece of food and a chance to play with the toy.
- *Time delay* is a procedure in which the child is shown a desirable object and prompted for a verbal or sign language response before being given the object. For example, a child might be shown an apple and prompted by a clinician or parent with the line "I want an apple." As the child acquires specific words and phrases, the adult reduces the use of prompts until the child asks for the item spontaneously.

Daily Living Skills.   Teaching of daily living skills focuses on self-care, as well as on community, vocational, and leisure activities. The goal is for children with autism or another pervasive developmental disorder to grow up to care independently for as many of their daily needs as possible. As in social skills training, daily living skills (such as getting dressed or using public transportation) are usually broken down into discrete tasks and then chained together. After these skills are mastered, they can be put together to enable the child to function independently in important areas of daily life.

Academic Competency. Academic competency includes fundamental competencies, such as reading, writing, and counting, as well as a broad set of skills (such as attention and gross and fine motor skills) that are necessary before such competencies can be acquired. Academic skills training is especially important for children with autism because of their tendency to focus on some aspects of their environment and to exclude others. Teaching in this area usually proceeds in steps. For example, a child might learn to sort blocks first by color, then by size, and later to arrange the blocks both by color and size.

Pivotal Areas. Skills in the five target areas just reviewed have often been taught independently of one another, usually by exposing the child to mass practice of each desired behavior in different settings. More recently, some researchers and clinicians have argued that many skills taught independently may in fact be components of a few **pivotal areas.** Pivotal areas are broad domains of functioning that are thought to be central to a child's adaptation because they control multiple skills and behaviors. Researchers have hypothesized that children with autism have significant deficits in four pivotal areas: motivation, attention, self-management, and self-initiation. Consequently, "intervention targeting certain core areas of the disorder may have more widespread effects across nontargeted behaviors than intervention that [focuses] on modifying a single targeted symptom" (Koegel, Koegel, & McNerney, 2001, p. 20). For example, because many children with autism lack motivation, they rarely initiate social interaction or language on their own. Increases in motivation should therefore facilitate social interaction and appropriate verbal exchange, and may also reduce disruptive behaviors that stem from limited language skills.

The pivotal approach differs in important respects from a more traditional approach that focuses on teaching specific skills. First, it seeks to respond to appropriate behaviors that the child initiates and to give the child as much control as possible, rather than to leave that control to the adult. Second, it allows the child to choose materials with which to play or work in a teaching situation, instead of imposing them. Third, it makes greater use of naturally occurring circumstances to reinforce the child's appropriate behaviors through praise and other natural consequences. Fourth, it seeks to ensure that the child experiences a high rate of success on a variety of tasks and is regularly reinforced in different contexts. A review of the findings of several studies provides preliminary support for the usefulness of this approach, although carefully controlled studies remain to be conducted to establish the extent to which this approach benefits children with autism (Koegel et al., 2001).

Specific Treatment Programs

Studies undertaken in the past thirty years show that children are most likely to benefit from treatment begun before age 4 (Harris & Handleman, 2000; Smith, Buch, & Gamby, 2000), and that the most promising treatment programs in this area are also the most demanding and most expensive (Gresham, Beebe-Frankenberger, & MacMillan, 1999). We summarize briefly three systematic programs for children with autism.

Any little improvement is a victory.

—Mother of a child with autism

UCLA Young Autism Project **(YAP; Lovaas, 1987).** This project is perhaps the most famous of the early autism intervention programs. As initially designed and implemented, YAP was an intensive, individualized behavioral treatment lasting for two years. Actually, the word "intensive" does not adequately reflect the demandingness of the program: children received over forty hours per week of one-on-one training from behavior therapists. Training was very directive and relied on massed practice of target skills in different environments. In addition, the children's parents were required to take a year off from work to learn how to administer the same training when professionals were not available. At the end of two years, 47% of children who participated in the program were functioning well in a regular classroom, compared to only 2% of comparison children. In addition, program participants had IQ scores up to thirty points higher than their control peers. Perhaps most important, follow-up research indicated that these gains were maintained throughout childhood and adolescence (McEachlin, Smith, & Lovaas, 1993).

Although impressive, these treatment gains must be interpreted with caution. Specifically, the design of the original YAP study was flawed, since children were not randomly assigned to the treatment and control groups. In addition, this and similar programs are limited in their generalizability because of costs. Most parents of children with autism would find it prohibitive to take a year off from work and to hire a full-time behavior therapist. However, researchers who have sought to remedy these limitations by modifying the YAP program have generally published encouraging results. For example, Smith and colleagues (2000) tested a modified version of the program that provided thirty hours of treatment per week and enabled parents to remain employed during treatment. This study, which randomly assigned subjects to groups, found that children who participated in the program made substantial gains, especially if their symptoms were less severe at the start of treatment.

***TEACCH Program* (Schopler, 1998).**   TEACCH stands for Treatment and Education of Autistic and Related Communication Handicapped Children. It is a statewide program providing services to children with autism in North Carolina. Like YAP, this program emphasizes the careful identification of each child's unique competencies and needs, in order to individualize the training the child receives. TEACCH has at least two unique features. First, the program relies heavily on visual prompts and cues in the environment, on the assumption that children with autism are much better at processing visual than auditory information. Second, it trains and makes use of parents as co-therapists for their children, and establishes a partnership between the child's home and preschool environment in order to facilitate generalization across settings. The TEACCH program has been evaluated in several studies. Results are generally positive, although controlled studies with random assignment to treatment and con-

trol groups are not available. For example, the program has been shown to reduce rates of institutionalization and to increase age-appropriate skills, by enabling program participants to make significant developmental gains in relatively short periods of time (Gresham et al., 1999).

***Learning Experiences . . . an Alternative Program (LEAP)* (Kohler, Strain, & Shearer, 1996).**   LEAP is an intensive preschool treatment program focusing on treating children with autism in a naturalistic setting. On the assumption that peers can be effective teachers of appropriate social and language skills, and that they can learn themselves from children with developmental disabilities, the program is delivered in a classroom where affected children interact throughout the day with average peers. Stressing that children show more progress when caregivers and therapists work as a team, LEAP, like TEACCH, trains parents in behavioral principles and skills, and actively involves parents in treatment. More generally, this program focuses on an integrated approach to treatment that emphasizes learning at home, at school, and in the community.

There is encouraging support for several of the components of LEAP, although there are no controlled outcome studies testing the entire program (Rogers, 1998). Such studies are urgently needed, not only to compare the relative strengths and weaknesses of the programs we have just reviewed, but also to show which of these programs is most likely to bring about positive, long-term gains for children with autism and other pervasive developmental disorders.

Pharmacological Interventions

No standard pharmacological treatment is available for the pervasive developmental disorders (Buitelaar & Willemsen-Swinkels, 2000). However, children with these disorders are often prescribed a variety of drugs that were not originally developed to treat their condition. In a survey of a large sample of persons with autism, researchers found that 31% took at least one psychotropic medication, 6% took two such medications, and 2% took three or more. Anticonvulsant drugs were prescribed in 13% of cases to control epileptic seizures; and a variety of drugs were prescribed in 12% of cases to control aggressive and self-injurious behaviors (Aman, Von Bourgondien, Wolford, & Sarphare, 1995). Although the efficacy of anticonvulsants to control seizures is well established, the effectiveness of drugs to control disruptive behaviors in this area has yet to be demonstrated in controlled studies (AACAP, 1999d). There are numerous reports of positive results but probably just as many findings of negative ones, either because a particular medication does not bring about desirable changes or because it has severe side effects. In addition, as noted in Chapter 3, medications that may be effective in reducing disruptive behaviors do so at times by lowering overall responsiveness to the environment and preventing learning. Finally, medications often prescribed to children with pervasive developmental disorders are better at alleviating associated than core symptoms of the disorder. In other words, the key social and communication challenges of affected children do not respond well to existing pharmacological interventions (Volkmar, 2001).

Alternative Treatments

The multiple problems and poor prognosis of children with pervasive developmental disorders often lead concerned, at times desperate, parents to turn to alternative treatments with little or no empirical support. Although their desire to try anything that might help their children is understandable, many of these treatments may be harmful, both because they may have serious side effects and because they may be pursued at the exclusion of better-established approaches. Alternative treatments lacking empirical support include:

- Mega-doses of vitamins or vitamins supposedly formulated specifically to treat autism. These preparations have not been shown to decrease autistic symptoms despite claims to the contrary (AACAP, 1999d).
- Administration of human secretin hormone, a hormone used to treat some gastrointestinal disorders. This form of treatment is not effective either (Sandler et al., 1999).
- Facilitated communication devices. These machines are meant to allow nonverbal individuals to communicate through the use of a specialized keyboard. However, whenever children with autism or another pervasive developmental disorder use these devices, the messages they communicate come from the normal adults who help them use the devices, rather than from the children themselves (Gresham et al., 1999).
- Auditory integration training and sensory integration therapy. These treatments are designed to stimulate children or adolescents with autism in different sensory areas in which they are assumed to have specific deficits. Here again, research does not support the effectiveness of these treatments, in spite of multiple testimonials to the contrary (Gresham et al., 1999).

Prevention

Unfortunately, no methods have yet been devised for preventing autism and other pervasive developmental disorders, largely because their etiologies remain unknown. Currently, early diagnosis and intervention are as close to prevention as can be achieved.

Web Links

5

Childhood-Onset Schizophrenia

Nobody realizes that some people expend tremendous energy merely to be normal.

—Albert Camus

Schizophrenia is one of the most serious and complex psychological disorders known to affect humans. In a majority of cases, the disorder begins at the end of adolescence or at the beginning of adulthood, although it can begin earlier. In this chapter, we use the term *childhood-onset schizophrenia* (COS) to describe the disorder when it begins in childhood or adolescence, and to differentiate affected youth from adults who develop the disorder in their twenties or thirties. Like the pervasive developmental disorders we considered in Chapter 4, COS is a persistent and generally chronic condition. When it affects young people, it usually interferes with their cognitive, social, and emotional development and functioning; it distorts and disturbs perception, attention, memory, language, thought, will, judgment, emotions, and more. The nature and severity of the disorder vary considerably from one person to the next, but the common denominator is that all affected children and adolescents appear to have lost touch with reality: their speech is disorganized or incoherent, their beliefs are bizarre or irrational, and many of their actions do not make sense to those around them. For example, they may be convinced that walls, furniture, or appliances talk to them, or they may

take refuge in a closet at home or under a desk in school, fearing that evil forces are plotting against them. In short, the disorder is devastating because it disturbs "the structuring of relationships with people and things, as with oneself" (Messerschmitt, 1990, p. 24).

COS is receiving considerable research attention, but its precise nature remains poorly understood. This is so for at least three reasons:

1. COS is pervasive; it affects all areas of functioning and development.
2. Its symptoms vary considerably from one person to another, making it difficult to determine which symptoms should be considered "core" or key identifying features.
3. COS forms part of a group of serious disorders known as the **childhood psychoses.** Psychoses, which include the pervasive developmental disorders covered in Chapter 4, are characterized by major disturbances in cognitive, social, emotional, and motor functioning. However, they share overlapping features, so that differential diagnosis for the disorders is often difficult.

Historical Overview

Schizophrenia as Early Madness

The study of schizophrenia began in the early nineteenth century, although the disorder received its current name only a century or so later (Weckowicz & Liebel-Weckowicz, 1990). Philippe Pinel, a French physician famous for advocating the humane treatment of people with mental illness, published the first detailed descriptions of the disorder in 1801. A few years later, in 1809, the English physician John Haslam published similar findings in his *Observations on Madness and Melancholy.*

By 1860, another French physician, Bénédicte Augustin Morel, had observed that schizophrenia often began in the latter part of adolescence, in young people who were not otherwise ill and who did not have any obvious brain dysfunction. Morel named this early-onset disorder **dementia praecox.** This Latin term means, literally, to be out of one's mind early (i.e., before adulthood). The term proved useful, since it enabled physicians to distinguish between younger people with the disorder and older people afflicted with senility or dementia of old age. Morel postulated that this "early madness" resulted from genetic weaknesses. Specifically, like many of his contemporaries, he thought that youth with the disorder had inherited their bizarre behavior from their parents and/or grandparents.

Schizophrenia as Disruption in Processes of Association

It was not until 1911 that the Swiss psychiatrist Eugen Bleuler coined the term *schizophrenia.* Bleuler stressed the heterogeneity of the disorder and referred to it in the plural as the *schizophrenias.* However, he believed that the various manifestations of the disorder had a common denominator: they represented *disruptions in the processes of association that are essential to adaptive functioning.*

Bleuler assumed that the disorder was caused by a dysfunction within the brain that prevented the person from forming logical associations between thoughts, ideas, and experiences. For example, you undoubtedly *associate* flipping a light switch with turning a light on and off. This learned association has remained functional and stable for you over the years, and serves as a reliable guide for your behavior with light switches. You will be surprised and probably upset if the next time you flip a switch a voice comes out of nowhere to tell you that you are evil. But in schizophrenia that is often just what happens, because affected persons have **loose (illogical) associations** that may lead them to believe that switches and lights are not reliably associated. If a person cannot form reliable associations of this kind to negotiate the numerous challenges of daily life, normal contact with reality is lost.

Because Bleuler believed that disruptions in the processes of association resulted from "splits" in various mental functions, he renamed dementia praecox *schizophrenia,* which in Greek means "split mind." (The term is often used wrongly to refer to a very different disorder—namely, dissociative identity disorder, or what used to be called multiple personality disorder. The split that Bleuler wrote about refers to the psychological functions of the *same* person, not to the separation into various identities or personalities that is characteristic of dissociative identity disorder.)

From Bleuler to Current Diagnostic Systems

For much of the twentieth century, Bleuler's perspective dominated psychiatric and psychological research and practice with children and adolescents. Unfortunately, he relegated to the rank of secondary symptoms the most striking characteristics of schizophrenia: **delusions,** or persistent beliefs that others do not share and consider odd, exaggerated, irrational, or false; and **hallucinations,** or perceptual experiences that others do not share. Bleuler's failure to give prominence to these characteristics led to a definition of schizophrenia so broad that throughout much of the twentieth century researchers and clinicians often used it to describe very different forms of severely disturbed behavior. In a detailed review of the child and adolescent literature, Rutter (1972) concluded that, by the early 1970s, the concept of schizophrenia had become so vague as to be of little use in research or clinical work:

Childhood schizophrenia has tended to be used as a generic term to include an astonishingly heterogeneous mixture of disorders with little in common other than their severity, chronicity, and occurrence in childhood. To add to the difficulty, the term has been employed in widely different ways by different psychiatrists. . . . A host of different syndromes have been included in the general category of "childhood schizophrenia. . . ." The diagnostic situation can only be described as chaotic (p. 315).

This diagnostic chaos is much less of a problem today than it was a few decades ago. Systematic research by pioneers in the field has made it possible to distinguish schizophrenia from other childhood psychoses, in particular from autism and other pervasive developmental disorders (Kolvin, 1971; Rutter, Greenfeld, & Lockyer, 1967). This and more recent research has also shown that key features of the disorder are generally comparable in childhood, adolescence, and adulthood; that delusions and hallucinations are primary, not secondary, symptoms at all ages; and that the age of the child at the time of onset of the disorder is a critical factor in prognosis.

In line with the progress of research in this area, the last three editions of the DSM distinguish schizophrenia from autism and other pervasive developmental disorders, instead of grouping all these conditions under the broad category of childhood psychoses. This distinction represents a major change in the definition of the disorder (Asarnow, 1994; Volkmar, 1996). *What is now called COS is not the same disorder as it was thirty years ago.* This relatively new—or newly defined—disorder is still very complex, however, and considerable research remains to be conducted to establish its diagnostic boundaries and its empirical validity.

Definitions, Diagnostic Criteria, and Major Characteristics

COS is a devastating disorder in which the child or adolescent's entire functioning is adversely affected. The disorder is characterized by disturbances or distortions in perception, thought, emotion, and motor behavior. In a majority of cases, COS:

1. Leads to a significant deterioration in the child or adolescent's prior level of adjustment.
2. Limits the child or adolescent's adaptive functioning in many areas essential to everyday life.
3. Jeopardizes the child or adolescent's long-term development in major ways, resulting in a relatively chronic disorder that typically persists into adulthood.

COS affects the development of children and adolescents at the very core of their being—disturbing *all* their relationships, not only with others but also with themselves. Although these disturbances are profound, affected youth generally remain aware of themselves and of the world around them. It is only during acute phases of the disorder that their connection with the world can be lost.

The DSM-IV-TR diagnostic criteria for schizophrenia are shown in Table 5.1. The major symptoms of the disorder can be grouped into three broad categories: *positive symptoms, symptoms of disorganization,* and *negative symptoms.* These categories are obviously not independent, although they are relatively distinct (Andreasen, Arndt, Alliger, Miller, & Flaum, 1995).

Positive Symptoms

Positive symptoms consist of delusions and hallucinations. As mentioned already, these symptoms reflect excesses or distortions in an individual's cognitive or perceptual functioning (Russell, 1994). When present, they are the most striking features of the disorder.

> *Madness is always fascinating, for it reveals the ungluing we all secretly fear: the mind taking off from the body, the possibility that the magnet that attaches us to a context in the world can lose its grip.*
>
> —Molly Haskell

Delusions.   Delusions are persistent beliefs that others consider odd, exaggerated, irrational, or false. For example, children or adolescents with COS may believe that they are inhabited by spirits who enable them to transmit their thoughts; or that their thoughts or ac-

TABLE 5.1 *Schizophrenia: DSM-IV-TR Diagnostic Criteria*

A. *Characteristic symptoms:* Two (or more) of the following, each present for a significant portion of time during a 1-month period (or less if successfully treated):

(1) delusions

(2) hallucinations

(3) disorganized speech (e.g., frequent derailment or incoherence)

(4) grossly disorganized or catatonic behavior

(5) negative symptoms, i. e., affective flattening, alogia, or avolition

Note: Only one Criterion A symptom is required if delusions are bizarre or hallucinations consist of a voice keeping up a running commentary on the person's behavior or thoughts, or two or more voices conversing with each other.

B. *Social/occupational dysfunction:* For a significant portion of the time since the onset of the disturbance, one or more major areas of functioning such as work, interpersonal relations, or self-care are markedly below the level achieved prior to the onset (or when the onset is in childhood or adolescence, failure to achieve expected level of interpersonal, academic, or occupational achievement).

C. *Duration:* Continuous signs of the disturbance persist for at least 6 months. This 6-month period must include at least 1 month of symptoms (or less if successfully treated) that meet Criterion A (i.e., active-phase symptoms) and may include periods of prodromal or residual symptoms. During these prodromal or residual periods, the signs of the disturbance may be manifested by only negative symptoms or two or more symptoms listed in Criterion A present in an attenuated form (e.g., odd beliefs, unusual perceptual experiences).

D. *Schizoaffective and Mood Disorder exclusion:* Schizoaffective Disorder and Mood Disorder with Psychotic Features have been ruled out because either (1) no Major Depressive, Manic, or Mixed Episode have occurred concurrently with the active phase symptoms; or (2) if mood episodes have occurred during active phase symptoms, their total duration has been brief relative to the duration of the active and residual periods.

E. *Substance/general medical condition exclusion:* The disturbance is not due to the direct physiological effects of a substance (e.g., a drug of abuse, a medication) or a general medical condition.

F. *Relationship to a Pervasive Developmental Disorder:* If there is a history of Autistic Disorder or another Pervasive Developmental Disorder, the additional diagnosis of Schizophrenia is made only if prominent delusions or hallucinations are also present for at least a month (or less if successfully treated).

Classification of longitudinal course (can be applied only after at least 1 year has elapsed since the initial onset of active-phase symptoms): *Episodic with Interepisode Residual Symptoms* (episodes are defined by the reemergence of prominent psychotic symptoms); also specify if: *With Prominent Negative Symptoms*

Episodic with No Interepisode Residual Symptoms

Continuous (prominent psychotic symptoms are present throughout the period of observation); also specify if: *With Prominent Negative Symptoms*

Single Episode in Partial Remission; also specify if: *With Prominent Negative Symptoms*

Single Episode in Full Remission

Other or Unspecified Pattern

Source: American Psychiatric Association, *Diagnostic and Statistical Manual of Mental Disorders, Fourth Edition, Text Revision* (Washington, DC: American Psychiatric Association, 2000a). Copyright 2000 American Psychiatric Association. Reprinted with permission.

tions are manipulated by the police, a supernatural power, or other forces beyond their control. They may also believe that they are victims of forces that want to harm them or to compel them to behave in certain ways. Or they may have grandiose delusions, in which they have an exaggerated sense of their own importance, power, or identity, or believe that they are entrusted with a special mission that will have important consequences for others (e.g., the elimination of poverty). Affected youth also may have **ideas of reference** that lead them to attribute great personal significance to trivial or unimportant events (for instance, they may believe that television programs send them messages that nobody else receives). We present several examples of delusions in Box 5.1.

Delusions vary considerably from one child to another and tend to change with age, both in nature and in complexity. In a review of the literature, 55–63% of children with COS were found to have experienced delusions (Russell, 1994). Delusions of persecution (in which children fear that others want to harm them) and somatic delusions (in which children are convinced, for example, that they are inhabited by a foreign spirit) are among the most frequent (Russell, Bott, & Sammons, 1989).

Hallucinations.   Whereas delusions are cognitive experiences, hallucinations are perceptual experiences that only the child or adolescent perceives. They can affect any sensory modality (i.e., auditory, visual, tactile, and somatic—especially taste and smell), but auditory hallucinations are most common. Typically, children and adolescents report hearing one or more negative or threatening voices that monopolize their attention and cause intense feelings of anxiety. For example, Green and colleagues reported on a child who heard a voice telling him to kill his friend if he did not want to be killed himself; the child slept with a knife under his pillow for protection (Green, Padron-Gayol, Hardesty, & Bassiri, 1992). Less frequently, the voice is neutral or even benevolent.

In most cases, the voice comments, challenges, answers, or threatens the child. Or the voice talks with another voice, thus placing the child in the role of a

---

BOX 5.1 • *Delusions in Children with COS*

The following are examples of delusions reported by children with COS. They are grouped by theme.

Bizarre Delusions

A 7-year-old boy believed that there were "memory boxes" in his head and body and reported that he could broadcast his thoughts from his memory boxes using radar tracking.

A 9-year-old boy was convinced he was a dog (his parents were German Shepherds) and was growing fur, and on one occasion refused to leave a veterinarian's office unless he received a shot.

Persecutory Delusions

An 11-year-old boy believed his father had escaped from jail and was coming to kill him. When he saw food missing from the refrigerator, he knew his father had come to kill him.

A girl believed that the "evil one" was trying to poison her orange juice.

Somatic Delusions

One 7-year-old boy believed that there were boy and girl spirits living inside his head; "They're squishing on the whole inside, they're touching the walls, the skin."

An 11-year-old boy described "waste" produced when the good and bad voices fought with each other; the "waste" came out of his feet when he swam in chlorinated pools.

Ideas of Reference

An 8-year-old girl believed that people outside of her house were staring and pointing at her trying to send her a message to come outside. She also believed that people on the TV were talking to her because they used the word "you."

Grandiose Delusions

An 11-year-old boy had the firm belief that he was "different" and able to kill people. He felt that when "God zooms through me [him]," he became very strong and developed big muscles.

Source: Russell (1994, p. 635). (The U.S. National Institute of Mental Health does not currently authorize or endorse any foreign translation of any material contained in any NIMH publication and bears no responsibility for the accuracy of any translation or reproduction.)

Imaginative play and imaginary friends are a normal part of development. A major challenge in diagnosing COS is to distinguish accurately between fertile imagination and loss of contact with reality.

third party to a conversation that nobody else can hear. The content of hallucinatory voices varies considerably, so that generalizations are impossible. In many cases, children are unable to explain clearly what they hear. Hallucinations can occur at regular or irregular intervals, and in some places more than others (e.g., in the child's bedroom). Youth who suffer from hallucinations reject all attempts to prove to them that they have no basis in reality—sincerely believing that these voices or sounds are real. To be considered pathological, however, hallucinatory experiences must clearly be out of the ordinary and occur when the child is fully awake. Children who, from time to time, hear somebody call their name or experience a somatic sensation that surprises them—such as a buzz in the head or a strange sensation in part of the body—do not suffer from hallucinations. Examples of auditory, visual, tactile, and somatic hallucinations are shown in Box 5.2 (p. 122).

In three major studies, 80–84% of children with COS had auditory hallucinations and 30–47% had visual hallucinations (Russell, 1994). Auditory and visual hallucinations often co-occurred. Hallucinations involving tactile or olfactory sensations were much rarer and, in a majority of cases, were also accompanied by auditory hallucinations. Almost 70% of children who had auditory hallucinations heard voices that ordered them to do or not do something, whereas 23–34% heard voices that described or commented on what the child was doing or conversed in the child's presence (Russell et al., 1989).

Delusions and hallucinations can be difficult to diagnose before adolescence for three major reasons. First, these symptoms do not occur continuously, even when the child is in an **active phase** of the disorder (i.e., in a phase in which all symptoms required for a diagnosis are present). Therefore, delusions or hallucinations may not be actively occurring at the time of examination, and clinicians often have to rely on the child's memory to establish their presence. Second, language is less well developed in childhood than it is in adolescence and adulthood, and children with COS often have serious communication problems that limit their clinical evaluation and can make a diagnosis tenuous. Finally, a clinician has to determine whether symptoms are truly pathological, rather than merely bizarre or odd; and, even with experience, this judgment can be difficult to make—especially when the child's descriptions are vague or change during the evaluation, or when the child describes events or beliefs that reflect

BOX 5.2 • *Hallucinations in Children with COS*

The following are examples of hallucinations reported by children with COS. As these examples show, hallucinations can affect auditory, visual, tactile, and somatic modalities.

Auditory Hallucinations

Neutral Comments

An 8-year-old girl reported hearing multiple voices including the voice of a dead baby brother saying "I love you sister," "Sister, I am going to miss you."

A 7-year-old boy stated "everything is talking, the walls, the furniture. I just know they're talking."

Commands

An 8-year-old boy states "I once heard a noise coming from the south and the east; one told me to jump off the roof and one told me to smash my mom."

An 11-year-old boy heard both "good" and "bad voices." The bad voices tell him to hit others and that they will kill the good voices if he does not obey. The "good" voices say things like "help your mom with dinner."

Another 11-year-old boy heard a man's voice saying "murder your stepfather" and "go play outside."

Conversing Voices

An 8-year-old boy stated "I can hear the devil talk—God interrupts him and the devils says 'shut up God.' God and the devil are always fighting."

An 11-year-old boy described voices of various animals talking softly with each other (about child).

Commenting Voices

A boy described voices commenting on how he was feeling or what he was doing, for example, "You're feeling excited today."

An 8-year-old girl reported an angel saying things like "You didn't cry today" and "You've been a very nice girl today."

Religious Voices

An 11-year-old boy heard God's voice saying "Sorry D., but I can't help you now. I'm helping someone else." He also reported hearing Jesus and the devil.

Persecutory Voices

A boy described monsters calling him "Stupid F.," and saying they will hurt him.

A 9-year-old boy reported voices calling him bad names, and threatening that if he doesn't do what he is told something bad will happen to him.

Visual Hallucinations

A 12-year-old boy saw a ghost (man) with red, burned, scarred, and cut face on multiple occasions and in different locations. He had been seeing this since age 5.

A 9-year-old girl reported, "If I stare at the wall I see monsters coming toward me. If I stop staring, they'll come faster."

Tactile Hallucinations

An 8-year old boy felt the devil touching him and moving his body "so he can make me come and live with him."

A 5-year-old felt snakes and spiders on his back (and was so convincing he was taken to the emergency room by his parents).

Somatic Hallucinations

An 8-year-old reported feeling an angel, babies, and devil inside her arm, and that she could feel them fighting.

Source: Russell (1994), pp. 634–635. (The National Institute of Mental Health does not currently authorize or endorse any foreign translation of any material contained in any NIMH publication and bears no responsibility for the accuracy of any translation or reproduction.)

social, cultural, or religious practices (such as visions of angels or demons) that are not accepted by the community at large.

The presence of delusions or hallucinations can be established only when (1) they are inconsistent with the social, cultural, or religious context in which the child lives; (2) they are clearly bizarre or unbelievable, not only in the eyes of the clinician but also of the child's caregivers; (3) they persist in spite of evidence that they have no basis in reality.

Symptoms of Disorganization

As their name implies, **disorganized symptoms** are behaviors that lack organization or purpose. These symptoms are most obvious in the speech of affected children and adolescents, but can also occasionally be seen in their motor behavior (e.g., agitation or stereotypical movements). For example, affected youth may rock for hours or continuously grimace without being apparently aware of what they are doing. Others may slap or pinch themselves repeatedly, sometimes to the point of self-injury.

Conversations with children or adolescents with COS can be both moving and frustrating: moving because they want to communicate but repeatedly "fumble" their message or ignore what others are trying to tell them; and frustrating because they do not heed the implicit rules of human conversation. Despite efforts by both parties to have a conversation, the *illogical thinking* and *loose associations* of young people with COS prevent them from observing elements such as turn-taking, appropriate nonverbal behavior, and a focus on a connected theme or topic. The following example illustrates these characteristics:

> I used to have a Mexican dream. I was watching TV. . . . I disappeared outside of this world and then I was in a closet. Sounds like a vacuum dream. It's a Mexican dream. When I was close to that dream earth, I was turning upside down. Sometimes I have Mexican dreams and vacuum dreams. It's real hard to scream in dreams (Russell et al., 1989, p. 404).

This kind of speech is obviously disorganized and difficult to follow. If you compare a normal conversation to a train traveling smoothly from one station to another, disorganized speech is like a train running wildly out of control, stopping frequently at unplanned destinations, or derailing abruptly. In other words, disorganized speech consists more often of a juxtaposition of sentences than of a coherent communication. Moreover, even when their conversation is focused and logical, the speech of affected children resembles a monologue more than a conversation in which both parties are active participants. Because it lacks many of the qualities of normal speech, schizophrenic speech is often described as poor: it does not employ conventional linguistic tools—such as the conjunctions "and" and "but"—to connect sentences together; it does not tell a story that engages the listener; and it fails to take the listener's perspective into account, or to make sure that the listener can follow the story.

Between 40% and 100% of children with COS exhibit symptoms of thought disorganization (Russell, 1994). This very broad range reflects in large part the fact that these symptoms are particularly difficult to define and evaluate in a reliable manner. Disorganized symptoms are probably the clearest indicators of COS because they are very rare in children with other psychological disorders or in average children (Caplan, 1994a; 1994b).

Especially rare in unaffected youth is a form of disorganized behavior known as **catatonia.** Catatonic symptoms can range from complete immobility and rigidity to severe agitation and excessive motor movements. A most dramatic form of catatonia is waxy flexibility (or catalepsy), a condition in which muscles are semi-rigid or "waxy." In this state, affected youth tend to hold their arms or legs in unusual positions for prolonged periods—much longer than most people are able to do. Catatonic behaviors have been observed in as many as 25% to 30% of youth with COS (Green et al., 1984; Werry, McClellon, & Chard, 1991).

Negative Symptoms

Positive and disorganized symptoms often distinguish COS most clearly from other childhood disorders. By contrast, negative symptoms are often found in other conditions as well, such as mood and anxiety disorders (see Chapters 9 and 10). However, three negative symptoms—affective flattening, alogia, and avolition—are particularly frequent in schizophrenia.

The majority of youth with COS have limited or inappropriate emotions (Russell et al., 1989; Spencer & Campbell, 1994). **Affective flattening** is characterized by the expression of few, if any, emotions or by inappropriate emotions. Affected children and adolescents often appear indifferent: their face or entire body is motionless, and they show no emotion. At times they may also react in extreme or inappropriate ways to different situations: crying when those around them laugh or laughing at the announcement of sad news.

The processes accounting for symptoms of affective flattening remain unknown. Research with adults with schizophrenia suggests that these symptoms reflect major difficulties in understanding or expressing emotions appropriately, rather than a lack of emotions (Kring & Neale, 1996).

The speech of young people with COS is usually disturbed. They may be extremely talkative (see Elizabeth's autobiographical account below), but more often than not they speak very little—a phenomenon known as **alogia.** They rarely initiate a conversation, use few words to communicate when they do, and lack spontaneity in the way they talk. Similarly, their answers are short and offer limited information; or they are slow to answer, as if they had difficulty formulating what they wanted to say. In a small number of cases, youth with the disorder are mute for varying periods of time. Most people with schizophrenia probably have adequate skills to communicate with those around them, but for a variety of reasons they have considerable difficulties in doing so; and these difficulties are responsible for their limited communication and social withdrawal (Alpert, Clark, & Pouget, 1994).

Finally, youth with COS often seem unable to complete various daily tasks, especially tasks that require planning and organization (e.g., personal hygiene, chores, schoolwork). Psychologists describe this characteristic as a loss of will, or **avolition,** because the person was able to complete such tasks before the disorder occurred. In most cases, these young people do not lack the ability to complete daily tasks but, rather, are unable to "get going"—to organize themselves and persist until the task is done.

Case Study

The following case study is an autobiographical account written by Elizabeth, a 16-year-old adolescent with COS (Anonymous, 1994). Her report describes many characteristics of the disorder and their impact on development and family relationships.

I have schizophrenia. Actually I have childhood-onset schizophrenia. This is a rare form of schizophrenia, especially in girls.

I have had problems ever since I started school. I remember trying to hide under the tables in kindergarten so I wouldn't have to do any work. In first grade, I was in the top reading group, even though my mom and grandma had to come to school every day to make sure I got my work done. By the third grade I was in the bottom reading group. . . . But something happened in October. All of a sudden I couldn't read or write or do math anymore. Everything was so confusing because I couldn't understand anything that was going on around me. By November I was so sick I couldn't go to school anymore. On November 13 I went to the hospital and I stayed there for 2 months.

I got on a medicine . . . and that helped me on my way to recovery. . . . But getting better took me a long, long time. In the middle of the seventh grade, I was proclaimed to be in remission. . . .

Below I describe my experiences and difficulties in several of the areas that are affected by schizophrenia.

Interpersonal Relations

It has always been hard for me to have friends. I want friends, but I don't know how to make them. I always think people are being serious when they are just joking around, but I don't figure that out until a lot later. I just don't know how to adapt.

I get into fights with people all the time. I take their teasing seriously and get into trouble. I don't remember having as much trouble getting along with kids when I was little. They seemed to feel sorry for me or thought I was weird. I used to run away from kids and hide in the bathroom at school or under my desk.

After I got back from the hospital, I really couldn't get along with anyone. That was when kids first began calling me "retard." I am not retarded, but I get confused and I can't figure out what is going on. At first I couldn't figure out what they were saying to me. Finally one girl in my special education class became my friend. She kind of took care of me. I had another friend in junior high who was also nice and kind to me. But my best friend is my dog Cindie. Even though I give her a hard time she is always ready to love me.

I like to play by myself best. I make up stories and fantasies. My mother says it is too bad I have such a hard time writing, because with my imagination and all the stories I have created in my mind I could write a book.

Activities

I have trouble getting things done or even getting them started. For example, I bought some beads to make earrings for Christmas gifts. I bought the beads over 2 weeks ago, because I work slowly. But I haven't started on my project. Even though I had time during Thanksgiving break, I just couldn't make myself get started. And I even like to make earrings. . . .

One of the hardest things for me in high school has been trying to get all the extra work done. I managed to convince my junior high teachers that I couldn't do very much work. I would cry, or put my head on my desk, or act stressed out, or take lots and lots of time to do simple assignments. Now I have homework every night in algebra and nobody cares if I have trouble or not. This has been a hard semester, but I am happy because so far I have been able to stay up with my algebra class. My dad works with me every single night. . . .

Emotion

I have always had plenty of emotion. But a lot of my emotions, or how I show them, have been inappropriate. In fact my mother is always saying to me "Inappropriate" to let me know I am acting weird (I can't tell).

Sometimes I laugh too much, even when things aren't all that funny. I get too excited and upset about things too. One of my nicknames is Sarah Bernhardt (she was a famous actress who sometimes overacted) because my family thinks I overdramatize almost anything that happens to me. Sometimes I fall down and pretend to faint. . . .

One clue about the flat emotions might be my pictures during the years I was getting sick and then beginning to get better. I never smiled or had any expression on my face. I had a blank look on all my school pictures. . . .

Hallucinations

I certainly heard voices. They started in the fourth grade when I was really sick. At first the voices were friendly; then they got mean and scared me to pieces. I got so I couldn't even go into my bedroom because I was so scared that a voice who lived there might get me. Then for a while some other voices came, and they were good voices who protected me from the bad voices. . . .

It was 6 years ago that this happened, so I really don't remember what the voices said to me. But I do remember that it was a very bad experience. I always had a terrible headache when the voices came, so the doctors x-rayed my head to see if they could find anything wrong with my brain, but there was nothing wrong.

When I was the sickest, I could even see the voices. They were very weird. They were like ghosts (one of them had three heads). . . .

Now the voices seem like a bad dream. I don't ever, ever want them to come back. Schizophrenia is a very painful disease.

Thought Disorder

Sometimes I go on and on when I talk, and people have a hard time understanding what I am talking about. My family is always saying to me "You're going on and on." This is supposed to be a clue to me to stop talking, or that nobody is understanding what I am talking about. My brother says that nobody wants to hear all the things I have to say, but brothers talk that way to sisters all the time.

Actually that was one of the first clues my doctor had as to what was wrong with me. I had lots of problems, but they didn't have a name. My first psychiatrist thought I had attention deficit disorder because I had so much trouble paying attention and getting my work done. But one time when I was going on and on, my mother said that the listener had to share the experience with me to be able to understand what I was talking about, and even then it was hard. My doctor said that was a serious problem and then he asked if I was hearing voices. When I said yes, he said I needed to be hospitalized for evaluation, and that was a very serious problem. My parents were scared out of their wits. . . .

Conclusion

I have been in remission for over 2 years. Whenever we ask either my psychiatrist or my psychologist what my future will be, they say they just don't know. . . . But every night I pray that I will stay in remission. So far that has *worked along with my therapy, my medicine, and all the help I get from my family and some of my teachers.*

Diagnostic and Developmental Considerations

Even though the same criteria are used to diagnose schizophrenia at all ages, children, adolescents, and adults do not have the same symptoms. Therefore, a developmental perspective is essential to understand the disorder, particularly when the child's difficulties begin early (Rothstein, 1981). As we stress repeatedly throughout this chapter, (1) symptoms change with age, so that features that may be particularly diagnostic at one age may be less relevant at another; and (2) the developmental trajectory of the disorder and its long-term outcome depend both on the nature and on the age of onset of the first symptoms. We will focus on this first point here and return to the second one later (see Developmental Trajectories and Prognosis).

Distinguishing between Normal and Abnormal Childhood Experiences

It can be difficult to distinguish between normative experiences of childhood and schizophrenic symptoms. First, there is considerable overlap between reality and fantasy in early childhood. It is well known, for example, that young children often have imaginary friends with whom they talk and play. Second, the distinction between what adults label real and imaginary has to be established within the child's social and cultural context (Woolley, 1997). It follows that the line between a vivid imagination and an irrational belief or an unusual experience is not always clear. You may be absolutely convinced that walls do not talk, but many children may not be as certain as you are—especially when their cognitive and language abilities are limited because of age, and when strange beliefs or experiences relate to common childhood fears (e.g., dangerous animals, monsters) or reflect cultural or religious practices (e.g., visions, spiritual trances) (McClellan & Werry, 1992).

Distinguishing between normal and abnormal childhood experiences is further complicated by the fact that young children's thinking is often illogical. Adults frequently have to establish contextual "bridges" or links that children naturally omit (Caplan, 1994a). For example, a preschool boy may be asked what he likes to do. Instead of describing different activities, he may talk about his favorite games or his super-hero, leaving it to the adult to make the link to the original question. Since norms reflecting the development of thought and language in the course of childhood have yet to be developed, clinicians who are confronted with what might be evidence of irrational thinking must rely primarily on their judgment. In our preschooler's case, a clinician may have to decide whether a complicated discussion about how he travels in space with his hero to rescue lost children reflects a vivid, healthy imagination or a delusion. This task can be particularly difficult because diagnosis of the disorder depends heavily on language; that is, on what children *say* they believe or experience. Contrary to psychological disorders in which detailed observation of the child's behavior may be sufficient for a diagnosis, a diagnosis of COS depends heavily on ways of thinking and experiencing the world that the child must be capable of expressing verbally.

In one of the few studies on the development of illogical thinking and loose associations in children, these key symptoms followed different developmental patterns (Caplan, 1994a). As Figure 5.1 shows, both average children and children with COS engaged in illogical thinking. Illogical thinking decreased with age in both groups, but at all ages it remained more prevalent in the affected group. Loose associations followed a different developmental pattern: only children with the disorder exhibited loose associations, which decreased with age as well.

These results highlight the challenge of determining when specific symptoms truly reflect the presence of the disorder and when they are in keeping with normative development. When illogical thinking *and* loose associations are clearly evident in childhood, they are probably diagnostic of COS; when only illogical thinking is obvious, a diagnosis of COS is less likely to be appropriate.

Limitations of Using One Set of Diagnostic Criteria for All Ages

Although schizophrenia has major similarities in childhood, adolescence, and adulthood, there are significant

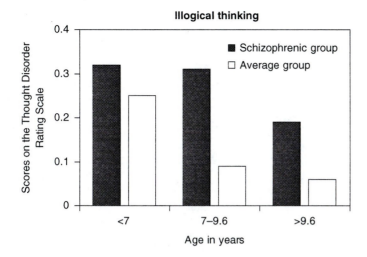

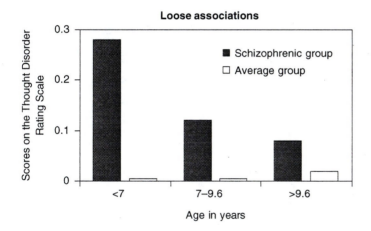

FIGURE 5.1 *Development of Illogical Thinking and Loose Associations in 31 Children with COS and 31 Average Children.* In all children, illogical thinking decreases with age. However, at any age, only children with COS exhibit loose associations, although these also decrease with age.

Source: Caplan (1994a), p. 675. (The National Institute of Mental Health does not currently authorize or endorse any foreign translation of any material contained in any NIMH publication and bears no responsibility for the accuracy of any translation or reproduction.)

limitations to using the same diagnostic criteria for all ages. Primarily, the criteria ignore important developmental changes and probably result in *underestimates* of the prevalence of the disorder—especially before the child has reached adolescence (see Developmental Trajectories and Prognosis). Specifically, younger children may show early signs of COS but not meet the criteria necessary for a diagnosis until much later (Asarnow, 1994). For example, when a child has language difficulties or does not speak, or when symptoms have not been present for the full six months required by the DSM-IV-TR, professionals run the risk of being unable to diagnose the disorder accurately and may diagnose a different condition—such as a communication, mood, or pervasive developmental disorder (Werry, 1992).

We know that age of onset provides important information in understanding the development of the disorder and in predicting its long-term consequences (see Developmental Trajectories and Prognosis). In younger children, the current diagnostic criteria make establishing precise age of onset difficult because positive, negative, and disorganized symptoms do not develop at the same time and at the same rate. Typically, negative symptoms appear first, often months or even years before positive symptoms. The use of a one-set-of-diagnostic-criteria-fits-all-ages strategy—especially the criterion that requires symptoms to be present for at least six months—probably contributes to the erroneous diagnoses often made in younger children, because the negative symptoms that appear first are not unique to schizophrenia; and it is only later, when positive symptoms are clearly present, that a correct diagnosis can be made (McKenna et al., 1994; Werry, 1992).

Empirical Validity

The empirical validity of schizophrenia is clearly established in adults (e.g., Sartorius, Jablensky, Ernberg, Leff, & Gulbinat, 1987). The number of studies conducted with children and adolescents is much smaller. Nevertheless, available evidence indicates that the disorder can occur before adulthood; that adult criteria can reliably diagnose the condition, at least in adolescents; and that COS predicts schizophrenia, rather than other disorders, in adulthood (Hollis, 2000; Remschmidt et al., 1994). However, as we have pointed out, important validity problems remain. First, the very nature of schizophrenia remains to be defined, especially during childhood and adolescence. Second, the validity of the one-set-of-diagnostic-criteria-fits-all-ages approach to diagnosis is questionable.

In Chapter 4, we stressed the importance of distinguishing COS from autism. Clinical, epidemiological, and developmental data clearly demonstrate that these two disorders are distinct (see Table 5.2)—especially when group data are examined. The distinction is not as clear in individual cases. It rests primarily on the clinical presentation, developmental history (when there is sufficient information available), and age of onset of the first symptoms. Typically, schizophrenia begins much later than autism and follows a relatively normal period of development, although some children exhibit significant delays in language, communication, and motor skills early in life without satisfying other diagnostic criteria for the disorder. For example, a retrospective study of eighteen children who developed schizophrenia before their tenth birthday found that 39% of them had symptoms of autism in early childhood, including disturbances of language and communication and limitations in behavioral repertoire

(Watkins, Asarnow, & Tanguay, 1988). Therefore, it is not surprising that in some cases a diagnosis of autism is made first and later modified to one of COS when disturbances in thought and speech become obvious (Dulcan & Popper, 1991).

Associated Characteristics; Comorbidity

Youth with schizophrenia often have multiple psychological disorders or symptoms, making comorbidity a common phenomenon in this area. Precise data are still lacking, but comorbidity is an especially important issue because the precise boundaries of the disorder remain uncertain.

Medical Conditions

Little is known about the links that may exist between COS and medical conditions. Some evidence indicates that a few children with the disorder suffer from epilepsy and that some children who suffer from epilepsy may later develop COS (Kolvin, 1971). As in the case of autism, the nature of this association is unclear.

Psychological Symptoms and Disorders

Between 50% and 75% of all youth with COS suffer from developmental delays. Delays in manual dexterity and language acquisition are among the most common (Werry, 1992; Watkins et al., 1988). Likewise, between 10% and 20% of children and adolescents with schizophrenia have a low IQ or suffer from mental retardation (Werry, 1992). It is unlikely that COS itself leads to intellectual deficits, since low IQ often precedes the appearance of the disorder (Werry et al., 1991). However, adolescents with the disorder often show significant decreases in IQ. Originally, researchers believed that these decreases resulted from pathological changes in the brain brought about by COS. Recent research suggests that that assumption may be erroneous. Rather, as Elizabeth described, it is more likely that affected adolescents manifest de-

TABLE 5.2 *Comparison of the Clinical, Epidemiological, and Developmental Characteristics of Childhood-Onset Schizophrenia and Autism*

Characteristics	Childhood-Onset Schizophrenia	Autism
Major symptoms	Hallucinations and delusions Illogical and disorganized speech Disorganized motor behavior Affective flattening (little or no emotional expression) Alogia (poverty of speech) Avolition (lack of will) or apathy	Severe deficits in reciprocal social interactions Severe deficits in language and communication Limited interests Repetitive, self-stimulating, or stereotypical behaviors
Intellectual functioning	Typically average or below average	Typically in the mentally retarded range, but can range from superior intellectual ability to severe mental retardation
Prevalence	1 per 10,000	5 to 10 per 10,000
Age of onset	Not before age 5	Before age 3
Sex ratio	1 to 2.5 boys per girl (this ratio is closer to 1:1 in adolescence)	4 to 5 boys per girl (this ratio is closer to 1:1 in the presence of more severe mental retardation)
Social status	More often found in lower socio-economic classes	Found in all socioeconomic classes
Progression	Typically, major symptoms follow a cyclical pattern, in which shorter active phases alternate with longer residual or remission periods. Prognosis depends on age of onset and whether onset was acute or insidious	Typically, major symptoms are continuous and chronic in nature. Complete remission is very rare. Prognosis depends on intellectual ability and the amount of language present before age 5.
Psychopathology of other family members	Schizophrenia is more common in first- and second-degree family members than in the general population.	Autism and other pervasive developmental disorders are more common in first- and second-degree family members than in the general population.

creases in IQ because of their limited ability to acquire new information (Bedwell et al., 1999).

Comorbid psychological difficulties are also common in COS. For example, a study of thirty-five affected children found that 69% met diagnostic criteria for at least one additional disorder. These disorders included attention deficit hyperactivity disorder (40%), conduct or oppositional defiant disorder (31%), mood disorders (37%), and elimination disorders (i.e., enuresis or encopresis) (14%) (Russell, Bott, & Sammons,

1989). (These figures add up to more than 69% because some children received more than one additional diagnosis.)

COS is also associated with an increased risk of suicide. Specifically, between 5% and 15% of youth with the disorder later commit suicide (Werry, 1992). Moreover, many children and adolescents with COS make one or more suicide attempts or have **suicidal ideation** (recurring thoughts about death and ways of dying) (see Figure 5.2, p. 130). For example, in a study

FIGURE 5.2 *Artwork by Harriet, an 18-Year-Old with Schizophrenia.* Harriet's drawing portrays a distorted face and a tombstone that reads: "Here lies one who died, but whose body wandered the earth."

Source: Naumberg (1950), p. 85. Reprinted by permission.

of twenty-one hospitalized youth, 38% had made at least one suicide attempt and 38% had expressed suicidal thoughts without actually attempting suicide (Asarnow, Tompson, & Goldstein, 1994).

Finally, by definition, COS limits adaptive development. The DSM-IV-TR states that when the disorder occurs prior to adulthood, it leads to a "failure to achieve expected level of interpersonal, academic, or occupational achievement" (APA, 2000a, p. 312). As Elizabeth's autobiographical account shows, the disorder disturbs the child's entire family and social relationships, limits academic progress, and requires one or more periods of prolonged hospitalization. Overall, these disturbances are profound and pervasive, and disrupt the child's development in most, if not all, areas of adaptive functioning (Asarnow, Tompson, & Goldstein, 1994).

Epidemiology

Prevalence; Age and Gender Characteristics

COS is very rare. Estimates of its prevalence before age 12 range from 0.19 to 1 child in 10,000 (McClellan &

Werry, 1992; Remschmidt et al., 1994; Thomsen, 1996). Precise prevalence estimates are not yet available, however, because few epidemiological studies have been conducted with youth. In addition, the more restricted diagnostic criteria used since the introduction of the DSM-III in the 1980s make comparisons with earlier studies difficult if not impossible (Werry, 1992).

Although the prevalence of COS has yet to be accurately determined, it is well known that the number of children with the disorder increases rapidly at the beginning of adolescence. In a comprehensive study of all children and adolescents hospitalized for a schizophrenic disorder in Denmark between 1970 and 1993, only 4 of 312 children received the diagnosis before age 13, but 28 received it before age 15 (Thomsen, 1996; see also Figure 5.3).

COS is more common in boys than girls. For example, a review of three U.S. studies found that the sex ratio varied from 2.2 to 2.7 boys per girl among children and adolescents between the ages of 5 and 15 (Russell, 1994). A review of three German studies reported a somewhat broader sex ratio, ranging from 2 to 4.5 boys per girl before age 14. However, that ratio was approx-

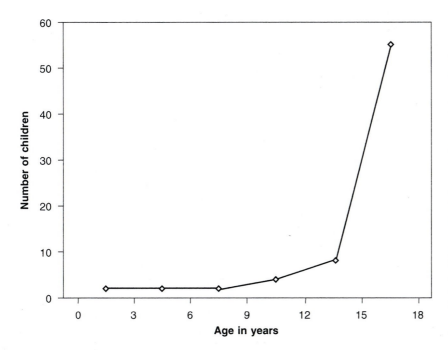

FIGURE 5.3 *Incidence of COS by Age.* This figure, which is based on 280 children and adolescents ranging in age from 7 to 21 years, shows that the *incidence* (the number of new cases of the disorder that develop over a specific period of time) of schizophrenia is very low in childhood but increases rapidly between the ages of 12 and 18.

Source: Remschmidt et al. (1994), p. 730. (The National Institute of Mental Health does not currently authorize or endorse any foreign translation of any material contained in any NIMH publication and bears no responsibility for the accuracy of any translation or reproduction.)

imately equal in adolescents and young adults between the ages of 14 and 21 (Remschmidt et al., 1994).

Social and Cultural Differences

A large number of studies conducted with adults show that:

1. Schizophrenia has been found in all countries and cultures, although observed symptoms and their developmental trajectory vary somewhat from one culture to another (Leff, Sartorius, Jablensky, Korten, & Ernberg, 1992).
2. Schizophrenia is particularly frequent among people from underprivileged socioeconomic backgrounds, especially in urban environments. This is the case, for example, among homeless adolescents (Mundy, Robertson, Robertson, & Greenblatt, 1990).
3. In the Western world, a diagnosis of schizophrenia is more often given to people of lower socioeconomic classes and to ethnic minorities than to middle- or upper-class individuals (Lewis, Croft-Jeffreys, & Anthony, 1990).

Comparable data are lacking for youth. Some investigators report that the disorder is more frequent in children from underprivileged families (Eggers & Bunk, 1997; Green et al., 1984, 1992), but others do not (Russell et al., 1989; Werry et al., 1991). These differences are difficult to interpret, however, for they are all based on clinical samples that are unlikely to be representative of the distribution of the disorder in the general population.

Developmental Trajectories and Prognosis

In a majority of cases—approximately 75–80%—onset of the disorder is insidious and progressive, rather than sudden and acute, especially before adolescence. For example, in a study comparing the disorder in youths ranging from 7 to 17 years in the United States and New Zealand, 60–78% had had an insidious onset, with a gradual increase in symptoms over a period of twelve weeks or more. Only a minority had had a sudden and acute onset (Werry, McClellan, Andrews,

& Ham, 1994). Preliminary data also suggest that onset may be more often insidious in boys than girls (Alaghband-Rad, Hamburger, Giedd, Frazier, & Rapoport, 1997).

The first signs of difficulties are often minor and can affect most areas of functioning. One child may be a "daydreamer" who has difficulty concentrating, appears lost in her thoughts, and behaves inappropriately or is withdrawn in social situations. Another child may have rapid or extreme mood changes, becoming angry or aggressive and then anxious or withdrawn for no apparent reason. A third may have odd ideas, based on trivial observations that others do not see as important. In clinical cases, these problems snowball as the child develops, such that "daydreaming" becomes social isolation and "odd ideas" become delusions or hallucinations.

Studies indicate that 54–90% of affected youth showed a variety of psychological symptoms or disorders prior to qualifying for a diagnosis of COS, especially when onset occurred during childhood (McClellan & Werry, 1992). Agitation, hyperactivity, and marked mood changes are common antecedents. As we mentioned earlier, in some cases symptoms of autism may also be present in early childhood (Watkins et al., 1988). More generally, developmental delays in language, motor skills, and social relationships provide the first signs that the child is not developing normally (Hollis, 1995).

The often insidious nature of COS is reflected in an intriguing study in which untrained observers were shown home movies of children who later developed symptoms of COS. After looking at the movies, which featured these children and their siblings, the observers could reliably distinguish between the children who developed the disorder in late adolescence or early adulthood and their siblings who did not—even though the movies were made before the participants were 8 years old; that is, long before they began to have significant symptoms that brought them to the attention of mental health professionals (Walker & Lewine, 1990).

As Elizabeth's story shows, schizophrenia typically affects *all* aspects of the child or adolescent's life. But symptoms usually are not continuously present. In one of the few studies examining the developmental trajectory of COS, 79–90% of affected youth experienced three acute episodes or more during a four-year period (Werry et al., 1994). In other words, the disorder is often cyclical: short, acute schizophrenic episodes are interspersed with longer periods of partial or complete remission or even recovery. In a majority of cases, acute episodes are replaced over time by a residual phase in which negative symptoms predominate (McClellan & Werry, 1992).

These findings illustrate the generally chronic nature of COS. However, its progression and long-term prognosis vary considerably from one person to another. Three overlapping factors play a particularly important role in determining the course of the disorder:

1. *Age of onset:* Progression and prognosis are worse when the disorder begins during childhood than when it appears for the first time at the end of adolescence or at the beginning of adulthood (Remschmidt et al., 1994);
2. *Level of adaptation before the first episode and level of recovery following it:* Progression and prognosis are worse when the child's personal and social adaptation was poor before onset of the disorder and when the amount of recovery after the first episode is limited (Werry & McClellan, 1992);
3. *Manner in which the disorder begins and manifests itself:* Progression and prognosis are worse when the disorder begins in an insidious rather than acute manner. Similarly, youth who have predominantly negative symptoms have a less favorable prognosis than those who have primarily positive symptoms (Eggers & Bunk, 1997; Remschmidt et al., 1994).

This last point is documented in a six-year follow-up of 113 hospitalized adolescents (Remschmidt et al., 1994). The researchers grouped the adolescents into three categories: (1) those with mainly positive symptoms (i.e., hallucinations, delusions, disorganized speech); (2) those with mainly negative symptoms (i.e., affective flattening, alogia, avolition); or (3) those with a combination of positive and negative symptoms. Adolescents in the primarily positive-symptom group had a better prognosis than their peers who had either predominantly negative symptoms or mixed symptoms. More precisely, 40% of primarily positive-symptom adolescents were in remission following their hospitalization. In contrast, only 4% of adolescents in the primarily negative- or mixed-symptom groups were in remission following their hospitalization. These figures must obviously be interpreted with caution, since they are based on a single study in which participants had had the disorder for varying periods of time and had been through one or more hospitalizations. Nevertheless, they highlight the complexity of the disorder—in symptomatology, progression, and prognosis—and stress the importance of a developmental and longitudinal approach to research in this area.

Unfortunately, for a considerable number of children and adolescents with schizophrenia, the prognosis remains grim in adulthood. In one of the rare longitudinal studies that followed children and adolescents for a long period of time (forty-two years on average), only 25% of participants achieved complete remission, whereas 25% continued to have moderate and 50% major difficulties in adulthood (Eggers, Bunk, Volberg, & Roepcke, 1999). Again, prognosis was more favorable for participants whose symptom development was acute. In fact, all participants in complete remission came from the acute-onset group. None of the participants with an insidious onset were in complete remission by the time of follow-up (see also Asarnow & Tompson, 1999).

Two shorter longitudinal studies obtained even more pessimistic results, reporting that 78–90% of youth who developed schizophrenia during adolescence still had major difficulties of adaptation in early adulthood (Gillberg, Hellgren, & Gillberg, 1993; Werry et al., 1994). For example, approximately four years after diagnosis, fewer than 30% of participants lived independently, and only a small minority (13%) had a job or were full-time students (Werry et al., 1994). This grim conclusion is similar to that found in many studies conducted with adults and generally confirms the continuity of the disorder over the life course.

Etiology

In COS, as in many other psychological disorders of childhood and adolescence, a transactional, biopsychosocial perspective currently dominates the work of a majority of researchers and clinicians. This perspective regards the disorder as the visible manifestation of a biological vulnerability, which is triggered by a high level of stressful life events. This vulnerability is expressed in diverse ways, depending on the nature and timing of these events and on the child or adolescent's own temperamental and personality characteristics.

Biological Factors

Genetic Factors. It has been known for a long time that schizophrenia tends to run in families. This is true whether one looks at young people (Green et al., 1992; Spencer & Campbell, 1994) or at adults with the disorder (Jay, Gorwood, & Feingold, 1997; Kendler et al., 1993). Twin, adoption, and family aggregation studies indicate that these results are due in part to genetic effects. Figure 5.4 (p. 134) illustrates the risk of developing schizophrenia as a function of genetic relatedness.

Landmark summaries of the genetic research (Gottesman 1991, 1996) show that:

1. Concordance rates for schizophrenia are approximately two and a half to three times higher in monozygotic or identical twins than in dizygotic or fraternal twins (averaging 45–50% in the former compared to 15–20% in the latter).
2. A person who has a first-degree relative with schizophrenia has a much greater risk of developing it than someone without such a relative (Kendler & Diehl, 1993). Furthermore, first-degree relatives, such as children of affected parents, run a higher risk of developing the disorder, and of developing it at an earlier age, than second- or third-degree relatives (e.g., grandchildren or cousins) (Jay et al., 1997).
3. The probability of developing the disorder increases with the number of affected relatives.

This last point is highlighted in a study of the families of sixteen children with COS. A full 33% had one or more family members with the disorder. This percentage is extremely high when one considers the prevalence of the condition in the general population. In addition, even when relatives did not have the

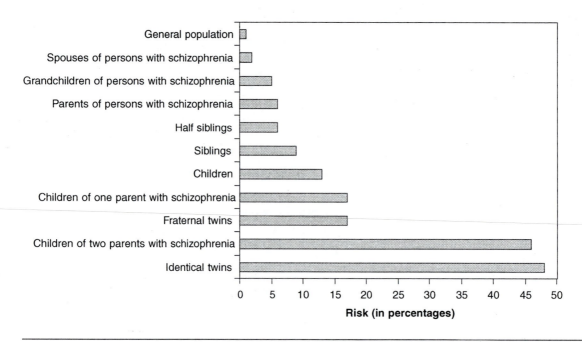

FIGURE 5.4   *Risk of Developing Schizophrenia as a Function of Genetic Relatedness.* A person's risk of developing schizophrenia increases as a function of genetic relatedness. For example, if a person's identical twin (who shares the same genetic makeup) has schizophrenia, that person has approximately one chance in two of developing the disorder. However, if one of the person's grandparents (who shares approximately one-fourth of the same genetic makeup) has the disorder, that person has one chance in twenty of becoming affected.

Source: Gottesman (1991), p. 96. Reprinted by permission.

disorder themselves, they often had other psychological difficulties, such as mental retardation or mood disorders (Spencer & Campbell, 1994). This finding suggests that the increased risk found in families of affected individuals is probably not specific to schizophrenia only, but also includes a more general risk of increased psychological disorders.

Adoption studies confirm the importance of genetic factors in the transmission of the disorder. There is strong evidence that children who were born to mothers with schizophrenia but who were adopted as infants run the same risk of developing the disorder as children born to and raised by mothers with the disorder. In addition, adopted children who develop schizophrenia as adolescents or adults tend to have large percentages of biological, but not adoptive, relatives with the disorder (Kety, 1988; Kety et al., 1994).

Genetic factors, then, play a major etiological role in the disorder. To date, however, schizophrenia has not been linked reliably to one or more genes, although researchers are actively pursuing several possible linkages (Kendler et al., 2000). Specific genetic abnormalities have also been reported in *some* children with COS (e.g., Kumra et al., 1998; Usiskin et al., 1999); but no firm conclusion can be drawn from such evidence, because these abnormalities are evident only in a minority of children and are rarely consistent from one child to the next. Possibly the disorder is caused not by a specific gene or genes but by an unknown number of genetic variations. In this perspective—which corresponds to the long-held view that schizophrenia is a group of disorders, rather than a single condition—different genetic variations may make certain individuals susceptible to develop schizophrenia.

Some of these variations may result in the disorder irrespective of environmental influences, whereas others may only contribute to the disorder in association with adverse life circumstances. In other words, some children may inherit the disorder directly (through genetic processes that remain to be uncovered), whereas others may inherit a genetic *vulnerability* to the disorder (but not the disorder itself) (Kendler, 1998).

The notion of vulnerability reflects a diathesis-stress model of psychopathology, in which adverse genetic and environmental factors act in transaction to produce dysfunction. In this etiological perspective, a child's genetic vulnerability is likely to be activated if the child becomes exposed to stressful life circumstances and does not have the personal and social resources necessary to cope effectively. Genetic vulnerability and stress may thus, in combination, result in the first signs of the disorder and set its developmental trajectory in motion. Numerous studies lend support to this transactional model. For example, children at high risk for schizophrenia—because their mothers are affected—are more likely to develop it if they suffered from adverse life circumstances in their growing years than if they did not (Olin & Mednick, 1996). Similarly, the risk for adopted children born to mothers with schizophrenia depends not only on the presence of psychological problems in their families of origin, but also in their adoptive families (Wahlberg et al., 1997).

Neurobiological and Neuropsychological Factors.
Numerous studies have focused on the neurobiological and neuropsychological characteristics that differentiate people with schizophrenia from people with other psychological disorders or without any psychopathology (R. F. Asarnow et al., 1994; Jacobsen & Rapoport, 1998). This research is based on various methods of investigation. Some of these methods make it possible to describe the structure or functioning of the brain through biochemical studies of specific neurotransmitters, electroencephalographs (EEGs), positron emission tomography (PET scans), magnetic resonance imaging (MRI), or cerebral blood flow. Other methods aim at comparing the performance of experimental and control children or adolescents on different experimental tasks that measure perceptual and cognitive

skills (e.g., attention, memory). We will briefly summarize the evidence.

Drugs that reduce schizophrenic symptoms (e.g., *chlorpromazine*) or increase them (e.g., *amphetamines*) were discovered in the 1950s. This discovery led to a considerable amount of research on the neurotransmitters that underlie these drug effects. Of these neurotransmitters, **dopamine** is the best studied and the most often implicated in the etiology of the disorder. The drugs that are most effective in controlling schizophrenic symptoms act by reducing dopamine activity in the transmission of nerve impulses; therefore, schizophrenia appears to reflect an excess of dopamine activity in the brain (e.g., Holcomb et al., 1996). However, dopamine alone cannot provide an adequate causal explanation for the various manifestations of the disorder; as years of research have shown, medications affecting this neurotransmitter do not reduce all schizophrenic symptoms (Carlsson, 1995). Typically, medications that decrease dopamine activity reduce mostly positive symptoms and social withdrawal but have only limited effects on other symptoms. In addition, these medications often provide little or no relief to children and adolescents with COS.

Some studies also suggest that certain brain abnormalities may account for the origin of the disorder (Buchsbaum, 1990). For example, magnetic resonance imaging (MRI) has shown that youth with schizophrenia have smaller cerebral blood volume than their average peers and that this decrease in volume is linked to negative symptoms (Alaghband-Rad et al., 1997; Frazier et al., 1996). In related research, neuropsychological investigations indicate that children and adolescents with COS have significant difficulties in information processing and, more particularly, in the management of attention (R. F. Asarnow et al., 1994; Strandburg, Marsh, Brown, Asarnow, & Guthrie, 1994; Zahn et al., 1998). Specifically, when sensory, perceptual, and language capacities are tested in a variety of experimental tasks, youth with the disorder obtain poorer results than comparison children—largely because they cannot process information quickly and efficiently.

Neurophysiological and neuropsychological studies offer particularly promising avenues of research by providing increasingly more precise links between biological and psychological processes and functions.

However, these studies do not make it possible to specify the etiology of the disorder at this time, because their findings have multiple explanations, only one of which is that brain abnormalities are the cause of schizophrenia. For example, these abnormalities could be the continuation of an abnormal developmental process that began before the onset of the disorder and was necessary for its appearance. Alternatively, they could be a consequence of the disorder itself, or a side effect of the various medications most research participants receive. Even though competing interpretations can be advanced to explain research results in this area, ongoing research will undoubtedly provide a growing number of hypotheses that will contribute to a better understanding of the factors that are at the origin of the disorder or contribute to its progression over time.

Factors Related to Development in the Course of Pregnancy.   Incidents during pregnancy and at birth are more frequent in persons with schizophrenia than in average individuals, according to some studies (e.g., Günther-Genta, Bovet, & Hohlfeld, 1994) but not others (e.g., Green et al., 1992). The role that such incidents may play in the etiology of the disorder is unclear, once again because potential risk factors are numerous and typically apply only to a minority of cases. However, we will briefly consider two intriguing hypotheses here.

The first one stems from evidence that some cases of schizophrenia may result from a slow viral infection that develops during the course of pregnancy or shortly after birth but becomes manifest only years later. Specifically, people who are born in the winter months—when viral infections are common—have a greater risk of developing the disorder than people born at other times of the year (Tam & Sewell, 1995; Torrey, Bowler, Rawlings, & Terrazas, 1993). The timing of infections appears important also, because the risk of schizophrenia is greatest when exposure to viruses occurs in the second trimester of pregnancy, as opposed to the first or third trimesters (Wright, Takei, Rifkin, & Murray, 1995). Although suggestive, these findings do not establish causality, because the virus or viruses that may be implicated have not been isolated (Battle, Martin, Dorfman, & Miller, 1999). However, in a diathesis-

stress model, a single virus may not need to be found, since infection at critical times in fetal or infant development may act to increase vulnerability, making it more likely that exposure to stressors will lead the child to develop the disorder in the course of childhood or adolescence.

The second hypothesis relating schizophrenia to fetal development has been proposed by Weinberger (1995). In this etiological model, abnormalities in the brain that develop before birth may have detrimental psychological effects that become evident only years later. Weinberger proposed that these effects do not appear fully until puberty, when they are activated by hormonal changes. Although a few case studies support this theory, a study of twenty-eight adolescents (fourteen boys and fourteen girls) with COS did not find any link between onset of the disorder and puberty (Frazier et al., 1997). However, this model remains important, not only because a single study is not enough to invalidate it, but also because it illustrates the complexity of the etiological processes that are likely to account for the disorder.

It is clear that theories that focus on single causal explanations will not explain the etiology of a disorder as complex as schizophrenia. Indeed, in this as in other psychological disorders, the appearance of symptoms is most likely the result of complex transactions among numerous risk factors *and* of the developmental period during which these factors are most active.

Family, Social, and Cultural Factors

Various psychological theories have been advanced to explain the etiology of COS. The common denominator of many of them is the assumption that the origin of the disorder lies in dysfunctional patterns of interaction or communication between the child and other family members. As we saw in Chapter 4 with respect to autism, a number of early psychoanalytic theories attributed the etiology of schizophrenia to pathological mother-child interactions (e.g., Fromm-Reichman, 1948). Clinicians who accepted these theories commonly spoke then of **schizophrenogenic** mothers. These mothers were supposed to be cold and rejecting women who dominated and controlled their children by depriving them of affection. Over time, their children withdrew from social contacts and sought refuge in a safer psychological inner world. As you might expect, there is no empirical support at all for such sweeping "mother-blaming" assertions.

Another influential theory, known as the **double-bind theory,** was proposed at approximately the same time (Bateson, Jackson, Haley, & Weakland, 1956). It states that the roots of the disorder are to be found in a discordant style of family communication (again, especially between mother and child). In this perspective, some children are unable to interpret correctly the messages they receive from family members because the messages are basically contradictory. Bateson and colleagues (1956) give this example of a young man who receives a double-bind message from his mother:

> A young man who had fairly well recovered from an acute schizophrenic episode was visited in the hospital by his mother. He was glad to see her and impulsively put his arm around her shoulders whereupon she stiffened. He withdrew his arm and she asked, "Don't you love me anymore?" He then blushed and she said, "Dear, you must not be so easily embarrassed and afraid of your feelings" (pp. 258–259).

Bateson's theory gave rise to considerable clinical work. However, the causal processes it postulates have been repeatedly questioned by empirical research. The theory has two major shortcomings: first, it is vague and does not clearly specify which family communication patterns, if any, are necessary and sufficient to bring about schizophrenic symptoms; and, second, since patterns of conflicted communication are found in many families without COS, the specific role these patterns may play in the etiology of the disorder is unclear (Jacob, 1975).

These conclusions have not put an end to research on family communication (Goldstein, 1987). Ongoing work in this area now aims at evaluating the *family's role in the progression of the disorder, rather than in its etiology.* Much of this research focuses on the concept of **expressed emotion,** or EE (Hooley, 1985; Leff & Vaughn, 1985).

EE is a measure of emotional quality or tone used to describe communication in families of persons with COS (or other disorders) and to compare it with that of other families. By sampling how parents speak about their children (typically in the child's absence), this measure gauges their tendency to be critical and controlling, by becoming overinvolved in the child's affairs or expressing strong negative emotions about the child. Box 5.3 (p. 138) provides examples of high and low EE.

Research on EE in COS is in its infancy. It is likely that EE—if it plays any role in schizophrenia—merely influences the course of the disorder, rather than causing it in the first place. There are no longitudinal studies establishing a causal link between high levels of EE and schizophrenia; moreover, since cross-cultural research shows that EE varies considerably from one culture to another, it is unlikely to play a causal role in the etiology of the disorder except in association with other variables (Jenkins & Karno, 1992). Finally, the etiological role of EE, if it can be established, would not be specific to schizophrenia, since high levels of EE are found in families of children and adolescents with other psychological conditions, such as disruptive behavior disorders and anxiety disorders (Hibbs et al., 1991; Stubbe, Zahner, Goldstein, & Leckman, 1993).

In short, there is no doubt that the communications and interactions between youth with COS and their families are often disturbed—sometimes seriously so. However, causal links are difficult to demonstrate, because the majority of published studies are based on cross-sectional analyses. In addition, other family members with disorders are often found in the homes of children with COS. These factors make it impossible to know with certainty whether negative family interactions lead to COS, whether COS causes these interactions, or whether these two variables are associated in noncausal ways (Werry, 1992).

Treatment and Prevention

No soul is desolate as long as there is a human being for whom it can feel trust and reverence.
—George Eliot

Although COS is a severe disorder with particularly poor prognosis, there is little literature on its treatment (Dulmus & Smyth, 2000; Kumra, 2000). However,

BOX 5.3 • *Expressed Emotion: Identifying Deviance in Family Communication*

Expressed emotion (EE) is a measure obtained by a researcher as he or she listens to family members (usually parents) talk about a close relative, such as a child or an adolescent with a psychological disorder. Critical comments and emotional overinvolvement by parents are strong predictors of relapse in persons with schizophrenia.

A *critical comment* is a "statement which, by the manner in which it is expressed, constitutes an unfavorable comment upon the behavior or personality of the person to whom it refers" (Leff & Vaughn, 1985, p. 38). In high EE, a parent says something negative about the child and does so in a critical tone of voice. The following are examples of high and low EE in parental comments:

High EE

This kid is a genuine con artist, believe me. I spent time in the service and I've been around con artists. This kid is a first-class, genuine con artist, bar none (Leff & Vaughn, 1985, p. 40).

I always say, "why don't you pick up a book, do a crossword or something like that to keep your mind off it." *That's* even too much trouble (Hooley, 1985, p. 134).

Low EE

It really annoys me when she does that but that's probably because I am an intolerant person (Hooley, p. 121).

Emotional overinvolvement of family members is also an important facet of EE. Researchers look here for evidence of a family member's attempt to overcontrol the child's behavior. In extreme cases, parents can become so involved in the child's life that they stop living their own life. Again, here are some examples:

High EE

I miss her; I miss her, I think about her all the time. See we've always been close, always been together. She seemed to be always "me and dad." She didn't like other people (Leff & Vaughn, 1985, p. 46).

I haven't been out with my husband. I could go out if I wanted to but I don't go because I'm looking after Johnnie [age 29 and working] you see, and I'm devoting my life to Johnnie because I think he needs me more (Hooley, 1985, p. 121).

Low EE

I just tend to let it go because I know that when she wants to speak she will speak (Hooley, p. 134).

I know it's better for her to be on her own, to get away from me and try to do things on her own (Hooley, p. 134).

---

researchers in this area generally agree that four considerations are essential to help youth with the disorder (McClellan & Werry, 1994; Clark & Lewis, 1998):

1. Establish an accurate diagnosis.
2. Rely on pharmacological intervention to control acute symptoms of delusions and hallucinations.
3. Develop a multidisciplinary treatment plan that includes skills training, family education and therapy, and educational and vocational instruction, in addition to pharmacological intervention.
4. Understand the course of the disorder.

Diagnosis

An accurate diagnosis of COS is difficult, especially in younger children. As McClellan and Werry (1994) note,

"[The] problem is distinguishing true psychotic phenomena from nonpsychotic idiosyncratic thinking and perceptions caused by developmental delays, exposure to traumatic events, and/or over-active imaginations" (p. 619). This problem is complicated by the fact that idiosyncratic thinking and perceptions, as well as delusions and hallucinations, are also found in children with other psychological disorders, such as autism (see Chapter 4) or mood disorders (see Chapter 9). For example, as many as half of all youth with bipolar disorder may initially be misdiagnosed as having schizophrenia (Carlson, 1990). These and other factors discussed earlier make correct diagnosis difficult. But research highlights the importance of an early and accurate diagnosis, because the longer that psychotic episodes remain untreated, or are treated inappropriately, the worse the prognosis becomes (Birchwood, McGorry, & Jackson, 1997).

Proper diagnosis depends on a comprehensive assessment of the child. This assessment must include a complete medical workup to rule out organic explanations for the child's symptoms; a thorough history of the child's symptoms; extensive interviews with the child and with family members; and consultation with school officials and mental health professionals who have previously been involved in the child's care (Clark & Lewis, 1998). Also useful in establishing a valid diagnosis are behavior-rating scales and structured interviews, such as the ones described in Chapter 2. This assessment should rule out other diagnoses that share a similar symptomatology and consider the cyclical nature of the disorder. Because children with schizophrenia experience periods of acute distress alternating with periods of remission, clinicians must take into account the child's level of functioning at different points in time; also, once a diagnosis is made, clinicians must continue to monitor the child, to meet his or her changing needs.

Pharmacological Interventions

Because schizophrenia is a rare disorder, there are few potential participants with whom to conduct controlled drug trials. In addition, such trials raise ethical questions, because they require random assignment to an experimental and a control group—and, therefore, the withholding of potentially beneficial drugs to control children. These factors are undoubtedly slowing the growth of knowledge in this area (Clark & Lewis, 1998). However, as the following two sections will show, it is already well established that neuroleptics can help many children and adolescents with COS, even though they are not a cure and need to be prescribed in most, if not all, active phases of the disorder.

Conventional Neuroleptics.   Unlike most psychological disorders of childhood and adolescence, COS is primarily treated with medication (Clark & Lewis, 1998; McClellan & Werry, 1994). **Neuroleptics** are usually the drugs of choice. They are part of a class of compounds that specifically target dopamine receptors and lead to an overall decrease in available dopamine in the brain. As mentioned, dopamine excesses have

been hypothesized to be an etiological factor in the development and maintenance of the disorder.

There is considerable evidence to support the efficacy of neuroleptics to control positive symptoms in adults. In fact, "the only *specific* treatment of documented efficacy in [adult] schizophrenia is antipsychotic [neuroleptic] medicine" (McClellan & Werry, 1994, p. 624, italics in original). Few controlled studies have assessed the effectiveness of neuroleptics in COS, however, although they generally lead to a similar conclusion. Specifically, neuroleptics such as *haloperidol* and *loxapine* usually improve the symptoms of approximately 70% of affected children and adolescents (Clark & Lewis, 1998).

The major drawback of conventional neuroleptics is their side effects. These effects are dose related; that is, they increase as drug dosage increases. Common side effects include sedation, hypotension (low blood pressure), gastrointestinal discomfort, and **extrapyramidal symptoms.** Extrapyramidal symptoms are potentially extreme muscle and motor disturbances, such as spasms of the tongue, neck, and head; Parkinson's disease; and tardive dyskinesia. Individuals with Parkinson's disease lose muscle control and walk in a stooped, shuffling gait with small steps. In addition, they often have visible tremors and drool. Individuals with tardive dyskinesia develop involuntary face, body, and limb movements and tremors as a result of taking neuroleptics for prolonged periods. The development of Parkinson's disease is not reversible. Tardive dyskinesia may be reversed after the use of neuroleptics is discontinued. Although research is sparse, between 8% and 51% of children treated with conventional neuroleptics may develop extrapyramidal symptoms (McClellan & Werry, 1994). Not surprisingly, anti-Parkinson's medications are often prescribed along with conventional neuroleptics to minimize the appearance and severity of these symptoms.

Atypical Neuroleptics.   A new class of drugs, called *atypical neuroleptics,* has been developed in recent years, in an attempt to treat schizophrenia without provoking the severe side effects just described. Like their conventional predecessors, atypical neuroleptics, such as *clozapine* and *risperidone,* target dopamine receptors but do not affect receptors associated with muscular and motor control. Consequently, the probability of someone's developing extrapyramidal symptoms is reduced. However, these new compounds can still have significant side effects, such as sedation and weight gain, and little is known about their long-term developmental effects (Kumra, 2000). Research on the use of atypical neuroleptics in the treatment of schizophrenia is ongoing. Current evidence suggests that they are more effective than conventional neuroleptics in reducing both positive and negative symptoms, and that they produce fewer side effects, especially severe extrapyramidal symptoms (Kumra et al., 1996; Toren, Laor, & Weizman, 1998).

Multidisciplinary, Multimodal Treatment

To be effective, treatment for COS must be both specific and general: it must control the most debilitating symptoms of the disorder, and it must meet the psychological, social, and educational needs of the child and family. Whereas symptom control relies almost entirely on medication, management of the psychosocial challenges associated with the disorder requires a multidisciplinary team of professionals focusing on different modes of service delivery (Dulmus & Symthe, 2000; McClellan & Werry, 1994). In other words, medication can usually reduce symptoms, but it cannot remedy the adaptation problems brought about by the disorder or prevent its recurrence when it is in remission.

Psychoeducation.   In hospital or in a day treatment program, the child and family members must be taught about medications and their side effects. The family also must receive support to ensure that the child takes all prescribed medications and attends follow-up appointments, since failure to adhere to treatment recommendations complicates the disorder. Given that neuroleptics have many adverse side effects, failure to take them as prescribed is a common occurrence and a major cause for relapse (McClellan & Werry, 1994).

Family members may also need to develop strategies to manage their child's disruptive or withdrawn behavior—possibly through a **token economy.** A token economy is a behavior modification technique that allows children to earn points for positive behavior and to lose them for inappropriate behavior. Points

earned can then be exchanged for desired goods or activities such as treats and playtime.

Social Skills Training.   As is true of youth with other psychological disorders, youth with COS may benefit from social skills training. This training can take the form of role-playing to rehearse effective communication skills or of direct instruction in grooming, self-management, and interpersonal problem-solving skills. No study has tested the effectiveness of social skills training with affected youth, but evidence collected with adults suggests that participation in this form of treatment predicts a higher level of adaptive functioning and fewer relapses (Dulmus & Symth, 2000).

Educational and Vocational Training.   A comprehensive treatment plan generally includes important educational and vocational components. Youth with COS require specialized education programs to reduce the limitations and disruptions caused by the disorder. As we saw in Chapter 3, educational services and individualized education plans require close collaboration between the child's family, the school, and mental health and social service professionals. Likewise, in adolescence, vocational training becomes a critical component of a youth's move toward greater independence and requires collaboration of all involved to bring about this transition and help the adolescent cope with new developmental challenges.

Family Therapy.   Another important component of a multidisciplinary treatment approach is family therapy, to deal with the major disruptions in families who have to live with and care for an affected child. Family intervention may focus on managing the youth's behavior; on helping the caregivers handle their responsibilities for the child; and on improving family communication and expressed emotion. As we saw earlier, high EE or negative and overinvolved comments by family members predict relapse in adults with schizophrenia (Leff, 1991). To date, this issue has only begun to be explored in children and adolescents, although past work with adults suggests that it may be a useful component of a family therapy program (Dulmus & Symth, 2000).

Understanding the Course of the Disorder

Slowly I worked free from the past, from the web. . . . A whole lifetime could be spent making, outside oneself, webs to match how one is inside. To go into madness, to start to come out, to leave the web, is to fight to get free, to live.

—Mary Barnes

As you know, COS is characterized by short, acute schizophrenic episodes and longer periods of partial or complete remission or even recovery. Inpatient hospitalization is often necessary in an *active phase* of the disorder, because inpatient treatment provides children with a safe, therapeutic setting in which they can be monitored around the clock. Hospitalization also allows medication to be initiated or changed, and side effects to be monitored. Duration of inpatient hospitalization varies considerably. It can be relatively long, however, because neuroleptics usually take four to six weeks to bring about a clear improvement in symptoms.

Most youth with COS remain disorganized and confused for some time, even when their acute symptoms are brought under control by medication. During this *maintenance phase,* youth may be involved in a partial hospitalization or day treatment program but return home at night. Partial hospitalization usually provides a variety of psychosocial and educational ser-vices in addition to medication management. The goals of this phase of treatment are to help the child return to a normal pattern of activities and to minimize the chances of relapse (Kumra, 2000).

As symptoms and adaptive functioning improve, and the disorder moves into *remission,* transition back into the home and community is usually warranted. Prevailing wisdom in schizophrenia treatment is that children should remain at home whenever possible. However, in many cases, aggressive, disruptive, or bizarre behavior, or a chaotic home environment, makes at-home care impossible. Unfortunately, youth with COS are at high risk not only for relapse but also for long-term out-of-home placements (Asarnow, 1994).

Prevention

Because COS is a rare disorder of largely unknown etiology (or etiologies), prevention efforts are exceedingly difficult and are not conducted on a large scale. However, a number of researchers are working in this area, trying to develop reliable methods of assessing known risk factors and to determine whether these factors can predict the onset of the disorder (Tsuang, Stone, & Faraone, 2000; Yung et al., 1998). These studies may one day provide the foundation for early interventions that may delay the onset or lessen the severity of an initial episode of the disorder.

Web Links

www.schizophrenia.com (Not-for-profit information, support, and education center; provides links to researchers and families)

mhsource.com/narsad.html (National Alliance for Research on Schizophrenia and Depression; provides scientific information on the disorder)

vaxxine.com/schizophrenia (Schizophrenia Digest; commercially supported information about schizophrenia)

6

Learning Disorders

Learning is not compulsory . . . neither is survival.
—W. Edwards Deming

Learning disorders—or learning disabilities, as they are more commonly called—are a varied group of developmental disorders in which children's achievement in reading, writing, and/or mathematics is not at the expected level given their intellectual ability. Typically, these disorders affect children's self-concept and the attitudes of others toward them. For these children, school becomes a particularly trying experience, and later employment opportunities are seriously limited. Karen, a 17-year-old with a reading disorder, forcefully describes her reaction to her disability:

> Words have always bullied me around. I have been afraid of words as long as I can remember. Not afraid of saying them, but seeing them and hearing them. Maybe I've been afraid of thinking them too because they never seemed as comfortable inside my head as pictures, music and feelings did (Lyman, 1986, p. xi).

The DSM-IV-TR lists three major learning disorders: **reading disorder, disorder of written expression,** and **mathematics disorder.** Reading disorder is the most common. Alone or with a comorbid learning disorder, it accounts for approximately 80% of all learning disabilities (APA, 2000a; Lyon, 1996).

Learning disorders, especially severe difficulties in reading and writing, are frequently accompanied by significant language and communication problems.

Although children in most industrialized countries receive specialized educational services for learning disabilities, these problems remain poorly understood. In fact, their nature, definition, and classification are among today's most hotly debated topics in abnormal child and adolescent psychology. Some authors even question their very existence or their place in a classification system of psychological disorders, because many aspects of learning disorders are educational rather than psychological in nature. Controversy around this topic reflects five important issues that we discuss throughout this chapter (see also Lyon, 1994, 1996):

1. *There is no generally agreed-upon definition of learning disorders.* Systematic research in this area has been conducted only for the past twenty to thirty years. In spite of important progress, researchers still do not have a largely accepted definition of learning disorders or detailed information about the core characteristics and likely etiologies.

2. *The field of learning disabilities is diversified but not truly multidisciplinary.* Professionals in areas such as psychology, education, psychiatry, neurology, and speech pathology have made and continue to make key contributions to knowledge in this area. However, they all employ different approaches and focus on overlapping issues that are not always defined or assessed in the same manner. Moreover, these professionals are often unaware of the work conducted in adjoining disciplines. This lack of a truly multidisciplinary orientation has repeatedly condemned the field to advance more slowly than would otherwise be possible.

3. *Diagnosis is made difficult by a lack of well-validated assessment tools.* It is almost impossible to create adequate assessment measures until what they must measure is clearly defined. Because no instrument has established itself as the "gold standard" for assessing learning disabilities, school psychologists—who evaluate children with learning difficulties—often rely on criteria that vary from state to state and even from school district to school district.

4. *Most interventions for learning disabilities are created as needed and are rarely evaluated.* Therefore, data on the developmental trajectory of these disorders are difficult to interpret, and a useful prognosis is often impossible to establish.

5. *Research in this field is heavily influenced by administrative decisions.* In a majority of industrialized countries, a large number of children and adolescents receive specialized services aimed at remedying their learning difficulties. These services, which are very expensive and often of unknown effectiveness, are frequently modified in response to social, political, or economic concerns—rather than in light of empirical research.

Historical Overview

More than a century ago, people began to observe that some children had learning difficulties that could not be explained by unsatisfactory schooling (inadequate teaching or prolonged school absences); intellectual or sensory impairment (mental retardation, blindness, or hearing loss); or family or social difficulties (poverty or neglect). Many people today are surprised to hear that Albert Einstein, Thomas Edison, Leonardo da Vinci, Woodrow Wilson, Cher, Walt Disney, Whoopi Goldberg, Winston Churchill, Tom Cruise, George Bush, and George Burns, among others, struggled with learning problems as they grew up (Dyslexia: The gift, 2002).

The Concept of Minimal Brain Damage

Medicine was the first discipline to focus on the very specific challenges that some children face as they go through school (see Box 6.1, p. 144). In the first half of the twentieth century, the origin of learning disabilities in the absence of other difficulties in functioning was explained by the concept of **minimal brain damage** (Strauss & Lehtinen, 1947). Researchers commonly believed then that learning disabilities resulted from minor brain damage in individuals who in all other respects were functioning normally. The concept of minimal brain damage gave rise to a considerable amount of research. However, it proved too vague to explain the etiology of learning disabilities. The presumed "minimal" damage was, by definition, difficult to detect; therefore, if an empirical study found no evidence of brain damage, the researcher could not conclude that the damage did not exist, since it may have been so minimal that it was not detected. Furthermore, years of research showed that the majority of children and adolescents with learning disabilities did *not* have any detectable brain damage or neurological disorder that could explain the origin of their difficulties (Keogh & Sears, 1991). The concept of minimal brain damage, then, is not precise enough to account for any biological factors that may contribute to learning problems (see Etiology).

Educational Interest in Learning Disorders

Education specialists are interested primarily in the cognitive and behavioral characteristics of young people with learning disorders, and in the development of educational methods to help them (Lyon,

BOX 6.1 • *An Early Case of Reading Disorder*

The social and scientific spotlight on learning disabilities is relatively new, but physicians, psychiatrists, and educators knew about them more than a century ago. For example, in 1896 the English physician W. Pringle Morgan wrote a detailed case study of a 14-year-old with reading disorder.

> Percy . . . is the eldest son of intelligent parents, the second child of a family of seven. He has always been a bright and intelligent boy, quick at games, and in no way inferior to others his age.
>
> His great difficulty has been—and is now—his inability to learn to read. . . . He has been at school or under tutors since he was 7 years old, and the greatest efforts have been made to teach him to read, but, in spite of this laborious and persistent training, he can only with difficulty spell out words of one syllable. . . . He knows all his letters, and can write them and read them.

In writing from dictation he comes to grief over any but the simplest words. For instance, I dictated the following sentence: "Now you watch me while I spin it." He wrote: "Now you word me wale I spin it." . . . In writing his own name he made a mistake, putting "Precy" for "Percy," and he did not notice the mistake until his attention was called to it more than once. . . .

I next tried his ability to read figures, and found he could do so easily. . . . He says he is fond of arithmetic, and finds no difficulty with it, but that printed or written words "have no meaning to him," and my examination of him quite convinces me that he is correct in that opinion. . . .

I may add that the boy is bright and of average intelligence in conversation. His eyes are normal . . . and his eyesight is good. The schoolmaster who has taught him for some years said that he would be the smartest lad in the school if the instruction were entirely oral (p. 1378).

1996). Samuel Kirk, an educator, actually coined the term *learning disabilities*. In 1963, he wrote:

> I have used the term learning disabilities to describe a group of children who have disorders in development in language, speech, reading, and associated communication skills needed for social interaction. In this group I do not include children who have sensory handicaps such as blindness or deafness, because we have ways of managing and training the deaf and the blind. I also exclude from this group children who have generalized mental retardation (pp. 2–3).

Kirk's work and that of other educators contributed greatly to the recognition of learning disabilities as an educational issue and, over time, as a major social concern. Together with strong political pressure from parent and teacher groups, their work led to the establishment of specialized educational programs mandated by law to serve children and adolescents with learning disabilities (see Box 6.2).

To date, the history of learning disabilities is primarily the history of reading disorder. Until recently, most researchers believed that major writing difficul-

ties were a physical problem—a by-product of motor disturbances; therefore, these researchers paid more attention to disturbances in reading than in writing skills. Likewise, mathematics disorder has only recently come to the attention of researchers, probably because most societies put more emphasis on learning to read and write than on learning to handle numbers, illiteracy being considered a much more serious problem than math incompetence.

The concept of learning disabilities is largely accepted today (at least in industrialized countries). A major advantage of the concept is that diagnosis of a learning disorder is less stigmatizing than one of minimal brain damage or dysfunction. The concept has also the advantage of specifying that these disorders are not due to mental retardation, sensory limitations, or emotional or behavioral problems. Consequently, each diagnosed child—as well as parents and teachers—has reason to hope that learning difficulties can be overcome through the provision of favorable learning conditions in a supportive environment (Lyon, 1996). Nonetheless, the fundamental questions that have been the focus of attention for more than a century remain: How should these disabilities be defined, and how should they be distin-

BOX 6.2 • *Learning Disabilities and the 1975 Education for All Handicapped Children Act*

As you read this chapter, you will see that we often stress the importance of social and political issues in the diagnosis and treatment of learning disabilities. This is because they, unlike most other psychological disorders, have a clinical *and* a legal definition. The 1975 Education for All Handicapped Children Act defines "specific learning disability" as follows:

> Specific learning disability means a disorder in one or more of the basic psychological processes involved in understanding or in using language, spoken or written, which may manifest itself in an imperfect ability to listen, think, speak, read, write, spell, or do mathematical calculations. The term does not include children who have learning problems that are primarily the result of visual, hearing, or motor handicaps, mental retardation, emotional disturbance, or environmental, cultural, or economic disadvantage.

Before passage of this act, learning disabilities were hardly known outside of educational circles and were not defined in clinical classification systems. Although they presented a major challenge for countless children and adolescents, they were not labeled as disorders. Consequently, most children and adolescents with learning disabilities did not receive specialized educational services. The 1975 act compelled schools to identify children in need of help early, in order to provide them with services to enable them to gain the most from their school years. It also ignited a continuing controversy over funding for these expensive services.

guished from the wide range of individual differences that characterize learning?

Definitions, Diagnostic Criteria, and Major Characteristics

As their names imply, learning disorders involve specific and significant weaknesses in one of three domains:

- *Reading:* The child has difficulty decoding and recognizing words, reading fluently, and understanding what is read. Some authors refer to such challenges as **dyslexia.**
- *Writing:* The child has difficulty with handwriting, vocabulary, spelling, and organizing written compositions. These challenges are referred to at times as **dysgraphia.**
- *Mathematics:* The child has difficulty carrying out basic arithmetic operations (addition, subtraction, multiplication, division) and solving mathematical problems. Some authors speak of **dyscalculia** when referring to challenges in this area.

Learning disorders are *not* the result of an intellectual deficit, a sensory or neurological disorder, or an inadequate home or school environment (APA, 2000a), although they are often influenced by such factors. In all cases, learning disabilities interfere with the child's progress in school and with activities that require the ability to read, write, or calculate. In many cases, the child encounters challenges well beyond the academic realm, as Dayle's story illustrates.

[Dayle] had been a leader among her preschool friends; both boys and girls wanted her to join their groups. The first week of first grade was great—just what she had imagined. Then came the second week, when her classmates began to learn the letters of the alphabet with their corresponding sounds, and how to combine them to read. The little girl didn't understand what was going on. . . . Every day, schoolwork grew harder. She didn't understand how other kids learned to read and write! She stopped being the leader and began to feel left out. She didn't want the teacher to call on her to read because she couldn't do it . . . and finally the teacher stopped calling on her. Sometimes, she worked alone with the teacher after school; but she still could not solve the mystery of reading and writing. She decided to skip school once [in] a while. . . .

Oh no, another assignment! Writing can be a daunting task for some children, even though they are functioning well in other areas.

As she grew older, the little girl fell farther and farther behind her classmates. She tried to be good in school so that everyone would like her, but she could never seem to satisfy anyone. Sometimes, she became so angry that she would beat up another child. . . . She could prove her strength by beating someone up—at least she could do something well.

Her teachers and parents did not know what to do. They decided . . . it would help if she repeated a grade. But staying back didn't help at all; instead, the girl just felt dumb, and believed she was just being punished for not learning [to read] as quickly as the other children. . . . When she finally went on to junior and senior high, she found the one thing she could do well was play sports . . . but even that backfired. Without good grades she couldn't remain on the team! . . . What's the use of trying to succeed at anything? She was just a "loser" (Upham & Trumbull, 1997, pp. 1–2).

For countless children like Dayle, a learning disability represents a lifelong struggle with basic skills that most people take for granted. If you wonder whether Dayle's learning problems were simply a reflection of limited intellectual abilities and not a disorder, we will add that she went on to complete her Ph.D. in special education.

Only the curious will learn and only the resolute overcome the obstacles to learning. The quest quotient has always excited me more than the intelligence quotient.

—Eugene S. Wilson

Table 6.1 lists the DSM-IV-TR diagnostic criteria for reading disorder. The diagnostic criteria for disorder of written expression and mathematics disorder are not

TABLE 6.1   *Reading Disorder: DSM-IV-TR Diagnostic Criteria*

A. Reading achievement, as measured by individually administered standardized tests of reading accuracy or comprehension, is substantially below that expected given the person's chronological age, measured intelligence, and age-appropriate education.

B. The disturbance in Criterion A significantly interferes with academic achievement or activities of daily living that require reading skills.

C. If a sensory deficit is present, the reading difficulties are in excess of those usually associated with it.

Source: American Psychiatric Association, *Diagnostic and Statistical Manual of Mental Disorders, Fourth Edition, Text Revision* (Washington, DC: American Psychiatric Association, 2000a). Copyright 2000 American Psychiatric Association. Reprinted with permission.

reproduced here, since they are essentially the same as those for reading disorder but specify writing or mathematics as the focus of difficulties. With all three disorders, a diagnosis can be made only when the child's achievement falls below expectation, considering the child's age, intellectual abilities, health, and schooling. The DSM-IV-TR specifies that achievement must be "substantially below" what is expected of the child and states that this level of achievement is usually defined by a *discrepancy* of at least two standard deviations between achievement testing results and IQ scores (American Psychiatric Association, 2000a).

Limitations of the Concept of Discrepancy

The discrepancy requirement, although it makes sense in many individual cases, lacks empirical validity as a diagnostic criterion (Fletcher et al., 1994; B. Shaywitz, Fletcher, Holahan, & S. Shaywitz, 1992), because it assumes that children with average or above-average intelligence and learning disabilities differ in significant ways—neurologically, cognitively, or behaviorally—from children who are slow learners in all academic areas and who have below-average IQ scores. However, systematic differences between these two types of children are rarely found. In other words, there is little evidence that a discrepancy between IQ and achievement reflects underlying differences in neurological or psychological functioning. For example, in a follow-up study of children from kindergarten to the end of elementary school, children with an IQ-achievement discrepancy performed much the same as slow learners who did not have such a discrepancy. Children in both groups had comparable language, visual, and motor skills, and made similar academic progress when IQ scores were controlled in the analyses (B. Shaywitz et al., 1992).

A number of studies confirm these results and show that one must look for variables other than a discrepancy between IQ and achievement to predict learning problems. For example, some researchers have used cognitive and linguistic measures of comprehension and phonological awareness and have found that these measures did differentiate between children with reading problems—whether or not they showed this discrepancy—and children who could read without difficulty (Fletcher et al., 1994). In other words, the discrepancy criterion that is central to the DSM-IV-TR definition of reading disorder does not systematically distinguish between diagnosed children and children who read normally (Pereira-Laird, Deane, & Bunnell, 1999). That is also the conclusion of research with children who have significant difficulties in writing or mathematics (Hooper et al., 1994; Siegel, 1989).

Reading Disorder

Box 6.3 (p. 148) illustrates some of the challenges that reading would present for you if you had reading disorder. The difficulties of children and adolescents with reading disorder appear in two closely related domains: decoding (identification and recognition of single words) and comprehension (understanding of the meaning of words in context).

Research has shown that, from the first stages of learning, skills in decoding and comprehension develop simultaneously (Gaillard, 1997). Children do not learn to decode first and understand later. However, although these skills progress together, it is the ability to decode that appears to be impaired in most affected children. Youth with reading disorder have considerable difficulty in understanding that words can be broken down and identified by means of relatively consistent phonological rules. The case of 14-year-old Terry illustrates this challenge.

Pertinent History: *There were three children in the L. family. Two older sisters were doing very well in school, while Terry always had a hard time with his work. The parents were both college graduates and stressed the value of a good education. . . .*

Mrs. L. noted that Terry always wanted to make a top score in school or on the athletic field. . . . According to his parents, he had a number of friends and aside from his worries about school lived a "normal" life.

School History: *. . . Kindergarten and first grade were recalled as hard years for him, and he repeated first grade. It must be noted, however, that Terry was a December baby, and being retained a year placed him with children only slightly younger than himself. Mrs.*

BOX 6.3 • *Imagine That You Have Reading Disorder*

Read the following lines and count how long it takes you.

IMAGINEHOWCONFUSINGITWOULDBEIF
EVERYTHINGYOUREADLOOKEDLIKE THIS!
ORIFTH EWOR DSBE GINA NDEN DI NPLAC ESTH
ATDON'TM AKES ENSET OY OU?
TAHW FI EHT SRETTEL EREW DESREVER or
OTU FO ODRER?

Now imagine being called on to read aloud and the *words seem to dance all over the place,* like this:

```
    w   o       e       o   d       n       e
    a       l       e       h       c
            r   s   e   t           a           l
        o           r       t           l       e.
    ds      m                       c
  v                   e   p   a
```

These two exercises can give you only a glimpse of some of the difficulties that youth with reading disorder face whenever they have to make sense of written text.

Source: Comfort (1992), p. 23. Reprinted by permission.

L. viewed the retention as a sensible move, but in spite of the extra year of primary school, in second grade a reading problem was recognized. Reading scores at that time were approximately one year below grade level.

During the third and fourth grades, Terry received special tutoring, but at the end of the fourth grade his reading test scores were still one year below grade level. The school was not especially concerned about these results since group intelligence tests over a period of several years had consistently indicated an IQ of 88. The below-average reading scores were viewed as consistent with his potential, and no additional remedial work was provided.

Junior high school seemed to be fairly successful academically for Terry, with the exception of Eng-lish. His other grades were in the 70s and 80s, and although the guidance counselor observed that he appeared to be tense, he was holding his own. . . .

Intellectual Abilities: The Wechsler Intelligence Scale for Children was administered and a Full Scale quotient of 107 was obtained, which fell within the average range. Verbal and Performance quotients were 97 and 115, respectively. . . . Discrepancy between the two scales grossly confirms Terry's relative comfort with nonverbal tasks and indicates his vulnerability in language related areas. . . .

Reading Performance: Reading aloud did not appear to be a chore for Terry. He read the easier paragraphs quickly, confidently, and accurately, only occasionally asking for the meaning of words. As the *words became more difficult, his reading became less accurate, and he began to make errors with small sight words and endings as well as with the multisyllable words. He obviously lost track of meaning, and although he struggled to apply his phonic skills to words such as "habitually" and "profusion" he was hampered by not recognizing the words once he produced the syllables. The resulting sentences, while always correct syntactically, were full of nonsense words and substitutions. . . .*

Summary: *Terry had a history of reading difficulties, for which he had received remediation in elementary school. . . . He was a youngster of average intellectual abilities whose comprehension of reading material depended heavily upon use of context. . . . As a result, Terry experienced reading as both tedious and frustrating and viewed himself as stupid and incompetent in his academic work (Raim, 1982, pp. 223–230).*

As Terry's case shows, youth with reading disorder cannot decode and identify words quickly and reliably, because they do not understand the **phonological rules** underlying language—that is, "the rules for combining and selecting speech sounds of a language." For example, in English, "words cannot begin with the 'ng' sound and . . . sounds 'b,' 'n,' and 'f' cannot occur continuously" (Cantwell & Baker, 1991, p. 1).

These rules help children who are learning to read sound out new words. Without an understanding of these rules, most children cannot establish the necessary bridge between the letters on the page and the sounds they hear. This lack of understanding is particularly evident when children participate in game-like tasks such as Pig Latin (see Box 6.4). It is also evident when they are asked to remove a **phoneme** from a word and to combine and pronounce its remaining elements. (Phonemes are the smallest units of speech—for instance, "sh" in show and "o" in boat.) In such an exercise, the child may be given the word *computer* and asked to say it again without its first, middle, or last syllable. The answer would be "puter," "comter," or "compu" (Lecocq, 1986). This process seems simple to most readers but is very challenging for children with limited phonological awareness. More generally, with-

BOX 6.4 • *Pig Latin*

Pennington and associates (1993) used Pig Latin to assess the phonological skills of school-age boys with and without reading disorder. In Pig Latin, children create a new language by taking the first letter of a common word, moving it to the end, and adding "ay" to the new word. Thus, "house" becomes "ousehay" and "boy" becomes "oybay." The study found that boys with reading disorder had significantly more difficulty creating and pronouncing words in Pig Latin than their average peers. Specifically, out of forty-eight words, boys who had reading disorder pronounced an average of fourteen Pig Latin words correctly, compared to thirty for boys who read without difficulty. Try it. Translate the following words into Pig Latin, and then read them quickly and fluently. It is not as easy as it may seem.

| hat | train | phone | carpet | pants |

out such awareness, children have great difficulty going from the spelling of a word to its pronunciation and meaning, and then from the meaning of each word to that of the sentence, the paragraph, and the text as a whole (Aaron et al., 1999). These difficulties repeatedly slow down and interrupt their reading and, by absorbing their entire attention, limit or even prevent their comprehension.

Disorder of Written Expression

Like reading, writing depends on multiple skills: it requires fine motor coordination, a working vocabulary, and knowledge of spelling, grammar, and composition. Given the number of skills involved, it is not surprising that children with disorder of written expression form a very heterogeneous group (Berninger, 1994).

Descriptive accounts of the skills necessary to write well highlight the fundamental behavioral differences between children who can write and their peers who have significant problems in this area (Hooper et al., 1994). Children and adolescents who write relatively well have a comprehensive understanding of what they want to achieve. Having or knowing where to obtain the information they need, good writers

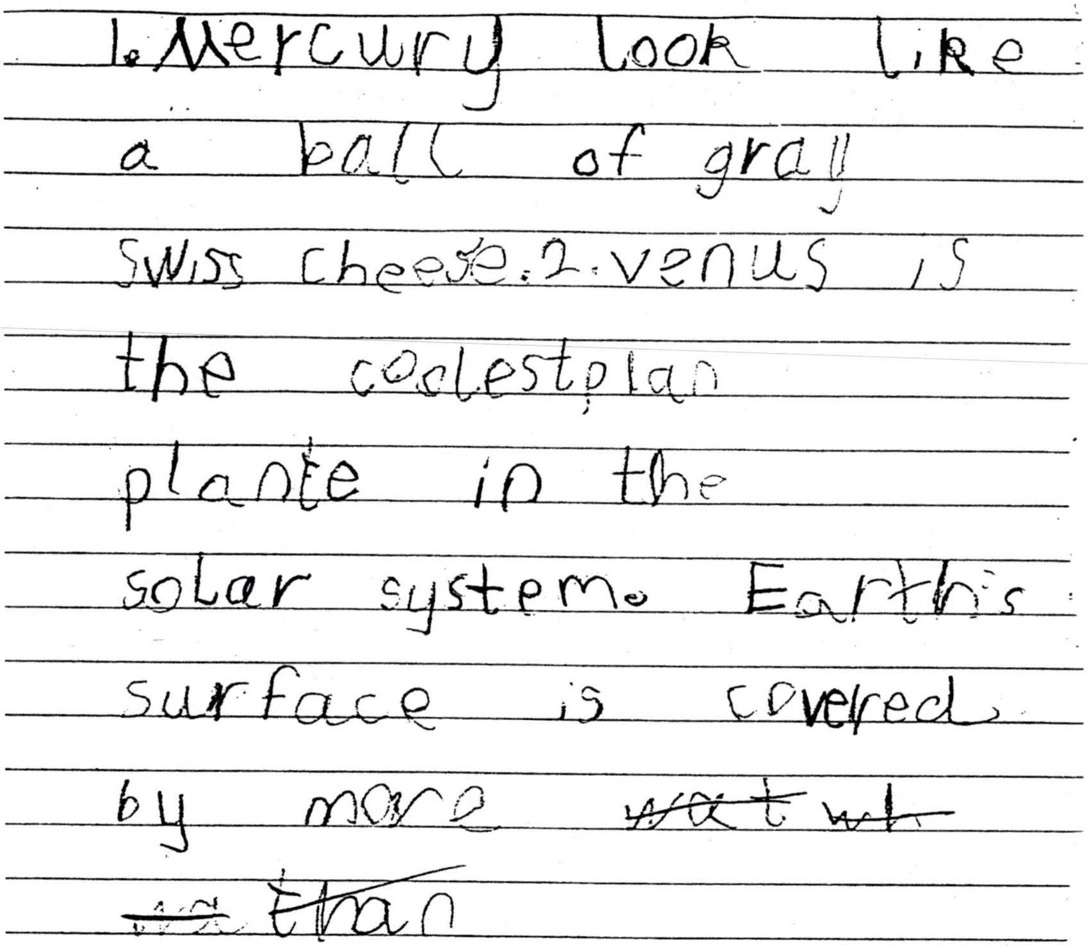

> 1. Mercury look like
> a ball of gray
> Swiss cheese. 2. venus is
> the coolestplan
> plante in the
> solar system. Earth's
> surface is covered
> by more *wat wt*
> *than*

FIGURE 6.1   *A Handwriting Sample.* Copying simple sentences can be very difficult for children with disorder of written expression. In this sample, the child was asked to copy the following sentences and to indicate whether each sentence was true or false.

1. Mercury looks like a ball of gray Swiss cheese.
2. Venus is the coolest planet in the solar system.
3. Earth's surface is covered by more water than dirt.

Note the child's spelling, spacing, and punctuation errors. Note also that the child turned in this assignment as complete. However, item 3 was never completed and the child did not indicate whether each sentence was true or false.

present their ideas clearly as they compose a coherent text. They are also able to anticipate how their writing will be interpreted and call repeatedly on their knowledge of spelling, grammar, and punctuation to make sure that their text conforms to the rules of the language. By contrast, their peers with disorder of written expression are unable to develop an overall plan and to integrate the various aspects of the task. They do not take into account or are unaware of their readers' perspective, and usually have major problems with handwriting, spelling, grammar, and punctuation. These mechanical and functional aspects of the writing process are often a source of distraction that contributes further to the poor quality of their work. As a result, they produce short, poorly organized texts, in which important information is lacking, ideas are badly developed or difficult to follow, the rules of the language are often ignored, and handwriting is unsatisfactory (see Figure 6.1).

The DSM-IV-TR diagnostic criteria for disorder of written expression do not reflect the complexity of the skills involved in the process of writing. Researchers and clinicians generally agree that these criteria are too broad. They say little about the nature of the child or adolescent's challenges, and thus provide only limited guidance in research or clinical work (Lyon, 1996).

Mathematics Disorder

The DSM-IV-TR diagnostic criteria also do not adequately reflect the multiple difficulties of children and adolescents with mathematics disorder. As the DSM itself states:

> A number of different skills may be impaired in Mathematics Disorder, including "linguistic" skills (e.g., understanding or naming mathematical terms, operations, or concepts, and decoding written problems into mathematical symbols), "perceptual" skills (e.g., recognizing or reading numerical symbols or arithmetic signs, and clustering objects into groups), "attention" skills (e.g., copying numbers or figures correctly, remembering to add in "carried" numbers, and observing operational signs), and "mathematical" skills (e.g., following sequences of mathematical steps, counting objects, and learning multiplication tables) (APA, 2000a, p. 53).

When reasoning difficulties are added to this long list, it becomes clear that a child or adolescent with mathematics disorder can be affected in one or more areas that are essential to all academic learning: language, perception, attention, memory, the organization and manipulation of numbers and symbols, and logical reasoning. In actuality, however, the major features of the disorder are significant difficulties with arithmetic operations and mathematical reasoning (Lyon, 1996). The following case illustrates these features:

Vivian was referred to our clinic by her parents because of her unsatisfactory academic progress, especially in math.

Vivian is in fourth grade at the time of her initial assessment. Smiling and talkative, she explains that her parents decided to bring her to the clinic "because they had a meeting with my teacher and she said that I wasn't very good in math. . . . I really love school. I love all the things I do in school, especially math, but I don't understand everything and I try, but when we have a test—like a test with long problems with lots of numbers—I don't do very well." Vivian says that she does not have problems in other subjects, except social studies. In order to assure the clinician that she is a serious student, she mentions on several occasions that she does her homework with her father every day. She reports also that she gets along well with her parents, her older brother (who is 12), and her friends.

Her parents confirm Vivian's reports and emphasize that she is a pleasant child with an active social life. But they are concerned by her lack of progress since the beginning of the current school year. Her father explains:

> *She has a great deal of difficulty with anything having to do with math. I don't know, she seems to not understand even the simplest problems, and she is lost when it comes to numbers. . . . She's a hard worker—it's not that—she does her homework with me every night and the teacher does not have any behavior problems with her. . . . When someone is by her side and helps her follow the logic or tells her that her numbers are in the right column and things like that, you know, she follows along well enough. . . . But afterwards, when she has to apply what she has just learned to another problem, it's as if everything was brand new to her. Then she can stare at the paper for hours without making any progress. Or the tears start rolling down her cheeks and she's completely lost. And there are times when she is so frustrated that she gets mad, along with me, to tell you the truth. . . .*

According to her mother, Vivian has had academic difficulties since second grade:

And now, I think we're seeing the culmination of these last years. Her difficulties are catching up with her. The work is becoming more difficult and she can no longer follow as she used to. . . . But what really concerns me most is the negative effect on her. It's heart-breaking to see her cry every night over her homework, not because she doesn't succeed—though that's certainly important—but because she's so clearly unhappy and I don't want to lose my happy little daughter. She has always been so full of joy, so full of life, and I don't want this problem to get worse and to make her unhappy. This would be terrible for her and for the whole family.

Vivian's intelligence is within the normal range (IQ = 102 on the Wechsler Intelligence Scale for Children, Third Edition), but she shows considerable variability in her cognitive skills. Her general knowledge is good, as is her understanding of social situations and relationships. She has no deficits in attention. However, she performs below average on tasks requiring memory, symbol manipulation, and problem solving. When she is confronted with such tasks, her tendency is: (1) to continue to apply the same incorrect solution instead of trying a new approach; and (2) to slow down in her work, become lost in details, and forget the overall goal of the task. At these times, she can become very frustrated and give the impression that she is inattentive or unmotivated.

Treatment is conducted simultaneously at home, at school, and at the clinic. Specifically, treatment provides her with a working method that enables her, through self-talk, to identify the nature of the problem to be solved, set up the steps to follow, and verify her results after each step. Though Vivian still works very slowly in math, she is now capable of solving the majority of problems she encounters. It is very likely that she will always find mathematics particularly challenging and that she will need more help in this area than most of her classmates throughout her education.

More generally, treatment contributes to raising Vivian's self-esteem and self-confidence. Her mother confirms these observations, by noting that her daughter is more relaxed and positive than she was at the time of referral.

Diagnostic and Developmental Considerations

Advances in the understanding of learning disorders have been hampered by important diagnostic and developmental issues that persist to this day. We will outline four of them here, because they provide the context within which to consider their empirical validity, as well as their epidemiology, developmental course, and etiology.

1. *Learning disabilities have traditionally been divided into three categories (reading, writing, and mathematics).* These categories correspond to the breakdown of key subject matters in elementary education but do not reflect observed symptom patterns. In the current state of knowledge, a diagnosis of a learning disability lacks precision and rarely reflects the child or adolescent's specific difficulties. This lack of precision should not be surprising, since the perceptual, motor, and cognitive skills required to read, write, and solve math problems overlap—as do the disorders themselves. Furthermore, within each disorder, the challenges of affected children can vary greatly.

2. *Learning disabilities may reflect an inadequate family or school environment more than the child's inherent difficulties.* To a greater extent than other psychological disorders, learning problems can be the result of an inadequate family or school environment. For example, in neglectful homes or in classrooms where teaching is inadequate, some children may have all the symptoms necessary for a diagnosis of learning disability without being disabled. It is often impossible to know whether these children would have the same difficulties if they came from different homes or had an adequate school environment, or if the teaching methods at their school were more suitable to their particular style of learning (Carnine, 1991).

3. *There is no clear-cut distinction between normal performance and dysfunction in the area of learning disabilities.* Although the line between

what is normal and what is not can be difficult to draw in other areas of psychological functioning (e.g., mental retardation), a diagnosis of learning disability depends heavily on nonpsychological factors, such as administrative decisions regarding eligibility for specialized educational services (S. Shaywitz, Escobar, Shaywitz, Fletcher, & Makuch, 1992). In the United States, for example, in the six years following passage of the Education for All Handicapped Children Act (a law requiring specialized services for persons with learning disabilities; see Box 6.2), the number of children said to have such disabilities increased by 130% (Torgesen, 1991). In this country, as elsewhere, a diagnosis gives a child access to specialized services that must be provided by law. The diagnostic requirements a child must meet to receive these expensive services vary from state to state and reflect budgetary, social, and political considerations as much as psychological ones. A diagnosis of learning disability is therefore always to some extent "shared": it depends not only on the challenges the child or adolescent presents, but also on the administrative context in which the diagnosis is made.

4. *The existence of the concept of learning disability reflects in part our society's emphasis on school success.* For most youth, schooling and education have a positive impact on psychological or social functioning. But growing social pressures to succeed in school can compound the struggles some children face academically. This emphasis on academic success is relatively recent. Prior to the 1960s, many schools focused on the teaching of vocational skills and stressed the importance of responsible citizenship, rather than of academic excellence. Although the emphasis on school success is not sufficient to explain all learning problems, learning disabilities are most obvious in cultures that regard academic excellence as evidence of a child's personal worth and as a requirement for later social and occupational success. Beyond the child, academic ability reflects positively on the entire family. As Durning (1995) puts it, "the child's school success . . . is frequently regarded as evidence of the effectiveness of the family's educational methods" (pp. 111–112). Or, as the mother of a child with a learning disability notes, "Mothers wear their child on their sleeve in this town. . . . A smart and accomplished child is the ultimate status symbol" (Weiss, 1989, p. 100). In other words, children who struggle to read, write, or do math are often "failures," not only in their own eyes and in those of their immediate family but also in those of society.

> *I taught school in the early days of my manhood and I think I know something about mothers. . . . They want three things only; for their children to be fed, to be healthy, and to make the most of themselves.*
> —Lyndon Baines Johnson

Empirical Validity

The empirical validity of learning disorders has not been established. The broad diagnostic categories that are used to define learning disorders are inadequate because they (1) do not account for the heterogeneity of these disorders, (2) do not predict their developmental trajectories, (3) do not reliably distinguish between children who have a learning disorder and children who are merely slow learners, and (4) provide little useful information on how to design effective interventions.

These sweeping conclusions are neither rash nor new (Ysseldyke, Algozzine, Shinn, & McGue, 1982). Several research programs suggest that strong evidence of empirical validity may never be obtained for the three learning disorders currently in the DSM-IV-TR. Rather, more precise disorders may have to be defined to replace the existing ones. Potential candidates include *nonverbal learning disabilities* and *phonological reading disability* (see Box 6.5, p. 154). If ongoing research confirms the existence of such disorders, they may provide a better understanding of the processes underlying the difficulties faced by children with learning problems and, over time, replace the current reliance on three disorders that reflect the three basic areas of learning in elementary school.

BOX 6.5 • *Nonverbal Learning Disabilities and Phonological Reading Disability*

A better understanding of learning disabilities will probably come in large part from a better understanding of the key characteristics of subgroups of children with significant challenges in reading, writing, or mathematics. Two ongoing research programs illustrate the approach taken by a number of scientists to define new disorders in which learning problems are central.

Nonverbal Learning Disabilities. We discussed nonverbal learning disabilities (NLD) in Chapter 4. Originally thought to be a subtype of mathematics disorder, NLD can be found in children who receive other diagnoses (such as Asperger syndrome). Children with NLD have difficulties in mathematical skills and reasoning, and in the processing of nonverbal information (Rourke, 1995). These deficits limit their understanding of the information needed to solve mathematical problems or to succeed in social situations (such as the nonverbal cues essential for conversational turn-taking). Children with NLD also have problems in visual-spatial organization, coordination, and touch sensation. However, they usually have excellent rote memories and strong reading abilities, and can be very talkative (although the tone of their speech is often poorly modulated and its content repetitive).

Rourke believes that this symptom pattern is related to problems in the right hemisphere of the brain. More specifically, he hypothesizes that NLD results from the destruction of white matter that facilitates communication within the brain. This theory is promising because it specifies an expected pattern of strengths and weaknesses, and provides an explanation for the observed link between seemingly diverse areas of functioning (i.e., mathematic and social skills). If ongoing research confirms the existence of NLD, this research program will make it possible to define a learning disability with precise diagnostic criteria, a particular developmental trajectory, and a likely etiology.

Phonological Reading Disability. Another research group has spent the last decade exploring a subtype of reading disorder called phonological reading disability (PRD) (Bradley & Shankweiler, 1991; Liberman & Shankweiler, 1991). Children with PRD have significant difficulty understanding the phonological rules of language: they are unable to connect and combine sounds and letters rapidly, and consequently find reading particularly challenging. With training, these children can memorize a large number of words by sight, but most continue to be unable to decode new words without considerable effort. Children with PRD are of average or above-average intelligence, however, and do not have learning difficulties in areas that do not require much reading (e.g., mathematics).

Like its NLD counterpart, PRD is interesting because it describes a pattern of specific strengths and weaknesses in the child's behavior. If ongoing research confirms the existence of this pattern of functioning, it will provide a better understanding of the difficulties faced by many children with reading disorder. It should also lead to the development of more precise diagnostic criteria than are currently available, and encourage new etiological and treatment research.

Associated Characteristics; Comorbidity

Comorbidity among Learning Disorders

Learning disabilities are often associated (APA, 2000a). For example, in a study of children with a variety of learning challenges, one research team could not find many subjects who had significant difficulties in reading alone (Ozols & Rourke (1988). Most of the children with reading problems had deficits in other academic areas as well. Although this comorbidity is well known, the nature of the associations among the learning disorders remains unclear. Most researchers believe that they are at least somewhat distinct conditions for two reasons. First, learning disabilities do not show perfect overlap. For example, a child with reading disorder does not invariably also have disorder of written expression. Second, although many children and adolescents have difficulties in multiple areas, it is not possible to predict their skills in one area (e.g., their math scores) on the basis of their skills in another (e.g., their reading scores) (Berninger, 1994).

Medical Conditions

Research on the association between specific medical conditions and learning disabilities is sparse. The DSM-IV-TR notes that these disorders can be associated with birth complications, and with conditions such as fetal alcohol syndrome and fragile X syndrome (APA, 2000a). However, in a large majority of cases, a link between a medical condition and a learning disability is never established (Keogh & Sears, 1991).

Attention Deficit Hyperactivity Disorder (ADHD)

ADHD is common in children with learning disorders (Chadwick, Taylor, Taylor, Heptinstall, & Dankaerts, 1999), as are learning disorders in children with ADHD (see Chapter 7). However, it is important to distinguish between these conditions. Specifically, studies of **executive functions**—the capacities necessary "to engage successfully in independent, purposive, self-serving behavior" (Lezak, 1995)—suggest that there may be differences in basic cognitive processes between ADHD and learning disabilities (see Etiology). For example, children with ADHD have executive function deficits in planning, monitoring, and self-regulation, whereas children with reading disorder have nonexecutive deficits in phonological awareness or understanding (Pennington, Groisser, & Welsh, 1993). This finding suggests that deficits in executive functions may be specific to ADHD and that, when they are observed in children with learning disorders, they probably reflect the effect of comorbidity with ADHD.

Other Disruptive Behavior Problems and Adjustment Difficulties

In approximately 30% of affected youth, learning disorders are accompanied by disruptive and aggressive behavior problems (see Chapter 8). Studies indicate that different causal pathways may account for this association (Spreen, 2001). As Figure 6.2 (p. 156) shows, (1) some children may have underlying biological vulnerabilities and/or be exposed to adverse environmental factors that contribute to learning and behavioral problems; (2) oppositional and aggressive behaviors may disturb the acquisition of knowledge in children with average learning capabilities and result in comorbidity; or (3) the academic and social challenges posed by a learning disability may lead some children to become disruptive and aggressive.

Whether they are disruptive or not, youth with learning disabilities often face important difficulties beyond the classroom. Chronic academic failure can lead to negative evaluation by teachers, parents, and peers, and result in harmful psychological consequences that act to make learning even more challenging (e.g., by undermining self-confidence, motivation, and interest). Like Dayle, whom we described earlier, children and adolescents who have significant challenges in reading, writing, or mathematics are acutely aware of their difficulties. They doubt their own abilities and are ashamed of a problem that can be misunderstood by teachers, family, and friends. Not surprisingly, most want to hide their lack of progress and develop an intense fear of revealing their difficulties to others (e.g., by having to read aloud in class). In middle school, they tend to show lower achievement than their peers and are more often absent. More generally, low self-esteem, frustration, and discouragement are common among youth with learning disorders, as are symptoms of anxiety and depression, and peer rejection (Hooper et al., 1994). In keeping with such evidence, some research suggests that many youth with learning disabilities are "inactive learners," who are frequently passive, disorganized, or convinced that they will always fail in school (Torgesen, 1982).

People who do not face the challenges posed by learning disabilities tend to misunderstand the child's difficulties, attributing them to poor motivation or downright laziness, rather than to a psychological disorder. In a teacher's words: "[This child] acts . . . a little . . . well, irresponsible. She doesn't seem to care about the mistakes she makes on her papers, and most every one of them is caused from sheer carelessness" (Schwarz, 1992, p. 109). Mistakes that children and adolescents with learning disorders make in their academic work are generally not the result of "carelessness," "laziness," or "irresponsibility," but of a genuine inability to master basic skills that others take for granted. When their environment fails to recognize this fundamental point and to provide genuine help, these

Pathway 1

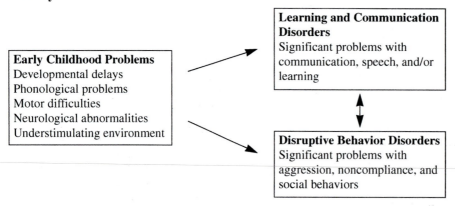

Early problems lead to learning, communication, and behavior disorders.

Pathway 2

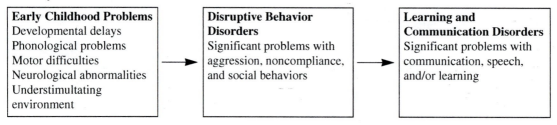

Early problems lead to behavior problems that then disrupt learning and communication.

Pathway 3

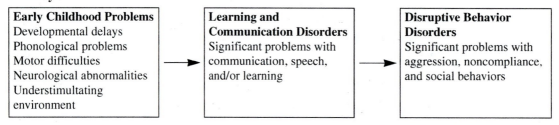

Early problems lead to learning and communication problems that, in turn, lead to disruptive conduct.

FIGURE 6.2   *Possible Pathways Accounting for the Link between Learning Disorders and Disruptive Behavior Problems.* There are at least three possible pathways to account for the link between learning disorders and disruptive behavior problems, especially oppositional defiant disorder and conduct disorder. In pathway 1, adverse biological or developmental factors in early childhood predict both learning and disruptive behavior problems. In pathway 2, early childhood factors result in the development of a disruptive behavior disorder, which in turn disrupts learning. In pathway 3, early childhood factors predict the onset of learning difficulties. These difficulties cause frustration and anger, and a general attitude of defeat at school that is displayed as disruptive conduct. In all three pathways, learning problems may be compounded by significant communication difficulties.

BOX 6.6 • *Common Strategies Used by Children to "Escape" from a Learning Disability*

Learning disorders are associated with behavior problems and adjustment difficulties that may be a consequence of growing up with a disability that is often misunderstood. Lyman (1986), who has a learning disability, describes three strategies used by affected children to "escape." Although these "escapes" reflect his personal experience rather than empirical research, they highlight the fact that chronic academic difficulties can affect a child's entire life. He writes:

I developed an intense determination to turn school into a nice place for me. I could have chosen to escape. Three routes were open to me. I could have become the clown to escape, diverting attention from my difficulty to my "funny" personality. I can remember James C., who did this successfully. He clowned his way from third grade through eighth grade and then dropped out. He had terrible grades, but his tactics worked. So he escaped from school with an intact self-image. . . .

Another escape open to me was the delinquency route. I could have started to skip school, break windows, get into fights, and cause trouble any way I could imagine. . . . Adults would think I was bad, kids would

think I was tough and fearless: nobody would think I was stupid. Marty D. chose this route. . . . Once he had to read, "What is your name?" and he read "What is your man?" Nobody laughed at Marty, not if he wanted to survive recess. . . . I learned that he earned a long suspension from school midway through tenth grade and never went back. . . .

Charlie J. chose the final escape route. . . . Charlie actually chose to be stupid. Everybody felt sorry for him and tried to help him. Even though Charlie was a big rugged guy, he became the class pet. . . . Apparently, Charlie was just playing a "survival" game in school, for his self-image also remained intact. He dropped out of school after the eighth grade graduation (pp. 8–9).

Lyman's description does not mean, obviously, that all children and adolescents with a learning disability attempt to escape from their condition by developing some type of adjustment problem; only that emotional and behavioral difficulties are often associated with learning disorders and can aggravate them—very seriously in some cases.

children feel deeply misunderstood and yearn to "escape" from this painful reality (see Box 6.6).

Epidemiology

Prevalence; Age and Gender Characteristics

Prevalence. In the United States, approximately 10–20% of school-age children have reading disorder, if one includes *all* children and adolescents with significant reading difficulties (whether or not they show a discrepancy between IQ and achievement). However, in many cases this disorder is of relatively short duration, since this range is only half as large for youth whose difficulties persist for three or more years (S. Shaywitz et al., 1992). Hooper and associates (1994) found that approximately 15% of a community sample of children obtained scores more than two standard deviations below the mean on different measures of written expression. Other estimates place the prevalence of disorder of written expression at 10%

(Lyon, 1996). The prevalence rate of mathematics disorder is about 6% among school-age children (Fleishner, 1994).

The rates just summarized are based on studies conducted in the United States and are relatively high, partly because significant numbers of children and adolescents receive a diagnosis of learning disability to give them access to specialized educational services, rather than because they meet DSM-IV-TR diagnostic criteria (Torgesen, 1991). In other words, the prevalence rates reported in different studies probably depend in part on administrative considerations. For example, much lower rates of reading, mathematics, and comorbid reading and mathematics disorder were reported in a British study of more than 1,200 children between 9 and 10 years old. We present the results of that study in Table 6.2 (p. 158).

Age of Onset. Learning disabilities are seldom identified before third grade (Lyon, 1996). Before that age, most children have only a limited mastery of reading,

TABLE 6.2   *Prevalence Rates of Reading Disorder, Mathematics Disorder, and Comorbid Reading and Mathematics Disorders in a Large British Epidemiological Study*

Rates are presented separately for children with and without a discrepancy between IQ and achievement.

	Children of Average Ability (Discrepancy between IQ and achievement)	Children of Below-Average Ability (No discrepancy between IQ and achievement)
Reading Disorder Alone	3.9%	2.0%
Mathematics Disorder Alone	1.3%	1.8%
Comorbid Reading and Mathematics Disorder	2.3%	5.3%

Source: From C. Lewis, G. J. Hitch, and P. Walker, "The Prevalence of Specific Reading Difficulties in 9- to 10-Year-Old Boys and Girls," *Journal of Child Psychology and Psychiatry, 35* (1994), p. 289.

writing, and mathematics, so that educators cannot distinguish clearly between true problems and normal differences in individual performance. Consequently, little is known about the specific age of onset of learning disorders. In many cases, diagnosis follows a request for professional assistance from the school or the family—typically after a relatively prolonged period of academic failure.

Gender Differences.   Educational and clinical statistics indicate that reading disorder and disorder of written expression are three to five times more frequent in boys than girls. Comparable data on the sex ratio of mathematics disorder are equivocal. Statistics from studies of community samples generally present more balanced sex ratios—for example, 3.2 boys and 1.5 boys per 1 girl for reading and writing disorder, and close to 1 to 1 for mathematics disorder (Lewis, Hitch, & Walker, 1994; S. Shaywitz, Escobar, Shaywitz, & Fletcher, 1990). It is likely that boys are overrepresented in educational and clinical statistics because their learning difficulties are more often associated with adjustment problems (disruptive behaviors in particular) than they are in girls (APA, 2000a).

Social and Cultural Differences

Empirical data are sparse on the social and cultural factors associated with learning disabilities. Some studies report that these disorders are often linked to poverty (Keogh & Sears, 1991) and to cultural misunderstandings between families and schools (Comfort, 1992). However, these associations are not specific to learning disorders; similar social and cultural factors are related to a host of psychosocial difficulties. Only a few studies have attempted to isolate the variables that account for the link between socioeconomic factors and learning disabilities, but those that have been conducted point to the importance of exposure to language and communication in the early years (Hecht, Burgess, Torgesen, Wagner, & Rashotte, 2000). Specifically, children raised in poverty are less likely than children from middle- and upper-income homes to be stimulated linguistically and intellectually, in part because their caregivers often have multiple psychosocial stressors to contend with (e.g., working multiple, low-paying jobs), and have limited time and resources to help their children learn from a very young age.

Other studies have focused on the relationship between ethnicity and learning disorders. In a developmental study of reading skills, Wood, Felton, Flowers, and Naylor (1991) followed nearly five hundred European American and African American children through elementary school. Results showed that ethnicity and reading ability were not associated in first grade, but that they were two years later. By that time, African American children had more reading difficulties on average than their European American peers.

This association between ethnicity and reading ability could not be explained by socioeconomic differences between the two groups (e.g., poverty, level of parental education, single- or two-parent family). Wood and colleagues speculate that the **"whole language" approach** to teaching reading, which was used with the majority of children in their sample, may have been detrimental to African American children. This method teaches children to infer the meaning of unknown words from the context of the sentence, rather than to decode them with the help of phonetics. Children who are familiar with and use a dialect form of English, in which spoken and written words do not correspond as closely as they do in standard English, may not benefit from this teaching method. In other words, prevalence rates for specific learning disorders may vary across different ethnic groups in the United States because the methods used to teach basic academic skills to young children tend to favor some groups over others, rather than because of inherent differences in ability across groups.

Comparable differences in prevalence rates among children from different socioeconomic or ethnic groups have been reported in studies of disorder of written expression and of mathematics disorder. However, they are difficult to interpret, because most studies do not control for important variables—such as the teaching methods to which participants were exposed—that might explain these results.

Developmental Trajectories and Prognosis

Learning disabilities must be distinguished from the temporary, although serious, difficulties that some children encounter when they first learn to read, write, or do math (Lyon, 1994). By definition, learning disorders are persistent and can have a negative effect on a person's functioning throughout life (Polloway, Schewel, & Patton, 1992). In a detailed review of longitudinal studies undertaken since the 1950s, Kavale (1988) concluded that:

1. Difficulties persist (at some level) for a majority of children and adolescents with learning dis-

abilities, even though many of them make remarkable progress.
2. Progress is directly related to intelligence and, probably, family socioeconomic status; that is, more intelligent youth make better progress in acquiring skills in their problem area than less intelligent peers, as do youth from more privileged backgrounds.
3. Throughout development, learning problems are often associated with emotional and behavioral challenges (e.g., communication deficits, hyperactivity, poor self-concept).
4. In adulthood, the social and professional status of persons with learning disabilities is lower on average than that of individuals without such difficulties, although many of them are able to overcome their disability in creative ways.

> *I believe that I became an actor because memorizing was for me a long-time survival skill. It was a way of pretending that I could read when I could not.*
>
> —Adult who had a learning disability as a child

These broad generalizations tell us little about the developmental trajectories of learning disabilities. Most follow-up studies highlight the heterogeneity of affected children and adolescents and show that the challenges they face evolve in the course of development as the demands that are placed on them change (Keogh & Sears, 1991). Precise information on the developmental trajectory of each learning disorder is still lacking, however, in large part because little is known about the developmental trajectory of the acquisition of reading, writing, and mathematic skills in average children (Francis, Shaywitz, Stuebing, Shaywitz, & Fletcher, 1994).

From Developmental Challenges to Disorder

Longitudinal studies are not available to outline the developmental trajectory (or trajectories) of reading disorder. Clinically, it has been observed that many children with the disorder have communication problems from the earliest stages of development (see Box 6.7, p. 160). They often learn to speak late and face a

BOX 6.7 • *Communication Disorders*

As learning to read and write depends closely on a child's verbal abilities, it is not surprising to find that communication and learning disorders are often associated (Lyon, 1996). Typically, youth with a communication disorder have difficulty producing age-appropriate speech sounds, and combining and manipulating the various components of language (i.e., phonemes, syllables, and words) for fluent, effective communication. The DSM-IV-TR describes four communication disorders: *expressive language disorder, mixed receptive-expressive language disorder, phonological disorder,* and *stuttering.* The first three are most closely linked to learning disabilities and will be described here. We do not cover these in depth because historically, these disorders have been less the province of clinical psychology than that of speech pathology and psycholinguistics—that is, of researchers interested in the psychological factors associated with speech and language.

Expressive Language Disorder. From their first attempts to acquire speech, children with expressive language disorder experience significant difficulties communicating verbally. These difficulties occur even though these children are able to understand spoken language and have no hearing difficulties. The following example conveys the difficulty associated with an expressive language disorder. Imagine the phone ringing. As you answer it, you hear an unfamiliar voice, begging: "An Mamma, an Mamma, . . . 'tackn for the floor, 'tackn real bad, real bad 'tackn! Mamma hapin comin' a hel . . . merchee, merchee . . . now!" (Schwarz, 1992, p. 70). What would you do? This is what an operator heard when Lucille called for help as her mother was having a heart attack. Her cries were in vain, because unfortunately she was unable to communicate this critical information effectively. This example illustrates the key symptoms of expressive language disorder: pronunciation and vocabulary errors, limited amount of speech, unusual word order, simplified sentence structure, and omission of important parts of the message. Many children with expressive language disorder also have limited memory for verbally presented information and have considerable trouble remembering the words they want to use as they speak and composing complete sentences to tell a coherent story (APA, 2000).

Mixed Receptive-Expressive Language Disorder. Children with mixed receptive-expressive language disorder have difficulties speaking and understanding spoken language. The expressive difficulties of children with the disorder are similar to those that are characteristic of expressive language disorder. Problems in receptive abilities may range from mild to severe and are usually apparent from the first years of life. In severe cases, children are unable to understand simple words and sentences, and have difficulty processing most kinds of auditory information. As in expressive language disorder, children with mixed language disorder often have pronunciation or articulation difficulties and deficits in verbal memory (APA, 2000a).

Phonological Disorder. Children with phonological disorder have difficulties producing age-appropriate speech sounds. Unlike other communication disorders, phonological disorder is very often associated with a physical condition, such as a hearing impairment, a physical malformation (e.g., cleft palette), or a neurological condition (e.g., cerebral palsy). Children with the disorder are difficult to understand, for example, substituting one speech sound for another (e.g., saying "thithorth" for "scissors" or "fum" for "thumb"), and/or transposing sounds inside a word (e.g., "aminal" for "animal" or "teller" for "letter"; Cantwell & Baker, 1991). In more serious cases, the child will omit some phonemes completely, saying, for example, "Rember what happened yesterday" or "I didn't do noten" (Lyman, 1986, p. 79). The severity of the disorder varies considerably; some children are relatively easy to understand, whereas others are practically unintelligible.

Comorbidity. An understanding of the communication disorders is essential for mental health researchers and clinicians because communication disorders are often comorbid with other psychological problems. For example, one study found that 45% to 90% of children with communication disorders were found to have significant academic problems that have been indicative of a learning disability (Beitchman & Brownlie, 1996), while more than 80% of children who have major challenges in reading also have significantly delayed communication skills (Fletcher et al., 1994). Further, 19% of youth enrolled in a study of communication disorders qualified for a comorbid diagnosis of ADHD, 10% an anxiety disorder, and 7% either oppositional defiant or conduct disorder (Cantwell & Baker, 1991).

variety of difficulties in the process (APA, 2000a; Lyon, 1996). Others learn to speak at the same time as their peers, but have significant expressive or receptive difficulties (e.g., they are unable to pronounce or to recognize certain sounds or words). Still others do not have noticeable difficulties until they have to learn to read.

Similarly, little is known about the development of disorder of written expression. A diagnosis is usually made in elementary school, although the first signs of the disorder may be obvious as soon as the child starts to write. Children who have persistent difficulties forming letters and numbers between the ages of 4 and 6 have a high probability of facing major challenges when they learn to write, as well as to read and count (Simner, 1996). Figure 6.3 shows that, when these children are asked to copy letters or numbers from sight or memory, they often add or remove essential elements, or give them unrecognizable shapes. To write well, a child must obviously be able to do more than form letters and numbers properly. However, marked difficulties in handwriting and copying could be the first signs of the disorder in many children.

Although major weaknesses in mathematics can be identified relatively early, diagnosis of the disorder depends on a variety of factors besides the child's performance in this area. These factors include the child's ability to hide or compensate for some of these weaknesses (e.g., by performing better orally than in writing).

The first signs of a learning disorder are often minor: the child struggles to master the alphabet, recognize letters, match letters and sounds correctly, write simple sentences, or complete basic counting and computation. Later, these skills become painfully slow, frequently interrupted, and accompanied by repeated errors, such as addition, omission, substitution, distortion, and transposition. These problems can rapidly lead to significant difficulties in comprehension. For example, children with reading disorder may not understand or remember what they just read, and may be unable to solve even simple problems when the solution depends on an ability to follow written instructions. These difficulties may be less obvious, or take longer to be noticed, in children of higher intelligence, who may be able to solve problems or answer questions by recalling facts they know rather than by relying on reading, writing, or math. However, even in gifted children, compensatory mechanisms become insufficient as school requirements increase.

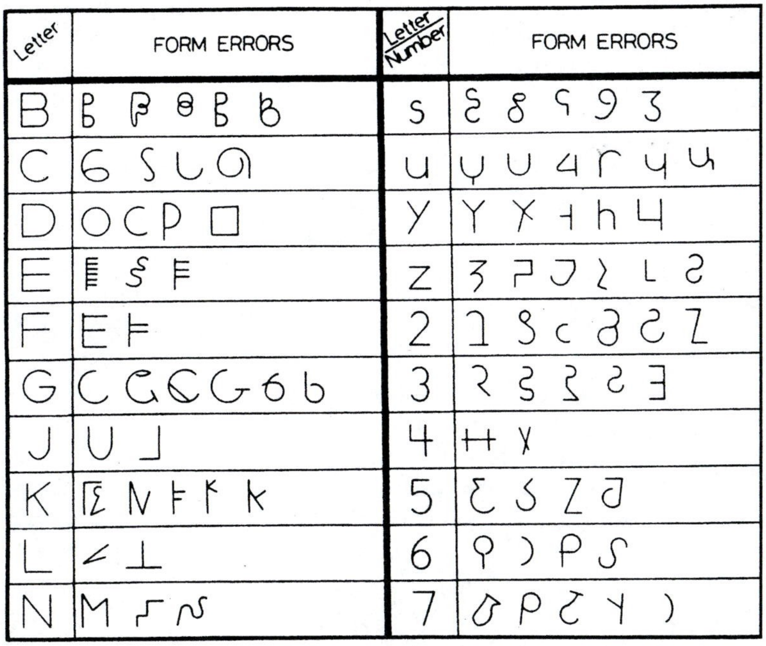

FIGURE 6.3 *Examples of Form Errors Observed in Children's Writing of Letters and Numbers.* As these examples show, when young children with disorder of written expression (or its early symptoms) are asked to copy letters or numbers from sight or memory, they often add or remove essential elements, or give them unrecognizable shapes.

Source: From L. M. Simner, "Estimating a Child's Learning Potential from Form Errors in a Child's Printing." In J. Wenn, A. M. Wing, and N. Sovik (Eds.), *Development of Graphic Skills* (London: Academic Press, 1991), p. 206. Reprinted by permission of Academic Press London.

Evolution and Prognosis

When they are diagnosed with one or more learning disorders, children often participate in intervention programs designed to help them. But since most of these programs are never evaluated, little is known about their impact on the progression of these disorders. What is known, however, is that a large number of children continue to have significant difficulties in adolescence and beyond. Prognosis is particularly poor for children whose difficulties persist for several years. Longitudinal studies indicate that three-quarters of children with reading disorder in third grade still have the same diagnosis six years later (Lyon, 1996). Consequently, children with this disorder often repeat one or more grades (Kavale, 1988), drop out of school in adolescence (Simner & Barnes, 1991), and are unemployed (or underemployed) in early adulthood (Shapiro & Lentz, 1991).

> *When I got to high school I really wanted to be in the choir. I finally got in. I was so proud. Then one day at a rehearsal the choir teacher pointed me out as not being able to read the words. This really embarrassed me. I quit the choir and quit school! Now I wish I could go to community college, but I don't have the money. . . . I have four kids and it's rough!*
>
> —Adult who had a learning disability as a child

Mathematics disorder is often a persistent condition also, affecting a large number of children and adolescents for the duration of their schooling and into adulthood (APA, 2000a; Lyon, 1996). The disorder is much less obvious in adulthood, however, because persons who have major difficulties in mathematics avoid situations in which they must calculate—something that is much easier to do than to avoid situations that require reading or writing.

Etiology

Biological, psychological, educational, and social factors are implicated in the etiology of learning disorders (Hooper et al., 1994; Lyon, 1996). Although this generalization is vague and applicable to the etiology of most psychological conditions of childhood and adolescence, it summarizes the current state of knowledge. Etiological data pertain mainly to reading disorder, which has been the focus of most research.

Biological Factors

Genetic Factors.   Twin studies and studies of the relatives of children with a learning disability indicate that genetic factors are probably implicated in the etiology of these disorders, reading disorder in particular (Pennington, 1999). These studies show that phonological difficulties tend to run in families (Lewis, 1990) and are more likely to be found in identical than in fraternal twins (DeFries, Olson, Pennington, & Smith, 1991). Similarly, genetic factors are involved in spelling difficulties, probably also because of difficulties in phonological processing (Noethen, Schulte-Koerne, Grimm, Cichon, & Vogt, 1999). However, since not all children with learning disabilities have family members with similar conditions, other factors also must play a role in their etiology.

Neurobiological and Neuropsychological Factors. As we mentioned earlier, in the first half of the twentieth century, most researchers and clinicians assumed that learning disabilities had their origin in minimal brain damage. Opposing this traditional view, Samuel Orton (1937) advanced a neurobiological theory of reading disorder that hinged on the relative dominance of each brain hemisphere. Orton was well aware that, in most people, the left hemisphere dominates language processing (both speech and hearing). Relying on this knowledge, he proposed that a lack of left-hemisphere dominance was responsible for **dyslexia**—that is, the tendency of some children to transpose or reverse some letters, numbers, and words, such as b and d, p and q; 2 and 5; and "was" and "saw." Although Orton's theory was ultimately rejected, it had a considerable impact in clinical and educational circles, and led to a large amount of research aimed at understanding how cerebral dominance develops. Much of this work focused on the process of cerebral lateralization; that is, on the development of right- or left-handedness. We know today that cerebral lateralization plays a major role in the acquisition of perceptual, language, and motor skills throughout childhood. However, strong dominance by

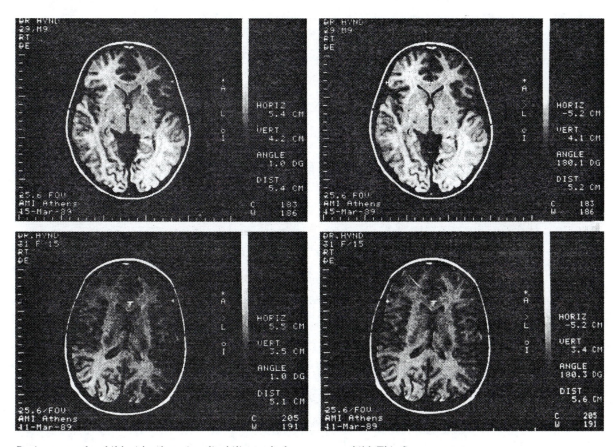

*Brain scans of a child with a learning disability and of an average child. This figure compares
the brain scans obtained by magnetic resonance imaging (MRI) of a child with reading disorder
(top photos) and of an average child (bottom photos). In average children, the left side of the
frontal region of the brain is generally larger than the right side, whereas the opposite is often
true in children with reading disorder.*

the left hemisphere is not what distinguishes between
good readers and readers who have trouble mastering
this skill. Rather, language depends on complementary
right- and left-hemisphere processes (Beeman &
Chiarello, 1998); and children who read best are those
who, after a developmental period of lateralization, are
capable of performance that relies on interaction between the two cerebral hemispheres (Gaillard & Converso, 1988). This work illustrates the importance of a
developmental perspective in understanding the abilities of both good and poor readers, since knowledge of
normal development informs our understanding of specific dysfunctions.

In recent years, advances in our understanding of
the neurobiological characteristics that may differentiate individuals with learning disorders from average individuals have come from research that relies on a
variety of investigative techniques, such as positron
emission tomography (PET) scans, magnetic resonance imaging (MRI), and the tracing of cerebral blood
flow. Research using these techniques shows that,
when subjects engage in reading tasks that call on specific phonological skills, some areas of the brain (in
particular the angular gyrus in the left hemisphere)
are less active in some children and adults with reading disorder than they are in individuals without such

difficulties (Pugh et al., 2000; Wood et al., 1991). Studies of the brain structure of persons with reading disorder reveal abnormalities in similar areas (Bennington et al., 1999). Such abnormalities may be specific to reading disorder, for they are seldom found in ADHD only or control children (Hynd, Semrud-Clikeman, Lorys, Novey, & Eliopulos, 1990). Deficits associated with the right hemisphere of the brain have also been reported in persons with mathematics disorder (Rourke, 1995).

The results just summarized are promising but preliminary; important developments will undoubtedly occur in coming years. Caution in interpreting them is particularly important because the majority of children and adolescents who receive a diagnosis of learning disorder do *not* have any detectable neurological abnormality. In addition, because most studies are not developmental in nature, it is not possible to determine whether an abnormality caused or was caused by the disability, or whether the two were unrelated (Lyon, 1996; Torgesen, 1991). Finally, published studies are often difficult to interpret because they usually do not take into account the effects of comorbidity. For example, in one study, restricted blood flow in specific brain areas was associated with significant language difficulties. However, the majority of children who participated in the study were also hyperactive, so that it was impossible to associate these findings specifically with their language problems (Lou, Henriksen, & Bruhn, 1984).

Executive Functions.   A growing number of neuropsychological studies focus on executive functioning in children with learning disabilities. Children who read, write, or do math fluently are able to coordinate the visual, cognitive, and motor activities that these tasks require (Berninger, 1994). For example, they can recognize common words and decode unfamiliar ones rapidly. They can also spell simple words and follow common grammatical rules without effort, while keeping track of the overall purpose of what they are doing. With time and practice, these processes become automatic, and children can give their full attention to the cognitive requirements of the task. In contrast, some studies suggest that when executive functions do not develop normally, children

may show the characteristic symptoms of learning disorders (Pennington et al., 1993). However, as we mentioned earlier, abnormal development in this area may simply reflect the comorbidity of these disorders and ADHD.

Family, Social, and Cultural Factors

Some clinical studies assume that psychological or family factors are at the origin of learning disabilities, but empirical evidence goes against this assumption. It is likely that the family difficulties found in clinical samples are more often a consequence than a cause of the child or adolescent's problems (Konstantareas, 1991). In other words, family difficulties may aggravate learning disabilities, but they are unlikely to cause them unless other adverse factors (e.g., biological vulnerability or educational neglect) are present. Nonetheless, a favorable family environment encourages learning, and adverse family circumstances are associated with learning difficulties. For example, poverty and lack of parental education predict the appearance of learning disabilities (Keogh & Sears, 1991). Such factors probably do not have a specific etiological role in learning problems, but they exert a general effect that may be reflected in the child or the adolescent's overall functioning.

Teaching Methods and Materials.   In some cases, learning disorders may be promoted by inadequate teaching methods or materials, rather than by anything in the child or adolescent's immediate environment. For example, a detailed review of how mathematics are taught in American schools concludes that many teaching methods and textbooks do not allow enough time for a majority of students to understand key mathematical concepts; do not organize learning so as to maintain the students' attention and to allow them to understand how these concepts are related; and do not provide students with enough opportunities to apply the concepts (Carnine, 1991).

In other words, by covering the vast and complex field of mathematics rapidly and with limited opportunities for practice, many approaches may provide superficial teaching of most topics and contribute to the difficulties that students often face in this area. We cannot conclude, however, that these factors alone are the

BOX 6.8 • *America: The Land of Mathematics Disorder?*

Cross-cultural research consistently shows that Chinese children and adolescents outperform their American counterparts on mathematical tests. On average, kindergarten, first-grade, sixth-grade, and twelfth-grade students obtain comparable IQ scores in both countries, but American youth in all grades score significantly lower in math than their Chinese peers (Geary et al., 1997). In other words, when the average level of achievement of Chinese and American students is compared, the Americans score lower in mathematics than what would be expected given their level of intelligence. But when the cross-cultural performance of older adults (Chinese and American adults age 60 to 80 years old) is examined, the math achievement is comparable (Geary, Bow-Thomas, Liu, & Siegler, 1996). Geary's research team concludes that today's Chinese students are not smarter or more mature than their American peers, but that the discrepancies found in their math performance are the result of educational differences in the two countries that were not apparent two or three generations earlier. In short, Geary and colleagues (1997) note that "the Chinese advantage . . . is due to a cross-generational decline in [math] competencies in the U.S. and a cross-generational improvement in China" (p. 425). In other words, these researchers conclude that China has improved the way that it teaches math over the last sixty years, but the United States has not (or may even have adopted less effective methods in the same time interval). Could this be evidence of a "cultural mathematics disorder"? What do you think?

cause of mathematics disorder, since most American students are able to learn mathematics no matter what kind of teaching they receive. (However, see Box 6.8 for a cross-cultural comparison of mathematics performance in China and the United States.)

Social and Cultural Expectations. As we stressed in the first part of this chapter, learning disabilities are more likely to develop in some social and cultural contexts than others. All industrial societies highly value academic success and measure much of a person's worth in terms of such success. The downside of this emphasis on success is that people who fail to "measure up" are often passed by from an early age. In other words, in societies that give pride of place to academic success, family and community expectations may increase the challenges that reading, writing, and mathematics present for many children, and contribute at times to the development and/or maintenance of a learning disorder.

Treatment and Prevention

Because diagnosis of a learning disability requires a discrepancy between IQ and achievement, children are rarely identified as having such a disability before sec-ond or third grade, essentially because it takes time for their achievement to clearly lag behind their IQ. When learning disabilities are diagnosed, they are rarely treated in clinical settings. Rather, children and adolescents usually receive treatment within their school system, because most interventions focus less on psychological issues than on remedial educational services. Irrespective of where services are offered, a multidisciplinary assessment is always necessary and, in the United States, typically involves an *individualized education plan* (IEP) (see Chapter 3). This plan is the culmination of an assessment process that usually takes into account (1) the child's intellectual and academic functioning; (2) vision, hearing, or other physical challenges that may be present; and (3) behavioral or emotional issues that may limit the child's adaptive functioning. For example, children with learning disabilities who have trouble paying attention and following directions, or who are aggressive and rejected by their peers, often need a behavior management program at school and at home if they are to benefit from classroom instruction and to succeed academically and socially.

The bulk of the research to date has focused on reading disorder; therefore, the following discussion applies mainly to that disorder, rather than to all learning disabilities.

Direct and Strategy Instruction

In reviews of the literature, Swanson and colleagues (Swanson, Carson, & Sachse-Lee, 2000; Swanson & Sachse-Lee, 2000) contrast two approaches to the treatment of reading disorder in early elementary school: **direct instruction,** which "emphasizes fast-paced, well-sequenced, highly focused lessons"; and **strategy instruction,** which "focuses less on the acquisition of specific skills than on teaching students to deal effectively with the many aspects of learning, such as how to organize material and ask questions that facilitate their understanding" (Swanson & Sachse-Lee, p. 115). The direct instruction approach concentrates mainly on the content of the materials that students find difficult to master. For example, lessons help children with reading disorder develop appropriate decoding skills—skills such as letter recognition and phonological awareness—that will enable them to become more fluent readers. Evidence suggests that direct instruction is most effective with children of average or above-average intelligence (IQ > 90) but below-average reading skills.

Strategy instruction is less about helping students acquire specific reading skills than about teaching them to deal effectively with the reading process. This form of instruction, either one-on-one or in groups, is most effective for children who can read a paragraph or two of text but cannot understand what they have just read. As we noted earlier, when children have to devote all their energy and attention to decoding each word they read, instead of recognizing most common words automatically, they often have comprehension problems. Strategy instruction is most effective with children whose intelligence and reading skills are in the low-average range. This approach has the following key features (see Swanson and Sachse-Lee, 2000, p. 116):

- *Organization*—Encourages students to regularly assess their understanding of the material to ensure that they are following what they are reading.
- *Advanced organizers*—Give students strategies to organize the information they have already, in order to improve their understanding or to build new understanding.

- *Elaboration*—Requires students to think about what they are reading and learning in ways that connect it to information or knowledge they have already.
- *Generative learning*—Teaches students to actively process the material they are learning by summarizing it and asking questions about it, and by developing general study strategies, such as underlining and note taking.
- *Metacognition*—Encourages students to think about the process of learning in order to better control it.
- *Attributions*—Invite students to evaluate their work and understanding, and the effectiveness of their learning strategies.

No matter which approach one chooses, regular and intensive remedial work is needed for students with reading disorder to succeed. Specifically, what Swanson and Sachse-Lee (2000) call "drill-repetition-practice-review" are essential elements of successful interventions. However, not all youth benefit from intensive intervention efforts, and many of those who do may never become fluent readers. For example, one study found that only one-quarter of students who participate in remedial reading programs may benefit from them (S. Shaywitz et al., 1992). This very low success rate does not necessarily indicate that these programs are ineffective. In some cases programs may begin too late—after several years of frustrating attempts to learn on the part of the child. In others, the child, the school, and the family may not be willing or able to make the sustained effort required by the program. Or a particular program may not be suitable for the child's specific learning needs.

Psychosocial Treatment

Clinicians are often called to work with youth with learning disabilities because of their many comorbid difficulties. Vivian's case study, presented earlier, illustrates the potential benefits of a psychosocial approach in this area. More generally, many children with learning disabilities have behavior problems that interfere with their ability to pay attention and to participate in class; and these problems need to be dealt with before the children can benefit from any remedial instruction. Similarly, adolescents with learning disabilities often develop an incapacitating anxiety about their difficulties. This anxiety prevents them from attending fully to what they have to learn, contributes to their disorganization, and leaves them feeling helpless. The American Academy of Child and Adolescent Psychiatry (1998b) suggests that clinicians take an active role not only in providing services to children with a learning disorder, but also in coordinating and monitoring these services. This role is particularly important when children need psychosocial and/or pharmacological intervention, and when families have to consider different treatment options and choose the one which is most likely to be successful.

Pharmacological Interventions

There are no drugs designed specifically to treat learning disabilities. However, affected children and adolescents are often prescribed a variety of stimulant medications that were initially developed to treat youth with ADHD (see Chapter 7). These medications can help children with comorbid attentional problems, as well as some children who do not have such problems. For example, a review of the literature found that the use of stimulant medications by youth with learning disorders without attentional problems resulted in increases in IQ scores, as well as in improvements on measures of mathematic and reading skills (DeLong, 1995). Although these results are encouraging, there is little evidence that medication provides long-term academic benefits for children with learning disorders (Beitchman & Young, 1997). Medication

may help affected children in the short term—by enabling them to pay attention and to concentrate—but it does not appear to have beneficial effects on learning over time.

Prevention

Systematic efforts to prevent learning disorders have only begun, and little knowledge is available in this area. Programs aimed at prevention attempt to help young children who are at risk of developing specific learning difficulties in the preschool years. For example, Torgesen (2000) describes a prevention program for kindergarten children who have phonological processing difficulties and are thus at risk of developing reading disorder. The program administrators found that children who received almost ninety hours of one-on-one instruction in phonological and word recognition skills over a two-year period showed significant gains in their ability to read single words. Unfortunately, at the end of the intervention, there was no significant difference in reading comprehension between children who had participated in the program and children who had not.

Other programs continue to work in the area of prevention, often using games to promote phonological awareness in preschoolers. These projects include rhyming and listening exercises, as well as age-appropriate identification of phonemes, syllables, and words. Although prevention efforts have the potential to reduce risk in this area, much remains to be learned in order to limit the number of children who begin elementary school with learning difficulties that are likely to develop into learning disorders.

Web Links

www.ldanatl.org (Learning Disabilities Association of America)

www.interdys.org (International Dyslexia Association)

www.ncld.org (National Center for Learning Disabilities)

www.kidsource.com/ASHA/index.html (American Speech-Language-Hearing Association)

7

Attention Deficit Hyperactivity Disorder

Every morning he runs around the house looking for a shoe. I mean every morning. He always seems to have one but to be missing the other . . . and when he finally finds it, he often can't put it on because he is too agitated by then.

—Mother of a child with ADHD

Attention deficit hyperactivity disorder (ADHD) is a condition in which children and adolescents face major disruptions in the normal development of social, emotional, and academic skills because of high levels of hyperactivity, impulsivity, and/or inattention. To understand ADHD, you must understand normal development. As children grow up, they rapidly acquire social, emotional, and instrumental skills that help them negotiate the daily demands and expectations of their environment. With time, these skills bring them increasing amounts of autonomy, but also new demands and responsibilities. Before they begin first grade, children are expected to feed and dress themselves without help; to follow simple instructions and obey reasonable rules; to deal with minor frustrations without crying, complaining, or becoming angry; and to know colors, letters, their addresses and phone numbers, and more. They are also expected to entertain themselves for short periods of time, and to play or work constructively with others. In short, to succeed in

first grade—that is, to get along well with adults and peers, and to learn—children must be able to "behave," something that would not have been expected of them when they were younger.

To behave well has both social and temporal aspects. Socially, children must be able to weigh personal needs and wishes against consideration for others and adult limits. Temporally, they must learn to forgo immediate advantages or rewards for future, often more important, accomplishments or gains. They must take other people's point of view into account, listen carefully, and follow directions; and they must ignore immediate distractions and temptations in order to make the sustained, prolonged efforts that are likely to have important personal and social benefits. Learning to read and write, to get along well with peers, or to succeed in sports, music, or art is impossible without such abilities. In short, children must learn to act *and* to refrain from action, to speak *and* to listen, to lead *and* to follow directions or instructions, to forge ahead *and* to reflect calmly.

Developing these skills represents a major challenge for some children. When they enter school, or even earlier, these children stand out from their peers: they are noisy and disruptive, easily agitated and rash, and inattentive and disorganized. Not surprisingly, their behavior often puts them on a collision course with parents and teachers, as well as peers (see Figure 7.1). This behavior often is severe enough to qualify for a diagnosis of attention deficit hyperactivity disorder. Unfortunately, contrary to some popular reports you may have seen in the media, ADHD is a serious disorder that can have harmful consequences throughout childhood and adolescence, and even into adulthood. It is not a minor developmental delay from which most affected children catch up in time. Nor is it—as some people claim—an invention of parents, teachers, or professionals who are unable or unwilling to deal with lively children (International Consensus Statement on ADHD, 2002).

Historical Overview

The behaviors that are characteristic of ADHD have attracted considerable interest for a long time. The first detailed descriptions of these behaviors can be found in the writings of Heinrich Hoffmann in Germany (1845/ 1995). Hoffmann was a pediatrician who used skillful artwork (in the form of comic strips) and rhymes to illustrate many of the behaviors he observed in his young patients. Although many of these stories would be considered offensive today, because they make light of children with serious disorders, the story of Fidgety Phil in Hoffmann's *Der Struwwelpeter* (*Shock-Headed Peter*) shows that the symptoms of ADHD as described more than 150 years ago were very similar to what they are today (see Box 7.1, p. 170).

Early researchers speculated that ADHD had biological origins. Large epidemics of encephalitis in the United States and Canada at the end of World War I (1917–1918) played a major role in this biological perspective. Studies showed then that some children who had recovered from the disease had been left with a behavioral syndrome that greatly resembled what we now call ADHD. Many researchers and clinicians therefore assumed that children who were severely hyperactive, impulsive, and inattentive suffered from brain abnormalities brought about by disease or by other causes that could have similar effects on the brain (e.g., complications during pregnancy or at birth). However, in most cases, an organic origin for the child's difficulties

FIGURE 7.1 *From Activity to Hyperactivity.* It is very common for young children to be active and, at times, disruptive. ADHD is often diagnosed when the child's behavior is clearly excessive and when one or more adults can no longer tolerate it.

Source: Cartoon courtesy of Ed Schelb (2002). Reprinted by permission.

BOX 7.1 • *The Story of Fidgety Phil*

Let me see if Philip can
Be a little gentleman;
Let me see, if he is able
To sit still for once at table:
Thus Papa bade Phil behave;
And Mamma look'd very grave.
But fidgety Phil,
He won't sit still;
He wriggles
And giggles,
And then, I declare,
Swings backwards and forwards
And tilts up his chair,
Just like any rocking horse;
"Philip! I am getting cross!"

See the naughty restless child
Growing still more rude and wild.
Till his chair falls over quite.
Philip screams with all his might.
Catches the cloth, but then
That makes matters worse again.
Down upon the ground they fall.
Glasses, plates, knives, forks and all.
How Mamma did fret and frown.
When she saw them tumbling down!
And Papa made such a face!
Philip is in sad disgrace.

Source: Hoffmann (1845/1995). Reprinted by permission.

was never found. Consequently, some researchers proposed broader causal explanations that remained essentially biological but no longer sought to trace the origin of the disorder to specific harmful events, such as a disease. As they did in the field of learning disabilities, a number of authors speculated that ADHD resulted from minimal brain damage or dysfunction (Strauss & Lehtinen, 1947). However, as we saw in Chapter 6, these concepts had to be abandoned eventually, because no brain dysfunction or damage was ever detected in most children who exhibited these symptoms.

As we will see later in this chapter, current theories about the origin of ADHD continue to put considerable emphasis on biological factors. Briefly stated,

these theories speculate that the brain dysfunction that may affect children with the disorder stems from deficits in behavioral inhibition (see Chapter 2 and Etiology).

Definitions, Diagnostic Criteria, and Major Characteristics

Children with ADHD show a persistent pattern of conduct, in which inattention and/or hyperactivity and impulsivity predominate. These behaviors are common in childhood. However:

- They are more frequent and severe in affected children than in the majority of their peers.
- They limit the development of adaptive skills.
- They result in considerable difficulties for the child and for adults at home and in school.

To meet DSM-IV-TR criteria, symptoms must begin before age 7, persist for a minimum of six months, and be evident in multiple settings. The age criterion is somewhat flexible, in that the disorder can be diagnosed after age 7 as long as the child's difficulties were clearly present before that age. Even though the symptoms that are most characteristic of the disorder tend to decrease with age, ADHD often has enduring adverse consequences well beyond childhood (see Developmental Trajectories and Prognosis). The DSM-IV-TR lists the symptoms of the disorder in two distinct groups: inattention and hyperactivity-impulsivity (see Table 7.1, p. 172).

Inattention

Children with attentional difficulties are unable to pay careful, sustained attention to daily activities such as games, meals, schoolwork, and chores, and to follow even simple rules. Their difficulties cannot be fully explained by tiredness, lack of interest, or disobedience, because they are often obvious even in activities that the children enjoy. In addition, children with ADHD find it very difficult to organize themselves, and to follow simple routines that they have practiced on numerous occasions and that are well within the range of their abilities. For example, getting dressed without the presence of an adult is an impossible task for some school-age children with ADHD. Repeatedly faced with such difficulties, these children often fail to complete what they set out to do, so that others often accuse them of losing interest quickly and giving up easily. Over time, children with ADHD also learn to avoid a growing number of tasks that require attention and organization, such as homework, and may become oppositional when parents or teachers insist that they complete them (APA, 2000a).

Although clinical descriptions of children with ADHD emphasize the importance of inattention in the symptomatology of the disorder, empirical research suggests that these children are usually as capable of sustained attention as are nonaffected children or children with other psychological disorders (Halperin, Matier, Bedi, & Sharma, 1992), particularly when they are interested in the tasks they undertake. For example, many parents of children with ADHD complain that they cannot complete ten to fifteen minutes of uninterrupted homework but that they can play videogames for hours. (See Box 7.2, p.173, which lists key factors that affect the attentional capabilities of children with the disorder.)

Hyperactivity and Impulsivity

Children with ADHD display a level of activity that is both excessive and disruptive. They move constantly either by going from one place to another or by fidgeting, squirming, or swinging different parts of their body. They find it very challenging to sit still, remain calm, or keep quiet when it is expected of them, such as at mealtime, in class, or in other social activities. In addition, they often speak without waiting their turn or thinking about what they want to say, make inappropriate noises or comments, and interrupt the conversation or butt into the activities of others without reason (APA, 2000a).

Difficulties across Settings

The DSM-IV-TR specifies that a diagnosis can be made only when the child's symptomatology is obvious in two or more settings. However, some children with ADHD have significant difficulties only at home or at school or daycare, whereas others have more pervasive difficulties that markedly limit their adaptive functioning in all settings. In addition, symptoms are much less obvious or even nonexistent when children are absorbed in activities they enjoy or when they have the full attention and support of an adult. In contrast, symptoms generally worsen when the same children must concentrate and organize themselves for sustained periods of time, or when the situation is uninteresting or no longer novel. Common examples of such situations include schoolwork that is difficult to understand, boring, or poorly presented; chores and routines that the child is expected to complete independently;

TABLE 7.1 *Attention Deficit Hyperactivity Disorder: DSM-IV-TR Diagnostic Criteria*

A. Either (1) or (2):

   (1) six (or more) of the following symptoms of inattention have persisted for at least 6 months to a degree that is maladaptive and inconsistent with developmental level:

Inattention

    (a) often fails to give close attention to details or makes careless mistakes in schoolwork, work, or other activities

    (b) often has difficulty sustaining attention in tasks or play activities

    (c) often does not seem to listen when spoken to directly

    (d) often does not follow through on instructions and fails to finish schoolwork, chores, or duties in the workplace (not due to oppositional behavior or failure to understand instructions)

    (e) often has difficulty organizing tasks and activities

    (f) often avoids, dislikes, or is reluctant to engage in tasks that require sustained mental effort (such as schoolwork or homework)

    (g) often loses things necessary for tasks or activities (e.g., toys, school assignments, pencils, books, or tools)

    (h) is often easily distracted by extraneous stimuli

    (i) is often forgetful in daily activities

   (2) six (or more) of the following symptoms of hyperactivity-impulsivity have persisted for at least 6 months to a degree that is maladaptive and inconsistent with developmental level:

Hyperactivity

    (a) often fidgets with hands or feet or squirms in seat

    (b) often leaves seat in classroom or in other situations in which remaining seated is expected

    (c) often runs about or climbs excessively in situations in which it is inappropriate (in adolescents or adults, may be limited to subjective feelings of restlessness)

    (d) often has difficulty playing or engaging in leisure activities quietly

    (e) is often "on the go" or often acts as if "driven by a motor"

    (f) often talks excessively

Impulsivity

    (g) often blurts out answers before questions have been completed

    (h) often has difficulty awaiting turn

    (i) often interrupts or intrudes on others (e.g., butts into conversations or games)

B. Some hyperactive-impulsive or inattentive symptoms that caused impairment were present before age 7 years.

C. Some impairment from the symptoms is present in two or more settings (e.g., at school [or work] and at home).

D. There must be clear evidence of clinically significant impairment in social, academic, or occupational functioning.

E. The symptoms do not occur exclusively during the course of a Pervasive Developmental Disorder, Schizophrenia, or other Psychotic Disorder and are not better accounted for by another mental disorder (e.g., Mood Disorder, Anxiety Disorder, Dissociative Disorder, or a Personality Disorder).

Code based on type:

Attention Deficit Hyperactivity Disorder, Combined Type: if both Criteria A1 and A2 are met for the past 6 months

Attention Deficit Hyperactivity Disorder, Predominantly Inattentive Type: if Criterion A1 is met but Criterion A2 is not met for the past 6 months

Attention Deficit Hyperactivity Disorder, Predominantly Hyperactive-Impulsive Type: if Criterion A2 is met but Criterion A1 is not met for the past 6 months

Coding Note: For individuals (especially adolescents and adults) who currently have symptoms that no longer meet full criteria, "In Partial Remission" should be specified.

Source: American Psychiatric Association, *Diagnostic and Statistical Manual of Mental Disorders, Fourth Edition, Text Revision* (Washington, DC: American Psychiatric Association, 2000a). Copyright 2000 American Psychiatric Association. Reprinted with permission.

BOX 7.2 • *Factors Affecting Attention in Children with ADHD*

Parents and teachers often express considerable frustration at the fleeting nature of attention in children with ADHD. They may one day watch a movie for two uninterrupted hours, but be unable to attend to ten consecutive minutes of class. The next day they may do both quite successfully, but be very inattentive to most things a day—or even a few hours—later. Barkley (1996) describes six common factors that can limit the attention of children with ADHD. As you will see, these factors interfere with most children's performance—although average children tend not be affected to the same extent or are better able to compensate.

1. *Fatigue.* The attention of children with ADHD is very limited when they are tired. At times, homework is particularly challenging for them, especially if they are expected to do it an hour or so before bedtime.
2. *Task complexity.* Tasks that require planning, organization, and sustained effort (e.g., multi-step tasks, such as cleaning one's room or completing a classroom assignment) can easily disrupt the attention of children with ADHD.
3. *Restraint.* Children with ADHD usually attend poorly when they feel confined or restrained (e.g., when they must sit still and concentrate in class).
4. *Level of stimulation.* The attention of children with ADHD is usually comparable to that of their average peers in highly stimulating environments, such as when watching an enjoyable movie or playing a favorite game. It tends to be much poorer in less stimulating environments, such as that of the classroom.
5. *Reward immediacy and frequency.* Children with the disorder are best able to pay attention when they expect to be rewarded immediately and frequently, such as when playing a videogame. Their attention fluctuates, however, when rewards are delayed and uncertain—for example, when they have to take a test.
6. *Adult presence.* The presence of an adult consistently improves the attention of children with ADHD, probably because adults encourage them regularly, help them organize themselves and remain on task, and redirect their attention when it strays.

and activities in which the child is expected to be calm, quiet, and patient, such as waiting in a restaurant (Barkley, 1996).

Variability

That a child or adolescent's symptoms can vary considerably from one situation or even one moment to the next is true of most of the disorders we cover in this book. However, this variability is particularly striking in ADHD. For example, Zahn, Kruesi, and Rapoport (1991) found that the performance of children with ADHD on different laboratory tasks varied much more from task to task than that of average children, especially when these tasks were complex (e.g., when they required a choice between two responses rather than always the same response). Parents and teachers often report that symptoms of the disorder come and go for

no apparent reason, even in the absence of significant changes in the child's environment. For example, children who are easily distracted and disruptive in class will occasionally be able to concentrate and complete assignments that they had been unable to complete the previous day. Similarly, children who are hyperactive and inattentive, rather than inattentive only, can be happy one minute and sad or mad the next—swinging rapidly between extremes of positive and negative emotions and behaviors (Maedgen & Carlson, 2000). Such mood swings are particularly evident in children who have high levels of comorbid aggressive and disruptive problems (Melnick & Hinshaw, 2000). This variability probably contributes to a common misperception among parents and teachers of children with ADHD that, all too often, "They do it on purpose," "They lack motivation," or "They could do better if only they tried harder."

Sociability

In spite of their frequent disruptions, many children with ADHD are very sociable, affectionate, and endearing. Consequently, even though they regularly irritate their parents, many of them still enjoy relatively positive family relationships (Buhrmester, Camparo, Christensen, Gonzalez, & Hinshaw, 1992). Bobby's case illustrates this important point, as well as the general symptomatology of ADHD.

Bobby is 6. In our first interview with them, his parents describe the many facets of his behavior. "I don't know where to start," says his mother. "He turns the house upside-down and he never obeys me. . . . O.K, I am probably exaggerating a little. But it's true that he often doesn't obey me and that he doesn't obey his dad either."

Bobby's parents go on to report a series of incidents that highlight the child's difficulties: hyperactivity, inattention, impatience, and, above all, a total lack of organization bordering on panic when he is faced with complex tasks that he is expected to complete quickly and efficiently—such as getting dressed and eating breakfast in order to leave for school on time. His parents also note that Bobby is defiant and that he deliberately provokes his mother and 4-year-old sister. "He aggravates his sister so much," his mother says, "that the poor thing often has just had enough—I can understand that—and she hits him or bites him, and it turns into a fight or a screaming match."

Bobby's father intervenes at this point to describe his son's many positive qualities, especially the fact that he is a very affectionate child, and to make sure that his wife does not portray him as a "monster." "I know he's not a monster," she says, "but it's just that he drives me crazy! He's very affectionate and really a little charmer. And he can be adorable. . . . But he also knows how to be horrible! His unpredictable swings just kill me. One minute everything's fine, sometimes an entire day goes by without problems, but then all of a sudden everything's upside-down. And then there is no telling for how long. He becomes agitated, runs back and forth without hearing a thing, disobeys, or hits his sister, and this can last for a few minutes or an hour or a day. . . . What you need to understand is that *when he is in such a state, all his behavior seems disorganized, his emotions, everything. . . . It's not just that he is irritating but, I don't know, he just loses it—I don't know how else to put it—and then he is totally unhappy . . . and us with him!"*

Detailed information obtained from the child, his parents, and his teachers, and direct observations at home and at school, lead to a diagnosis of ADHD accompanied by symptoms of oppositional defiant disorder (see Chapter 8). It is likely that Bobby's difficulties began very early. His mother had a normal pregnancy but a long and trying delivery; and his parents report that he "never really settled." . . . Also, unlike his sister, Bobby has always been very active and unable to concentrate for any length of time. For example, he does not enjoy listening to children's stories and rarely sits in front of the TV. His mother reports an incident that stands out in her memory: "He must have been a little over 4. I can see him as if it were yesterday. He was sitting on the kitchen floor and trying to make a puzzle he had already put together many times before. But he was getting frustrated; he was insisting on putting a piece where it didn't belong, and suddenly, all at once, bang, it was as if a gun went off. He went mad. He threw everything in the air and just ran and ran around the house—it took everything I had to calm him down."

Both parents agree that Bobby is a difficult child, but often disagree on how to deal with him. For example, his mother feels that he needs discipline and firmness to help him learn to be better organized and to control his outbursts, whereas his father believes that this type of behavior is quite normal for boys and will pass. He explains: "I was a little bit like him when I was his age, at least if you believe my mother. It's funny, we were at her house for a big family reunion a few weeks back and Bobby had done something wild, I don't remember what exactly, and it struck me because my mother looked at him and said, 'You're just like your father.'"

Coordinated treatment at home and school helps Bobby make considerable progress and greatly improves the overall family climate. From the outset, emphasis is placed on helping the parents set and enforce consistent goals for their son, and on working with Bobby's teacher to ensure that comparable goals are implemented in school. After almost a year of treatment, Bobby remains an active child, who requires firm limits to control his behavior; but he is better able to organize himself than he used to be and is now rarely aggressive or destructive when frustrated.

Additional Difficulties

Many children with ADHD have important motor, language, emotional, and/or cognitive difficulties in addition to the behavior problems that are reflected in the disorder's diagnostic criteria (Barkley, 1996). These difficulties vary from case to case, both in number and intensity. For example, children with ADHD often find it difficult to control their motor activity, especially when they are involved in complex tasks that require planning, organization, and well-coordinated motor skills (Shue & Douglas, 1992). Studies of the speech and language of children with the disorder show also that they tend to speak excessively (Cunningham & Siegel, 1987), but that they are less likely than average peers to talk to themselves to monitor and control their behavior (Berk & Potts, 1991). In addition, they have difficulties organizing and expressing their thoughts when they are prompted, but not when they are speaking spontaneously (Zentall, 1988). Finally, they control their emotions poorly, especially when the emotions are negative (Cole, Zahn-Waxler, & Smith, 1994), and have problems resisting temptation and delaying gratification (Hinshaw, Heller, & McHale, 1992).

The common denominator of the difficulties just described is that they are all self-regulatory. In other words, they are *executive* difficulties. As discussed in Chapter 6, executive functions are the neuropsychological processes underlying self-regulation. Executive functions include:

- Volition; planning; and purposive, goal-directed, or intentional action.
- Inhibition and resistance to distraction.
- Problem-solving and strategy development, selection, and monitoring.
- Flexible shifting of actions to meet task demands.
- Maintenance of persistence toward attaining a goal.

- Self-awareness across time. (Barkley, 2000, p. 1065)

These functions enable individuals to coordinate their behavior in flexible ways, so that they can adapt to the varying demands of their environment, as well as to their own changing needs and states. In a meta-analysis, Pennington and Ozonoff (1996) found that children with ADHD scored lower than comparison children on two-thirds of measures of executive functioning, and higher on none. For example, children with the disorder had greater difficulty completing experimental tasks in which they had to sort cards or to match familiar figures. They also lacked flexibility and adaptability as they approached such tasks. In particular, they were more likely to continue to rely on the same course of action when the problems they had to solve changed, and thus to make errors of **perseveration**— by continuing to respond in the same way even when the responses proved counterproductive. These results support the assumption that inattention, hyperactivity, and impulsivity reflect, at least in part, significant deficits in executive functioning and, more precisely, in processes of behavioral inhibition that are necessary for the smooth execution of a host of daily tasks (Barkley, 1997, 2000). We will return to this assumption later (see Etiology).

Subtypes

The DSM-IV-TR describes three subtypes of ADHD (see Table 7.1). These subtypes reflect the nature of the dominant symptoms. In **ADHD, predominantly inattentive type,** the child has at least six symptoms of inattention, but fewer than six symptoms of hyperactivity and impulsivity. In **ADHD, predominantly hyperactive-impulsive type,** the reverse applies: the child has at least six symptoms of hyperactivity and impulsivity, but fewer than six symptoms of inattention. In **ADHD, combined type,** the child has both six or more symptoms of inattention and six or more symptoms of hyperactivity and impulsivity. Research supports the existence of the predominantly inattentive and combined types (Neuman et al., 1999). There is also some evidence for the predominantly hyperactive-impulsive type, but in young children only (Applegate et al., 1997). For the majority of children with hyperactive and impulsive behaviors, however, inattention is also an issue.

Diagnostic and Developmental Considerations

Diagnosis of any psychological disorder in childhood or adolescence is always made within an evolving developmental and social context. In ADHD in particular, diagnosis is often hampered because (1) our knowledge about the development of attention in children in general remains limited; (2) symptoms vary greatly according to age and gender, and to the social context in which the child is observed; and (3) social considerations largely determine the extent of the child's difficulties.

Limited Knowledge about the Development of Attention

The DSM-IV-TR defines an essential aspect of ADHD—inattention—in largely negative terms: as a failure to pay attention to details, to sustain attention in various activities, to listen, to follow through on instructions and complete tasks, and to organize oneself (see Table 7.1). But these multiple shortcomings might also be found in other children in the course of their development. More generally, the diagnosis of any behavior problem is significantly affected by comparisons of that behavior with normal development; and at present clinicians and researchers have only a limited knowledge of how attention usually develops in children of the same age (Halperin, 1996).

Symptom Variability According to Age, Gender, and Context

Diagnosis of ADHD can also be made difficult because its symptoms depend to a large extent on the age and gender of the child being evaluated, as well as on the social context in which this evaluation takes place. DSM-IV-TR symptoms of hyperactivity and impulsivity apply primarily to preschool and school-age children, and to boys more than girls. In contrast, symptoms of inattention are relevant to a broader period of development, and generally to girls as much as boys (Willoughby, Curran, Costello, & Angold, 2000).

The symptoms of ADHD tend to be more frequent and severe in boys than in girls (Szatmari, 1992), and are not always manifested in the same manner by both genders. For example, Cole and colleagues (1994) exposed 4- and 5-year-old children to a short disappointment, by promising them a prize that they did not receive when they expected it. The researchers observed the children's emotional reactions to this disappointment, first in the presence of an adult and later when the child was left alone for a short time. Results showed that boys with high levels of ADHD and oppositional symptoms reacted with signs of anger in the presence of the adult but not when they were alone; girls reacted by minimizing all signs of negative emotions, especially when they were alone. These results show that, from a young age, children with behavior problems including ADHD manage their emotions differently according to their gender and to the context in which they are observed.

The DSM-IV-TR recognizes the importance of the social context in ADHD by requiring that children exhibit significant difficulties in at least two different settings—typically home and school—before a diagnosis is made. It is sound clinical and research practice to evaluate children in different situations. However, multiple sources of information do not always present the same picture and can complicate the diagnostic process. This is true of all psychological disorders of childhood and adolescence but is particularly evident in disorders such as ADHD, in which symptoms can vary considerably from one setting to another. For example, parents and teachers do not always identify the same children as having ADHD and, when they do, are not necessarily alarmed by the same symptoms. More precisely, parents tend to describe affected children as having moderate levels of ADHD accompanied by several symptoms of oppositional defiant disorder (see Chapter 8). In contrast, teachers generally describe the *same* children as having more severe levels of ADHD, but not necessarily with comorbid symptoms of opposition (Costello, Loeber, & Stouthamer-Loeber, 1991; Mitsis, McKay, Schulz, Newcorn, & Halperin, 2000).

Social Considerations

The fact that ADHD symptoms vary greatly in frequency and intensity from one context to another implies that diagnosis of the disorder always reflects considerable input from important adults in the child's life. In most cases, parents and/or teachers request a professional evaluation once they come to the conclusion that challenging behavior limits the child's adaptive functioning and creates significant disturbances at home and/or school. As the following case illustrates, a diagnosis reflects not only the child's problems but also the social expectations of those requesting and making the evaluation.

Enrique is 10. His mother, who referred him to our clinic, eloquently describes the problems that she and her partner are having with her son. She notes that these problems have been apparent for several years, but that, until recently, she thought that Enrique "was just a boy" who would outgrow his difficulties "sooner or later."

Enrique has been in a special education classroom since kindergarten because of hyperactivity, aggression, and oppositional behavior. According to his teachers, his progress has been slow. He continues to have multiple symptoms of ADHD and to be prone to angry and aggressive outbursts. Furthermore, because he has considerable difficulties organizing his work and completing it satisfactorily, he has recently been diagnosed as having a learning disability. At the beginning of fifth grade, he barely reads at a third-grade level and his writing is comparable to that of a second grader.

Enrique's mother acknowledges his many challenges at school but explains that she never sought treatment until now because she was convinced that his behavior was a consequence of his learning problems. She adds that she rarely has difficulties with him at home because she is able to "see his heart of gold." Pressed on this issue, however, she reluctantly describes several incidents in which Enrique has been particularly defiant—usually yelling obscenities when angry and walking out of the house when reprimanded. In one such incident, Enrique ran impulsively across a busy street and was almost killed. This near tragedy prompted his mother to seek treatment.

Enrique's teachers did not hesitate to describe him as having ADHD and oppositional defiant disorder (see Chapter 8), and reported that he had had these disorders since at least kindergarten. Two psychological evaluations conducted at the request of the school came to the same conclusion. However, Enrique's mother did not believe that he had significant difficulties—besides his learning problems—until his impulsivity got him almost killed. In other words, a diagnosis of ADHD—and of many other psychological disorders—is not simply an objective summary of reality. It also reflects how significant adults interpret that reality.

Three key points sum up the preceding discussion:

1. Developmental issues play a major role in ADHD. The DSM-IV-TR recognizes this fact but minimizes its importance by providing a single list of symptoms that are meant to reflect accurately the various manifestations of the disorder at different ages. This list does not fully account for developmental changes in ADHD. Specifically, current diagnostic criteria do not always detect the disorder in older children—not because these children do not have significant difficulties, but in large part because their challenges do not map precisely onto current criteria (see also Epidemiology).

2. The fact that these criteria are meant to apply equally to girls and boys may partly explain why the majority of children with the disorder are males. Again, this result does not necessarily mean that boys are always at greater risk of developing ADHD; it may mean simply that current criteria describe boys' difficulties in this area better than girls' (Barkley, 1996).

3. The DSM-IV-TR criteria are heavily weighted with hyperactivity and impulsivity items, whose diagnostic relevance diminishes with age. This weighting of items may explain why ADHD is easier to diagnose during childhood than adolescence; why it is often diagnosed at the beginning of elementary school—when children move from the more flexible and individualized behavioral standards of the home to the more structured and standardized demands of the classroom; and why many symptoms of ADHD decline in frequency

and severity during adolescence or at the beginning of adulthood (Costello et al., 1991). This decline probably occurs because older adolescents and young adults have a greater say in what they do and how they structure their time than they had when they were in school.

Empirical Validity

There is no doubt that a significant number of children and adolescents have high levels of inattention and/or hyperactivity-impulsivity that limit their adaptive functioning. Consequently, the central issue in the empiri-cal validity of ADHD has more to do with how the disorder should be classified than with demonstrating its existence (Barkley, 1996, 1997). A summary of the evidence for the empirical validity of ADHD and its subtypes is presented in Table 7.2.

Statistical Evidence

Data from the *Child Behavior Checklist* (see Box 2.5) and other behavior rating scales show that behaviors mainly observed in children with ADHD tend to cluster into two main features: inattention and disorganization, and hyperactivity-impulsivity. These findings are valid: they have been obtained with different rating

TABLE 7.2 *Evidence for the Empirical Validity of ADHD and Its Subtypes*

	ADHD, Predominantly Hyperactive-Impulsive and Combined Type	ADHD, Predominantly Inattentive Type
General level of functioning	Poor; or poor to fair.	Fair to good.
Age at onset	Develops early, but usually not distinguishable from normative behavior until age 3 or 4.	Develops in the early school years.
Behavioral impressions	"Difficult," "unruly," "hard-to-manage" children.	"Dreamers."
Developmental trajectory	Tends to be chronic, especially when other disruptive behaviors such as aggression and noncompliance are present. During the school years, school delays and special education are common, as is school dropout in adolescence. Approximately 20% of affected children develop antisocial personality disorder in adulthood.	Is rarely chronic but involves learning difficulties and school delays. Often decreases in adolescence.
Comorbidity with oppositional defiant and conduct disorder	Common; found in approximately 50% of affected children.	Not common.
Comorbidity with anxiety and mood disorders	Not common.	Fairly common.
Family characteristics	Family history of ADHD, antisocial behavior, and substance abuse common.	Family history of anxiety and depression common.
Peer relations	Often socially isolated because of active rejection by peers.	Social isolation, when present, is usually the result of the child's withdrawal rather than of peer rejection.

scales and in normative and clinical samples from countries such as Japan (Kanbayashi, Nakata, Fujji, Kita, & Wada, 1994), France (Pry, 1998), and the United States (Neuman et al., 1999). Within North America, these findings are also supported by evidence that they apply across different cultural groups (Beiser, Dion, & Gotowiec, 2000).

Longitudinal Evidence

Longitudinal studies also support the empirical validity of these two dimensions and, more specifically, of two of the subtypes of the disorder described in the DSM-IV-TR: a predominantly inattentive type on one hand, and a predominantly hyperactive-impulsive on the other. (The combined type is usually grouped with the hyperactive-impulsive subtype.) As you will see, these two subtypes have different developmental trajectories (see Developmental Trajectories and Prognosis). Briefly stated, when hyperactive and impulsive symptoms predominate, they predict a disorder that is likely to affect many areas of functioning and to be chronic in nature, often persisting into adolescence and even adulthood—especially when hyperactivity and impulsivity are accompanied by opposition, defiance, aggression, or other disruptive behaviors (Mannuzza & Klein, 1992). In contrast, early problems of attention alone are rarely the precursors of antisocial conduct, but rather of learning difficulties and school delays (Fergusson, Horwood, & Lynskey, 1993).

Descriptive Evidence

Descriptive studies lend further support to the empirical validity of the disorder and to the distinction between these two subtypes. Children with marked levels of hyperactivity are impulsive and often lack the ability to sustain attention. In contrast, children with significant levels of inattention are more often "dreamers," who lack concentration and have difficulty processing information in a fast and efficient manner. The functioning of children in the hyperactive group is also more impaired. They find it difficult to regulate their emotions, often fluctuating rapidly between extremes of positive and negative emotional states and behaviors. They are more aggressive as well, and more likely

to be actively rejected by their peers. Children who are primarily inattentive, however, tend to be socially passive and aloof, and to have a limited knowledge of social rules and expectations. When they have peer problems, they are isolated or withdrawn more often than rejected (Maedgen & Carlson, 2000). In addition, when broader characteristics are assessed, inattention is associated with personal and family histories of anxiety and depression, whereas hyperactivity and impulsivity are associated with personal and family symptoms of antisocial conduct and drug abuse.

Experimental Evidence

Experimental studies suggest that hyperactivity and impulsivity are core characteristics of the disorder. For example, in a study that compared children with ADHD, children with other psychological conditions, and a control group of children, the children with ADHD had higher levels of activity than peers in the other two groups and higher levels of impulsivity than peers in the control group. Interestingly, inattention was more pronounced in the two clinical groups than in the control group, but children with ADHD did not have more inattentive symptoms than children with other disorders (Halperin et al., 1992). These results indicate that high levels of hyperactivity and impulsivity may be specific to ADHD, whereas high levels of inattention may be found in other psychological disorders as well.

To sum up, the studies just reviewed suggest that, as it is currently defined, ADHD may not be one disorder with two or three subtypes, but two separate conditions that have different characteristics and developmental trajectories, and, in many cases, distinctive family antecedents. These studies also highlight the fact that diagnostic systems are works in progress. The disorders they define are not unchangeable descriptions of an objective reality, but temporary categories that evolve in light of ongoing research findings.

Associated Characteristics; Comorbidity

The difficulties of young people with ADHD are often accompanied by other disorders or problems that further limit their adaptation. For example, an epidemiological study of more than 7,000 first- through fourth-grade children found that 61% of children with ADHD had one or two other diagnoses—usually oppositional defiant disorder, conduct disorder, and/or an anxiety disorder (August, Realmuto, MacDonald, Nugent, & Crosby, 1996).

Psychological Symptoms and Disorders

Oppositional Defiant and Conduct Disorders. As noted earlier, many children and adolescents with ADHD have comorbid symptoms of opposition and aggression, or oppositional defiant or conduct disorder (Gresham, MacMillan, Bocian, Ward, & Forness, 1998). Clinical studies show that between one-third and two-thirds of children who receive professional care for ADHD also have oppositional defiant disorder and that 30–50% have conduct disorder (Barkley, Fischer, Edelbrock, & Smallish, 1990; Biederman, Faraone, & Lapey, 1992). Rates of comorbidity are lower but still important in studies of normative samples. For example, August and colleagues (1996) reported that 32% of the 6- to 10-year-olds diagnosed with ADHD qualified for a diagnosis of oppositional defiant disorder, and 12% for one of conduct disorder. In a majority of cases, ADHD precedes these comorbid disorders by a few years and hastens their onset.

Anxiety Disorders. ADHD and anxiety disorders are often comorbid also, especially in childhood. Overlap has been found to range from 27% to 30% in clinical samples, and from 8% to 26% in normative samples (Biederman et al., 1992). This comorbidity decreases with age. During adolescence, the prevalence of anxiety disorders among youth with ADHD is often not higher than in the general population; however, anxiety disorders may often appear among children and adolescents with the predominantly inattentive type of ADHD (Russo & Beidel, 1994).

Mood Disorders. A number of children with ADHD develop a mood disorder, especially around puberty or during adolescence. However, reported rates of comorbidity vary considerably. Rates range from 25% to 75% in clinical samples, and from 15% to 19% in nor-

mative samples (Biederman et al., 1992). Not surprisingly, rates are typically higher in children who have other problems in addition to ADHD (Treuting & Hinshaw, 2001). The part played by depressive symptoms or a mood disorder in the presentation and course of ADHD still remains to be specified. This comorbidity might reflect to a large extent the reaction of children with ADHD to the social and school problems that their disruptive behaviors provoke (Hoza, Pelham, Milich, Pillow, & McBride, 1993). Some researchers speculate also that ADHD is common in youth with bipolar disorder—a disorder in which the child's mood fluctuates between periods of depression and emotional agitation (see Chapter 10). For example, in a clinical study, Biederman, Wozniak, Kiely, and Ablon (1995) found that 60% of children with mania had multiple symptoms of inattention, hyperactivity, and distractibility. These authors believe that this finding is evidence that the two disorders are often comorbid, but others (e.g., Barkley, 1996) explain the findings by pointing out that there is considerable overlap among the diagnostic criteria for the two disorders.

Learning and Communication Disorders. Many children with ADHD have significant learning problems that can result in major academic difficulties, especially when the disorder persists for several years. Here also, rates of comorbidity vary greatly—ranging from less than 10% to more than 90%, largely because of sampling and other methodological differences across studies. When strict criteria are used, comorbidity averages 20–25% (Pliszka, 2000). Research shows also that in elementary school the work produced by children with ADHD is inferior (in both quantity and quality) to that of average children, and that by age 11 nearly 80% have accumulated a delay of two years or more in school (Cantwell & Baker, 1992). Many of them are placed in special education classrooms for extended periods of time and frequently fail to complete high school (Weiss & Hechtman, 1993).

Given these difficulties, it should come as no surprise that the intellectual performance of children with ADHD is generally lower than that of average children, especially when it is assessed with verbal measures of IQ. Lower intellectual performance is most likely to be evident in children who are primarily hyperactive and impulsive (Lynam, Moffitt, & Stouthamer-Loeber, 1993), and who have comorbid oppositional defiant or conduct disorder (Frick et al., 1991).

Tic Disorders.   ADHD and **tic disorders** also can co-occur. We define these disorders and briefly discuss their association with ADHD in Box 7.3.

General Adaptation

Medical Problems.   It was long thought that many children with ADHD had chronic health problems, such as allergies, asthma, and elimination problems (i.e., poor bladder or bowel control). Early research on ADHD and allergies tended to support this association. However, longitudinal studies using careful research designs have shown that such an association is unlikely. The same is true for asthma. A stronger case can be made for the existence of a link between ADHD and poor bladder control or enuresis: clinical

studies show that some 30% of children with ADHD do not have full bladder control by the time most of their average peers do (Biederman et al., 1995). However, this link may not be specific to ADHD, as enuresis is associated with a variety of other disorders (see Chapter 13).

Accident-Proneness.   Youth with ADHD have an elevated risk of having accidents or serious injuries, because their excessive activity and their impulsivity often lead them to act without thinking of the consequences (Szatmari et al., 1989a). Accident-proneness is especially obvious in school-age children, but remains evident throughout adolescence and into young adulthood (Weiss & Hechtman, 1993). Susan's case illustrates this risk:

Susan is 16. She is referred to our clinic because of difficulties managing her insulin-dependent diabetes (see Chapter 13). Susan was diagnosed with ADHD,

BOX 7.3 • *ADHD and Tic Disorders*

A small number of children with ADHD also have a comorbid tic disorder. Tics are rapid, repeated, nonrhythmical motor movements or vocalizations that have no apparent purpose. Motor tics include twitches, grimaces, head jerks, eye blinks, and limb or whole-body movements. Vocal tics involve grunts and other throat noises, as well as repetitive saying or shouting of words or phrases out of context. Typically, tics appear in short series or "bursts," and tend to be worsened by stress and lessened by situations that require attention or concentration. It is most likely that youth with ADHD are not at greater risk of having a tic disorder than youth in the general population, but that a link between the two conditions is reported in some cases because children with both disorders are more likely to be referred for mental health services than children who have only one (Barkley, 1996).

In contrast, youth who have a tic disorder are much more likely than their average peers to have ADHD. Clinical studies show that 40–50% of children with a tic disorder actually have ADHD (Towbin & Riddle, 1993). Furthermore, children with a tic disorder who do not meet diagnostic criteria for ADHD often have behavioral diffi-

culties that are associated with the condition—such as problems with motor coordination and impulsivity (Baron-Cohen, Cross, Crowson, & Robertson, 1994).

Much about the association between tic disorders and ADHD is still unknown—for example, we do not know the nature of the neuropsychological processes underlying this comorbidity; nor do we know whether some psychostimulants used in the medical treatment of ADHD (e.g., Ritalin) can increase the frequency and severity of tics, or provoke symptoms in a child with a genetic vulnerability for tics. Some researchers report that psychostimulants increase the frequency and severity of tics (Bruun & Budman, 1993), but others do not (Gadnow, Sverd, Sprafkin, Nolan, & Grossman, 1999). What is clear already is that for children with both disorders, tics and symptoms of inattention and hyperactivity tend to aggravate each other. At home and school, these combined challenges can lead to feelings of failure, frustration, embarrassment, and shame, both in affected children and in their families, as well as to conflicts with parents, siblings, teachers, and peers (Dykens et al., 1990).

Children with ADHD are prone to have accidents. ADHD is associated with accident-proneness, especially during childhood, probably because young children with the disorder often fail to think of the consequences of their actions.

combined type, at age 6. Her mother notes jokingly that she never sat still during her entire childhood. When Susan entered school, her hyperactivity, impulsivity, and aggression caused her constant difficulties. In second grade, she was placed in a special education classroom. . . .

Susan's mother reports that her daughter's problems only became a concern when she began high school. "She is still in a special education classroom and doing quite well, but I don't know what it is, she often gets into fights and . . . recently she got in trouble, big time, for hitting one of her coaches. . . . She's very good in sports but she doesn't like to be told what to do." Susan's aggressive behavior has resulted in numerous suspensions and removal from her favorite sports teams. To complicate matters, Susan has diabetes but does a poor job of monitoring her blood sugar level and of following her diet, in spite of her mother's supervision and encouragement. Finally, three months before the family came for treatment, Susan was responsible for two automobile accidents only weeks apart. She was not seriously injured and did not injure anyone else, but she caused important property damage on both occasions.

Susan sees no reason to come for treatment and—though superficially pleasant—is uncooperative

from the outset. Her approach consists essentially of minimizing the seriousness of the concerns that adults have about the personal and social consequences of her conduct. She sees "no problem" in her management of her diabetes and says that her accidents and fights at school are "no big deal." She blames the principal and one particular coach for her disciplinary problems, stating that she has "never hurt anyone." She explains that her first accident occurred when she became distracted by a "neat song on the radio," and her second one when she "put [her] foot down" to cross a busy intersection as the lights were changing. Susan admits also that her diabetic problems result largely from her inattention to the monitoring procedures she has learned and from her impulsive eating. When the therapist points out to her that she has difficulty thinking about the consequences of her behavior, she laughs and says that she "lives for the moment."

Susan makes little or no progress in treatment and, after a few weeks, refuses to return. Her mother, who is very reluctant to impose any limit on her daughter, agrees that she should discontinue treatment, explaining that in time Susan will "outgrow" her impulsive and aggressive behavior, and learn to manage her diabetes.

Self-Concept. Given the nature of ADHD, you might think that affected youth have a poor self-concept, and often feel helpless or incompetent. Some studies support this assumption, but many do not. Specifically, when asked to rate their social or academic competence, or to predict their ability to solve problems or to succeed on a test, children with the disorder are often *more* positive about themselves than average children. This is especially true of boys. However, their positive self-reports are fragile. They are more likely than average peers to attribute their success on a variety of tasks to external factors, such as being lucky, than to personal characteristics, such as being a hard worker (Hoza, Waschbusch, Pelham, Molina, & Milich, 2000). Moreover, their positive self-evaluations disappear quickly when they are exposed to failure or when others evaluate their behavior *positively* (Diener and Milich, 1997). Their initially positive but unrealistic self-evaluations, Diener and Milich speculate, may serve a self-protective function by preventing them from seeing every new task as another occasion for failure. When others tell them instead that they succeeded, their need to protect themselves decreases, enabling them to evaluate themselves more accurately. Alternatively, children with ADHD may simply overestimate their ability, less to protect themselves than because they are unaware of how they actually perform. These competing hypotheses will have to be evaluated in further research.

Epidemiology

Prevalence; Age and Gender Characteristics

Large-scale epidemiological studies conducted in several countries during the past three decades show prevalence ranges for ADHD from 4.2% to 6.3% when DSM-III or DSM-III-R criteria are used to define the disorder (Szatmari, 1992). When DSM-IV-TR criteria are used, these rates are slightly higher (APA, 2000a). Studies show also that most affected youth have the predominantly hyperactive-impulsive or the combined type of the disorder. The predominantly inattentive type affects a little more than 1% of the population and is probably more common in adolescence than childhood (Szatmari, 1992).

These prevalence figures, however, hide important age and gender differences. Specifically, ADHD is diagnosed more frequently in children than in adolescents, and in boys than in girls. Szatmari and associates (1989b) report that between the ages of 6 and 12, ADHD affects approximately 6% to 9% of boys and 2% to 3% of girls, whereas in adolescence it affects 3% of boys and 1% of girls. This and other studies indicate that, in normative samples, the sex ratio is approximately 3 boys per girl (Fergusson et al., 1993). The overrepresentation of boys is more pronounced in clinical samples, especially for the hyperactive subtypes. Consequently, boys are much more likely to be treated for ADHD than girls are (Barkley, 1996).

Important gender differences are also found when one considers the prevalence of ADHD subtypes and of comorbid conditions in boys and girls. A large clinical study comparing children with and without ADHD found that the combined type was most prevalent in both genders (Biederman, Mick, et al., 2002). The study also found, however, that girls with the disorder were (1) twice as likely as boys to have the predominantly inattentive subtype of ADHD; (2) less likely than boys to have oppositional defiant disorder, conduct disorder, and major depressive disorder; (3) less likely than boys to have learning or school problems; and (4) at greater risk than boys for drug use and abuse problems.

More research is needed before gender differences in ADHD can be fully understood, but this important study suggests that, overall, girls with the disorder may be less disruptive and dysfunctional than boys, and consequently less likely to receive professional services, even though their difficulties clearly seem to require such services.

Some Unanswered Questions

Although the prevalence of ADHD decreases with age, this decrease may not represent an actual epidemiological change. A comparable decrease in prevalence might not be observed if the DSM-IV-TR diagnostic criteria reflected a developmentally more sensitive range of symptoms; instead, those criteria—especially for symptoms of hyperactivity and impulsivity—apply primarily to young children (Barkley, 1996). That is, symptoms such as "runs about or climbs excessively" and "often has difficulty awaiting turn" describe behaviors that are typical of early and middle childhood.

The same critique applies to gender differences. As Barkley (1996) notes, ADHD is more often diagnosed in boys than in girls in part because its diagnostic criteria apply best to boys. In the general population, behaviors such as running about, climbing, and being noisy are more typical of boys than girls. Therefore, the behavioral threshold needed to establish the presence of the disorder is not the same for both genders, because, to qualify for the diagnosis, girls have to engage excessively in behaviors that are most characteristic of boys. The disorder also may be more common in boys because of its frequent comorbidity with oppositional defiant and conduct disorder—two disorders that affect boys more often than girls (Szatmari et al., 1989b). Taken as a whole, these unanswered questions illustrate the limitations of the current diagnostic criteria and point to the need for careful developmental research in this area.

Social and Cultural Differences

ADHD is found in children and adolescents of different social status, ethnicity, and cultural backgrounds. The disorder has been described in comparable terms in studies conducted in Canada, China, Colombia, Germany, Japan, New Zealand, Puerto Rico, and the United States. For example, in a Japanese study of more than 1,000 children between 4 and 12 years old, Kanbayashi and associates (1994) reported an average prevalence rate of almost 8% and, like their North American colleagues, a marked reduction in symptoms with age. Similarly, in a study of over 2,700 children from different areas of China, Shen, Wang, and Yang (1985) reported rates of 3% in urban settings, 8% in suburbs, and 7% in rural areas.

Contrary to the Chinese study, some evidence suggests that ADHD is more frequent in urban environments and in socioeconomically disadvantaged groups (Szatmari, 1992). However, these associations are partly the consequence of the high rates of comorbidity between ADHD and antisocial behavior problems, which tend to be most prevalent in poor, urban settings. For example, August and associates (1996)

found that children whose ADHD was accompanied by conduct disorder were more likely to come from a disadvantaged background than children whose ADHD was not comorbid or was associated with a different disorder. The apparently contradictory findings reported by Shen and colleagues (1985) in China may reflect the fact that poverty is not distributed in the same manner across urban and rural areas in that country as it is in North America.

Developmental Trajectories and Prognosis

As is true in all psychological disorders of childhood and adolescence, the developmental trajectory of ADHD can vary greatly from one child to another. However, longitudinal studies make it possible to outline some of the key features of this trajectory. Most follow-up data have been collected with boys, although there is evidence that girls with ADHD are as likely as boys to have a troubled development (Klein & Mannuzza, 1991).

Outline of the Trajectory

You will recall that children with ADHD, predominantly hyperactive-impulsive or combined type, develop symptoms of excessive activity and impulsivity first, usually around age 3 or 4. These are followed two or three years later by symptoms of inattention (Barkley et al., 1990). In a majority of cases, symptoms decrease with age. Hyperactivity and impulsivity tend to decrease steadily with age, improving by the beginning of adolescence. Inattention is often more pronounced in the elementary school years than it is in early childhood and during adolescence. However, it often persists until the end of adolescence or the beginning of adulthood (Pineda et al., 1999). In spite of this reduction in symptoms, affected children may have long-term difficulties in adaptation. Specifically, 50–80% continue to manifest the disorder or its major symptoms until adolescence, and 30–50% until adulthood (Barkley et al., 1990; Mannuzza & Klein, 2000). Children whose symptoms include early and persistent hyperactivity and impulsivity, combined with oppositional defiant or conduct disorder, and whose parents also suffer from psychological and social difficulties, are particularly likely to have symptoms that persist (Gresham et al., 1998).

The Preschool Years

Although ADHD appears to develop relatively early, it is usually not diagnosed before the age of 4, because at an earlier age clinical levels of hyperactivity and impulsivity are difficult to distinguish from normal behavior. The first signs that these symptoms may constitute a disorder come when frequent conflicts at home or in preschool or daycare begin to interfere with the child's normal development and to cause major disruptions for others. Conflicts commonly arise when adults attempt to set limits to the child's behavioral excesses, to get the child to go from one activity or setting to another, or to impose a change in routine. Children with the disorder, or its early symptoms, tend to react to such impositions by becoming negative and oppositional, or even more hyperactive, setting the stage for a "battle of will" with their caregivers. More generally, young children with the condition stand out by the frequency, intensity, and persistence of their behavioral excesses, and by the fact that they are very difficult to calm down when agitated and do not respond to attempts to reason with them. For example, average 3- to 4-year-olds can play cooperatively with adults or peers, follow simple instructions, listen to a story and leaf through a picture book, or watch a children's program on television. Young children with ADHD cannot do these things, or they do them fairly well one day but very poorly the next.

The School Years

Whereas hyperactivity and impulsivity are of primary concern in the preschool years, difficulties of attention and organization become increasingly important in elementary school (Barkley, 1996). Children with ADHD find themselves unable to meet normal academic expectations, because they lack sustained attention, are poorly organized, and quickly forget what they have been asked to do or do it quickly and poorly. These difficulties often interfere with the acquisition of essential skills, such as reading, writing, and arithmetic. In some cases, to avoid labeling children early, teachers may attribute difficulties of attention and organization to "immaturity" and recommend that children repeat first or second grade to give them more time to catch up to their peers. Since lack of maturity is usually not the problem, this solution rarely works; and the child's difficulties worsen as academic expectations increase. It is often during the first years of school that a diagnosis of ADHD is made (APA, 2000a) and that the family requests mental health services for the first time. In many cases, this first professional contact is prompted not by the symptomatology of the disorder itself, but by its academic and social consequences for the child and others.

The multiple difficulties of children with ADHD in the elementary school years have negative ramifications for more than their academic progress. Their hyperactivity, impulsivity, and short attention span lead to regular disruptions, and cause conflicts with teachers and peers, especially when they are accompanied by aggressive outbursts (Cunningham & Siegel, 1987). For example, in an eight-year longitudinal study, Barkley and colleagues (1990) found that children with ADHD had much higher rates of school failure, suspension, or expulsion than their average peers, especially when they had comorbid conduct problems. Specifically, children with ADHD and conduct problems had twice the rate of school suspensions and more than fourteen times as many school expulsions as children with ADHD only.

Late Adolescence and Early Adulthood

A number of children with ADHD continue to have significant problems beyond the school years. In general, they are less likely to complete high school than their average peers, and more likely to have difficulties developing and maintaining satisfactory intimate relationships and employment. In one study, 90% of the subjects who had been diagnosed with ADHD in their youth were employed as young adults, but their level of education and their professional status were lower than those of control subjects (Mannuzza, Klein, Bessler, Malloy, & LaPadula, 1998). More generally, when difficulties persist beyond adolescence, individuals with

ADHD do not have an increased risk of developing other conditions, except for antisocial personality disorder and alcohol or drug abuse problems (see Figure 7.2). They also run an elevated risk of being arrested as young adults and, especially, of having multiple arrests, convictions, and incarcerations (Mannuzza, Klein, Konig, & Giampino, 1989; Weiss & Hechtman, 1993).

Not surprisingly, problems are most likely to persist beyond adolescence when youth with ADHD face other challenges, especially ongoing conduct problems and disturbed family relationships (Weiss & Hechtman, 1993). In the absence of such challenges, young people with the disorder are not problem-free, but their adjustment is better in adulthood than it was earlier in their development. The story of 27-year-old Ian Murray highlights some of the challenges of growing up with this common disorder.

My . . . kindergarten experience passed relatively unnoticed. . . . The complaints didn't start until my first year of grade school. The Grade 1 teacher, Mr. Roach, was a particularly severe disciplinarian, who had a va-

riety of techniques for punishing misbehavior. . . . That year with Mr. Roach I spent most of my time in the corridors. . . .

I start Grade 1 over, and Rosemary wants to know why I flunked. She thinks "it's weird," and so do the other kids. I don't know what to answer, so at lunch I tell my mother that the kids at school are teasing me. She instructs me to tell them that "it's none of their business." For me it's easier to just punch them out. . . . Mrs. Rowe is my new Grade 1 teacher. . . . I like her a lot as she encourages every success and I feel proud helping her when I can. Arithmetic is going much better because now I understand most of the concepts being taught. . . .

Throughout grade school some teachers made sincere efforts to help, others opted to pass me over, demanding little, expecting even less, and hoping for my eventual classroom conformity which would not undermine the rights of others. Rote phrases I hear throughout my childhood are "Slow down, Ian," or "Now remember, Ian, you are fooling nobody but yourself." They were wrong. I never wanted to fool myself and I did not know how to slow down. . . .

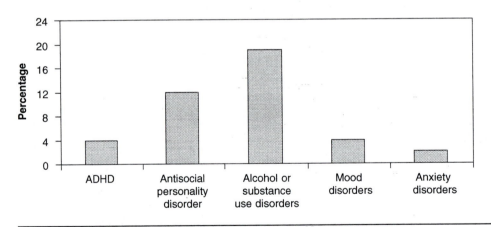

FIGURE 7.2 *Adult Adjustment of Youth with ADHD.* This figure illustrates the adult adjustment of 85 children who grew up with ADHD. A total of 28 participants continued to qualify for one or more diagnoses in adulthood. These diagnoses were most likely to be of antisocial personality disorder and/or alcohol or substance use disorder, rather than of ADHD or of mood or anxiety disorder.

Source: From S. Mannuzza, R. G. Klein, A. Bessler, P. Malloy, and M. LaPadula, "Adult Psychiatric Status of ADHD," *American Journal of Psychiatry* 155 (1998), p. 495. Copyright 1998 by American Psychiatric Association. Reprinted by permission.

My dignity and self-esteem rested on my ability to conceal from anyone that there was something wrong with me. . . . Unfortunately, my hyperactivity precluded being able to slip by unnoticed. The calls home would inevitably start coming by the first week of October. I still could not read phonetically and my teacher offered to help me after school. The boys at school were into the Hardy Boys books and talked about their adventures. I asked my mother to read to me in the evening so I could know what they were talking about. I pretended I read the same books. . . . Eventually, teachers stopped expecting me to do homework, and for better or worse the tension eased. . . .

I was on my ten-speed bike not long ago. I rode past my old high school. Slowing down, I noticed my former biology teacher. For an instant I was startled to see how much he had changed. I realized how much I had changed too, inside I mean. I wanted to say hello, to tell him what I've been doing and still hope to do. But I doubt he would have recognized me—it's been a long time (Weiss & Hechtman, 1993, pp. 302–317).

Etiology

A comprehensive account of the manner in which ADHD develops and evolves over time is not yet available. However, etiological findings converge on three major points.

1. Because children with ADHD form a very diverse group, their difficulties probably have different, and often overlapping, etiologies.
2. Both biological and psychosocial factors play important roles in the development of the disorder, which will be clearly understood only when the complex transactions that occur among these factors over time are better known.
3. In a majority of clinical cases diagnosed today, the etiology of the child's difficulties is unclear. Known etiological factors can be difficult to establish in individual cases and, when they are established, typically apply only to a minority of children with the disorder.

Biological Factors: Genetic Studies

Family Aggregation Studies. There is little doubt that the etiology of ADHD has a genetic component (Kuntsi & Stevenson, 2000). For example, ADHD is five to six times more prevalent in families of boys with the disorder than in families of control children (Biederman, Faraone, Keenan, Knee, & Tsuang, 1990), and three times more prevalent in families of girls with the disorder (Faraone et al., 2000). Similarly, biological parents of children with high levels of inattention and hyperactivity often had comparable problems when they were children (Loney, Paternite, Schwartz, & Roberts, 1997) or have such problems as adults (Epstein et al., 2000). Siblings of children with ADHD are also more likely to have the disorder than siblings of average children (Barkley, 1996). In sum, a child with ADHD is much more likely than an average child to have a relative who also has ADHD. This finding does not demonstrate genetic transmission, obviously; it could conceivably reflect nongenetic influences, such as the fact that parents with the disorder tend to raise children who behave like them. However, twin and adoption studies indicate that this familial contribution is not simply environmental.

Twin Studies. Monozygotic (identical) twins have a concordance rate for the disorder that is two to three times higher than that of dizygotic (fraternal) twins. In a study conducted by Gilger, Pennington, and DeFries (1992), 81% of monozygotic twin pairs had ADHD, in comparison to 29% of dizygotic pairs. Likewise, when measures of inattention, hyperactivity, and impulsivity are used to assess the severity of the disorder (instead of whether the disorder is or is not present), the symptomatology of identical twins is more similar than that of fraternal twins (Hudziak, Rudiger, Neale, Heath, & Todd, 2000).

Adoption Studies. When they present symptoms of inattention, hyperactivity, and impulsivity, adopted children tend to resemble their biological parents to a greater extent than their adoptive ones. Similarly, adopted children of biological parents who have significant antisocial behavior problems have a higher probability of having symptoms of ADHD than adopted children of biological parents without a history of anti-social conduct (Thapar, Holmes, Poulton, & Harrington, 1999). This increased risk probably does not point to a direct link between the biological parents' antisocial problems and their children's ADHD symptoms; instead it is probably the result of the comorbidity of ADHD and aggressive and disruptive behaviors. This association is particularly strong when children of antisocial parents are adopted by families of low socioeconomic status or by families in which someone has a psychological disorder (Cadoret & Stewart, 1991). Thus, children who may be biologically vulnerable or at risk to develop the disorder are more likely to do so when they are raised in an environment where they are exposed to significant sources of stress (e.g., as a result of poverty or of living with someone with a mental illness).

Possible Genetic Mechanisms.   Faraone and colleagues (1999) looked for genetic similarities in parents with ADHD who had children with the disorder. They found evidence suggesting that the disorder may, in some cases, be transmitted on the gene that is responsible for the production of **dopamine.** Dopamine is a neurotransmitter that has been implicated in movement disorders, such as Parkinson's disease, alcoholism, and other psychological conditions. However, even though these researchers found the target dopamine gene more often in children with ADHD and in their parents than in control families, 58% of participants who had been diagnosed with ADHD did not have this gene. These results suggest that the dopamine gene, if it plays any role in the etiology of the disorder, does so in some cases only. This is a fruitful area of research that will undoubtedly contribute to a better understanding of the disorder as further advances are made. It is unlikely to show, however, that a single gene causes ADHD. Instead, several genes may compound their effects to make some children particularly vulnerable to the disorder, but the likelihood that this vulnerability will express itself in ADHD depends on the psychosocial environment in which these children grow up.

Biological Factors: Neurophysiological Studies

For more than two decades, various research teams have concentrated on the neurophysiological and neuropsychological characteristics of children with ADHD. Research has made great advances in this area, primarily because of modern neurological methods of investigation. These include tracing of **evoked potentials** and cerebral blood flow, and magnetic resonance imaging (MRI). These techniques make it possible to measure brain activity "live," as the child or adolescent completes a particular task known to require certain attentional, cognitive, or motor skills.

Evoked potentials are measurements of brain electrical activity in response to different stimulations. When children with ADHD are asked to complete tasks requiring sustained attention, such as watching for a light to appear on a computer screen, they show smaller evoked potentials than nonaffected children do. These differences, which are thought to indicate deficits in the prefrontal regions of the brain, are observable behaviorally in poor task performance among children with the disorder. Interestingly, task performance generally improves when these children are treated with *methylphenidate* (Ritalin), a medication commonly used to treat ADHD (see Treatment and Prevention) (Pliszka, Liotti, & Woldorff, 2000).

Magnetic resonance imaging (MRI) also is contributing to important advances in understanding of brain structures in children with ADHD. This technology allows researchers to take three-dimensional pictures of the brain and to compare them in children with and without the disorder. Results show that some areas of the brain differ in the two groups. For example, the *plana temporale* area of the right hemisphere, which identifies sounds and conducts analyses of auditory information, is often smaller in children with ADHD, as is the *corpus callosum* (the band of neurons that connects the right and left hemispheres) and the *caudate nucleus* (a region of the frontal lobes in which lesions lead to symptoms that closely resemble those of ADHD) (Hynd, Semrud-Clikeman, Lorys, Novey, & Eliopulos, 1990; Hynd, Semrud-Clikeman, Lorys, & Novey, 1991; Hynd et al., 1993). Similarly, some children with ADHD have decreased blood flow to the prefrontal area of the brain and, more specifically, to the caudate nucleus (Lou, Henriksen, & Bruhn, 1984).

Although neurophysiological studies are contributing to a greater understanding of the disorder, many of the reports available today are based on small sample sizes, and their results apply only to some of the children or adolescents studied. In addition, studies in this area have often failed to control for comorbidity. For example, Lou and colleagues (1984) found evidence of restricted blood flow in the frontal lobes of children with ADHD. However, the majority of their subjects also had significant language difficulties, thus making it impossible to attribute observed differences in these children specifically to their ADHD symptoms. Finally, and perhaps most important, this line of research does not allow us to establish cause and effect. ADHD may be as much the cause as the consequence of reported neurophysiological differences. This is an important point to remember, since subjects who participate in such studies have often had the disorder for several years and, in many cases, are taking (or have taken) different medications to manage their symptoms.

Biological Factors: Neuropsychological Studies

In a perspective that complements a neurophysiological approach, a number of neuropsychological studies suggest that the genetic vulnerability of some children with ADHD is not expressed directly, through the observable symptoms of the disorder; instead, it may be expressed indirectly, through significant deficits in behavioral inhibition. Different etiological models implying such deficits have been proposed. The two major models are those of Quay (1997) and of Barkley (1997, 2000).

Quay's Model. Herbert Quay (1997) proposed a popular neuropsychological model to explain the origin of ADHD and other disruptive behavior problems. This model applies only to the predominantly hyperactive-impulsive type and to the combined type of ADHD. It assumes that the individual differences among children in social, emotional, and instrumental situations reflect the complementary activity of three neurobiological systems: a **behavioral activation system,** a **behavioral inhibition system,** and a nonspecific arousal system (see Chapter 2). According to Quay, a dysfunctional behavioral inhibition system is responsible for the symptoms of children with ADHD. Under normal circumstances, this system enables children to stop what

they are doing and increases their level of nonspecific arousal, so that they can pay attention to their surroundings and plan their behavior accordingly. In children with ADHD, however, the behavioral inhibition system is "weak" or underperforming. Consequently, they fail to slow down or to stop regularly to scan their environment and, if necessary, redirect their attention and activity onto relevant stimuli (Quay, 1997).

Support for Quay's model comes mainly from experimental tasks in which children have to respond quickly and correctly to computer-generated stimuli (e.g., Cepeda, Cepeda, & Kramer, 2000; Schachar, Mota, Logan, Tannock, & Klim, 2000). As they work to complete such tasks, they have to pay attention to an auditory signal that tells them either to stop responding temporarily and wait for another signal (stop-signal procedure) or to change task (change-signal procedure). Compared to average children, children with ADHD, predominantly hyperactive-impulsive type, find it much more difficult to stop rapidly what they are doing or to change task in response to the auditory signal. This is particularly true of children who have problems at home and school, rather than in one setting only, suggesting that inhibition difficulties may be related to symptom severity. Results show also that these difficulties (1) cannot be explained by lack of attention on the part of children with the disorder, since they attend to events on the screen as well as their average peers do; (2) cannot be explained by a lack of motivation, because these difficulties are obvious even when affected children are rewarded each time they succeed in inhibiting their response; and (3) are specific to children with ADHD only (the same difficulties are not found in average children, or in children with conduct disorder, or in children with ADHD and comorbid conduct disorder).

Barkley's Model. Russell Barkley (1997, 2000) also proposed a neuropsychological model to explain the diverse symptomatology associated with the predominantly hyperactive-impulsive and the combined types of ADHD. According to Barkley, symptoms of ADHD stem from deficits in four executive functions. Specifically, the model assumes that, to adapt to the varying demands of their environment and to respond to their own changing needs and states, children rely on complementary processes of behavioral activation and in-hibition. That is, to meet the daily challenges they en-counter in a prosocial manner, children must know not only when and how to act (behavioral activation), but also when and how not to act (behavioral inhibition).

Barkley's model is built on the same premise as Quay's. However, it is more complex, in that it at-tempts to specify how dysfunctional processes of inhi-bition manifest themselves in observable symptoms. Barkley believes that functional inhibitory processes enable children not to respond as they would normally do under similar circumstances. Thus, there is a *delay* between an event—such as an environmental stimulus, a thought, or a feeling—and the child's reaction to it. Barkley hypothesizes further that inhibitory processes allow children to keep this delay free from distractions or other interferences, and to use it to plan what they will do next. For example, in a classroom setting, in-hibitory processes are at work whenever children have to respond orally to a series of questions. Some will blurt out answers without thinking, often interrupting and making mistakes. Others will want to respond as

quickly but will instead stop to consider what to say and check their answer to make sure it is correct before they ask to speak.

Figure 7.3 outlines Barkley's model. As this fig-ure shows, inhibitory processes are assumed to control four executive functions, which in turn determine the extent to which people's behavior runs smoothly and in a manner that is responsive to their needs and goals, and to the demands of the environment. These complex processes develop gradually as a result of maturation, experience, and the acquisition of language. The exec-utive functions they control are essential to the social-ization of all human beings, because they enable children and adults to regulate and coordinate their ver-bal and motor behavior—in short, to manage what they say and do. These executive functions have the follow-ing features:

1. *Prolongation/working memory* holds current in-formation about the self and the environment in memory. It enables us to remember events long enough to anticipate the consequences that dif-

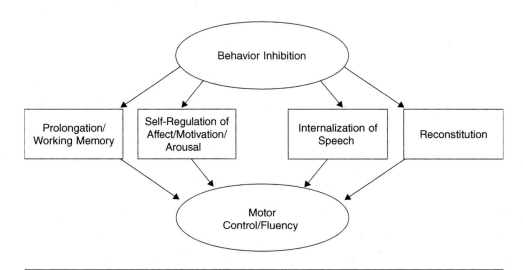

FIGURE 7.3   *Etiological Model Linking Behavioral Inhibition to Four Executive Functions Necessary for Smooth Coordination and Control of Motor and Verbal Behavior.* Evidence suggests that these functions are impaired in children with ADHD, in part because deficits in behavioral inhibition limit their ability to manage effectively what they say and do.

Source: From R. A. Barkley, "Behavioral Inhibition, Sustained Attention, and Executive Functions," *Psychological Bulletin 121* (1997), p. 73. Copyright 1997 by the American Psychological Association. Reprinted by permission.

ferent courses of action may have. In other words, working memory allows us to put a time delay—a prolongation—between action and reaction, and thus to avoid behaving automatically and often impulsively.

2. *Self-regulation of affect/motivation/arousal* has its roots in the prolongation created by behavioral inhibition. During the time delays that separate events and our reactions to them, this function enables us (a) to take some cognitive and emotional distance from these events; (b) to control our feelings instead of responding to them immediately; and (c) to take into account the desires and feelings of others as we consider how to respond. Also, by regulating our level of emotion and arousal, this function allows us to undertake tasks that require sustained efforts or in which rewards are delayed—in short, to be motivated.

3. *Internalization of speech* provides us with a complex tool for monitoring and managing what we do, thereby helping us plan, organize, and carry out our various activities. As they grow up, children learn to control much of their behavior by talking to themselves, first aloud and later through private, internalized speech. Over time, internalized speech becomes crucial for the development of problem solving and moral reasoning.

4. *Reconstitution* enables us to analyze various elements of a situation and to combine them in different ways to adapt our behavior to the changing requirements of our environment. This executive function, which operates in close cooperation with the other three, "consists of two interacting processes: analysis (taking apart) and synthesis (recombining)" (Barkley, 2000, p. 1067). Reconstitution allows us to analyze events cognitively in order to weigh the risks and benefits of possible courses of action.

The evidence presented throughout this chapter shows that children with ADHD face major difficulties in each of these four areas. In addition, a growing number of studies provide direct support for the model. For example, Clark, Prior, and Kinsella (2000) found that

executive function deficits were specific to adolescents with ADHD; these authors did not find such deficits in average adolescents or in adolescents with conduct disorder or with ADHD and comorbid conduct disorder. Comparable results have been obtained with children (Schachar et al., 2000). However, as Barkley (1997, 2000) is careful to stress, this evidence does not yet provide a systematic evaluation of the links between the four executive functions central to the model and ADHD symptoms. In other words, the model remains to be rigorously tested.

Biological Factors: Toxins and Foods

The role that toxic products, such as lead, may play in the development and evolution of the disorder has drawn considerable attention (e.g., Fergusson, Fergusson, Horwood, & Kinzett, 1988). Evidence shows that there is a small but statistically significant link between lead poisoning and ADHD. However, this link has been found only in a small minority of cases and in the presence of other variables, such as poverty and inadequate housing. In other words, lead poisoning may play a causal role in the symptoms of some children with ADHD, but the majority of them do not have elevated lead levels. Similarly, most children who suffer from lead poisoning do not have the disorder (Barkley, 1996).

Many people believe also that ADHD is linked to certain foods or to an unbalanced diet. For example, Feingold (1975) and his followers claimed for years that a diet too rich in sugar or in foods containing artificial colors, additives, or preservatives caused the disorder. This and similar theories tend to attract considerable attention in the popular press, because they offer an appealingly simple solution to families who are distressed by their children's complex problems. However, research does not support these theories. For example, in a detailed review of studies investigating the possible link between sugar and hyperactivity, Milich, Wolraich, and Lindgren (1986) reported that a majority of controlled studies did not find a significant association between sugar and hyperactivity, and those that did often obtained results showing that sugar may improve the behavior of children with ADHD as often as it worsens it.

Biological Factors: Prenatal and Birth Complications

Some clinical accounts note that mothers of children with ADHD experienced more complications in the course of pregnancy or at the time of delivery than mothers of average children. However, this association is found in only a small subset of children with the disorder (Gross-Tsur, Shalev, & Amir, 1991).

Family Factors

Coercive Family Processes.   The neuropsychological evidence reviewed above may inadvertently give the impression that psychosocial factors play little or no etiological role in ADHD—that the disorder is essentially a biological condition. This would be mistaken. For example, the interactions between children with ADHD and their immediate family have been the focus of much research. The family interactions of children with the disorder closely resemble those of children with oppositional defiant disorder (see Chapter 8), especially in early childhood. Studies generally agree on several points (Johnston & Mash, 2001):

1. Conflict is common in families of children with ADHD, in large part because these children are agitated, noisy, and demanding, and require constant direction and supervision. Conflict is often aggravated by the fact that children with ADHD do not accept limits easily and disobey frequently, provoking anger and other negative reactions in parents and siblings.
2. Mothers of children with ADHD are more directing, more critical, less encouraging, and less affectionate than mothers of average children. These mothers tend also to ignore children with ADHD when they act appropriately, probably because they fear that any attention may provoke misbehavior.
3. Mother-child conflicts are particularly frequent in structured situations in which children are expected to complete a specific task, such as homework. Conflicts occur less often when the same children are engaged in free play or in other activities in which fewer limits are imposed. In such situations, mother-child conflicts are probably not more frequent than they are in families of average children.
4. Mothers tend to be more directive and negative toward boys with ADHD, but reward them more often than girls with the disorder. Otherwise, there are few differences in family interactions as a function of the child's gender.
5. Although family conflicts tend to decrease over time, they remain more frequent in families of adolescents with the disorder than in average families, especially when oppositional defiant problems are also present (Barkley, Fischer, Edelbrock, & Smallish, 1991; Edwards, Barkley, Laneri, Fletcher, & Metevia, 2001).

A Family System in Conflict.   The presence of a child with ADHD usually disturbs the entire family system. You will recall that Bobby's parents often disagreed on how to respond to his outbursts—his mother believing that he should be handled firmly, his father advocating a more lenient approach because he remembered being like his son when he was a child. Such disagreements regularly lead to numerous inconsistencies in the way that children with ADHD are raised, further aggravating their difficulties. In a study of boys with the disorder, Buhrmester and associates (Buhrmester, Camparo, Christensen, Gonzalez, & Hinshaw, 1992) illustrate how such inconsistencies can disturb the entire family. As you would probably expect, the mothers of these boys were often coercive as they attempted to control them. The same was true of their fathers, but only when mothers were also present. In such triadic situations—when mother, father, and son were together—fathers tended to demand as much, if not more, of their children than their partners did. When mothers were absent, however, fathers were much less coercive toward their sons. In other words, this study suggests that mothers of sons with the disorder have a more negative relationship with them than fathers when they are observed in pairs (that is, when mother and son, or father and son, are together); but that this is not true when all three of them are observed together. Such inconsistencies can only contribute to the difficulties of children with ADHD, or at least boys.

Such family conflicts are particularly severe and most likely to be chronic when children with ADHD are also oppositional, defiant, and aggressive. In his review of the literature, Barkley (1996) actually concludes that these conflicts stem more often from a comorbid oppositional defiant or conduct disorder than from ADHD itself. This conclusion is supported by the findings in a study of elementary school children, which showed that youth with ADHD and a comorbid disruptive behavior disorder caused higher levels of parenting stress (as reported by mothers) than youth with ADHD only or average children (August et al., 1996).

The Family as a Developmental Context. Children with ADHD play an active role in family conflict—often from an early age. Specifically, early temperamental characteristics—such as poor attentional focus, demandingness, and irritability—predict development of the disorder, especially in children who are also exposed to adverse psychosocial factors in their growing years. For example, in a longitudinal follow-up of children from birth to 11, Carlson, Jacobvitz, and Sroufe (1995) studied the variables that best predicted high levels of distractibility at age 3½, and of hyperactivity between ages 6 and 8 and at age 11. Results showed that development of the disorder in middle childhood depended closely on the child's early temperamental characteristics, as well as on the quality of maternal care and on the social and emotional support that mothers received from other adults.

Besides the child's own characteristics and the family's daily interactions, environmental factors can cause or intensify conflict in families of children with ADHD. These factors include parental antisocial behavior (especially in fathers), drug or alcohol abuse, marital conflict and domestic violence, parental psychopathology, and maternal social isolation. Mash and Johnston (1990) showed that mothers of children with the disorder are often highly stressed and have marked feelings of depression and low self-esteem. In many cases, these feelings are chronic; these mothers continue to express them even when their children become adolescents (Barkley et al., 1991).

Parental, especially maternal, stress probably reflects and also contributes to the behavior problems of children with ADHD, as do other adverse factors often observed in their families. For example, in an eight-year longitudinal study of families of children with the disorder, Barkley and associates (1990) found that fathers had changed employment twice as often as in average families; that mothers had separated or divorced three times as often; and that the families themselves had moved four times as often. It would obviously be naïve to conclude from this or similar studies that family instability by itself causes ADHD, since children with the disorder probably contribute to that instability as much as they are affected by it. Rather, researchers and clinicians generally agree that the family serves as a major developmental context for *all* of its members. In that context, these and other psychosocial factors influence and are themselves influenced by child characteristics and by daily family interactions—thus determining together whether the disorder will manifest itself and, if it does, how it will evolve.

Social and Cultural Factors

As we showed earlier, children who manifest several symptoms of ADHD or the disorder itself rapidly face two new challenges in first grade and beyond: peer rejection and learning difficulties (see Associated Characteristics; Comorbidity). Although these challenges are a consequence rather than a cause of the child's problems, they invariably contribute to their aggravation. In many cases, they also lead to a referral for psychological evaluation and to a formal diagnosis of the disorder.

Treatment and Prevention

I do not love him because he is good, but because he is my little child.

—Rabindranath Tagore

Considerable efforts have been made to develop treatments for ADHD, but professionals still do not agree on which approach (or combination of approaches) is most effective (AACAP, 1997a). This lack of agreement reflects two important facts, which apply to other psychological disorders as well. First, because children and adolescents with ADHD have symptoms that vary considerably in nature, frequency, and intensity, it is unlikely that they would all respond favorably to only one or two types of intervention. Second, clinical psychologists, psychiatrists, family therapists, and other professionals working in this area bring different perspectives to bear on intervention, and thus contribute to the development of different treatments for the disorder.

Knowledge is also limited because most treatment and prevention studies include elementary school–age boys who (1) have the predominantly hyperactive-impulsive or combined type of ADHD and (2) have at least one comorbid psychological disorder (MTA Cooperative Group, 1999). Only a few such studies are relevant to the inattentive type of ADHD, which may be more common in girls, or to adolescents and young adults (National Institutes of Health Consensus Development Conference, 2000). Thus, although there is a vast literature on the treatment of ADHD, its findings are most relevant only to a subgroup of children with the disorder.

We will describe four types of treatment commonly prescribed for children with ADHD: (1) parent training, (2) intensive behavior modification, (3) pharmacological interventions, and (4) alternative treatments.

Parent Training

One of the most widely studied interventions for children with ADHD is **parent training** (Barkley, 1998). This intervention, which has its roots in a behavioral approach to the etiology and treatment of psychological disorders, is designed to teach caregivers to modify the *antecedents* and *consequences* they provide for their children's desirable and undesirable behavior. For example, parental reports and home observations may show that a 9-year-old boy with ADHD is allowed to stop doing his homework whenever he becomes frustrated and starts to fidget. Parent training would teach parents to recognize that this consequence rewards their son's inappropriate behavior. It would also provide them with alternatives designed to reduce the child's fidgeting and other hyperactive symptoms, and to teach him to complete his homework in a certain amount of time. For example, parents

may be instructed to break a thirty-minute homework period into five-minute segments, to check the child's progress after each segment, to help the child as needed, and to praise the child for consistent attention and effort. Parents may also be trained to respond to procrastination, arguing, and other negative behaviors by removing playtime and other privileges, and by punishing the child.

A common punishment used in parent training is **time-out.** The purpose of time-out is to remove the child from pleasurable activities and from the company of others for a brief period of time. The child is asked to sit quietly in an area of the house where there is little or no stimulation, and parents and siblings are instructed to ignore the child until time-out is complete. If the child goes to time-out without fussing and sits there quietly, the punishment is over as soon as the specified time has expired. If the child refuses to go to time-out or fusses in the time-out area, time is added to the procedure until the child calms down and sits quietly as instructed. Once time-out is complete, parents may briefly discuss the events that led to the punishment, to help the child avoid future time-outs by behaving appropriately. Although time-out can be difficult to implement in households in which parents and children are not used to consistent rules and discipline, this form of punishment is very effective in reducing the symptoms of ADHD (Herbert, 1989).

Effective parent-training programs do not focus only on implementing clear and predictable consequences for desirable and undesirable child behavior. They also attempt to modify the environmental conditions that precede such behavior—that is, the commands or instructions parents give to children with ADHD (Barkley, 1998). These parents often complain that they have to ask their children to do the same things over and over again because they ignore or deliberately disobey them. However, in such cases, careful observation commonly shows that parents do not command effectively. For example, the mother of a 7-year-old boy with ADHD complained that she had to get him up at 5:00 A.M. on school days because she had "to remind him a thousand times of all the things he has to do to get ready for school." Observations conducted on three separate mornings showed that this mother gave her son long lists of ineffective commands, which she often screamed from another room: "Are you getting dressed? Oh, and don't forget to make your bed and to get your school bag ready. Hurry up, you're going to be late for breakfast." Her son, who was only half awake then, ignored most of these commands, in large part because he was too disorganized to stay on task for any length of time. For several weeks in the parent-training program, the mother worked on issuing one-step commands, avoiding chains of commands, and making sure that she had her son's full attention whenever she issued an instruction. Over time, the child became more compliant with the morning routine and took less time to complete it. These positive changes were reinforced daily and weekly through small rewards, such as playing a game with Mom, watching a special video with Dad, or choosing a special dessert. In this and in many other cases, parent training has the threefold effect of reducing parental stress, giving children a chance to succeed at tasks at which they have failed in the past, and improving the overall quality of the parent-child relationship.

Finally, with school-age children, parent-training programs often include a classroom component. In many cases, clinicians work directly with the child's parents and teacher to develop an intervention plan in which desirable behavior is rewarded and undesirable behavior is ignored or punished. This plan seeks to implement consistent rules at home and school, and often includes the use of a **daily report card** (see Figure 7.4, p. 196). As its name implies, this is a simple form to track a child's progress on a limited number of treatment goals. At the end of each day, the teacher completes the form and sends it home in the child's assignment folder. The card allows for regular communication between home and school, and enables parents to reward the child's positive school behavior as part of their overall behavior management plan.

Although parent training is one of the most effective psychosocial interventions available today, it has some significant limitations. First, parent-training programs take a considerable amount of time and energy. They often involve a minimum of ten to twenty weekly sessions, as well as some follow-up appointments, and require caregivers to monitor their children's behavior and to provide them with consistent, appropriate consequences on a daily basis (Barkley, 1998). Not surprisingly, almost 50% of parents drop

out of parent training against professional advice (Pelham & Waschbusch, 1999). Second, most programs are not free, and most health insurance plans provide only limited coverage for psychological disorders; as a result, the cost of such programs may further discourage families from remaining in parent training for an extended period of time (Smith, Waschbusch, Willoughby, & Evans, 2000).

Intensive Behavior Modification

Parent training may not be enough to help children with severe and chronic ADHD symptoms. To meet the needs of these youth, intensive ADHD treatment programs have been developed. One of the best known is the Summer Treatment Program developed by Pelham and associates (1996). This 45-hour-per-week, eight-week program is based on the premise that intensive summer intervention followed by clinical services during the school year is likely to be most effective for youth with persistent difficulties. The program is run like a summer camp. However, it offers an unusually high staff-to-child ratio (5 staff members for every 12 children) and provides each participant with two hours of individualized classroom instruction every day. In addition, trained staff members monitor each child's activities throughout the day as part of a **contingency management program.** Contingency management programs are intensive behavior modification plans that are individually tailored to enable participants to earn points for appropriate target behaviors (and usually to lose points for inappropriate behaviors). Points can later be exchanged for group activities, such as field trips, as well as for privileges and other rewards. Furthermore, because the peer interactions of children with ADHD are often problematic, participants in the Summer Treatment Program take part in social skills training and in group activities that require them to work or play cooperatively with other campers. Finally, to ensure that gains made at camp are maintained after the children go home, parents of youth in the program are involved in a parent-training program. Each family is then followed through an outpatient clinic during the school year; and, if necessary, steps are taken to work with the child's teacher to set up a behavior management program in the classroom.

		Goal Met?	
Child's name	Today's date: _____		

Homework goals:

Brings assignment book home*   Yes   No

Brings home necessary materials to complete assignments*   Yes   No

Evening goal:

Between 8:00 pm and 9:00 pm, when told by a parent   Yes   No
to "occupy himself," he does so

Comments:

*If [child's name] is off school due to illness or school closing, he can earn up to **two "yes"** by doing two of the following in the place of his regular daily goals:

1. Does his homework (if he has homework to do)   Yes   No

2. Spends 1/2 hour studying and practicing spelling   Yes   No

3. Spends 1/2 hour reading   Yes   No

X_____   X_____
        Teacher   Parent

FIGURE 7.4 *A Daily Report Card.* This is an example of a daily report card used in the treatment of a 12-year-old boy with ADHD. The child had significant attentional and organizational problems, and was repeatedly in conflict at home and school for failing to complete his homework. This simple card helped him to become better organized, and facilitated clear communication between home and school. Unlike similar daily report cards, this one also included a home component to teach the child to occupy himself appropriately in the evening. At the end of every week, the child tallied the number of times he had met each of the goals on the card. He earned a reward, such as going out to eat with his family, if he had met the program goals a predetermined number of times.

Children with ADHD who participate in the Summer Treatment Program are involved in daily group activities designed—among other things—to teach them to work and play cooperatively with their peers.

Not surprisingly, the Summer Treatment Program is expensive, in terms of the time and financial investment required of families. (In 1997, the program cost $2,500 per child.) Consequently, it is not an option for many children with ADHD. However, for those who take part in it, results show that it is almost twice as effective as parent training alone and that, unlike less intensive programs, the dropout rate is extremely low (Pelham & Waschbusch, 1999). Although this result is encouraging, this study also found that the behavior of a majority of participants still remains significantly worse than that of average youth. In other words, the best-developed and researched programs in this area bring important benefits to many affected children but do not always bring them to a normal level of functioning.

Pharmacological Interventions

Stimulants are the medication of choice for youth with ADHD (AACAP, 1997a; NIH, 2000). The most common of these medications are *methylphenidate,* sold under the brand name Ritalin, and *amphetamine,* sold under brand names such as Adderall and Dexedrine. They are members of a class of drugs known as **psychostimulants.** These drugs increase central nervous system activity in parts of the brain where youth with ADHD may be understimulated. A considerable amount of research conducted over the past sixty years highlights the effectiveness of stimulants in reducing impulsivity and inattention in children and adolescents with ADHD (Barkley, 1998). This conclusion was confirmed in a large-scale treatment study that took place in several research centers across the United States (MTA Cooperative Group, 1999). The study, which worked intensively with almost 600 children for fourteen months and then followed them up longitudinally, compared their responses to one of four interventions:

- *Medication treatment.* Children in this condition began with a 28-day, *double-blind, daily-switch placebo trial,* to determine which type of stimulant medication and dosage were most appropriate for them. This procedure ensured that parents, teachers, and researchers did not know on which day the children were receiving a stimulant and on which day they were receiving a placebo. At the end of the trial, records of the children's behavior on drug and placebo days were compared, in order to select the most appropriate medication and dosage for each child.

Children in this condition received no additional treatment, except that they saw their prescribing physician for half-hour monthly meetings to review their response to medication.

- *Behavioral treatment.* Children in this condition participated in intensive behavioral programming that included parent training, school-based intervention, and the eight-week summer treatment program described above.
- *Combined treatment.* Children in this condition received the components of the behavioral and medication treatments.
- *Community treatment.* In this condition, children were assessed by the researchers, but their families were then sent into the community to seek whatever treatment they deemed appropriate. Most children in this group received stimulant medication (67%). Some families sought psychosocial treatments in addition to or instead of medication, although the exact nature of these treatments was not specified.

Results of this landmark study show that children who received stimulant medication or the combined treatment improved as much as or more than children receiving behavioral treatment alone on nineteen measures tracked by the researchers. The MTA group's long-term follow-up of these children should permit more definitive conclusions to be drawn about the efficacy of each of these interventions. However, these results have clearly come as a surprise to proponents of behavioral interventions for youth with ADHD, who did not expect children in the medication condition to do as well as children who participated in the much more intensive psychological intervention. It is possible that treatment gains made by children in the behavioral or combined conditions may ultimately surpass and outlast those made by children in the medication condition. In addition, some evidence suggests that parent-training and behavior modification programs may reduce the amount of stimulant medication children with ADHD need to show significant behavioral improvements (e.g., Kolko, Bukstein, & Barron, 1999). For the time being, however, this study shows that psychostimulants are as effective as more demanding behavioral interventions to reduce the symptoms of youth with the disorder.

Psychostimulants are not only effective in decreasing impulsivity and inattention; they tend also to improve academic performance and to reduce oppositional and aggressive symptoms that are often comorbid with ADHD (Connor, Barkley, & Davis, 2000). In fact, according to the American Academy of Child and Adolescent Psychiatry (1997a), stimulants reduce hyperactivity, distractibility, impulsivity, talking, off-task behavior, anger, verbal aggression and bossiness with peers, and noncompliance and oppositional behavior with adults. They also improve attention (especially to boring tasks), short-term memory, academic accuracy, amount of work completed, handwriting, fine motor control, peer social status, and parent-child interactions.

Nonetheless, the use of stimulant medications to treat ADHD does raise questions. First, approximately 30% of youth with ADHD do not respond to stimulants. Nonresponders are often prescribed other medications, but there is little evidence that those medications are appropriate or effective. Second, many youth who are prescribed stimulants do not take them or take them irregularly. Third, psychostimulants can lead to reduced sleep and appetite and other undesirable effects. In particular, they can have a **rebound effect,** in which children show "increased excitability, activity, talkativeness, irritability, and insomnia, beginning 4 to 15 hours after a dose" (AACAP, 1997a, p. 95S; Sherman & Hertzig, 1991). This effect can usually be countered with a small dose of stimulants after school or with another medication to help calm the child's evening agitation, although many parents are understandably reluctant to give their children drugs to control their behavior throughout the day. Fourth, stimulant medications do not teach children with ADHD to behave appropriately. They only control several of their symptoms as long as they are taken consistently. Most important, the changes in behavior brought about by stimulants do not appear to improve the long-term prognosis of children and adolescents with the disorder, leading many researchers and clinicians to argue that they are useful, but only in combination with intensive psychosocial intervention (Weiss & Hechtman, 1993).

Finally, a growing number of professionals and social critics are raising concerns that too many children and adolescents are medicated to control their behavior—many of them with psychostimulants. In support of such concerns, data show that sales of Ritalin and other psychostimulants increased substantially during the 1990s, and that they are prescribed much more often in the United States than in any other country (see Figure 7.5). For example, a survey of almost 7,000 parents in one North Carolina county found that psychostimulants were widely used to treat both boys and girls with ADHD. However, they were more likely to be prescribed to European American than to African American or Hispanic children with the disorder. This discrepancy may reflect a variety of factors that remain to be studied, such as socioeconomic disparities among these different groups or cultural differences in the acceptability of medication to control behavior (Rowland et al., 2001).

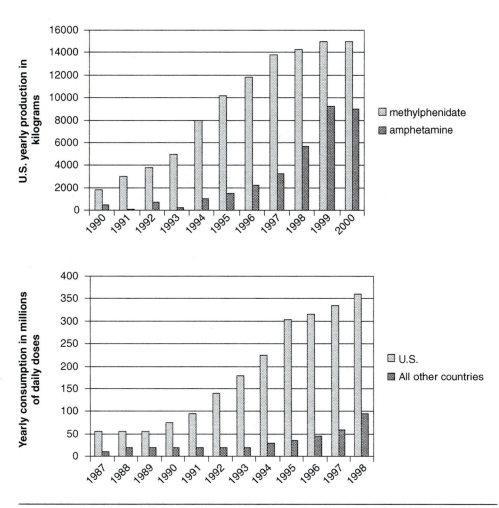

FIGURE 7.5 *Documenting the Widespread Use of Psychostimulants in the United States.*
The first graph shows the rise in production and use of methylphenidate and amphetamine in the United States from 1990 to 2000. The second graph shows that the United States produces and consumes about 85% of the yearly world production of methylphenidate (1987–1998 figures).
Source: U.S. Drug Enforcement Agency (2000), p. 3.

More generally, the U.S. Drug Enforcement Agency (2000) reports that there has been a fivefold increase in the number of prescriptions written for ADHD between 1991 and 2000. Many of them are apparently written for very young children, even though these drugs are not approved for use in children under the age of 6.

It would be a mistake to use this evidence to question the effectiveness or safety of psychostimulants. Rather, what must be questioned is the common practice of prescribing stimulants to control behavior on the basis of only a limited evaluation of how the child actually behaves. When a carefully conducted assessment shows that a child meets diagnostic criteria for ADHD, the weight of the evidence indicates clearly that stimulant medication may be able to alleviate the child's difficulties.

Alternative Treatments

Given that children with ADHD can be very disruptive and that their symptoms are often chronic, it is not surprising that many families turn to alternative treatments for help. They may seek such treatments because they are dissatisfied with conventional treatment approaches, or are unwilling to participate in an intensive behavioral intervention, or are reluctant to have their children take prescription medications. Advocates of "natural," homeopathic, and other unresearched alternatives abound, and many unsubstantiated claims have been made and continue to be made in this area (AACAP, 1997a; Waschbusch & Hill, 2001). We are regularly consulted by parents who spent large sums of money on such treatments before seeking professional advice.

Mega-doses of vitamins are often prescribed as an alternative treatment for ADHD as well. Unlike most dietary programs, which generally do little good but cause little harm, vitamins taken far in excess of recommended daily allowances are not only ineffective but can also be toxic (AACAP, 1997a; Waschbusch & Hill, 2001).

Prevention

At present, no one knows how to prevent ADHD. However, a number of researchers are actively working with young children who are at risk of developing the disorder, as well as with their parents, in order to gain much-needed knowledge in this area. For example, in a community study conducted with at-risk preschoolers and their families, Barkley and associates (2000) found that an intensive school intervention improved the children's classroom behavior. Unfortunately, this improvement was not accompanied by an increase in academic achievement or by comparable gains in other settings. Furthermore, this research team had great difficulty getting families to attend a free parent-training program. In fact, only 13% of caregivers attended a majority of the fourteen sessions offered. These findings suggest that, to be successful, prevention programs will have to devise effective ways of engaging caregivers in intervention efforts on behalf of their children, and of encouraging them to remain engaged throughout the program. Considerable work with at-risk children and their families remains to be done to create successful models of prevention.

Web Links

www.add.org (ADDA: National Attention Deficit
    Disorder Association)
www.chadd.org (CHADD: Children and Adults with
    Attention-Deficit/Hyperactivity Disorder)

www.nimh.nih.gov/publicat/adhd.cfm (National
    Institute of Mental Health Website for ADHD)
www.additudemag.com (Magazine for persons with
    ADHD)

8

Oppositional Defiant Disorder and Conduct Disorder

Conduct is three-fourths of our lives and its largest concern.
—Matthew Arnold

Children and adolescents with oppositional defiant disorder (ODD) and conduct disorder (CD) disturb, annoy, hurt, or victimize people around them in significant ways. Together with ADHD, discussed in Chapter 7, these conditions form the **disruptive behavior disorders.** The word *disruptive* can be used in a broad, descriptive sense, or in a narrower, clinical one. Descriptively, the word refers to behavior problems that are common in most children and adolescents. For example, at some time during development, most youth argue, disobey, provoke, fight, lie, and are verbally or physically aggressive. Such antisocial acts are unacceptable in most situations, but are not in themselves indicative of a psychological disorder. Clinically, the word *disruptive* refers to the presence of the same behaviors, but carried out to such extremes that they are indicative of a disorder. The word refers also to antisocial behaviors—such as repeated theft, assault, and rape—that are extremely rare or nonexistent in most young people.

Diagnosis of a disruptive behavior disorder requires the presence of several relatively well-defined behaviors for a minimum amount of time, as well as a clear indication that these behaviors are affecting not only others but also the child or adolescent's own development and adjustment. Because of these requirements, only a fairly small number of youth display a pervasive pattern of disruptive conduct severe enough to warrant a clinical diagnosis.

Children with **oppositional defiant disorder** display a pattern of opposition, disobedience, and defiance that usually leads to conflict with parents, siblings, teachers, and peers. **Conduct disorder** encompasses all of these behaviors, but also includes repeated violations of the basic rights of others and of social norms, standards, and rules. Consequently, CD is much more serious than ODD, because it often has major developmental *and* legal repercussions. Broadly speaking, ODD includes behaviors that, to a lesser degree, most children and adolescents exhibit in the course of development, whereas CD covers socially and legally proscribed behaviors that are not observed in a majority of children or adolescents.

For decades, these two disruptive behavior disorders—oppositional defiant disorder and conduct

Aggressive behavior is common in young children. However, in most cases it decreases with age. When aggression is severe or continues into adolescence, children may be identified as having disruptive and antisocial behavior problems.

disorder—have been the subjects of considerable research. Consequently, more empirical evidence is available in this area than in most others, although the bulk of this evidence pertains to boys; much less is known about these disorders in girls.

Historical Overview

The first accounts of what are now called disruptive and antisocial behavior problems date back to antiquity. Descriptions of undisciplined children can be found in religious and secular sources, such as the biblical books of Leviticus and Deuteronomy, and ancient Greek legends. For example, the Greek god Hermes had scarcely emerged from the womb when he began plotting to steal Apollo's cattle. Much more recently, in the New World, the Puritans regularly complained about the evil ways of youth, whose infractions were common given the strictness of their moral codes. And in classic English and American literature, Charles Dickens and Mark Twain gave prominent roles to resourceful but often delinquent characters in some of their best-known stories (see Box 8.1).

Disruptive and antisocial behaviors were also described in detail in the first textbooks of child and ado-

lescent psychopathology. In 1888, in a work entitled *La folie chez les enfants* (*Madness in Children*), the French physician Paul Moreau de Tours described several children who had what he called a "pathogenic character"— that is, a disorder that was as harmful to those around them as it was to themselves. One of them would likely meet our modern diagnostic criteria for CD:

E. D. is 13½ years. He was born in 1871. . . . The child was born easily, but he was small, weak, and sickly. Adequate care and country air made him quickly into a healthy child. At age 2, almost as soon as he started to walk and to speak, he developed an abnormal tendency towards spitefulness and teasing. . . . He enjoyed tormenting his parents. To worry them, he made them look for him everywhere, hid objects, or screamed so loud when his whims were not satisfied that he brought the neighbors running. These instincts only worsened until he was 6. At that time, he started to go to school, but after a few days, his unpleasant and malevolent character . . . was such a problem that it took all the teacher's energy to handle him and keep him under control. . . .

From his seventh year on, he started to profess ideas of independence that were inappropriate for his age. He took long walks instead of going to school. . . . Then little by little, his absences became longer, until

BOX 8.1 • *Two Famous Delinquent Characters: The Artful Dodger and Huckleberry Finn*

Charles Dickens's *Oliver Twist* and Mark Twain's *Huckleberry Finn* provide interesting perspectives on youth and delinquency in the nineteenth century. Dickens's Artful Dodger is a shrewd young fellow who makes his living picking pockets and stealing in the city of London. His American counterpart, Huckleberry Finn, has a solid reputation for disobedience, lying, stealing, and truancy. The Dodger and Huck undoubtedly would qualify for a diagnosis of CD today, since they both engage in a pervasive pattern of antisocial activities that harm others and limit their own functioning.

These characters are interesting for two reasons. First, they confirm that disruptive behaviors are not new and that the complaints many adults have about the youth of today are similar to what they were a century or so ago. Second, Dickens and Twain make it clear that their characters' antisocial conduct has its roots in what remains a major risk factor for many youth today: poverty. A mistreated orphan, the Dodger has never had a normal family life. His antisocial conduct is adaptive, allowing him to navigate through a treacherous world in order to survive. He is quick to assess Oliver Twist's own survival skills in that world: "You've been brought up bad. . . . Fagan [the head thief] will make something of you" (Dickens, 1837–8/1949, p. 132). Huck's story is similar. "Huckleberry Finn, son of the town drunkard . . . was idle, lawless, and vulgar, and bad. . . . Huckleberry came and went at his own free will. He slept on door-steps in fine weather, and in empty hogsheads in wet; he did not have to go to church or school, or call any being master" (Twain, 1884/1959, p. 35).

As we emphasize throughout this chapter, behavior regarded as disruptive and antisocial may be adaptive in certain situations. For the Dodger, a life of crime was probably far better than one of misery and starvation in a

HUCK AND HIS FATHER.

workhouse. For Huck, a life on the run was undoubtedly safer than one in the house of a drunken, abusive father at a time when children were considered their parents' property. Clearly, there are other ways—besides resorting to delinquency and crime—to survive in such circumstances; but much of what we judge to be disruptive and antisocial—and, more generally, abnormal—does depend to a large extent on the context in which we make that judgment.

Source: From M. Twain, *Adventures of Huckleberry Finn,* ed./ trans. V. Fische (Berkeley: University of California Press, 1987). Copyright 1987/2001 the Mark Twain Foundation. Reprinted by permission.

it was necessary in the evening to look for him outside. . . . This child, as I said, was malicious. Indeed, when he was very small, he sought to bite or scratch the people who tried to dress him or wanted to hug him. When he became older, he readily fought with other children of his age and sometimes even attacked older children. . . . One day . . . he had fun drowning small ducks one by one in a fountain. . . . At school everyone feared him. A consummate liar, he invented stories designed to disrupt and upset people wherever he could.

Heredity is unlikely to be involved: E. D. has two sisters—one older, the other younger—who enjoy perfect health. . . . His mother is very healthy and does not know anybody in her family who has a nervous or intellectual disorder. His father also has no hereditary antecedent. Rather, it is by hard work that his family has risen to an honorable position in Paris, where they are successful merchants (pp. 58–59).

A few years later, the famous American psychologist G. Stanley Hall devoted an entire chapter of his book on adolescence to "juvenile faults, immoralities, and crimes." He wrote:

> In all civilized lands, criminal statistics show two sad and significant facts: First there is a marked increase in crime at the age of 12 to 14, not in crimes of one kind, but of all kinds. . . . The second fact is that the proportion of juvenile delinquents seems to be everywhere increasing and crime is more and more precocious (1904, p. 325).

Hall's summary still applies today. Over the past decades, crime and delinquency among young people increased at an alarming rate in the United States, and did not begin to taper off until the late 1990s (U.S. Department of Justice, 1999). Although less extreme, the situation is hardly more encouraging in other Western countries, such as England, France, and Germany (Pain, Barrier, & Robin, 1997). We will emphasize throughout this chapter that only a minority of children and adolescents who engage in criminal or delinquent conduct have ODD or CD; however, the prevalence of these disorders has risen significantly over the last decades also, in parallel with the increases in aggression and violence just mentioned.

Definitions, Diagnostic Criteria, and Major Characteristics

Oppositional Defiant Disorder

> *Getting hit motivates me. It makes me punish the guy more. A fighter takes a punch, hits back with three punches.*
>
> —Roberto Duran, prizefighter

Table 8.1 presents the DSM-IV-TR diagnostic criteria for ODD. These criteria describe behaviors that are common in the course of social development, especially around ages 2 and 3, and again during adoles-

TABLE 8.1   *Oppositional Defiant Disorder: DSM-IV-TR Diagnostic Criteria*

A. A pattern of negativistic, hostile, and defiant behavior lasting at least 6 months, during which four (or more) of the following are present:

    (1) often loses temper

    (2) often argues with adults

    (3) often actively defies or refuses to comply with adults' requests or rules

    (4) often deliberately annoys people

    (5) often blames others for his or her mistakes or misbehavior

    (6) is often touchy or easily annoyed by others

    (7) is often angry and resentful

    (8) is often spiteful or vindictive

Note: Consider a criterion met only if the behavior occurs more frequently than is typically observed in individuals of comparable age and developmental level.

B. The disturbance in behavior causes clinically significant impairment in social, academic, or occupational functioning.

C. The behaviors do not occur exclusively during the course of a Psychotic or Mood Disorder.

D. Criteria are not met for Conduct Disorder, and, if the individual is age 18 years or older, criteria are not met for Antisocial Personality Disorder.

Source: American Psychiatric Association, *Diagnostic and Statistical Manual of Mental Disorders, Fourth Edition, Text Revision* (Washington, DC: American Psychiatric Association, 2000a). Copyright 2000 American Psychiatric Association. Reprinted with permission.

cence. Therefore, the disorder can be challenging to diagnose, since one cannot define precisely where normal conduct ends and ODD begins (see Empirical Validity). In most clinical cases, however, the child's disruptive behaviors are clearly excessive because of their frequency, severity, or duration—as Jackie's case illustrates.

Jackie is 6. She is referred to our clinic because she "rules the house" and refuses to go to bed at night. According to her parents, Jackie objects to most rules and instructions, even when they are very reasonable, and is hard to manage at home and at school. "She didn't come with an owner's manual," jokes her father, "so we came to see if by chance you can help us."

Two separate visits to the family's home illustrate the nature and extent of the child's difficulties. Jackie ignores many of her parents' commands or does the opposite of what they ask. At dinnertime, for example, she continues to watch television instead of coming to table as requested. After her mother's third, exasperated command to turn the television off, her father does so himself without a word. Jackie gets up immediately and, also without a word, turns the television back on. At that point, her mother tells her that she may watch the end of her show, as long as she comes to table as soon as it is over. Her parents begin eating and Jackie joins them a few minutes later without fussing. However, she refuses to eat what has been prepared, complaining instead and playing with her food. As her parents ignore her, she leaves the table and goes to the refrigerator, where she takes a yogurt that she begins eating while standing in the middle of the kitchen. Her parents exchange sighs of despair but do not intervene to get Jackie back to the table or to make her eat her meal.

Later that evening, Jackie takes her bath without problem, talking and singing happily while playing in the water. She takes a considerable time to get ready for bed, however, making up multiple excuses to delay the process. Obviously frustrated, her father tells her that she will not have her radio to fall asleep, as she does usually. Jackie loses her temper almost instantly and throws her slippers at her father in anger, while howling, "I want my radio, I want my radio." She finally goes to bed—without brushing her teeth, as she had been asked—but continues to whine and scream about her radio. Her parents attempt to ignore her angry tears. However, after approximately ten minutes, her father turns her radio on "to allow her to fall asleep." He explains to the observer that if he had not given in, Jackie would have continued to scream "for hours" to get her way.

A school observation and an interview with her teacher show that, although Jackie is not entirely rejected by her peers, she is often alone. The teacher explains that this is "because she always wants to be in charge. She is very bossy. . . . She often complains bitterly that nobody wants to play with her . . . but as soon as somebody does not do exactly what she wants, she becomes upset or starts calling the child names, and I must quickly intervene to calm things down. . . . I isolate her; I put her in the corner for a few minutes or at her desk. She obeys me. Personally, I don't have problems with her. . . . But it starts again the following day or a couple of days later. I don't want to exaggerate. She has good days when she plays well with the other kids. But she often gets the conflicts going. . . . She already has a bad reputation in the school, well deserved for the most part, unfortunately." . . .

Treatment focuses later on helping Jackie's parents to set clear behavioral goals for their daughter and to modify their parenting practices to achieve them. After multiple attempts to sabotage her parents' new approach, Jackie learns to go to bed without fuss and to obey a number of simple household rules. Thanks to her teacher's cooperation, Jackie makes similar progress at school, but over a longer period of time. Treatment ends after approximately eight months. As her father puts it, "I think we can do it alone, because she knows now who's the boss."

A diagnosis of ODD requires the presence of at least four negative or hostile behaviors. These behaviors reflect two overlapping problem areas: opposition and defiance.

Opposition.   Imagine the following scene, which we witnessed in our clinic:

Cynthia, who is 5, is playing nicely with her father. When her father asks her to pass him a small toy truck well within her reach, she refuses. Repeated requests are met with continued refusal and lead quickly to a temper tantrum, which lasts for 45 minutes. During her tantrum, Cynthia screams, punches, spits, kicks, and cries until she is too tired to continue.

Children with ODD actively resist restrictions or limitations on their activities, or even simple requests, no matter how reasonable or unavoidable they might be. For example, they may refuse to come to table, to go to bed, or to put on a heavy coat when it is snowing.

They also fail to take other people's perspective or wishes into account and to compromise. And when they are forced to obey or prevented from doing what they would like, they frequently have prolonged temper tantrums.

Defiance.   Children with ODD "test the limits" constantly, by ignoring or questioning what they are asked to do (or not do), and by deliberately contradicting or provoking others. They also seem to take pleasure in disturbing, annoying, teasing, or irritating others. Some authors talk of **aggression-related happiness** to describe a characteristic observed in highly aggressive children: from a young age, these children often appear happy and gleeful as they taunt or fight with adults or peers (Arsenio, Cooperman, & Lover, 2000). As a distressed mother once put it to us in tears:

You know the way boxers move their arms and fists in front of their opponents before they actually start fighting, like they're pumping themselves up and baiting and teasing the other guy. Well, that's Rusty! He reminds me all the time of a boxer. He's on the lookout for an argument and he will provoke you, like being rude or saying something nasty, or he'll just ignore you or do the opposite of what you want, and he'll keep it up, man, he'll keep it up until you fight with him. . . . It's so sad, you know, because he's not a monster, he's my son.

Not surprisingly, children with ODD can be particularly touchy and resentful, and often react very negatively when they themselves are provoked or teased. In addition, they lack tolerance and patience, and are easily frustrated by minor aggravations. Again, frustration results in frequent temper tantrums and in other disruptive behaviors, such as prolonged arguments or explosive verbal outbursts.

Most children with ODD blame others for their difficulties. They do not accept responsibility for their extreme actions, which they justify by claiming that others are unreasonable, unfair, or unkind. Their aggressive and disruptive behaviors, like the hostile interpretations they often make of the behaviors or intentions of others, usually lead to conflicts at home and beyond, as well as to social rejection. In each case, this pattern of conduct

has immediate negative repercussions on social and adaptive functioning, and compromises long-term development (Coie & Dodge, 1997).

As with many other disorders, the nature and extent of ODD depend on the social context in which the child is observed, and evaluations made in different situations or by different people often show little agreement. Thus, it is important to obtain information from multiple sources and to base a diagnosis of ODD on a comprehensive assessment of the child, if possible in two or more settings.

Conduct Disorder

> *Temper gets you in trouble. Pride keeps you there.*
> —Anonymous

Table 8.2 lists the DSM-IV-TR diagnostic criteria for CD. Read this table carefully; then look for symptoms of the disorder in Bob's case study.

Bob is 11. He is referred to our clinic by his mother, following an argument in which he punched her in the stomach. His mother describes him as "out of control" and explains that words, threats, or punishments do little to change his behavior. He ignores her more often than he fights with her openly, stays out late at night, and spends time with older boys, with whom his mother complains that he "skips school or gets up to no good." Bob is actually in danger of being expelled from school for truancy and repeated outbursts of aggression and violence toward other students.

A detailed history of his development indicates that Bob's problems go back to early childhood. His mother reports that he was a difficult, "fussy" baby and that, as a preschooler, he had to leave multiple daycare facilities because of his disobedient, defiant, and aggressive behavior. "He has always had trouble following instructions or doing what he is told, you know, as far back as I can remember, really." Bob has also had academic and behavior problems at school since kindergarten. He repeated third grade and is presently failing fifth grade. He was arrested for the first time at age 9, for assaulting a neighbor's child, with whom he had had an argument. He has since been arrested on two other occasions, once for assaulting

TABLE 8.2 *Conduct Disorder: DSM-IV-TR Diagnostic Criteria*

A. A repetitive and persistent pattern of behavior in which the basic rights of others or major age-appropriate societal norms or rules are violated, as manifested by the presence of three (or more) of the following criteria in the past 12 months, with at least one of these criteria present in the past 6 months:

Aggression to people and animals
(1) often bullies, threatens, or intimidates others

(2) often initiates physical fights

(3) has used a weapon that can cause serious physical harm to others (e.g., a bat, brick, broken bottle, knife, gun)

(4) has been physically cruel to people

(5) has been physically cruel to animals

(6) has stolen while confronting a victim (e.g., mugging, purse snatching, extortion, armed robbery)

(7) has forced someone into sexual activity

Destruction of property
(8) has deliberately engaged in fire setting with the intention of causing serious damage

(9) has deliberately destroyed others' property (other than by fire setting)

Deceitfulness or theft
(10) has broken into someone else's house, building, or car

(11) often lies to obtain goods or favors or to avoid obligations (i.e., "cons" others)

(12) has stolen items of nontrivial value without confronting a victim (e.g., shoplifting, but without breaking and entering; forgery)

Serious violations of rules
(13) often stays out at night despite parental prohibitions, beginning before age 13 years

(14) has run away from home overnight at least twice while living in parental or parental surrogate home (or once without returning home for a lengthy period)

(15) is often truant from school, beginning before age 13 years

B. The disturbance in behavior causes clinically significant impairment in social, academic, or occupational functioning.

C. If the individual is age 18 years or older, criteria are not met for Antisocial Personality Disorder.

Code type based on age at onset:
Conduct Disorder, Childhood-Onset Type: onset of at least one criterion characteristic Conduct Disorder prior to age 10 years

Conduct Disorder, Adolescence-Onset Type: absence of any criterion characteristic Conduct Disorder prior to age 10 years

Conduct Disorder, Unspecified-Onset Type: age at onset is not known

Specify severity:
Mild: few if any conduct problems in excess of those required to make the diagnosis *and* conduct problems cause only minor harm to others

Moderate: number of conduct problems and effect on others intermediate between "mild" and "severe"

Severe: many conduct problems in excess of those required to make the diagnosis *or* conduct problems cause considerable harm to others

Source: American Psychiatric Association, *Diagnostic and Statistical Manual of Mental Disorders, Fourth Edition, Text Revision* (Washington, DC: American Psychiatric Association, 2000a). Copyright 2000 American Psychiatric Association. Reprinted with permission.

another child and the other for dropping his pants in front of an elderly woman. Bob acknowledges each incident but reports no feelings of guilt or remorse, and adamantly maintains that he was not at fault, as he had been provoked every time. He minimizes also the seriousness of these incidents, stating repeatedly that "grownups love to exaggerate" and that "it's no big deal; I mean, the old lady freaked out, so what?"

Bob has problems in multiple areas but his mother believes that his relationship with her husband—Bob's stepfather—is at the heart of his difficulties. Bob's biological father suffered from schizophrenia and left the family when Bob was very young. Bob's mother remarried soon afterward. She reports that Bob has never liked his stepfather and that he tries to provoke him "at every chance possible. It's like his goal is to get Lance to hit him so he can get him out of the house. . . . He'll provoke him, he really will, and he'll yell, like 'go ahead and hit me so that I can get you out of here.' " [Bob's stepfather was actually removed from the house for a year for child abuse after he struck Bob in the stomach shortly after his eighth birthday.] *"So you see I feel like I am being pulled between the two of them and I am almost ready to give up on him [Bob]. It's sad, but it's the truth."* . . .

Bob makes minimal progress in therapy, stating bluntly that he does not want or need help, and that treatment is a "waste of time." He is placed in juvenile detention shortly after his twelfth birthday, following a gang arrest.

As this case illustrates, CD often has its origins in a pattern of oppositional and defiant behavior dating back to early and middle childhood. However, its scope and consequences are much worse than those of ODD—especially after puberty, when physical and sexual maturation create added opportunities and incentives for disruptive and antisocial behavior. As was true in Bob's case, fights, threats, and intimidation are frequent at home, at school, and in the community, as are callousness and cruelty to people and animals. Also common are theft, fraud, vandalism, and willful destruction of property (such as joyriding and damaging stolen property). Finally, youth with CD are often *not only perpetrators but also victims* of acts of violence, such as aggravated assault, rape, and murder. In the United States, violent acts such as these have particularly devastating—and deadly—consequences because of easy access to guns and other firearms (U.S. Department of Justice, 1999).

Like ODD, CD can be difficult to diagnose, for several reasons. First, some of its diagnostic criteria include covert behaviors, such as lying and stealing, that others cannot always identify reliably. Second, as Bob did, young people with CD are likely to minimize or deny their difficulties. Third, the disorder can vary considerably over time and from one context to another. As we remarked earlier, one must obtain information from different sources before making a diagnosis, even though the child or adolescent may not be trustworthy, and the family and school may have only limited knowledge of the extent of the problems.

Personality Characteristics of Youth with CD. The personality characteristics of young people with CD are similar to those of children with ODD. They lack patience and tolerance for frustration, and can be particularly touchy and resentful. They are proud, do not take kindly to criticism, and are prone to anger and violent outbursts. Their behavior can also be unpredictable and explosive, especially youth who are both aggressive and rejected by peers. They often blow up at minor aggravations that others do not find upsetting; and, in conflict situations, they do little to calm things down but instead heighten tension further (Coie & Lenox, 1994). More generally, youth with CD fail to take responsibility for their actions: they blame others for the conflicts they cause, or explain their outbursts by saying that others simply get what they deserve. An adolescent girl with CD may explain that another girl's remark started the fight, even though she threw the first punch and continued punching long after her opponent had given up. Afterward, she may add that even if she started the fight, "That little slut never shuts her f—— mouth; she had it coming and she knew it!"

As this last quote shows, children and adolescents with behavior problems in general, and CD in particular, often appear tough and heartless. They lack empathy from an early age, especially if they are boys (Hughes, White, Sharpen, & Dunn, 2000). They have little consideration for others, and show no remorse or guilt when confronted with the consequences of their actions. When they appear remorseful, their sincerity is frequently called into question, for they are often more concerned with avoiding punishment than with changing their attitudes and behavior.

Major Breakdown in the Socialization Process. The multiple problems associated with CD appear when adults who exercise control over young people— typically at home and at school—are unable to do so. The parents have little or no influence on the behavior of children and adolescents with CD. These youth ignore parental instructions and rules, and often leave home and stay out without permission. The same is true of the school. Teachers and peers reject youth with CD, because they are afraid of them and disapprove of their conduct, especially when they are aggressive. Not surprisingly, most of them do poorly in school and, when they are not suspended or expelled for their disruptive and antisocial conduct, are often truant (Coie & Dodge, 1997).

Subtypes. The DSM-IV-TR specifies age and severity criteria for CD, giving a developmental and dimensional aspect to its categorical approach. The age-of-onset criterion establishes whether the disorder began during childhood or adolescence. This distinction is important in determining the developmental trajectories and prognosis of the disorder, because it is widely recognized that children who manifest a number of CD symptoms before age 10 run a high risk of continuing to have serious antisocial problems in adolescence and beyond (Moffitt, 1993). The severity criterion makes it possible to specify whether the disorder is mild, moderate, or severe. This criterion has not been subjected to systematic validity research and lacks precision, calling primarily on the subjective judgment of the person making the diagnosis.

From "Fledgling Psychopath" to Antisocial Personality Disorder. Insensitivity, harshness, and lack of remorse are particularly prominent characteristics of a small subset of children with severe, early-onset CD. These children exhibit disruptive, impulsive, and aggressive conduct *in combination with* callous and unemotional personality traits, such as a disturbing lack of empathy and consideration for others. For example, they may justify their cruelty to people or animals by saying that they "just wanted to have a good time" or that it was "fun" to hurt them. These "fledgling psychopaths," as Lynam (1996) calls them, do not represent a recognized subtype of the disorder. However, they are the focus of growing interest on the part of researchers and clinicians, because their callousness may develop regardless of the quality of parenting they receive, something that is not true for a majority of children with CD (Wootton, Frick, Shelton, & Silverthorn, 1997); in addition, their psychological profile may correspond to that of adults with antisocial personality disorder (Blair, Colledge, Murray, & Mitchell, 2001; Frick & Ellis, 1999). This disorder cannot be diagnosed before 18 because it is believed to reflect a chronic and pervasive personality style not present in childhood or adolescence. "Fledgling psychopaths" are

rare, fortunately. However, as the case of Lucas illustrates, their difficulties begin early and can have devastating consequences for them and their victims.

Lucas is 4. He is referred to us by the preschool he has been attending. A detailed evaluation based on different sources of information (such as parent and teacher interviews, questionnaires, and school observations) results in a diagnosis of early-onset CD accompanied by multiple symptoms of ADHD (see Chapter 7).

Lucas's teacher is extremely worried by his hyperactivity, impulsivity, and daily acts of aggression toward his peers, the classroom assistant, and herself. "I have been in this business [teaching preschool] a long time and, honestly, I have never seen such an aggressive and disturbed youngster. It's scary." According to his teacher, Lucas hits, bites, or kicks without apparent cause or provocation. "And he has the foulest language I've ever heard. . . . I believe he swears in almost every sentence and, if he is upset, he will call you all sorts of names; doesn't matter that you are three times as big as he is, nothing is rude enough for him." Lucas also seems to take pleasure in making people around him suffer. His teacher goes on to explain that "he is not afraid of anyone and will strike an adult as quickly as a child. . . . And, I hesitate to say it, but I believe that he likes to hurt. It sounds terrible, I know, but I believe he likes to see another child crying. It is the only time when he seems attentive, in fact, I would even say calm. Yesterday, he took a toy from a small girl, who, of course, began to cry. Lucas took the toy but he didn't play with it. He looked at the poor little girl crying for a long time, as if he wanted to see her in tears. . . . Obviously, with that kind of behavior he has no friends. He often complains that nobody wants to play with him, but I understand why the other kids avoid him." Finally, Lucas is in trouble because he regularly steals in class. "If he sees something that he likes, he takes it. It's that simple. . . ."

The teacher reports also that Lucas regularly disturbs group activities. He has difficulty occupying himself constructively and rarely finishes craft or other group projects. In addition, unlike the other children, he seldom listens to the stories that the teacher reads, preferring instead to walk aimlessly from one end of the classroom to the other. His learning appears com-

promised already: "I have eighteen children this year. He is the only one, besides a little girl who is developmentally delayed, who does not know his colors and alphabet yet. And he cannot write his name."

A classroom observation confirms the teacher's disturbing report. In the course of forty-five minutes, Lucas hits or pushes five children—four without provocation. Two incidents leave the victims in tears. Also, Lucas obeys only 25% of commands issued by the teacher and her assistant, ignoring or disobeying the others without consequences. For example, in spite of clear instructions not to play with scissors, he destroys a picture that he had colored by cutting it into small pieces.

At 4, Lucas is already known to the authorities. Shortly after his third birthday, he set fire to the family's trailer, which was entirely destroyed. At 3½ years, he used a live electrical cord to shock a cat. The animal was severely burned and had to be put to death. Far from showing any remorse, he attempted to do the same to a babysitter a few weeks later. The sitter was also burned and required medical attention. "I could give you other examples," his mother says. "It's always been like that. Each morning, when I get up, I don't know what he will be up to that day, who he will attack or what he will do; there's no way of knowing. . . . If he is upset, no matter what it is, he screams and he threatens people, like his father, using bad language. . . . I cannot tell you how many times he has told me he was going to kill me. . . . I do not know if he realizes what he does, I doubt it. I can be nice to him, or mad, or try to speak calmly, but it doesn't make a difference really. If he cries it's because he got hurt or got a good whipping, never because he has a bad conscience."

Lucas lives with his mother and his two older brothers, who have similar but reportedly less serious problems. His father is in prison—for the second time—for breaking and entering, and signing bad checks. Family life is precarious and chaotic, because of chronic poverty, unstable housing, and maternal depression and bouts of alcohol abuse. An intervention is set up to attempt to contain Lucas's behavior at school, and to ensure the safety of his peers and of the teaching staff. From the outset, his mother is invited to take part in this intervention. She agrees to do so and to have weekly home visits from a clinician to support her

and help her in her parenting task. However, after a few weeks, she fails to keep most of her appointments and the intervention fails. Lucas is later expelled from school following an act of serious aggression against another child.

Though Lucas's case is no doubt exceptional—both in age of onset and severity—it shows that CD can occur in very young children. Some of these children may, before grade school, show the first signs of what might develop over time into an antisocial personality disorder. However, as we will see later, early disruptive problems have multiple developmental trajectories, so that it would be a mistake to believe that all children like Lucas will grow up to be ruthless, violent adolescents and criminal adults, and that nothing can be done to help them.

Diagnostic and Developmental Considerations

The Sociological and Criminal Perspective

The best way to describe and understand the disruptive behaviors of many young people is a subject of considerable debate. Researchers outside of psychology and psychiatry do not use the terms *oppositional defiant disorder* and *conduct disorder* to describe disruptive youth; instead, they describe these youth as delinquent. **Delinquency** is a *legal* concept used to label an array of antisocial behaviors that generally begin and end during adolescence. Adolescents (and younger children) become officially delinquent when they are arrested and convicted of engaging in illegal activity. Consequently, delinquent conduct depends on current laws in a particular society or jurisdiction, and on the manner and extent to which the police and other officials enforce those laws. In addition, delinquency refers only to illegal behavior, not to socially inappropriate behavior such as lying or cheating. Finally, the concept applies to a wide range of children and adolescents, from those who have been arrested for a single, minor offense (such as drinking alcohol at a party) to youth who have a long history of arrests and convictions for serious, violent crimes.

In contrast, ODD and CD are *clinical* concepts used to label a broad array of disruptive and antisocial behaviors in youth, irrespective of their legality. Diagnosis of ODD or CD requires careful psychological or psychiatric evaluation to determine whether a particular child or adolescent's disruptive behaviors have harmful consequences for the youth and others. Consequently, CD and, to a lesser extent, ODD refer to youth who usually display a much more serious and harmful pattern of conduct than most juvenile delinquents do, because the concept of delinquency does not take into account the frequency or severity of the offenses committed or the overall mental health of the offender. Therefore, although most young people who receive a diagnosis of CD are delinquents who are known to the juvenile justice system, many delinquents do not have a conduct disorder—that is, they do not show a serious, pervasive pattern of disruptive behaviors that is harmful to themselves and others. We explore this issue in Box 8.2 (p. 212).

Heterogeneity of the Disorders

Describing and understanding antisocial behavior is further complicated by the extreme heterogeneity of the disruptive disorders themselves. In many instances, the only thing that youth with these disorders have in common is that they are very troublesome for parents, teachers, law enforcement agents, or other adults. This heterogeneity is evident in the symptoms listed in the DSM-IV-TR to diagnose ODD and CD, as well as in the different facets of disruptiveness that characterize these disorders. For example, there are obvious developmental differences between repeated disobedience and defiance at age 3 or 4, fighting at age 7, lying and stealing at age 10, vandalism and cruelty at age 12, rape at age 16, and armed robbery or even murder at age 19—but all of these behaviors can be diagnostic of ODD and later CD. In addition, children of the same age do not necessarily present the same problems. A 12-year-old with CD may have a history of lying, stealing, and disregard for authority, whereas another may already have committed one or more violent crimes.

A number of important distinctions are helpful to make sense of this behavioral diversity. First, it is useful to distinguish between **overt** and **covert behav-**ior problems. Overt problems are generally observable behaviors, such as defiance, opposition, and verbal and physical aggression. Covert problems are more secretive or deceptive behaviors, such as lying, stealing, skipping school, and fraud. These two types of problems have different family antecedents and developmental consequences, and are associated with distinct parenting practices (see Developmental Trajectories and Prognosis, and Etiology) (Willoughby, Kupersmidt, & Bryant, 2001).

Second, aggression itself can take different forms. **Instrumental aggression** is intended to achieve a goal that the child is unable or unwilling to achieve by other means. In contrast, **hostile aggression** is not a means to an end but is designed solely to inflict harm. Instrumental aggression occurs frequently during the first years of life, when young children push, hit, grab, or bite to obtain something they want, to assert their growing autonomy, or to establish their place among siblings or peers. These behaviors usually decrease with the development of language and social skills in the preschool years, at approximately the same time as verbal and hostile aggression tend to increase (Patterson, Reid, & Dishion, 1992).

Physical aggression typically follows a similar developmental pattern. In some children, however, physical aggression persists and often increases in the first years of elementary school, and is accompanied by high levels of hostility and impulsivity (Atkins & Stoff, 1993). Longitudinal studies show that *physical aggression is the most important risk factor for severe and persistent conduct problems* (Loeber, Green, Lahey, & Kalb, 2000). Specifically, this factor predicts (1) persistence of ODD and development of early-onset CD, especially in boys; (2) persistence and aggravation of numerous disruptive and antisocial behaviors in late childhood and adolescence (especially covert problems such as lying and stealing); and (3) in extreme cases, development of a criminal career in late adolescence and adulthood.

A distinction can also be made between reactive and proactive aggression. **Reactive aggression** reflects a hostile interpretation of the behavior of others; that is, a tendency to interpret the intentions of another child or adult as hostile, when these intentions are actually neutral or ambiguous. This type of aggression is generally exhibited in response to a perceived threat but does not

BOX 8.2 • *Distinguishing Conduct Disorder from Delinquency in a Young Offenders Group*

If you obey all of the rules, you miss all of the fun.
—Katharine Hepburn

Our clinical work brings us in contact with young offenders (12 to 17 years of age) who have been arrested and are in the juvenile justice system. These adolescents participate in a group intervention designed to help them explore what may have led them to offend and develop prosocial coping strategies to avoid future offending. A brief look at one of these groups shows that adolescent offenders engage in a variety of disruptive and antisocial behaviors, and highlights some of the difficulties in distinguishing between CD and delinquency. By definition, all group members are delinquent, because they have been arrested and convicted of one or more illegal acts. However, they do not all have a psychological disorder. Look at the diagnostic criteria for CD in Table 8.2 and, as you read each vignette, ask yourself if you would give these adolescents a diagnosis of CD.

- A 14-year-old girl was arrested at a party. There was alcohol at the party, but she had not been drinking. She reports that she never uses drugs or alcohol, attends school regularly, and has good grades. She comes from a family without history of drug or alcohol use.
- A 16-year-old girl was arrested at the same party. She had been drinking but was not intoxicated. When the police arrived, she was spray-painting her initials on the patio. She reports that she enjoys graffiti and often draws on public property because "it beautifies the world and doesn't hurt anyone." A frequent social drinker, she describes herself as "a bit of a con artist" who knows how to avoid responsibilities with ease and to talk people into doing what she wants. She has several truancy violations dating back to middle school, and a history of shoplifting and other petty theft, but no other delinquent or criminal record.
- A 16-year-old boy, also at the party, had to be taken to hospital by ambulance in a state of alcoholic stu-

por. He is the star of the high school football team but has a history of drug and alcohol use, and is often truant from school. He has no history of aggression or other illegal activities, but suffers from bouts of depression and made a suicidal gesture six months earlier.

- A 17-year-old boy has a history of binge drinking, physical aggression, and auto theft. His aggressive problems date back to elementary school. He says that he has always done poorly in school and is often truant. Group members who know him say that they are afraid of him, especially when he is drunk. His father is an alcoholic who is regularly in trouble with the law.
- A 13-year-old boy was arrested for shoplifting a $100 stereo. He admitted to a long history of petty theft, but this was his first arrest. He attends school regularly and is an average student. He does not use drugs or alcohol. He lives at home with his mother. His father died in an automobile accident two years earlier.
- A 13-year-old boy was arrested for breaking and entering into a neighbor's home. He did not steal anything but had already been arrested twice, each time for theft. He has a history of aggressive behavior at home and school and, although he appears to be of normal intelligence, he has expressive language disorder. He reports that he often skips school and uses alcohol and marijuana "for fun." He lives with his mother and two younger sisters.

Three of these youth had a DSM-IV-TR diagnosis of CD: the 17-year-old binge drinker, the 13-year-old with a record of multiple arrests and expressive language disorder, and the 16-year-old graffiti artist. The last one may come as a surprise. Many clinicians will probably argue that the two boys need psychological help and that their future is bleak, but that this may not be true of the "artist," who may outgrow her problems in late adolescence or early adulthood. What do you think?

always have a precise goal. Reactive aggression is accompanied by negative emotions—especially anger—and central nervous system activation, such as rapid

heart rate and shallow breathing. In contrast, **proactive aggression** is more deliberate, and involves fewer negative emotions and less central nervous system activation. It usually has an instrumental or hostile goal and requires some planning. Boys who are proactively aggressive have a higher probability of developing CD than boys whose aggression is primarily reactive (Vitaro, Gendreau, Tremblay, & Oligny, 1998), probably because proactively aggressive boys believe—often on the basis of prior experience—that aggression "pays," that it is an effective tool to solve problems (Smithmyer, Hubbard, & Simons, 2000).

Finally, a distinction can be made between **direct** and **indirect aggression.** Some children choose to confront their opponents or to attack their victims directly, whereas others attempt to achieve their aggressive ends in indirect ways. Children who start a fight or "get in someone's face" use direct aggression. Children who spread false rumors, plot in secret, or incite other children to attack their victims employ indirect aggression. Indirect aggression is poorly represented in the diagnostic criteria for ODD and CD and, because of its "sneaky" nature, is more difficult to assess than other forms of aggression. Girls are more often perpetrators and victims of indirect aggression than boys (Crick & Bigbee, 1998). This may explain, in part, why ODD and CD are more often diagnosed in males than in females—a point to which we will return later (see Epidemiology).

Social Norms and Expectations

By definition, disruptive and antisocial behaviors antagonize others, infringe on their rights, and violate social rules. However, social norms and expectations are not always the same across contexts. A child may be faced with different sets of rules at home, at school, and in the neighborhood. For example, ODD is often diagnosed in first or second grade, when behaviors that may have been tolerated or even encouraged at home are judged unacceptable at school. The mother of an ODD boy may find him "difficult at times," but his teachers may complain that he is "out of control."

To complicate matters further, antisocial behaviors can be acceptable, even adaptive, in contexts in which violence is common (see Box 8.1). For example, gangs encourage delinquency, but they also give many youth access to peers who provide them with support and protection at times when they feel or are objectively in danger (Fergusson, Woodward, & Horwood,

1999). Similarly, students who are confronted daily with verbal and physical violence at school may prefer to be offenders rather than victims or may choose to skip school because they feel safer at home or on the streets (Pain et al., 1997).

Cultural Norms and Expectations

ODD and CD must also be considered in the light of cultural expectations. In the United States and other industrial countries, deviant and antisocial behaviors are common in youth—so much so that isolated incidents of delinquency are almost "normal": they are a part of what many young people do. Figure 8.1 (p. 214) illustrates this point by summarizing some of the results of the 1997 National Longitudinal Survey of Youth.

Likewise, open manifestations of aggression and hostility in young people are actively encouraged and even glorified in American culture—especially in sports and in different forms of entertainment, such as movies, videogames, and wrestling (Cairns & Cairns, 1994). Boys in particular are expected to be "loud" and "boisterous," whereas girls are more likely to be complimented for being "nice" and "sweet." A classical experiment illustrates these deep-rooted cultural expectations. Condry and Ross (1985) asked college students to watch a video of two children playing roughly in the snow and to rate how aggressive they were. The children—a girl and a boy—were dressed in heavy winter clothes that made it impossible to distinguish their gender. Students who had been led to believe that the children were boys rated their play as *less* aggressive than students who thought that they were girls, or were a boy and a girl—probably because "boys will be boys" but "nice girls don't fight." This study illustrates the importance of cultural factors in the assessment of disruptive and antisocial behaviors, and by extension the role that they may play in their development.

Empirical Validity

Oppositional Defiant Disorder

ODD begins on average two to three years earlier than CD, and the two disorders do not follow the same

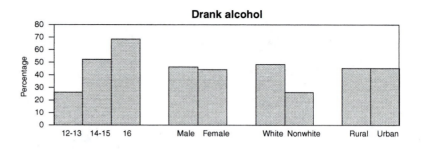

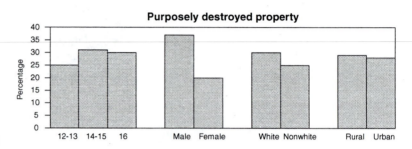

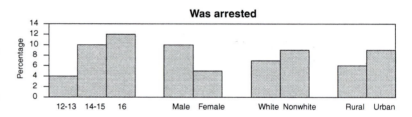

FIGURE 8.1   *Percentages of Youth Who Reported That They Had Drunk Alcohol Purposely, Destroyed Property, or Been Arrested in the 1997 National Longitudinal Survey of Youth.* The data are based on a nationally representative sample of 9,000 youth and broken down by age, gender, ethnicity, and urban/rural residence.

Source: U.S. Department of Justice (1999), pp. 58–59.

developmental trajectory (see Developmental Trajectories and Prognosis). Although such evidence would seem to support the empirical validity of ODD as a separate condition from CD, it can also be argued that ODD is an early manifestation of CD in some children, rather than a truly distinct condition. Findings bearing on this issue come from research conducted within categorical and dimensional approaches.

Categorical Research.   Cross-sectional studies show that more than 80% of youth with CD also meet diagnostic criteria for ODD (Spitzer, Davies, & Barkley, 1990). Similarly, longitudinal studies report that a majority of youth who develop CD qualified for an earlier diagnosis of ODD (Loeber, Green, Lahey, Frick, & McBurnett, 2000). This finding suggests that symptoms of the two disorders overlap considerably and that

ODD is a common precursor of CD—thereby calling into question the validity of describing them as distinct conditions. However, longitudinal evidence shows also that a majority of children who qualify for a diagnosis of ODD do *not* go on to develop CD. For example, Lahey and associates (1990) found that 75% of boys who had ODD at the beginning of their study did not have CD three years later. In other words, cross-sectional and retrospective data show that a majority of young people with CD also meet diagnostic criteria for ODD (or met them in the past), whereas prospective data show that only a minority of children with ODD go on to develop CD.

Dimensional Research.   Data collected within a dimensional approach do not provide a clearer picture of the empirical validity of ODD as a separate condition from CD. For example, Keenan and Wakschlag (2000) found that children with ODD and CD scored significantly higher on the *Child Behavior Checklist* than children without those disorders. However, in this and similar studies, these children were difficult to distinguish on the basis of the nature or severity of their symptoms—a finding that calls into question the validity of ODD as a separate disorder.

To sum up, the empirical validity of ODD has not been clearly established. Researchers who are interested in the early identification and prevention of severe conduct problems often argue that ODD should be regarded as a distinct entity from CD, since it permits early identification of children with developmentally inappropriate levels of oppositional, defiant, and aggressive behaviors early, and thereby enables intervention programs to be set up to prevent CD (see Treatment and Prevention). Researchers who are interested in empirically based diagnostic research more than in prevention stress that few children with ODD present symptoms serious enough to constitute a psychological disorder—even though their behavior can be highly disruptive at home and/or school. In this perspective, a single diagnostic category such as CD is enough to identify children who display major behavior problems in early or middle childhood, and to track the progression of their symptoms over time (Achenbach, 1993).

Conduct Disorder

The social validity of CD is not in doubt. In all societies and cultures, physical and sexual aggression, property destruction, lying, stealing, fraud, and firesetting are strongly condemned and proscribed by explicit laws and customs. However, the clinical validity of the disorder is more difficult to establish—essentially because many of its diagnostic symptoms may limit a child or adolescent's functioning and have negative consequences for others without necessarily being clear signs of psychological dysfunction.

As several longitudinal studies show, the clinical validity of the disorder depends primarily on age of onset and chronicity (Moffitt, 1993). Children and adolescents who exhibit chronic disruptive behaviors from an early age—especially repeated physical aggression—and who have comorbid psychological problems

have a valid psychological disorder. However, the presence of CD is questionable in youth who engage in delinquent conduct in adolescence, even though their behavior may be both disruptive and illegal. In other words, there are considerable differences between a child who sets fires at 4, is repeatedly aggressive and cruel throughout childhood, and is arrested twice for car theft before age 13; and an adolescent who, from about age 13, shoplifts, is occasionally truant from school, lies to parents and teachers, smokes, and is arrested for drinking and disorderly conduct at a football game. Diagnosis is very likely to be appropriate and valid in the first case, but may not be in the second one.

Associated Characteristics; Comorbidity

Since ODD often precedes CD and youth with CD have many symptoms of ODD, the two conditions are often associated, but they are never comorbid because a diagnosis of CD takes precedence over one of ODD in the DSM-IV-TR. In other words, if a youth qualifies for a diagnosis of CD, then the behavior is too severe to be labeled ODD by DSM criteria.

ADHD

ODD and CD are often associated with symptoms of ADHD or with the disorder itself (Hinshaw, Lahey, & Hart, 1993; Willcutt, Pennington, Chabildas, Friedman, & Alexander, 1999). For example, the Ontario Child Health Study, a large epidemiological study conducted in Canada, found comorbidity rates of 59% in boys and 56% in girls during childhood, and of 30% in boys and 37% in girls during adolescence (Offord, Alder, & Boyle, 1986).

This association is significant for at least two reasons. First, children with a dual diagnosis have more severe difficulties than children with either ADHD alone or ODD or CD alone. They are more disruptive and physically aggressive, and more impulsive and hostile; they also have more social and school challenges, such as peer rejection and learning problems (Atkins & Stoff, 1993). Second, a dual diagnosis predicts a faster and more problematic evolution of the child's difficulties. In particular, children with ODD and ADHD who go on to develop CD do so, on average, 3½ years earlier than children with ODD alone (Loeber, Green, Keenan, & Lahey, 1995), and have a much higher probability of committing antisocial and violent acts in adolescence and adulthood (Moffitt, 1993).

Drug and Alcohol Abuse

Disruptive behavior disorders are also associated with the early and abusive use of legal and illegal drugs, as well as with the development of various drug addictions. In a longitudinal study of a community sample of boys evaluated in first, fourth, and seventh grade, Van Kammen, Loeber, and Stouthamer-Loeber (1991) found high rates of tobacco and alcohol use as early as first grade, and these rates increased tenfold in the course of the study (both in quantity and diversity of drug use). This increase was particularly pronounced in youth who had several antisocial symptoms.

Wills, Vaccaro, McNamara, and Hirky (1996) reported comparable increases in drug and alcohol use in a longitudinal study of almost twelve hundred adolescents evaluated from seventh through ninth grade. This study confirms the finding that disruptive behavior problems and drug abuse often co-occur and aggravate each other, and that adolescents with more severe behavior problems are also more likely to abuse drugs. Finally, longitudinal evidence indicates that disruptive behaviors generally precede and are a reliable predictor of drug use in adolescence. For example, in a follow-up of over seven hundred 12- to 16-year-olds who were part of the Ontario Child Health Study, CD was the only psychological disorder that predicted the use of marijuana and other drugs four years later (Boyle et al., 1992).

Mood Disorders

ODD and CD are also frequently associated with depressive symptoms or mood disorders. This is true throughout development, for boys as well as girls. Specifically, mood and anxiety disorders are three to five times more frequent in children and adolescents with CD than in other youth (Zoccolillo, 1992). CD is also an important risk factor for suicide. In a retrospective study of sixty-seven adolescents who had committed suicide and matched controls who had died from other causes, Brent and associates (1993) found that there were six times as many youth with CD in the suicide group than in the control group. High comorbidity rates have also been found among incarcerated youth (Pliszka, Sherman, Barrow, & Irick, 2000).

To explore the link between depression and conduct problems, Seeley, Lewinsohn, and Rohde (1997) studied a community sample of predominantly European American adolescents up to their twenty-fourth birthdays. The subjects who had both CD and major depressive disorder were more likely than other subjects to abuse drugs and attempt suicide in adolescence, and to have adjustment difficulties at the beginning of adulthood. Comparable results have been found in two other follow-up studies, one of African American adolescents (Miller-Johnson, Lochman, Coie, Perry, & Hyman, 1998), the other of British adolescents (Harrington, Fudge, Rutter, Pickles, & Hill, 1991). A number of researchers believe that adolescents who meet diagnostic criteria for CD and a mood disorder do not necessarily have two distinct psychological conditions, but a "mixed" one, called *depressive conduct disorder.* This disorder is not in the DSM-IV-TR. Future research may show that it has its own characteristics and developmental trajectory, and that it is a separate condition or a subtype of CD.

Anxiety Disorders

Before puberty, boys who have CD and a comorbid anxiety disorder are less aggressive and have more positive peer relationships than boys with CD only (Walker et al., 1991). Similarly, boys with high levels of impulsiveness and anxiety at age 5 run less risk of presenting a chronic pattern of disruptive and antisocial conduct between ages 10 and 13 than boys who are impulsive but not anxious (Tremblay, Phil, Vitaro, & Dobkin, 1994). However, this seemingly protective effect of anxiety may not last beyond childhood. In a follow-up of the prepubertal boys studied by Walker and associates (1991), Lahey and McBurnett (1992, cited by Hinshaw et al., 1993) found that the level of aggression of boys with CD and anxiety increased in adolescence until it was comparable to or higher than that of boys with CD only.

Less is known about girls, although girls with a history of oppositional and conduct problems are at risk of developing different anxiety disorders, especially in later childhood and adolescence. However, rates of comorbidity with such disorders do not appear to be higher in girls than in boys (Keenan, Loeber, & Green, 1999).

General Adaptation

Social Rejection.   As mentioned, aggressive and other disruptive behaviors frequently lead to adult and peer rejection. Aggression is particularly frowned upon by peers, especially when it comes from girls (Keenan et al., 1999). Irrespective of gender, aggressive youth face major social challenges. In particular, they tend to pay *selective attention* to negative signals or cues in the course of social interactions, and consequently to interpret them wrongly. When the intentions of another child or adult are ambiguous or unclear, aggressive children often interpret them as hostile and conclude that the other person is mean, or intends to provoke or spite them. This **hostile attributional bias** is associated with frequent use of aggressive solutions to interpersonal conflicts and with high levels of social rejection (Dodge, 1993).

When it is associated with ODD or CD, social rejection is significant for at least two reasons. First, social rejection is both a common comorbid characteristic of disruptive behavior and a major predictor of how it will evolve over time. For example, a study of a community sample of over five hundred boys and girls found that 50% of children who, by age 8, had already been rejected by peers for at least two years (but only 9% of children who had not been rejected) had clinically significant symptoms of CD in adolescence (Dodge, 1997). Second, children who are rejected in childhood are likely to associate with disruptive peers in adolescence, because social rejection tends to foster the development of relationships between disruptive youth. In most cases, these relationships increase the intensity and chronicity of antisocial problems, and encourage aggression and violence, especially in youth who join a gang (Keenan, Loeber, Zhang, Stouthamer-Loeber, & Van Kammen, 1995).

School Difficulties.   Many children with ODD or CD have cognitive and language delays and do poorly in school (Fergusson & Horwood, 1995)—possibly because, in childhood at least, the relationship between disruptiveness and school problems reflects the co-occurrence of ADHD with ODD or CD (Hinshaw, 1992). For example, in a follow-up of boys from preschool to the end of elementary school, Gagnon, Craig, Tremblay, Zhou, and Vitaro (1995) found that early symptoms of hyperactivity and impulsivity (but not inattention), as well as low IQ, predicted high levels of aggression. A related explanation is that some children with CD have deficits in executive functions (Morgan & Lilienfeld, 2000). (For a definition of these deficits, see Chapter 7, Diagnostic Criteria and Major Characteristics.)

Self-Esteem.   In keeping with the tough image they like to convey, children and adolescents with ODD and CD generally have high levels of self-esteem and do not see themselves as particularly aggressive. As you know, high levels of self-esteem are also common among children and adolescents with ADHD and are probably an important characteristic of all disruptive behavior disorders. Although the nature of the association between self-esteem and aggression is unclear, research with highly aggressive adults suggests that they often use aggression as a means of preserving their favorable view of themselves when this view is threatened by criticism or rejection (Baumeister, Bushman, & Campbell, 2000).

Epidemiology

Prevalence; Age and Gender Characteristics

Oppositional Defiant Disorder.   Prevalence rates of ODD vary considerably from one published report to another. In a review of five epidemiological studies, Rey (1993) found an average prevalence rate of almost 6%. Rates ranged from 2% to 10%, depending on the characteristics of the sample and on the methods used to calculate them. These figures are based on older diagnostic criteria than the current ones and may be somewhat elevated, since today's criteria are stricter than their predecessors. Some studies indicate that the prevalence of the disorder increases with age (e.g., Pelham et al., 1992), whereas others report that it decreases (e.g., McGee et al., 1990).

Average age of onset for ODD is around 7 (Lahey, Loeber, Quay, Frick, & Grimm, 1992). The disorder typically develops earlier in boys than in girls and, until age 12, also occurs more frequently in boys than in girls (approximate sex ratio 2 : 1). In adolescence, ODD is evenly distributed or slightly more frequent in girls (Rey, 1993). This increase in frequency among girls has a double explanation. First, the disorder begins later in girls, so that the number of affected girls grows over time (Lahey et al., 1992). Second, a number of boys diagnosed with ODD in childhood develop CD in adolescence, and are then no longer counted in studies assessing the prevalence rate of ODD (Achenbach, McConaughy, & Howell, 1987).

Conduct Disorder.   In a review of research conducted in different countries, Zoccolillo (1993) found prevalence rates for CD ranging from 2% to 8% in boys and 0% to 2% in girls during childhood, and from 3% to 10% in boys and 1% to 7% in girls during adolescence. In the Ontario Child Health Study, Offord and colleagues (1986) reported an average rate of 5% in youth from 4 to 16 years, with marked increases in older children and adolescents (6% in boys and 2% in girls from 4 to 11 years, and 10% in boys and 4% in girls from 12 to 16 years). In many cases, CD develops at the end of childhood or at the beginning of adolescence; but it can appear earlier, as in Lucas's case. Typically, although they often have early antecedents, the more serious forms of the disorder have a relatively narrow window of onset. They rarely begin before late childhood or after early to mid-adolescence (Robins, 1966).

Boys are more likely to have CD than girls are— at least in childhood. Possibly the disorder occurs less frequently and appears later in girls; or the diagnostic criteria used to define CD are sex-biased, in that they include more aggressive behaviors that are more typical of males than of females, especially before adolescence (Zoccolillo, 1993). This last possibility is supported by the fact that the increases in prevalence of CD in adolescent girls are due primarily to increases in

covert, nonaggressive behaviors (such as lying, stealing, and running away from home) (McDermott & Schaefer, 1996). In other words, the CD symptoms that are most likely to get girls in trouble are covert problems and not the aggression and destruction common in affected boys. In addition, antisocial girls often associate with boys who are already in trouble for aggressive behavior problems, further heightening the risks they face in adolescence and beyond, including exposure to physical violence, teenage pregnancy, and school failure (Caspi, Lynam, Moffitt, & Silva, 1993).

Social and Cultural Differences

Cross-Cultural Findings.   Overall, ODD and CD are more prevalent among children and adolescents from underprivileged and ethnic minority groups. The association between these disorders and ethnic membership reflects the fact that many minorities are socially and economically disadvantaged. For example, Lahey and colleagues (1995) found that the association between ethnicity and disruptive behavior was no longer significant when they controlled for socioeconomic status in their analyses.

Most studies of ODD and CD come from North America, Western Europe, Australia, and New Zealand, and show that these disorders have comparable rates of prevalence in these countries. In a rare epidemiological study coming from Asia, Matsuura and associates (1993) compared the prevalence of disruptive symptoms among several thousand elementary school children from Japan, China, and Korea. In each country, boys were more disruptive than girls. However, in thirteen of their sixteen cross-cultural comparisons, Japanese boys and girls were found to be less disruptive than their Chinese and Korean peers. This single study does not make it possible to draw firm conclusions on the epidemiology of disruptive symptoms in these countries. However, it highlights the importance of cross-cultural research to understand the role that different cultures may play in their manifestation.

Cohort Effects.   As you know, disruptive and antisocial behaviors in general, and ODD and CD in particular, have increased dramatically since the 1960s in most industrialized countries. Consequently, epidemiological data collected today may not correspond to similar data collected earlier because of cohort effects—namely, effects that depend less on the nature of the disorder being studied than on the historical period in which a particular sample was recruited to study it. We will return to these effects in the following section.

Developmental Trajectories and Prognosis

In spite of important individual differences in their progression, (1) disruptive and antisocial behavior problems—especially early-onset CD—are among the most stable of all psychological conditions of childhood and adolescence in boys and girls; and (2) in severe cases,

CD is often preceded by ODD and follows a predictable developmental trajectory, which is striking considering the marked heterogeneity of its manifestations. Our discussion focuses primarily on CD. Box 8.3 complements this discussion by outlining Sidney's development from early-onset CD to armed robbery, rape, and incarceration. Sidney grew up in Chicago in the 1920s, but his delinquent "career" was similar to that of many youth today.

Distinguishing between Early- and Late-Onset CD

As we noted earlier, there are fundamental differences between early- and late-onset CD. We summarize these differences in Table 8.3 (p. 220). Most youth who have

---

BOX 8.3 • *Sidney: A Case Study in Delinquency*

In his book *Natural History of a Delinquent Career,* the famous criminologist Clifford Shaw (1931) tells the story of Sidney Blotzman, an 18-year-old juvenile delinquent who grew up in Chicago in the early part of the twentieth century. This classical case study sheds important light on the world of disruptive children who become serious and violent juvenile offenders. Sidney's contacts with the juvenile justice system included the following:

Age 7—Placed in a home for dependent children. Escaped two months later with an older boy.

Age 7½—Arrested on three different occasions for shoplifting with older boys.

Age 8½—Charged with truancy. Placed in a juvenile home where he remained for six months.

Age 9½—Charged with truancy. Placed in a juvenile home where he remained for six months.

Age 10¼—Arrested on three different occasions for shoplifting with older boys.

Age 10¼—Placed in a juvenile home where he remained for one year.

Age 11½—Charged with truancy. Placed in a juvenile home where he remained for 1½ years. Escaped twice during his stay, but was returned each time within a month.

Age 15¼—Arrested for auto theft. Placed in a foster home.

Age 15¼—Arrested for fighting and breaking a window.

Age 15½—Arrested for stealing from his employer. Placed in a juvenile home for six months. Escaped on two different occasions, but was returned each time within a month.

Age 16—Arrested for armed robbery, auto theft, and attempted rape. Placed in juvenile detention.

Age 16½—Escaped from detention.

Age 16¾—Arrested for armed robbery and rape, and later incarcerated.

This record gives a sense of the scope of Sidney's behavioral problems, and of their devastating consequences. However, his parents' descriptions of their home life provide an essential context to understand Sidney's growing years. When asked about her family, his mother said:

The old man [Sidney's father] is always bad. If he kisses me one day, he hits me the next. He was always bad to the kids. . . . When Sidney was six years old, he asked the old man for a penny to get candy. The old man hit him so hard about a quart of blood came out of his nose and mouth. . . .

(continued)

BOX 8.3 • Continued

When Sidney was 3 and 4 years old, he was sickly and I felt sorry for him and petted him. I bought lots of candy and ice cream for him. When I refused to do this he would cry until I bought it for him, and this I always did. He could always get his own way by crying. . . .

Sidney got bad with other boys. It cut my heart when the boys would come to the house to take him away when he was so little. He never had any home. Nobody ever cared for him because I worked all the time until Abe [his older brother] was old enough to work. He never had any good friends. He was bad when he was seven and the old man only beat him up.

I tell you the truth, maybe you think I blame everything on my husband, but when Abe was a child I didn't take my eyes off him. But when Sidney was a child, I had so much trouble with my husband, he was drinking so heavily, I didn't know who to watch first and I had to go out and go to work because my husband didn't support me. I kept Abe always with me and Sidney was freer because I wasn't always home to take care of him (p. 48).

Sidney's father had an entirely different view of his family. He noted:

[Sidney] was born bad like his mudder. All that is no good in him comes from her. She is sneaky and so is he and she lies to protect him but not to protect me. The boy was born to die on the gallows. I know this because when a boy has been hit as much as I hit Sidney and he is still bad, there can be no good end. Ever since he was old enough, I say seven years old, to know better he stole everything and lie and go with bad bunch and beg on street. . . .

One day when he was about twelve, he brought a stolen bicycle home. I said, "Where did you get it?" and he said, just like a real thief, "I stole it." I hit him so hard one of his teeth fell out and then Sidney, sneak, had the nerve to say, "That is not any worse than what you did today." He said I bought some suits that were stolen property. Well, it was true, maybe, maybe not, that was business (p. 49).

These excerpts provide a long list of family and social factors that, in addition to his own personality characteristics, undoubtedly contributed to Sidney's multiple, chronic problems: poverty, child abuse, domestic violence, parental criminality, and parental alcoholism, among others. We discuss these factors in the text, where we show that their effects are most harmful when they occur for extended periods of time and in combination, rather than in isolation.

TABLE 8.3 *Developmental Characteristics of Early- and Late-Onset Conduct Disorder*

	"Early starters"	*"Late starters"*
Age of onset	Approx. 4 to 8 years	Late childhood, early adolescence
Major features	Multiple aggressive and nonaggressive problems exhibited in a variety of contexts	Predominantly nonaggressive antisocial acts, such as theft, vandalism, and truancy
Associated features	Limited social skills and ability to regulate emotions, poor peer relationships, academic difficulties, drug use	Few except drug use
Epidemiology	More severe but less frequent than late-onset CD	Less severe but more frequent than early-onset CD
Developmental course	Low remission and high innovation	High remission and low innovation
Etiology	Adverse temperamental characteristics, ineffective parenting and disturbed family relationships, adverse social and economic conditions	Negative peer influences

the disorder—or many of its symptoms—are of the second type ("late starters") and include girls as often as boys. These youth are not particularly oppositional or aggressive as children, and follow an uneventful developmental trajectory similar to that of their peers until the teenage years. Their first problems appear in adolescence, when they are not aggressive and violent offenders, but rather delinquents: they steal, commit acts of vandalism, or use alcohol or other drugs, and consequently often become involved with the juvenile justice system. The developmental trajectory of these "late starters" is generally characterized by a *low level of innovation* and a *high level of remission.* That is, their antisocial behaviors tend to be of one or two types only; to be limited in scope; to appear at irregular intervals; and to disappear entirely after a few months or years. For example, "late starters" may engage in shoplifting or in vandalism at sporting events, but present no major problems at home or school. Although their delinquency can be very serious, it tends to be irregular and seldom persists beyond adolescence (Moffitt, 1993). It is also rarely highly aggressive (Brame, Nagin, & Tremblay, 2001).

In contrast, the developmental trajectory of early-onset CD is more common in boys than girls, and typically includes repeated acts of aggression and violence. This trajectory is characterized by a *high level of innovation* and a *low level of remission.* Youth on this trajectory manifest disruptive and antisocial behaviors that are varied; occur in multiple contexts (home, school, neighborhood); and tend to escalate over time, continuing in many cases into adulthood. Early-onset CD affects 4–6% of all youth, but this group inflicts a disproportionate amount of harm on others. "Early starters" are responsible for at least half of all delinquent and criminal acts committed by young people, as well as for a majority of aggressive and violent offenses (Farrington, Lambert, & West, 1998).

Developmentally, the trajectories of early- and late-onset CD overlap. This overlap results in a rapid increase in the incidence of antisocial, violent, and criminal conduct around age 12, followed by a corresponding decrease in late adolescence and early adulthood. Figure 8.2 illustrates this developmental trend. It shows that self-reports of serious and violent offending are at their highest in the teen years. Practically, this means that more people engage in antisocial conduct in adolescence than at any other time in their development; and when they do, they commit more offenses, on average, than earlier or later in life.

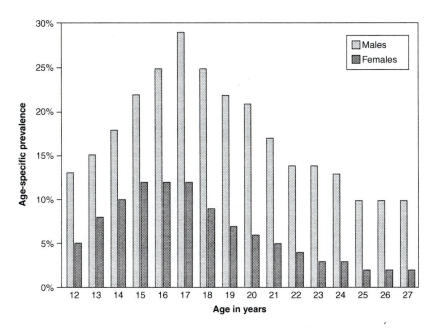

FIGURE 8.2 *Prevalence of Self-Reported Acts of Serious Violence by Age and Gender.* Violent offending—aggravated assault, robbery, or rape—peaks for both boys and girls between the ages of 16 and 18. It is rare before age 12 but then rises sharply through age 18. Although the overall trend is comparable for males and females, gender differences in prevalence are striking.

Source: From J. D. Coie and K. A. Dodge, "Aggression and Antisocial Behavior." In W. Damon and N. Eisenberg (Eds.), *Handbook of Child Psychology,* vol. 3: *Social, Emotional, and Personality Development* (5th ed.). (New York: Wiley, 1997), p. 792. Copyright 1997 by John Wiley and Sons, Inc. Reprinted by permission.

Although this adolescent peak in antisocial behaviors has often been reported, it is at least partly a generational phenomenon. For example, Farrington and colleagues (1998) kept track of the criminal records of four hundred men from childhood to age 40, and the records of their immediate family members. As Figure 2.3 shows, offending peaked sharply in adolescence, but only in the youngest generation—namely, that of the study subjects and their brothers. In their parents' generation, offending increased in adolescence also but tended to remain more constant overall. These intergenerational findings illustrate the cohort effects we mentioned earlier, showing that what is true of a developmental trajectory at one period of time may not be at another. More generally, these findings highlight the importance of social and cultural factors in the development and evolution of disruptive and antisocial behavior problems, and caution against hasty explanations that attempt to account for them in terms of individual psychopathology only.

Stability of Early-Onset CD

Longitudinal studies show that early-onset CD is a particularly stable disorder. For example, in a four-year follow-up of a clinical sample of boys, 50% of subjects met diagnostic criteria for CD every year, and 88% met them at least once during the follow-up period (Lahey et al., 1995). Stability is particularly evident among boys who, from an early age, have a high level of physical aggression, multiple and varied disruptive symptoms, and comorbid difficulties, such as hyperactivity/impulsivity, social rejection, and learning and communication problems (Maughan, Pickles, Rowe, Costello, & Angold, 2000). CD has also been found to be highly stable in girls (Côté, Zoccolillo, Tremblay, Nagin, & Vitaro, 2001).

Given this stability, it is not surprising that disruptive behaviors in early childhood are one of the most reliable predictors of the frequency, severity, and duration of antisocial conduct—especially aggression and violence—in adolescence and beyond. A Swedish study illustrates the disastrous ramifications that early disruptiveness can have on adult adjustment (Kratzer & Hodgins, 1997). This study followed over six thousand men and six thousand women born in Stockholm in

1953 from birth to age 30. By age 30, 75% of men and 30% of women who had exhibited disruptive behavior problems in childhood had committed one or more crimes and/or had a psychological disorder (in a majority of cases, drug or alcohol abuse). In addition, men with a history of disruptiveness in childhood had a much higher risk of dying before age 30. Although it may seem that women generally fared better than men, the authors believe that their data did not capture the fact that many of them had major marital, family, and work difficulties that were not documented in the official government statistics they consulted.

Even though disruptive and antisocial behaviors are particularly stable, it would be mistaken to attribute this stability to the child alone, because children who present chronic conduct problems are also repeatedly exposed to multiple risk factors at home, at school, and in the community. Thus, *their behavior is stable for environmental as much as individual reasons* (Loeber & Farrington, 1998). Environmental stability undoubtedly influences the developmental trajectory of other psychological disorders of childhood and adolescence, but probably to a lesser degree.

Development of Early-Onset CD

Early-onset CD develops in a relatively predictable fashion from childhood to late adolescence and adulthood. Specifically, the work of pioneering researchers in this area, such as Gerald Patterson (e.g., Patterson et al., 1992) and Rolf Loeber (e.g., Loeber, Green, Lahey, & Kalb, 2000), shows that in spite of important individual differences (1) disruptive and antisocial behaviors have staggered ages of onset, in which milder problems, such as opposition and defiance, generally precede more serious aggression and violence, often by several years; (2) problems that appear later do not replace earlier ones but compound them, typically adding to the child or adolescent's difficulties over time; and (3) the longer problems persist and the more complicated they become, the less likely is the child or adolescent to desist from an antisocial career.

An antisocial career brings a host of challenges in addition to conduct problems. Youth who remain antisocial into the teenage years run a high risk of using alcohol and other drugs, dropping out of school, being unemployed, and becoming teen parents—and thus of further perpetuating problems across generations. As young adults, they are also at risk of developing other psychological disorders and, for males, of dying young (Cairns & Cairns, 1994). This bleak picture must be tempered by two important considerations, however. First, psychological intervention can help disruptive youth and their families, especially if it begins early in the developmental trajectory (see Treatment and Prevention). Second, adjustment in late adolescence and early adulthood depends greatly on life circumstances. Youth with a history of persistent conduct problems can make a positive transition to adulthood with the support of other, nonaggressive adults and the resources of a regular job (Zoccolillo, Pickles, Quinton, & Rutter, 1992).

Etiology

Countless observations of children and adolescents show that some of them are at greater risk than others of displaying disruptive, antisocial behaviors because of adverse circumstances—such as a difficult temperament, a dysfunctional family, or a violent neighborhood. On the strength of such observations, many etiological studies speak of risk factors and **protective factors** in the development of these disorders (Loeber & Farrington, 2000). As their names imply, risk factors are variables that increase the risk for ODD or CD, whereas protective factors are variables that lower the same risk. The risk/protective approach is less interested in determining the cause or causes of disruptive behavior disorders than in establishing the *probability* that children exposed to specific, measurable influences will develop either of these conditions. For example, Loeber and associates (1995) found that 70% of boys who had three risk factors (a diagnosis of ODD, low socioeconomic status, and parental drug abuse) developed CD, compared to 12% of boys without any of them. This does not mean, obviously, that these variables are the causes of CD; only that they increase the likelihood that boys who are exposed to them will develop the disorder. In general, the greater the number of risk factors and the lower the number of protective factors, the more likely a disorder is to develop and to become resistant to change (Dumas & Wahler, 1983).

The risk/protective approach has the advantage of stressing that ODD and CD can develop in several ways in the presence of different factors, but the disadvantage of not explaining fully how these factors exert their influence. It is one thing to know that low socioeconomic status predicts CD, but another to know why. How does being poor relate to becoming disruptive and antisocial? Lack of money cannot alone be the cause of aggression, since the vast majority of poor people are not aggressive. In other words, we know a lot today about factors that reliably predict the development of ODD and CD, but much less about the processes that explain their influence.

Biological Factors: Genetic Studies

Twin and adoption studies support the existence of a genetic link in the etiology of CD in later adolescence and of antisocial personality disorder in early adulthood, especially in severe and chronic cases. However, this link is less clear in childhood and adolescence (Rutter et al., 1990). In a statistical analysis of the results of multiple studies, known as a **meta-analysis,** Mason and Frick (1994) report evidence for a genetic link in the etiology of some of the most serious disruptive behaviors. For example, there is greater genetic correspondence in school-age twins for extreme behaviors such as cruelty to animals and firesetting than for more common acts of disobedience and provocation.

Though evidence suggests that genetic factors play a role in the etiology of the most serious disruptive behaviors, it does not specify what may be passed from one generation to the next. Most researchers believe that children do not inherit antisocial behaviors directly. Rather, they inherit broad behavioral tendencies, which in the presence of other risk factors, make them particularly vulnerable to develop ODD and early-onset CD (see below).

Biological Factors: Neuropsychological and Neurophysiological Studies

Considerable research focuses on neurobiological and neuropsychological characteristics that distinguish children with ODD or CD from other children (e.g., Baving, Laucht, & Schmidt, 2000). Generally speaking, evidence shows that the behavioral tendencies some children probably inherit include a high level of motor activity and irritability, a lack of tolerance for frustration, and difficulties in emotion regulation; when these temperamental characteristics operate in transaction with other risk factors, they increase the likelihood that the child will present multiple ODD or CD symptoms. We describe important findings from three overlapping areas.

Behavioral Activation and Inhibition.   Quay (1993) proposed a theoretical model to explain the etiology of ADHD, ODD, and CD, which we presented in Chapter 7 (see Etiology). This model assumes that individual differences in the management of social, affective, and instrumental situations reflect the complementary activity of three neurobiological systems: a *behavioral activation system;* a *behavioral inhibition system;* and a *general arousal system.* According to Quay, children with severe early-onset CD suffer from an imbalance in the first two of these systems: their behavioral activation system is overactive, at the expense of their inhibition system. More precisely, their activation system repeatedly leads these children to seek immediate positive reinforcement, while minimizing or dismissing the negative consequences of such behavior (in the form of failure, punishment, or social disapproval).

There is considerable evidence to support Quay's model. In particular, experimental studies show that children with high levels of disruptive symptoms have a marked tendency to act to maximize immediate rewards, even when these rewards become less and less frequent in the course of the experiment; that is, when their own behavior leads them to experience an increasing number of failures over time. This perseverance in the face of increasing failure was illustrated by Daugherty and Quay (1991), who compared five groups of children ranging in age from 8 to 13: a disruptive group, a hyperactive/impulsive group, a mixed disruptive and hyperactive/impulsive group, an anxious/withdrawn group, and a control group. They asked subjects to complete a computer-controlled task in which they had to open a door that appeared on the screen to discover if they would receive a reward token

or lose a token they had already earned. The probability that a token was hidden behind the door decreased gradually from 90% to 0% in the course of the experiment. Subjects were allowed to stop playing at any time and to keep the rewards they had earned. The researchers could then determine the point at which each child decided to stop when confronted with mounting losses. Results showed that children in the disruptive and mixed disruptive/hyperactive groups persisted longer—and thus lost more—than their peers in the other groups. Other studies have shown that this perseverance is not the result of inhibition problems; that is, disruptive children persevere on this and similar tasks because of possible gains, not because they are unable to prevent themselves from responding (Schachar, Tannock, & Logan, 1993).

Neurochemical and Hormonal Regulation of Activation.   Aggression, dominance, and violence in general, and early-onset CD in particular, are also associated with low autonomic nervous system activity and low HPA axis responsivity (Van Goozen, Matthys, Cohen-Kettenis, Buitelaar, & van Engeland, 2000). Specific neurochemical and hormonal dysregulations include low serotonin activity, which is linked to hypersensitivity and hyperresponsiveness to aversive stimuli; high testosterone activity, which promotes dominance and aggression in situations of frustration, especially when individuals are in a negative mood; and low cortisol activity, which disrupts the organism's ability to modulate stress effectively (McBurnett, Lahey, Rathouz, & Loeber, 2000). However, the etiological role of such characteristics remains to be established. A review of the neurophysiological factors associated with CD generally supports and broadens Quay's predictions (Lahey, Hart, Pliszka, Applegate, & McBurnett, 1993). Specifically, this review leads to an intriguing conclusion—namely, that the biological processes underlying early-onset, aggressive CD may operate in generally opposite ways to those that underlie late-onset, nonaggressive CD. Relatively low levels of physiological activation and autonomic nervous system reactivity may characterize aggressive CD; and relatively high levels of activation and reactivity may characterize nonaggressive CD. If this speculation is correct, children in the first group would be expected to seek to increase their level of activation by engaging in behaviors that they find stimulating and rewarding but, because of low reactivity, to minimize or ignore signs of trouble or danger, and thus to underestimate the probability that these behaviors will have negative consequences—just as children and adolescents with early-onset CD are known to do.

Early Temperament. Research on the temperament of children who are aggressive and disruptive from an early age generally reports complementary findings. For example, in a study of more than 2,400 children followed from infancy to age 8, Sanson and associates (Sanson, Smart, Prior, & Oberklaid, 1993) compared the early temperamental characteristics of subjects who were later identified as aggressive, hyperactive, or both. On average, children who later became aggressive or both aggressive and hyperactive were more difficult in infancy than children who became hyperactive (but not aggressive). Even as babies, these children were easily irritated and often in a negative mood. Differences among the three groups became more pronounced as time progressed. By age 8, the aggressive and especially the combined aggressive and hyperactive groups could be clearly distinguished from the hyperactive and control groups by their difficult temperament and by their disruptive behaviors at home and later at school. Although these results may seem rather straightforward, Sanson and colleagues caution that the link between early temperament and aggressive and disruptive behavior problems is complex. In particular, this link is strongest when the child is not only aggressive but also hyperactive; when maternal discipline is inadequate; when the family environment is characterized by multiple social and financial difficulties; and/or when the child is rejected by peers (Bates, Pettit, Dodge, & Ridge, 1998; Olson, Bates, Sandy, & Lanthier, 2000).

Psychological and Family Factors

The Family. The disruptive and antisocial behaviors of a majority of children with ODD or early-onset CD appear initially within the context of the family. Studies indicate that, in early childhood, persistent oppositional and aggressive conduct reflects a pattern of disturbed family relationships as much as a child's own behavior problems (Dumas & LaFreniere, 1993; Patterson et al., 1992). The mother-child relationship is the family relationship that has been most often studied and that is best understood. However, the father-child and sibling-child relationships also play important roles in the development and maintenance of disruptive behavior problems (Aguilar, O'Brien, August, Aoun, & Hektner, 2001; DeKlyen, Speltz, & Greenberg, 1998).

The relationship problems in the families of young children at risk of developing ODD or CD (or who have one of these disorders already) are evident in a number of specific risk factors: (1) lack of parental responsiveness and an insecure or disorganized attachment from the first months of life; (2) reciprocal exchanges that involve high levels of coercion and low levels of positive activities and affectionate gestures; (3) parental discipline that is harsh and inconsistent, and often reflects parental mood more than child behavior; (4) limited opportunities and encouragement to develop appropriate social and emotional skills before school entry—so extreme in some cases as to amount to neglect.

Discipline and Aggression. Each of the risk factors just listed has complex origins and effects that we can only illustrate here. In the discipline area, aggressive, antisocial children are less likely to comply with maternal requests than other children are. And their mothers often issue vague, unclear instructions that make it difficult for them to comply (Dumas & Lechowicz, 1989). Such encounters tend to invite harsh and inconsistent discipline. Specifically, a mother may sometimes react to the misdeeds of her disruptive child by scolding, severely punishing, or even abusing him; at other times, by lecturing or threatening him with dire consequences that she does not enforce; and at still other times, by ignoring or even encouraging his inappropriate conduct (e.g., by laughing when he misbehaves) (Patterson et al., 1992). Mothers who use inconsistent discipline often describe themselves as wavering between feelings of frustration and anger and feelings of defeat and helplessness. These ambivalent thoughts and feelings work against more positive interactions and affectionate exchanges, such as hugs, kisses, and compliments, and can, in extreme cases, push mothers to withdraw from or even reject their children (Dumas & Wahler, 1985; Pinderhughes, Dodge, Bates, Pettit, & Zelli, 2000).

Coercion and Balance of Power.   Most children usually know that their parents have the last word when it comes to discipline: more often than not, they will have to obey, whether they like it or not. As shown in Chapter 2, however, in families with disruptive children, the children often have the last word (see Box 2.5). In direct observations of mothers and their preschool children in a structured play setting, Dumas, LaFreniere, and Serketich (1995) found that the balance of power between aggressive children and their mothers tended to favor the children. Specifically, aggressive children regularly resorted to a variety of disruptive or coercive behaviors to obtain what they wanted, while their mothers were inconsistent and failed to impose effective limits, especially when they were faced with particularly coercive child demands. Dumas (1997) speculates that when coercive interactions within the family occur repeatedly over prolonged periods of time, aggression can be so well practiced that it becomes an automatic mode of communication—making aggressive exchanges common occurrences among *all* family members and providing a fertile terrain on which aggressive children develop and refine their disruptive repertoire.

Parenting Practices and Child Outcomes.   Different parenting practices are associated with different child outcomes. Specifically, parents who are harsh and physically aggressive are likely to have children who are also aggressive, whereas parents who show little affection (without being particularly harsh in their discipline) are likely to have children who are oppositional (Stormshak et al., 2000). However, comparable parenting practices do not always have the same consequences for every child, or even for the same child at different developmental stages (Grusec, Goodnow, & Kuczynski, 2000). In the United States, for example, severe and overreactive discipline in early childhood predicts the appearance of disruptive and antisocial behaviors in European American, but not in African American, children (Deater-Deckard et al., 1996). A similar conclusion comes from research on the link between child maltreatment and disruptive behavior disorders. Physically abused or neglected children have a higher probability of becoming aggressive than children who are not mistreated, even when possible mediating variables such as socioeconomic status are considered (Widom & Maxfield, 2001). However, the link between maltreatment and aggression is complex, making straightforward statements about causes and effects impossible (see Chapter 12).

Other Family Challenges.   Discipline difficulties play a major role in the etiology of ODD and early-onset CD, but these disorders are more likely to develop when (1) children present adverse temperamental dispositions or hyperactivity from an early age; (2) parents have chronic mental health problems, such as depression; or (3) the family faces multiple socioeconomic problems, such as poverty, inadequate housing, and unemployment.

More generally, disruptive and antisocial behavior problems are associated with family risk factors such as parental criminality, marital conflict, drug and alcohol abuse, social isolation, and family instability (Bates et al., 1998; Dumas & Wekerle, 1995). Family instability can involve frequent changes in the intimate relationships of parents, as well as repeated moves that require adjustment to new neighborhoods and schools (Ackerman, Kogos, Youngstrom, Schoff, & Izard, 1999). Two examples illustrate how these factors may operate.

It stands to reason that children who are regularly exposed to high levels of disagreement and conflict between their parents or other adults run the risk of developing a variety of problems themselves. The effect of such conflict was explored in a follow-up study of children who, at age 4 to 5, had parents who were experiencing high levels of marital discord. Discord predicted disruptive behavior problems in the children three years later, but only when adult conflict was mutually hostile—that is, when there was reciprocal antagonism and resentment, and a high level of maternal anger toward her spouse (Katz & Gottman, 1993).

Children are also affected by the social and psychological resources available to their parents outside the home. Dumas (1986) studied fourteen mothers who had particularly challenging, aggressive children. These mothers also lacked adequate social support and often felt isolated. The study compared mother-child interactions at home on days when the mothers had had positive, supportive social contacts with adults outside the home ("good days") and on days when they had not ("bad days"). Not surprisingly, the children's behavior did not differ much from day to day. However, their mothers were more likely to be harsh and inconsistent with them on "bad" than on "good" days. This finding shows that the quality of the mother-child relationship reflects complex social circumstances, which do not all involve the child directly.

A final word of caution: Young children are often victims of adverse life circumstances over which they have little or no control. However, they are not puppets unable to influence their environment. As we emphasize again in Box 8.4, they are active agents who shape their daily world as much as they are shaped by it.

BOX 8.4 • *Could Disruptive Children Push Their Parents to Drink?*

In a clever experiment, Pelham and associates (1997) trained four boys aged 10 to 12 to play one of two roles: (1) a cooperative child without behavior problems; (2) a disruptive child who manifested various behaviors diagnostic of ADHD, ODD, and CD. Then they invited sixty parents to take part in a series of laboratory games and tasks with either a cooperative or a disruptive actor. Following these activities, the authors offered the parents their preferred alcoholic drink, which they could consume freely while completing a series of questionnaires evaluating their reactions to the experiment. Parents who had been paired with a disruptive child found the experience much more stressful and reported higher levels of parental ineffectiveness, anxiety, depression, and hostility than did parents who had carried out the task with a cooperative child. Most important, the parents who had just spent time with a disruptive child also consumed 30% more alcohol than the other parents did! Thus, there is no doubt that parenting difficulties make an important contribution in the etiology of all disruptive behavior disorders, but this study highlights the fact that children themselves always play an active part in how they behave, and that they influence their environment as much as they are influenced by it.

Beyond the Family.   Children who begin elementary school with numerous symptoms of ODD or CD run a high risk of developing additional difficulties that will aggravate the ones they exhibit already. As we showed earlier, children who act aggressively toward peers, or regularly disturb class and other group activities, find themselves quickly rejected and cut off from the normative influence of other children that is essential to the development of many social and emotional skills.

The same applies to learning difficulties. Children whose behavior is aggressive and disruptive often start school with a lack of basic knowledge and skills that are essential to early school success. These problems, together with their tendency to disrupt and disobey, result in numerous negative interactions with teachers and greatly increase the probability that these children will exhibit important academic delays, or one or more learning disorders (Glassberg, Hooper, & Mattison, 1999). To make matters worse, such school factors often have a negative impact on the child's functioning at home, when teachers complain to parents about the child's conduct or lack of progress. Strained communication between home and school can set in motion a vicious cycle, in which aggression and disruptiveness in both contexts lead to social rejection by teachers and peers, and often by parents as well. With time, such a cycle can lead adults and peers to expect that the child will disrupt and fail, and to focus almost exclusively on the child's *mis*behavior. As one adolescent with CD remarked bitterly: "Everybody notices when I screw up. When I get it right, nobody cares."

Social and Cultural Factors

> *The child was diseased at birth, stricken with a hereditary ill that only the most vital men are able to shake off. I mean poverty—the most deadly and prevalent of all diseases.*
>
> —Eugene O'Neill

Many theories and empirical studies from different fields—psychology, sociology, criminology—emphasize the importance of social and cultural variables in the development of aggression and delinquency. However, because data are almost exclusively correlational, it is impossible to establish a clear etiological role for the many social or cultural risk factors that often are associated with disruptive behavior problems. Moreover, the majority of children exposed to such factors never develop ODD or CD, suggesting that when they play an etiological role, these factors do so only in interaction with other variables. Although many of the risk factors in this area are beyond the scope of this chapter, we will briefly mention four of them here: poverty, racism, neighborhood, and exposure to violence. There is little doubt that each of these factors can have harmful effects on children and adolescents.

Poverty.   The role played by poverty in the etiology of ODD and CD is difficult to evaluate, because poverty is itself associated with a number of variables often implicated in the development of these disorders. Variables such as ethnicity, lack of parental education, unemployment, poor housing and school conditions, and—in countries such as the United States—limited access to medical care and social services co-occur with poverty, so that their individual effects are hard to untangle. When these variables are taken into account in data analyses, the effect of poverty is strongly reduced or disappears entirely. In addition, the relationship between poverty and child behavior varies according to factors such as parenting practices and family social support (Elder, Eccles, Ardelt, & Lord, 1995). In spite of these important considerations, however, the relationship between poverty and disruptive and antisocial behavior problems is not in doubt. Even when it is not chronic, poverty is related to the appearance of various disruptive behaviors, particularly violence in boys (Bolger, Patterson, Thompson, & Kupersmidt, 1995). Poverty also predicts later aggression toward peers, delinquency, and criminality (Farrington & Loeber, 1998).

Racism.   In many families, the adverse effects of poverty are associated with ethnic minority status, and are aggravated by racism and discrimination. Kennedy (1997) gives a striking example of how racist remarks can trigger aggressive outbursts in at-risk youth. This is a short dialogue between the author and Iesha, a 14 year-old African American adolescent:

> **Author:**   *Tell me what somebody would say to you that triggered the "fight" on your part.*

> **Iesha:**   *Okay, there was this boy, we were in science and it was the last period of the day. And this boy said, "Iesha." I said, "What?" He said, "How come you are black and your mom is white?" It just stunned me for a minute and I didn't pay no attention to him. I said, "Cause my dad is black." He said, "Your mom is a nigger lover?" and I just seen a chair that looked handy, and so I just picked it up and started throwing it at him. And the teacher tried to grab me and I smacked him with a book. . . . I just cannot stand nobody talking about the color somebody is. I mean, just when somebody say something about me I don't like . . . at first I just look at them and start laughing. And then I start getting real mad. And the next thing I know I be yelling and then I end up hitting them (pp. 195–196).*

Neighborhood.   Disruptive and antisocial behavior problems are also linked to the area in which children live and to the school they attend. Severe aggression and delinquency are more frequent in urban than in rural environments, and tend to be concentrated in underprivileged neighborhoods where chronic social problems regularly disrupt the lives of children and families. Such environments are particularly likely to give rise to serious and violent offending, which is often associated with early-onset CD (Loeber & Farrington, 1998). Children who live in underprivileged neighborhoods run an increased risk of developing disruptive and antisocial behavior problems and of developing them earlier than children raised in more privileged neighborhoods (Kupersmidt, Griesler, DeRosier, Patterson, & Davis, 1995). This effect may be directly attributable to neighborhood quality, rather than simply reflecting child or family characteristics. Specifically, Kupersmidt and associates found that living in a relatively affluent neighborhood protected children who would otherwise have been at high risk for aggressive behavior problems because of individual or family risk factors.

Exposure to Violence.   In many societies, children who have regular access to television, movies, and video games are almost unavoidably exposed to high levels of violence under the guise of entertainment. Likewise, youth who live in disadvantaged neighborhoods are

American culture supports and in some cases actively encourages the development of aggression, especially in young boys. A few years after this picture was taken, Andrew Golden (age 11) and his friend Mitchell Johnson (age 13) opened fire on their classmates in Jonesboro, Arkansas, killing five people and wounding ten others.

BOX 8.5 • *Violence in the Media*

Children are inclined to learn from television [because] it is never too busy to talk to them, and it never has to brush them aside while it does household chores.

—National Commission on Causes and Prevention of Violence

The influence of media violence on young people has led to considerable research—and even more debate. To study this and other issues related to youth violence, the American Psychological Association set up a Commission on Violence and Youth in 1991. This panel of experts has published some highly regarded reviews in that area. In particular, the panel found clear research evidence that violence on television and in other media has four major effects:

1. An *aggressor effect* of increased meanness, aggression, and even violence toward others.
2. A *victim effect* of increased fearfulness and mistrust, and self-protective behavior (such as carrying a gun, which ironically increases one's risk of becoming a victim of violence).
3. A *bystander effect* of increased desensitization, callousness, and apathy toward victims of violence.
4. An *appetitive effect* of increased interest in violent material.

On a more positive note, the commission also found that exposure to prosocial behavior in the media has at least two effects:

1. A *prosocial effect* of increased helpful behavior toward others.
2. An *antiviolence effect* of decreased violence toward others.

These findings highlight the importance of considering youth violence within a broad social and cultural context as we search for explanations and solutions in this area.

Source: Donnerstein, Slaby, and Eron (1994), p. 240.

---

often exposed to high levels of violence in their immediate surroundings. A large body of research documents the negative effects of such exposure in early childhood (Farver & Frosch, 1996), middle childhood (Schwartz & Proctor, 2000), and beyond (Grossman & Kloske, 1996). Children and adolescents who are regularly exposed to violence tend to be more violent than peers without such exposure—probably because they see others relying on force to solve problems and are inclined to imitate them, believing that violence offers an effective solution to difficulties. In addition, children who are exposed to violence, directly or as bystanders, may suffer from posttraumatic stress that triggers or aggravates their disruptive behavior (Ford et al., 1999; see Chapter 10). We discuss this issue further in Box 8.5.

Exposure to violence probably has its most devastating consequences—for aggressors and victims—in communities where guns and other weapons are easily accessible (O'Donnell, 1995; U.S. Department

BOX 8.6 • *Seeing a Weapon Can Automatically Trigger Aggressive Thoughts*

Researchers have known for years that the mere presence of a weapon increases aggressive thoughts and behavior. However, the processes responsible for this increase remain a source of considerable debate. Anderson, Benjamin, and Bartholow (1998) relied on research concepts and methods from cognitive psychology to study the relationship between weapons and aggression. Specifically, they worked with two groups of participants who saw either pictures of weapons, such as guns, clubs, and swords (experimental group), or pictures of plants, such as fruit, trees, and flowers (comparison group). To make sure they attended to the pictures, participants in both groups were asked to name each item as it appeared on the screen. After they had seen all the pictures, participants were then asked to read a series of target words that appeared on the screen. The target words included 74 nonaggressive and 24 aggressive words. Based on extensive cognitive research on memory, the researchers hypothesized that the mere fact that the experimental group had seen weapons would make aggressive thoughts more accessible in their memory. Accessibility was then measured by how quickly the participants named each word on the screen. If the word was not immediately available in memory, the participants would have to think harder and longer to say the word. Results confirmed the researchers' hypothesis, indicating that the simple fact of seeing a weapon increased access to aggression-related thoughts and made it easier for experimental participants to name aggressive target words quickly. These findings suggest that the presence of weapons may *automatically* prompt people to think—and possibly behave—aggressively. This is not to say that people have little or no control of what they think or do whenever they see a weapon, but that the mere presence of weapons may facilitate thoughts and actions that can have violent consequences.

(Killias & Rabasa, 1997). These findings are particularly troublesome in a country like the United States, where youth who engage in many disruptive behaviors associated with CD—such as drug trafficking—are among the most likely to be armed *from an early age* in their community and at school (Puzzanchera, 2000). National statistics reflect the gruesome reality that many youth use guns to kill: from 1980 to 1997, 77% of youth who died at the hands of other youth were killed with a firearm (U.S. Department of Justice, 1999).

Treatment and Prevention

The treatment and, more recently, the prevention of ODD and CD have attracted considerable attention on the part of researchers and clinicians from different professional backgrounds, such as psychology, psychiatry, criminology, and public health. We will focus here on three psychosocial approaches to these disorders: parent training, **cognitive-behavioral therapy,** and **multisystemic therapy.**

Parent Training

> Dear God,
> What is the use of being good if nobody knows it.
> —Mark, in *Children's Letters to God*

As we noted in Chapter 7, parent training is designed to promote positive parent-child interactions through supportive parenting and consistent discipline. This form of treatment has proved effective in helping families of different cultural backgrounds who have children or young adolescents with aggressive and antisocial behavior problems (Kumpfer, Moolgaard, & Spoth, 1996; Myers et al., 1992). The most successful of these programs share some important features. Essentially, they teach parents to identify and reward appropriate behavior patterns (such as compliance with parental requests) and to specify clearly and ignore or punish inappropriate conduct (such as temper tantrums, aggressive outbursts, and lying and stealing). Parents are then helped to implement positive consequences whenever the child behaves appropriately, as

of Justice, 1999). This statement is supported by experimental research showing that the mere presence or mention of a weapon facilitates access to aggressive thoughts (see Box 8.6); and by criminological research linking access to firearms specifically to violent, rather than delinquent, behaviors, at least in adolescent boys well as negative (but nonaggressive) consequences whenever the child disobeys, fights, or behaves in an unacceptable manner. Some parent-training programs also make direct attempts to improve the overall quality of the parent-child relationship. For example, in her Parent-Child Interaction Training Program, Sheila Eyberg begins by training parents of young aggressive children to play with them in a nondirective manner called child-directed play (Eyberg & Boggs, 1998). Specifically, parents are instructed not to issue commands or directives but to follow their child's lead as they play together for brief periods of time every day. These regularly scheduled, short play periods allow parents and children to learn to interact positively and to enjoy sharing pleasurable activities. These play periods also allow disruptive children to learn to exercise positive control over their parents, rather than to rely on aggressive and antisocial means to force their parents to give in to their demands.

Parent training can be delivered to families individually or in small groups. Both approaches have advantages and drawbacks. Individual delivery allows clinicians to focus specifically on the family's concerns, to advance at the family's pace, and to deal with setbacks or unexpected challenges as they occur. Group delivery does not offer the same degree of flexibility but has the advantage of giving parents opportunities to share their common concerns and to support each other as they work to help their children. Irrespective of approach, most programs give parents homework assignments to complete between sessions. These assignments are designed to help parents and children learn to deal effectively with issues that are frequent sources of conflict. For example, in a group parent-training program developed by Dumas (2001) called *Parenting Our Children to Excellence,* parents receive a one-page sheet of Take Home Points at the end of each session (see Figure 8.3, p. 232). This sheet summarizes the material covered in the session. Parents are encouraged to display it prominently at home and to use it as a guide to complete their homework assignments.

A meta-analysis of twenty-six carefully selected studies on the effectiveness of parent-training programs showed that, on average, children whose parents participated in these programs were better adjusted at home after treatment than approximately 80% of children whose parents did not participate. In addition, children of participating parents were better adjusted at school after treatment than three-fourths of their peers whose parents did not. Similarly, participating parents were better adjusted themselves at the end of intervention than two-thirds of nonparticipating parents (Serketich & Dumas, 1996). These positive findings are commonly supported by direct observations showing that successful program participants display better parenting skills after treatment than parents of disruptive children who declined to participate or dropped out before completing treatment.

The parent-training approach, despite its proven effectiveness, has important limitations. First, as with ADHD, parent-training programs for ODD and CD have high levels of parent dropout and are less effective with families facing multiple sources of stress (Kazdin, 1997). These programs do not offer a "quick fix" for disruptive problems; they are time-consuming and require that parents be willing and able to change the manner in which they relate to their children and discipline them. In addition, the research on these programs does not indicate whether there are gender differences (since it has mainly featured boys) or age differences in treatment response to parent training. Some evidence suggests that it is most effective with younger children (Dishion & Patterson, 1992)—probably because the influence of the family generally declines in favor of peers and other social models as children get older.

Cognitive-Behavioral Therapy

> *When angry, count to ten before you speak; if very angry, a hundred.*
>
> —Thomas Jefferson

We will discuss cognitive-behavioral therapy (CBT) in detail in Chapters 9 and 10. We introduce it here because it offers another avenue in the treatment of ODD and CD. Generally speaking, cognitive-behavioral therapy attempts to change inappropriate behavior by modifying the thoughts or cognitions that are believed to control it. For example, assume that you are working with a young adolescent boy who gets extremely angry and abusive whenever his peers tease him or disagree

Setting Clear Limits for Our Children
Take Home Points

Why does everybody need limits, even adults?
- Life would be crazy and terribly stressful without limits.
- Life would be dangerous without limits.

Use effective commands to set limits. To give effective commands:
- Get your child's full attention by making eye contact; if your child is upset, give him or her the chance to calm down first.
- Give one clear command at a time, rather than chain commands; be firm, not sweet or angry.
- Be specific and direct; tell your child what to do, don't ask. For example, say: "Go brush your teeth," rather than "Go get ready for bed."
- Avoid "stop" and let's" commands. For example, say: "Lower your voice, please," rather than "Stop shouting!"
- Give your child 5–10 seconds to comply.
- Give warnings or reminders. For example, say: "In 5 minutes it will be time to go brush your teeth."
- Use "when-then" commands, going from less to more pleasant activities whenever possible. For example, "When you finish your dinner, then you can have dessert."
- Praise compliance to tell your child that you appreciate his or her cooperation.

Use effective consequences to set limits. Effective consequences are:
- Natural consequences that result from your child's own behavior and that can be used to change that behavior
- Logical consequences that you impose to change your child's behavior

---

FIGURE 8.3 *Example of a* **Take Home Points** *Sheet Used in a Group Parent-Training Program.* Parents receive this sheet at the end of a session in which emphasis is put on setting clear limits for children with disruptive and antisocial behavior problems. The sheet explains why limits are important and provides guidelines to give effective commands and effective consequences when setting limits. Parents also are given detailed homework assignments in which they have to set limits for their children. Parents are asked to display the sheet on their refrigerator or elsewhere, so that it can be easily seen, and to refer to it throughout the week to remind them of how best to proceed.

Source: Dumas (2001). Reprinted by permission.

with him. You could attempt to change his behavior directly, by teaching him to ignore rather than react to comments he dislikes, or by modeling and role-playing more adaptive ways of coping. Alternatively, you could choose a more indirect, cognitive approach by focusing on what the boy thinks whenever he loses his temper with peers. You may find that he explains most of his outbursts and justifies them to himself by saying that people who tease him or disagree with him do not respect him. This response would give you an avenue to

explore his cognitive processes in angry and aggressive situations, in order to help him consider more positive ways of solving problems.

CBT for youth with ODD or CD focuses on increasing their self-control in situations in which they are likely to become aggressive or otherwise disruptive. For example, Kazdin's (1996) Problem-Solving Skills Training Program teaches disruptive youth to generate alternative solutions to common interpersonal situations, and to consider the likely benefits and costs of each solution. This approach has three key characteristics:

1. It teaches youth with ODD or CD that the way they approach problems such as not viewing ambiguous behavior as hostile has important consequences for the manner in which they attempt to resolve them.
2. Through modeling, role-playing, and practice, it trains these youth to develop effective, non-aggressive solutions to personal and social problems.
3. It guides and encourages youth with ODD or CD to apply strategies and solutions developed in a treatment setting to real-world situations, in order to give them opportunities to practice and to change the way they think in these situations.

CBT has become an established treatment for older children and adolescents with ODD or CD, as well as for disruptive youth whose parents may be unwilling or unable to take part in a parent-training program. Evidence indicates that this treatment is effective. Specifically, it leads to positive changes in affected youth, to improvements in family functioning, and to decreases in parenting stress (Kazdin & Wassell, 2000).

Multisystemic Therapy

In its practice guidelines for youth with CD, the American Academy of Child and Adolescent Psychiatry (1997d) notes that "no single intervention is effective against severe CD. Multimodal interventions must target each domain assessed as dysfunctional and must be suited to the age and ethnicity of the patient" (p. 130S). Multisystemic therapy (MST) is designed to do just that. Developed by Scott Henggeler and colleagues, MST addresses the many problems disruptive youth present at home, at school, and in the community. In addition, MST considers the legal difficulties youth with CD often face, as well as the problems other family members may have that interfere with the youth's adaptive functioning (Henggeler, Schoenwald, Borduin, Rowland, & Cunningham, 1998). For example, parents with a history of delinquency may be actively

encouraging their children's antisocial activities. Likewise, parents who have marital difficulties may be unable to work as a team to set consistent limits, such as regular school attendance and curfews. MST seeks to influence the multiple systems of which youth with CD are a part. These techniques are guided by nine basic principles:

1. The primary purpose of assessment is to understand the fit between the identified problem and their broader systemic context.
2. Therapeutic contacts emphasize what is positive about the child and the family, and use their strengths as levers for change.
3. Interventions are designed to promote responsible behavior and decrease irresponsible behavior.
4. Interventions are present-focused and action-oriented, targeting specific, well-defined problems.
5. Interventions target sequences of behavior within or between multiple systems.
6. Interventions are designed to meet the developmental needs of the youth.
7. Interventions are designed to require daily or weekly effort by family members.
8. Intervention effectiveness is evaluated continuously from multiple perspectives, with providers assuming accountability for overcoming barriers to successful outcomes.
9. Interventions are designed to promote treatment generalization and long-term maintenance of therapeutic change by empowering caregivers to address family members' needs across multiple systemic contexts (Henggeler et al., 1998, p. 23).

Specific techniques used by multisystemic therapists vary but may include parent training to help caregivers set limits and establish appropriate consequences, and CBT to teach participants effective problem-solving skills. In addition, multisystemic therapists work mostly in homes and schools, rather than in clinical settings, so that they can observe directly how multiple systems operate, and can help bring about change in the youth's own natural environments. Also, by working in homes and schools, they have lower dropout rates than other treatment approaches do (Cunningham & Henggeler, 1999).

MST outcome studies have focused primarily on youth with a history of delinquency, arrest, and incarceration, often for serious offenses. In a review, Kazdin (1997) found that MST resulted in greater reductions in delinquency, behavior problems, and emotional distress than more common forms of intervention, such as probation and individual psychotherapy. In line with the stated principles of this approach, MST also improved family functioning. Perhaps most important, MST resulted in lower rates of recidivism than other interventions, a finding that is particularly impressive given the initial severity of the problems of many youth treated with this approach.

Pharmacological Interventions

There is no pharmacological intervention of choice for youth with ODD or CD, unless they also have ADHD. The American Academy of Child and Adolescent Psychiatry (1997d) suggests that medication be used to treat severe disruptive behavior only in times of crisis or as a short-term intervention. Medications that can be used in such cases include the atypical neuroleptics described in Chapter 5, as well as mood stabilizers, such as *lithium carbonate* (see Chapter 9). Neuroleptics tend to reduce aggressive and impulsive behavior largely because they decrease general activity level. Mood stabilizers may be beneficial because they moderate the tendency of some youth with CD to go through dramatic mood swings, in which they change rapidly from a neutral or positive mood to a very angry one. Although case studies document the effectiveness of these medications, their use must be considered tentative until well-controlled studies are conducted.

Prevention

> *For every complex problem, there is a solution that is simple, neat, and wrong.*
>
> —Henry L. Mencken

Interest in the prevention of youth violence and delinquency is not new. The Greek philosopher Plato discussed the issue some twenty-five centuries ago, as have countless authors ever since (Tremblay, LeMarquand, &

Vitaro, 1999). This interest remains high today, fueled by mounting social pressures to reduce incidents of school and neighborhood violence, as well as other acts of aggression on the part of young people. Prevention programs have a wide range of intervention targets: some are designed to modify child behavior directly, whereas others focus on parents, teachers, peers, or even entire communities. Thus, comprehensive programs aim not only to prevent disorder but also to promote the development of child coping-competence, help children to succeed in school, and reduce the likelihood that they will smoke, drink alcohol, and abuse drugs. We will briefly describe three such programs here.

Fast Track. Begun in the early 1990s across four different sites in the United States, Fast Track works with youth who were initially selected because they presented high levels of aggressive behavior in kindergarten. This intensive program offers social, emotional, and interpersonal skills training, as well as academic tutoring, both in small groups and in the children's regular classroom. As participants grow older, the focus of the program changes to provide them with support and individualized help in early and middle adolescence. In addition, parents and teachers participate in the program. Parents receive group and individual parent training and support, and teachers are trained to deliver key aspects of the program in schools. Early results indicate that Fast Track is helpful in increasing children's social, emotional, and academic skills, as well as in reducing parenting stress and increasing the use of more consistent, less physical forms of punishment (Conduct Problems Prevention Research Group, 1999). However, results are not yet available on the program's ability to prevent ODD and CD and, more generally, to reduce the risk of aggressive and antisocial behavior in adolescence.

Early Alliance. Early Alliance is similar to though more modest than Fast Track. It began in 1997 in South Carolina and is designed to prevent the development of conduct disorder, substance abuse, and school failure in children with high levels of aggressive behavior in kindergarten. Specifically, the program aims to develop coping-competence as a means of reducing the participants' reliance on antisocial solutions to solve the unavoidable challenges they will encounter as they row up.

To promote the ability to cope with all three types of challenges, Early Alliance works with children, families, and teachers. At-risk children in the program receive training to develop effective communication and to get along well with peers. They also participate in a reading enrichment program with high school reading mentors. Their parents participate in a parent-training program at home, and receive professional support and advocacy to address family issues that may or may not concern the target child. Teachers are trained to manage their entire classroom with a communication skills curriculum and to administer a daily school-home communication system, which is similar to a daily report card (see Chapter 7). Early Alliance has not been in effect long enough to demonstrate if it is able to prevent the adverse outcomes it targets. However, its results should in time contribute to much-needed knowledge in this area.

The Safe Schools Initiative. In the late 1990s, the U.S. Departments of Justice, Education, and Health and Human Services launched the Safe Schools Initiative in response to growing public concern about school safety in the wake of a number of tragic school shootings. This initiative focuses on preschoolers, school-age children, and adolescents and their families who are at risk of violence as perpetrators, victims, or witnesses. Several model projects have been set up to provide students, schools, and communities with comprehensive educational, mental health, social, and law enforcement services to promote healthy childhood development and prevent violence, drug abuse, and school failure. The results of this initiative are still being evaluated. However, this large undertaking promises to provide important information on working through schools to promote child competence and prevent violence, and on the feasibility of implementing significant social changes on a national scale.

Web Links

www.aacap.org/publications/factsfam/conduct.htm (American Academy of Child & Adolescent Psychiatry; information about conduct disorder)

www.iay.org (University of Toronto, Institute for the Study of Antisocial Behaviour in Youth)

www.cdc.gov/ncipc/ncipchm.htm (U.S. Centers for Disease Control and Prevention; National Center for Injury Prevention and Control)

www.conductdisorders.com (Support group for parents of children with ODD or CD)

9

Mood Disorders

It's hard to be a person who never gives up.
—Babe Ruth

Sooner or later, everyone is confronted with painful life events—such as the death of a loved one or the loss of a dream. These events invariably provoke feelings of distress and despair, not only in adults but in children and adolescents as well. For some youth, feelings of distress and despair become so overwhelming that they severely disrupt their lives. All they see is a bleak and hopeless future, if they see any future at all. As Ben, a teenager who attended our clinic, noted: "It's as if I were dead, but I am still alive. . . . I wake up every morning with the light of day thinking, feeling deeply, so deeply, that that light could have waited. The night could have gone on and on, without end, and I could have gone on sleeping, just sleeping." Children and adolescents for whom psychological daytime turns to night often have a mood disorder.

As their name implies, **mood disorders** are characterized by prolonged and severe negative emotions that include feelings of depression, hopelessness, and despair. These disorders are also accompanied by numerous symptoms that further interfere with the youth's daily functioning and relationships. The most common are irritability, feelings of worthlessness or guilt, agitation or lethargy, and fatigue. These symptoms are reflected in a lack of interest in pleasurable activities and in a decline in academic performance. In some youth, periods of normal mood or depression alternate with episodes of *mania*—phases of "abnormally and persistently elevated, expansive, or irritable mood" (APA, 2000a; p. 357). Manic episodes are accompanied by increases in activity and reduced need for sleep, and, in many cases, by an inflated sense of self-worth and an overestimation of one's own abilities or importance. Mood disorders are often chronic, but their severity usually varies over time, with periods of near normal functioning fluctuating with periods of dysfunction. In the most serious cases, these disorders continue into adulthood or end in suicide.

The DSM-IV-TR uses the same criteria to define and diagnose mood disorders in children and adolescents as those employed with adults. It describes three primary mood disorders: **major depressive disorder** (or MDD), **dysthymic disorder** (or dysthymia), and **bipolar disorder.**

Historical Overview

The first modern descriptions of mood disorders date back approximately 150 years. In 1860, Sir James

Most unhappy children, such as these girls, are not depressed, but we have known for a long time that young children can be very unhappy to the point of being depressed. However, the study of mood disorders in childhood and adolescence only began relatively recently.

Crichton-Browne, a physician, observed that depression "appears incompatible with early life . . . [but that] it is so only in appearance, for the buoyancy and gladness of childhood may give place to despondency and despair, and faith and confidence may be superseded by doubt and misery" (cited in Parry-Jones, 1995, p. 7). A few years later, the British researcher Harold Maudsley (1867) included melancholia—an earlier label for depression—as one of seven forms of child insanity. Isolated cases of what we would now call bipolar disorder in children were also reported in the medical literature. However, without a coherent theoretical framework, these brief descriptions remained isolated and ignored for more than a century. In fact, it was only in 1975, at a National Institute of Mental Health Conference on Depression in Children, that depression prior to adulthood was first recognized as an important health concern (Schulterbrandt & Raskin, 1977). Thus, mood disorders in children and adolescents have only been systematically studied for approximately three decades—an interesting paradox, given that many influential theorists had long believed that adult depression had its roots in painful childhood experiences (e.g., Freud, 1917/1961b).

At first, researchers hypothesized that before adulthood, depression was often masked; that is, it showed up primarily in the form of other problems, such as aggression, hyperactivity, or anxiety (Glaser, 1967). Thus, the concept of **masked depression** was introduced, and these other symptoms were referred to as **depressive equivalents.** These problems supposedly reflected an underlying depressive condition. This perspective had the advantage of bringing together diverse symptoms under the umbrella of a single disorder. However, it quickly ran into two logical problems:

1. A clear definition of what constituted a depressive equivalent was never established. Consequently, these equivalents ended up covering almost all the psychological disorders of childhood and adolescence (except for disorders such as autism and schizophrenia). This overinclusiveness meant that depression had no unique symptoms prior to adulthood but merely mimicked the symptoms of other conditions.
2. Attempts to establish a list of commonly recognized depressive equivalents failed because a child or adolescent could always exhibit a new "masked" symptom that had not yet been recognized as a sign of depression. (This second problem is similar to the logical problem created by the concept of minimal brain dysfunction, which was advanced to account for learning disabilities and ADHD; see Chapters 6 and 7.)

Over time, these problems led to a theoretical shift away from the concept of masked depression. However, theorists who worked in this area contributed greatly to our knowledge of the diverse symptoms that often accompany depressive phenomena in childhood and adolescence, as we will show later (see Associated Characteristics; Comorbidity).

Definitions, Diagnostic Criteria, and Major Characteristics

Major Depressive Disorder

> *Ask yourself whether you are happy and you cease to be so.*
>
> —John Stuart Mill

Depressive Episodes. Table 9.1 presents the DSM-IV-TR diagnostic criteria for a *depressive episode.* Major depressive disorder (MDD) is characterized by the occurrence of one or more depressive episodes (with symptoms reported by the youth or observed by caregivers), each lasting at least two weeks.

Initially, it can be difficult to determine whether the child or adolescent has a single depressive episode or recurrent episodes, because symptoms tend to fluctuate from one day or week to another. The DSM-IV-TR specifies that, for a depressive episode to have ended, there must be a two-month period in which the youth has not met diagnostic criteria (APA, 2000a). The duration, frequency, and severity of depressive episodes—as well as adjustment between episodes—vary considerably. Some youth are free of symptoms between episodes, but others continue to

---

TABLE 9.1 *Depressive Episode: DSM-IV-TR Diagnostic Criteria*

A. Five (or more) of the following symptoms have been present during the same 2-week period and represent a change from previous functioning; at least one of the symptoms is either (1) depressed mood or (2) loss of interest or pleasure.

Note: Do not include symptoms that are clearly due to a general medical condition, or mood-incongruent delusions or hallucinations.

(1) depressed mood most of the day, nearly every day, as indicated by either subjective report (e.g., feels sad or empty) or observation made by others (e.g., appears tearful). *Note:* In children and adolescents, can be irritable mood.

(2) markedly diminished interest or pleasure in all, or almost all, activities most of the day, nearly every day (as indicated by either subjective account or observation made by others)

(3) significant weight loss when not dieting or weight gain (e.g., a change of more than 5% of body weight in a month), or decrease or increase in appetite nearly every day. *Note:* In children, consider failure to make expected weight gains.

(4) insomnia or hypersomnia nearly every day

(5) psychomotor agitation or retardation nearly every day (observable by others, not merely subjective feelings of restlessness or being slowed down)

(6) fatigue or loss of energy nearly every day

(7) feelings of worthlessness or excessive or inappropriate guilt (which may be delusional) nearly every day (not merely self-reproach or guilt about being sick)

(8) diminished ability to think or concentrate, or indecisiveness, nearly every day (either by subjective account or as observed by others)

(9) recurrent thoughts of death (not just fear of dying), recurrent suicidal ideation without a specific plan, or a suicide attempt or a specific plan for committing suicide

B. The symptoms do not meet criteria for a Mixed Episode (see text).

C. The symptoms cause clinically significant distress or impairment in social, occupational, or other important areas of functioning.

D. The symptoms are not due to the direct physiological effects of a substance (e.g., a drug of abuse, a medication) or a general medical condition (e.g., hypothyroidism).

E. The symptoms are not better accounted for by Bereavement, i.e., after the loss of a loved one, the symptoms persist for longer than 2 months or are characterized by marked functional impairment, morbid preoccupation with worthlessness, suicidal ideation, psychotic symptoms, or psychomotor retardation.

Source: American Psychiatric Association, *Diagnostic and Statistical Manual of Mental Disorders, Fourth Edition, Text Revision* (Washington, DC: American Psychiatric Association, 2000a). Copyright 2000 American Psychiatric Association. Reprinted with permission.

show some symptoms without meeting full diagnostic criteria. In the latter case, it can be difficult to determine whether the person suffers from MDD in partial remission or from dysthymia (see below).

Bob is 14. He attends our clinic with his family. His mother describes him as very unhappy, irritable, and withdrawn. Bob agrees with this description, but insists that he is not irritable, just responding to "unreasonable demands from unreasonable people." These people include almost everyone in Bob's environment—parents, brother, teachers, peers, and the therapist.

Bob was "a normal child" until approximately eight months ago. His mother cannot explain his present state but notes that his maternal uncle died just before he became depressed. Bob says that he was not close to his uncle and that his death did not bother him. However, he acknowledges that a few weeks after his uncle's passing, he began to "think a lot about death," and to eat and sleep much more than he had previously. He has also gained fifty pounds in the last months and is clearly overweight. He is still going to school but says in a monotone voice that "nothing is worth the energy" and that he would not leave the house if he did not have to. Bob has no history of depression. However, his mother has suffered from depression all her life, and her brother—Bob's uncle—had been diagnosed with bipolar disorder.

Bob is treated with a combination of cognitive-behavioral therapy and medication (see Treatment and Prevention). Therapy focuses on changing his negative automatic thoughts and on getting him involved in social activities with family and peers. He makes good progress, in spite of his initial opposition and open dislike for the therapist. After six months, he reports that his depression "is a thing of the past," something that parents, teachers, and peers all confirm.

Irritability vs. Depressed Mood.
Although the same criteria are used to diagnose MDD at all ages, the DSM-IV-TR specifies that, unlike adults, children and adolescents may appear to be more irritable than depressed (APA, 2000a). This developmental distinction is important because it makes it possible to base a diagnosis less on direct observation of depressed feelings than on the child's presumed reaction to these feelings.

In other words, instead of complaining that they are depressed, children with MDD are often cranky and irritable, presumably because they feel down. Although this distinction bears a striking resemblance to the "depressive equivalents" described earlier, clinical and research findings support the existence of a link between depression and irritability in young people. For example, in a study of two clinical samples of youth, Ryan and associates (1987) found that 83% of subjects with a depressive disorder had symptoms of irritability and anger.

Age Differences.
The core symptoms of MDD are found equally often in children and adolescents with the disorder. However, the frequency of other symptoms varies with age. Young children often look sad and depressed and have frequent physical complaints, such as headaches and stomach pains. They can also be particularly irritable. In contrast, adolescents are more likely to express feelings of sadness and hopelessness and to experience changes in sleep, energy, appetite, and weight. Likewise, children with MDD are often very anxious, whereas adolescents are more likely to experience severe **anhedonia,** which is a pathological lack of interest or pleasure in normally enjoyable activities (Kashani & Carlson, 1987; Ryan et al., 1987).

Vegetative Symptoms.
Many young people with MDD suffer from multiple somatic or **vegetative symptoms,** especially in adolescence. These symptoms include hypersomnia (sleeping too much) or insomnia (sleeping too little or disturbed sleep), weight gain or loss, changes in appetite, and fatigue (Mitchell, McCauley, Burke, & Moss, 1988). Vegetative symptoms are often one of the major complaints of parents who bring their children for professional consultation, probably because changes in sleep, appetite, and similar daily activities are easier to track than internal feelings of hopelessness and worthlessness or changes in interests.

Endogenous Symptoms.
Approximately half of the children and adolescents with MDD have **endogenous symptoms** (Mitchell et al., 1988; Ryan et al., 1987). These are emotional and behavioral characteristics that cannot be explained by observable changes in the

environment and that are assumed to result from internal, presumably biological, factors. Endogenous symptoms include daily changes in mood (mood is usually worse in the morning), mood that fails to respond to changes in the child's life and environment, and blunted or flat affect. These symptoms are among the most serious of the disorder. They generally predict rapid relapse between episodes and poor long-term prognosis (McCauley et al., 1993).

Psychotic Symptoms.   A significant number of children and adolescents also exhibit psychotic symptoms during depressive episodes. Auditory hallucinations are most frequent (Ulloa et al., 2000). Visual and olfactory hallucinations are rarer, as are delusions, although these symptoms are difficult to evaluate reliably before adolescence. In clinical samples, 30–50% of youth with MDD have hallucinations, and 6–7% have delusions (Mitchell et al., 1988; Ryan et al., 1987). Psychotic symptoms probably decrease with age. For example, Mitchell and associates (1988) found that 31% of depressed children had hallucinations and that 13% had delusions; in depressed adolescents, the corresponding figures were 22% and 6%. However, in any event, despite any such decrease, psychotic symptoms accompany mood disorders in children and adolescents more often than they do in adults and are usually a sign of poor prognosis (see Developmental Trajectories and Prognosis). Lydia's story illustrates the presence of psychotic features in some youth with MDD.

Lydia is 15. She was referred to our clinic after a teacher found a "hit list" she had written. This list, labeled "People to kill," contains the names of several students. The list is apparently the culmination of a difficult year at school. Lydia started her freshman year very depressed, socially isolated, and often teased by peers. She has since dropped out of all her usual activities (especially school sports, in which she had been very active), lost contact with longtime friends, and seen her grades decline. Most days she oversleeps and is late for school. After school, she often takes "naps" that last well into the evening.

Most dramatically, Lydia hears a voice telling her to kill herself and other students at school. "The voice tells me their names and I put them on the list."

Lydia is extremely distressed by this voice, which she can hear at times almost constantly. However, she insists that she has no plan to harm herself or others and even manages to laugh at what she calls "such a silly idea." Similarly, her parents and teachers report that she has no history of violence, and has never been aggressive at home or school.

Lydia is removed from school and begins psychotherapy and medication for her depression. Within a few weeks the voice stops and Lydia begins to "feel better, more like myself." She returns to school after a two-month absence and, at follow-up, continues to do well.

Dysthymia

During depression the world disappears.
Language itself. One has nothing to say.
Nothing. No small talk, no anecdotes.
Nothing can be risked on the board of talk.
Because the inner voice is so urgent in its own discourse:
How shall I live? How shall I manage the future?
Why should I go on?

—Kate Millett

Table 9.2 lists the DSM-IV-TR diagnostic criteria for dysthymic disorder (or dysthymia). This condition is often described as a "low-grade" form of depression, because symptoms are less severe but more chronic than in MDD. In addition, fluctuations between depressive periods and periods of remission are less marked, making it often difficult to establish clinically when these periods begin and end. The disorder must last a minimum of one year without any period of improvement of more than two months during that time. In other words, most youth with dysthymia have fewer symptoms of depression than youth with MDD who are in the middle of a depressive episode. However, they often go for months without any significant improvement in mood (APA, 2000a). Joseph's story illustrates the chronic nature of the disorder and the sad fact that many youth with dysthymia become so used to being depressed that they may not recognize their mood as abnormal.

Joseph is 14. He is an only child. Mrs. Smith, his mother, reports that he was doing well at school until

TABLE 9.2   *Dysthymic Disorder: DSM-IV-TR Diagnostic Criteria*

A. Depressed mood for most of the day, for more days than not, as indicated either by subjective account or observation by others, for at least 2 years. *Note:* In children and adolescents, mood can be irritable and duration must be at least 1 year.

B. Presence, while depressed, of two (or more) of the following:

   (1) poor appetite or overeating

   (2) insomnia or hypersomnia

   (3) low energy or fatigue

   (4) low self-esteem

   (5) poor concentration or difficulty making decisions

   (6) feelings of hopelessness

C. During the 2-year period (1 year for children or adolescents) of the disturbance, the person has never been without the symptoms in Criteria A and B for more than 2 months at a time.

D. No Major Depressive Episode has been present during the first 2 years of the disturbance (1 year for children and adolescents); i.e., the disturbance is not better accounted for by chronic Major Depressive Disorder, or Major Depressive Disorder, In Partial Remission.

Note: There may have been a previous Major Depressive Episode provided there was a full remission (no significant signs or symptoms for 2 months) before development of the Dysthymic Disorder. In addition, after the initial 2 years (1 year in children or adolescents) of Dysthymic Disorder, there may be superimposed episodes of Major Depressive Disorder, in which case both diagnoses may be given when the criteria are met for a Major Depressive Episode.

E. There has never been a Manic Episode, a Mixed Episode, or a Hypomanic Episode (see text).

F. The disturbance does not occur exclusively during the course of a chronic Psychotic Disorder, such as Schizophrenia or Delusional Disorder.

G. The symptoms are not due to the direct physiological effects of a substance (e.g., a drug of abuse, a medication) or a general medical condition (e.g., hypothyroidism).

H. The symptoms cause clinically significant distress or impairment in social, occupational, or other important areas of functioning.

Specify if:

Early Onset: if onset is before age 21 years

Late Onset: if onset is age 21 years or older

last year, when his grades began to decline very rapidly and "he lost total interest in school." She feels that he may not be challenged intellectually, because "he is very quiet in school and does not really show his teachers what he can do." However, she does not attribute his difficulties to his high intelligence alone, noting that he has emotional problems at home and at school—where he is frequently teased by peers.

Mrs. Smith describes a family history of depression, which she refers to as the "family curse." However, she remembers Joseph as a "happy and joyful preschooler." She believes that "he lost all this joy during his years in school," so much so that family members often characterize him now as "Eyeore" (the unhappy donkey in Winnie the Pooh*'s children's stories). Inter-*

estingly, she is persuaded that Joseph can have fun but that "he brings himself down all the time, like he was preventing himself from really living for the moment."

Assessment shows that Joseph has numerous depressive symptoms, especially depressed mood, anhedonia, feelings of hopelessness, and low self-esteem. However, IQ testing confirms that he is of superior intelligence. Joseph denies any difficulty with depression, stating instead that "This is how I am and I have always been." He acknowledges that many of his peers seem to have more enjoyable and rewarding lives than he does, but then adds almost defiantly, "Well, what do you want me to do about it?"

Joseph is treated with a cognitive-behavioral approach. Given his superior intelligence, he quickly *grasps the concept of cognitive errors (see Treatment and Prevention) and rapidly changes his thinking style to reduce his reliance on negative automatic thoughts. At his one-year follow-up appointment, Joseph reports doing well in school and at home, something which his mother and school counselor confirm. . . . He remains a "serious person" but is no longer withdrawn or depressed, and is better able to deal with daily challenges in a positive manner.*

As in MDD, the DSM-IV-TR specifies that children and adolescents with dysthymia often appear irritable rather than depressed. Besides a disturbed mood, the DSM-IV-TR requires at least two of six symptoms before a diagnosis can be made. These include lack of interest or pleasure in usual activities, fatigue or low energy, sleep and appetite disturbances, poor self-confidence, inability to concentrate or make decisions, and feelings of pessimism and hopelessness. Obviously, when present for long periods of time, these symptoms can significantly limit a young person's daily functioning. However, as in Joseph's case, symptoms are usually less severe than they are in MDD, although they may be so chronic that they come to be seen as the child's character or personality, rather than as signs of a psychological disorder.

As in MDD, some symptoms of dysthymia are more common than others. For example, in a follow-up of a clinical sample of fifty-five youth for periods ranging from three to twelve years, Kovacs, Akiskal, Gatsonis, and Parrone (1994) found that depressed mood, poor self-image and self-esteem, brooding about being unloved or not having friends, anger, temper tantrums, disobedience, and concentration difficulties were very common. Social withdrawal, loss of interest and pleasure, guilt, suicidal ideation, and sleep and appetite disturbances were less common and, by their absence, could often help to distinguish youth with dysthymia from youth with MDD.

Bipolar Disorder

Manic Episodes.   The key characteristic of bipolar disorder is the presence of one or more manic episodes. These episodes are phases of extreme elation or euphoria, often mixed with irritability, and excessive ac-

tivity. Youth with bipolar disorder alternate between periods of mania and of average or depressed mood. Although many adolescents appear excited and overly joyous during manic periods, this consists of much more than being in a good mood. Carlson (1994) reports the case of a 12-year-old boy who had a "perpetually silly grin," even though he had been separated from his family because of the severity of his emotional problems. In the child's words, "I don't know if I have family or a place to live, but I suddenly feel like it doesn't matter anymore. I feel like all my troubles are gone; it doesn't make sense 'cause none of that stuff has changed" (p. 48). His euphoric state, which contrasted with his previously depressed condition, had no basis in reality. As this example illustrates, mania is an abnormal mood state that places affected children and adolescents at risk, because their emotions are not in keeping with what is happening in their lives, thus cutting them off from their loved ones, or leading them to act dangerously or with little appreciation for the likely consequences of their actions.

Josh is 10. He has been having troubles with mood swings and aggressive behavior for two years. His mother notes that he has always been "sensitive," but that lately it seems that anything can set him off into long periods of extreme agitation and anger. These periods usually come to an end as quickly as they begin, but not without distressing the entire family first. When agitated, Josh rails at his family about the "injustices" he believes he suffers, and proclaims that everything is "unfair." His mother also reports that during these periods Josh talks "non-stop" about topics that are of little consequence to those around him—"I mean, not relevant to anything or anybody," she says. When Josh is not in this agitated and angry state, he often expresses feelings of hopelessness and guilt, as well as suicidal ideation.

Josh was adopted as an infant, and little is known about his biological family. His parents are able to find out, however, that his biological mother had suffered from severe depression and that his maternal uncle had been diagnosed with bipolar disorder. No information is available about his biological father or the paternal side of his family of origin.

Because of his extreme agitation and fears that he might act dangerously at home or at school, Josh is hos-

pitalized. Within a week of the start of lithium medication to stabilize his mood, Josh begins to show signs of improvement and, after five weeks, is able to be discharged.

Table 9.3 lists the DSM-IV-TR diagnostic criteria for *manic episode.* Only one episode is required for a diagnosis of bipolar disorder, essentially because most persons who have one will have another. In addition to the often rapid change in mood that is characteristic of the disorder, the DSM-IV-TR requires that the child or adolescent exhibit three or more associated symptoms (or four if the manic mood is primarily irritable), which we describe briefly here.

Pressured Speech, Racing Thoughts, and High-Risk Behavior.

Mood changes in bipolar disorder are generally accompanied by an *increase in energy* and activity level; a *decreased need for sleep,* at times to the point of total exhaustion (Biederman et al., 2000); and *racing thoughts.* Children and adolescents with the disorder often seem to be in "high gear": they talk at a rapid rate, almost as if they were under pressure to speak. An older adolescent seen in our clinic would begin her therapy sessions by breathlessly announcing, "I have so much to tell you" and then proceed to relate all she had done in the preceding week in a five-minute "race." The therapist found that the only way to interrupt her was to stand up and motion for "time-out." Pressured speech is the external sign of racing thoughts, or what clinicians call **flight of ideas.** Affected youth "are not able to get anything done because their [racing] thoughts keep interrupting" them (Geller & Luby, 1997, p. 1168). In keeping with this behavioral style, youth with mania are frequently involved in *high-risk pleasurable activities* such as sex and drug use (Weller et al., 1995). Many of them engage in such behavior while proclaiming that they are sure that no harm will come to them, so much so that they may need to be hospitalized for their own protection.

Exaggerated Sense of Self and Psychotic Features.

Manic episodes also are often accompanied by an

TABLE 9.3 *Manic Episode: DSM-IV-TR Diagnostic Criteria*

A. Distinct period of abnormally and persistently elevated, expansive, or irritable mood, lasting at least 1 week (or any duration if hospitalization is necessary).

B. During the period of mood disturbance, three (or more) of the following symptoms have persisted (four if the mood is only irritable) and have been present to a significant degree:

  (1) inflated self-esteem or grandiosity

  (2) decreased need for sleep (e.g., feels rested after only 3 hours of sleep)

  (3) more talkative than usual or pressure to keep talking

  (4) flight of ideas or subjective experience that thoughts are racing

  (5) distractibility (i.e., attention too easily drawn to unimportant or irrelevant external stimuli)

  (6) increase in goal-directed activity (either socially, at work or school, or sexually) or psychomotor agitation

  (7) excessive involvement in pleasurable activities that have a high potential for painful consequences (e.g., engaging in unrestrained buying sprees, sexual indiscretions, or foolish business investments)

C. The symptoms do not meet criteria for a Mixed Episode (see text).

D. The mood disturbance is sufficiently severe to cause marked impairment in occupational functioning or in usual social activities or relationships with others, or to necessitate hospitalization to prevent harm to self or others, or there are psychotic features.

F. The symptoms are not due to the direct physiological effects of a substance (e.g., a drug of abuse, a medication, or other treatment) or a general medical condition (e.g., hyperthyroidism).

Source: American Psychiatric Association, *Diagnostic and Statistical Manual of Mental Disorders, Fourth Edition, Text Revision* (Washington, DC: American Psychiatric Association, 2000a). Copyright 2000 American Psychiatric Association. Reprinted with permission.

exaggerated or *grandiose sense of self* that has no basis in reality. For example, a teen with failing grades may confidently announce that she is going to become a lawyer. Another may deliberately fail a test to show a teacher that the material was taught incorrectly (Geller & Luby, 1997). Carlson (1994) notes that sense of self during manic periods "often reflects and magnifies the person's premorbid conflicts, life-style, preoccupations, and other concerns. Thus, literary people are more likely than truck drivers to feel that they are writing the world's greatest novel. Those with strong religious backgrounds are more likely to hear from God than are atheists" (p. 49). In some cases, this exaggerated sense of self may be confirmed by the youth's *hallucinations or delusions.* For example, an adolescent boy who begins a manic period believing that he has a special religious calling may have hallucinations that God is talking to him and develop the delusion that he is a divine messenger. Carlson and Strober (1979) found that 50% of the adolescents with bipolar disorder they assessed had hallucinations, and that 66% had delusions. As in MDD, psychotic features have been shown to predict poor outcomes, at least in adults. However, longitudinal research with children and adolescents is lacking.

The DSM-IV-TR describes **mixed episodes,** in which the child or adolescent meets diagnostic criteria for manic and depressive episodes, and rapidly cycles between periods of mania, major depression, and normal mood; and **hypomanic episodes,** in which full criteria for mania are not met, but the person has enough manic symptoms to disturb functioning.

Suicide

Mood disorders are often accompanied by **suicidal ideation**—that is, persistent thoughts about death or plans to commit suicide—as well as by suicide attempts. Suicidal ideation is common in youth in general, and particularly in youth who are clinically depressed, with rates varying little throughout childhood and adolescence (Kashani & Carlson, 1987; Mitchell et al., 1988). For example, in a community sample of more than 1,700 adolescents, Roberts, Lewinsohn, and Seeley (1995) found that 41% had thought about suicide; this percentage is significantly higher in clinical samples, often affecting more than 75% of depressed

children and adolescents (DiFilippo & Overholser, 2000). Tragically, thoughts of suicide disturb the lives of even young children with MDD. Rita, a 4-year-old girl who attended our clinic, stated quite bluntly that she wanted to die "to go in the ground and never have to live again." This comment makes it clear that she understood the permanence of death, even though she did not have an actual plan to harm herself.

Box 9.1 lists the signs of increased suicidal potential in a suicidal person. In the general population,

---

BOX 9.1 • *Signs of Increased Suicidal Potential in a Suicidal Person*

I believe that when all is said and done, all you can do is to show up for someone in crisis, which seems so inadequate. But then when you do, it can radically change everything. Your there-ness, your stepping into a scared person's line of vision, can be life giving, because often everyone else is in hiding.

—Anne Lamott

Recent decades have seen significant increases in suicidal behavior in adolescents and young adults. The following is a list of behaviors indicating that a person is at an elevated risk of suicide and may actually be contemplating it:

- Previous attempts or gestures
- Suicidal plan
- Lethal plan, especially involving firearms
- Availability of firearms and potentially lethal medication in home
- Plan for suicide is combined with alcohol use
- Precautions against rescue
- Evidence of putting affairs in order
- High frequency of ideation
- Desire to join dead loved one
- Suicidal communications, written or oral
- Consideration of suicide as a viable alternative
- Failure to establish rapport with clinician
- Inability to abide by no-suicide contract
- Inadequate parent support, supervision, or judgment

Source: Carlson and Abbott (1995), p. 2389.

approximately 1% of children (Pfeffer, Lipkins, Plutchik, & Mizruchi, 1988) and between 1% and 7% of adolescents make at least one suicide attempt (Birmaher et al., 1996). Rates are considerably higher among young people with MDD. For example, in a clinical study, Ryan and associates (1987) found that 13% of children and 26% of adolescents with the disorder had made one or more attempts to kill themselves. Maria, an older teen in our clinic, swallowed a large quantity of cold tablets. After the incident, she said that she had wanted to die but knew she would not, because the tablets she had taken were not strong enough to kill her.

In the United States, approximately 7% of all suicides are committed by youth who are 19 or younger (U.S. Department of Justice, 1999). This figure, though alarming, may be underestimating the scope of the problem, because many youth suicides are registered as accidental rather than self-inflicted deaths. Suicide attempts in adolescence are generally more successful than in childhood. Older youth are more likely to have access to and choose lethal methods, such as firearms or overdoses. Also, many of them genuinely want to die (see Box 9.2). Brent and associates (1993) reported findings from a **psychological autopsy** of cases of completed suicide. Relying on a

BOX 9.2 • *Why Do Some Adolescents Attempt to Commit Suicide?*

Suicide attempts and completed suicides have risen dramatically among adolescents in recent decades, leaving researchers, clinicians, and concerned citizens to ask why so many young people try to end their lives. To find answers to this question, Boergers, Spirito, and Donaldson (1998) asked 120 adolescent suicide attempters exactly that question. Surprisingly, many of the reasons they gave do not support the widespread belief that young people who attempt suicide do it to call attention, not to die. As you can see below, about two-thirds of respondents cited a wish to die as one of the reasons for their suicide attempt.

Reason	Number (%) of participants who endorsed it as *one* reason	Number (%) of participants who endorsed it as the *primary* reason
To die	67 (56)	34 (28)
To get relief from a terrible state of mind	68 (57)	22 (18)
To escape for a while from an impossible situation	66 (55)	16 (13)
To make people understand how desperate you are feeling	34 (28)	11 (9)
To make people feel sorry for the way they've treated you; frighten or get someone back	35 (29)	5 (4)
To try and influence someone or get them to change their mind	16 (13)	1 (1)
To show how much you loved someone	25 (21)	2 (2)
To find out whether someone really loved you or not	32 (27)	6 (5)
To seek help from someone	22 (18)	2 (2)
Other	23 (19)	21 (18)

Source: From J. Boegers, J. Spirito, and D. Donaldson, "Reasons for Adolescent Suicide Attempts," *Journal of the American Academy of Child and Adolescent Psychiatry 37* (1998), p. 1289. Copyright 1998 by Lippincott, Williams & Wilkins. Reprinted by permission.

postmortem, in-depth examination of the child or adolescent's psychological functioning from clinical records and interviews with family, friends, and teachers, they found that depression was the greatest risk factor for committing suicide. However, nearly half of the youth who committed suicide had been depressed for only a few months. They were in the midst of their first depressive episode, rather than struggling with chronic distress, as might have been expected.

Diagnostic and Developmental Considerations

Diagnosis of mood disorders in young people can be made difficult because (1) the term *depression* has different meanings, and (2) the symptomatology of mood disorders changes with age, often in significant ways.

From Normal Feelings to Disorder

In its broadest sense, the term *depression* summarizes the feelings of distress and despair that people experience at different points in life. By themselves, these feelings are normative rather than pathological, since they are frequent in human beings in general and in young people in particular, specifically during adolescence. For example, Achenbach (1991) found that 40% of adolescents report feelings of depression, and that 10% to 20% of parents of adolescents describe them as depressed.

Finally, the term *depression* has a diagnostic meaning. It refers to a psychological disorder whose presence can be established by specific criteria such as those of the DSM-IV-TR. In this case, the term does not only describe a set of specific symptoms. It also specifies that the syndrome has reached a certain level of severity, has lasted for a minimum period of time, and is significantly interfering with the child or adolescent's ability to function normally. The diagnostic use of the term assumes that there are relatively distinct mood disorders and that these disorders can be differentiated from other psychological conditions by their symptoms and developmental trajectories. It was difficult until relatively recently to diagnose different

mood disorders in children and adolescents reliably. However, considerable progress has been made in this area with the publication of structured diagnostic interviews for children, such as the *Diagnostic Interview Schedule for Children* (see Box 2.6) and the *Dominic-R* (see Box 9.3).

Changes in Symptoms over the Course of Development

Carlson and Kashani (1988) compared depressive symptoms of preschoolers, school-age children, adolescents, and adults. They found little variation in the course of development in symptoms such as depressed mood, poor concentration, sleep disturbance, and suicidal ideation. However, lack of interest in pleasurable activities, marked changes in mood in the course of the day, despair, psychomotor retardation, and psychotic symptoms increased with age; and irritability, sad appearance, poor self-concept, and somatic complaints decreased with age. Symptoms also change with age in bipolar disorder. For example, irritability and extreme emotional variability are most common under age 9, but feelings of euphoria, elation, and grandiosity are most often found in adolescence (Weller, Weller, & Fristad, 1995). These findings highlight the fact that developmental differences do not affect the core symptoms of mood disorders, but that they influence their presentation in the course of development (see Developmental Trajectories and Prognosis).

Empirical Validity

Major Depressive Disorder and Dysthymia

The empirical validity of MDD and dysthymia in adulthood is clearly established. Research leads to a comparable, but somewhat more cautious, conclusion in childhood and adolescence.

Use of Adult Diagnostic Criteria.   Adult criteria elicit valid diagnoses of MDD and dysthymia (Hammen & Rudolph, 1996), as the following findings make clear: (1) As long as irritability is accepted as an equivalent of sad or depressed mood, current criteria

BOX 9.3 • *The* **Dominic-R:** *A Pictorial Clinical Interview*

Most researchers and clinicians rely on standardized interviews or behavior checklists to determine the presence of symptoms in children and adolescents, and, when appropriate, to make a diagnosis. Each method can be very informative but has its drawbacks, especially with young children. Clinical interviews require participants to be able to attend to different questions for an extended period of time, and to have sufficiently developed language skills to answer them. Self-report checklists require them to be able to read and follow instructions. These requirements are often major obstacles in the assessment of elementary school children. To overcome them, Valla, Bergeron, and Smolla (2000)

developed the *Dominic-R,* a pictorial interview to diagnose psychological disorders in children between the ages of 6 and 11.

The *Dominic-R* is a structured interview that allows children to identify their own symptoms on the basis of drawings. Each drawing includes a young child named Dominic, portrayed alone or with adults or peers, and corresponds to a DSM-IV-TR psychological symptom. The interviewer shows each drawing to the child being assessed, asking the child each time whether he or she behaves or feels like Dominic. The two examples below come from the male version of the instrument (in the female version, Dominic is portrayed as a girl). As you can

DO YOU DO THINGS ON PURPOSE TO GET ON THE NERVES OF OTHER PEOPLE, LIKE DOMINIC?

(continued)

BOX 9.3 • Continued

DO YOU FEEL SAD MOST OF THE TIME, LIKE DOMINIC? EVEN WHEN OTHERS ARE HAVING FUN?

see, the first one corresponds to a symptom of oppositional defiant disorder and the second one to symptoms of
MDD or dysthymia.

The *Dominic-R* is a relatively new instrument, but
it has already been shown to provide reliable symptom
reports from school-age children. Its unique pictorial design overcomes some of the difficulties researchers and
clinicians have had in the past when they wanted to assess

children directly, rather than relying only on parental or
teacher reports.

Source: From J. P. Valla, L. Bergeron, and N. Smolla, "A Pictorial Interview for 6- to 11-Year-Old Children, *Journal of the American Academy of Child and Adolescent Psychiatry 39* (2000), fig. 1.
Copyright 2000 by Lippincott, Williams and Wilkins. Reprinted
by permission.

adequately describe the behavior of children or adolescents with depression. (2) Youth identified on the basis of these criteria are also identified by other methods, such as self-report measures and questionnaires completed by parents, teachers, or peers. (3) Although there is some variability in the intensity and frequency of symptoms with age, children and adolescents generally exhibit the same core depressive features as adults. (4) A mood disorder in childhood or adolescence represents a specific risk for adult psychopathology; in other words, MDD and dysthymia significantly increase the probability of depressive disorders in adulthood, rather than of other psychological conditions.

MDD vs. Dysthymia. Evidence for the empirical validity of MDD and dysthymia comes also from the fact that the two disorders can be distinguished from each other before adulthood. They have distinct symptom patterns (in spite of considerable overlap in actual symptoms), different ages of onset, and different developmental trajectories (see Epidemiology and Developmental Trajectories and Prognosis).

Bipolar Disorder

The existence—and, hence the empirical validity—of bipolar disorder in childhood and early adolescence is a subject of considerable debate (Biederman et al., 2000; Silva, Matzner, Diaz, Singh, & Dummit, 1999). This debate does not question the validity of the disorder in adolescence, when symptoms are very similar to those found in adulthood (Carlson, 1994). However, some researchers believe that true mania is rare in children and young adolescents, if it exists at all. At that age, affected youth do not manifest clearly alternating periods of mania and depression (or normal mood); instead, they make rapid transitions between agitation, irritability, aggression, depression, and normal mood (Klein, Pine, & Klein, 1998). Like Josh, described earlier, most affected children have brief periods of agitation or extreme irritability lasting usually for a few hours, rather than for a minimum of one week as specified in the diagnostic criteria. Many more youth would qualify for a diagnosis of bipolar disorder if a minimum of a week of symptoms were not required (Carlson & Kashani, 1988).

Associated Characteristics; Comorbidity

Of all disorders of childhood and adolescence, mood disorders are among those most often associated with other psychological symptoms or conditions. For example, in a clinical study of 275 children and adolescents, Kolvin and associates (1991) found that almost 90% of the participants diagnosed with a mood disorder had another disorder as well. However, evidence on comorbidity is limited because participants are often described simply as "depressed" youth, rather than youth with MDD, dysthymia, or bipolar disorder. Therefore, with some exceptions, most investigations do not make it clear whether comorbid conditions are linked to mood disorders in general, or specifically to MDD, dysthymia, or bipolar disorder.

As Figure 9.1 (p. 250) shows, mood disorders tend to become "purer" through adolescence, with rates of comorbidity highest during childhood (Anderson & McGee, 1994; Petersen et al., 1993). Comorbidity is often related to gender. Girls and boys have comparable rates of comorbidity, but mood disorders in girls are related to anxiety and eating disorders (especially in adolescence), whereas in boys they are often associated with disruptive behavior disorders.

Double Depression

MDD and dysthymia are often comorbid. For example, when Joseph was diagnosed at our clinic, he met diagnostic criteria for dysthymic disorder only. However, his mother reported that his mood had been much worse earlier in the year. His sleep and appetite had been disturbed, and he talked frequently about wanting to die. In other words, if he had been assessed a few months earlier, Joseph probably would have been diagnosed with both MDD and dysthymia. Clinically, the simultaneous presence of both disorders is called **double depression.** Double depression is quite common, with one research team reporting that between 38% and 69% of their depressed youth qualified for both diagnoses (Kovacs et al., 1994).

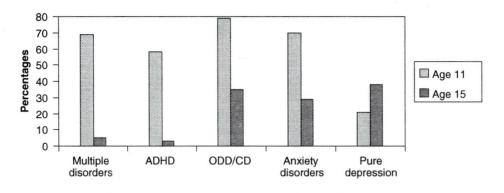

FIGURE 9.1 *Comorbidity in Mood Disorders as a Function of Age.* Mood disorders are often comorbid—but more so in childhood than in adolescence. Longitudinal data, such as this comparison of the same children in late childhood and mid-adolescence, show that comorbidity decreases with age, making mood disorders "purer" in the teenage years than they are earlier.

Source: Anderson and McGee (1994), p. 587. Reprinted by permission.

Anxiety Disorders

MDD and dysthymia (but not bipolar disorder) are also often associated with anxiety disorders (Geller & Luby, 1997; McCauley et al., 1993). Between 33% and 66% of depressed children and adolescents have symptoms of anxiety or an anxiety disorder (Kovacs, 1990). These high rates have led some researchers to hypothesize that anxiety can be a significant risk factor for the development of a mood disorder. Longitudinal research supports this assumption, finding that children with high levels of anxious symptoms at age 9 run an elevated risk of becoming depressed in adolescence (Reinherz et al., 1989).

Disruptive Behavior Disorders and Eating Disorders

As mentioned above, mood disorders are associated with disruptive behavior problems and, specifically, with oppositional defiant disorder (rates range from 0% to 50%), conduct disorder (17% to 79%), and attention deficit hyperactivity disorder (0% to 57%) (Fleming & Offord, 1990; Kovacs & Pollock, 1995). The reverse association also holds, as was shown in Chapter 8. Depressive symptoms or disorders are often comorbid in adolescent girls with eating disorders also

(see Chapter 11). Some evidence actually suggests that negative thoughts about one's appearance and disordered eating can lead to depression in adolescence (see Developmental Trajectories and Prognosis).

General Adaptation

Not surprisingly, mood disorders are associated with major challenges in daily functioning, including learning problems and relationship difficulties with family and peers (Hammen, 1991). For example, youth with high levels of depressive symptoms often perform worse academically than their nonaffected counterparts and have high rates of absenteeism. This is true of children and adolescents from different ethnic backgrounds (Steele, Armistead, & Forehand, 2000).

Youth who are depressed also have pronounced difficulties managing their emotions and resolving conflict with peers (Rudolph, Hammen, & Burge, 1994); and teenage girls have a higher probability of becoming pregnant (Horwitz et al., 1991; cited in Petersen et al., 1993). Interestingly, between depressive episodes youth often make satisfactory academic and social progress, although peer relationships often take longer to improve than academic performance (McCauley, Mitchell, Burke, & Moss, 1988).

Epidemiology

Prevalence; Age and Gender Characteristics

Mood disorders are among the most common psychological conditions of childhood and adolescence (Fleming & Offord, 1990). However, their exact prevalence remains unknown, largely because reported rates vary considerably depending on the samples studied (i.e., normative vs. clinical), the criteria used to define depression, the manner in which mood was assessed (e.g., questionnaires or clinical interviews), and the sources of information consulted (i.e., children, parents, teachers, or peers).

Large-scale epidemiological studies illustrate these difficulties. In a community sample of over 1,700 older adolescents, Roberts and associates (1995) found that the prevalence of MDD ranged from less than 3% to almost 30%, depending on how restrictive the definition of "disorder" was. Similarly, in another large community sample of children and adolescents, Fleming, Offord, and Boyle (1989) found that significant differences in prevalence appeared when data were obtained from different people. For example, adolescent self-reports were six times more likely to yield a diagnosis of depression than parental reports.

Although these studies indicate that care must be taken in interpreting available data, epidemiological research reports prevalence rates for MDD and dysthymia combined ranging from less than 1% to 9%, with a median rate of approximately 5% (Angold & Costello, 1995; Fleming & Offord, 1990). These rates, which estimate either the prevalence at a specific point in time or over periods ranging from six to twelve months, differ primarily according to age and, probably, gender. Epidemiological data on bipolar disorder in youth are not available, although mania is much less frequent than depression in adults.

Age Differences.
Depressive disorders affect fewer than 1% of preschoolers (Kashani et al., 1987). Between ages 6 and 12, rates increase to 2–3%, and reach 6–9% by adolescence. In addition, as many as 20% of adolescents report elevated levels of depressive symptoms. However, many of them do not meet diagnostic criteria for a mood disorder and, when they do, may never come to the attention of professionals (Birmaher et al., 1996). Finally, as is true of suicide, the prevalence of mood disorders—particularly MDD—has been increasing in recent decades, especially among adolescents and young adults. As Box 9.4 (p. 252) shows, this increase is real. It is not simply a reflection of the increase in the proportion of adolescents in the general population since the 1950s or of growing knowledge about mood disorders.

Few epidemiological studies make a distinction between MDD and dysthymia, although available data generally show that the prevalence of MDD is higher than dysthymia during adolescence (Lewinsohn, Hops, Roberts, Seeley, & Andrews, 1993). Childhood data are less clear. Some studies find no difference in prevalence rates between these two disorders in children (Anderson et al., 1987), whereas others find that dysthymia is the more frequent of the two disorders (Costello et al., 1988).

Gender Differences.
The prevalence of mood disorders increases with age in girls, so that adolescent females run a risk of developing depression approximately twice as high as males (Lewinsohn et al., 1993). These differences persist into adulthood. Although gender differences in adolescence are well established, data on younger children are less clear. For example, some studies show that before age 12 mood disorders—especially dysthymia—are more common in boys than girls (Costello et al., 1988); but others do not (Fleming et al., 1989). These contradictions arise in part because the assessment methods and samples on which these studies are based are not always comparable. For example, the results obtained by Costello and associates (1988) are based on structured diagnostic interviews, whereas those of Fleming and colleagues (1989) come from questionnaires completed by children, parents, and teachers.

A study by Angold, Costello, and Worthman (1998) may help clarify the timing of gender differences in depression. These researchers evaluated the link between depression and puberty in a large sample of children aged 9, 11, and 13. They found that increases in depressive disorders were strongly related to puberty for both boys and girls, but that the direction

BOX 9.4 • *Secular Increases in Rates of Major Depressive Disorder*

As Chapter 8 showed, aggressive and antisocial behaviors in general, and ODD and CD in particular, have increased dramatically in recent decades in most industrialized countries. The same is true of MDD. A study of the siblings of children with MDD shows that depressive symptoms and disorders have become more prevalent in recent generations (Ryan et al., 1992). As you can see in the graph below, siblings born before 1970 had a lower cumulative lifetime risk of developing MDD than siblings born after that date. Interestingly, this secular increase applies only to mild and moderate cases of MDD, and not to dysthymia (Birmaher et al., 1996).

Reasons for this secular increase have yet to be uncovered. However, it is most likely to reflect environmental factors, rather than changes in the genetic makeup of the population, simply because the gene pool cannot change significantly in the course of two or three generations. Moreover, there is little evidence for a secular increase in severe cases of MDD, which are presumed to reflect the contribution of genetic factors to a greater extent than mild or moderate ones (Birmaher et al., 1996).

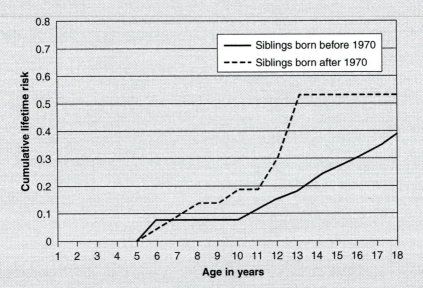

Source: From N. D. Ryan et al., "A Secular Increase in Child and Adolescent Onset Affective Disorder," *Journal of the American Academy of Child and Adolescent Psychiatry 31* (1992), p. 603. Copyright 1992 by Lippincott, Williams and Wilkins. Reprinted by permission.

of this relationship was different for the two sexes. Specifically, girls showed an increase in depressive disorders in mid-puberty. In contrast, boys showed a decrease in these disorders at the beginning of puberty, even though they had been more likely to have such disorders than girls prior to puberty. These findings indicate that puberty, rather than age, may be most important in understanding gender differences in the epidemiology of mood disorders, even though the processes accounting for pubertal changes remain to be established.

Social and Cultural Differences

Epidemiological evidence comparing the prevalence of mood symptoms or disorders in people of different socioeconomic status or ethnicity provides contradictory data that are difficult to interpret. Some studies report that prevalence is not associated with socioeconomic status, whereas others find that youth from disadvantaged backgrounds tend to have elevated levels of depression. The same is true of ethnicity. For example, in their review of the literature, Fleming and Offord (1990) found that depressive symptoms and disorders were more common among African American than European American adolescents, whereas Nettles and Pleck (1994) came to the opposite conclusion.

These discrepancies indicate that socioeconomic status and ethnicity do not reflect the complexities inherent in this area. For example, young people chronically exposed to adverse social circumstances such as poverty and racism have a high risk of developing psychological disorders, including mood disorders. However, it is inappropriate to generalize findings to an entire socioeconomic or ethnic group, because such a generalization ignores important *within-group differences* that can greatly affect a child's outcomes. Factors such as supportive family and temperamental characteristics are as important in determining outcomes as broader variables such as socioeconomic status and ethnicity (Beardslee, Versage, & Gladstone, 1998).

Nonetheless, members of groups that face widespread discrimination are decidedly at risk for depression. For example, in a longitudinal study conducted in New Zealand, Fergusson, Horwood, and Beautrais (1999) found that gay, lesbian, or bisexual adolescents have much higher rates of mood disorders and suicide attempts than heterosexual youth. Specifically, over 71% of the gay, lesbian, and bisexual teenagers they studied qualified for a diagnosis of MDD. In addition, these teens were five to six times more likely than their heterosexual peers to have thought about suicide and to have made one or more suicide attempts. The reasons that explain these findings are undoubtedly complex, but Fergusson and colleagues hypothesize that they often reflect the specific challenges that nonheterosexual teenagers face as they approach adulthood in societies in which homophobic attitudes prevail.

Developmental Trajectories and Prognosis

As is true of other conditions covered in this book, the developmental trajectories of mood disorders are complex and vary considerably from one case to another. In general, depressive symptoms are not continuous but tend to be recurrent, so that young people who experience an initial period of dysfunction have a high probability of experiencing others (Hammen & Rudolph, 1996). For example, a study of adolescents followed for up to twenty-five years found that high levels of depressive symptoms during adolescence predicted similar problems in adulthood, as well as challenges such as drug abuse and employment difficulties (Kandel & Davies, 1986). In addition, adolescent depression had a long-term negative impact on intimate relationships in adulthood. Rao, Hammen, and Daley (1999) found also that young women who were depressed during adolescence faced significant difficulties in their intimate and social relationships in early adult life.

Major Depressive Disorder

Although MDD can affect preschoolers (Kashani & Carlson, 1987), it usually begins in older childhood and adolescence, most often between the ages of 10 and 17. Average age of onset varies as a function of the population studied. It is 11 in clinical studies (Kovacs et al., 1994), 12 to 13 in studies of children of depressed mothers (Hammen, 1991), and 14 or older in community studies (Lewinsohn et al., 1993). The first episode lasts an average of seven to nine months (Kovacs et al., 1994; McCauley et al., 1993). Approximately 80% of youth who have a depressive episode recover within a year, and more than 90% within two years. However, risk of relapse is high, particularly among youth who have been hospitalized. Between 18% and 35% of affected children and adolescents will have a new episode within a year; 40–45% within two years; 54–61% within three years; and more than 70% within five years (Kovacs, Obrosky, Gatsonis, & Richards, 1997; McCauley et al., 1993). A follow-up of hospitalized adolescents actually found that *all participants* had one or more additional depressive episodes within eight years of their initial hospitalization (Garber, Kriss, Koch, & Lindholm, 1988).

Evolution.   Not surprisingly, prognosis is worst when symptoms are severe and begin early, and/or when endogenous or psychotic symptoms are present (Birmaher et al., 1996). For example, Strober, Lampert, Schmidt, and Morrell (1993) found that adolescents with psychotic features tended to have more chronic symptoms, and also that 28% of them developed mania during a two-year follow-up. (None of the depressed youth without psychotic symptoms developed mania over the same period.) These findings suggest that MDD, especially when it is accompanied by psychotic symptoms, may signal the beginning of a developmental trajectory that could evolve into bipolar disorder. This evolution is probably specific to children and adolescents with MDD, since it is seen much less frequently in adults with the disorder.

Adult Outcomes.   As we just noted, the difficulties of children and adolescents with MDD often persist into adulthood. However, the trajectory of the disorder after adolescence depends on the presence of comorbid conditions. For example, an eighteen-year follow-up of an English clinical sample found that youth who had a depressive disorder that was not comorbid with other psychological difficulties were likely to be depressed in adulthood (Harrington, Fudge, Rutter, Pickles, & Hill, 1991). In contrast, youth with comorbid mood and conduct problems were more likely to be involved in antisocial activities than to be depressed as adults.

Dysthymia

Dysthymia begins, on average, two to three years earlier than MDD and is characterized by longer periods of dysfunction. Reported ages of onset vary between 6 and 13 years, with an average age of 9 in clinical studies (Kovacs et al., 1994) and of 11 in community studies (Lewinsohn et al., 1993). The initial period of dysthymia lasts for approximately four years (Birmaher et al., 1996). The majority of children recover with time but, like their counterparts with MDD, have a high risk of relapsing. For example, in a three- to twelve-

year follow-up of a clinical sample of children and adolescents, Kovacs and associates (1994) found that they were free of depressive symptoms only half of the time during the follow-up period, and free of any psychological problems only one-third of the time. In addition, 76% of them developed MDD in the course of follow-up, 13% had at least one episode of mania, 40% were diagnosed with an anxiety disorder, and 31% developed conduct disorder. Kovacs and associates describe dysthymia as a "gateway" to other disorders, rather than as a condition that follows a persistent course from childhood through adolescence. In other words, dysthymia tends to develop into other disorders in a majority of affected children; and these disorders, in turn, determine the long-term nature of the difficulties they are likely to face in adolescence and adulthood.

Bipolar Disorder

As you know, bipolar disorder is usually a cyclical and more or less chronic condition. Before adulthood, manic episodes are of relatively long duration and are mostly *mixed*—with rapid cycles of mania, major depression, and normal mood lasting from a few hours to a few days. In adulthood, in contrast, discrete manic episodes lasting for several days alternate with depressive episodes or periods of normal mood (Carlson, 1994). Geller and associates (2001) highlight the long duration of manic or mixed episodes in young people. These authors found that only 37% of eighty-nine children and adolescents diagnosed with bipolar disorder had recovered within a year of initial diagnosis, and that almost 40% of those who had recovered later relapsed.

Hyperactivity and Mania.   Prepubertal cases of bipolar disorder may first begin with signs of hyperactivity or with ADHD (Geller & Luby, 1997). Similarly, some children with ADHD may have a comorbid bipolar disorder. In a four-year follow-up of children with ADHD and comparison children, Biederman and associates (1996) found that 11% of children with ADHD qualified for a diagnosis of bipolar disorder at initial assessment and that an additional 12% did so at follow-up. Thus, over 20% of subjects in the clinical group had a history of bipolar disorder. In sharp contrast, none of the comparison children had bipolar disorder at initial assessment or follow-up, even though this group contained subjects with many other diagnoses, such as MDD, anxiety disorders, oppositional defiant disorder, and conduct disorder. This link between ADHD and bipolar disorder is generally found only in youth with a family history of bipolar disorder (Faraone, Biederman, Mennin, Wozniak, & Spencer, 1997).

Adult Outcomes. Little is known about the long-term outcomes of youth with bipolar disorder. Since studies of adult samples show that the disorder is associated with multiple impairments, many affected youth probably face significant challenges in adulthood, even when they recover from the disorder.

Etiology

Biological Factors: Genetic Studies

MDD and Dysthymia. It is well known that MDD and dysthymia often affect members of the same family, partly because of genetic vulnerability. Genetic factors account for 50% or more of the variance associated with the transmission of these disorders (Birmaher et

al., 1996), and concordance rates are approximately two to four times higher for monozygotic than for dizygotic twins (see Figure 9.2).

Family aggregation studies show that between 15% and 45% of children of depressed parents are likely to develop a mood disorder (Birmaher et al., 1996). This rate is highest for youth with two affected parents and increases with age. A review of the genetics literature found that a child of a depressed parent has a 40% chance of becoming depressed by age 20, and that by age 25 this rate reaches 60% (Beardslee et al., 1998). Offspring of depressed parents also have an elevated risk of developing other disorders. For example, in one study, children of depressed mothers qualified for an average of 2.6 diagnoses, not all of which were mood disorders (Hammen, Burge, & Stansbury, 1990). Similarly, in another study, a diagnosis of depression in grandparents and parents was a significant predictor of both mood and anxiety disorders in grandchildren (Warner, Weissman, Mufson, & Wickramaratne, 1999).

Comparable findings emerge from family aggregation studies that looked at the relatives of affected children. Thus, 20–46% of first-degree relatives of depressed children also have a mood disorder (Mitchell et al., 1989). Rates are probably higher when the child's difficulties have an earlier age of onset (Birmaher et

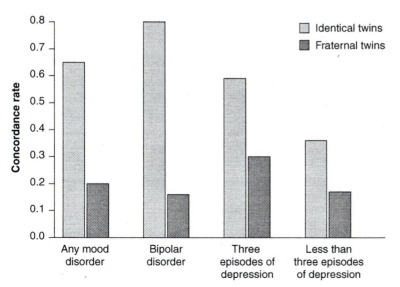

FIGURE 9.2 *Concordance Rates for Mood Disorders among Danish Twins.* This graph shows that concordance rates for mood disorders are much higher in identical than in fraternal twins. Note the especially high concordance rate for bipolar disorder.

Source: Based on data from Bertelsen, Harvald, and Hauge (1977), p. 332.

al., 1996), and when the child presents with dysthymia rather than MDD (Klein et al., 1998).

Bipolar Disorder.   Monozygotic twins are also significantly more likely to be concordant for mania than dizygotic twins are (55% vs. 5%) (Vehmanen, Kaprio, & Loennqvist, 1995). In fact, this last study as well as the study we summarize in Figure 9.4 suggest that genetic influences may be stronger in bipolar disorder than in other mood disorders.

In family aggregation studies, children whose parents have bipolar disorder can be differentiated from children of control parents by higher rates of depression and irritability, and increased difficulty regulating their mood (Chang, Steiner, & Ketter, 2000). Not surprisingly, these children have high rates of psychological problems in general, especially when both parents are affected (Beardslee et al., 1998). The disorder is also frequently found in first-degree relatives of affected youth. For example, Faraone and associates (1997) showed that the risk of finding bipolar disorder in a first-degree relative increased fivefold when there was an affected child in the family. This risk is unlikely to be specific to bipolar disorder, however, since relatives of youth with bipolar disorder were also at increased risk for other mood disorders.

Biological Factors: Neurobiological Studies

Following important advances in adult research, several investigators have focused on the neurobiological processes associated with mood disorders in childhood and adolescence. Important progress has been made in recent years, but interpretation of findings is often made difficult because normative developmental data are sparse—that is, because relatively little is known about neurobiological processes in normally developing children and adolescents (Emslie, Weinberg, Kennard, & Kowatch, 1994). The neurobiological processes most thoroughly studied focus on neurotransmitters, hormones, and sleep cycles.

Neurotransmitters.   Research into the role that neurotransmitters may play in the etiology of mood disorders has a long history, which closely parallels the development of psychotropic drugs to treat these dis-

orders. Two neurotransmitters have received particular attention: norepinephrine and serotonin. Data collected for the most part with adults suggest that (1) a deficiency of norepinephrine in some brain pathways is linked to depression, and an excess of this neurochemical to mania; and (2) a reduction in brain **serotonin** levels can trigger a fall in norepinephrine levels and thus contribute to depression also (Nemeroff, 1998). Support for these processes of neurotransmission comes from several sources. For example, drugs that reduce depression or produce mania increase brain norepinephrine levels. Conversely, drugs that have the opposite effects decrease norepinephrine levels. Similarly, antidepressants that act on serotonin increase synaptic levels of this neurotransmitter by inhibiting its reuptake (see below and Figure 2.2). Finally, children who have MDD or have a high risk of developing the disorder show abnormal responses to drugs that affect serotonin levels (Birmaher et al., 1997).

Hormones.   One way in which neurotransmitter imbalances may affect mood is through the dysregulation of brain pathways that control hormone production. The hypothalamus is particularly likely to be implicated in the etiology of mood disorders. This brain structure plays a central role in emotion regulation, through its control of hormone secretion and the HPA axis. Depressed adults—particularly those who are suicidal and/or have endogenous and psychotic symptoms—often show enlarged adrenal and pituitary glands (two glands controlled by the hypothalamus) and abnormal hormone levels (Nemeroff, 1998). For example, depressed adults produce abnormally high levels of **cortisol,** a hormone secreted by the body during times of stress, and have an abnormal response on the **dexamethasone suppression test** (DST). Dexamethasone is a cortisol-like chemical that, once in the bloodstream, ordinarily suppresses cortisol secretion for twenty-four hours or more. Many depressed adults fail to show this pattern of suppression, as do some depressed children and adolescents, especially when their symptoms are severe (Nelson & Davis, 1997). But although overproduction of cortisol may be linked to mood disorders, it is unlikely to be a unique or sufficient cause of these disorders, because cortisol imbalances and abnormal DST responses have been found in other psychological conditions.

Other hormones may play a role in the etiology of mood disorders, including growth hormone, thyroid-stimulating hormone, and testosterone and estrogen. For example, the last two hormones have been implicated in the rapid increase in prevalence of depression in girls at the time of puberty (Angold, Costello, Erkanli, & Worthman, 1999). Similarly, decreases in thyroid hormone produce depression-like symptoms in adults, and thyroid hormone replacement decreases these symptoms. In general, it is safe to conclude that, at this stage, adult findings are more consistent than those obtained with children and adolescents. Furthermore, if these hormones have an etiological role to play in mood disorders before adulthood, it is only in complex transaction with other biological and non-biological factors.

Sleep Patterns.   Given that sleep disturbances occur frequently in mood disorders, neurobiological studies have also focused on sleep patterns in search of possible etiological explanations. Findings show that depressed adolescents and adults have different patterns of brain activity during sleep than control individuals, and that similar differences are often found among their relatives also (Giles, Kupfer, Rush, & Roffwarg, 1998). This finding suggests that specific sleep abnormalities may be inherited and may predispose some youth to later depression, although the etiological processes involved are undoubtedly complex and involve more than sleep difficulties.

Psychological Factors

Attachment Theory.   John Bowlby's (1973) attachment theory points to disturbances in the attachment that very young children develop with their caregivers, primarily their mothers, as a key factor in the etiology of mood disorders. Developmental studies show that children who cannot establish a close, secure attachment with their primary caregiver are at risk for later psychological difficulties, including depressive symptoms and mood disorders (see Chapter 2 for an overview of attachment theory).

Although attachment disturbances are thought to be a factor in the etiology of mood disorders, attachment theory does not predict a specific association between these disorders and the quality of the early parent-child relationship. Empirical findings show also that attachment disturbances are nonspecific. In other words, they increase the risk of psychological problems throughout development; but the nature of these problems varies from one child to another (Greenberg, Cicchetti, & Cummings, 1990), because attachment is influential only in transaction with other factors, such as the child's temperamental disposition, family relationships, and life events. Furthermore, the impact of such transactions depends not only on their contents but also on their timing in the child's development (Reinherz et al., 1989).

Cognitive Perspective: Beck's Cognitive Triad Model.   As shown in Chapter 2, Aaron Beck proposed that depression results from a cycle of **negative automatic thoughts** *about the self, the world,* and *the future.* These thoughts, which occur automatically in individuals who engage in them repeatedly, form what Beck calls a negative **cognitive triad** (see Figure 9.3, p. 258). This triad predisposes to depression and, once the disorder occurs, helps to maintain it because, whatever affected individuals look at, all they see is grim and negative. For example, youth who do well on a test are usually happy about it. They feel good about themselves and are secure in the knowledge that they can succeed if they work hard. In contrast, youth who feel depressed are much more likely to dismiss good performance on a test with negative automatic thoughts. They may say to themselves, "I was lucky this time" or "That was an easy test." Similarly, if they failed the test, they are likely to think in ways that will set them up for future failure by saying to themselves, "I'm really stupid" or "I'll never learn this subject, it's just too hard."

This cycle of negative automatic thoughts influences immediate feelings and behavior and also affects the future by setting up negative **self-fulfilling prophecies,** in which youth will actually fail because of their beliefs. Thus, an adolescent may not study for a test because she "knows" that she will never get a good grade; and another will not ask a girl for a date because he "knows" that no girl will ever want to go out with him. In addition to this negative cognitive triad, Beck and other theorists point out that depressed young

Beck's model

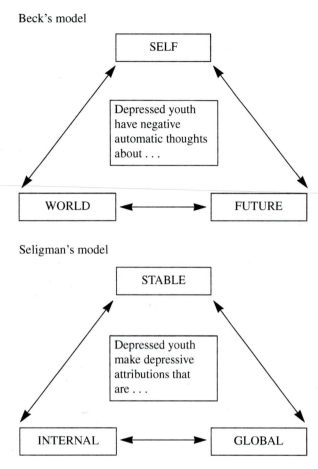

Seligman's model

FIGURE 9.3 *Schematic Representation of Beck's and Seligman's Etiological Models of Depression.* In each model, the child or adolescent's thought processes are assumed to play key roles in bringing about and maintaining depression.

people tend to remember bad experiences and other negative events more readily than positive ones—further aggravating their depressed mood and grim outlook on the future.

Support for Beck's theory comes from findings that depressed youth make more cognitive errors than their nonaffected peers, and that they are quick to engage in negative automatic thinking or to make pessimistic or otherwise negative judgments about themselves and others (Hammen & Rudolph, 1996). Thus,

longitudinal evidence shows that, in adolescent girls, negative beliefs about their physical appearance, in combination with eating disturbances, predict elevated levels of depression over time. This evidence suggests that negative thoughts, such as "I am fat and ugly," may play a causal role in the onset of mood disorders in adolescence (Stice & Bearman, 2001). However, for the most part, the evidence in this area is correlational in nature, so that one cannot establish whether cognitive disturbances actually lead to mood disorders or whether the disorders themselves result in the cognitive errors and negative automatic thoughts that are common in depressed children and adolescents.

Cognitive Perspective: Seligman's Learned Helplessness. Martin Seligman's (1975) **learned helplessness** model is another cognitive approach to depression that has received considerable attention. The model was originally a behavioral one, with roots in animal research. It hypothesized that depression arises from repeated experiences with uncontrollable, noncontingent events. Specifically, Seligman and colleagues found that dogs exposed to electric shocks from which they could not escape were very slow to learn to escape from such shocks when they later had the opportunity. Generalizing to human experience, Seligman proposed that individuals who learn that they are helpless to change the situations in which they find themselves give up in the face of challenges and become depressed.

Seligman later revised the model to emphasize not only the importance of such experiences but also the cognitions associated with them (Abramson, Seligman, & Teasdale, 1978). He and his associates assumed that exposure to uncontrollable events leads to the development of a characteristic belief system—a **depressive attributional style.** Persons who have such a belief system attribute negative outcomes to *stable, internal,* and *global* characteristics in themselves (see Figure 9.3). In this perspective, a child with a depressive attributional style is likely to explain his poor performance on a test by invoking negative personal characteristics that are stable ("I am stupid"), internal ("I just can't learn that stuff"), and global ("I hate tests and I always flunk them").

Support for Seligman's model comes from studies of clinical and community samples that have shown that depressive youth tend to attribute negative life events to stable, internal, and global causes over which they have little or no control. However, here also, the correlational nature of most studies does not generally permit the conclusion that a depressive attributional style is at the origin of mood disorders.

In one of the rare longitudinal studies published to date, Nolen-Hoeksema, Girgus, and Seligman (1992) assessed a sample of young people's depressive symptoms, negative life experiences, and cognitive styles every six months for five years. During the first two years of the study, only negative life events predicted depressive symptoms. In the third year, a pessimistic explanatory style became a significant predictor of depressive symptoms. In addition, the explanatory style of children who suffered from periods of depression in the course of the study remained pessimistic even when their mood improved substantially, thus putting them at risk for relapse. These results suggest that early depressive symptoms are more likely to reflect negative life events than a dysfunctional cognitive style. However, over time such a style may contribute to the maintenance of depressive symptoms and, when these improve, to later relapse.

Limitations of the Cognitive Perspective. Beck and Seligman's theories have given rise to ongoing research programs that demonstrate the importance of cognitive variables in mood disorders. However, these theories have significant limitations. First, both theories overlap to a large extent, and it is not always possible to distinguish clearly between the etiological processes they propose. Development of a single cognitive model regrouping key elements of each theory would be desirable (Gotlib & Hammen, 1992). Second, similar cognitive models have been developed to explain the etiology of other psychological conditions, especially anxiety disorders (see Chapter 10). Consequently, negative automatic thoughts and depressive attributions may not be specific to the etiology of depression; possibly, cognitive errors are merely important correlates of different conditions, rather than key etiological factors in mood disorders only.

Finally, both models assume that the cognitive processes they highlight are mistaken, that they are cognitive *errors* or attributional *biases* that distort a child or adolescent's understanding of reality. However, *the interpretations that affected youth make of their reality may actually be correct* (Weisz, Rudolph, Granger, & Sweeney, 1992), since youth who are depressed often live in a world in which many of their daily experiences are negative and they feel helpless to control them. Thus, if cognitive errors are not errors at all, the validity of the cognitive perspective is called into question, with major consequences for all treatment approaches that attempt to modify the manner in which depressed individuals think of themselves and their world. Instead, it would seem essential—and ethical—to change their world, rather than to attempt to get them to view it differently. As the biologist Robert Sapolsky (1994, p. 36) notes: "The cornerstone of the cognitive approach is that depression and distortion are intertwined, and that the clearing of distorted perceptions and interpretations will ameliorate depression. But what if there are no distortions? What if the depressive's reality is one of unremitting sadness, say, at being a refugee or a homeless streetperson?"

Sapolsky had adults in mind, but his question applies to children and adolescents as well. Many youth in the grip of depression may feel terrible because their parents are constantly fighting or struggling with alcohol, because they are mocked by peers who do not approve of their looks or of their sexual orientation, because they live in chronic poverty, or because of other distressing circumstances. In short, they may be depressed not because their perception of reality is mistaken but because it is accurate and hopeless.

Behavioral Perspective

Behavioral theories look for the causes of mood disorders in the interpersonal relationships that children or adolescents maintain with those around them (e.g., Lewinsohn, 1974). From this point of view, these disorders arise from a lack of positive social reinforcement. Some children may lack reinforcement because they are not valued or appreciated by family and friends, who ignore, neglect, or reject them. Others may lack the emotional, social, or instrumental skills that would enable them to obtain the social reinforcement they need to feel wanted and appreciated. Deprived of social reinforcement, these youth may withdraw and develop depressive symptoms or a mood disorder. For example, Bob, the 14-year-old with MDD we described earlier, claimed that he had withdrawn from his friends and family because they did not understand how he felt. By the time he came to the clinic, he rarely interacted with those around him, and, when he did, he was irritable and short-tempered. It is likely that Bob's difficulties started in part because of a lack of positive social reinforcement; but his behavior over time alienated those around him. If this negative pattern had continued, Bob might have failed to develop appropriate teenage social and interpersonal skills, and would have become even more isolated and depressed.

Several studies clearly show that depressive symptoms, and especially mood disorders, are associated with important characteristics described in the behavioral perspective. For example, depression often appears in social contexts that provide little reinforcement or are filled with stressful life events (Kashani et al., 1987; McCauley et al., 1993). Similarly, depressed children and adolescents often lack the emotional, social, and instrumental skills required to interact adequately with peers and adults. For example, they tend to be submissive or oppositional, instead of asserting themselves appropriately. These characteristics contribute to their isolation at home and school (Lewinsohn et al., 1994).

Although available information confirms the importance of behavioral variables and interpersonal relationships in mood disorders, the questions raised earlier concerning the cognitive perspective apply here also. Briefly, it is difficult to distinguish between environmental and behavioral variables that may play an etiological role in the development of depression, and variables that are only associated characteristics. In addition, many of these characteristics are not specific to mood disorders. They are also implicated in the etiology of other disorders, such as anxiety and disruptive behavior disorders. Finally, the etiological role of behavioral and interpersonal variables remains to be established. A growing number of longitudinal studies support important aspects of these models (Lewinsohn et al., 1994; Nolen-Hoeksema et al., 1992); however, many researchers today adopt a transactional model, in which negative events and poor skills are both the cause and consequence of depressive symptoms. In this per-

spective, stressful life events, limited skills, and depressive symptoms feed on each other to disturb the emotional, social, and instrumental functioning of affected children and adolescents, leading many of them to develop an actual mood disorder.

Family Factors

Numerous studies conducted in different theoretical perspectives show that family interactions are often disturbed in families in which parents or children have a mood disorder (Gotlib & Hammen, 1992; Sheeber, Hops, & Davis, 2001). Specifically, "families with depressed members are perceived as less cohesive and adaptable, less open to emotional expressiveness, less democratic, more hostile and rejecting, more conflictual and disorganized, and less likely to engage in pleasant activities" (Hammen & Rudolph, 1996, p. 179). However, whether disturbed family relationships can actually cause mood disorders has not been established. Such relationships are a risk factor for many psychological disorders; therefore, some relational patterns may not be specific to mood disorders. In addition, as with other disorders, disturbances in family functioning may be as much a consequence as a cause of a child's psychological problems. In other words, findings again support a transactional model in which depressive symptoms and disturbed family relationships reciprocally aggravate each other.

Depressed Caregivers.   Families with a depressed parent expose children to patterns of interaction and communication that place them at high risk of developing or maintaining depressive symptoms (Jones, Forehand, & Neary, 2001). For example, mothers with postpartum depression are less positive with their infants, who in turn are less positive with them. More generally, mothers with high levels of critical expressed emotion (see Chapter 5) have children with elevated levels of depressive symptoms (Asarnow, Tompson, Woo, & Cantwell, 2001). Two aspects of maternal behavior seem to contribute to the development of depressive symptoms: high levels of negative critical communication and a lack of positive attention to the child. Even though findings in this area often come from longitudinal research, it would be naive to conclude that these maternal behaviors invariably cause childhood depression; instead, *both* parents *and* children—over time—develop inappropriate patterns of communication that contribute to their personal feelings of distress (Burge & Hammen, 1991).

Depressed Children.   Studies also show that relationships are often disturbed in families of depressed children and adolescents. Observations of these families find a high level of critical communication and hostility and a low level of affection, demonstrated either by withdrawal and rejection or lack of emotional support (Dadds, Sanders, Morrison, & Regbetz, 1992). Unfortunately, these patterns of interaction and communication rarely improve when the child recovers from a depressive episode; therefore, they represent a risk factor for additional episodes.

Depressive symptoms may also serve to protect youth from some negative exchanges with family members. Sheeber and colleagues (Sheeber, Allen, Davis, & Sorensen, 2000; Sheeber, Hops, Andrews, Alpert, & Davis, 1998) found that mothers of depressed adolescents attended to their child's depressive behaviors more often than mothers of control youth,

and that fathers of affected adolescents generally reacted to depressive behavior in a passive way by withdrawing and avoiding any aggressive reactions. Thus, in some cases at least, depressed adolescents may use their symptoms to moderate negative family relationships.

Beyond the Family

Several studies document the existence of a link between adversity and mood disorders in childhood and adolescence. Specifically, mood disorders have been linked to child abuse and neglect (Kashani & Carlson, 1987); marital conflict, separation, and divorce (Block, Block, & Gjerde, 1986); parental drug abuse and alcoholism (Mitchell, McCauley, Burke, & Moss, 1989); death of a relative (Reinherz et al., 1989); and socioeconomic factors such as poverty and unemployment (Daniels & Moos, 1990). As Box 9.5 shows, stressful life events have particularly negative effects when they are chronic and when youth lack the physical and psychological resources to cope with them adequately.

The links between mood disorders and negative life events are complex, and the role that these variables

---

BOX 9.5 • *Negative Life Events and Depression: Depressive Symptoms in Adolescent Refugees*

Negative life events are related to the development of mood disorders and other psychological problems—especially when stressful experiences are (1) chronic, (2) uncontrollable, and (3) beyond a young person's coping skills. Michel Tousignant and colleagues (1999) studied the psychological adaptation of over two hundred adolescent refugees (aged 13 to 19) who had settled in Canada with their families. In many cases, families had fled their country of origin and faced significant challenges adjusting to life in a new land.

Study participants had high rates of psychological disorders. Specifically, almost twice as many refugee youth met diagnostic criteria for MDD and dysthymia when compared with their Canadian peers (approximately 8% vs. 5%). Many of the refugees also reported that they had attempted to commit suicide. Interestingly, the level

of adaptation of these refugees was not related to their parents' education, to a drop in socioeconomic status because of their immigration to Canada, to parental mastery of the host language or culture, or to the families' country of origin. Only the number of residences since birth, parental separation, and changes in family structure were related to observed disorders in refugee youth.

This study illustrates the link between negative life events and mood disorders, but it also documents the lack of specificity between such events and adolescent adaptation. In addition to high rates of depression, participants had high rates of anxiety and conduct disorders—showing that negative life events predispose young people to a variety of problems as they attempt to cope with challenges that are often beyond their own, and their families', skills and resources.

play in the etiology of depressive phenomena remains poorly understood. Simple causal relations are probably the exception rather than the rule. For example, no one doubts that the death of a relative is a tragic event, but the limited data available indicate that girls are more affected than boys (Reinherz et al., 1989). Even then, this generalization is too broad, for the impact of a loved one's death also depends on the child's stage of social, emotional, and cognitive development. In short, current knowledge about the relationship between life events and mood disorders cannot point to any single factor or group of risk factors that appear to be specific to mood disorders.

Treatment and Prevention

If depression is creeping up and must be faced, learn something about the nature of the beast: You may escape without a mauling.

—Dr. R. W. Shepherd

Unlike several of the treatments we described in earlier chapters, the approaches used to treat mood disorders were not developed specifically for children and adolescents. Instead, these approaches are downward extensions of interventions developed for adults (AACAP, 1998a).

Theoretically, the downward extension of adult treatments is questionable because it fails to take into account developmentally specific aspects of mood disorders in youth. For example, the cognitive focus of some psychological treatment approaches may be developmentally inappropriate for children, because many children do not exhibit the cognitive errors that cognitive therapies are designed to address (Stark et al., 1996). Moreover, even when such errors are present, children are usually unable to reflect and talk about the way that they think, since thinking about one's thinking is very difficult for most preadolescents.

These theoretical problems are compounded by important methodological limitations. The major one is that there are few well-controlled studies in this area. Also, those that have an experimental design do not adequately report the extent to which their subjects had other psychological problems besides a mood disorder

and do not examine the effect of comorbidity on treatment outcome. Thus, the small number of studies and the fact that they do not usually control for comorbidity limits our knowledge of which treatment approach is most effective in the presence or absence of comorbid problems (AACAP, 1998a).

Major Depressive Disorder and Dysthymia

Cognitive-Behavioral Therapy. You will recall from Chapter 8 that cognitive-behavioral therapy (CBT) attempts to change inappropriate behavior by modifying the thoughts or cognitions that are believed to control it, rather than by focusing on it directly. In other words, the goal of this approach is to change erroneous beliefs in order to have a positive influence on behavior. In addition, many advocates of this approach rely on modeling and role-playing activities in sessions or through weekly homework assignments to put into practice what the child or adolescent has learned cognitively. For example, CBT helped 14-year-old Ray learn that other children's failure to say hello to him at school did not mean that nobody cared about him. Over time, he came to understand that, most often, lack of greeting simply meant that others were distracted or did not notice him. More important, Ray learned that his habit of looking down when he walked, instead of making eye contact, limited the amount of interaction he had with others. The behavioral component of his therapy sought to help him look at people and make eye contact, and to say hello first instead of waiting for others to greet him. Overall, CBT enabled Ray to question many of his erroneous beliefs and, as he gained courage to act differently, to feel much more positive about himself and others.

The greatest discovery of my generation is that human beings can alter their lives by altering their attitudes of mind.

—William James

CBT has been shown to be effective for a majority of youth with MDD, dysthymia, or mild depressive symptoms (Asarnow, Jaycox, & Tompson, 2001). Immediately following treatment, 54–87% of young people treated with CBT show significant improvement when compared to youth on a waiting list or to youth treated only with relaxation training or with **supportive psychotherapy**—a form of treatment in which the therapist listens and provides support but does not challenge erroneous beliefs or teach youth to behave differently. These results are encouraging. However, follow-up studies are needed to evaluate the long-term effectiveness of CBT, especially with youth presenting severe forms of depression or significant comorbid problems.

Interpersonal Therapy.   As we mentioned earlier, some theorists believe that depression arises from a lack of positive social reinforcement, especially in interpersonal interactions. The role of **interpersonal therapy** (IPT) is to help distressed and withdrawn children and adolescents gain access to positive sources of reinforcement in order to combat their depression (Mufson, Moreau, Weissman, & Klerman, 1993). As in CBT, therapy is conducted through direct instruction, role-playing, and modeling in sessions, as well as through weekly homework assignments. For example, 13-year-old Sarah was depressed because she had no friends and the ones she had often avoided her. In therapy, Sarah came to realize that she did nothing to keep her friendships and to develop new ones. Specifically, she complained about being alone but never called or invited anyone, waiting instead to be called or invited. Furthermore, when she was with friends, she overwhelmed them with her attention and resented having to share them with anybody else. Treatment focused on helping Sarah meet new people and develop a list of friends she could call on when she needed social interaction. Role-playing and direct instruction were used to teach her to interact effectively and to deal with peer and family conflict, and served as preparation for weekly homework exercises in which she had to put in practice what she had learned in therapy.

There is preliminary evidence to show that IPT is effective in reducing depressive symptoms and in improving social functioning in adolescents (Mufson, Weissman, Moreau, & Garfinkel, 1999). However, here also, follow-up studies are needed to evaluate the long-term effectiveness of this approach, as well as to establish whether it can help youth presenting severe forms of depression or significant comorbid problems.

Family Therapy.   Given that many youth with MDD or dysthymia have depressed parents and/or live in families in which there are frequent conflicts, some researchers and clinicians have long thought that treatment of the entire family was important. However, research on family therapy for youth with depression does not support this hypothesis (Asarnow et al., 2001). For example, Brent and associates (1998) found that CBT was significantly more effective in reducing depressive symptoms, especially in adolescents with comorbid anxiety disorders, than an extensive family therapy program. Similarly, Clarke, Rhode, Lewinsohn, Hops, and Seeley (1999) reported that adding a parental component to their CBT treatment for adolescents did not result in any further reduction of depressive symptoms or in a greater percentage of youth showing improvement. Although many family therapists would still argue that their approach is crucial to the successful treatment of depression in children and adolescents, some families are reluctant to get involved in family therapy and may refuse treatment or look for other, non-family alternatives. For example, Brent and associates (1998) found that 60% of the families who refused to be randomly assigned to a treatment condition in their study did so because they did not want to participate in family therapy.

Summary and Integration of Findings.   A meta-analysis of psychological interventions for depression summarizes and expands on the findings just reviewed (Michael & Crowley, 2002). Specifically, this analysis found that:

1. On average, children and adolescents receiving a psychological intervention for depression were better adjusted after treatment than approximately 76% of untreated youth.
2. Treatment gains were generally maintained when participants were followed up over time (although several studies did not report follow-up data).
3. The most commonly used psychological intervention was CBT, delivered individually or in families or small groups.
4. Adolescents often benefited more from treatment than children, possibly because their better-

developed cognitive skills allowed them to gain most from cognitively oriented interventions.

5. There was some indication that girls benefited more from treatment than boys, although more research is needed to determine the role that gender may play in treatment outcome.

Pharmacological Interventions. Recent years have seen a dramatic increase in the number of children and adolescents taking antidepressant medications (Safer, 1997), in spite of the fact that the Food and Drug Administration has not approved any of these medications for use before age 18. Even preschoolers are being prescribed these medications in growing numbers (see Figure 9.4).

The widespread use of antidepressant medications before adulthood is not supported by empirical findings. Specifically, the meta-analysis we just summarized found that, on average, youth taking antidepressants were not functioning better than youth taking placebo medications (Michael & Crowley, 2002). More generally, most of the medications they are regularly prescribed have only been tested with adults (Wagner & Ambrosini, 2001). Consequently, little is known about their safety for children and about the long-term developmental consequences

they may have for physical development and psychological adjustment.

Many researchers and clinicians agree that antidepressant medication should be used with children only in conjunction with a psychological intervention (AACAP, 1998a). For example, the Texas Consensus Panel on Medication Treatment of Childhood Major Depressive Disorder recommends that, in most cases, a psychological approach be attempted before any medication is prescribed (Hughes et al., 1999). Antidepressants are recommended only when psychological treatment has failed, when the depression includes psychotic features or is so severe as to impair the child or adolescent's ability to participate in treatment, or when the youth is suicidal.

Antidepressants increase a class of brain chemicals called **monoamines.** Neurotransmitters such as serotonin, norepinephrine, and dopamine are monoamines. Antidepressants are classified according to the monoamine or monoamines on which they act. Older medications, called **tricyclic antidepressants** (TCAs), increase serotonin and norepinephrine by blocking their removal at the level of the synapse. TCAs are effective in adults but are not superior to placebos in children or adolescents. Furthermore, youth taking these medications can easily overdose and require close

FIGURE 9.4 *Antidepressant Medications and Children.*
Antidepressant medications are commonly prescribed, even to very young children. Specifically, there was an approximately twofold increase in antidepressant use in preschool children in the United States between 1991 and 1995 (Zito et al., 2000).

Source: Rob Rogers (2000). Reprinted by permission.

monitoring; in some cases, TCAs have been associated with sudden, unexplained death, possibly because of side effects on the cardiovascular system (AACAP, 1998a).

Newer antidepressants, called **selective serotonin reuptake inhibitors** (SSRIs), increase serotonin in the brain by increasing its availability in the synapse. They are called reuptake inhibitors because they reduce the reabsorption of serotonin into the neuron once it has been released. SSRIs are appealing because they target a fairly specific neurotransmitter process, produce fewer side effects that TCAs, and have not been associated with unexplained fatalities. Because SSRIs are a relatively new class of medications, there is little information about their efficacy in treating depressive symptoms before adulthood. However, available research suggests that they are more promising than

TCAs. For example, one study examined the effect of one SSRI, *fluoxetine* (Prozac), on the functioning of one hundred children and adolescents with MDD (Emslie et al., 1997). The researchers found that subjects taking Prozac showed greater improvement than subjects receiving a placebo. However, this improvement was not always synonymous with cure, since only 31% of youth taking Prozac showed a complete remission of their symptoms during the eight-week duration of the study (see Figure 9.5). This percentage compared favorably with, but was not very different from, the 23% remission rate of children and adolescents treated with a placebo. Finally, this study did not find any difference between the two groups in other psychological symptoms or in adaptive functioning at the end of treatment. These findings suggest that SSRIs may be an effective treatment component for some youth with

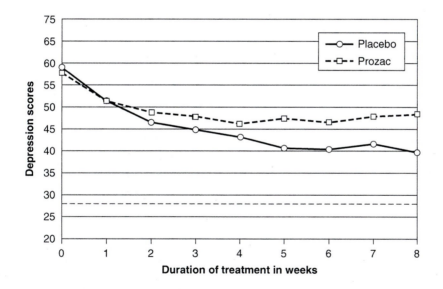

FIGURE 9.5 *Reduction in Depressive Symptoms in Response to an Eight-Week Treatment with Antidepressant Medication.* This figure compares improvement in depressive symptoms in children who received Prozac or a placebo. Both groups of children improved over the course of the study, but the medication group had significantly fewer symptoms at the end of treatment than the placebo group. Note that the dotted line at 28 on the Children's Depressive Rating Scale–Revised (CDRS-R) is the clinical cutoff for a depressive disorder. This line shows that the average child in either group did not improve enough to be considered depression-free at the end of treatment.

Source: Emslie et al. (1997), p. 1035. Reprinted by permission.

depression, but they are not the wonder drugs that some had hoped for. More research is needed in this area also. Specifically, follow-up studies of medicated youth are necessary to evaluate the long-term effectiveness and side effects of different medications, and to determine whether they can help youth with significant comorbid problems.

Bipolar Disorder

To treat bipolar disorder, the American Academy of Child and Adolescent Psychiatry recommends "a multimodal treatment plan, combining medications with psychotherapeutic interventions" (1997c, p. 143). In such a plan, medication is designed to control the core symptoms of mania that are characteristic of the disorder, whereas psychological intervention is used to deal with the child or adolescent's inevitable impairments in functioning. Psychological intervention can also be useful to treat comorbid symptoms and disorders, and to promote medication compliance. Medication compliance is promoted through psychoeducation about the disorder and the role of medication in reducing manic symptoms and preventing relapse.

Traditionally, the medication of choice in the treatment of bipolar disorder has been **lithium,** a naturally occurring alkali metal. Considerable research conducted with adults shows that this medication reduces manic symptoms and, when taken regularly over long periods of time, can prevent future manic episodes. Because bipolar disorder is believed to be a chronic disorder, treatment usually lasts at least eighteen months, long after the initial symptoms have been brought under control. At that time, medication may be tapered off, but the child and family must watch for a return of the disorder. If the child remains symptom-free, medication may be withdrawn indefinitely. If a relapse occurs, medication must resume immediately. Although there are no specific guidelines for the treatment of children and adolescents who relapse after medication is withdrawn, some youth may need to rely on lithium for extended, possibly lifelong, management of their condition (AACAP, 1997c).

The rationale for the use of medication to treat bipolar disorder before adulthood relies again on a downward extension of the adult treatment literature.

However, a growing number of studies provide support for the efficacy of lithium in the treatment of early-onset bipolar disorder, especially in adolescence. This result is encouraging, but more research is needed. Of particular concern is the fact that lithium is a highly toxic agent, which can have serious, even fatal, side effects. For example, long-term lithium treatment has been linked to structural changes in the kidneys, to thyroid problems, and to significant cardiovascular changes that may not be reversible once medication is stopped (Alessi, Naylor, Ghaziuddin, & Zubieta, 1994). In short, although lithium is a highly effective drug, it can have serious side effects and, like the neuroleptics used in the treatment of schizophrenia, requires careful monitoring, as well as an exhaustion of alternative forms of treatment.

Mood stabilizers are another class of drugs used to treat bipolar disorder. Mood stabilizers are anticonvulsants (i.e., antiseizure medications) that are effective in reducing manic symptoms and in preventing future manic episodes. Controlled studies of the effectiveness of mood stabilizers in youth have not been conducted, although case studies and noncontrolled investigations have found support for their use in adolescents. Like lithium, these medications present considerable risks or at least risks that have not been properly studied in children and adolescents. For example, long-term treatment with mood stabilizers is related to blood and liver disorders in adults, as well as to increases in ovarian disease in women (American Association of Child and Adolescent Psychiatry, 1997c).

Prevention

> *Nothing is certain in life, but generally the chances of happiness are greater if one has multiple areas of interest and involvement. To juggle is to diminish the risk of depression, anxiety, and unhappiness.*
>
> —Faye J. Crosby

Prevention generally focuses on youth at risk of developing a mood disorder, either because they already have mild depressive symptoms or because they have parents with a mood disorder. Prevention programs are delivered in schools, in small groups of same-age peers, using modified treatment approaches such as CBT, IPT, relaxation training, and psychoeducation. Findings to date are fairly encouraging. For example, Clarke and associates (1995) found that group CBT with mildly depressed adolescents decreased their symptoms and reduced the rate of onset of MDD and dysthymia over a one-year period. Similar findings have been obtained with younger children (Gillham & Reivich, 1999). Likewise, Beardslee and colleagues (1992) relied on family and individual psychoeducation to teach at-risk children and adolescents about their parents' mood disorder and to help parents understand the impact of family factors on their children's development and ability to cope with stress. Although the participants' mood was not directly measured in this study, they found this preventive intervention helpful because it increased family communication about mood disorders.

Little is known about the effectiveness of prevention efforts with youth who do not have significant depressive symptoms. In an evaluation of one such prevention program for adolescents, Clarke, Hawkins, Murphy, and Sheeber (1993) found no benefits at a three-month follow-up. However, in another preventive program for adolescents, Shochet and colleagues (2001) found that participants reported significantly lower levels of depressive symptoms and hopelessness at the end of the program and at a ten-month follow-up than adolescents who had not participated in the program. Results from this last study are encouraging, although additional research of this kind is urgently needed to reduce the potential suffering of youth at risk for mood disorders.

Web Links

www.depression.org (National Foundation for Depressive Illness)

www.nimh.nih.gov/publicat/depressionmenu.cfm (U.S. National Institute of Mental Health Mood Disorders Website)

www.depressionalliance.org (Depression Alliance, British charity offering help to people with depression)

www.bpkids.org (Child and Adolescent Bipolar Foundation)

www.ndmda.org (National Depressive and Manic-Depressive Association)

10

Anxiety Disorders

To suffering there is a limit, to fearing, none.
—Sir Francis Bacon

All human beings are naturally predisposed to fear and avoid objects and situations that may harm them. Sudden noises, animals, and strangers often startle young children and make them cry. Children can become panic-stricken when the wild creatures that fill their storybooks and imagination disturb their sleep (see Box 10.1). And adolescents can be excessively concerned about their appearance, their school performance, or their relationships with friends.

Feelings of apprehension are universal reactions to unsafe situations and threats. In most cases, these reactions are adaptive. They act to keep us alive in a world often filled with danger, and they motivate us to overcome challenges and learn. As such, fear and anxiety are an integral and healthy part of normal development. In a minority of children and adolescents, however, fear and anxiety become excessive and impair functioning.

Studies of the development of fear and anxiety in childhood and adolescence began with the pioneering research of Jersild and Holmes (1935). These and many other researchers who have followed in their footsteps have shown that most children and adolescents go through periods of relatively intense fears; these fears change over the course of development, typically decreasing in number but increasing in complexity with age; in spite of important cultural influences, the content of fears follows a relatively universal developmental trajectory as children mature cognitively and emotionally.

Development of Normal Fears and Worry

Table 10.1 summarizes the development of normal fears and worry from infancy to adolescence. This table shows that the fearful concerns of children change as they grow older. New fears replace earlier ones at different developmental stages, but certain fears remain relatively frequent and stable across ages: fears of accidents, being kidnapped, death and dead bodies, embarrassment, and school failure (Muris, Merckelbach, Gadet, & Moulaert, 2000).

However, even though fears are normal in young children and subside with age, anxiety disorders do occur frequently in childhood and adolescence. As you will see throughout this chapter, the perception that such disorders are rare is mistaken but often difficult to change, largely because these disorders are "quiet" conditions in which the majority of affected young people seek to avoid drawing attention to themselves and often suffer in silence (Albano, Chorpita, & Barlow, 1996).

BOX 10.1 • *Franklin in the Dark: A Story about a Common Childhood Fear*

All children have fears as they grow. A common fear in preschool and school-age children is fear of the dark. Franklin the turtle, a popular children's book character, tells his young readers about this fear:

> Franklin could slide down a riverbank all by himself. He could count forwards and backwards. He could even zip zippers and button buttons. But Franklin was afraid of small, dark places and that was a problem because . . . Franklin was a turtle. He was afraid of crawling into his small, dark shell. And so, Franklin the turtle dragged his shell behind him.
>
> Every night, Franklin's mother would take a flashlight, and shine it into his shell.
>
> "See," she would say, "there's nothing to be afraid of."
>
> She always said that. She wasn't afraid of anything. But Franklin was sure that creepy things, slippery things, and monsters lived inside his small, dark shell (Bourgeois & Clark, 1986, pp. 2, 7).

Franklin's fear of dark places leads him to run away from home in a desperate attempt to find a solution to his problem. Along the way he meets a duck who is afraid of water, a polar bear who fears cold, a lion who is scared of loud noises, and a bird who is afraid of heights. His journey makes him realize that all creatures are afraid of something and that the only way to get rid of a fear is to face it. When his mother, terribly worried, finds him, Franklin returns home to crawl bravely into his shell and overcome his fear.

Source: Selection from P. Bourgeois, *Franklin in the Dark* (Toronto: Kids Can Press, 1986), p. 7. Copyright 1986 by Context, Inc. Illustration copyright 1986 by Brenda Clark Illustrator, Inc. Used by permission.

From Normal Fears and Worry to Psychological Disorders

Excessive fear or anxiety is maladaptive. **Anxiety disorders** are a heterogeneous group of problems characterized by intense and persistent feelings of fear or anxiety. These feelings (1) are extreme given the child or adolescent's developmental stage; (2) interfere with daily functioning or the attainment of developmental milestones; and (3) cannot be dispelled through reassurances or appeals to reason or logic.

TABLE 10.1   *Outline of the Development of Normal Fears and Worry from Birth to Adolescence*

At birth	Unexpected events, such as sudden noises and fast-moving objects
Around 6 months	New people and situations; separation from familiar adults or siblings
Around 2 years	Animals such as dogs; being left alone, especially in the dark
Around 5 years	Fantasy creatures such as ghosts and monsters; wild animals
From 7 years	Death of loved ones; accidents; natural disasters; wars; punishment at home and school
In adolescence	Negative peer evaluation and social rejection; embarrassment and failure in school and beyond

The DSM-IV-TR classifies several conditions under the heading of anxiety disorders. We will present seven of them in this chapter: **separation anxiety disorder (SAD), specific phobia, social phobia, obsessive-compulsive disorder (OCD), panic disorder, posttraumatic stress disorder (PTSD),** and **generalized anxiety disorder (GAD).** Separation anxiety disorder is the only anxiety disorder that the DSM-IV-TR classifies under those conditions usually first diagnosed in infancy, childhood, or adolescence. The other anxiety disorders are diagnosed by means of criteria established for adults. However, in an attempt to take developmental differences into account, the DSM allows some modifications of these criteria when they are applied to children or adolescents.

Historical Overview

The scientific study of anxiety disorders in childhood and adolescence did not begin until the late 1970s and early 1980s. Consequently, much less is known about them than about their corresponding conditions in adulthood. However, the classical case studies of two children with significant fears—Little Hans (Freud, 1909/1961a) and Little Albert (Watson & Rayner, 1920)—played an important role in the development of modern psychiatry and psychology.

Freud and Psychoanalytic Theory

Sigmund Freud believed that anxiety arises from conflicts between unconscious impulses and urges and the demands of reality (see Box 1.1). In a famous case study of a child, Freud (1909/1961a) described the symptoms and treatment of a 5-year-old boy named Hans, who had separation anxiety disorder and a severe phobia of horses (which was problematic in the years before automobiles). Hans had come to Freud's attention because he refused to be separated from his mother or to leave the house. Working entirely by correspondence with Hans's father, Freud interpreted the child's symptoms as expressions of **oedipal conflict.** Specifically, he assumed that the child's anxiety stemmed from an unconscious urge to kill his father in order to have sexual relations with his mother. Freud

thought that Hans's phobia of horses represented his unconscious fear that his father might castrate him because of his desire for his mother, and that this phobia, together with his separation anxiety, enabled him to stay home, close to her (Klein & Last, 1989). Because these conflicts operate unconsciously, Freud's interpretation is not open to scientific scrutiny. However, the case of Little Hans remains important historically, because it was the first to point to the existence of anxiety disorders in early childhood and to the complications they can cause for development.

Watson's Radical Behaviorism

Freud's work was based entirely on drives and conflicts resulting from unseen, unconscious urges and impulses. In contrast, behaviorists such as John Watson contended that the science of psychology had to be based on processes that could be directly observed (see Box 1.2). Convinced that all behaviors are learned, Watson relied on the principles of classical conditioning to create a specific phobia in a young child. Watson and Rayner (1920) taught Little Albert, an 11-month-old boy, to fear a white rat by making a loud, clanging noise that startled the child every time he approached the animal. After consistent pairing of rat and noise, Albert soon developed a pathological fear of rats, which later generalized to other animals and many light-colored, furry objects. Although important in the history of childhood anxiety, this study was highly unethical by today's standards, since it is obviously inappropriate to deliberately create a disorder in a child. Not surprisingly, Watson and Rayner did not get a chance to treat Albert for his phobia after they had created it, as they apparently intended to. His mother removed him from their care when she realized what they had done (Klein & Last, 1989).

A few years later, Mary Cover Jones (1924) used the principles of classical and operant conditioning, as well as **modeling,** to treat a specific phobia in a 3-year-old boy named Peter. Like Albert, Peter was afraid of small, furry animals, especially rabbits. Alone or with other, nonanxious children, Peter was placed in a playroom where he was exposed to a rabbit in progressive steps. At first, the rabbit only appeared in its cage and at a safe distance from the child. Later, the animal was brought closer to the child, let out of its cage, and allowed to roam freely around the room. Peter was rewarded each time he approached the rabbit. He also saw his peers do the same successfully on many occasions, and thus learned quite quickly to overcome his phobia.

Bowlby and Attachment Theory

In spite of Freud and the early behaviorists' interest in anxiety, for decades most researchers in this area focused on the development of normal fears, rather than on the study of anxiety disorders in childhood and adolescence. Systematic investigation of these disorders began with John Bowlby (1973) and Mary Ainsworth's (1982) work on attachment, which focused attention on the influence of pathological anxiety in the developmental process. Their work stresses that anxiety acts as an alarm in situations of potential or actual danger. Under normal circumstances, this alarm allows organisms to learn to respond appropriately—for example, by teaching them to overcome some dangers and to avoid others. In this perspective, a positive, secure relationship between mothers (and other trusted adults) and young children is essential for this learning to proceed normally. A secure attachment serves two functions: it teaches children that familiar adults will protect them in potentially dangerous situations; and it provides them with a secure base from which they can explore their environment and develop social, emotional, and cognitive skills in relative safety. Conversely, an insecure attachment leaves young children vulnerable to overwhelming feelings of fear and anxiety when they are faced with unavoidable challenges. Such feelings can result in limited skill development and, if they are prolonged, in behavioral or emotional problems—a point to which we will return later (see Etiology).

Definitions, Diagnostic Criteria, and Major Characteristics

Separation Anxiety Disorder

Children with separation anxiety disorder (SAD) have an excessive fear of being separated from their care-givers. This fear arises when parents leave the child at home or when they drop the child off somewhere, such as school. Most children with SAD fear that something terrible will happen to them or to their parents when they are separated: they may fear that they will be abducted and never see their family again or that their parents will be killed in a car crash.

Feelings of anxiety related to separation are very common in infancy and early childhood; therefore, a diagnosis of SAD can be made only when symptoms are persistent and clearly excessive, given the child's developmental level and cultural context. In addition, the fear must center on the actual separation and not on something at the place where he is left. For example, when he is dropped off at school, a 7-year-old boy must not be afraid of something or someone there. Rather, he must fear that his mother might be killed or that he might never see her again for some other reason. Finally, the child's anxiety must be so severe as to limit social or academic development. In many cases, the disorder interferes with school attendance, since children are so worried about being separated from one or more loved ones that they refuse to leave them. In such instances, the disorder is often referred to as school phobia or refusal (see below).

Table 10.2 (p. 272) presents the DSM-IV-TR diagnostic criteria for SAD. As these criteria indicate, it is extreme and persistent distress in anticipation or at the time of separation that distinguishes SAD from the short-lived outbursts of tears associated with parting from caregivers that are common in early childhood. Older children are less likely to cry or to show other obvious signs of distress; instead, they often manifest severe physical symptoms, such as headaches and nausea. As in all other anxiety disorders, reassurances or appeals to reason do not lessen the child's fears. Children with SAD may spend an entire day at school in inconsolable fear, crying persistently or complaining of stomachaches, headaches, or other physical discomforts. Although symptoms of SAD vary with age and from one child to another, they are evident at the behavioral, cognitive, and physiological levels. They include, among other things, avoidance of separation through clinging and other demanding behaviors, irrational fears of separation, and physical symptoms such as nausea, hyperventilation, rapid heart rate, and light-headedness.

TABLE 10.2 *Separation Anxiety Disorder: DSM-IV-TR Diagnostic Criteria*

A. Developmentally inappropriate and excessive anxiety concerning separation from home or from those to whom the individual is attached, as evidenced by three (or more) of the following:

   (1) recurrent excessive distress when separation from home or major attachment figures occurs or is anticipated

   (2) persistent and excessive worry about losing, or about possible harm befalling, major attachment figures

   (3) persistent and excessive worry that an untoward event will lead to separation from a major attachment figure (e.g., getting lost or being kidnapped)

   (4) persistent reluctance or refusal to go to school or elsewhere because of fear of separation

   (5) persistently and excessively fearful or reluctant to be alone or without major attachment figures at home or without significant adults in other settings

   (6) persistent reluctance or refusal to go to sleep without being near a major attachment figure or to sleep away from home

   (7) repeated nightmares involving the theme of separation

   (8) repeated complaints of physical symptoms (such as headaches, stomachaches, nausea, or vomiting) when separation from major attachment figures occurs or is anticipated

B. The duration of the disturbance is at least 4 weeks.

C. The onset is before age 18 years.

D. The disturbance causes clinically significant distress or impairment in social, academic (occupational), or other important areas of functioning.

E. The disturbance does not occur exclusively during the course of a Pervasive Developmental Disorder, Schizophrenia, or other Psychotic Disorder and, in adolescents and adults, is not better accounted for by Panic Disorder With Agoraphobia.

Specify if:
Early Onset: if onset occurs before age 6 years

Source: American Psychiatric Association, *Diagnostic and Statistical Manual of Mental Disorders, Fourth Edition, Text Revision* (Washington, DC: American Psychiatric Association, 2000a). Copyright 2000 American Psychiatric Association. Reprinted with permission.

In severe cases, children with SAD may become so agitated in anticipation of separation that they vomit or otherwise become ill (American Psychiatric Association, 2000a).

Other Anxiety Symptoms. In the preschool and early school years, the distress brought about by SAD often results in tearful outbursts, screams, temper tantrums, or other oppositional behaviors aimed at avoiding or postponing separation. Away from home, younger children with SAD remain unhappy until they are reunited with their caregivers. Typically, they keep to themselves, crying or whining almost continuously, and refusing to talk or to be comforted by concerned adults attempting to reduce their distress. In most cases, they are unable to give voice to their fears, noting only that they want to be reunited with their caregivers. As small Kristina repeated inconsolably after her mother dropped her off at daycare, "I just want to be with Momma."

Older children with SAD may call home regularly or try to return home in the middle of the day to make sure that their loved ones are safe and well. Many of them carry cell phones to monitor their caregivers' whereabouts throughout the day. These symptoms often affect these children's school performance, because they cannot concentrate or work productively for long periods of time. In addition, even when older children endure school without showing obvious signs of fearfulness, their refusal to participate in extracurricular activities or to spend time at anyone else's house hinders the development of social relationships.

General Adaptation. Most children with SAD claim that everything would be just fine if they were never away from their caregivers, but this is rarely true.

Separation anxiety disorder. Some children find separation from their loved ones extremely painful and resist it by all means at their disposal.

At home, preschoolers are often "clingy," shadowing their caregivers and becoming upset when they get out of sight. The mother of 5-year-old Olivia noted that her daughter had to be in the bathroom with her whether she was taking a shower, putting on makeup, or even toileting. Asking Olivia to leave her alone—even for a moment—resulted in a major tantrum. In addition, many children with SAD constantly seek their caregivers' approval and seem unable to play or work independently. At bedtime, these children often refuse to get ready for bed and to fall asleep alone. As a result, many parents find it easier to let the children sleep with them. In short, children with SAD have multiple symptoms that disrupt their lives and the lives of those around them, even when they do not face any imminent separation. It is often disruptive symptoms, rather than anxiety, that lead parents to seek professional advice, as in Sarah's case.

Sarah is 6. She was referred to us by her pediatrician. She has missed almost half of the first two months of elementary school. When she attends school, she usually arrives late and in tears, and often disturbs the class by crying inconsolably for hours. In a conference with her parents, Sarah's teacher notes that, even when she is quiet in class, she is unable to concentrate on her schoolwork or to participate in class activities, preferring to sit alone in a corner of the room. In our initial interview with the family, Sarah's mother notes that "It is a battle to get her out of bed each morning. As soon as she wakes up, she cries and moans because she does not want to go to school or because she does not feel well. . . . She has it all: headaches, stomach cramps, and tears. Oh my, she can cry! It's not funny, because I am a nurse and I swear to you that she is truly a small hypochondriac. She complains about pains everywhere. . . . She always gets dressed slowly and I must often help her because she wastes so much time. . . . She can spend 10 or 15 minutes on the toilet just to pee, all curled up in a ball, her head on her knees, as if she had just had a terrible operation. . . . Then she eats hardly anything for breakfast, even if I offer her her favorite cereals or a chocolate roll. She will devour them on weekends but not during the week. . . . And finally, of course, it's time to leave and then the real battle starts, especially if my husband has already left for work. She has the worst temper tantrums: crying, howling, stomping her feet, and refusing to go to the car. If I don't watch her even for a second, she will hide somewhere. . . . On occasions she gets herself in such a state that she ends up vomiting. Once this year, she even vomited at school and they phoned me to come and get her. . . . As soon as she saw me, all was well, like nothing had ever happened. . . . The same is true if I allow her to stay home, like when I don't have to go to work. That drives my husband insane. He says she is just manipulating us. I don't know. . . . But it's true, she is fine as soon as she can stay home." Sarah's parents report that they have tried everything—firmness, punishments, lectures on the virtues of education, and promises of rewards—to no avail. Every morning they face the same battle to get their daughter to school.

Compared to her younger brother, "who is never afraid of anything," Sarah has always been a "shy and timid" child, according to her mother. For this reason her parents kept her home until she was 5. Then they put her in kindergarten "to get her used to going to school." After a difficult start marked by several weeks of tears whenever she had to leave her mother, Sarah liked kindergarten and attended regularly—in large part, her mother believes, because she had "a charismatic teacher, who did lots of projects with the children and who could reassure them when something went wrong."

Sarah's first obvious symptoms of anxiety date back to the summer before preschool, when her mother was hospitalized for a minor surgical procedure. "She took it really badly," explains her father, "and I sometimes feel a little guilty because with only two children at home I should have recognized it. . . . She was very calm and spoke very little when we went to the hospital, but at home she asked endless questions. I guess that was her way of saying that she was concerned for her mother. . . . Then, when her mother was back home, Sarah became very 'clingy' and, before we knew it, she would not let us leave home anymore. . . . And every night, I mean every night, she slips into our bed and usually wakes her mother up deliberately. If I try to get her back into her own bed, she returns a little later or lies down and falls asleep in our doorway like a small watchdog."

Sarah recognizes that her behavior makes her unhappy and worries her parents but she justifies it by explaining that she often feels sick in the morning. She also notes that she does not like her peers or her new teacher, whom she describes as an "old witch." When someone points out to her that she does not have any physical symptoms on days off or that several of her neighborhood friends are in her class, she shrugs without answering.

Intervention focuses on two areas: (1) Counseling with Sarah's parents explores their educational priorities and the family circumstances that may have fostered their daughter's difficulties. This work uncovers significant marital tensions, which are addressed

before working with Sarah directly. (2) A precise morning routine is implemented to teach Sarah to get ready for school and to separate from her mother with a minimum amount of distress. Over a five-week period, this routine reduces the child's symptoms significantly, enabling her to attend school on a regular basis. After six months, Sarah attends school without difficulty. However, she remains a timid young girl who withdraws easily and has few friends.

Specific Phobia

> *To him that is in fear everything rustles.*
>
> —Sophocles

Table 10.3 lists the DSM-IV-TR diagnostic criteria for specific phobia. The disorder is characterized by marked and persistent fear of a particular object or situation. Paradoxically, specific phobia is both the broadest type of anxiety disorder—since, theoretically, any object or situation can be the focus of a specific phobia—and the most restrictive type—since fear can occur only in relation to a specific stimulus. Given that fears are common in the growing years, specific phobia can be diagnosed only when the child or adolescent's fear is clearly excessive, both developmentally and culturally.

Specific phobias cause extreme distress, which cannot be reduced by reassurance or appeals to reason, is not under voluntary control, leads to avoidance or escape from the feared stimulus, is persistent (rather than a passing, developmental phase), and limits adaptive functioning. Phobias of animals (especially dogs and insects), the natural environment (darkness, lightning, and thunder), and injections are common in childhood and adolescence (Essau, Conradt, & Petermann, 2000). Kathy, an adolescent we treated for a phobia of hypodermic needles, refused to go to the dentist to have cavities filled because she was afraid of injections. She also avoided medical visits because she feared that she would have blood drawn. Over time, her phobia became so intense that she began fearing all illnesses and shunned contact with people to avoid "germs" and the injections that they might force her to have. As you can easily imagine, her avoidance caused her multiple problems at school, both socially and academically.

TABLE 10.3 *Specific Phobia: DSM-IV-TR Diagnostic Criteria*

A. Marked and persistent fear that is excessive or unreasonable, cued by the presence or anticipation of a specific object or situation (e.g., flying, heights, animals, receiving an injection, seeing blood).

B. Exposure to the phobic stimulus almost invariably provokes an immediate anxiety response, which may take the form of a situationally bound or situationally predisposed Panic Attack. *Note:* In children, the anxiety may be expressed by crying, tantrums, freezing, or clinging.

C. The person recognizes that the fear is excessive or unreasonable. *Note:* In children, this feature may be absent.

D. The phobic situation(s) is avoided or else is endured with intense anxiety or distress.

E. The avoidance, anxious anticipation, or distress in the feared situation(s) interferes significantly with the person's normal routine, occupational (or academic) functioning, or social activities or relationships, or there is marked distress about having the phobia.

F. In individuals under age 18 years, the duration is at least 6 months.

G. The anxiety, Panic Attacks, or phobic avoidance associated with the specific object or situation are not better accounted for by another mental disorder, such as Obsessive-Compulsive Disorder (e.g., fear of dirt in someone with an obsession about contamination), Posttraumatic Stress Disorder (e.g., avoidance of stimuli associated with a severe stressor), Separation Anxiety Disorder (e.g., avoidance of school), Social Phobia (e.g., avoidance of social situations because of fear of embarrassment), Panic Disorder With Agoraphobia or Agoraphobia Without History of Panic Disorder.

Specify type:
Animal Type

Natural Environment Type (e.g., heights, storms, water)

Blood-Injection-Injury Type

Situational Type (e.g., airplanes, elevators, enclosed places)

Other Type (e.g., fear of choking, vomiting, or contracting an illness; in children, fear of loud sounds or costumed characters)

Source: American Psychiatric Association, *Diagnostic and Statistical Manual of Mental Disorders, Fourth Edition, Text Revision* (Washington, DC: American Psychiatric Association, 2000a). Copyright 2000 American Psychiatric Association. Reprinted with permission.

Other Anxiety Symptoms. Agitation, feelings of dread, muscle tension, and multiple somatic symptoms can often be triggered in youth with specific phobia by the mere mention of the feared stimulus. In extreme cases, exposure to the object or situation they dread provokes a **panic attack** (see Table 10.3). More often, contact with the phobic stimulus causes affected children to scream and to try to run away, no matter how much adults or peers attempt to comfort, reassure, or reason with them. Older youth may be able to control their more extreme reactions, but never fully or for any length of time. Common in the conversation of young people with specific phobia and other anxiety disorders are *"what if . . ."* statements (Silverman & Rabian, 1993). Most of these statements are catastrophic predictions of what might occur if the child or adolescent came into contact with the feared object or situation. For example, Kathy often asked, "What if they miss

the vein with the needle and puncture a bone or a muscle?" Invariably, she provided her own irrational answers to such questions, predicting excruciating pain and permanent injuries, and refusing to consider much more realistic alternatives.

General Adaptation. When they are not directly confronted with what they fear, children and adolescents with specific phobia tend to be apprehensive and hypervigilant, especially if they believe they may suddenly have to face the phobic stimulus. These youth are constantly scanning their environment to make sure they do *not* come into contact with the object or situation they dread—often at the expense of more positive activities, such as social relationships and schoolwork. In some cases, affected children refuse to take part in certain activities, such as going to school. Joelle was referred to us following a parent-teacher conference in

Specific phobia. Most children love animals, and many of them have pets. However, children with specific phobia of animals are extremely fearful and almost constantly on the lookout to make sure they do not come in contact with the animal they fear.

which her teacher expressed concerns that she was often missing school and falling behind academically, and that she was increasingly rejected or ignored by her peers because of her odd behaviors.

Joelle is 8 and is pathologically afraid of severe weather—thunder and lightning in particular. She spends nearly an hour a day consulting various weather information sources, such as radio, television, and newspapers, for news of any impending storms. She has actually acquired exceptional knowledge in this field for a child of her age. Her parents affectionately call her "Miss Weather Channel" and she does not hide her pride at the fact that she knows more about the subject than most grown-ups. However, pride and fear are two facets of the same reality for Joelle.

At home, Joelle repeatedly asks what might happen if the weather turns bad. "What can I do on the school bus if it starts raining?" "Will all the children be killed if lightning hits the bus?" These are typical of the many "what if . . . " questions that plague Joelle's waking hours. In the morning she often refuses to leave for school when the weather or the forecast is bad. At night she has considerable difficulty falling or staying asleep. When it actually rains, she clutches her mother or father in distress or takes refuge behind a mattress

that her parents have allowed her to place upright at an angle next to a wall.

At school, Joelle often gets up to look out for signs of ominous changes in the weather. Her teacher reports that on one occasion she took refuge under her desk after she mistook the sound of a door banging for thunder. Reassurances and appeals to reason do not work. For example, when her father once pointed out to her that other children on the bus were not afraid of being struck by lightning, she simply replied: "Yes, but they don't realize!"

As Joelle's reply illustrates, children with specific phobia often fail to recognize the extreme and irrational nature of their fears. Diagnostically, this lack of insight is acceptable in children but not in adolescents. The DSM-IV-TR requires that adolescents must be aware that their fears are excessive before a diagnosis can be made.

Subtypes of Specific Phobias.   There are four subtypes of specific phobias: the *animal type* (fear of animals or insects), the *natural environment type* (fear of specific aspects of the environment, such as storms, heights, or water), the *blood-injection-injury type* (fear of blood, wounds, or injections), and the *situational type* (fear of a particular situation, such as airplanes, dentists' offices, or elevators). Data to validate the existence of these subtypes in childhood are limited. In adolescence and adulthood, however, evidence indicates that people with the blood-injection-injury type of specific phobia often have a distinct **vasovagal response** when they are confronted with the stimuli they dread most (American Psychiatric Association, 2000a). That is, they experience a brief increase in heart rate, followed by a significant drop in heart rate and blood pressure. This response is the opposite of that provoked by most other phobias, which usually involve a rapid increase in heart rate and blood pressure. Behaviorally, this vasovagal response often results in fainting at the sight of the phobic stimulus (e.g., blood).

Social Phobia

Table 10.4 lists the DSM-IV-TR diagnostic criteria for social phobia—a disorder manifested by marked and

TABLE 10.4   *Social Phobia: DSM-IV-TR Diagnostic Criteria*

A. A marked and persistent fear of one or more social or performance situations in which the person is exposed to unfamiliar people or to possible scrutiny by others. The individual fears that he or she will act in a way (or show anxiety symptoms) that will be humiliating or embarrassing. *Note:* In children, there must be evidence of the capacity for age-appropriate social relationships with familiar people and the anxiety must occur in peer settings, not just in interactions with adults.

B. Exposure to the feared social situation almost invariably provokes anxiety, which may take the form of a situationally bound or situationally predisposed Panic Attack. *Note:* In children, the anxiety may be expressed by crying, tantrums, freezing, or shrinking from social situations with unfamiliar people.

C. The person recognizes that the fear is excessive or unreasonable. *Note:* In children, this feature may be absent.

D. The feared social or performance situations are avoided or else are endured with intense anxiety or distress.

E. The avoidance, anxious anticipation, or distress in the feared social or performance situation(s) interferes significantly with the person's normal routine, occupational (academic) functioning, or social activities or relationships, or there is marked distress about having the phobia.

F. In individuals under age 18 years, the duration is at least 6 months.

G. The fear or avoidance is not due to the direct physiological effects of a substance (e.g., a drug of abuse, a medication) or a general medical condition and is not better accounted for by another mental disorder (e.g., Panic Disorder With or Without Agoraphobia, Separation Anxiety Disorder, Body Dysmorphic Disorder, a Pervasive Developmental Disorder, Schizoid Personality Disorder).

H. If a general medical condition or another mental disorder is present, the fear in Criterion A is unrelated to it, e.g., the fear is not of Stuttering, trembling in Parkinson's disease, or exhibiting abnormal eating behavior in Anorexia Nervosa or Bulimia Nervosa.

Specify if:
Generalized: if the fears include most social situations (also consider the additional diagnosis of Avoidant Personality Disorder)

Source: American Psychiatric Association, *Diagnostic and Statistical Manual of Mental Disorders, Fourth Edition, Text Revision* (Washington, DC: American Psychiatric Association, 2000a). Copyright 2000 American Psychiatric Association. Reprinted with permission.

persistent fears of one or more social situations in which negative evaluation or embarrassment could occur. These fears lead to social avoidance, and over time limit the child or adolescent's development and adaptive functioning in significant ways. Youth with social phobia are not simply shy; they actively avoid social situations whenever they can. When they cannot, they "put up" with them at great psychological costs—often experiencing intense physical symptoms of distress and discomfort and, in extreme cases, panic attacks.

Social and specific phobias obviously share common characteristics. However, in social phobia, uncontrollable anxiety does not stem from a particular object or situation, but from situations calling for social interactions. Specifically, children and adolescents with social phobia fear negative social evaluation and embarrassment on the part of adults and peers, even though they have no objective reason to do so. For example, 15-year-old Jeff felt strongly that if he talked to another boy in his grade—any boy—he would immediately be deemed "weird" and rejected, even though this fear was totally unfounded.

To be diagnosed with the disorder, a child or adolescent must have obvious difficulties in interactions with adults and peers. As in specific phobia, adolescents must realize that their social fears are excessive and irrational, whereas children may not have the cognitive ability to see their symptoms as anything other than appropriate means of coping with reality (APA, 2000a).

Other Anxiety Symptoms.   Social phobia causes extreme distress. Physiologically, the disorder is

Social phobia. When they are unable to avoid social situations, youth with social phobia endure them in considerable discomfort.

tend to be less impressive or dramatic than those of specific phobia, essentially because it is much harder for children or adolescents to avoid all social interactions than it is to avoid a specific object or situation. Typically, they seek to hide their fear and to go unnoticed, or to run away if the situation permits. When they have to interact, they avoid eye contact and speak as little as possible and with hesitation. In severe cases, they may actually be unable to speak.

Social Behavior.   Parents, teachers, and peers usually describe children and adolescents with social phobia as loners who live on the sideline of the social world. Besides their family and one or two good friends with whom they may interact, their social contacts are very limited. In school, they dread talking to teachers, participating in group activities, or having to speak in class. They also avoid busy corridors, gym class, and the cafeteria, and eat alone or with one or two friends who are also withdrawn. In adolescence, few of them have age-appropriate, intimate relationships (Ballenger et al., 1998). In addition, many of them have social skills deficits, probably in large part because they rarely practice these skills with adults or peers (Spence, Donovan, & Brechman-Toussaint, 1999). When their difficulties persist, as they often do, their limited social skills may give some substance to their social phobia, that is, their social ackwardness may bring about the very reactions they fear—negative evaluations and embarrassment.

characterized by a racing heart, trembling hands, shortness of breath, nausea, and perspiration, as well as by panic attacks in more extreme cases. Cognitively, youth with social phobia often have difficulty concentrating and producing satisfactory academic work. In stressful social situations, some even report that their head becomes empty and that they can no longer think. Like all overanxious youth, they also perceive ambiguous events as more threatening, more likely to happen to them, and more likely to have bad outcomes than their nonaffected peers (Muris, Merckelbach, & Damsma, 2000; Suarez and Bell-Dolan, 2001). However, the behavioral manifestations of social phobia

Kevin is 14. He lost his mother at the age of 5 and lives with his father and younger sister. Since he was 11, Kevin has been driven to school by his father. He refuses to ride the school bus even though it stops at his house. By way of explanation, Kevin notes: "I don't like it when people look at me on the bus and anyway there's far too much noise." Every morning, he insists on leaving home early, to arrive at school before the buses do. This allows him to get to his locker when the hallways are still almost empty. From there, he runs to the bathroom, where he locks himself up until the morning bell rings.

Kevin's academic performance is satisfactory. He attends class regularly but, in the words of a teacher, "as a shadow more than as a participant."

Most classes go well for him unless someone asks him a question. Through the years, by remaining silent and avoiding all eye contact, he has trained his teachers and peers not to call on him. At lunchtime, Kevin eats rapidly, usually with a younger boy who is also very withdrawn. Then he waits for classes to resume, either in a corner of the playground with one or two other solitary friends or in the library where talking is prohibited. The following dialogue with his therapist illustrates Kevin's difficulties:

> **Therapist:**   *Kevin, tell me something. Would you like to have contact with people at school if you did not have this fear or do you just not care about them?*
>
> **Kevin:**   *I would like . . . I believe, yes, I would like . . . The other day I waited to leave class [Kevin always leaves class last to avoid any scuffling] and I heard these two guys speaking about this video game. They could not reach the next level and were discussing what it would take to make it. I know the game, I have it, and it was clear that they didn't have much of a clue.*
>
> **Therapist:**   *So, did you give them the solution?*
>
> **Kevin:**   *No, not exactly . . . I, I don't know, I hesitated . . . and anyway they left.*
>
> **Therapist:**   *Tell me exactly what went through your head while you hesitated.*
>
> **Kevin:**   *I don't know. I asked myself what they would say, like if I told them. . . . And then very quickly, I don't know, I was afraid and I didn't think about it anymore.*

Kevin clearly wants to be accepted. However, according to his father and a teacher who has known him from elementary school, he has always been a loner. For years, nobody paid much attention to his behavior, because he was always easy-going at home and made satisfactory progress at school. It was on the insistent recommendation of his gym teacher that Kevin's father brought him in for a psychological consultation. Kevin, who is a very good swimmer, had agreed to take part in a swimming competition at another school. A few minutes before his first race, Kevin panicked when he saw how many people had come to watch. In fear, he fled to the locker room, where the gym teacher found

him "very agitated and almost disoriented." The teacher calmed him down before taking him home. Kevin recalled the incident a few weeks later: "I don't know what happened. When I saw all these people, suddenly I was afraid to let down the team. I panicked, and it was stronger than me. I had to leave."

On a day-to-day basis, most of Kevin's behaviors are not extreme. Rather, they go unnoticed or are dismissed as mere shyness. However, youth like Kevin suffer in silence, cut off from many experiences that are essential to healthy emotional, social, and academic development. More than their peers with other anxiety disorders, they fear the social world, a world to which they would like to belong fully but that causes them great distress (La Greca & Lopez, 1998).

Subtype of Social Phobia.   The DSM-IV-TR specifies that social phobia should be described as of a *generalized type* when symptoms occur in a majority of social situations. This subtype is probably the most frequent form of the disorder, although epidemiological data before adulthood are sparse (Albano et al., 1996).

School Refusal.   Youth with social phobia are at times described as school refusers. The same is true of children with SAD and specific phobia (Last & Strauss, 1990). **School refusal** refers to extreme reluctance or outright refusal to attend school on the part of a child who has no objective reason to fear school. School refusers attend school intermittently (for part of the day or on some days but not others) or refuse to attend altogether. Research on school refusal shows that most affected children are of average or above-average intelligence and do not avoid school because of failing grades. School refusal is not listed as a disorder in the DSM-IV-TR, probably in large part because it is a very heterogeneous condition that does not have a unique symptomatology. Rather, the condition can be associated with fear of social evaluation (as in social phobia), of separation from loved ones (as in SAD), or of uncontrollable events at school (as in specific phobia; recall that Joelle often refused to go to school in bad weather because she was pathologically afraid of thunder and lightning). In some instances, parents may bring about school refusal by inadvertently or deliberately encouraging the child to stay home. Some parents may give considerable attention to a child who claims to be unwell just before going to school and, for example, allow the child to stay in bed late or to watch television. Over time, this treatment may reinforce the child's physical symptoms to the point of school refusal. Other parents may be overprotective and overinvolved in their child's care, and may imply that they are distressed whenever the child leaves them alone during the day (Kearney, 2001).

Obsessive-Compulsive Disorder

Obsessive-compulsive disorder (OCD) is one of the most serious anxiety disorders. Children and adolescents with OCD have recurrent and intrusive anxiety-provoking thoughts and impulses that mobilize their attention (**obsessions**). In addition, they perform repetitive, ritualistic behaviors (**compulsions**) to reduce anxiety associated with obsessions. Often all-consuming, obsessions and compulsions provoke considerable distress and, in most cases, interfere greatly with adaptive functioning. These unwelcome behaviors must be clearly distinguished from the bedtime stories, bath routines, and other rituals many children enjoy, especially at a younger age. The latter are experienced as reassuring and fun, whereas the former always give rise to anxiety (American Psychiatric Association, 2000a).

Table 10.5 presents the DSM-IV-TR diagnostic criteria for OCD. These criteria clearly reflect the intrusive and debilitating nature of the disorder, since obsessions and compulsions cannot be voluntarily controlled; require a considerable amount of time (over one hour a day to be considered pathological); and are experienced as unwelcome, painful intrusions that must be endured because they offer the only means of temporarily relieving an ever-threatening anxiety.

Obsessions and compulsions tend to change in the course of development and often vary considerably from one child to another. However, the former are always intrusive and the latter rigid and demanding: obsessions *must* be attended to and compulsions *must* be carried out exactly the same way each time. Consequently, any attempt to ignore obsessions or to resist compulsions produces a rapid increase in anxiety.

Obsessions.   Obsessions are thoughts or impulses that children or adolescents see as their own but that they cannot "get out of their head." They usually appear as ideas, images, or irresistible urges that reflect an irrational fear or an emotionally charged topic, often of a sexual, aggressive, or religious nature. For example, one child may become obsessed with thoughts of killing and death; another, with pornographic images. Still another may have unceasing worries or doubts that he or she has not performed some schoolwork or chores "just the right way." By definition, obsessions are always extreme; they are "not simply excessive worries about real-life problems" (APA, 2000a, p. 462); and caregivers cannot control or reduce the obsessions by reasoning or taking adequate measures to alleviate the child's concerns (Henin & Kendall, 1997).

Compulsions.   As their name implies, compulsions are repetitive, ritualistic acts that are coercive in nature: they force affected individuals to act against their will. Washing rituals are most common in children and adolescents with OCD, although a significant number of them have checking, sorting, or arranging compulsions. Others have compulsions that require them to perform a series of gestures or movements in a particular order. Maria, an 8-year-old child in our clinic, had to make a complicated series of skipping steps whenever she entered or left a room. For many children, compulsions are thematically related to the obsessions that trigger them; for example, an unrealistic fear of contamination can be used to justify compulsive hand washing. For other children, such as Maria, there is no logical connection between obsessions and compulsions. In all cases, however, compulsions act as a means of getting rid of obsessive anxiety (Henin & Kendall, 1997).

In some cases, encouraging children or adolescents to "take your mind off it" or preventing them from engaging in their rituals can provoke a full-blown panic attack (Albano et al., 1996). In others, interruption of a compulsion can result in crying or screaming. For example, when Maria's brother interrupted her skipping pattern, as he often did because he was easily irritated by it, she would have a short but noisy tantrum and then begin skipping all over again. In her case, as in many other cases of OCD, compulsions can take the

TABLE 10.5   *Obsessive-Compulsive Disorder: DSM-IV-TR Diagnostic Criteria*

A. Either obsessions or compulsions:

Obsessions as defined by (1), (2), (3), and (4):

(1) recurrent and persistent thoughts, impulses, or images that are experienced, at some time during the disturbance, as intrusive and inappropriate and that cause marked anxiety or distress

(2) the thoughts, impulses, or images are not simply excessive worries about real-life problems

(3) the person attempts to ignore or suppress such thoughts, impulses, or images, or to neutralize them with some other thought or action

(4) the person recognizes that the obsessional thoughts, impulses, or images are a product of his or her own mind (not imposed from without as in thought insertion)

Compulsions as defined by (1) and (2):

(1) repetitive behaviors (e.g., hand washing, ordering, checking) or mental acts (e.g., praying, counting, repeating words silently) that the person feels driven to perform in response to an obsession, or according to rules that must be applied rigidly

(2) the behaviors or mental acts are aimed at preventing or reducing distress or preventing some dreaded event or situation; however, these behaviors or mental acts either are not connected in a realistic way with what they are designed to neutralize or prevent or are clearly excessive

B. At some point during the course of the disorder, the person has recognized that the obsessions or compulsions are excessive or unreasonable. *Note:* This does not apply to children.

C. The obsessions or compulsions cause marked distress, are time consuming (taking more than 1 hour a day), or significantly interfere with the person's normal routine, occupational (or academic) functioning, or usual social activities or relationships.

D. If another Axis I disorder is present, the content of the obsessions or compulsions is not restricted to it (e.g., preoccupation with food in the presence of an Eating Disorder; hair pulling in the presence of Trichotillomania; concern with appearance in the presence of Body Dysmorphic Disorder; preoccupation with drugs in the presence of a Substance Use Disorder; preoccupation with having a serious illness in the presence of Hypochondriasis; preoccupation with sexual urges or fantasies in the presence of a Paraphilia; or guilty ruminations in the presence of major Depressive Disorder).

E. The disturbance is not due to the direct physiological effects of a substance (e.g., a drug of abuse, a medication) or of a general medical condition.

Specify if:

With Poor Insight: if, for most of the time during the current episode, the person does not recognize that the obsessions and compulsions are excessive and unreasonable

Source: American Psychiatric Association, *Diagnostic and Statistical Manual of Mental Disorders, Fourth Edition, Text Revision* (Washington, DC: American Psychiatric Association, 2000a). Copyright 2000 American Psychiatric Association. Reprinted with permission.

form of true choreographed rituals, elaborated in minute, individual detail, which must be repeated until the child or adolescent is temporarily satisfied (APA, 2000a).

General Adaptation.   About 50–60% of youth with OCD face major problems of adaptation at home, at school, and in the community (Albano et al., 1996). By definition, obsessions monopolize attention and compulsions take a lot of time—time that could be devoted to more productive pursuits. In addition, the struggles that children and adolescents with OCD feel between resisting and giving in to their symptoms often lead

them to feel exhausted and further disturb their emotional state. In severe cases, they can become school refusers, both to have enough time for their disorder and to avoid being humiliated in front of friends. Even in relatively mild cases, the disorder can cause significant disturbances at home, because youth with OCD often involve other family members in their rituals. For example, 6-year-old Jaquil could not leave a room without flipping the light switch five times. As his symptoms worsened, he began requiring all family members to perform this ritual and had severe tantrums when his wishes were not met. Many families also become involved in the disorder through their attempts to

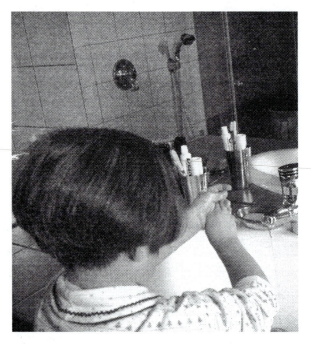

Obsessive-compulsive disorder. Many youth with OCD have irresistible compulsive rituals that interfere considerably with their ability to relate to others, learn, and enjoy life.

hide the child's problems and save themselves considerable embarrassment. Anne's story illustrates just how many areas of functioning OCD can disrupt.

Anne is 13. She is in hospital for the second time for OCD. Her parents report that her difficulties began in early childhood, with ritualistic arranging of almost everything she could reach around the house. For example, her clothes and all dishes and kitchen utensils had to be folded or arranged precisely as she demanded, and any untidiness provoked marked agitation and anger. Over a period of several years, these rituals were replaced by compulsions associated with washing and cleanliness. By age 10, Anne washed her hands more than ten times a day for several minutes each time and insisted that anything she touched be clean—an insistence that made her keep her hands to herself most of the time. At that point, her symptoms worsened rapidly. At first, she began refusing to dry her

hands after washing them. Then she kept them wet all the time, by wrapping them in soaked handkerchiefs or towels, or by licking and spitting on them. Since age 12, she has been bandaging her hands in wet towels and keeping them in plastic bags at all times—day and night. She takes them out of the bags only to eat, get dressed, go to the toilet, or wash. A few months later, she also began wetting her feet. She continued to attend school until her hospitalization, but kept her hands in her pockets to hide them, unable to write anything or to take part in many school activities.

Anne arrived at the hospital with her hands in plastic bags and her feet in large, wet cotton socks. She was very agitated, alternatively crying and begging her parents to take her home. Her hands and feet were grayish-white, entirely wrinkled by the water, and had several large sores that had developed from constant moisture and lack of air circulation.

Anne is very oppositional and controlling, and refuses to take an active part in any intervention. She recognizes the extreme nature of her behavior but cannot explain it in terms of obsessions. She only repeats that she "must" wet her hands and feet to avoid a "terrible itching."

Panic Disorder

Panic disorder is characterized by sudden and intense panic attacks—that is, unexpected and uncontrollable attacks of anxiety. Panic attacks can occur in a variety of situations but are not brought about by life-threatening events, medical conditions, or other disorders (such as drug addiction). Although these attacks cause extreme fear and anxiety, they are always time-limited. They usually reach their peak within a few minutes and subside shortly afterward. Children and adolescents with panic disorder often believe that their attacks are the result of some terrible physical or mental condition. Their catastrophic beliefs lead them to believe that they will suffer other, perhaps more severe, attacks. Over time, this fear causes them to constantly "listen to their body" for signs that a new attack is about to occur. For example, common bodily sensations, such as a temporary increase in heart rate or mild stomach pains, may be interpreted as signs of an impending attack. Figure 10.1 outlines the links between the behavioral, cogni-

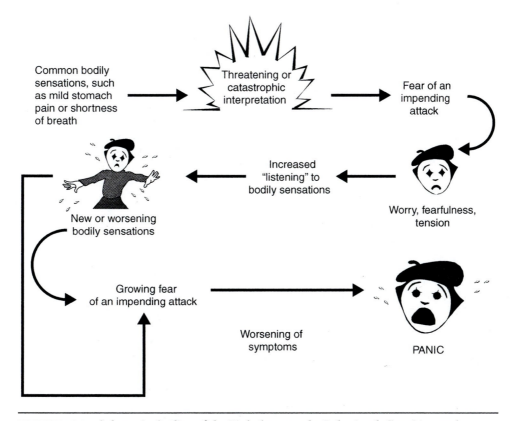

FIGURE 10.1 *Schematic Outline of the Links between the Behavioral, Cognitive, and Physiological Components of Panic Attacks.* Panic attacks are believed to result from a positive feedback loop among behavioral, cognitive, and physiological processes.

tive, and physiological components of panic attacks. By definition, the initial panic attack occurs unexpectedly. Over time, however, attacks often come to be linked—sometimes erroneously—to places, events, or circumstances that the child or adolescent associates with past attacks (American Psychiatric Association, 2000a).

Table 10.6 (p. 284) lists the DSM-IV-TR diagnostic criteria for a panic attack. These criteria focus not on panic disorder per se but on the attacks that are central to the disorder. The disorder can only be diagnosed in children or adolescents who have had at least two panic attacks, and who remain persistently concerned that they will have others. In addition, the disorder cannot be diagnosed if the attacks occur solely in situations of real threat or as part of another anxiety

disorder, of a mood or drug disorder, or of a medical condition such as asthma (APA, 2000a).

Agoraphobia. When panic attacks persist, they can lead to increasingly avoidant behaviors. For example, the child or adolescent may refuse to remain alone or to leave the house unaccompanied for fear of having an attack in a situation where immediate help would not be available. Thus, panic disorder can result in **agoraphobia,** a pathological anxiety about being outside of a safe place and helpless. Frequently, anywhere outside of the home is considered unsafe. In the most extreme cases, the youth becomes house-bound. In such cases, a diagnosis of panic disorder with agoraphobia is made.

TABLE 10.6   *Panic Disorder: DSM-IV-TR Diagnostic Criteria*

Note: A Panic Attack is not a codable disorder. Code the specific diagnosis in which the Panic Attack occurs.

A discrete period of intense fear or discomfort, in which four (or more) of the following symptoms developed abruptly and reached a peak within 10 minutes:

1. palpitations, pounding heart, or accelerated heart rate
2. sweating
3. trembling or shaking
4. sensations of shortness of breath or smothering
5. feeling of choking
6. chest pain or discomfort
7. nausea or abdominal distress
8. feeling dizzy, unsteady, lightheaded, or faint
9. derealization (feelings of unreality) or depersonalization (being detached from oneself)
10. fear of losing control or going crazy
11. fear of dying
12. paresthesias (numbness or tingling sensations)
13. chills or hot flushes

Source: American Psychiatric Association, *Diagnostic and Statistical Manual of Mental Disorders, Fourth Edition, Text Revision* (Washington, DC: American Psychiatric Association, 2000a). Copyright 2000 American Psychiatric Association. Reprinted with permission.

General Adaptation.   As is true of all anxiety disorders, the severity of panic disorder varies considerably. However, for a majority of youth with the disorder, fear of future attacks interferes with social and academic development. As one teen noted, "I can't even go to a movie or on a date anymore because I'm so afraid that I will have an attack!" The distress associated with the disorder comes primarily from the anxiety aroused as the child anticipates an imminent attack and from the fear that such attacks are signs of serious physical or psychological problems (Albano et al., 1996). For example, 10-year-old Alexis was convinced that the shortness of breath and hyperventilation she experienced during her panic attacks were proof that she had lung cancer. Adolescents often attribute their symptoms to severe mental illness. As a 16-year-old girl in our clinic noted, "It was terrible; it was as if I had lost my mind. I believed, really I believed, for one moment that I was going to go completely crazy."

Can Children Really Panic?   At first, many authors believed that children did not have the cognitive capacities necessary to interpret bodily sensations of panic in catastrophic ways. But research has shown that this is not the case. Many children not only meet diagnostic criteria for panic disorder; they also show a pattern of symptoms that corresponds quite closely to that of adults. However, contrary to adults who interpret symptoms of panic as evidence that they might die, lose control, or go crazy (Barlow, 1988), many children and even some adolescents interpret the same symptoms as indications that they are "going to get sick" or that they will "throw up" (Mattis & Ollendick, 1997). This difference is illustrated in Figure 10.2, which shows that children with the disorder tend to experience high levels of nausea but not of **depersonalization** (i.e., out-of-body sensations or feelings of unreality). In other words, unlike adults, children with panic disorder tend to experience physical symptoms. However, they rarely have a sense of loss of their personal identity or feelings that they are somebody else when they are in the midst of an attack.

Eve is 15. Her mother, who requested services at our clinic because of Eve's recent suicide threats, reports that her daughter has an intense fear of vomiting. "She has been home-schooled for the last three years because of it. . . . She has only left the house three times in the past year to visit relatives." Eve is shy but quite talkative with her therapist on the phone (see below). She believes that her problems started when she was 12. She remembers that a child in her class had thrown up and that she thought it was "disgusting." Her reaction was apparently very noticeable, as other children began to tease her about it. Within a few weeks, she felt more and more often nauseated and started to spend long hours each day at the nurse's office. Eve remembers also that she began "scanning her stomach" for

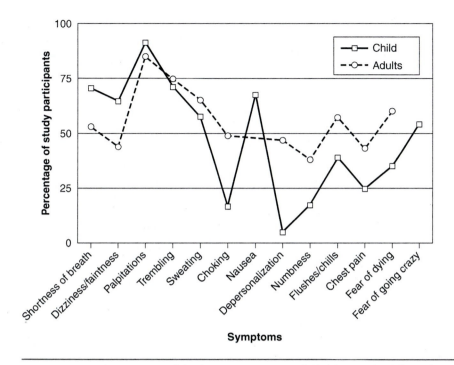

FIGURE 10.2 *Comparison of the Symptom Patterns of Children and Adults with Panic Disorder.* This figure shows that children and adults with panic disorder tend to experience a similar pattern of symptoms. However, in children, the disorder is unlikely to be associated with feelings of depersonalization.

Source: From J. Biederman et al., "Panic Disorder and Agoraphobia in Consecutively Referred Children and Adolescents," *Journal of the American Academy of Child and Adolescent Psychiatry 36* (1997) p. 218. Copyright 1997 by Lippincott, Williams, and Wilkins. Reprinted by permission.

signs of impending illness and that she became very careful about her diet, monitoring her food intake to avoid any stomach upset.

At the end of the school year, Eve's mother decided to home-school her, because she was now spending more time in the nurse's office than in class. In Eve's own words, "Only at home was my stomach at peace." Her initial reaction to this important change was positive; her complaints of nausea became far less frequent and her mood generally improved. However, she became more and more concerned that she might feel sick if she left the house and invented countless reasons to stay home. By age 14, any trip required considerable advance planning, because Eve had to take two aspirins and drink water but eat no food for at least six hours prior to leaving the house. When out, she kept aspirin and water within reach at all times. More importantly, she was miserable and, in her mother's words, "made the rest of us just as miserable," because she was anxious for the entire trip. "I don't know what it is, like when I am out my heart starts beating real fast and pounding and I start shaking and sweating and I know I am going to throw up or I'll just faint." Within six months, Eve was confined almost entirely to her home and began at times feeling nauseated even there. She also became more and more helpless and made several verbal threats of suicide.

Cognitive-behavioral therapy was used to treat Eve, along with medication prescribed to control anxiety. At first, her therapist worked with her by phone, *since Eve was unable to come to the clinic. Therapy focused initially on helping Eve understand that her symptoms were indicative of panic disorder and not of a serious physical disease, as she believed. After a few weeks, Eve began coming to the clinic for very brief visits. These visits allowed her to realize repeatedly that the nausea she experienced when she left the house never had the catastrophic results she dreaded: never did she throw up or faint. By the end of the third month of therapy, Eve was enrolled in a small private school for disabled youth, which she attended regularly and with growing self-confidence. Finally, by the end of the sixth month, Eve returned to her regular school—a large, local public high school, where she was not treated differently from other students. A one-year follow-up interview showed that she had remained panic-free and was no longer housebound.*

Posttraumatic Stress Disorder

Posttraumatic stress disorder (PTSD) is an anxiety disorder that develops after exposure to a traumatic event, such as child abuse, a natural disaster or war, an accident, or the serious injury or violent death of a loved one. By definition, the traumatic event at the origin of PTSD must be such that it provokes a response of "intense fear, horror, or helplessness" (APA, 2000a, p. 424). PTSD must be distinguished from short-term, negative responses to trauma, such as the natural death of a loved one. Although these responses may be severe, they are essentially normal because they do not provoke the anxiety associated with PTSD, nor do they disrupt adaptive functioning, as PTSD always does (APA, 2000a; Davis & Siegel, 2000).

Intrusive Symptoms.   Table 10.7 presents the DSM-IV-TR diagnostic criteria for PTSD. **Intrusive symptoms** are key characteristics of the disorder. These symptoms consist of "recurrent and intrusive distressing recollections of the event, including images, thoughts, or perceptions" and, especially in younger children, repetitive play that reenacts aspects of the trauma (APA, 2000a, p. 468). Intrusive symptoms allow the memories of the trauma to remain alive and powerful, and thus to continue traumatizing youth with PTSD, even when they are safe. Sarah, who was

raped at 15, relived the scene of her victimization like a movie every time she closed her eyes. For years, 4-year-old Chantell saw her mother beaten by her father; she often played games in a state of extreme anxiety, beating and killing her dolls again and again. Intrusive symptoms can also include nightmares of the trauma or **flashbacks,** in which the youth relives the event, often in a near-panic state. José came to our clinic after his friend had died in a car crash in which he, José, had been driving. Time and again, he said, "I am back in that spinning car, hearing the tires squeal and my friend scream." This experience was so real for him that he often screamed aloud before waking up, shaking and sweating. In some cases, mere reminders of the trauma can lead to intrusive symptoms. After his apartment had been burglarized, 6-year-old J. R. became extremely agitated when his mother did not bolt the front door or left a window open, because he remembered how vulnerable he and his family were to intruders.

Avoidance Symptoms.   PTSD is also associated with active avoidance of the memories or emotions surrounding the trauma. Traumatized children and adolescents may deliberately avoid thoughts, places, people, or events that remind them of the trauma; or they may exhibit partial or total memory loss for the trauma. Memory problems are more likely in adolescents and adults than in younger children (Fletcher, 1996). In addition, youth with PTSD may show little interest in most activities and may feel detached from others. After her rape, Sarah could no longer relate to her friends and said that the things they had done together in the past did not seem pleasurable anymore. In keeping with these symptoms, young people with PTSD have a restricted range of affect: they appear emotionally flat and distant, unable to experience the highs and lows of life as their peers do. In particular, victims of prolonged trauma, such as repeated sexual abuse, often give the impression of suffering from "emotional anesthesia" (APA, 2000a, p. 464). Many youth with PTSD also have a sense of foreshortened or limited future. José's contemplation of his future adequately describes this symptom: "I used to plan for college and my career. Now I just get through each day. Why bother to think about the future, who knows

TABLE 10.7 *Posttraumatic Stress Disorder: DSM-IV-TR Diagnostic Criteria*

A. The person has been exposed to a traumatic event in which both of the following were present:

   (1) the person experienced, witnessed, or was confronted with an event or events that involved actual or threatened death or serious injury, or a threat to the physical integrity of self or others.

   (2) the person's response involved intense fear, helplessness, or horror. *Note:* In children, this may be expressed instead by disorganized or agitated behavior.

B. The traumatic event is persistently reexperienced in one (or more) of the following ways:

   (1) recurrent and intrusive distressing recollections of the event, including images, thoughts, or perceptions. *Note:* in young children, repetitive play may occur in which themes or aspects of the trauma are expressed.

   (2) recurrent and distressing dreams of the event. *Note:* in children, there may be frightening dreams without recognizable content.

   (3) acting or feeling as if the traumatic event were recurring (includes a sense of reliving the experience, illusions, hallucinations, and dissociative flashback episodes, including those that occur on awakening or when intoxicated). *Note:* in young children, trauma-specific reenactment may occur.

   (4) intense psychological distress at exposure to internal or external cues that symbolize or resemble an aspect of the traumatic event.

   (5) physiological reactivity on exposure to internal or external cues that symbolize or resemble an aspect of the traumatic event.

C. Persistent avoidance of stimuli associated with the trauma and numbing of general responsiveness (not present before the trauma), as indicated by three (or more) of the following:

   (1) efforts to avoid thoughts, feelings, or conversations associated with the trauma

   (2) efforts to avoid activities, places, or people that arouse recollections of the trauma

   (3) inability to recall an important aspect of the trauma

   (4) markedly diminished interest or participation in significant activities

   (5) feeling of detachment or estrangement from others

   (6) restricted range of affect (e.g., unable to have loving feelings)

   (7) sense of a foreshortened future (e.g., does not expect to have a career, marriage, children, or a normal life span)

D. Persistent symptoms of increased arousal (not present before the trauma), as indicated by two (or more) of the following:

   (1) difficulty falling or staying asleep

   (2) irritability or outbursts of anger

   (3) difficulty concentrating

   (4) hypervigilance

   (5) exaggerated startle response

E. Duration of the disturbance (symptoms in Criteria B, C and D) is more than 1 month.

F. The disturbance causes clinically significant distress or impairment in social, occupational, or other important areas of functioning.

Specify if:
Acute: if duration of symptoms is less than 3 months

Chronic: if duration of symptoms is 3 months or more

Specify if:
With Delayed Onset: if onset of symptoms is at least 6 months after the stressor

Source: American Psychiatric Association, *Diagnostic and Statistical Manual of Mental Disorders, Fourth Edition, Text Revision* (Washington, DC: American Psychiatric Association, 2000a). Copyright 2000 American Psychiatric Association. Reprinted with permission.

what will happen?" More generally, PTSD is often accompanied by low self-esteem, guilt feelings, and pessimism, because the world has come to be regarded as an unpredictable and dangerous place that is difficult to control and in which one can seldom trust adults.

Hyperarousal.   PTSD is also associated with symptoms of hyperarousal. These include difficulties falling or staying asleep, irritability, limited attention and concentration, hypervigilance to threats, and an exaggerated reaction to sudden noises or surprises, known as an abnormal **startle response.** The adoptive mother of an 18-year-old girl who had a long history of abuse described her daughter as very easily aroused, both behaviorally and emotionally, and as being always on the lookout for signs of danger. For example, this mother had to whistle wherever she went around the house to avoid startling her daughter by appearing unexpectedly. Ashley, whose case is described here, also had PTSD as a consequence of abuse.

Ashley is 5. She has been living with her paternal grandparents since she was 3. Her father is serving a prison sentence for having repeatedly abused her sexually. Her mother, who has a history of drug addiction, visits her now and then but does not play an active role in her life. Her grandparents, whom she loves very much, treat her lovingly also but find it difficult to deal with the problems she presents. For example, during her first visit to our clinic, her grandmother describes Ashley's extreme fear of men: "I decided to come to you because she refuses to go to school. . . . A few weeks ago, on the first day [of school], she was ready to leave, feeling a little timid, but that's normal at this age. But as soon as she saw that it was a man driving the school bus, she refused to get on, clinging to me and starting to howl something terrible, as if somebody was trying to strangle her. . . . Same thing the following day. My husband had to take us to school. She agreed to come in with me but she was gripping my hand, not just holding it. . . . The school was very busy. She looked all around, like a hunter almost, if you know what I mean. Now, as luck would have it, she saw the custodian, who was cleaning windows. She immediately started to howl and the principal came running to see what was happening. I was so embarrassed. But she was very nice. I mean, she spoke to Ashley very nicely and encouraged her to calm down, but there was nothing she could do. The poor child was still screaming, I felt so sorry for her and for the poor custo-

dian! . . . I had to take her back with me to the house and she has not been back to school since."

With the exception of her grandfather, whom she trusts, Ashley has an extreme fear of men of all ages. According to her grandmother, Ashley's first symptoms appeared around 3 and have worsened since. She started by being very "clingy" and constantly looking around to make sure that her grandmother was near. She then developed sleep difficulties, demanding that her grandmother remain in her bedroom every evening until she fell asleep, and awakening two or three times a week crying from nightmares. She also refused to be in the presence of men without her grandmother being right beside her. Finally, she started reenacting her abuse through sexual play. In her grandmother's words, "It's often embarrassing, but for about a year now she has been lying down on a cushion and twisting her hips and making noises. At times, she will just strip to rub herself sexually. . . . Recently, I even caught her trying to do sexual things with a little boy I sometimes watch at the house."

Ashley does not recognize her problems and is unable to speak about her abuse. She knows, however, that her father is in prison: "They put him in a house very, very far from here and he cannot come out. But I am still scared." No amount of reassurance can calm her fears.

An intervention program lasting for more than a year was set up, initially to make it possible for Ashley to separate from her grandmother. Through activities with Ashley and her grandmother, initially in the home and later outside, her separation anxiety decreased and she learned how to trust her female therapist. After a few months, the therapist introduced her to "a friend of mine" who was a male therapist. For several weeks, he attended all the sessions, but was not active—often sitting in the back of the room and just observing. This period of habituation to a man gradually made it possible for Ashley to trust him and, through play and then excursions, to realize that not all men wanted to harm her. The intervention also enabled her to go to school, initially with her grandmother and later in the school bus, which was still driven by a man. Finally, the female therapist withdrew gradually, letting Ashley complete treatment with the male therapist.

Generalized Anxiety Disorder

> *Anxiety is the space between the "now" and the "then."*
>
> —Richard Abell

Generalized anxiety disorder (GAD) is a disorder in which children or adolescents have severe, uncontrollable anxiety or worry about a range of activities, events, or skills. For example, they may constantly worry, not only about the weather but also about family finances, world peace, and grades. These worries are accompanied by one or more physiological symptoms, such as tension, agitation, or restlessness, and by stomachaches, headaches, or other physical pains. Because of the extent of their worries, children with GAD are often described as "carrying the whole world on their shoulders" by parents and teachers, and as "worry-warts" by peers. However, these expressions do not adequately sum up

the seriousness of their difficulties. Generally, youth with GAD do not show the disruptive symptoms associated with OCD or panic disorder, but the chronicity and severity of their anxiety affect their entire behavior (American Psychiatric Association, 2000a).

Table 10.8 lists the DSM-IV-TR diagnostic criteria for GAD. Prior to publication of the DSM-IV, children and adolescents with symptoms of GAD were diagnosed with **overanxious disorder,** which was listed in the DSM-II, DSM-III, and DSM-III-R as one of the disorders usually diagnosed in childhood or adolescence. Compared to other anxiety disorders, GAD in childhood and adolescence remains poorly understood, not only because of this change in the DSM classification but also because it is very broad and its boundaries are difficult to specify.

Excessive Worry. Unlike the majority of children, who live for the moment and enjoy life fully, children

---

TABLE 10.8 *Generalized Anxiety Disorder: DSM-IV-TR Diagnostic Criteria*

A. Excessive anxiety and worry (apprehensive expectation), occurring more days than not for at least 6 months, about a number of events or activities (such as work or school performance).

B. The person finds it difficult to control the worry.

C. The anxiety and worry are associated with three (or more) of the following six symptoms (with at least some symptoms present for more days than not for the past 6 months). *Note:* Only one item is required in children.

    (1) restlessness or feeling keyed up or on edge

    (2) being easily fatigued

    (3) difficulty concentrating or mind going blank

    (4) irritability

    (5) muscle tension

    (6) sleep disturbance (difficulty falling or staying asleep, or restless unsatisfying sleep).

D. The focus of the anxiety and worry is not confined to features of an Axis I disorder, e.g., the anxiety or

worry is not about having a Panic Attack (as in Panic Disorder), being embarrassed in public (as in Social Phobia), being contaminated (as in Obsessive-Compulsive Disorder), being away from home or close relatives (as in Separation Anxiety Disorder), gaining weight (as in Anorexia Nervosa), having multiple physical complaints (as in Somatization Disorder), or having a serious illness (as in Hypochondriasis), and the anxiety and worry do not occur exclusively during Posttraumatic Stress Disorder.

E. The anxiety, worry, or physical symptoms cause clinically significant distress or impairment in social, occupational, or in other important areas of functioning.

F. The disturbance is not due to the direct physiological effects of a substance (e.g., a drug of abuse, a medication) or a general medical condition (e.g., hyperthyroidism) and does not occur exclusively during a Mood Disorder, a Psychotic Disorder, or a Pervasive Developmental Disorder.

Source: American Psychiatric Association, *Diagnostic and Statistical Manual of Mental Disorders, Fourth Edition, Text Revision* (Washington, DC: American Psychiatric Association, 2000a). Copyright 2000 American Psychiatric Association. Reprinted with permission.

with GAD worry excessively. As 10-year-old Mike said, "All the kids and teachers ever say is 'lighten up' or 'just chill out.' They should know it's not that easy." The focus of the many fears of children and adolescents with GAD changes over the course of development, but the fact that their worries are always extreme and unrealistic remains constant. In short, they overestimate the probability that something bad is going to happen, while underestimating their own ability or that of others to cope (Bögels & Zigterman, 2000).

Most youth with GAD worry about health (their own or that of family members), school, or changes in family routines (such as going on vacation). They also worry about adult concerns, such as their parents' job stability or family finances (see Figure 10.3). In addition, they often doubt their own abilities but are

FIGURE 10.3 *Generalized Anxiety Disorder.* The development and psychological adjustment of children with GAD is compromised by almost constant worries about a host of issues, and about their ability to cope.

Source: Cartoon courtesy of Ed Schelb (2002). Reprinted by permission.

perfectionists—a combination of characteristics that can leave them feeling like failures because their standards are too high and their self-esteem too low. Their high standards and perceived lack of competence also lead them to fear that others will judge them as severely as they judge themselves.

Physiological and Cognitive Symptoms. Like their peers with other anxiety disorders, youth with GAD mull over their worries. Although the amount of time they spend ruminating fluctuates, it takes up a significant part of each day and is generally accompanied by physiological symptoms, such as tension, restlessness, sleep difficulties, and unexplained physical complaints (Werry, 1991). Not surprisingly, children and adolescents with GAD also report difficulties in concentration and attention, because the focus of their thoughts is often on their worries rather than on the topic at hand. As one child aptly put it, "How can I pay attention to the teacher when I am sure all these [bad] things are going to happen?" In keeping with their many preoccupations, affected youth have an excessive need for reassurance and may repeatedly ask parents or teachers if their performance is up to standard. However, reassurance does not lessen their worries.

Kathy is 11. She was diagnosed with a chronic illness two year ago, but her pediatrician is concerned that most of her symptoms are not a result of her disease. She suffers from unexplained stomach pains and occasional vomiting, as well as from frequent headaches and neck and back pains.

In her initial interview, Kathy reports that she worries about "a lot of things," and that her doctor thinks that her worrying increases her pains. She also says that she often feels overwhelmed at school. However, she believes that this is realistic because she is "not good enough." Interestingly, Kathy is an A-average student and excels at many sports. When asked about the exact focus of her worries, she remains vague. She mentions grades, friends, sports, weather, and accidents. She is particularly afraid that her parents will die in a car crash. She also expresses concerns about how much therapy will cost and about her mother's health. Surprisingly, however, Kathy does not mention her own health as a source of worry.

In a separate interview, Kathy's mother notes that her daughter " has always been a worrier, like me. . . . Ever since she was a small child, Kathy has been concerned about things that most children her age are not." For example, her father reports that she watches the weather channel in the morning before school to make sure that she dresses appropriately and "to be prepared for the worst." However, according to both parents, her most profound worries focus on her own performance, at times to the point of almost paralyzing her. "She will often check and recheck her homework so many times that she will not get all of the work done at a reasonable hour," her mother says. "Then I have to sit with her and talk her through her work step by step, even though she is perfectly capable of doing the work. It's just that she doesn't believe in herself." Her father adds that Kathy's worries are often accompanied by physiological symptoms: "Her back and neck pain always grows worse before tests, and her vomiting always occurs when she is behind in a subject or just thinks she is behind."

Treatment for Kathy focuses on:

- Teaching her relaxation techniques to control her anxiety and reduce her physical symptoms.
- Helping her learn to recognize and modify her thoughts (i.e., self-talk) in order not to overestimate the probability of negative events or underestimate her skills.
- Teaching Kathy's parents to encourage their daughter's positive coping skills and to discourage her worrying.

Kathy progresses well and at the end of six months asks for therapy to be terminated. She still worries about many things that do not preoccupy her peers, but this no longer causes her to have unmanageable physical symptoms.

Diagnostic and Developmental Considerations

Impact on Functioning and Development

Anxiety problems often represent an exaggeration of normal developmental fears, rather than qualitatively distinct psychological disorders. Consequently, to determine whether a disorder is or is not present, one must assess the severity of the symptoms and the impact of these symptoms on the child's daily functioning. For example, consider two boys who both fear cars to the point of not wanting to ride in them. One of them lives in a large city, in a family that does not own a car but gets around by foot or public transportation. His fear is clearly excessive but not necessarily pathological, because it does not hinder his functioning or limit his development in significant ways. The other child lives in a suburb of the same city, in a family that owns a car and must rely on it because public transportation is limited. His fearfulness is not more intense than that of the first child. However, in this setting, it is pathological because it interferes with important daily tasks, such as attending school. In other words, the same symptoms of anxiety can have a different impact on functioning and development because of circumstances.

Interplay of Behavioral, Physiological, and Cognitive Processes

Anxiety and fear responses manifest themselves through three overlapping response systems: behavioral, physiological, and cognitive. At the behavioral level, anxiety results in avoidance or escape from the feared object or situation. Physiologically, anxiety expresses itself in a variety of physical responses, including changes in heart rate or breathing, sweating, stomach upset, and nausea. At the cognitive level, worries, ruminations, misinterpretations of bodily symptoms, and feelings of fear, tension, panic, and distress are common anxiety responses. Although they are closely related, these processes do not overlap completely. For example, one child may experience multiple physiological and behavioral symptoms of anxiety without reporting subjective feelings of fear. But another child may seem to worry almost constantly without showing corresponding signs of physiological activation. These differences can hinder diagnostic work, not only because the same disorder may manifest itself differently in different children, but also because the behavioral, physiological, and cognitive processes characteristic of anxiety change with age, and are influenced by social and cultural factors that remain poorly understood.

Complementary Perspectives from Different Informants

Diagnostic work can be made difficult because there is usually only partial correspondence between symptoms reported by different informants. For example, in a clinical sample of three hundred children aged 7 to 11, Benjamin, Costello, and Warren (1990) found that parents, teachers, and the children themselves presented differing images of the children's anxiety, and also described the children's symptom patterns and comorbidity in different ways.

These discrepancies show that anxiety problems tend to be perceived differently according to each informant's perspective. For example, children who have recurring fears of social interaction may avoid most contacts with peers and unfamiliar adults, and their self-descriptions would meet the diagnostic criteria for an anxiety disorder. At school, teachers are likely to describe these students as lacking in social skills, preoccupied, and often disorganized, but not necessarily as anxious. At home, where they have fewer opportunities to compare their children with children of the same age, parents may describe them as shy, quiet, and emotional, but well behaved and not socially unskilled. These different but complementary perspectives illustrate the difficulty of diagnosing disorders whose primary symptoms are internal.

Empirical Validity

As currently defined, most of the anxiety disorders of childhood and adolescence lack empirical validity (Hagopian & Ollendick, 1997). Because systematic research in this area began only two decades ago, a solid body of empirical knowledge has not yet been amassed. In any event, past research is not always relevant to the current understanding of these disorders, because the most recent editions of the DSM introduced significant changes in their diagnostic criteria.

Therefore, these symptoms still have not been adequately categorized into specific disorders.

Lack of Specificity

To be considered empirically valid, as you know, a psychological disorder must have specificity. It must have a distinctive set of symptoms and a unique developmental trajectory. Questions of empirical validity arise in this area because, as a group, anxiety disorders share a variety of symptoms and have overlapping developmental trajectories (Albano et al., 1996). For example, SAD has symptoms in common with specific phobia, and many children who have SAD will develop panic disorder in adolescence or early adulthood (Mattis & Ollendick, 1997).

Overlap between Anxiety and Mood Disorders

The high degree of comorbidity between anxious and depressive phenomena, which we discussed in Chapter 9, is a major threat to the empirical validity of anxiety disorders as they are currently defined. In line with research on this comorbidity in adults, a number of authors believe that anxiety and depression are part of a broad group of conditions characterized by **negative affectivity**—that is, by subjective feelings of tension, fear, hostility, sadness, and distress. To explain the relationship between these conditions, Clark and Watson (1991) devised a three-factor model. In this model, the three factors—negative affectivity, positive affect and experiences, and physiological hyperarousal—are assumed to interact to cause either mood or anxiety disorders. Specifically, when negative affectivity is paired with lack of positive affect and experiences, a mood disorder is likely to develop; when it is paired with physiological hyperarousal, an anxiety disorder is more probable. There is some support for this model (Chorpita, Albano, & Barlow, 1998; Murphy, Marelich, & Hoffman, 2000). Should additional evidence become available, this model would go a long way towards establishing empirical validity and accounting for the high degree of comorbidity between anxiety and depression.

Associated Characteristics; Comorbidity

Medical Conditions

Since physical symptoms are part of the diagnostic criteria of all anxiety disorders, it should come as no surprise that these disorders are often associated with medical complications. For example, washing rituals in OCD can lead to serious skin conditions, and chronic exposure to stress can provoke gastrointestinal problems in GAD. In fact, physical complaints are often what alarm families initially and lead to professional consultation—as you saw in Kathy's case. However, only a minority of affected youth have a well-established medical condition (American Psychiatric Association, 2000a). Clinically, children and adolescents with an anxiety disorder should receive a thorough medical examination to rule out any medical condition or physical abnormality that might explain their psychological symptoms.

Psychological Disorders

Anxiety Disorders. In clinical samples, two-thirds or more of children and adolescents with significant anxiety problems have at least two comorbid anxiety disorders (Biederman et al., 1997). Overanxious disorder, SAD, and specific and social phobias have most often been found to be comorbid. In community samples, comorbidity rates average approximately 37% in children and 14% in adolescents (Anderson, 1994). Comparable rates have been published in reviews of the OCD and PTSD literature (Fletcher, 1996; Henin & Kendall, 1997). In addition, youth who have an anxiety disorder often have multiple symptoms of other anxiety disorders, even though they may not meet all criteria necessary for another diagnosis.

Mood Disorders. Anxiety disorders are often associated with depressive symptoms and disorders. Although comorbidity rates vary considerably from one study to another, they are higher in adolescence than in childhood, and among young people who have multiple anxiety disorders rather than one only (Curry &

Murphy, 1995). Unfortunately, rates reported in many studies group all the anxiety disorders together, thereby hiding the fact that some of them—particularly SAD and overanxious disorder (Kovacs, Gatsonis, Paulauskas, & Richards, 1989)—are more often associated with depressive symptoms than others. However, this association is partly the result of the diagnostic overlap between SAD and overanxious disorder and the mood disorders—major depressive disorder in particular (Seligman & Ollendick, 1998).

Disruptive Behavior Disorders. Anxiety disorders can also be associated with ADHD, ODD, and CD (e.g., Biederman et al., 1997). Here again, average rates are most often reported and hide the fact that some anxiety disorders are more likely to be associated with these disruptive behavior disorders than others. Given this limitation, comorbidity rates ranging from 20% to 33% have been reported for ADHD, and from 15% to 40% for ODD and CD. For ADHD, rates are highest in younger samples, primarily because of the overall decrease in the prevalence of ADHD in adolescence (Andersen, 1994). For ODD and CD, in contrast, rates tend to remain stable or to increase somewhat from childhood to adolescence (Anderson, 1994; Curry & Murphy, 1995).

General Adaptation

As the case studies presented earlier clearly show, anxiety disorders can be debilitating and invariably limit adaptive functioning. Although child, parental, and teacher reports often describe different areas of functioning as most disturbed, all respondents usually agree that social interactions are affected, at times severely (La Greca & Lopez, 1998). Specifically, children with anxiety disorders are less competent socially—both in their own eyes and according to their peers—probably because they tend to withdraw rather than seek out interaction with peers and, consequently, receive less positive reinforcement from peers (Spence et al., 1999).

Unfortunately, these social deficits not only limit current functioning but also reinforce the child's anxiety through a process of self-fulfilling prophecy. Remember what Kevin said when he was asked why he did not help his peers solve their video game problem: "I asked my-self what they would say, like if I told them. And then very quickly, I don't know, I was afraid and I didn't think about it anymore." Escape from this stressful sit-uation only reinforced Kevin's social anxiety, further convincing him that he should avoid all social contacts. Not surprisingly, many children who live through simi-lar situations every day develop a poor self-concept and feelings of loneliness and despair that further aggravate their symptoms.

Epidemiology

Prevalence; Age and Gender Characteristics

Overall, anxiety disorders affect 6–18% of children and adolescents, prevalence rates varying with age and with the methods and informants used to assess their disorders (Costello & Angold, 1995b). For example, Kashani and Orvaschel (1988) found that 17% of their sample reported significant symptoms of anxiety, but that only 9% qualified for an actual diagnosis. Given that many anxiety symptoms are not readily observ-able, it is not surprising that rates are usually higher when data are obtained from the youth themselves, rather than from parents or teachers (Benjamin et al., 1990).

In community samples, anxiety disorders tend to affect girls more often than boys, with an approximate sex ratio of 2 : 1. This gender difference is apparent as early as age 6 and is most likely to be found in studies based on self-report data (Lewinsohn, Gotlib, Lewin-sohn, Seeley, & Allen, 1998). In clinical samples, the preponderance of girls appears clearly only in adoles-cence (Hagopian & Ollendick, 1997). It is also impor-tant to note that females are not overrepresented in all anxiety disorders. For example, social phobia and OCD tend to be equally distributed or slightly more frequent in boys than girls (Hagopian & Ollendick, 1997; Hanna, 1995).

Separation Anxiety Disorder.   In eight studies of community samples reviewed by Anderson (1994), the prevalence of SAD ranged from less than 1% to nearly 13%, with an average of 4% to 5%. More recent stud-ies indicate that these rates may be somewhat higher (Kashdan & Herbert, 2001). The disorder affects girls more often than boys. It is particularly frequent before puberty and decreases with age. These findings are supported by the clinical literature, which also indi-cates that average age of onset is about 7 years (Last et al., 1992).

Specific Phobia.   Community sample studies from around the world indicate that specific phobias are found in an average of 3–5% of children and adoles-cents, with rates ranging from less than 3% to almost 18%. Specific phobias are more frequent in girls than boys (Essau et al., 2000; Muris & Merckelbach, 2000). Not surprisingly, rates are higher in clinical samples. It is estimated that approximately 15% of children and adolescents who are referred for professional consulta-tion have specific phobia. However, in a majority of cases (approximately 60–75%), their phobia is accom-panied by another disorder, which is often the present-ing problem and the focus of intervention (Ollendick, Hagopian, & King, 1997). Clinical data indicate that the average age of onset for specific phobias is 8.4 years (Last et al., 1992).

Social Phobia and School Refusal.   Social phobia is rare, especially before adolescence. It affects ap-proximately 1% of children and adolescents and be-gins, on average, around age 10 or 11. In adolescence, girls are as often affected as boys. However, in child-hood, the sex ratio probably favors boys, who tend to have an earlier age of onset than girls (Albano et al., 1996; Last et al., 1992). School refusal overlaps with but is more prevalent than social phobia, affecting ap-proximately 5% of youth. Boys and girls are equally likely to be school refusers. School refusal usually be-gins in kindergarten or first grade, or around ages 10 to 11 (Kearney, 2001). It may be that these two peak ages of onset represent different underlying anxiety disor-ders—namely, SAD in the early school years and spe-cific or social phobia in later childhood. Additional research is needed to test this hypothesis.

Obsessive-Compulsive Disorder.   OCD probably affects fewer than 1% of children, and between 1% and 2% of adolescents, although epidemiological data are sparse. On average, the disorder begins between the ages of 10 and 13, probably earlier in boys than girls (Hanna, 1995). In clinical samples, the disorder is equally distributed across gender or slightly more frequent in boys, depending on the studies one considers (Hanna, 1995; Last et al., 1992).

Panic Disorder.   Isolated panic attacks are rare in children but may affect 40–60% of adolescents between the ages of 12 and 19 (King, Gullone, Tonge, & Ollendick, 1993; Macaulay & Kleinknecht, 1989). However, panic disorder is relatively rare. Depending on age and diagnostic procedures, prevalence rates range from 1% to 5% in community samples (Lewinsohn, Hops, Roberts, Seeley, & Andrews, 1993; Macaulay & Kleinknecht, 1989), and from 5% to 15% in clinical studies (Alessi & Magen, 1988). For yet unidentified reasons, the prevalence of the disorder greatly increases around the onset of puberty. In keeping with this finding, the disorder begins later than other anxiety disorders, on average between 12 and 14 years (Biederman et al., 1997; Last et al., 1992). The disorder affects girls more often than boys.

Posttraumatic Stress Disorder.   Data on the epidemiology of PTSD before adulthood are sparse, although evidence shows that children and adolescents run considerable risk of being exposed to at least one traumatic event during their growing years (Weine, Becker, Levy, Edell, & McGlashen, 1997). In a study of more than five thousand young people (from 9 to 19 years) exposed to Hurricane Hugo, a natural disaster that struck the east coast of the United States, Shannon and associates (1994) found that 5% of them met DSM-III-R criteria for the disorder three months after the event. This rate was similar in different ethnic groups, but higher in girls than boys (7% versus 4%). Importantly, this average rate hides the fact that children were more often affected than adolescents (ages 9–12: rate 9%; ages 13–15: rate 4%; ages 16–19: rate 3%).

Generalized Anxiety Disorder.   Much of our knowledge about the epidemiology of GAD relies on studies of its diagnostic predecessor, overanxious disorder. The disorder affects approximately 3% of children and

6% of adolescents (Anderson, 1994). Although its first symptoms often appear during early childhood, the disorder itself usually begins several years later (Westenberg, Siebelink, Warmhoven, & Trefffers, 1999). In a clinical study, Last and associates (1992) found that the average age of onset was 8.8 years and that girls were more commonly affected than boys. Werry's (1991) review reports that the sex ratio is balanced during childhood but that in adolescence the number of affected girls significantly exceeds the number of affected boys.

Social and Cultural Differences

Available evidence indicates that the overall prevalence of anxiety disorders differs little by social status or ethnicity (Benjamin et al., 1990; Last et al., 1992) and that when differences are found, they usually pertain only to specific disorders. However, this conclusion is limited by the fact that it is based almost exclusively on North American samples and that cross-cultural comparisons are rare.

Cross-cultural studies conducted to date have focused on the distribution of anxiety symptoms—rather than disorders—in different populations (Matsuura et al., 1993; Ollendick, Yang, King, Dong, & Akande, 1996). For example, Matsuura and associates (1993) compared the prevalence of worry, sadness, and fear among several thousand Japanese, Chinese, and Korean children aged from 6 to 12. They found that all three symptoms were as common in boys as in girls, but that they were significantly more frequent among Korean than among Japanese or Chinese children. In addition, Japanese boys and girls tended to worry more than their Chinese peers. These comparisons illustrate the importance of cross-cultural research to explore the extent to which anxiety symptoms and disorders manifest themselves differently in different cultures.

Developmental Trajectories and Prognosis

Given that anxiety manifests itself in very different disorders, it should come as no surprise that the developmental trajectories of these disorders vary, often considerably. We will begin with some broad developmental generalizations, before focusing more closely on SAD and OCD.

Change, Stability, and Chronicity

Even though adolescents tend to report more anxiety symptoms than children with similar problems (Werry, 1991), developmental data indicate that the symptomatology of anxiety disorders generally improves with age. In community samples, approximately 60% of those initially assessed with an anxiety disorder no longer qualify for a diagnosis four years later (Anderson, 1994). However, some anxiety disorders are much more stable than others. For example, Pine, Cohen, Gurley, Brook, and Ma (1998) found that panic disorder and GAD tended to change over time; youth initially diagnosed with one of these disorders might have another anxiety disorder, major depressive disorder, or no disorder at all at follow-up. In contrast, the same authors reported that social and specific phobias were much more stable diagnoses, so that youth diagnosed with either of these conditions would still have that disorder or none at all at follow-up.

Some anxiety disorders are also much more chronic than others. For example, a long-term follow-up of children with OCD found that over two-thirds of them (68%) continued to meet diagnostic criteria seven years later (Flament et al., 1990). PTSD has a similarly chronic trajectory, but only when trauma continues over an extended period of time, such as war, community violence, or child abuse (e.g., Beitchman et al., 1992). PTSD that develops in response to one-time traumatic events, such as natural disasters, tends to improve considerably or disappear over time (Shannon et al., 1994). Finally, stability and chronicity are most apparent in girls. In a review of the literature, Costello and Angold (1995b) found that the odds of a childhood anxiety disorder predicting an anxiety disorder in adolescence were almost twice as high for girls as compared to boys.

Fear and the Fear of Fear

A major element in the developmental processes underlying many cases of anxiety disorders is the appearance of a fear of fear—a phenomenon known as **anxiety sensitivity.** Youth with high levels of anxiety sensitivity fear the negative feelings and sensations that they associate with what they objectively fear. That is, youth with anxiety disorders not only fear one or more objects or situations; they also fear what might happen if they are confronted with what they dread. Anxiety sensitivity is believed to be a risk factor in the development of anxiety disorders, especially panic disorder, and to contribute to the chronicity of these disorders once they manifest themselves (Silverman & Weems, 1999). For example, many adolescents with panic disorder are continuously on the lookout for physiological signs of an impending attack and may gradually avoid all situations that they believe could trigger attacks. Likewise, children who are pathologically afraid of dogs do not simply have to contend with that objective fear. Many of them also spend time scanning their environment in anticipation that a dog might suddenly appear, at the expense of other activities essential to their development.

With time, this fear of fear supports the development of cognitive errors or biases. These are mistaken beliefs that promote anxiety and helplessness because they are based on false but unchallenged negative predictions (Suarez & Bell-Dolan, 2001). Eve, the adolescent with panic disorder we described earlier, was convinced that leaving her home would cause her to vomit and embarrass her in public. When we asked if she had ever tested this theory by going out, she said that she had not and appeared puzzled that anyone would ask her that question. Because of her fear of fear—her anxious anticipation of a disaster in public—she greatly overestimated the likelihood that she would have a panic attack if she left home; and, correspondingly, she underestimated her ability to cope with this and other stressful situations. As long as they remain unchallenged, cognitive errors obviously contribute to the maintenance of pathological anxiety and avoidance. As you will see below, modern treatment approaches often challenge these errors directly, in an attempt to help youth confront their fears and realize that the dreadful consequences they have been anticipating for so long never occur.

Two Specific Developmental Trajectories

The developmental trajectories of anxiety disorders are very diverse, and precise developmental research is lacking. There is considerable agreement on two points, however. First, in a majority of cases, anxiety disorders develop gradually—starting with relatively harmless behaviors that parents, teachers, and other adults can often accept or ignore for several years. Panic disorder and, to a lesser degree, PTSD are exceptions, however; their onset is often very sudden. Second, once a disorder is established, the severity and intensity of its symptoms do not remain constant. Generally, acute phases, when symptoms are most severe, alternate with periods in which symptoms are less prominent and debilitating. The exception to this generalization is specific phobia, in which symptom severity tends to remain fairly constant over time.

We will now focus more specifically on SAD and OCD, to describe how these disorders develop. SAD usually begins during periods of transition in the child's life, such as starting school or returning to school after a long break or illness. Onset is rarely associated with an actual trauma in which the child is confronted with the real possibility of being separated from loved ones. However, as in Sarah's case, a parent's hospitalization or other absence may be experienced as traumatic. During such periods of transition, children who tend to be anxious already may refuse to go to school, forcing a parent to stay home to care for them. Alternatively, at critical times of day, often bedtime, symptoms of illness may appear (or reappear), making it possible for the child to delay bedtime or to sleep with one or both parents. These harmless beginnings are rapidly reinforced, both through avoidance of a feared situation (going to school, going to bed) and through positive parental attention and care. Parents who realize early that this cycle of avoidance and positive reinforcement may become detrimental to the child's development can usually prevent the appearance of SAD by sending the child to school or to bed in spite of protests, or by otherwise refusing to attend to the child's symptoms. However, in many cases, parents do not realize that a maladaptive pattern may be developing and actively contribute to it, giving the child more and more attention as symptoms become more severe and extreme. With time, symptoms become unmanageable and begin to interfere with the child's own development and the entire family's functioning.

OCD often has similar apparently harmless beginnings. The child is somewhat rigid and does a few "odd" things that the family considers unusual or eccentric, but not alarming. No one protests when the child insists on arranging her socks or underwear in neat rows. It is "just something she does"—something quite helpful, actually, at least in families that value order and tidiness. Over time, the child's orderliness becomes more extreme and widespread, often during or after periods of family stress or conflict. She is now arranging all of her belongings in a particular order and insisting that the same be done in the living room and kitchen. At this point, what were once odd behaviors become an entrenched part of the child's daily activities. And any attempt to disrupt them causes such distress that families often continue to ignore them, to explain them away, or to accommodate them by conforming to the child's wishes. In the end, obsessions and compulsions occupy so much of the child's life that they can no longer be ignored, not only because the child is obviously suffering but also because the entire family is disrupted (Albano et al., 1996; Waters & Barrett, 2000).

Etiology

Scientific interest in the etiology of anxiety disorders dates back at least to the late nineteenth century, when Alfred Binet, the famous developer of the intelligence test, proposed that fear in children resulted from such diverse causes as illness, overexcitement, imagination, and heredity, as well as from traumatic experiences, especially child abuse and domestic violence. Binet's theoretical speculations have largely been confirmed by modern research, especially his assumption that anxiety disorders can have multiple and often very diverse origins.

Biological Factors: Genetic Studies

Twin Studies.   Vulnerability to different forms of anxiety is partly inherited. Specifically, monozygotic twins are more likely than their dizygotic counterparts to share personality characteristics or traits, such as loneliness, that can predispose them to develop anxiety disorders (McGuire & Clifford, 2000). Similarly, concordance rates for anxiety disorders are higher in monozygotic than dizygotic twins, although members of the same pair of twins do not necessarily have the same anxiety disorder (Kendler, Davis, & Kessler, 1997). This finding supports the conclusion that specific anxiety disorders are not inherited as such. Rather, it is more likely that some individuals are genetically vulnerable to become anxious and to develop one or more of these disorders as a function of multiple factors, only some of which are genetic. Kendler and associates (1992) hypothesize that, in women at least, this vulnerability may be even broader and encompass both anxious and depressed symptoms—thus accounting, in part, for the high levels of comorbidity among anxiety and mood disorders. Specifically, their twin study yielded data showing that some girls are particularly vulnerable to manifest both types of symptoms, but that the manner in which they evolve into one or more specific disorders depends in large part on environmental factors. In situations of loss, in which the child has little or no control, depression is likely to develop, whereas in situations of threat, in which the child has limited and uncertain control, anxiety is likely to be the outcome. This developmental model is consistent with research on negative affectivity, as reviewed above.

Family Aggregation Studies. Anxiety disorders also tend to run in families. For example, children of parents with panic disorder (with or without major depression) are more likely to suffer from an anxiety disorder in adolescence than children of parents with depression or children of control parents (Biederman et al., 2001). Conversely, parents of anxious, school-refusing children have high rates of anxiety disorders themselves (Martin, Cabrol, Bouvard, Lepine, & Mouren-Simeoni, 1999).

In keeping with the evidence just discussed, first-degree relatives probably share a general vulnerability to fearfulness and anxiety, rather than a specific risk to develop the same disorder. For example, children of parents with social phobia may have the disorder also, but they are equally as likely to have GAD, SAD, specific phobia, or PTSD (Mancini, van Ameringen, Szatmari, Fugere, & Boyle, 1996). Panic disorder and OCD

may be the only two anxiety disorders that have a statistically significant tendency to be found within the same families (Last, Hersen, Kazdin, Francis, & Grubb, 1987).

Biological Factors: Neurophysiological Studies

As is the case in mood disorders, dysregulation in central nervous system activity is implicated in the maintenance, if not in the etiology, of anxiety disorders. Research in this area relies on different methods of investigation, such as the tracing of brain electrical activity in response to a task or other stimulation (i.e., evoked potentials), as well as studies of neurotransmitters and brain morphology.

In a different line of research, studies of brain receptors show that serotonin and norepinephrine are involved in anxiety disorders, as do studies in which participants are given medications that are known to act on these neurotransmitters. Thus, highly anxious individuals have increased levels of norepinephrine, and experimental administration of this neurochemical provokes anxiety symptoms in nonanxious participants (Krystal, Deutsch, & Charney, 1996). This neurotransmitter may be particularly significant to the study of anxiety because the HPA axis, of which it is a part, is believed to be central to the sensory processing of environmental information and to emotion regulation.

Adults with PTSD secondary to severe physical and/or sexual abuse in childhood have a smaller hippocampus, on average, than adults without such a history (Bremner et al., 1997). As you know, the hippocampus is a brain structure that plays a central role in learning, memory, and emotion regulation.

Biological Factors: Neuropsychological Studies

A major line of research on the etiology of anxiety disorders focuses on early neuropsychological factors that differentiate anxious children from those who are not. This research is particularly important because it provides a link between the genetic and neurophysiological evidence just reviewed and the observable manifestations that are characteristic of anxiety. The work of Kagan and his colleagues on **behavioral inhibition** is best known in this area (e.g., Kagan, 1989). This work overlaps somewhat with the etiological research we described in the context of the disruptive behavior disorders (see Chapters 7 and 8). However, behavioral inhibition refers here to a temperamental style rather than a neurobiological system. The construct describes key characteristics of a group of children (approximately 15–20% of European American children in the United States) who are irritable as infants and later become shy, fearful, and usually extremely cautious. At the physiological level, they have a generally elevated heart rate that varies little over time and tends to increase further in the presence of unfamiliar stimuli or mild stressors, such as a stranger entering the room. At the behavioral level, inhibited children, especially when they are young, tend to react to unexpected situations by crying and increasing their motor activity, or by showing other signs of fearfulness and agitation. When they are older, the same children rarely talk spontaneously in unfamiliar surroundings, do little exploration of their environment, and avoid contact with unknown adults or children. These characteristics are stable throughout childhood. They cannot be explained in terms of environmental factors, such as birth status, chronic illness, family stress, or poverty, and may represent an inherited vulnerability to anxiety.

Most important from an etiological perspective, inhibited temperament in early childhood predicts the later development of anxiety disorders (Chorpita & Barlow, 1998; Kashdan & Herbert, 2001). For example, Prior and associates (2000) found that children who were rated by their mothers as inhibited or shy children over a thirteen-year period were more likely to have an anxiety disorder than children who were rated as less inhibited. Similarly, Rosenbaum and colleagues (1992) reported that 85% of the children whose parents had panic disorder with agoraphobia were significantly inhibited. In contrast, only 50% of the children of depressed parents and 15% of the children of control parents had comparable levels of inhibition. Finally, Rosenbaum and associates (1991) showed that parents of inhibited children were more likely to have suffered or still be suffering from an anxiety disorder than parents of noninhibited children.

Although research on behavioral inhibition is very convincing when considered as a whole, "behavioral inhibition and psychopathology are not synonymous" (Biederman, Rosenbaum, Chaloff, & Kagan, 1995, p. 74). Since approximately 70% of inhibited children do *not* have an anxiety disorder, inhibition is likely a significant risk factor only in association with other factors—such as relatives who suffer or have suffered from an anxiety disorder, or exposure to major stressors at home or beyond.

Psychological, Family, and Social Factors

Many psychological models have been proposed to explain the etiology of anxiety disorders. These models share common features with those we presented in Chapter 9 on mood disorders.

Behavioral Approaches. Behavioral theorists have long relied on principles of classical and operant conditioning to explain the origin of anxiety disorders (see Box 1.2). Mowrer's (1960) two-factor model of anxiety is among the best-known etiological theories proposed to date and has been the focus of considerable experimental research. Essentially, Mowrer assumes that phobias develop after an event or object has become associated with unconditioned feelings of fear. For example, Mowrer would say that Little Albert became afraid of white furry objects after he was made to experience strong fear (produced by a loud noise) in the presence of a white rat. Following initial conditioning, Mowrer believes that now-fearful individuals deliberately attempt to avoid the object or situation they fear in order not to experience again overwhelming feelings of anxiety and the many symptoms that accompany them. Unfortunately, every time children or adolescents successfully avoid what they fear most, their avoidance is reinforced—so that, over time, they develop a full-blown disorder. The feared stimuli that are the focus of anxiety in Mowrer's model can vary almost indefinitely—dogs, social interactions, panic attacks, flashbacks, etc., thus allowing the model to explain the heterogeneity that is characteristic of this area.

Behavioral theorists and clinicians have also paid considerable attention to social information and modeling in the etiology of different forms of anxiety. Many children may come to fear spiders, mice, and other small creatures because they have been told that these creatures are dangerous or have seen a parent scream and run from a spider or a mouse. Processes of modeling and imitation are able to account for the etiology of some anxiety disorders (e.g., specific phobia) much better than others (e.g., PTSD). Nevertheless, numerous studies highlight the role that imitation and reciprocal reinforcement between parents and children play in the maintenance—and possibly the etiology—of many anxiety disorders (e.g., Gerull & Rapee, 2002). We explore this issue and the importance of family interactions in shaping fearful child behavior further in Box 10.2.

Cognitive Approaches.   Cognitive approaches stress the importance of negative affectivity, cognitive errors, and limited controllability in the etiology of anxiety disorders (Barlow, 1988). Specifically, a number of cognitive theorists assume that children and adolescents—when they have repeatedly had life experiences that left them feeling helpless or unable to exercise effective control over their environment—will have a tendency to exhibit anxiety symptoms in stressful situations, because they will again anticipate that they will be unable to cope. This anticipation could obviously develop in a variety of ways. Thus, young children who are suddenly overwhelmed with fear in the presence of a large animal or of a stranger, but who are not comforted when they cry, may come to believe that the world is a dangerous place where adults may not protect them. The same could happen to older children who are regularly bullied in school and left to fend for themselves, or who find it difficult to make progress in a particular subject and are regularly scolded by overcritical parents, rather than helped. In a review of the literature, Chorpita and Barlow (1998) found considerable evidence for this perspective and, more precisely, for the assumption that feelings of inadequate control play a key role in the etiology of anxiety disorders. In this model, early experience with uncontrollable stimuli is assumed to lead to low perceived control at the cognitive level and to inhibition at the behavioral and psychophysiological levels. Inhibition and lack of control, in turn, contribute to tension, agitation, and other bodily sensations often found in anxious individuals. As time progresses, low perceived control facilitates the development of cognitive errors and the many behavioral symptoms commonly associated with various anxiety disorders.

Attachment Theory.   As shown in Chapter 2 and earlier in this chapter, attachment theory proposes that children who are unable to develop a secure attachment to a trusted caregiver may be vulnerable to develop an anxiety disorder later in life. This theory remains largely speculative. However, as more longitudinal data become available, it may be able to account for the vulnerability of some children to anxiety disorders.

Dysfunctional Family Relationships.   Direct observations of parents (mostly mothers) and their children have repeatedly pointed out the importance of dysfunctional family relationships in the etiology of anxiety disorders. For example, young children with high levels of anxiety often have excessively controlling mothers who grant them little autonomy and who tend to express little affection toward them (Dumas, LaFreniere, & Serketich, 1995; Whaley, Pinto, & Sigman, 1999). However, in this context, excessive control and lack of affection are probably the result of the relationship itself, since the mothers behaved this way only when they interacted with their *own* children; when they were asked to play with a child they did not know (this child was always of the same age and gender as their own), these mothers did not overcontrol and were very affectionate (Dumas & LaFreniere, 1993). Similar findings have been obtained in retrospective studies of adults asked to describe how they were parented. In a meta-analysis of several such studies, Gerlsma, Emmelkamp, and Arrindell (1990) found that adults with phobic disorders reported that they had been subjected to parenting marked by excessive control and lack of affection.

Stressful Life Events.   Like many psychological disorders of childhood and adolescence, anxiety disorders (except PTSD) are related to a history of stressful life events. For example, children who are exposed to high levels of community violence have significantly more anxious and depressive symptoms than control children, especially when they lack social support either within their family or in the community (Kliewer, Lepore, Oskin, & Johnson, 1998).

BOX 10.2 • *The FEAR Effect: How Some Parents May Actively Contribute to Their Children's Fears*

The following is an excerpt of a conversation between a 10-year-old boy, referred because of marked anxiety, and his parents. The family has been asked to imagine that the child notices a group of children laughing as he approaches them to play handball with them, and to discuss what the child should do in this situation:

Boy: I'd just ask them; just go up and say "Can I please join in?"

Mother: Do you reckon maybe they'd let you?

Boy: Maybe . . .

Father: Do you think they would let you if it was handball?

Boy: No.

Mother: Why?

Boy: I'm not that good at it . . .

Mother: Why is this?

Boy: Because I can't run fast enough . . .

Mother: Would you be brave enough to go and ask them in the first place?

Boy: I wouldn't bother.

Mother: No?

Father: Why wouldn't you bother?

Boy: Because I know what the answer would be. It's always "no."

Mother: You don't think they would be laughing at you before you even turned up, thinking "He's going to ask."

Boy: Oh. Yes.

Mother: They might do that?

Boy: Yes.

Mother: So what do you think you would do? Just avoid these situations or would you really like to play?

Boy: Handball I'd like to play.

Mother: But you've got to learn more ball skills.

Boy: Yes.

Mother: It's hard, isn't it?

Boy: Yes.

Mother: (Comforts boy) (Dadds, Barrett, Rapee, & Ryan, 1996, p. 716).

As this family conversation shows, mother and father undermine their son's initial willingness to ask his peers to join in their game of handball, because the questions they ask him chip away at his shaky confidence and raise doubts about his skills to play the game. Note that their questions are far from critical or negative. Rather, they offer so many supportive reservations that they effectively magnify the child's fearful and maladaptive behavior.

Barrett, Dadds, and associates have labeled this interactive phenomenon the *FEAR effect*. To study it, they asked three groups of families—those with average children, those with anxious children, and those with aggressive children—to take part in brief conversations such as the one you just read. When these families talked about potentially challenging situations, children in the anxious group were more likely to develop avoidant solutions if their parents—especially their mothers—reinforced the children's avoidant statements in the conversation. Such family discussions increased avoidance, instead of helping the children cope with the challenge. Interestingly, children in the aggressive group often favored aggressive solutions to the same situations after discussing them with their parents. Only in the average group did family discussions lead to a reduction in both avoidant and aggressive solutions. This research does not imply that some parents cause their children's symptoms of anxiety or aggression. However, the study shows that parents, in everyday conversations, may contribute to their children's fears and self-doubts, or to their aggressiveness, instead of encouraging them to cope more effectively (Barrett et al., 1996).

Exposure to marital conflict is another form of stress implicated in the etiology of anxiety disorders. In a longitudinal study focusing on the impact of marital conflict on child development, Katz and Gottman (1993) found that marital interactions in which husbands exhibited high levels of anger during conflict and tended to withdraw rather than communicate were associated with teacher ratings of anxiety and depression in children three years later.

Several theoretical models have been proposed to account for the role of stressful life events in the development and maintenance of anxiety disorders. The majority of them hypothesize that an optimal level of stimulation is necessary to allow people, whatever their age, to face the challenges of everyday life. In situations of stress, this stimulation increases to the point of disruption: attention, memory, communication skills, and decision-making all become ineffective in the face of overwhelming negative circumstances over which one has little or no control. Although stress models are useful, most of them fail to specify which stress factors, alone or in combination, predict which anxiety disorder(s). In addition, these models are limited by the fact that stressful life events only play an etiological role in a minority of cases, if they do at all, because most young people who are confronted with such events do not develop an anxiety disorder. Moreover, these disorders generally develop over a period of several years, and their onset can rarely be linked to particularly stressful life events. Consequently, most researchers and clinicians consider these events more as risk than as etiological factors. Specifically, threatening life events, such as physical trauma or threat of loss of a loved one, best predict high levels of anxiety symptoms in children. In contrast, life events involving loss, such as school failure or actual loss of a loved one, best predict depressive symptoms (Eley & Stevenson, 2000).

Researchers currently working in this field recognize that the origin of these disorders is complex and explain it by relying on theoretical models in which developmental, familial, and environmental factors work in synergy. Figure 10.4 presents such a model. Proposed by Barlow (1988) to account for the etiology of specific phobia, this model illustrates the many factors that are assumed to be involved and the processes that interconnect them. It also shows that the same disorder may develop along different pathways, because the factors at play are unlikely to have the same weight and to operate in the same manner in each case. Finally, it makes it clear that these factors should not be expected to exert their effects alone but only in transaction with one another.

Treatment and Prevention

Do what you fear and fear disappears.
—David Schwartz

You gain strength, courage, and confidence by every experience in which you really stop to look fear in the face. . . . You must do the things you cannot do.
—Eleanor Roosevelt

Cognitive-Behavioral Treatments and Exposure

In general, anxiety disorders respond better to intervention than many other disorders covered in this book. The psychological treatments that have been found to be most effective are cognitive-behavioral in nature. The specifics of these treatments differ depending on which disorder is the focus of intervention; but most of them help children and adolescents modify their anxious cognitions as well as their avoidant behaviors through psychoeducation, modeling and role-playing, and homework assignments. In addition, most empirically studied treatments have an **exposure** component. As the name suggests, this treatment consists of exposing anxious children to the situations or stimuli they fear most. Exposure is a critical component of intervention because youth with anxiety disorders avoid what they fear or, at best, endure it with dread.

Exposure gives fearful youth opportunities to learn new ways of coping with the situations or stimuli that scare them. Over time, exposure leads to **habituation**—that is, to a reduction of the child or adolescent's fearfulness and eventually to its extinction. Exposure usually proceeds gradually along a **fear hierarchy,** developed in consultation with the child or adolescent, in which the fearful situations or stimuli are approached in order of increasing severity. For example, an adolescent girl with social phobia might start by making eye contact with friends and acquaintances and end with asking a boy to a school dance. This hierarchy is then used as a guide to determine the steps to follow in treatment until the child or adolescent has been systematically exposed to what he or she fears most.

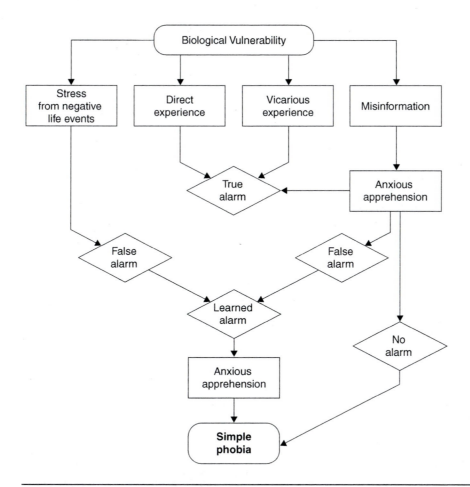

FIGURE 10.4 *Etiological Model of the Development of Specific Phobia.* This model assumes that phobias develop in people who have an underlying biological vulnerability. As susceptible individuals grow up, they are exposed to a variety of experiences, both positive and negative. Negative experiences can lead vulnerable children and adolescents to develop fear responses or alarms. Alarms can be either false alarms, in which fears arise when there is little or nothing to be afraid of, or learned alarms, in which anxiety responses are conditioned from past experience. Over time, vulnerable children and adolescents begin to fear the anxiety associated with their feared stimulus. At that point, they begin avoiding situations where they might encounter that stimulus; they then qualify for the diagnosis of a phobia.

Source: Barlow (1988), p. 484. Reprinted by permission.

Separation Anxiety Disorder, Social Phobia, Generalized Anxiety Disorder: Individual Intervention. Cognitive-behavioral treatments for SAD, social phobia, and GAD are very similar, even though their focus depends on the youth's presenting prob-

lems. For example, the treatment for SAD is designed to help children learn to feel comfortable when they are away from their parents or other loved ones. These children are taught age-appropriate coping skills and are exposed to actual separations; and their parents are shown how to promote effective as opposed to anxious coping skills, and how to deal with their own fears about their child's problems (Eisen, Engler, & Geyer, 1998). Children learn coping skills by planning more adaptive responses to anxiety-provoking objects or events than the avoidant responses they are typically using. Coping skills can also be strengthened through relaxation training to reduce muscular tension, stomachaches, and other physical symptoms (see Box 10.3). As they develop better coping skills, children with SAD are separated from their loved ones for increasingly longer periods of time. For example, they may progressively return to school, spend time at a friend's house, and eventually go to an overnight camp. The case of 8-year-old Saul highlights these simultaneous processes.

Saul has been attending school very irregularly for several months. His mother believes that it may be best to home-school him, "to avoid the daily battles of trying to get him ready and off to school, as well as the fact that when he goes he almost always comes home early with a headache or an upset stomach." However, she wants Saul to be assessed first to make sure that she is making the right decision. Initially, treatment focuses on psychoeducation about anxiety for Saul's parents. Much time is spent helping his mother realize that home-schooling may help her son academically but will only

BOX 10.3 • *Relax!*

Everybody knows that it is impossible to be anxious and relaxed at the same time. This common observation serves as the rationale for teaching relaxation to children and adolescents who struggle with debilitating anxiety disorders. Relaxation training is useful to reduce the physiological symptoms associated with anxiety, as well as the cognitive errors people often make when they are tense and worried, because stomachaches, sweaty palms, hyperventilation, and other physiological symptoms are not only triggered by anxious thoughts but also trigger those thoughts.

Like adults, youth can learn to relax with the help of **progressive muscle relaxation,** a procedure designed to teach a person to tense and relax different muscles systematically. This procedure teaches systematic muscle relaxation and also helps anxious youth learn to recognize when they are becoming tense. The following is a portion of a script showing how children and young adolescents can be taught progressive muscle relaxation.

> *Hands and arms.* Pretend you have a whole lemon in you left hand. Now squeeze it hard. Try to squeeze all the juice out of it. Feel the tightness in your hand and arm as you squeeze. Now drop the lemon. Notice how your muscles feel when they are relaxed. Take another lemon and squeeze it. Try to squeeze this one harder than you did the first one. That's right. Real hard. Now drop your lemon and relax. See how much better your hand and arm feel when they are relaxed. Once again,

take a lemon in your left hand and squeeze all the juice out. Don't leave a single drop. Squeeze hard. Good. Now relax and let the lemon fall from your hand. (Repeat the process for the right hand and arm.) . . .

Shoulder and neck. Now pretend you are a turtle. You're sitting out on a rock by a nice, peaceful pond, just relaxing in the warm sun . . .

Face and nose. Here comes a pesky old fly. He has landed on your nose. Try to get him off without using your hands. That's right, wrinkle up your nose. Make as many wrinkles in your nose as you can. Scrunch your nose up real hard. Good. You've chased him away. Now you can relax your nose. Oops, here he comes back again. Shoo him off. Wrinkle it up hard. Hold it just as tight as you can. Okay, he flew away. You can relax your face. Notice that when you scrunch up your nose that your cheeks and your mouth and your forehead and your eyes all help you, and they get tight, too. So when you relax your nose, your whole face relaxes too, and that feels good. Oh-oh. This time that old fly has come back, but this time he's on your forehead. Make lots of wrinkles. Try to catch him between all those wrinkles. Hold it tight, now. Okay, you can let go. He's gone for good. Now you can just relax. Let your face go smooth, no wrinkles anywhere. Your face feels nice and smooth and relaxed.

Source: Koeppen (1974), pp. 18–19. Reprinted with permission of Elementary School Guidance Counseling/American School Counselor Association.

reinforce his avoidance and make it more difficult for him to learn to face his anxiety. Once his parents are convinced that Saul has a psychological disorder in which avoidance is key, treatment switches to Saul. He learns to identify situations that make him anxious and to generate more adaptive coping responses than the ones on which he has been relying for months. For example, when he feels scared while waiting for the school bus, Saul learns to distract himself by thinking of the friends he will see at school or by practicing deep breathing to relax. These coping responses allow him to face many of his fears and, relatively quickly, to return to school, initially for brief periods of time only. His parents are also taught to be much firmer with Saul at home and to expose him to what he fears there also. At first, the parents make Saul sleep in his own bed, rather than in his parents' bed, as he has been doing for years. Sometime later, his parents begin going out once a week in the evening and leaving Saul with a baby-sitter. After a month of treatment, Saul spends his first night away from home at his grandmother's and, shortly afterward, begins to attend school again full time.

One of the better-evaluated treatments for SAD, social phobia, and GAD is Kendall's *Coping Cat Program* (Kendall & Treadwell, 1996). This CBT program is designed to teach youth to identify the physiological, cognitive, and behavioral components of their anxiety and to learn effective coping skills with the help of the acronym FEAR, which children must commit to memory:

F—Feeling frightened? Recognize the physiological signs of your anxiety.

E—Expecting bad things to happen? Identify the negative predictions that are at the heart of your anxiety.

A—Actions and attitudes that help. Instead of avoiding what you are afraid of, call on strategies that help you master your anxiety.

R—Rate and reward. After completing the first three steps, rate how well you did and praise yourself for your progress.

The *Coping Cat Program* is structured, but therapists work individually with affected children and

tailor the contents of the intervention to meet each child's needs. Sessions focus on the acquisition of effective coping skills and on homework assignments designed to promote exposure and regular practice of these skills at home and school. These assignments also include developmentally sensitive exercises, such as drawing pictures and writing coping stories, to reinforce the work conducted in session. Two clinical studies in which 9- to 13 year-olds were randomly assigned to the program or to a control condition obtained very positive results. Program participants were much more likely to be without a diagnosis at the end of treatment and at a twelve-month follow-up than control participants were. Preliminary examination of the role played by different treatment components showed that exposure was critical to treatment success (Kendall, 1994; Kendall et al., 1997). Not surprisingly, exposure is also believed to be critical to treat school refusal. Experts generally agree that affected children should be returned to school as soon as possible and that the problems that led to the child's refusal to go to school be dealt with in treatment. This last point is essential, since treatment has been found to be most effective when it specifically addresses the reasons that led to school refusal in the first place (Kearney, 2001).

Separation Anxiety Disorder, Social Phobia, Generalized Anxiety Disorder: Group Intervention. Cognitive-behavioral treatments for SAD, social phobia, and GAD can also be effectively delivered in small groups. Empirically evaluated group programs bring together children and adolescents with similar difficulties, and rely on psychoeducation (for youth and parents), social skills training, and exposure to help affected young people develop coping skills and reduce their anxiety. In a clinical study of youth aged 6 to 16 years, 64% of participants in a group cognitive-behavioral intervention were without a diagnosis at the end of treatment, compared to 13% in a wait-list condition. These impressive results were maintained through a twelve-month follow-up (Silverman et al., 1999). Comparable results have been obtained in independent studies conducted in Australia by Barrett and colleagues (Barrett, 1998; Shortt, Barrett, & Fox, 2001). The most recent of these studies worked with 6- to 10-year-olds who participated in a program called

FRIENDS. This program, which was initially modeled after the *Coping Cat Program,* helps participants make friends and thereby develop a supportive social network. *FRIENDS* appears to be very effective, in that 69% of group participants were without a diagnosis at the end of treatment, compared to 6% in the wait-list condition. These results were again maintained at a twelve-month follow-up.

Obsessive-Compulsive Disorder. As you know, OCD is a particularly severe anxiety disorder that is often resistant to treatment. However, encouraging results have been obtained with a cognitive-behavioral program developed by March and associates (March & Mulle, 1996). This comprehensive program, called *How I Ran OCD Off My Land,* has several components:

- *Psychoeducation.* Information about the disorder is provided to the entire family. They are taught that OCD is a bossy error message in the brain that interferes with normal development by taking up too much time and energy. Specifically, to "run OCD off their land," affected children and adolescents must learn to "boss back OCD." To do so, they are taught to give their symptoms names or nicknames and to describe how OCD dominates their life. By naming symptoms and highlighting how "they" have come to control the child's life, all involved can begin to see that the disorder is an intruder, something external to the child and the family. In other words, rituals and compulsions are not behaviors that are turned on and off at will, or performed just to irritate family members. This realization allows the family to come together in support around a mutual enemy, OCD.
- *Response prevention.* **Response prevention** prohibits children or adolescents from engaging in the compulsions they have developed to relieve their anxiety. It is a form of exposure, since it forces them to confront their obsessions without having recourse to their usual compulsions. In other words, response prevention brings youth with OCD face to face with their anxieties, allowing habituation and eventually extinction to take place. For example, 11-year-old Sue used to

wash her hands as many as fifty times a day. As part of treatment, she was allowed to do so only prior to meals and at bedtime. On occasions, she was also deliberately exposed to dirt and prevented from washing her hands, in order to help her realize that the consequences she dreaded if she did not wash repeatedly never materialized.
- *Anxiety management training.* Coping strategies designed to help affected youth reduce their anxiety as they learn to beat back OCD are also part of the program. These strategies, which therapists describe as a "tool kit," include relaxation exercises and positive self-talk ("bossing OCD"). They are used during role-plays and response prevention procedures.

Although controlled studies have not yet established the efficacy of this OCD treatment program, preliminary evidence indicates that it is effective (American Academy of Child and Adolescent Psychiatry, 1998c; March, Franklin, Nelson, & Foa, 2001).

Panic Disorder. Research on the treatment of youth with panic disorder is in its infancy, in large part because it was long thought that panic was extremely rare or nonexistent before adolescence. However, Panic Control Treatment (PCT), an empirically validated cognitive-behavioral approach for panic in adults, has been adapted for use with adolescents (Ollendick, 1995). PCT is based on the hypothesis that panic is a pathological response to normal physiological sensations (Barlow, 1988). To overcome their panic, affected individuals must be exposed to these sensations and learn to see them as normal occurrences, rather than as signs of impending doom. Exposure is conducted in sessions through previously established fear hierarchies and between sessions through homework. For example, an adolescent boy who is fearful that a racing heart may signal an impending panic attack may be exposed to strenuous exercise to accelerate his heart rate. Like other cognitive-behavioral programs for anxiety disorders, PCT also includes cognitive restructuring and relaxation training. This approach appears well suited to treat panic and agoraphobia, but its effectiveness with children and adolescents will need to be established in carefully controlled studies.

Posttraumatic Stress Disorder. Treatments for PTSD in childhood and adolescence are available mainly for youth who have experienced physical or sexual abuse and are again downward extensions of programs initially developed for adults. Different treatments have been found to be effective in reducing many of the symptoms of PTSD. However, none has been empirically tested with the kind of rigor required to know what works best in this area (AACAP, 1998d).

Cognitive-behavioral therapy for children and adolescents exposed to trauma usually focuses on psychoeducation, cognitive restructuring, and effective coping skills (Cohen, Mannarino, Berliner, & Deblinger, 2000). Cognitive restructuring is designed to modify the tendency of victims to blame themselves for what happened ("I should have . . . ," "If only I had not . . . ") or to feel guilty that they survived the trauma when others did not or suffered more severely. Cognitive restructuring is also designed to challenge the negative worldview of youth with PTSD, who often believe that their environment is unsafe and that most people cannot be trusted. Relaxation training is often used to combat the physical symptoms of anxiety and address the sleep problems associated with PTSD. Finally, discussion of the traumatic events at the origin of the disorder is seen as an essential part of treatment by some but not all clinicians and researchers. Work on PTSD in adult rape victims shows that exposure to the trauma in the form of discussions of what actually happened is a critical component of treatment (Foa, Rothbaum, Riggs, & Murdock, 1991). However, some professionals believe that having children or adolescents recount their physically or sexually abusive experiences again and again is more threatening or embarrassing than therapeutic in many cases (Cohen et al., 2000). Systematic research remains to be conducted to determine how best to proceed in this important area.

Family Involvement

Several of the individual and group programs just described have a parent-training component. Given that anxiety tends to run in families and that parents of anxious children often reinforce their symptoms (see Box 10.2), clinicians and researchers usually agree that a family component is crucial for successful treatment of anxiety disorders—particularly if one or both of the child's parents are anxious or have a psychological disorder themselves (Berman, Weems, Silverman, & Kurtines, 2000). In Saul's case, his mother was helped to cope with her own anxiety, especially about losing her "little boy." More generally, research has shown that including parents in treatment results in lower anxiety levels and better use of coping strategies in their children (Barrett, Dadds, & Rapee, 1996).

Pharmacological Interventions

Selective serotonin reuptake inhibitors (SSRIs) are commonly used to treat anxiety disorders (AACAP, 1997b, 1998c, 1998d). However, as in the case of mood disorders, little systematic research has been conducted on the efficacy of these medications with children and adolescents. Furthermore, we do not know whether SSRIs are more or less effective than psychological intervention or whether pharmacological and psychological interventions in combination are more effective than either is alone. For example, the Research Unit on Pediatric Psychopharmacology Anxiety Study Group (2001) found that the SSRI *fluvoxamine* (Zoloft) was effective in reducing anxiety symptoms in 76% of children and adolescents studied; in comparison, only 29% of participants who received a placebo had a reduction in symptoms. Unfortunately, this study did not show whether medication was more effective with some anxiety disorders than others, nor did it compare the effectiveness of medication with that of cognitive-behavioral therapy, which has proved to be very effective.

The use of medications may be more warranted in some anxiety disorders than others. For example, research on the treatment of OCD suggests that SSRIs be included as a standard component of treatment to help reduce the intrusive obsessions associated with the disorder (Grados & Riddle, 2001). However, in a condition such as PTSD, medication may be more helpful to control sleeplessness and other associated symptoms, and to reduce the adverse effects of comorbid disorders, than to treat the disorder as such (Donnelly, Amaya-Jackson, & March, 1999).

Prevention

Little empirical attention has been paid to the prevention of anxiety in childhood and adolescence. In a review of the available literature, Donovan and Spence (2000) note that prevention can occur at many levels and at different points in time. Some prevention programs focus on children who are at risk of developing an anxiety disorder because they already have high levels of anxiety. For example, in a prevention program for anxious and withdrawn preschoolers, LaFreniere and Capuano (1997) found that children in both the control and the treatment groups showed significant improvement, but that changes were greater in the treatment group. Other prevention programs work with children of different ages who do not necessarily have high levels of anxiety. Typically, these programs are offered in schools, often as a part of the regular curriculum, and are adaptations of effective treatment programs. For example, promising results have been obtained in preventive applications of the *Coping Cat* and *FRIENDS* programs described earlier (Dadds, Spence, Holland, Barrett, & Laurens, 1997; Lowry-Webster, Barrett, & Dadds, 2001). These programs are encouraging and show that large-scale prevention efforts with children at risk for anxiety disorders may have more favorable results than do efforts for many other conditions.

Web Links

www.adaa.org (Anxiety Disorders Association of America)

www.anxietynetwork.com (Anxiety Network International; provides information on social anxiety, panic/agoraphobia, and generalized anxiety)

www.npi.ucla.edu/caap/anxieties/anxiety_problems.htm (University of California at Los Angeles, Child and Adolescent Anxiety Program)

www.rcpsych.ac.uk/info/help/anxiety/index.htm (UK Royal College of Psychiatrists Website on anxiety disorders)

11

Eating Disorders

Here's what I did until [I learned to feed myself]: I ate, starved, binged, purged, grew fat, grew thin, grew fat, grew thin, binged, purged, dieted, was good, was bad, grew fat, grew thin, grew thinner.

—Anne Lamott

Food is a central part of our lives—biologically, psychologically, and socially. Under normal circumstances, we eat as much to maintain close relationships with others as to relieve hunger. Food also paces our lives, bringing us together as family and friends to celebrate holidays and to share in important events such as births, weddings, and funerals. Consequently, eating disorders severely disturb not only the health of children and adolescents who are affected by them, but their social relationships as well.

The psychological disorders related to food are generally grouped into two broad categories: **feeding disorders** and **eating disorders.** Feeding disorders are characterized by disturbances in the food-intake process. For example, the child eats nonedible substances or eats but fails to put on weight as expected. Eating disorders are characterized by major dysfunctions in several behaviors associated with eating, rather than with food intake. Young people with eating disorders are able to eat and digest food, but they follow an inappropriate diet, force themselves to vomit after each meal, or otherwise disrupt the normal eating process.

Feeding and eating disorders are also distinguished by different ages of onset. Feeding disorders generally occur in young children, whereas eating disorders are most frequent during adolescence and early adulthood. Their unifying feature, however, is that all children and adolescents who present them face serious health risks. This chapter focuses exclusively on the eating disorders: anorexia nervosa, bulimia nervosa, and binge-eating disorder. We will not cover feeding disorder in any detail in this book.

Historical Overview

Anorexia

The first reliable accounts of **anorexia nervosa,** or anorexia for short, date back to the Middle Ages. During that period, the symptoms of people with the disorder were often described in religious terms and were not considered as signs of a psychological dysfunction. Specifically, fasting is a practice followed in all major religions, and self-starvation was then seen as an extreme form of that practice—the selfless denial of bodily needs in search of spiritual discipline and fulfillment.

Medical interest in anorexia dates back to the seventeenth century. However, the disorder was not recognized as such until the second half of the nineteenth century, when two physicians, Charles Lasègue in France (1873) and William Gull in England (1874), simultaneously but independently described the common characteristics of young women who were deliberately starving themselves. Both authors chose the word *anorexia*, which means "loss of appetite" in Latin, to refer to this condition. The following excerpts highlight what Lasègue (1873/1964) saw as the major characteristics of the disorder and its usual developmental trajectory and prognosis.

A young girl, between fifteen and twenty years of age, suffers from some emotion which she avows or conceals. Generally it relates to [the fact that her feelings were hurt], or to some more or less conscious desire. . . . At first, she feels uneasiness after food, vague sensations of fullness. . . . The same sensations are repeated during several days, but if they are slight they are tenacious. The patient thinks to herself that the best remedy for this indefinite and painful uneasiness will be to diminish her food. Up to this point, there is nothing remarkable in her case. . . . Gradually she reduces her food, furnishing pretexts, sometimes in a headache, sometimes in temporary distaste, and sometimes in the fear of a recurrence of pain after eating. At the end of some weeks there is no longer a supposed temporary repugnance, but a refusal of food that may be indefinitely prolonged. The disease is now declared. . . . Woe to the physician who, misunderstanding the peril, treats as a fancy without object or duration an obstinacy [i.e., refusal to eat] that he hopes to vanquish by medicines, friendly advice, or the still more defective resource, intimidation. . . . Ever on the watch for the judgments concerning themselves, especially such as are approved by their family, [young women with anorexia] never pardon; and considering that hostilities have been commenced against them [i.e., to try to make them eat], they attribute to themselves the right of em-ploying these [behaviors to avoid eating] with implacable tenacity. . . .

The family has but two methods at its service which it always exhausts—entreaties and menaces [i.e., pleading and threats]. . . . She is besought, as a favor, and as . . . proof of affection, to consent to even an additional mouthful to what she has taken; but this excess of insistence begets an excess of resistance. . . . The anorexia gradually becomes the sole object of preoccupation and conversation. The patient thus gets surrounded by a kind of atmosphere, from which there is no escape during the entire day. . . .

What dominates in the mental condition of the hysterical patient is, above all, a state of quietude—I might almost say a condition of contentment truly pathological. Not only does she not sigh for recovery, but she is not ill pleased with her condition. . . . [She has] an inexhaustible optimism, against which supplications and threats are alike of no avail (pp. 145–152).

Lasègue's description remains current, not only because it carefully summarizes the disorder, but also because it emphasizes the role of the family in its development. What is missing in his description is the person's obsessive fear of becoming fat. This obsession is central to our understanding of the disorder. Does that mean that the cases described by Lasègue did not have anorexia? Probably not. A review of the history of the disorder suggests that the patients treated by Lasègue did have the disorder, but that obsessive preoccupation with thinness is a relatively recent addition to its symptomatology (van Deth & Vandereycken, 2000).

Bulimia

Whereas anorexia has been the focus of medicine, psychiatry, and psychology for over one hundred years, **bulimia nervosa** (or bulimia for short) is a much more recent "discovery." Bulimia was formally described for the first time by Gerald Russell in 1979. Although bulimic behavior had been observed before then, episodes of **binge eating** and deliberate vomiting were generally considered a luxury that only the rich could afford, rather than a disorder. For example, in ancient Rome, upper-class people who had eaten too much made use of the *vomitorium,* a public vomiting area where they could purge themselves before they ate again. Such a practice was unthinkable for the vast majority of their fellow citizens, who struggled every day to find enough food to survive. And it remained unthinkable for centuries afterward.

In Western societies in the last decades, however, the incidence of anorexia and bulimia has increased dramatically (see Figures 11.1 and 11.2). This increase has much to do with the Western cultural emphasis on thinness. As we note in Box 11.1 (pp. 312–313), ideals of beauty in Western societies have shifted over the past century: the buxom women of the Victorian days have given way to the super-slim models of the 1990s. For example, bust-to-waist ratios dropped from 1909 to 1929 and again from 1949 to 1981 (Silverstein, Perdue, Peterson, & Kelly, 1986) and have probably continued to drop since these studies were published. Although recent increases in the incidence of the disorder cannot

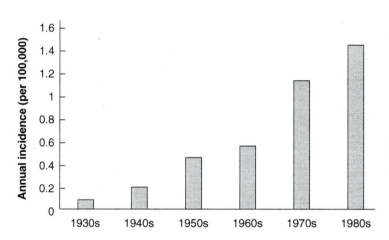

FIGURE 11.1 *Increases in the Incidence of Anorexia over Time.* Research from different Western countries shows that anorexia increased dramatically in the twentieth century, making it a major mental health problem in many Western societies. Rates reported below reflect increases in the average number of new cases per year. The rates for the 1930s through the 1950s come from data collected in Sweden (Theander, 1970), whereas the more recent rates come from data collected in Switzerland (Willi & Grossman, 1983; Willi et al., 1990). Comparable increases have been found in studies not summarized here.

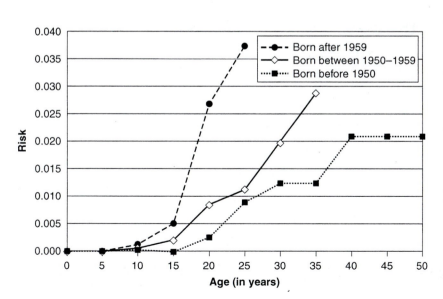

FIGURE 11.2 *Increases in Lifetime Risk for Bulimia over Time.* This figure, which is based on data from female twins, shows that women born after 1959 face a much greater risk of developing bulimia in their lifetime—and of developing it earlier—than women born before 1959.

Source: K. S. Kendler et al., "The Genetic Epidemiology of Bulimia Nervosa," *American Journal of Psychiatry, 148* (1991), p. 1631. Copyright © 1991 by the American Psychiatric Association. Reprinted by permission.

BOX 11.1 • *The Thinning of America*

In an interesting study of the phenomenon of thinness, Brumberg (1997) documents how the shape of the ideal woman has changed over time. For centuries, the prevailing culture in America and other Western countries looked favorably on what we would call heavy women today. Women needed the protection that weight afforded to survive in cold winters and during long stretches when food was scarce or not available. A full figure was also seen as a good indicator of a woman's ability to bear children and to deliver them without complications, and was an unmistakable sign that her husband was a good provider.

In the 1920s, rapid cultural changes made thinness fashionable. The decline of feminine modesty and more revealing flapper clothing reflected an easing of the strict moral and sexual codes of earlier decades. These changes were accompanied by a growing preference for a slender, long-legged, and flat-chested look over the traditional, Victorian "hourglass" figure with substantial busts and hips. By the 1960s, cultural emphasis was no longer merely on thinness but often on extreme slimness. Miniskirts and hip-hugger jeans allowed all to observe much of a woman's body and to freely imagine what they could

What we consider to be a beautiful woman has changed considerably over the years.

be accounted for exclusively by cultural factors (see Etiology), there is little doubt that these factors are important in societies in which it is widely believed that thin is beautiful.

Binge-Eating Disorder

Binge-eating disorder (BED) was formally described for the first time in the DSM-IV under the broad category of *eating disorders not otherwise specified* (APA,

1994). The concept of BED developed out of research on bulimia. Specifically, work on bingeing and purging showed that many people had serious problems with binge eating; however, they did not meet diagnostic criteria for bulimia because they did not show any purging or compensatory weight control behaviors, and were not overconcerned about their body shape (Devlin, Walsh, Spitzer, & Hasin, 1992).

Interestingly, more than three decades earlier, Stunkard (1959) had described a syndrome similar not see. The fashion model Twiggy became the image of the female ideal—long thin legs, tiny waist, and small chest—and a "gold standard" in the entertainment and advertising industries.

This preoccupation with slimness has continued to increase in recent decades. By the 1990s, middle-class European American girls described the "ideal" body size as 5'7" tall and 110 pounds. Today, the average weight of fashion models—who are seen by many as standards of American beauty—is lower than the weight of over 95% of women! We illustrate this discrepancy between "ideal" and actual body weight in the diagram below. Many adolescent girls and young women struggle to maintain a healthy weight, which is lower than the average weight of the population; and most of them will never meet the culturally ideal weight that is conveyed to them daily through entertainment, advertising, and other models of success. Many researchers believe that this is an important factor in the increase in eating disorders, as more and more adolescent girls and young women attempt to achieve the impossible.

As Brumberg (1997) writes, "The fitness craze can aggravate adolescent self-consciousness and make girls desperately unhappy . . . about their own bodies, particularly if it is combined with unrealistic expectations drawn from airbrushed and retouched photographs in advertising, and the seductive camera angles and body doubles so common in television and movies. . . . Although eating disorders . . . are not caused by visual images alone, these pathologies thrive in an environment in which so many 'normal' people work so hard (and spend so much money) in pursuit of the perfect body" (p. 124).

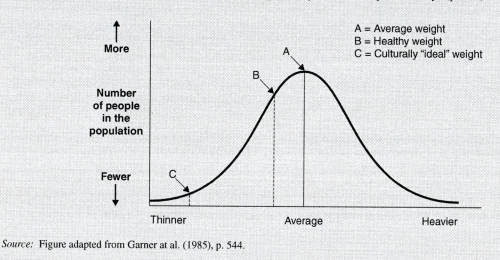

A = Average weight
B = Healthy weight
C = Culturally "ideal" weight

Source: Figure adapted from Garner at al. (1985), p. 544.

to BED in a group of obese patients. The syndrome remained overlooked for years in the psychological literature, probably in large part because it is most common in obese individuals. Obesity has traditionally been considered as a physical rather than a psychological condition, and research in this area focused for a long time on the medical problems of obese persons much more than on their behavior around food (Wilson, Heffernan, & Black, 1996).

Definitions, Diagnostic Criteria, and Major Characteristics

Anorexia

Anorexia is characterized by persistent refusal to maintain a healthy body weight and by extreme **compensatory behaviors** aimed at losing weight—including dieting and extreme exercise, self-induced vomiting, and unnecessary use of laxatives. In addition, adolescents with anorexia have an intense and irrational fear of gaining weight. Many have a distorted image of their own body and see themselves as fat, even though they are extremely thin, even emaciated by most standards. The disorder primarily affects adolescent females and young adult women. However, it does occur in males and can begin before puberty (APA, 2000a).

Table 11.1 presents the DSM-IV-TR diagnostic criteria for anorexia. Lori Gottlieb's (2000) story, *I Wanted to Be the Thinnest Girl on the Planet*, illustrates these criteria from the perspective of an 11-year-old with the disorder.

Winter

Tonight Mom, Dad, and my brother David, and I went to visit Uncle Lou. . . . He likes to brag about my cousin Kate and how pretty and popular she is. . . . We all went in the dining room for dinner. That's when I found out that I eat much more than Kate does. . . . I asked Kate if she lost weight from not eating very much, but Kate said she's not on a diet. Which made no sense, since she hardly ate anything at dinner. Then Kate explained how that's not a diet, it's just how you eat when you grow up. . . .

I hardly ate anything yesterday, and by lunchtime today I felt kind of dizzy. . . . I mean, I was hungry, but it felt neat, like I was flying. Besides, if I stop eating from now on, I can make my legs look as skinny as Kate's.

Spring

Mom took me to see Dr. Katz my pediatrician. . . . Dr. Katz asked why I lost six pounds since my last check-up in December . . . I told Dr. Katz that Mom and Dad are making a big deal over nothing . . . I mean everyone is watching what they eat . . . He said that a girl my age should be gaining weight, not losing it; that I'm supposed to gain more weight than usual over the next few years because I'm starting to develop (into what—a fat person?). . . .

But today at breakfast . . . we got into a big argument . . . I wanted to know why . . . [my mother] could put nonfat milk in her coffee when I'm not allowed to drink nonfat milk. Naturally, Mom got mad at me for asking and said I can drink all the nonfat milk I want when I become a woman . . . I wish I was a woman already so I could diet and people would think it's normal. . . .

[A]t lunch everyone at our table noticed I was losing weight and got pretty interested in how I did it. "What do you eat for breakfast?" Leslie wanted to know. "Exactly nineteen flakes of Product 19 cereal,

---

TABLE 11.1 *Anorexia: DSM-IV-TR Diagnostic Criteria*

A. Refusal to maintain body weight at or above a minimally normal weight for age and height (e.g., weight loss leading to maintenance of body weight less than 85% of that expected; or failure to make expected weight gain during period of growth, leading to body weight less than 85% of that expected).

B. Intense fear of gaining weight or becoming fat, even though underweight.

C. Disturbance in the way in which one's body weight or shape is experienced, undue influence of body weight or shape on self-evaluation, or denial of the seriousness of the current low body weight.

D. In postmenarcheal females, amenorrhea, i.e. the absence of at least three consecutive menstrual cycles.

(A woman is considered to have amenorrhea if her periods occur only following hormone, e.g., estrogen, administration.)

Specify type:

Restricting Type: during the current episode of Anorexia Nervosa, the person has not regularly engaged in binge-eating or purging behavior (i.e., self-induced vomiting or the misuse of laxatives, diuretics, or enemas).

Binge-Eating/Purging Type: during the current episode of Anorexia Nervosa, the person has regularly engaged in binge-eating or purging behavior (i.e., self-induced vomiting or the misuse of laxatives, diuretics, or enemas).

Source: American Psychiatric Association, *Diagnostic and Statistical Manual of Mental Disorders, Fourth Edition, Text Revision* (Washington, DC: American Psychiatric Association, 2000a). Copyright 2000 American Psychiatric Association. Reprinted with permission.

with two ounces of nonfat milk," I said, but I made it sound like it was no big deal . . . Then everyone started crowding around me and asking me questions all at once, like I was a movie star or something . . . Which is why I never ate my own lunch. I mean if I ate a bologna sandwich with mayonnaise on Wonderbread, everyone would definitely think I was a phoney. . . .

Today was my first appointment with Dr. Gold (the psychiatrist) . . . Dr. Gold . . . asked me to draw my "ideal" of what I want to look like . . . So I picked up the pencil and drew a girl I want to look like. She was tall and skinny, but with my face and hair . . . "This is a stick figure," he said, like I didn't understand the assignment the first time. "Try to draw a realistic picture of how you'd like to look" . . . I tried explaining how that was exactly the way I want to look. . . .

Dinner was brisket in a disgusting sauce . . . I dished out half a piece . . . and scraped all the sauce off, then blotted it with a paper towel, just in case I missed some. Then I put seven peas and eight carrot squares on my plate, but I didn't like the number eight because it sounds like "ate," so I took one off.

Dr. Gold talked to Dr. Katz, who said that if I didn't "shape up," they'd put me in the hospital. I said I wanted to shape down, not up . . . I said I'd do anything—go to high school early, go away to boarding school if I made everyone too nervous—anything, if I didn't have to go to the hospital . . . Dr. Gold wanted to know what I meant by "anything." He asked if it meant eating, but I never meant that. I can't eat if I'm this fat. It was obviously a trick question.

Summer

"This isn't a game anymore," Dr. Katz said when he came in this morning. . . . Dr. Katz started examining me . . . Every time he found something wrong, he'd say it out loud like there was another doctor in the room taking notes . . . "Acute dehydration," . . . "Osteoporosis," he said . . . and sighed right into my face. . . . Today his breath smelled like chewed-up sausage—210 calories per serving. I figured maybe about a third of it went up my nose, so I'd have to give up my slice of bread for lunch to make up for the 70 calories. . . .

[T]oday's my half-birthday . . . I usually make a wish on my half birthdays, so I was thinking that I'd wish to be the thinnest girl at school, or maybe even the

thinnest eleven-year-old on the planet. Then I'd never have to worry about dieting anymore . . . but I sort of wondered what I'll have left to wish for on my real birthday, if I finally get that thin. I mean, what are girls supposed to wish for, other than being thin? . . . I didn't know what to wish for, because even if you are thin, you still have to worry that you won't get fat . . . I wished being thin didn't matter so much to everyone, even me.

Dr. Katz had a huge smile on his face when he came to see me today. He said the whole treatment team is thrilled that I ate part of my breakfast and lunch . . . Yesterday I was "uncooperative," but today everyone likes me all of a sudden, like I'm a completely different person because I ate a half a turkey sandwich. . . .

The first thing I saw when I walked into the bathroom was a really skinny girl [in a mirror] . . . She was a stick figure . . . but when I turned around to look, I was the only person in the bathroom. Except the girl couldn't be me because she was so skinny . . . I walked closer to the sink to get a better look, but the skinny legs in the mirror moved at the same time as mine. Then I smiled, and so did the mouth in the mirror . . . That's when I knew for sure it was me. I couldn't believe it! I looked disgusting. I used to want to be a stick figure, but now I'm not so sure (pp. 55–208).

As Lori's story makes clear, a diagnosis of anorexia presupposes the presence of the following characteristics: a refusal to maintain normal weight, an intense fear of gaining weight, and significant disturbances in body perception.

Refusal to Maintain Normal Weight. Youth with anorexia suffer from self-imposed starvation. Quite simply, they refuse to maintain a normal, healthy weight. By most definitions, "normal" here means no more than 15% below optimum body weight based on current height and weight standards. For example, the optimal weight for a 5'4" teenage girl is approximately 120 pounds. Consequently, a weight of less than 102 pounds is generally considered to be abnormally low in adolescent girls of that height. This cutoff is somewhat arbitrary, since it is necessary to consider a person's body shape, health, and history to determine when weight loss is becoming dangerous, both physically and psychologically (APA, 2000a). Starvation is associated with a host of physical and psychological changes that are not only dangerous, but also make treating someone with an eating disorder especially difficult (see Box 11.2).

Intense Fear of Gaining Weight. Youth with anorexia have an obsessive fear of putting on weight and becoming fat. Consequently, they choose an "ideal" weight that is much lower than that of the majority of their peers and threatens their health. Moreover, even when they reach their "ideal" weight, children and adolescents with anorexia continue to see

themselves as fat or in need of slimming further, and generally continue to starve themselves, often putting their lives in danger. It is not unusual to hear severely emaciated youth say things such as "But I still have thunder thighs!"

This irrational fear of gaining weight results in the avoidance of a number of foods that affected youth regard as "fattening." Over time, their diet becomes highly restricted and, in general, totally inadequate to maintain an optimal state of health. Besides restrictive dieting, many youth with the disorder rely on extreme behaviors to lose weight, such as self-induced vomiting and unnecessary use of laxatives, physical exercise, or both. Far from relieving their fear of gaining weight,

BOX 11.2 • *Starvation and Its Effects*

In 1950, Keys, Brozek, Henschel, Mickelsen, and Taylor published the results of an unusual experiment undertaken at the University of Minnesota (see also Garner, 1997). A group of thirty-six physically and psychologically healthy young men were recruited to study the effects of semi-starvation. These volunteers lived together in a dormitory setting for six months. Their diet was restricted to half of their normal food intake and, on average, they lost 25% of their body weight. The most interesting finding was that almost all the men exhibited dramatic cognitive, emotional, and social changes during their long period of food deprivation. Cognitively, they found that concentrating on anything besides food became almost impossible. The authors, who observed their subjects' behavior in considerable detail, wrote: "Those who ate in the common dining room smuggled out bits of food and consumed it on their bunks in a long drawn-out ritual. . . . Cookbooks, menus, and information bulletins on food production became intensely interesting to many of the men who had previously had little or no interest in dietetics or agriculture. . . . Toward the end of starvation some of the men would dawdle for almost two hours over a meal which previously they would have consumed in a matter of minutes" (p. 833). Not only did the men think about food almost constantly, but some of them found opportunities to binge. Interestingly, their bingeing was followed by vomiting and episodes that the researchers described as full of "disgust and self-criticism."

Although their preoccupation with food was greater than most would have predicted, the emotional changes that these previously healthy men underwent in the course of the study were probably most striking. Many of them experienced mood swings, with alternating periods of elation and depression. These swings were also coupled with increased irritability and anger. The severity of the mental health problems was such that some of the volunteers had to be admitted to a psychiatric hospital for treatment. One of these admissions was for a man who felt "a compulsive attraction to refuse [i.e., garbage] and a strong, almost compelling, desire to root in garbage cans" (p. 890). Another was admitted because of violent emotional outbursts paired with intense thoughts of self-harm.

The men's social and sex lives also changed dramatically. They spent much of their time alone and often reported that engaging in social activities (even dating) was just "too much trouble." Sexual activity was also curtailed, so much so that one man reported that he had "no more sexual feeling than a sick oyster" (p. 840).

This landmark study highlights the pronounced effects that almost constant hunger can have on all aspects of one's functioning. Keep these effects in mind as you read further about eating disorders, because they illustrate how severe food restrictions and preoccupations may account for some of the more extreme behaviors often seen in these disorders.

such strategies only aggravate their concerns and serve to maintain their never-ending search to lose yet more weight.

Significant Disturbances in Body Perception.
Children and adolescents with anorexia can accurately gauge the weight and body shape of others, but often not their own (Smeets, Ingleby, Hoek, & Panhuysen, 1999). Even when they are very thin, many youth with anorexia persist in believing that they are fat and refuse to admit that their physical state can have serious, even fatal, medical consequences. Others acknowledge their thinness but remain concerned that various parts of their body, such as their stomach, buttocks, or thighs, still "need to be trimmed." Many of them spend inordinate amounts of time weighing themselves and measuring different parts of their body to ensure that they are losing their "excessive" weight or at least not gaining any pounds or inches.

These body image disturbances explain why the large majority of persons with anorexia maintain that they are in good health and rarely seek professional help of their own accord. Usually their refusal to eat causes family members to intervene—first by trying to get the child or adolescent to eat and later by asking for professional assistance. However, youth with anorexia rarely accept any kind of intervention, thereby aggravating major family conflicts centered around food and weight.

Self-Esteem and Weight.
The self-concept of persons with anorexia depends closely on the extent to which they succeed in controlling their weight. They regard weight loss as a sign of personal control and self-worth, and weight gain as unmistakable evidence of personal weakness and failure.

Biological Changes.
Anorexia is accompanied by major physiological and hormonal disruptions. These disruptions can lead to severe health complications and even death. After puberty, most females with anorexia have **amenorrhea** (i.e., they do not have a normal ovulation cycle). Amenorrhea is usually considered to be present when at least three consecutive menstrual periods have been missed. In prepubertal girls, development of breasts and other secondary sexual characteristics, as

well as onset of menstruation, are delayed. Like prepubertal girls, prepubertal boys with anorexia often exhibit delayed genital development.

Subtypes.
The DSM-IV-TR describes two subtypes of anorexia based on the presence or absence of bingeing and purging behavior. Persons with **anorexia, restricting type** rely exclusively on restricted food intake and excessive exercise to lose weight—namely, exercise that ignores medical advice or common sense, or interferes with social or academic activities. Persons with **anorexia, binge-eating/purging type** restrict their food intake and also exercise excessively. However, in addition, they regularly engage in binge-eating and/or purging behaviors (i.e., self-induced vomiting, misuse of laxatives, diuretics, or enemas). These two subtypes are approximately evenly distributed among people with anorexia (Agras, 1987). As we will emphasize below (see Empirical Validity), youth with anorexia, binge-eating/purging type resemble persons with bulimia more than persons with anorexia, restricting type do. The majority of them purge themselves following a binge. However, some do not engage in regular binge eating, but vomit or purge themselves after eating. The frequency with which persons with this subtype of anorexia binge or resort to self-induced vomiting or other forms of purging varies considerably. The DSM-IV-TR notes that the majority of affected youth engage in binge eating or purging at least weekly.

Bulimia

Life itself is the proper binge.

—Julia Child

Bulimia is characterized by regular bingeing episodes in which affected individuals consume an unusually large amount of food in a specific time period (generally two hours or less). These episodes are often accompanied by feelings of loss of control. Many individuals with the disorder report that they cannot stop eating during a binge, no matter how much they try. Like anorexia, bulimia brings about compensatory behaviors designed to avoid weight gain. However, whereas persons with anorexia lose weight as their disorder progresses, the weight of the majority of persons with bulimia remains within normal limits.

The DSM-IV-TR specifies that a diagnosis of bulimia can be made only when the person does not meet all criteria for anorexia. Table 11.2 lists the diagnostic criteria for bulimia, which Kathy's story tragically illustrates.

Kathy is a university freshman. She was brought in for help at our clinic by her fiancé. Kathy is an attractive young woman who looks like a fashion model. However, her striking appearance hides a very shy and withdrawn person. She reports that she talks only to her fiancé, whom she met two months earlier. Her fiancé, who is very concerned about Kathy's well-being, reports that he has never seen her binge or purge, but that she has told him about her troubled eating and about the periods of depression that accompany it.

Speaking in a distant, monotone voice, Kathy recalls that she began being teased by her peers for being fat when she was 14 and that she decided then that she had to purge to lose weight. At approximately the same time, she suffered from a severe bout of depression,

which was relieved by antidepressant medication. She remembers "really liking" the medication because it decreased her appetite and helped her lose weight. Her weight loss brought her new friends and popularity—until she stopped needing the medication and gained weight again. Desperate, Kathy began vomiting after each meal. This apparent solution worked "very well" at first; she lost weight rapidly, but after some time she became obsessed with food and started bingeing.

Kathy recalls that, on average, she binged five or six times a week and vomited daily. In addition, she exercised excessively. A binge ranged anywhere from eating a box of cookies to eating four quarts of ice cream and a cake. Kathy felt totally out of control when bingeing and terribly depressed and hopeless afterward. The only thing that seemed to relieve her feelings of helplessness was to vomit after bingeing (or even eating at all). Because she kept "the problem" secret, she had nobody to talk to and often thought about suicide. Kathy often mentions that if she had been a "stronger" or "better" person, she would have had anorexia and not bulimia. "Only weak people cannot control what they eat and stick to a diet."

TABLE 11.2   *Bulimia: DSM-IV-TR Diagnostic Criteria*

A. Recurrent episodes of binge eating. An episode of binge eating is characterized by both of the following:

   (1) eating, in a discrete period of time (e.g., within any 2-hour period), an amount of food that is definitely larger than most people would eat during a similar period of time and under similar circumstances

   (2) a sense of lack of control over eating during the episode (e.g., a feeling that one cannot stop eating or control what or how much one is eating)

B. Recurrent inappropriate compensatory behavior in order to prevent weight gain, such as self-induced vomiting; misuse of laxatives, diuretics, enemas or other medications; fasting; or excessive exercise.

C. The binge eating and inappropriate compensatory behavior both occur, on average, at least twice a week for 3 months.

D. Self-evaluation is unduly influenced by body shape and weight.

E. The disturbance does not occur exclusively during episodes of Anorexia Nervosa.

Specify type:

Purging Type: during the current episode of Bulimia Nervosa, the person has regularly engaged in self-induced vomiting or the misuse of laxatives, diuretics, or enemas.

Nonpurging Type: during the current episode of Bulimia Nervosa, the person has used other inappropriate compensatory behaviors, such as fasting or excessive exercise, but has not regularly engaged in self-induced vomiting or the misuse of laxatives, diuretics, or enemas.

Source: American Psychiatric Association, *Diagnostic and Statistical Manual of Mental Disorders, Fourth Edition, Text Revision* (Washington, DC: American Psychiatric Association, 2000a). Copyright 2000 American Psychiatric Association. Reprinted with permission.

Kathy thinks that her family has known about her disordered eating for a long time. She reports that her parents have often suggested that she stop her bingeing and purging, but that their interventions have never been very insistent. Only her fiancé expresses genuine alarm at the effects of bulimia on her physical and mental health.

Sadly, Kathy drops out of school and moves to another state with her fiancé after several months of unsuccessful therapy. She has made no progress in controlling her symptoms and continues to struggle with feelings of depression and worthlessness. During her last meeting with her therapist, she says honestly that she has come to therapy only to please her fiancé and because the therapist was willing to listen to her when she had nobody else to talk to.

Recurrent Binge Eating. Binge eating is always limited in time but can occur in more than one place. For example, a binge may start at a restaurant and continue at home. In most cases, affected youth eat a variety of foods during a binge, rather than one preferred food. Binge foods often include snacks and desserts, such as potato chips and ice cream—foods generally considered "forbidden" because they are fattening. Binge-eating episodes are generally accompanied by intense feelings of loss of control and are followed by feelings of shame and guilt. Affected youth feel they are unable to control what or how much they eat or to stop eating once they start.

Unlike their counterparts with anorexia, youth with bulimia recognize that their behavior is extreme and are ashamed of it. In most cases, they try desperately to hide their disordered eating. The fact that episodes of binge eating are secretive, and that bingeing and purging do not affect physical appearance in any extreme way, explains to a large extent why adolescents with bulimia can often hide a very severe problem for a long time.

Recurrent Compensatory Behaviors. To avoid gaining weight, persons with bulimia rely on a variety of compensatory behaviors after eating. Approximately two-thirds of them induce vomiting, and one-third use laxatives, diuretics, enemas, or other pharmaceutical preparations (Mitchell & Pyle,

1988). Many also accompany their bulimic eating with excessive exercise. In addition, some youth with bulimia may alternate between bingeing and periods of fasting lasting a day or more. And others may neglect a necessary medical treatment that they believe may make them "fat," such as insulin injections for diabetes (Powers, 1997).

Although compensatory behaviors are usually very demanding, they are not particularly effective. For example, vomiting immediately after a meal only reduces by half the caloric intake of the food consumed (Kaye, Weltzin, Hsu, McConaha, & Bolton, 1993), and laxative abuse results primarily in dehydration rather than in weight loss (Mitchell, Pomeroy, & Adson, 1997). Moreover, these measures bring only temporary psychological relief. In every case, this relief is quickly replaced by feelings of personal weakness and hopelessness, and by a constant preoccupation with food and weight.

Self-Esteem and Weight. Like their counterparts with anorexia, adolescents with bulimia have an intense fear of gaining weight and base their self-worth almost exclusively on the shape and weight of their body.

Subtypes. The DSM-IV-TR describes two subtypes of bulimia, according to the presence or absence of purging. Persons with **bulimia, purging type** engage regularly in self-induced vomiting or misuse laxatives, diuretics, or enemas following an episode of eating. Persons with **bulimia, nonpurging type** do not regularly engage in vomiting or laxatives, but employ fasting or excessive exercise to control their weight. Of those diagnosed with bulimia, approximately two-thirds are of the purging type, and one-third of the nonpurging type (Agras, 1987).

Binge-Eating Disorder

As mentioned, BED was described for the first time in the DSM-IV. This disorder is characterized by bingeing, without attempts at controlling weight through the extreme compensatory behaviors associated with bulimia. Like people with bulimia, people with BED eat large amounts of food in a discrete time period (generally within two hours); report that they have no control over their eating when bingeing; and binge in secret and feel disgusted, depressed, and guilty or ashamed of themselves afterward. Unlike youth with bulimia, who are generally of average weight, individuals with BED tend to be overweight or obese. In such cases, it is not unusual for individuals with the disorder to binge for prolonged periods, at times for an entire day (Marcus, 1997). Affected youth are often unhappy about their tendency to binge but do not show the profound concern about their body shape and weight that is characteristic of persons with other eating disorders.

Empirical Validity

Distinction between Anorexia and Bulimia

There is considerable agreement that anorexia and bulimia are distinct disorders; however, current definitions may blur that distinction. In a study of over 950 women with anorexia, bulimia, or an atypical eating disorder, Gleaves, Lowe, Greene, Cororve, and Williams (2000) found that the restricting type of anorexia was most clearly distinct from bulimia, but that the binge-eating/purging type was on a continuum with the purging type of bulimia. This finding suggests that (1) the restricting type of anorexia stands apart from the other forms of eating disorder; and (2) there may be two types of young people who engage in bingeing and purging: those who are of average or above-average weight and those who are underweight. The underweight type would include adolescents who are currently diagnosed as having the bingeing and purging type of anorexia. In other words, what is now called "anorexia, bingeing and purging type" may need to be renamed, since it may be closer to bulimia than it is to anorexia.

Validity of the Bulimia Subtypes

Research supports the empirical validity of the bulimia subtypes. For example, in a study conducted in England of a large representative sample of women who met diagnostic criteria for recurrent binge eating, Hay, Fairburn, and Doll (1996) were able to distinguish three groups on the basis of the symptoms these women reported. The first group were particularly concerned about their physical appearance and weight. They followed a very restricted diet, relied on self-induced vomiting, and regularly abused laxatives after a binge. The second group binged frequently but, instead of purging, relied on restrictive dieting to control their weight. The third group included women who also binged frequently but did little purging, fasting, or excessive exercise. Comparable subtypes were found by Gleaves and associates (2000) in the study described earlier. The results of these and other validity studies are encouraging, since they point to important distinctions between and within the eating disorders. However, they will have to be confirmed in future research, particularly longitudinal studies, to describe the developmental trajectory of these disorders and their subtypes, and to establish with precision how they differ (Wilson et al., 1996).

Validity of Binge-Eating Disorder as a Diagnostic Category

Wilson and associates (1996) note that "the wisdom of identifying BED as a new diagnosis has been widely debated" (p. 546). Some studies support its validity as a distinct diagnostic category, but others do not. For example, Fairburn and associates (Fairburn, Cooper, Doll, Norman, & O'Connor, 2000) found that BED follows a different developmental course from bulimia, and that their prognoses differ. These authors also observed little movement between the two conditions. Specifically, participants in their study either fully recovered or continued to suffer from BED or bulimia, but usually did not switch from one disorder to the other over time.

In contrast, Hay and colleagues (1996) and Joiner, Vohs, and Heatherton (2000) found no support for the validity of BED. In both studies, participants with the disorder could not be reliably distinguished from those with the nonpurging type of bulimia. Further research is needed, obviously, because current definitions of most eating disorders (with the exception of anorexia, restricting type) overlap, often hindering diagnostic work and treatment planning.

Objective versus Subjective Binges

As mentioned earlier, the DSM-IV-TR requirement that bingeing must involve the consumption of objectively large amounts of food is questionable. Many youth with bulimia report "binges" in which they do not eat excessively. Rosen, Leitenberg, Fisher, and Khazam (1986) found that one-third of the participants in their study did not meet all of the criteria for bulimia, solely because their binges were small. However, these participants felt as anxious and depressed when they binged as participants who clearly ate far in excess of what would be considered normal in a binge. It is likely that these negative feelings are more important in bingeing than the actual amount of food consumed, but here also further research will need to determine the amount of food and the level of self-control required to designate an eating episode as a binge.

Associated Characteristics; Comorbidity

Considering the close link between food and health, it is not surprising that eating disorders are usually accompanied by medical problems, as well as by other psychological symptoms or disorders. We describe many of the problems commonly associated with eating disorders below. However, almost all of the literature on comorbidity is based on adult samples, and its applicability to children and adolescents remains to be established.

Anorexia

Medical Conditions.   Medical conditions that are likely to affect youth with anorexia depend mainly on the stage and subtype of their disorder. Besides amenorrhea, the following physical problems are common: general weakness; cardiovascular problems, such as rapid or irregular heartbeat and low blood pressure; gastrointestinal and kidney problems; dehydration and electrolyte imbalances (from misuse of laxatives and diuretics); and appearance of **lunago,** a covering of fine, downy hair on the face and body.

These problems tend to become more severe over time and, in extreme cases, can lead to death (Mitchell et al., 1997). As many as 10% of persons with anorexia die from suicide or medical complications associated with the disorder (APA, 2000a)—*making it probably the most fatal of all of the psychological disorders* (Beumont, Russell, & Touyz, 1995). In anorexia, binge-eating/purging type, repeated self-induced vomiting also results in problems such as erosion of dental enamel, swelling of salivary glands, and hand calluses. All these medical difficulties are made worse because most youth with anorexia refuse professional care and resist any changes in their activity or diet designed to protect their health.

Comorbidity with Bulimia.   Diagnostic criteria prevent the same person from having anorexia and bulimia simultaneously, but over time many affected youth switch from one disorder to the other. In the study that introduced bulimia into the modern clinical literature, Russell (1979) described it as an alternative to anorexia, reporting that 57% of the compulsive eaters he had studied also had a history of anorexia. More recently, Keel and colleagues (Keel, Mitchell, Miller, David, & Crow, 2000) found that almost 36% of their participants with bulimia had qualified for a diagnosis of anorexia at some point in their life.

Mood Disorders.   Adolescents with anorexia often have depressive symptoms or a mood disorder. They may be sad, withdrawn, and irritable, and have difficulty sleeping—especially when they are emaciated and, in many cases, even when anorexia is in remission. Reported rates of comorbid mood disorders vary widely, however, ranging from 21% to 91%, depending on the samples studied and on the criteria used to establish comorbidity (Kaye, Weltzin, & Hsu, 1993). The high rates of depression in youth with anorexia probably are related to malnutrition rather than to a true comorbid condition, since starvation is associated with depressive symptoms even in psychologically healthy volunteers (see Box 11.2).

Anxiety Disorders.   Anxiety is also common in anorexia. Approximately 40% of individuals with anorexia qualify for a comorbid diagnosis of anxiety disorder, and between 60% and 65% of them have a lifetime history of such disorder (Halmi, 1995). Common anxiety disorders are social phobia and obsessive-compulsive disorder. For example, many adolescents with anorexia worry constantly about food, obsessively collect kitchen recipes, or become experts in food preparation and nutrition. More generally, they often have a strong need for symmetry and exactness, and may be obsessed with ordering and arranging things. Obsessive-compulsive disorder can only be diagnosed as a comorbid condition when its symptoms are not solely centered on eating and food, but involve other obsessions or compulsions (American Psychiatric Association, 2000a; Hsu, Kaye, & Weltzin, 1993).

Personality Disorders.   Youth with chronic anorexia often have symptoms of one or more personality disorders. These disorders, which describe pervasive and entrenched methods of coping and problem solving, are generally not diagnosed under the age of 18 because they are presumed to reflect a relatively unchanging, maladaptive personality style. However, evidence of such a personality style can be observed earlier. Specifically, the restricting type of anorexia is often associated with the avoidance of social interactions, especially close relationships and intimacy, and with a strong need to control one's environment. In the binge-eating/purging type, socially avoidant traits are also common, as are traits of interpersonal and emotional instability.

Clinical reports have long described adolescents with anorexia as having paradoxical personality characteristics (Beumont et al., 1995). On the one hand, they want to conform to their parents' and society's wishes, and are very dependent on their approval. Thus, many of them work hard to succeed in school and please their families, and obviously try to embody what they see as the ideal of beauty. On the other hand, most of them are skillful manipulators who have an extreme need for control. Promises, lies, blackmail, and outright resistance alternate with a desire to please those around them, except, of course, when it comes to eating. These conflicting characteristics make many youth with anorexia untrustworthy in the eyes of family, friends, and professionals, and often very difficult to treat (see Treatment and Prevention).

Alcohol and Substance Abuse.   Alcohol and substance abuse are frequently comorbid with anorexia,

particularly of the binge-eating/purging type. Between 7% and 23% of individuals with anorexia may actually qualify for a diagnosis of alcohol or substance abuse (Wilson, 1991). Alcoholism and anorexia have much in common. In particular, both disorders may serve initially to decrease anxiety and progress until they result in impaired self-control. In addition, both disorders are marked by eating or drinking compulsions that are highly resistant to change and that often follow a chronic course marked by frequent relapses.

Bulimia

Medical Conditions.   As in the case of anorexia, the medical conditions associated with bulimia depend on the stage and subtype of the disorder. In general, however, these conditions are less severe than those that accompany anorexia, primarily because persons with bulimia do not usually suffer from malnutrition. Serious complications, such as tears in the esophagus or stomach, or cardiac abnormalities, are rare but can be fatal. More commonly, adolescents with chronic bulimia present all the physical problems associated with self-induced vomiting and laxative or diuretic abuse found in their counterparts with the binge-eating/purging type of anorexia (APA, 2000a). Some also develop amenorrhea because of their chaotic eating.

Mood Disorders.   Between 24% and 88% of individuals with bulimia—especially the purging type—have a lifetime history of mood disorder (Wilson et al., 1996; Halmi, 1995). The nature of this association remains poorly understood. In particular, studies have not established whether these disorders are truly comorbid or whether their association is nonspecific—simply reflecting the fact that depressive symptoms accompany many disorders of childhood and adolescence. Tentative support for a specific association between bulimia and mood disorders comes from twin studies showing that in a significant number of cases these disorders appear to share a common hereditary origin (Walters et al., 1992).

Anxiety and Personality Disorders.   Anxiety disorders are commonly associated with bulimia, as they are with anorexia. However, comorbidity varies among studies, in large part because of differences in sample characteristics and criteria used to establish the presence of comorbid conditions. Not surprisingly, obsessive-compulsive disorder appears to be particularly frequent among individuals with bulimia, who are often preoccupied with order and symmetry in the midst of their chaotic eating habits (von Ranson, Walter, Weltzin, Rao, & Matsunaga, 1999).

Personality disorders or pervasive maladaptive personality traits are also common in individuals with bulimia, even though, here again, prevalence rates vary considerably among studies (Halmi, 1995). The purging type of bulimia is often associated with personality characteristics that include impulsiveness and instability in social relationships, emotions, and self-perception. Clinical reports regularly describe youth with bulimia as manipulative, secretive, and untrustworthy, but usually not to the same extent as youth with anorexia.

Alcohol and Substance Abuse.

As early as 1945, Otto Fenichel described the bingeing and purging cycles of bulimia as a "drug addiction without drugs." This assertion is supported by the fact that approximately one-third of adolescents and young adults with bulimia regularly misuse alcohol or other drugs (APA, 2000a), and that many of them qualify for a diagnosis of one or more substance abuse disorders (Wilson, 1991).

Binge-Eating Disorder

BED is associated with many of the comorbid psychological conditions that commonly accompany bulimia (Walsh & Kahn, 1997). However, the disorder most often mentioned in conjunction with BED is obesity. Studies show that as many as one-third of obese people seeking treatment to lose weight meet diagnostic criteria for BED. Currently, the relationship between these conditions is unknown, although bingeing and chaotic eating patterns may precede obesity, rather than the other way around (Mitchell & Mussell, 1995).

Epidemiology

Although much remains to be learned about the epidemiology of eating disorders, several authors stress that the prevalence rates summarized here are likely to underestimate the true extent of the problem (Wilson et al., 1996), because these rates exclude a large number of people with significantly disordered eating who do not meet all current diagnostic criteria and, more simply, because the shame associated with eating disorders causes affected individuals to be very secretive about them. Specifically, many of these individuals—possibly those with the most severe eating problems—refuse to participate in epidemiological studies.

Prevalence; Age and Gender Characteristics

Anorexia. Epidemiological studies conducted in several industrialized countries over the past twenty years indicate that prevalence rates of anorexia range from 0.5% to 1.0% and that the highest rates are generally found in samples of middle- to upper-middle-class European American females (American Psychiatric Association, 2000a; Herzog, 1988). A much higher proportion of adolescents—approximately 3%—manifest many symptoms of the disorder without meeting all criteria required for diagnosis (Johnson-Sabine, Wood, Patton, Mann, & Wakeling, 1988).

Anorexia begins most often in adolescence. Over 90% of individuals with the disorder are adolescent girls or young women. In childhood, however, approximately 25% of those diagnosed with anorexia are boys (Lask & Bryant-Waugh, 1997).

As you know, Western societies have seen rapid increases in the incidence of anorexia in the second half of the twentieth century (see Figure 11.1). In Switzerland, for example, Willi and Grossmann (1983) found that the number of 12- to 25-year-old females hospitalized for anorexia averaged only 4 per 100,000 between 1956 and 1958, but that the number quadrupled to reach a rate of 17 per 100,000 between 1973 and 1975. This increase could not be explained by variables such as the age of the patients at the time of hospital admission or the use of different admission criteria from one period to another. Similar increases have been reported in countries such as Spain (Bosch, 2000) and the United States (Lucas, Beard, O'Fallon, & Kurlan, 1991).

Bulimia. Epidemiological studies on bulimia are sparse, but we know that it occurs more frequently than anorexia and begins later, usually in late adolescence or early adulthood. Reported rates of prevalence vary from 1% to 5% in Western countries (APA, 2000a; Fairburn & Beglin, 1990), and often exceed this range in high-risk groups, such as young college women (Schlundt & Johnson, 1990). About 90–95% of individuals with bulimia are in their late teens or early twenties. The incidence of bulimia has also increased rapidly in recent decades (see Figure 11.2).

Binge-Eating Disorder. Epidemiological data on the prevalence of BED are rare, given the newness of the diagnosis. In community samples, the disorder probably affects between 2% and 4% of the population. Not surprisingly, rates are much higher among people who participate in weight-loss programs or attend Overeaters Anonymous or similar support groups (Hsu, 1996; Mitchell & Mussell, 1995). Like other eating disorders, BED is more common in females, although the ratio of women to men is only 1.2 to 1 (Hsu, 1996). Like bulimia, BED usually begins in late adolescence and early adulthood.

Social and Cultural Differences

Cross-cultural comparisons of the characteristics and epidemiology of eating disorders are rare. However, the highest prevalence rates are found in societies where there is an abundance of food and where the cultural ideal of feminine beauty places major emphasis on thinness. In the United States, anorexia and bulimia often affect white female adolescents and young women from privileged backgrounds (Smith & Krejci, 1991). However, minority youth are by no means immune from these conditions. Striegel-Moore and colleagues (2000) examined longitudinal data from approximately three thousand girls aged 11 to 16. Results showed that all of the key symptoms of eating disorders increased with age in both African American and European American girls. However, European American girls—especially older girls (after age 13) and girls with a higher body mass index (a common measure of body fat)—were more likely to report dissatisfaction with their body and a desire to be thin than their African American peers. This finding suggests that African American girls are more satisfied with

their body and, when they are not, that their judgment is more realistic—that is, that they admit more readily than European American girls that they are overweight.

In an often-cited study, Nasser (1986) compared the incidence of eating disorders among sixty young Egyptian women attending university in Cairo and their compatriots attending university in London. Whereas none of the women living in Egypt described behaviors indicative of an eating disorder, 12% of those living in England suffered from bulimia. Comparable findings have been reported in cross-cultural comparisons conducted in Australia and China (Gunewardene, Huon, & Zheng, 2001). These results suggest that processes of acculturation—especially acceptance of the Western ideal of thinness—may place youth who are consistently exposed to that ideal at increased risk for developing eating disorders.

The major characteristics of eating disorders are generally similar across cultures. However, in cultures where thinness is less central to the definition of beauty than it is in Western societies, other physical attributes may be associated with eating disorders. Box 11.3 highlights some important predictors of anorexia in China.

Developmental Trajectories and Prognosis

Early Feeding Problems and Obesity

Although eating disorders usually appear during adolescence or early adulthood, they often have much earlier precursors. For example, children of parents with an eating disorder have a much higher risk of developing comparable problems than children of parents without such a disorder, a point to which we will return later (see Etiology). Likewise, early feeding problems have been found to be predictive of later eating disorders. In a ten-year follow-up of over eight hundred young children, Marchi and Cohen (1990) discovered that problematic eating behaviors were relatively stable. Obesity during childhood also is predictive of future eating disorders. For example, Epstein and colleagues (Epstein, Valoski, Wing, & McCurley, 1994) studied a group of children who had been in treatment

BOX 11.3 • *Eating Disorders in China: Do You Have to Fear Fat to Have Anorexia?*

In America and other Western societies, one of the hallmark symptoms of anorexia is a morbid fear of becoming fat. The Chinese researcher Sing Lee reports that this symptom is not routinely observed in China. In fact, in one sample of Chinese youth with anorexia, almost 60% of participants did not show any fear of fatness during the course of their disorder. If fear of fatness does not drive anorexic symptoms in many Chinese youth, what does? The Lee research team presents case studies suggesting that the anorexic symptoms of many Chinese adolescents develop as a result of disturbances in facial or body image not associated with weight (Lee, Hsu, & Wing, 1992; Lee, Leung, Wing, Chiu, & Chen, 1991). For example, anorexia may begin after a change in diet in response to severe acne, as in the following case:

> Ms. D, age 18, height 160 cm, ideal body weight 47.5 kg . . . was referred for weight loss of 24% from 49 kg to 37 kg over the past six months. The elder of two girls from a middle class family, she was described unanimously as having been "a nice and quiet girl." . . .
> One year previously, she was embarrassed by the development of moderate amount of facial acne, which did not improve with medical treatment. She felt

ashamed, became socially withdrawn, and walked with her face down in the street. Upon advice from her mother and a dermatologist, she significantly increased her intake of fruits and vegetables to the exclusion of meat and fat. In a Chinese restaurant, she was coaxed by her mother to eat "cooling" food and was not allowed to order "hot" food, so that the acne could heal. In the next six months this resulted in amenorrhea and marked weight loss, which, to her delight, made most of her acne disappear. Her mother's advice to increase her intake of meat and rice was ignored (Lee et al., 1991, p. 135).

Note that nowhere in this report do the researchers mention a fear of being fat and a corresponding drive for thinness. Instead, Ms. D's weight loss resulted from dietary changes intended to help her become more attractive. Probably regardless of culture, anorexia reflects a youth's strong desire to be attractive, but in each culture attractiveness is defined somewhat differently. In China, facial appearance may be most critical to being beautiful, whereas in America and many other Western countries, thinness may be key.

---

for obesity between the ages of 6 and 12 years. In spite of the extensive services these children received, a ten-year follow-up showed that 4% of the girls had developed bulimia. Western children who are overweight obviously face major developmental challenges as they strive to meet the standards of thinness deemed desirable in their culture.

From Dieting to Eating Disorders

Dieting during childhood and adolescence also contributes to the development of eating disorders. Generally speaking, the growing emphasis on thinness and dieting to which youth in the United States and other Western countries have been exposed in recent decades parallels the increase in eating disorders seen over the same period (see Box 11.4, p. 326). More specifically, research by Patton and colleagues (1990), among others, shows that dieting adolescents are much more likely to

develop an eating disorder than adolescents who are not attempting to control their weight.

Anorexia

As Lasègue (1873) had noted, persons with anorexia often start by eliminating one or two foods they consider "fattening" from their diet. This initial step leads to a growing number of dietary restrictions, and ultimately to an extremely limited and totally inadequate diet. Unfortunately, as you know, dieting—no matter how extreme—never calms the fear of being fat. It has the opposite effect, setting in motion a vicious cycle in which the more weight the older child or adolescent loses, the more she or he becomes concerned about weight.

Once present, anorexia often lasts for several years. However, the disorder can evolve in very different ways. Some adolescents recover fully after a single

BOX 11.4 • *Striving to Be Thin*

Striving to be thin is a daily fact of life for countless Americans—children and adolescents, as well as adults. The American drive for thinness is so intense that a large percentage of first- through third-grade girls are dissatisfied with their bodies, are afraid of being fat, and want to be thinner (Lucero, Hill, & Ferraro, 1999). Dietary and weight concerns are actually so common among American youth that they have become almost normative.

A survey of over 16,000 boys and girls ages 9 through 14 illustrates the extent to which dieting is often a part of everyday life in early adolescence (Field et al., 1999). As the table below shows, a significant number of children at that age believe that they are overweight—even when they are not—and many are on a diet. Furthermore, dieting increases with age, as do other attempts to lose weight. Given these statistics, it should come as no surprise that eating disorders have rapidly become a major social and mental health problem in America. However, the American obsession with weight has not been paralleled by an increase in healthy eating and physical exercise, leaving more and more youth concerned about their bodies but doing little to improve them in healthy ways.

	Age					
	9	10	11	12	13	14
Girls						
Actually are overweight	23%	23%	18%	19%	16%	15%
Think they are overweight	15	21	23	28	31	33
Not overweight, but think they are overweight	4.2	7.0	9.4	13	17	19
Trying to lose weight	20	24	27	35	40	44
Exercise daily to lose weight	5.9	5.9	7.1	8.3	11	12
Always on a diet to lose weight	1.1	1.5	1.2	2.0	4.2	5.0
Purge (i.e., use vomiting or laxatives) at least monthly	0.9	0.5	0.4	0.8	2.1	2.5
Binge at least monthly	0.4	0.9	1.5	1.8	2.9	3.6
Boys						
Actually are overweight	29	26	26	27	26	22
Think they are overweight	16	21	22	26	24	20
Not overweight, but think they are overweight	2.3	4.6	4.6	6.0	6.3	5.3
Trying to lose weight	17	19	19	23	21	19
Exercise daily to lose weight	5.1	4.8	7.2	6.5	8.9	8.4
Always on a diet to lose weight	0.8	0.9	1.1	1.3	1.7	1.3
Purge (i.e., use vomiting or laxatives) at least monthly	1.1	0.6	0.5	0.6	0.6	0.3
Binge at least monthly	0.8	0.5	0.8	1.1	0.9	0.8

Note: Values represent percentages.

Source: Table from A. E. Field at al., "Overweight, Weight Concerns, and Bulimic Behaviors among Girls and Boys," *Journal of the American Academy of Child and Adolescent Psychiatry 38* (1999), table 3. Copyright 1999 by Lippencott, Williams, & Wilkins. Reprinted by permission.

episode. Others alternate, often for years, between periods of anorexia and partial remission. When they are not in remission, these youth often have to be hospitalized for varying lengths of time because of the medical and psychological consequences of their emaciation. You will recall from Lori's description of her disorder that hospitalization often takes place against the child or adolescent's will and becomes itself a major source of contention. Still other youth regain weight after a period or more of anorexia, but then develop bulimia. Finally, some never recover from anorexia. Approximately 10% of people who have the disorder die from it—some from suicide and the others from medical complications brought about by starvation (APA, 2000a). In a 7.5-year longitudinal investigation of young women with anorexia, Herzog and colleagues (2000) found that one-third had fully recovered during the study period, and that an additional 50% had made a partial recovery. However, almost 20% of the sample showed little or no sign of recovery during the entire follow-up period, and 7 of the original 246 women (2.8%) had died during that period.

Bulimia

In more than 80% of cases, bulimia also starts with a prolonged period of dieting (Fairburn, 1994, cited in Wilson et al., 1996). The remaining cases develop after an initial period of anorexia (Mitchell & Pyle, 1988). Unlike their counterparts with anorexia, adolescents with bulimia are often overweight at the onset of the disorder (Patton, Johnson-Sabine, Wood, Mann, & Wakeling, 1990). To lose weight, they usually attempt to follow one or more diets. Dieting and weight loss quickly become a source of constant preoccupation and set in motion the vicious cycle that is characteristic of the disorder. This cycle—or "infernal merry-go-round," as one of our clients aptly called it—is marked by alternating episodes of binge eating and purging, fasting, or other compensatory behaviors. In many cases, this situation worsens quite rapidly, in large part because the more that affected adolescents try to control what they eat, the greater their risk of bingeing.

Bingeing generally begins a year or so before purging does and is associated with acute feelings of loss of control and extreme anxiety, particularly at the onset of the disorder (Fairburn & Cooper, 1984). In a large majority of cases, bulimia is chronic, usually alternating between periods of disorder and remission. However, once bulimia is present, it does not tend to develop into other forms of psychopathology.

Binge-Eating Disorder

Knowledge of the developmental trajectory of BED is very limited. Some evidence indicates that many of its antecedents are similar to those of bulimia. In a five-year follow-up of women with BED, Fairburn and associates (2000) found that the recovery rate for BED was high. Approximately 18% of their participants qualified for a diagnosis of eating disorder at the end of the study, even though only 3% of them had received treatment.

Etiology

Biological Factors: Genetic Studies

Family Studies. Eating disorders tend to run in families. For example, first-degree female relatives of persons with anorexia run a risk eleven times higher than the general population of developing an eating disorder. That risk is four times higher for female relatives of persons with bulimia (Strober, Freeman, Lampert, Diamond, & Kaye, 2000). These figures do not necessarily imply a genetic etiology, since members of the same family might conceivably develop similar eating disorders exclusively as a function of living together. However, other studies indicate that this explanation is insufficient and that genetic factors are important in the etiology of the disorder.

Twin Studies. Concordance rates for eating disorders range from approximately 20% to 50% among monozygotic twins, but are typically below 10% among dizygotic twins (Kendler et al., 1991). Twin studies focusing specifically on anorexia or bulimia are rarer, but generally report comparable differences. For example, concordance rates for bulimia range from 8% to 47% for monozygotic twins, and from 0% to 9% for dizygotic twins (Bulik, Sullivan, & Kendler, 2000; Fairburn, Cowen, & Harrison, 1999).

Although this evidence shows that genetic factors play an important role in the transmission of eating disorders, what is actually inherited is unclear. As is the case for many of the disorders we cover in this book, a majority of researchers believe that it is not the disorders themselves that are inherited, but a vulnerability to them, which is expressed through behavioral tendencies such as impulsiveness or anxiety. These tendencies may make some children and adolescents particularly likely to react to stress by resorting to maladaptive forms of eating (Strober, 1995). It is also likely that a physiological predisposition to obesity can be transmitted from one generation to the next and lead many adolescents to become convinced—in line with their culture—that they are overweight. In some cases, this predisposition may indirectly contribute to the development of an eating disorder, as affected youth set themselves an "ideal" target weight that they cannot meet.

Biological Factors: Neurophysiological Studies

Several theorists hypothesize that the hypothalamus, a brain structure involved in the regulation of hunger, plays a major role in pathological eating through the neurotransmitters it modulates (especially serotonin and norepinephrine) (Kay & Weltzin, 1991). Support for this hypothesis comes from animal research and from clinical studies of neurotransmitters in women with anorexia and bulimia. Specifically, when compared to average women, women with bulimia show decreased serotonin activity when their disorder is active and increased serotonin activity after recovery. In contrast, women with anorexia show elevated levels of serotonin activity in the course of the disorder and after recovery (Ferguson & Pigott, 2000). These authors also report that **neuropeptides,** a class of hormone-like substances that act as neurotransmitters, are implicated in the complex regulation problems faced by women with eating disorders. Theoretically, difficulties in neurochemical and hormonal regulation are consistent with the obsessions around thinness and symmetry, as well as with the depressive symptoms that are so common in these disorders.

Although a number of neurophysiological studies describe important differences between women with

and without eating disorders, these differences are difficult to interpret, mainly because they are most often reported in one-time, cross-sectional studies, rather than in longitudinal research. In other words, when neurophysiological differences are found between people who have an eating disorder and people who do not, it is usually impossible to establish whether these differences were present before the onset of the disorder and could have played a role in its development, or whether the disorder itself was the cause of these differences. Because malnutrition and starvation are very detrimental to the human body, it is reasonable to assume that neurophysiological regulation problems may often be a consequence of the disordered eating of persons with anorexia or bulimia rather than a cause.

Psychological and Family Factors

Thin-Ideal Internalization. Adolescents with eating disorders are convinced that they are overweight and strive forever to be thin. In a systematic program of research, Stice and colleagues have shown that **thin-ideal internalization** plays a causal role in the etiology of eating disorders, especially bulimia (e.g., Stice, 2001). Thin-ideal internalization "refers to the extent to which an individual cognitively 'buys into' socially defined ideals of attractiveness and engages in behaviors designed to produce an approximation of those ideals" (Thompson & Stice, 2001, p. 181). In other words, in the course of development, many youth internalize widely shared cultural expectations about the way they ought to look and take active steps to look that way. Unfortunately, in many cases, these steps are extreme and result in disorder.

Dieting is probably the most common step initially taken by adolescents striving to be thin. In a longitudinal study of over two hundred adolescent girls, Stice's research team found that thin-ideal internalization predicted dieting, and that together these two factors were among the best predictors of the development of bulimia in girls who had no symptoms of the disorder nine months earlier (Stice, 2001). Dieting may thus be one of the processes accounting for the link between thin-ideal internalization and eating disorder. Dieting may be particularly important because it is not related to weight loss in a simple, linear fashion. In other words, it is incorrect to believe that the more people diet, the more they lose weight. Rather, low to moderate dieting predicts weight *gains;* only extreme dieting predicts weight loss in adolescence. Thus, contrary to what they intend to achieve, many adolescents who diet put themselves at risk of gaining weight and then resort to dysfunctional behaviors to reverse this process. This and similar research is important because it shows prospectively that thin-ideal internalization and dieting may play causal roles in the development of eating disorders (Byely, Archibald, Graber, & Brooks-Gunn, 2000). Once these disorders are set in motion, however, these factors may become both causes and consequences of disordered eating, maintaining and often aggravating each other in complex transactional processes.

Dysfunctional Parenting.

As Lasègue (1873) emphasized, family variables play an important role in the etiology of eating disorders. Considerable work has been conducted in this area. However, much of it is limited by serious methodological problems. Most important, because the vast majority of studies are correlational, it is impossible to establish cause and effect. In addition, many studies are based on clinical samples, which are seldom representative of persons with these disorders (Wilson et al., 1996).

In a careful program of research conducted in England, Stein and associates are avoiding these methodological limitations through longitudinal studies of a high-risk sample of young children (e.g., Stein, Woolley, Cooper, & Fairburn, 1994; Stein, Murray, Cooper, & Fairburn, 1996). This program follows the early development of children whose mothers have a history of eating disorder. Home observations have shown that when the children were 12 to 14 months old their mothers were already more negative during mealtime interactions than mothers of control children. For example, they were more critical when their children refused to eat or when they did not eat as much or as neatly as their mothers expected them to. In addition, their children generally weighed less than the children of average or depressed mothers, and their concerns about their own body shape were a better predictor of the children's weight at age 1 than the children's own weight at birth. These results do not demonstrate the existence of an etiological link between eating disorders and mother-child conflicts around food or maternal concerns about weight. However, they clearly suggest such a link, which a follow-up of these children to early adulthood might confirm.

Disturbances in the Family System.

Researchers focusing on families as dynamic systems of interaction have paid considerable attention to eating disorders as well. In different etiological accounts, these researchers postulate that some children and adolescents develop anorexia or bulimia in order to deflect attention from marital discord or other major issues that threaten the family's unity and stability. Thus, a young adolescent may limit her food intake and become overconcerned about her weight in order to force her parents to pay increasing attention to her, rather than to their own conflict. In pioneering work in this area, Minuchin and co-workers stated that anorexia typically develops within what they call "psychosomatic families." These families have three characteristics: "First, the child is physiologically vulnerable. . . . Second, the child's family has four transactional characteristics: enmeshment, overprotectiveness, rigidity, and a lack of conflict resolution. Third, the sick child plays an important role in the family's pattern of conflict avoidance; and this role is an important source of reinforcement for his symptoms" (Minuchin et al., 1975, p. 1033).

More specifically, Minuchin claims that these families put undue emphasis on maintaining social appearances at the expense of genuine and healthy communication about personal feelings, needs, and preferences. As a result, all family members attempt to keep true problems hidden: nobody outside the family must know that the family has problems, and nobody within the family must acknowledge these problems to other family members. This work has often been cited and has led to the development of treatments for eating disorders. However, it lacks empirical support (Eisler, 1995), because there are many more rigid, enmeshed, overprotective, and conflicted families than there are families with youth with eating disorders. Therefore, if these characteristics play an etiological role, it cannot be specific to these disorders. In addition, family researchers have not always considered the possibility that these family characteristics may be a consequence of living with a person with anorexia or bulimia, rather than a cause of these conditions.

Stress and Negative Life Events.   Women with bulimia report high levels of stress in the six months preceding onset of their symptoms (Raffi, Rondini, Grandi, & Fava, 2000), as well as elevated rates of childhood family conflict and abuse (Webster & Palmer, 2000). Such reports suggest that stress and negative life events, such as child abuse and trauma, may contribute to the later development of eating disorders.

   Although often reported as fact in the media, a link between child abuse and eating disorders has not been clearly established. Evidence indicates that a significant number of children (Wonderlich et al., 2001) and adults (Webster & Palmer, 2000) with anorexia or bulimia, or symptoms of these disorders, have a history of sexual abuse. The same is true for emotional abuse (Kent & Waller, 2000). However, these findings do not demonstrate causality, because child abuse predicts a variety of psychological problems in addition to eating disorders, and because evidence in this area is based almost exclusively on unrepresentative clinical samples. In a nonclinical study conducted in the United States, Austria, and Brazil, Pope and colleagues (Pope, Mang-

weth, Negrao, Hudson, & Cordas, 1994) compared community samples of women with bulimia with samples of control women and did not find a difference in reported rates of sexual abuse. Similarly, Fairburn (1994, cited in Wilson et al., 1996) found comparable rates of sexual abuse in samples of persons with bulimia and with other psychological disorders. These results indicate that sexual abuse and other traumatic events probably do not cause eating disorders but, instead, make children and adolescents vulnerable to various psychological disorders.

Social and Cultural Factors

Of all the psychological disorders of childhood and adolescence, anorexia and bulimia are among the ones that most clearly reflect a narrow but particularly powerful set of cultural expectations. We have already mentioned that these disorders are most frequent in affluent societies, where they have rapidly increased over the past decades. It is probable that this increase reflects, in part, an important paradox brought about by historical events. In Western countries, many young people are now confronted with excesses rather than shortages of food, and are often encouraged to eat well beyond their physical needs. Paradoxically, this abundance comes at

Daily temptations. In affluent societies, children and adolescents face numerous temptations to overeat and to exercise little.

a time when the cultural ideal of feminine beauty is to be thin—much thinner than beautiful women used to be a few generations ago (Brownell, 1991).

Changes in the cultural ideal of thinness have been documented in numerous studies. For example, reviews of popular U.S. magazines published from 1959 to 1989 showed that the weight of *Playboy* magazine's centerfold women, like that of the Miss America pageant candidates, has decreased over time. Moreover, the weight of 65% of the centerfold women and of 60% of the Miss America candidates met one of the diagnostic criteria for anorexia—namely, being at 85% of optimal body weight or below. During the same period, the number of articles praising the virtues of physical exercise or dieting increased significantly in the feminine popular press (Wiseman, Gray, Mosimann, & Ahrens, 1992). This evidence does not establish cause and effect, obviously. Other etiological factors are at work also, if only because the vast majority of children and adolescents who are influenced by these cultural expectations do not develop an eating disorder. Nevertheless, it is striking that from 1975 to 1986 the incidence of anorexia increased by approximately 10% in many industrialized countries, and that of bulimia by almost 150% (Garner & Fairburn, 1988).

Because adolescents—girls and boys—weigh more today, on average, than they did a few generations ago, many of them cannot easily conform to a cultural ideal of thinness (Garner, Garfinkel, & Olmsted, 1983). Moreover, the process of physical maturation, particularly in girls, works directly against this ideal—further increasing the pressure that many of them feel not to put on weight at any cost (Striegel-Moore, Silberstein, & Rodin, 1986).

Treatment and Prevention

As noted earlier, eating disorders—especially anorexia—are often difficult to treat. Beyond this broad generalization, little is known about the effectiveness of various treatments for eating disorders, largely because the available literature consists mainly of case studies of adults, although it is not always clear that findings obtained with adults can be adequately extrapolated to young people.

Anorexia

Overall, anorexia is a chronic disorder that is often resistant to change (Garner, Vitousek, & Pike, 1997). However, adolescents with the disorder may have a somewhat better prognosis than adults. Specifically, Strober, Freeman, and Morrell (1997) found that, although most of the almost one hundred adolescents they followed relapsed immediately after treatment, by the end of ten to fifteen years 76% had made a full recovery. Steinhausen, Seidel, and Metzke (2000) have reported similar results.

Inpatient Hospitalization. Treatment for anorexia often begins with inpatient hospitalization (APA, 2000b). Youth with the disorder may be hospitalized because they are suffering from severe malnutrition or from medical complications associated with malnutrition or dehydration; because they have not made progress in outpatient therapy; or because they have another psychological disorder that interferes with intervention. For example, some youth with anorexia may be severely depressed and may have to be hospitalized because they have suicidal ideations or have made one or more suicide attempts (Fisher et al., 1995).

The structure and control inherent in hospital settings make feeding youth with anorexia easier than it is at home. Specifically, hospitalization allows eating to be planned and monitored in systematic ways—for example, through a **behavioral contract.** The following contract between an adolescent and a psychologist or psychiatrist was prepared by Robin, Gilroy, and Dennis (1998). It specifies when and how much the person must eat each day. Once signed, the contract is considered a binding agreement and makes much of the youth's pleasurable activities contingent on her having eaten a minimum amount of food.

1. You will be given three meals and several snacks each day.
2. We expect you to eat 100% of your food.
3. You will be given an opportunity to exclude three aversive foods. We expect you to eat all other foods that are on your tray.
4. You will have 30 minutes to eat everything on your tray. You will eat in the play room

with a nurse present to monitor and encourage you.

5. You cannot have food brought in from outside the hospital.

6. If you are unable to eat all of your food within 30 minutes, you will be given 15 additional minutes to drink a nutritious milkshake equal to the amount of food remaining on your tray. If you cannot drink the milkshake, we will ask you to preserve your energy by staying on bed rest until the next meal. During bed rest, there are no activities or TV.

7. You will remain in the playroom with the nurse for 30 minutes following each meal.

8. If you eat breakfast completely, you have earned telephone privileges.

9. If you eat all three meals completely, you have earned one hour of visitation in the evening (p. 428).

Ideally, parents or other key family members are involved in treatment during and after hospitalization. In many cases, they are trained in the behavioral methods designed to help the child or adolescent gain a healthy weight, and are provided with support once the youth leaves hospital to ensure that treatment gains are maintained.

Outpatient Psychological Treatments. When a youth's health is not in immediate jeopardy because of starvation or suicidal behavior, outpatient psychological treatment is usually the intervention of choice. Treatment generally focuses on helping affected children or adolescents return to a healthy pattern of eating and enabling them to develop a more accurate image of themselves and their body. Although all treatments share these common goals, the principles and methods on which they rely vary considerably. The most common approaches used in this area are the psychoanalytic, cognitive-behavioral, and family systems approaches.

Psychoanalytic Treatment. Psychoanalytic treatment is one of the most commonly used interventions for anorexia, at least with adults (Herzog, 1995). In this perspective, children and adolescents with anorexia use their disordered eating to deal with anxiety-provoking and painful psychological or family conflicts. These conflicts often center on issues of identity, autonomy, and independence. Therapy focuses on strengthening the children or adolescents' ego through self-acceptance, to enable them to develop a sense of control and self-efficacy, and to choose healthier ways of coping with conflict than self-starvation.

Psychoanalytic treatment research is rare, but the few studies that have been conducted suggest that this approach may be effective with this difficult disorder. For example, Crisp (1997) reports that youth who participated in inpatient or outpatient psychoanalytic treatment had better outcomes than youth on a waiting list. Further, Robin and colleagues (1999) found that psychoanalytic treatment produced outcomes similar to those of family systems treatment (see below).

Cognitive-Behavioral Treatment. CBT for anorexia focuses on changing erroneous beliefs about body weight, shape, and size (Garner & Bemis, 1985). Affected young people's beliefs about their appearance are challenged through psychoeducation, problem solving, and homework assignments. These different facets of intervention are designed to teach the child or adolescent that physical appearance is not the same as self-worth and that maintaining a healthy weight does not mean being ugly, unloved, or unlovable. In addition, eating is closely monitored through the use of food diaries in which youth note their food intake, as well as the events and feelings that precede and follow their eating. Diary notes can then be used to monitor treatment progress and to challenge the erroneous beliefs that are believed to maintain the child's difficulties.

Research to test the effectiveness of CBT for youth with anorexia remains to be conducted. Research with young adults suggests that CBT is more effective than no treatment (Channon, deSilva, Hemsley, & Perkins, 1989). This result is promising, but Robin and colleagues (1998) warn that CBT may not be appropriate for severely emaciated youth with rigid and often obsessional thinking.

Family Systems Therapy. The goal of family therapy is to change the dysfunctional interaction patterns that are believed to maintain eating disordered behavior (Minuchin et al., 1975). Therapy usually proceeds in three stages:

1. Parents are helped to take control of their child's chaotic eating, whether family therapy begins in hospital or in an outpatient setting.
2. When parents are able to control their child's eating, the focus of therapy shifts to changing maladaptive family interactions, as well as to reducing the child's erroneous beliefs about body weight, shape, and size. Changing family interactions is essential because family systems theorists assume that the disorder often serves to divert attention away from troubling psychological problems within the family.
3. When the child's target weight is reached and family interactions improve, parents are helped to return control over eating to their child. Youth are also taught problem-solving and communication skills designed to prevent relapse and promote healthy coping with future challenges.

Family therapy is effective in increasing weight and decreasing depression and family conflict in youth with anorexia. This appears to be true whether parents and children are seen together or separately, as long as the family is involved (Robin et al., 1998, 1999).

Bulimia

Unlike youth with anorexia, youth with bulimia are rarely hospitalized, because there are fewer major health risks associated with the disorder. Outpatient CBT and interpersonal therapy are the best-established interventions in this area (Steiner & Lock, 1998). Overall, bulimia is easier to treat than anorexia (Peterson & Mitchell, 1999). Specifically, longitudinal research shows that bulimia is associated with faster recovery rates than anorexia, with almost three-quarters of those affected recovering within a 7.5-year period (Herzog et al., 2000).

Cognitive-Behavioral Treatment. CBT has yet to be systematically tested with youth. However, CBT has received considerable support in the treatment of adults with bulimia (APA, 2000b). CBT programs work to reduce cognitive errors about weight, size, and self-worth that are thought to be the core of the disorder (Wilson, Fairburn, & Agras, 1997). Again, treatment

includes psychoeducation, problem solving, and homework assignments, as well as a detailed food diary kept by the patient.

Interpersonal Therapy. Interpersonal therapy has proven effective with adults with bulimia (Fairburn, Jones, Peveler, Hope, & O'Conner, 1991), but has not yet been tested with a younger population. This treatment approach is derived from interpersonal therapy for depression. Focus is on interpersonal relationships that maintain or worsen bulimic symptomatology. They and their therapist can then identify specific interpersonal problems and decide to work on them to develop effective coping skills. Robin and associates (1998) suggest that, because of its effectiveness with adults, and the success of interpersonal therapy with depressed adolescents, this approach may be helpful to youth with bulimia.

Pharmacological Interventions

There is little controlled research on the effectiveness of medication in the treatment of anorexia. Overall, pharmacological interventions seem to be relatively ineffective at treating the core symptoms of the disorder. Specifically, benefits from medications have often been reported in uncontrolled studies, but beneficial effects are lacking in controlled investigations (Ferguson & Pigott, 2000). For example, Attia, Haiman, Walsh, and Flater (1998) found that weight changes, depressive symptoms, and attitudes about weight and body shape were equivalent in a group of thirty-one affected women who were either given *fluoxetine* (Prozac) or a placebo as an adjunct to psychotherapy.

There is some evidence that medication is effective in the treatment of bulimia, at least in adults. In their review, Ferguson and Pigott (2000) found that SSRIs and tricyclic antidepressants were both effective. However, the side effects and possibility of overdose associated with tricyclics favor the use of SSRIs in pharmacological intervention. Although these findings are encouraging, it is important to note that medication is not more effective than psychological treatment and does not appear to boost the effectiveness of that treatment. In fact, Ferguson and Pigott write that "combining CBT and medication may not offer clear advantages over CBT alone" (p. 253). For example, Goldbloom and colleagues (1997) compared treatment with CBT alone and with fluoxetine alone to an approach that combined CBT and medication. They found that CBT alone was more effective than medication alone and just as effective as the combined approach, suggesting that the combined group benefited primarily from CBT rather than from medication.

Prevention

I'm not into working out. My philosophy:
No pain, no pain.

—Carol Leifer

It is widely agreed that the most effective ways of preventing eating disorders would be to change Western culture's overemphasis on slimness, as well as to promote healthy exercise and improve the eating habits of many families (Brumberg, 1997). Since such changes are beyond the realm of psychological intervention alone, and are likely to take considerable time, researchers have begun to design prevention programs to teach children and adolescents healthy eating habits. Most of these programs take place in schools, primarily as informational sessions about eating disorders (e.g., Killen et al., 1993). Unfortunately, there is little evidence that these programs are successful. As O'Dea and Abraham (2000) note:

> The information-giving approach is likely to improve knowledge of eating disorders and problem eating, but is unlikely to affect the beliefs, attitudes, intent, and behaviors that influence the development of eating problems. . . . [It] also has the potential to create adverse effects such as the glamorization and normalization of eating disorders and to introduce young people to dangerous practices by providing

information about dangerous methods of weight control (p. 44).

Another approach to prevention focuses not on eating but on self-esteem. For example, O'Dea and Abraham (2000) conducted a nine-week, in-school prevention program with almost five hundred adolescents (aged 11 to 14). Delivered by the regular classroom teacher, the program targeted self-esteem, stress reduction, relationship skills, self-image and the effects of stereotypes, and communication skills. Results showed that this brief program produced changes in body image and attitudes that persisted at a one-year follow-up. Furthermore, youth who participated in the program gained weight more appropriately than youth in the control group. Although these results are promising, they will obviously need to be replicated and expanded to confirm the usefulness of such an approach to prevention.

A related approach to prevention seeks to reduce thin-ideal internalization and negative stereotypes about large body shapes. For example, a media literacy program taught high school girls to challenge media portrayals of female beauty (Irving, DuPen, & Berel, 1998). Results show that the program reduced thin-ideal internalization and made participants critical of media images promoting unhealthy standards of attractiveness. Similarly, a puppet program taught elementary school children to be accepting of different body shapes and to refrain from teasing children who look different (Irving, 2000). Preliminary results were also encouraging, showing that the program promoted greater acceptance of different body shapes and helped children learn not to tease each other about their weight. Longitudinal studies are now needed to see whether such programs can prevent eating disorders or, at least, delay their onset. To be most effective, however, prevention efforts will likely require changes in societal attitudes about weight and beauty.

Web Links

www.anad.org (National Association of Anorexia
   Nervosa and Associated Disorders)
www.edauk.com (UK Eating Disorders Association)
www.teenoutreach.com (Website for teens covering a
   broad range of social and mental health issues;
   includes personal stories)

www.eating-disorder.org (Support, concern, and
   resources for eating disorders; includes
   information of specific relevance to teenagers)

12

Child Abuse and Neglect

Dear God,
My father is mean. Please get him not to be. But don't hurt him.
—Sincerely, Martin, in *Children's Letters to God*

Unlike the other conditions discussed in this text, **child abuse** and **neglect** are not psychological disorders but are covered here because they are implicated in the etiology of many of the symptoms and disorders already discussed. For example, child and adolescent maltreatment is linked to disruptive, mood, anxiety, and eating disorders, as well as to numerous other psychological symptoms and conditions.

Even though abuse and neglect can have devastating consequences for their victims—and, in extreme cases, lead to death—we must acknowledge from the outset that abuse and neglect do not always have the same consequences for all victims. Many young people who are abused or neglected, even severely, grow up to lead productive lives. For example, Cicchetti and Rogosch (1997) reported that in a clinical sample of school-age children with a history of maltreatment, 12% made significant developmental strides in spite of their victimization. Obviously, this is not to say that we condone maltreatment in any way or wish to minimize its harmful effects. Like all serious researchers and clinicians who work in this field, we believe that *all* forms of maltreatment—whether they cause lasting harm or not—are wrong and should never be tolerated.

Types of Child Maltreatment

There are four major types of child maltreatment: **physical abuse** (nonaccidental or avoidable acts by a caregiver that lead to the physical harm of a child or adolescent), **sexual abuse** (sexual acts perpetrated by an adult or a much older youth on a child or adolescent), **emotional abuse** (nonaccidental or avoidable acts by a caregiver that are emotionally or psychologically harmful to a child or adolescent), and **neglect** (a caregiver's failure to provide a child or adolescent with a safe environment). To describe neglect with greater precision, some researchers break it down further into **emotional, physical,** and **educational neglect.**

Caregivers and Victims

By definition, abuse and neglect describe the behavior of parents or caregivers (and, in the case of sexual abuse, other adults or older youth), rather than the victims' behavior. In the 1997 report of the National Child Abuse and Neglect Data System, 75% of perpetrators were parents and 10% were other relatives. Only 2% were caregivers such as childcare providers and foster parents. The remaining 13% were classified as non-caregivers or unknown. Over 80% of all perpetrators were under age 40, and over 60% were female. Females were most likely to have been neglectful and males to have been sexually abusive (USDHHS, 1999). Other studies found that stepparents—especially stepfathers—are more likely to be maltreating, and often violent, toward children than biological parents are (Daly & Wilson, 1996).

Regardless of the type of maltreatment they suffer, all victims have three things in common. First, their basic rights are violated, since they are developing in an environment that does not provide adequately for their needs or protect them from harm. Second, they have little choice over the people they live with. Children are brought into a family by one or two parents and have to live in that family unless an outside agency intervenes. Third, because parents and other adults have physical power and authority over them, young people have few effective means of protecting themselves against victimization, especially in childhood and early adolescence. Victimized children cannot simply walk out in search of a home where they will not be beaten, assaulted, or uncared for, physically and emotionally. Quite simply and tragically, they are trapped.

With the exception of sexual abuse, most behaviors implicated in child maltreatment lie on a continuum of normal to abnormal conduct, making it often difficult to determine where appropriate care ends and where abuse or neglect begins. Thus, acts that are classified as abusive or neglectful in their more extreme forms are often observed to a much lesser degree in functional families. For example, a majority of American children are spanked when they misbehave, but only a minority are deliberately hit and bruised. Likewise, many children are sent to bed without supper once or twice by exasperated or overtired parents, but far fewer are deprived of food on a regular basis.

As we will emphasize repeatedly, there is considerable overlap between the different types of maltreatment. For example, it is almost impossible for a parent to abuse a child physically but not emotionally. Similarly, sexually victimized children and adolescents are often physically maltreated also, because of the violation of their bodily integrity and the pain associated with sexual abuse; and they are almost always emo-

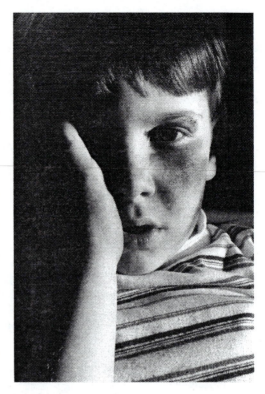

Abused children can rarely run away to escape from victimization.

tionally abused, because of the breach of trust and shame associated with sexual victimization.

Historical Overview

For centuries, children were viewed as the property of their caregivers and afforded very few civil rights (Wekerle & Wolfe, 1996). Consequently, it should come as no surprise to find countless instances of abuse and neglect throughout the history of humankind. We can provide only a few examples here, which we borrow mostly from Breiner (1990).

Early Evidence

The belief that children had no rights was widely shared in the ancient world. In Greece, young boys were often sold to the highest bidder. These youth were first their owners' concubines, or sexual partners, and later became their slaves. In Rome, a father was allowed to kill his children without fear of legal reprisals. Children were treated much the same in Far Eastern societies. In the eleventh century, infanticide was so common in China that the poet Su Shi created a "Save the Children" association. His association brought much-needed help to expectant mothers, in exchange only for the promise that the mothers would not kill their children.

Until recently, abuse and neglect were also rampant throughout Europe, even in societies that prided themselves on their enlightenment. For example, in 1739 a group of aristocratic English women prepared a detailed document about maltreatment for presentation to their government. They wrote: "No expedient [means] has yet been found out for preventing the murder of poor miserable infants at their birth, or suppressing the inhuman custom of exposing newly-born infants to perish in the streets; or the putting of such unhappy foundlings [orphans] to wicked and barbarous nurses, who undertake to bring them up for a small and trifling sum of money, do often suffer them to starve for want of due sustenance or care, or if permitted to live . . . turn them into the streets to beg or steal" (Hyde, 1986, p. 46).

Maltreatment in Early American Society

The New World was not exempt from cruelty toward children. Puritan settlers in America strongly believed that "sparing the rod would spoil the child" and often acted accordingly with religious zeal. Puritan values also made it very difficult for social and governmental agencies to intervene in the lives of maltreated children, because such intervention was seen as interference in family affairs. This perspective was seriously challenged for the first time in the second half of the nineteenth century, when in 1874 Mary Ellen Wilson became a tragic "poster child" for the early child welfare movement (see Box 12.1). Mary Ellen's plight drew the attention of enough concerned citizens that in 1885 the Society for Prevention of Cruelty to Children was formed to protect children from maltreatment. Although children still continued to be severely beaten, made to work long hours, or deprived of food as a form of punishment, the society was able to protect some

---

BOX 12.1 • *Mary Ellen Wilson and the Start of the Child Welfare Movement in the United States*

Costin, Karger, and Stoesz (1996) recount the story of Mary Ellen Wilson, an abused child who played an important role in the start of the child welfare movement in the United States.

While on her "errands of mercy," Mrs. Etta Angell Wheeler, variously termed a mission worker, a tenement visitor, and a social worker, was told of a child named Mary Ellen who frequently was left locked in an apartment by herself and at other times was cruelly beaten and mistreated by her caretakers, Mary and Francis Connolly. . . . Mrs. Wheeler tried to gain entrance to the Connollys' apartment. . . . Although her visit was very short, Mrs. Wheeler was able to see Mary Ellen, a pale, thin child the size of a five-year-old, although it was later established that she was nine. It was a bitterly cold December day, yet the barefoot child wore only a thin, tattered dress over one other ragged garment. A whip lay on a table, and the child's arms and legs bore many marks of its use. The saddest aspect, Mrs. Wheeler reported, was written on the child's face, the face of an unloved child who knew only misery and the fearsome side of life.

For several months, Mrs. Wheeler tried to find some means to have the child removed from the clutches of her foster parents, who, as the story was told, beat her with a whip of twisted leather thongs until her diminutive body was a mass of cuts and bruises. Mrs. Wheeler . . . sought the help of powerful charitable organizations and law enforcement officers. She met rebuffs at every turn. She was told that it was dangerous to interfere with parent and child and to leave it alone. Etta Wheeler was tempted to apply to the Society for the Prevention of Cruelty to Animals, but was reluctant to do what seemed to her incongruous. However, according to legend, when her niece suggested she go to Henry Bergh, the president of the animal society, since

(continued)

BOX 12.1 • Continued

the child was a "little animal surely," Mrs. Wheeler agreed. Within an hour she had presented her story of the wretched conditions under which Mary Ellen was living to Mr. Bergh. The legend continues with Mr. Bergh responding at once: "The child is an animal. If there is no justice for it as a human being, it shall at least have the right of the cur in the street. . . . It shall not be abused" (pp. 52–53).

Mary Ellen's tragic story is often seen as the beginning of the child welfare movement in the United States. However, social advocates had been calling for years for effective steps to protect children from abuse. For example, in 1867—seven years before Mary Ellen came to the public's attention—a *Home Journal* writer noted that "miserable children (animals we might call them) should be offered the same protection afforded to animals with the advent of the Society for the Prevention of Cruelty to Animals" (cited in Costin et al., 1996, p. 54).

So why does the case of Mary Ellen stand as a landmark in the history of child abuse? Costin and associates speculate that she became famous for three converging reasons. First, her case received considerable press coverage. Second, by 1874 the public was ripe for an investigation into child welfare. It was well known then that many children—often orphans—were bought and sold into cruel jobs, in which they were exploited and, at times, worked to death. Thus, the entire issue of how orphans and other unfortunate children were placed was attracting increasing public and political concern. Finally, the child welfare movement did not develop in isolation. The growing women's movement was focusing interest not only on the rights of women but also on other powerless members of society, as was the movement to protect animals from cruelty—making it almost impossible to ignore the plight of abused and neglected children.

---

of them and to challenge the belief that children could be considered—and treated—as their parents' or guardians' property.

Sexual Abuse and Early Psychiatry

In the second half of the nineteenth century, sexual abuse likewise became the focus of considerable attention in Europe. In 1886, Sigmund Freud proposed a controversial theory: he hypothesized that the psychological symptoms of some of his adult female patients were the result of childhood sexual victimization (Freud, 1886/1989). This theory was based on an observation commonly made by clinicians—namely, that women who seek therapy for a variety of psychological disorders often report that they were sexually abused as children. Freud's theory served initially to confront the medical profession with the reality of childhood sexual abuse and prompted debate on a highly sensitive topic that had been ignored in all segments of society. However, debate was soon squashed amid mounting cries of indignation, even outrage, at the theory's implications. Quite simply, the medical community of the time could not accept a fellow pro-

fessional's suggestion that respectable citizens, including some of their own colleagues, might be abusing their female children by fondling them or having incestuous intercourse with them.

The rejection of his theory forced Freud to change his position on childhood sexual abuse. Thirty years later, he no longer argued that some of his patients' psychological symptoms were the result of sexual victimization. Instead, he claimed that the victimization these women reported was a product of their imagination. Without any empirical evidence, Freud now said that most children fantasized about sexual encounters with their parents and often desired them unconsciously. And thus, when female patients reported having been victimized as children, they were actually recalling their most intimate fantasies rather than historical events (Olafson, Corwin, & Summit, 1993). Freud's stark reversal undoubtedly caused immeasurable harm to many victims of sexual abuse.

Throughout the first half of the twentieth century, psychoanalytically oriented clinicians pushed Freudian claims to extremes, stating that sexual abuse was generally harmless and in some cases actually beneficial to children, since it enabled them to explore their sexual fantasies in the "safety" of their home environment. For example, in 1937 Bender and Blau concluded: "The experience of the child in its sex relationship with adults does not seem always to have a traumatic effect. . . . The experience offers the opportunity for the child to test out in reality an infantile fantasy; it probably finds the consequences less severe, and in fact actually gratifying to a pleasure sense. . . . There was evidence that the child derived some emotional satisfaction from the experience" (pp. 516–517).

The Battered Child Syndrome

Current views about child abuse and neglect have gained ground only recently in the United States and other Western societies. It was only in 1962 that C. Henry Kempe and his colleagues published a now-classic article in which they exposed the reality of physical abuse in America (Kempe, Silverman, Steele, Droegenmueller, & Silver, 1962). Entitled "The Battered Child Syndrome," this article reported the results of a survey of seventy-one hospitals in which children had received treatment for serious injuries. The survey identified 302 victims of nonaccidental injuries—injuries that either did not match the accidents reported by the children's caregivers or that the caregivers admitted having inflicted themselves. Of these 302 victims, 11% had died and 28% suffered permanent brain damage. This study contributed to major changes in American attitudes about abuse and neglect by (1) showing that some caregivers were capable of harming their children deliberately and did so quite frequently; (2) challenging the age-old assumption that parents were essentially free to discipline their children as they saw fit; and (3) prompting calls for legislation to protect children from maltreatment.

In 1974, the U.S. Congress passed the Child Abuse Prevention and Treatment Act and funded a National Center on Abuse and Neglect. This groundbreaking legislation required all persons who come in contact with children—such as teachers, doctors, psychologists, school bus drivers, nurses, and others—to report any suspected cases of child maltreatment. The act also recognized for the first time that children had the fundamental right to have their basic developmental needs fulfilled and, by implication, that parents or other caregivers could not mistreat them without fear of legal sanctions (Wekerle & Wolfe, 1996).

Since the 1970s, other child abuse and neglect legislation has been passed by federal, state, and provincial legislatures throughout North America, and agencies have been set up to investigate alleged cases of maltreatment. Public and private agencies also sponsor programs designed to prevent abuse and neglect, and to teach children that maltreatment is not something to be silent about. Andrew's inability to look after his daughter's basic needs provides an example of a case that warranted investigation and intervention by a state agency in charge of protecting children from maltreatment.

Andrew is 31 when he comes to our clinic for help with severe depression and anxiety. He is a single parent. His wife left him a few months earlier. Since that time, Andrew has had difficulty sleeping at night. He usually falls asleep around 3 A.M. and does not wake up until noon the next day. When he sleeps, his 4-year-old daughter, Mary, is left to fend for herself. Mary has learned to turn on the television, to get her own breakfast, and to sit on her potty-seat to go to the bathroom.

In our first interview with Andrew, we learn that he lost his job three weeks earlier, because he is overwhelmed by distress and agitation and unable to meet his work responsibilities. He has no help from family or friends, no savings, and often no food in the house for himself or his daughter. He has not contacted any public or charitable agency to help him obtain food or childcare, but has gone out a few times to look for a job, each time leaving Mary alone at home, asking her "to be good."

Because of mandatory reporting laws, this sad situation was reported to the local **Child Protective Services** (CPS) agency. (CPS is charged with protecting children from abuse and neglect by investigating cases of possible maltreatment and, if necessary, arranging placements for these children outside the home.) The agency helped the family receive the services they needed, so that Mary would no longer be neglected.

Definitions, Diagnostic Criteria, and Major Characteristics

Defining Abuse

Unlike most of the psychological disorders covered in this text, child abuse and neglect were defined not by mental health professionals but by politicians and child welfare advocates to establish and protect some of the fundamental legal rights of minors. In the words of the 1988 Child Abuse Prevention and Treatment Act:

> The term "child abuse and neglect" means the physical or mental injury, sexual abuse or exploitation, negligent treatment, or maltreatment of a child under the age of eighteen, or the age specified by the child protection law of the State in question, by a person (including an employee of a residential facility or any staff person providing out-of-home care) who is responsible for the child's welfare under circumstances which indicate that the child's health or welfare is harmed or threatened thereby, as determined in accordance with regulations prescribed by the Secretary. . . .

As you can see, the legislation provides only broad guidelines to establish working definitions of child abuse and neglect. In practice, mental health professionals, lawyers, and researchers generally agree that maltreatment occurs whenever a minor is seriously harmed or endangered as a result of avoidable, nonaccidental acts of *omission* or *commission* on the part of a parent or other caregiver. This means that abuse or neglect takes place whenever an adult responsible for the child's welfare either fails to protect the child from actual or potential harm or acts in harmful ways toward the child. Acts of omission include a failure to obtain necessary medical care or to ensure that a young child is not left alone; acts of commission include such behavior as beating a child or exposing a child to sexual exploitation.

Maltreatment is difficult to define with precision for a number of reasons.

1. *Determination of abuse or neglect is rarely clear-cut.* Most cases of alleged child maltreatment

that come to the attention of authorities are not so blatant as to make the determination of abuse or neglect self-evident. The same acts of omission or commission may be considered unacceptable by one person but not by another, or deemed abusive or neglectful according to the rules of one governmental agency but not another. For example, most Americans would consider nonaccidental bone fractures or burns as abusive acts. However, little consensus would be found in describing spanking in similar terms.

Definitional issues are particularly challenging in the area of emotional abuse. Is it abusive to lock a child in a closet for hours to punish her for her "stupidity" because she received two Bs on her report card? Is it abusive to expose young siblings to repeated marital conflicts, in which their father belittles their mother on an almost daily basis, and occasionally hits her in fits of rage? Would you report any of these family situations to the authorities?

Problems of definition arise also in the areas of sexual abuse and of neglect. For example, can sexual abuse occur in the absence of physical contact between perpetrator and victim? Would you consider parents who watch pornographic videos and read pornographic magazines when their children are around to be abusive to them? Similarly, most Americans would consider parents who leave young children home alone for long hours to be negligent. However, the same may not be true for parents who refuse to vaccinate their children for religious or other reasons—even though a preventable disease contracted for lack of vaccination may have more harmful effects on a child than inadequate parental supervision.

2. *Abuse and neglect rarely occur in isolation.* Definitional issues are also complicated by the fact that few children are victims of "pure" abuse or neglect. In other words, few children suffer from only one or two isolated acts that can be clearly classified as physical abuse, sexual abuse, emotional abuse, or neglect (US-DHHS, 1996). Instead, most youth experience multiple forms of victimization.

3. *Abuse and neglect must always be considered in a developmental context.* Further definitional difficulties arise from the developmental context in which abuse or neglect takes place. What may be considered abusive or neglectful at one stage of development may not be at another. Most people would agree that 4-year-olds who, like Mary, are left to fend for themselves at home are being severely neglected. However, there would be less agreement in the case of 8- to 10-year-olds. Every day, countless American children return from school to an empty house, where they may be exposed to a variety of dangers. Are they equally as neglected as Mary was? They might be if they are regularly exposed to violent videogames, drug trafficking, or sexual exploitation on the part of older siblings or neighbors—although the determination of danger will vary considerably from one community context to another.

The role of development is particularly evident in the determination of maltreatment in adolescence, when a distinction between perpetrators and victims is not always clear-cut. First, many cases of abuse begin then, rather than in infancy or childhood, probably because key characteristics of adolescence—such as the tendency to rebel against parental authority—often provoke or aggravate family conflicts, leading some caregivers to resort to abuse in failed attempts to solve them (Kaplan, Pelcovitz, & Labruna, 1999). It can therefore be difficult to distinguish clearly between parental actions taken to curb adolescent rebellion or provocation, and abusive practices labeled by parents as necessary discipline. Second, adolescent abuse differs from abuse at earlier stages of development because teenagers are generally better able to resist their aggressors and even to initiate violence with family members. In fact, as many as 25% of cases of abuse in adolescence may follow an adolescent's alleged attack on a parent (Kaplan, Pelcovitz, & Weiner, 1994). Researchers and interventionists working for CPS agencies are often acutely aware that this issue can make judges hesitant to rule in favor of adolescents in abuse cases, unless victimization is severe and unmistakable. Tom's case illustrates this situation.

Tom was 14 when he was evaluated at our clinic. He had been removed from home following numerous incidents of what CPS and school officials labeled as abusive parenting. For example, he had been regularly beaten by his father in violent fistfights for disobeying house rules and for minor delinquency. However, the judge who heard the case refused to label it as abuse, explaining that Tom had such a "bad attitude" and was so disruptive at home that he provoked his own abuse as much as he was a victim of it. The judge ordered the family to undergo counseling and returned the adolescent to his parents' care.

Physical Abuse

Physical abuse consists of acts that "include scalding, beatings with an object, severe physical punishment, slapping, punching, and kicking" (Wekerle & Wolfe, 1996, p. 496). Physical abuse also includes acts such as pushing and shoving, especially when they cause injury, and deliberate exposure of a child or adolescent to harm or danger. For example, a caregiver who intentionally gives wheat to a child who has a severe allergy to this food would be considered physically abusive. The following case, reported by a member of the American Professional Society on the Abuse of Children, illustrates a clear-cut case of physical abuse:

The head nurse in the emergency room called me in for a consult when an x-ray of a two-month-old baby showed a leg fracture which the parents could not explain. My first steps were to order a skeletal survey and to call in the hospital social worker who had expertise in child abuse and neglect.

While the parents gave the social worker evasive and contradictory accounts of the cause of the presenting injury, I discovered 17 rib fractures in various stages of healing, and other unexplained fractures as well. When I presented this information to the parents, the mother asked to speak to the social worker alone. She disclosed ongoing abuse of the child by the father, and fear for her own safety as well. . . .

We immediately called in law enforcement and child protection services. Under expert interrogation by the officer, the father confessed. He was arrested and convicted. CPS stayed involved with the mother and child, who are together and doing pretty well now. Mom's getting some parenting instruction and is in a counseling group for victims of domestic violence. The baby's growing normally (American

Professional Society on the Abuse of Children, 1999, http://www.apsac.org).

Sexual Abuse

Sexual abuse consists of sexual contact between a child or adolescent and someone who is in a position of power because of age, physical size, or position of authority, or sexual exploitation of a child or adolescent by such a person (Briere, 1992; Wekerle & Wolfe, 1996). Sexual contact includes sexual touching or fondling, vaginal or anal intercourse, and other sexual acts, including having a minor perform any of these acts on the abuser. Sexual exploitation consists of exposure to or involvement in indecent acts (e.g., sexual rituals), child pornography, and child prostitution. Of all sexually abused children in the United States, approximately half are genitally molested (i.e., contact without penetration); another 32% suffer from oral, anal, or vaginal penetration or intercourse; and the balance are subjected to unknown or other forms of sexual abuse (e.g., breast fondling) (U.S. Department of Health and Human Services, 1988).

Sexual abuse of children and adolescents is sadly very common. Lisa was sexually abused by her stepfather for years—first the victim of inappropriate "cuddles" and, over time, of repeated sexual acts culminating in **incest** at gunpoint. Although incest is defined as sexual intercourse between close relatives, the term is commonly used in the child abuse area to describe sexual relations between a female child and a father or father figure.

Lisa was 16. She was brought to our clinic for a court-ordered psychological evaluation after she had been removed from home a few days earlier and placed in the custody of the Department of Human Services.

Lisa was a tall, attractive adolescent with short, blonde hair. She was well dressed, wearing carefully pressed jeans and a bright T-shirt and appropriate makeup. However, she had a distant look of sadness in her eyes. She chose to sit in the only armchair that had its back against a wall, feet off the floor, with her arms around her knees as if to protect herself.

Lisa had told her story to several people before and, with unusual candor, proceeded to tell it again.

She had been removed from her stepfather's custody because she had confided in her school counselor that he had abused her physically and sexually. She explained that she was an illegitimate child and that she met the man she called her father for the first time when she was 9. He had a daughter already, Kim, a year younger than Lisa, of whom he had obtained custody following divorce from his first wife. . . .

In a flat, distant tone of voice, Lisa described several incidents in which her father attacked her mother, apparently quite viciously. On one occasion her mother received severe blows to the head and was hospitalized for several days.

"It's when she was in hospital that he started messing up with me and Kim. . . . At the beginning, it was hardly nothing, like he made us sit on his knees and kissed us on the lips, but quickly it got worse. . . . He had all these dirty movies, you know, and he would make us watch them with him and then he'd take us upstairs and he'd make us take our clothes off and . . . we had to do all the things in those horrible movies."

Lisa's voice and posture changed rapidly as she began to talk about four years of abuse. She was now sitting in a tight fetal position, her face hidden in her knees and her arms wrapped around her ankles. Crying, shaking with fear, often choking on her words, Lisa went on to describe a terrifying progression in the abuse she and her sister suffered, from inappropriate kissing to fondling to forced oral sex and intercourse, not to mention regular, violent beatings with a switch (i.e., a thin, flexible branch).

"When my mom came back from the hospital, he would wait when she wasn't in the house to do it and that was easy 'cause she was never around, she was so scared of him. . . . And later he started to take us away in his car, always the two of us. He'd drive to some place in the country where there's no people, and he'd make us get in the back seat and take our clothes off to have sex with us. . . . He always left a gun and a knife on the dashboard so there was nothing we could do, like we couldn't run away. . . . So he was always able to get what he wanted. . . ."

With Lisa and her sister's full agreement, a judge ordered that they be placed in a group home until age 18 and, a few months later, terminated all parental rights.

Emotional Abuse

If the definitions of physical and sexual abuse are far from clear-cut, the definitional boundaries of emotional abuse are even more difficult to specify, because the parenting behaviors that constitute emotional abuse are not discrete acts that can be assessed in a straightforward manner. Briere (1992) described eight types of parenting behaviors that are indicative of emotional abuse.

- *Rejecting:* The child is avoided or pushed away; he or she is made to feel unworthy, unacceptable, and the like.
- *Degrading/devaluing:* The child is criticized, stigmatized, deprived of dignity, humiliated, made to feel inferior, and so on.
- *Terrorizing:* The child is verbally assaulted, frightened, threatened with physical or psychological harm.
- *Isolating:* The child is deprived of social contacts beyond the family, not allowed friends, kept in limited areas for long periods of time without social interaction.
- *Corrupting:* The child is "mis-socialized" . . . taught to behave in an antisocial manner, encouraged to develop socially unacceptable interests and appetites.
- *Exploiting:* The child is taken advantage of, used to meet the needs of his or her caregivers.
- *Denying essential stimulation, emotional responsiveness, or availability:* The child is deprived of loving, sensitive caregiving; his or her emotional development is stifled; the child is generally ignored or neglected.
- *Unreliable and inconsistent parenting:* Contradictory and ambivalent demands are made of the child, parental support or caregiving is inconsistent and unreliable, and family stability is denied the child (pp. 9–10).

This long list highlights the heterogeneity of the parenting behaviors that are indicative of emotional abuse, as well as the overlap between this form of abuse and neglect. Professionals in the field usually differentiate between emotional abuse and neglect by focusing on the caregiver's attitude toward the child, although this differentiation is never simple. Emotionally abusive caregivers actively reject their children or refuse to care for their emotional needs, whereas neglectful caregivers are more passive, often ignoring their children's basic needs rather than deliberately failing to provide for them. Marlene's story illustrates some of the harm that emotional abuse can cause.

Marlene is an 11-year-old girl referred to our clinic by her teacher, who reports that she is depressed and withdrawn at school. Marlene attends a special education classroom because of poor academic and social functioning. When asked to discuss any of these difficulties or to talk about life at home, she often hides her face in her hands or giggles nervously until the question is withdrawn.

Marlene is the oldest of four children. Her mother is disabled and has been confined to her house since Marlene was 5. For as long as she can remember, Marlene has been in charge of her younger siblings' care. She takes care also of cooking and cleaning for the family. Because of her mother's multiple problems, Marlene is never allowed to play or to have friends over, and must go home immediately after school to help care for her family. Her mother does not see any need for Marlene to be involved in after-school activities, explaining that even if these might be good for her she would not "deserve" them. Her teacher is able to get Marlene involved in some activities with other children from time to time, but only by talking with her mother weeks in advance and insisting repeatedly on the child's behalf.

Marlene describes her mother as "cranky." She gives examples to illustrate how she is treated at home, such as: "All the kids in my class they get presents at Christmas. My mother she always says like if I don't do something I will not get anything at Christmas or for my birthday. . . . Last Christmas, only my aunt gave me a present, she didn't." Home observations of the family confirm Marlene's report. Her mother rarely speaks to the children in a normal tone of voice and displays no affection toward them. Rather, she speaks harshly or yells at them in short phrases, often accompanied by obscenities or belittling comments. When asked in the course of the first home observation to describe Marlene, her mother says angrily that she is "lazy, just like her father" and proceeds to criticize her husband and children at length. She calls her daughter "stupid" in her presence and complains bitterly that "with her around, nothing much gets done around the house." She is not more positive about her other children and tells the therapist defiantly that "One of the best times in my life was when the lot of them were gone to a camp last summer; now that's the truth!"

Marlene and her siblings are eventually removed from home and placed in foster care because of their mother's illness and abusive behavior.

Neglect

As noted earlier, neglect stems from a parent or guardian's passive maltreatment of a child—from failure to ensure the child's safety and to meet the child's basic physical, emotional, and educational needs (U.S. Department of Health and Human Services, 1996). Many professionals make a distinction between physical, emotional, and educational neglect, although these three forms of neglect overlap considerably.

Physical Neglect.   As its name implies, physical neglect results from a parent or guardian's failure to provide the child with adequate shelter, food, clothing, hygiene, and/or medical care. Physical neglect also includes grossly inadequate supervision and abandonment. Mike's case illustrates this form of neglect and the important fact that it is very often associated with poverty.

Mike is brought to our clinic after his third arrest. He is 13. He is the second-oldest child in a family of six children who live with their mother. The children have four different fathers, none of whom lives with or supports the family at the time of the referral. Mike does not know his father and states categorically that he does not want to know "the jerk." Mike's mother is a bartender. She works six nights a week, explaining that she can make more money in a bar than in any other day job for which she may be qualified. Her schedule means that she sleeps during the day. On most days, she is asleep when her children have to leave for school and only sees them briefly in the afternoon—if they return from school before she has to go to work, some-

thing that Mike rarely does. The family lives in a run-down trailer park where crime is rampant. Like many other families in the neighborhood, Mike's family is very poor.

Mike was arrested two weeks earlier in an aborted burglary attempt. During his first visit to the clinic, he explains matter-of-factly that he needed money to buy clothes because the ones he has are too small or worn through. A quick glance at his attire supports his claim. His pants are torn and too short for his age, and he is wearing a dirty T-shirt, which provides inadequate protection against the cold weather of late fall. Although his mother denies that his need for clothes was the actual motive for her son's crime, she acknowledges that for some time she has been unable to provide her children with adequate clothing. She also admits that, because of her work hours, Mike is often unsupervised. She knows that he is regularly truant and that, in the evenings, he spends long hours roaming the streets or sleeps at his girlfriend's house. However, she explains that her current situation prevents her from working less than she does. She offers no alternative to provide adequate care for her children. "What do you want me to do?"

Emotional Neglect.   This form of neglect includes "inadequate nurturance or affection, chronic or extreme domestic violence in the child's presence, knowingly permitting drug or alcohol abuse or other maladaptive behavior, failure to seek needed treatment for an emotional or behavioral problem, and other inattention to the child's developmental and emotional needs" (USDHHS, 1996, p. 3–9). Emotional neglect is more difficult to define than almost all other forms of maltreatment, because the harm inflicted on the child leaves no obvious marks, such as bruises, and no easily observable signs, such as inadequate clothing. The following case highlights this issue and illustrates the central role played by social expectations and value judgments in the determination of emotional neglect.

Ken is 5. He attends a rural Head Start program. He is referred to us by the mental health coordinator of the program, following several aggressive outbursts at school. According to his teacher and teacher aide, Ken attempts almost every day to wrestle other boys to the ground and beats them, at times severely, in the process. His teacher explains that "Ken lives in a world of wrestle mania. He spends hours at home watching wrestling on television with his father and older brother, and thinks nothing of attacking other kids and beating them up, screaming like a mad man. The trouble is that he doesn't know the difference between a fake fight and a real one."

Ken's mother participates very reluctantly in the psychological evaluation requested by the school in order for her son to be allowed to remain in the program. This evaluation shows that Ken has severe aggressive behavior problems at school and at home, and points to important verbal deficits and possible hearing difficulties. In addition, Ken's mother reveals in the course of this evaluation that her husband is very abusive toward her—but not toward their children. She describes herself as a victim of chronic domestic violence and reports that her two boys witness their parents fighting "at least once a week." Steps are immediately taken to put her in contact with a domestic violence counselor and to provide her with practical means to ensure her own and the children's safety. Recommendations are also made to address Ken's behavior problems, to have his hearing checked, and to have him evaluated by a speech therapist.

The family does not return to the clinic for their second appointment. When Ken's mother is reached by phone, she evasively reports that everything is "fine." She adds that she and her husband have decided to withdraw Ken from Head Start and that they may or may not follow up on the clinic's recommendations, such as having Ken's hearing tested. Steps are taken to alert the local CPS agency. An agency worker makes a visit to the home but decides that there is not enough evidence to conclude that Ken is emotionally neglected. Specifically, Ken's mother denies any problem at home and refuses to acknowledge that she is a victim of domestic violence.

This outcome may surprise and even anger you. It illustrates some of the difficulties faced by CPS workers who are called to investigate allegations of emotional neglect. To be deemed neglectful, a parental action or inaction must cause serious, lasting harm to a child, or have a strong likelihood of causing such harm

in the future. However, the caseworker's investigation showed that the children were adequately cared for and concluded that the parents' decision not to follow up on our recommendations amounted to an unfortunate, but not to a neglectful, decision on their part.

Educational Neglect.   Educational neglect is the most commonly reported form of neglect, probably in part because it is the easiest one to define. Educational neglect occurs whenever a parent or caregiver fails to take steps for a child to attend school, by not registering the child for class, not getting the child up to go to school, or allowing the child to remain out of school for no valid reason. Kathy's story illustrates this form of neglect.

Kathy was 10 when she was evaluated at our clinic. She was in fourth grade but had missed a lot of schooling ever since she began grade 1. Kathy's mother called the school regularly to say that her daughter was sick. For the first three years, school officials thought little of these absences, except to note that Kathy never seemed sick or in poor health at school. In fourth grade, growing academic delays and several comments made by the child about her mother being ill led school officials to investigate the situation.

A court-ordered evaluation of Kathy's home life indicated that her absences were not illness-related. She stayed home as many as eight to ten days a month to care for her younger brother, to clean, and to cook when her mother, who suffered from chronic depression, was too ill to get out of bed. Kathy was put in her father's custody, thus enabling her to attend school on a regular basis for the first time in her life.

Diagnostic Criteria

The DSM-IV-TR does not provide criteria to diagnose the different forms of maltreatment and to differentiate among them. Maltreatment is mentioned only in an appendix labeled *Other Conditions That May Be a Focus of Clinical Attention.* This appendix lists three categories of child maltreatment: *physical abuse of child, sexual abuse of child,* and *neglect of child,* which "should be used when the focus of clinical attention is severe mistreatment of an individual by another through physical abuse, sexual abuse, and child neglect" (American Psychiatric Association, 2000a, p. 738). No definition or explanation of these terms is offered. As Box 12.2 shows, the DSM-IV-TR defines disorders in which child abuse is central, such as **factitious disorder by proxy** (also known as **Munchhausen's syndrome by proxy**) and **pedophilia.** However, focus in these conditions is on the abusers rather than on their victims.

BOX 12.2 • *Child Maltreatment in the DSM-IV-TR*

Some forms of child maltreatment are described in detail in the DSM-IV-TR. However, the focus of these descriptions is on the abuser rather than on the child victim. For example, the DSM-IV-TR describes **factitious disorder by proxy,** a condition in which a caregiver provokes or falsely reports physical or (more rarely) mental illness in a child in order to get the attention of medical or mental health professionals (APA, 2000a). For example, the perpetrator—who is typically the mother of a young child—may deliberately give the child something poisonous to eat, such as feces-tainted food. Later, she will deny any knowledge of the cause of the child's illness when the child has to be taken to an emergency room. This bizarre adult disorder was thought for a long time to be a very rare form of child abuse. However, more recent research suggests that many parents may deliberately induce or falsely report symptoms in their children. Factitious disorder by proxy is one of the least understood forms of child abuse. It is difficult to detect and confirm, and probably often goes unrecognized, in large part because most professionals find it inconceivable that a parent would deliberately induce or misreport illness in a child (Siegel & Fischer, 2001). Marguerite's abusive care of her son illustrates this complex disorder.

> Marguerite came to our attention during an evaluation that was conducted after she had asked for her estranged husband's visitation rights to be terminated. The request was based on her concern that he was mistreating her son, in that each time the boy visited his father he came home sick. Marguerite felt that her ex-husband was neglecting the child to the point of making him ill. Over time, her son's after-visitation illnesses had become worse and had even resulted in hospitalization.
>
> The court-ordered assessment of both parents' treatment of the child revealed the actual cause of the boy's illness. Prior to each visit, Marguerite exposed the child to foods that he was severely allergic to. On the morning of the visit, she would feed her son with these contaminants and then send him to his father's house to become sick. Over time, the boy's allergic reactions had become increasingly severe, and the medical staff involved in his care felt that his condition could have become life-threatening if it had gone undetected for much longer.

Pedophilia is another disorder listed in the DSM-IV-TR in which focus is on the abuser rather than on the child victim. Individuals with pedophilia are mostly males (older adolescents or adults) who find gratification in sexual activities with children who have not reached puberty. Harry's case highlights the behaviors associated with pedophilia and shows that the activities in which pedophiles engage amount to child sexual abuse.

> Harry is a 42-year-old man serving his second prison term for child molestation. He has been married for fourteen years and has two teenage children. He describes his marriage as good, except for the strain of his being in prison. Harry's first offense occurred ten years ago, while he was serving as a minister in a local church. He reports that he had fondled the genitals of a 4-year-old parishioner and incited her to stroke his penis. Harry maintains that this incident occurred on only one occasion, but in several statements obtained at the time the child insisted that it had happened many times.
>
> Harry's second offense occurred shortly after he was released from his first prison stay. He reportedly incited a neighborhood girl (age 6) to pull up her skirt and take down her underwear so that he could take a picture. In addition, Harry reportedly showed the child's brother (age 8) a pornography magazine while he masturbated himself in the boy's presence. According to the police report, Harry had spent a considerable amount of time with the children before these incidents and had invited them to his house when their parents were out. Harry maintains that these were isolated incidents, something which the victims both confirmed at the time. Harry denies ever sexually abusing his own children.

Empirical Validity

There is no doubt that child abuse and neglect are widespread, and that they are associated with severe and, in many cases, chronic psychological disorders. However, questions of validity arise because the different forms of abuse and neglect overlap, and because the distinctions made among them are essentially descriptive (rather than predictive) in nature. For example, the distinction between physical and emotional abuse is intuitively meaningful. But these two forms of maltreatment co-occur in countless cases, calling into question the empirical validity of physical and emotional abuse as distinct conditions. This is also true of the different forms of neglect. In other words, although many children and adolescents are victims of different forms of abuse and/or neglect, it is not clear that different forms of maltreatment predict distinct patterns of development in child and adolescent victims; therefore, the empirical validity of the descriptive distinctions commonly made in this area today is called into question (Wekerle & Wolfe, 1996). We will return to this point later (see Developmental Trajectories and Prognosis).

Empirical validity issues arise also from the lack of clear distinctions between inadequate parenting and maltreatment. For example, is a parent who hits a child a harsh disciplinarian or an abuser? Is there a difference between a slap with an open hand on the child's bottom and a blow with a closed fist on the child's face, and if so, why? Similarly, is a parent who, for religious reasons, refuses permission for a child to receive customary medical care acting in a neglectful or abusive manner? Should a distinction be made between parents who refuse to immunize their children and parents who withhold permission for necessary medical intervention, such as surgery or blood transfusion; and, if so, again why? These questions illustrate some of the issues that mental health professionals, CPS workers, judges, and child advocates struggle with every day, because they do not have answers that everyone can agree on. Even adults who were abused as children do not necessarily report that they were maltreated (see Box 12.3, p. 348).

Finally, like all disorders covered in this book, abuse and neglect are always defined within a cultural context. As mentioned, not long ago many American psychologists and psychiatrists believed that, in certain circumstances, sexual abuse was beneficial to children. A similar belief is still deeply rooted in parts of Africa, where it is common for female children to undergo a **clitoradectomy** when they reach puberty. This surgical procedure involves the removal of the young girl's clitoris, a part of the sexual organs that is extremely sensitive to stimulation. Cultures that promote the procedure justify it as an essential, celebrated rite of passage into womanhood. In Western cultures, however, the same procedure is seen as culturally sanctioned genital mutilation by parents and other community members who are knowingly and willingly abusing helpless female children.

Associated Characteristics

Medical Conditions

Many maltreated children suffer from a variety of medical conditions. These can range from relatively benign problems (e.g., hair lice resulting from neglectful care; respiratory infections from failure to give the child proper medical attention when needed), to serious diseases and malnutrition (e.g., syphilis and diseases transmitted by sexual abuse; see also Box 12.4, p. 349), to chronic disabilities (e.g., permanent hearing loss caused by repeated blows on the head; severe mental retardation from violent shaking in infancy), to life-threatening injuries (e.g., damage to one or more internal organs from violent blows), to murder. Similarly, neglect can aggravate serious but otherwise treatable conditions, such as asthma or diabetes.

As Chapter 10 indicates, posttraumatic stress disorder (PTSD) secondary to childhood physical and sexual abuse is associated with permanent changes in the hippocampus, a brain structure involved in learning, memory, and emotion regulation. More generally, abuse puts children at risk for later psychological disorders, such as major depression, partly because of the adverse effects of early trauma on brain development (Kaufman, Plotsky, Nemeroff, & Charney, 2000).

Psychological Symptoms and Disorders

Maltreatment is also associated with a variety of psychological symptoms and disorders, although the

BOX 12.3 • *Was I Abused or Not?*

Many abuse victims do not think of themselves as having suffered from abuse. In one study, researchers questioned more than 11,000 college undergraduates over a ten-year period about the punishment they received from early childhood through adolescence (Knutson & Selner, 1994). Participants were asked to state how many times they had been subjected to various forms of physical punishment, ranging from no physical punishment at all, to spanking, punching, kicking, choking, and being struck by objects. In addition, participants were asked which punishment, if any, had resulted in physical injuries.

More than 80% of the young adults who took part in this study reported that they had received some form of physical discipline as they grew up. More alarmingly,

34% of men and 27% of women reported that their parents had struck them with objects to discipline them, and 24% of men and 19% of women said that they had been physically injured as a result of parental discipline. However, few participants said they had been abused. As the accompanying figure shows, only slightly over half of the men and women who reported being injured three or more times in discipline encounters labeled themselves as victims of physical abuse. These findings highlight how difficult it is to define maltreatment in general, and physical abuse in particular, in part because persons who may have been maltreated in the past or who are still being maltreated may not see themselves as victims.

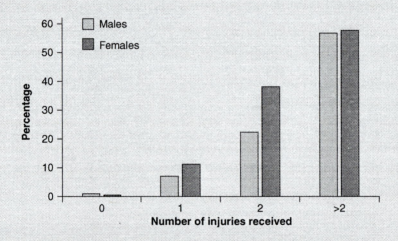

Source: Figure from J. F. Knutson and M. B. Selner, "Punitive Childhood Experiences Reported by Young Adults over a 10-Year Period." *Child Abuse and Neglect 18* (1994), p. 164. Copyright 1994 by Elsevier Science. Reprinted by permission.

actual problems observed in specific cases vary greatly, even in children who are victims of similar forms of abuse or neglect. In the words of an uncompromising critic of human violence: "Chronic childhood abuse takes place in a familial climate of pervasive terror, in which ordinary caretaking relationships have been profoundly disrupted. . . . The child trapped in an abusive environment . . . must find a way to preserve a sense of trust in people who are untrustworthy, safety in a situ-

ation that is unsafe, control in a situation that is terrifyingly unpredictable, power in a situation of helplessness" (Herman, 1992, pp. 98, 96).

The psychological symptoms and disorders that maltreated children develop often stem as much from these unsolvable dilemmas as from the abuse or neglect. Like other children, victims of maltreatment love their families and want, in turn, to be accepted and loved by them. Consequently, they are torn between

BOX 12.4 • *Failure to Thrive and Maltreatment*

In the DSM-IV-TR, failure to thrive (FTT) is described as a feeding disorder of infancy or early childhood. Children with this condition fail to gain weight and to reach important developmental milestones in early life. FTT can be caused by undiagnosed medical conditions, such as food allergies; by conflictual parent-child interactions, especially concerning eating; or by maltreatment. In the United States, malnutrition and undernutrition account for a large number of pediatric visits in low-income families; and 1–5% of young children who receive medical care in hospital settings do so because of insufficient weight gain that has no known organic cause (Breunlin, Desai, Stone, & Swilley, 1983).

It is very difficult to untangle the effects of food deprivation and of the lack of stimulation that comes from being inappropriately cared for in early life. As we noted with respect to eating disorders, being fed in infancy and eating independently later on are as much about social interaction as they are about nutrition. Thus, infants and children whose failure to thrive is the result of parental neglect or abuse are likely to suffer not only from the adverse developmental effects of malnutrition or undernutrition, but also from missed opportunities to form a secure attachment with a loving and responsive caregiver.

emotions that pull them both toward and away from their loved ones. These contrasting needs and feelings explain some of the problems associated with abuse and neglect. For example, a large community survey conducted in New York State and Puerto Rico found that 13% of physical abuse victims met diagnostic criteria for one or more disruptive behavior disorders, 10% for one or more mood disorders, and 19% for one or more anxiety disorders (Flischer et al., 1997). Similarly, a study of young victims of sexual abuse found significant levels of anxiety or depressive symptoms in 17% of preschoolers and 40% of school-age children (Gomes-Schwartz, Horowitz, & Cardarelli, 1990). Longitudinal data suggest that some of the disorders that maltreated children present develop as a consequence of their victimization rather than for other reasons (Dodge, Pettit, & Bates, 1997).

Disruptive Behavior Disorders or Symptoms. Disruptive behavior disorders or symptoms are frequent in maltreated children—particularly in physically abused boys (Feldman et al., 1995) and in physically and sexually abused girls (Green, Russo, Navatril, & Loeber, 1999). From an early age, boys are prone to angry outbursts in which they are verbally and/or physically aggressive toward parents, siblings, and peers. Girls are more likely to present covert symptoms of disruption, such as truancy, and to be both anxious and depressed. More generally, maltreatment—especially physical abuse—is associated in both genders with limited prosocial skills and with reduced compassion and empathy (Kolko, 1992).

Many physically abused children learn to act aggressively in their day-to-day interactions at home, and later generalize these skills to their school or neighborhood (Dodge, Bates, & Pettit, 1990). Such children begin grade school with multiple problems commonly associated with high levels of disruptiveness—such as poor emotional regulation and limited social and academic skills. Over time, these problems typically worsen and at times propel physically abused children, especially boys, on a developmental trajectory closely resembling that of conduct disorder (see Developmental Trajectories and Prognosis).

Anxiety and Mood Disorders or Symptoms. Anxiety and mood disorders or their symptoms are common in maltreated children also, especially children who have been victims of sexual abuse or neglect. Young victims of sexual abuse often suffer from generalized anxiety, sleep disturbances, depression, immature and age-inappropriate behaviors, social withdrawal, and PTSD. This symptom pattern, which differs from the predominantly oppositional and aggressive pattern associated with other forms of abuse, probably reflects the largely female makeup of most samples of sexually abused victims (Kendall-Tackett, Williams, & Finkelhor, 1993).

Like sexually abused children, victims of neglect are often withdrawn and sad, and avoid interaction with peers or unfamiliar adults. They also have difficulty expressing age-appropriate emotions. They appear distant, uninterested, or withdrawn, and do not laugh or giggle joyfully as most children do (Trickett

& McBride-Chang, 1995). For example, a 5-year-old girl who had been referred to our clinic after having been removed from the care of her heroin-addicted mother barely spoke and was unfamiliar with all of our playroom toys. She was fascinated by Play-doh but unable to make anything with it but a large, lumpy ball.

Cognitive and Language Deficits.   Maltreated children often present significant cognitive and language deficits that may stem from the children's limited opportunities to explore their surroundings and to learn, and/or from their parents' inattention to their need for appropriate stimulation (Cahill, Kaminar, & Johnson, 1999). Standardized achievement test scores show that developmental delays are particularly evident among neglected children. Typically, these children score lower than their physically abused peers, who in turn score lower than victims of sexual abuse or average children. Not surprisingly, a large number of maltreated children are referred for special services, such as speech and occupational therapy, or are retained a grade after kindergarten or in elementary school (Cicchetti & Toth, 1995).

Epidemiology

Incidence Estimates

Epidemiological studies of child maltreatment typically report incidence rates for various forms of abuse and neglect; that is, estimates of the number of new cases that are observed each year in the child and adolescent population. In the United States, most of these estimates are based on data from the National Incidence Studies (NIS) of Child Abuse and Neglect and the National Child Abuse and Neglect Data System (NCANDS), both sponsored by the U.S. Department of Health and Human Services. The NIS are periodic surveys of professionals working with children and adolescents, whereas the NCANDS collects and analyzes child maltreatment statistics provided annually by state CPS agencies.

Three NIS surveys have been published to date: NIS-1 in 1980, NIS-2 in 1988, and NIS-3 in 1996. According to the latest of these surveys, over 1.5 million children suffered some form of harm as a result of maltreatment in 1993. This figure corresponds to an annual incidence rate of 23.1 children per 1,000 (or 2.3%). When children in danger of being harmed (but for whom actual harm could not be confirmed) were added to this figure, the total climbed to over 2.8 million, amounting to an annual incidence rate of 41.9 children per 1,000 (or 4.2%) (USDHHS, 1996). As Wolfe and Jaffe (1991) write, these staggering numbers sadly make the American family "a violent institution, second only to the military and the police in terms of its accepted use of violent tactics to control others" (p. 284). On a more positive note, yearly comparisons of substantiated cases of child sexual abuse in the United States showed a steady 31% decrease from 1992 to 1998 (Jones & Finkelhor, 2001). Although several explanations for this trend are possible, it may represent both an actual decline in the incidence of sexual abuse and a decline in reported and substantiated cases of sexual abuse.

Reports from the states to the NCANDS typically yield lower incidence estimates. In 1997, CPS agencies investigated approximately two million reports of alleged maltreatment. These reports, which concerned approximately three million children, led CPS agencies to determine that just under one million of them were victims of substantiated or indicated abuse or neglect in 1997. ("Indicated" means here that there was strong evidence to suspect but not to substantiate maltreatment.) This figure corresponds to an annual incidence rate of 14 children per 1,000 (or 1.4%) (USDHHS, 1999). However, this is very likely an underestimate, since many cases of maltreatment are never reported and many others are difficult to substantiate (see below). For example, only 28% of children found to have been victims of abuse or neglect in the NIS-3 study were subjects of a CPS investigation.

Neglect is more frequent than abuse. Table 12.1 presents the NIS-3 estimates for all forms of child maltreatment. Of the total number of cases reported in 1993, 57% were for neglect and 48% for abuse. (These percentages add up to more than 100% because many children were identified as suffering from multiple forms of maltreatment.) Comparable percentages appear in NCANDS data. In 1997, 56% of CPS reports were for neglect and 43% for abuse (24%, physical

TABLE 12.1 *Third U.S. National Incidence Study (NIS-3) Estimates for All Forms of Child Maltreatment*

	Total No. of Children	Rate per 1,000 Children
All Maltreatment	1,553,800	23.1
Abuse:		
All Abuse	743,200	11.1
Physical Abuse	381,700	5.7
Sexual Abuse	217,700	3.2
Emotional Abuse	204,500	3.0
Neglect:		
All Neglect	879,000	13.1
Physical Neglect	338,900	5.0
Emotional Neglect	212,800	3.2
Educational Neglect	397,300	5.9

Note: These estimates represent only children and adolescents who were harmed in 1993. They do not include children and adolescents who were in danger of being harmed but for whom actual harm could not be confirmed.

Source: USDHHS (1996), p. 3-3.

abuse; 13%, sexual abuse; and 6%, emotional abuse) (USDHHS, 1996, 1999).

Death from Maltreatment. NCANDS statistics indicate that 1,196 children and adolescents died as a result of maltreatment in 1997. This is very likely a conservative estimate, since not all deaths from maltreatment are reported as such and known to CPS. Fatalities from all forms of abuse and neglect decrease significantly with age. Over three-quarters of the 1997 victims were children age 3 and under (USDHHS, 1999). This finding is in line with other research indicating that homicide is the most common cause of death in very young children (17% of deaths among children under age 1; USDHHS, 1999).

The Tip of the Iceberg. Official reports of child abuse and neglect represent only a percentage of victims of maltreatment. CPS agencies generally describe five levels of recognition of child abuse and neglect, ranging from "known to CPS" to "known to no one" (see Figure 12.1). For example, the NIS-3 study (see Table 12.1) estimates that sexual abuse has an incidence

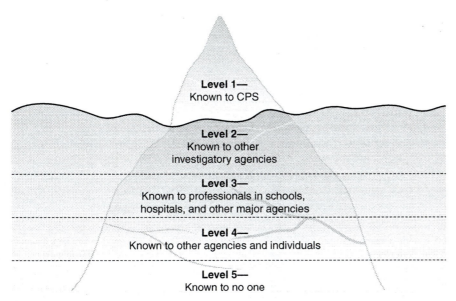

Level 1—
Known to CPS

Level 2—
Known to other
investigatory agencies

Level 3—
Known to professionals in schools,
hospitals, and other major agencies

Level 4—
Known to other agencies and individuals

Level 5—
Known to no one

FIGURE 12.1 *Levels of Recognition of Child Abuse and Neglect.* CPS agencies generally describe five levels of recognition of child abuse and neglect, to illustrate that officially known cases represent only the "tip of the iceberg."
Source: USDHHS (1996), p. 2.

rate of 0.32%; that is, that approximately 1 in every 300 children is sexually victimized in a given year. Obviously, this rate should be cause for considerable concern, but it is only the "tip of the iceberg." For example, retrospective research conducted with adults indicates that between 15% and 30% of women and 10% and 15% of men report that they were sexually abused as children (Briere, 1992). The accuracy of retrospective reports can be legitimately questioned in some cases. However, these very high percentages cannot be dismissed lightly, because a substantial majority of adults who report that they were sexually victimized as children say that they never revealed the fact to anyone.

Age and Gender Characteristics

Child maltreatment touches children from birth to adulthood. The 1997 NCANDS study showed that approximately 25% of abuse and neglect victims were from 0 to 3 years of age; 28% from 4 to 7; 22% from 8 to 11; and 25% from 12 to 18. Neglect was more frequent before age 8 and abuse after age 8. This study and the NIS-3 study found that maltreatment was equally likely to affect boys and girls, with one major exception: female children were three times more likely to be sexually abused than male children (USDHHS, 1996, 1999).

Changes in Incidence Rates over Time

Child maltreatment has increased in frequency *and* severity in recent decades. Comparison of the second and third NIS studies indicates that, from 1986 to 1993, the number of children harmed, or in danger of being harmed, doubled (from 1.4 to 2.8 million), while the number of children who were seriously injured as a result of maltreatment quadrupled (from 143,000 to 570,000 approximately) (USDHHS, 1996). Figure 12.2 illustrates the changes in incidence rates of physical, sexual, and emotional abuse across the three NIS studies (showing data from 1980, 1986, and 1993). Although these changes are dramatic, the same studies found that neglect increased even more significantly over the same period.

There are at least two explanations for these increases. First, because of mandatory reporting laws and widespread awareness of these laws among professionals and the general public, child abuse and neglect are now better identified than in the past. The 1997 NCANDS statistics show that over half of all reports of alleged maltreatment to CPS came from professionals. The remainder came from parents, relatives, or the victims themselves (18%), anonymous sources (12%), friends and neighbors (8%), and other sources (8%).

FIGURE 12.2   *Changes in Incidence Rates of Physical, Sexual, and Emotional Abuse across the Three U.S. National Incidence Studies.* These changes reflect consistent increases in *actual harm* to children. The data reported here include only cases of confirmed maltreatment; they exclude cases in which maltreatment was suspected but could not be clearly established.

Source: USDHHS (1996), p. 3-9.

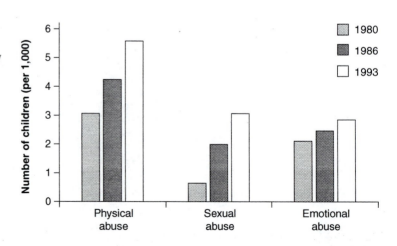

Second, these increases reflect an actual rise in the incidence of maltreatment. In other words, there is little doubt that American youth are abused and neglected in greater numbers than in the past. The NIS-3 study shows that, even when the definitions of abuse and neglect are held constant over time, rates of maltreatment have continued to rise faster than would be predicted by increases in education and awareness.

Social and Cultural Differences

Poverty.   Rates of abuse and neglect generally increase as socioeconomic status decreases (Lee & Goerge, 1999). For example, in the NIS-3 study, abuse was fourteen times more frequent, and neglect forty-five times more frequent, in families with yearly incomes of less than $15,000 than in families with yearly incomes greater than $30,000 (USDHHS, 1999). This association is likely to be accounted for by two major factors. First, low-income families are subjected to multiple, often chronic stressors that affect parenting, such as lack of social support, unemployment, limited educational opportunities, neighborhood violence, and crime (Belsky, 1993). Second, in the case of neglect at least, low-income families are limited in their ability to provide for their children's basic needs (Kerr et al., 2000; Wekerle & Wolfe, 1996). In other words, the common finding that abusive and neglectful parents are often young, unemployed adults who are poor may have more to do with the challenges these parents encounter in their daily lives than with the characteristics of a distinct, "maltreating" social group (Wolfe & McEachran, 1997) (see Etiology).

Ethnicity.   Whether ethnicity plays a role in child maltreatment is unclear (Kenny & McEachern, 2000). In all three NIS studies (1980, 1988, 1996), ethnicity was not a factor that differentiated children who were maltreated from children who were not. However, a reanalysis of the NIS-1 data showed that European American children were particularly likely to have been sexually, physically, and emotionally abused, as well as emotionally neglected, whereas African American children were most likely to have been educationally neglected (Ards, Chung, & Myers, 1998). In addition, a study of hospital reports found that shaken baby syndrome (a cluster of symptoms that occur when an infant is brain-injured after having been violently shaken) was more common in European American than African American families (Brenner, Fisher, & Mann-Gray, 1989). Finally, European American women are more likely to describe a history of sexual abuse than African American women (Wyatt, Loeb, Solis, Carmona, & Romero, 1999). Although these studies suggest that important ethnic differences may exist, others do not (Lee & Goerge, 1999; Mraovich & Wilson, 1999). Specifically, when differences are not found between ethnicities, it is when socioeconomic status is taken into account.

Cross-Cultural Comparisons.   Comparative studies of child maltreatment are rare, considering that children and adolescents are known to be subjected to abusive and neglectful treatment in all societies and cultures. Past epidemiological evidence indicated that rates of abuse and neglect in the United States tended to be generally higher than those reported in other countries, but more recent research suggests that this is not the case, at least for sexual abuse (Nilsen, 2001). Research from Canada, Europe, and Australia shows that rates of sexual abuse are comparable around the globe and that past discrepancies may be more the result of methodological differences among studies than actual differences in maltreatment.

Rates of other forms of maltreatment also appear to be comparable in many North American and European countries. However, with the exception of sexual abuse, which is somewhat easier to identify cross-culturally, the formulation of international definitions of physical or emotional abuse, and of neglect, is problematic because of differing cultural standards for the treatment and discipline of children and adolescents. For example, extreme poverty in some countries makes neglect a way of life for many parents—not because they are all maltreating their children but, rather, because they are unfortunate enough to live in a world in which they cannot provide for their family's basic needs.

Developmental Trajectories and Prognosis

Abuse and neglect cannot be understood apart from the developmental context in which they occur. Before we summarize the developmental evidence, however, it is important to note that maltreatment rarely affects children in the same manner. The research findings we present here must be considered with that important point in mind. They reflect broad developmental patterns that have often been observed, rather than patterns that apply to most victims of abuse or neglect.

Early Childhood

Disturbed Patterns of Attachment.   A stable and secure attachment is considered by many theorists to be critical to a child's healthy social and emotional development (see Chapter 2). Since acts of abuse or neglect violate the conditions necessary for the development of a secure attachment, it is not surprising to find that many maltreated infants and young children are insecurely attached to their caregivers (Barnett, Ganiban, & Cicchetti, 1999).

Indiscriminate Affection and Sexualized Behaviors.   An important consequence of a disturbed pattern of attachment often observed in young maltreated children—particularly children who have been physically or sexually abused, rather than neglected—is a tendency to be indiscriminate in their affection. Paradoxically, maltreated children who can be aggressive and hostile toward adults (see below) often crave adult approval and encouragement (Cicchetti & Toth, 1995) and may be indiscriminately affectionate toward them. For example, they may hug strangers, jump on their laps, or ask to follow them without hesitation.

In addition, young victims of sexual abuse often engage in inappropriate sexual conduct that appears to be related to their victimization. Sexualized behaviors, which are rarely found in children without a history of sexual abuse, include attempts to involve young peers in play activities with obvious sexual overtones, masturbation in the presence of adults or children, and "flirting" or other provocative approaches that are clearly inappropriate given the child's age (Cahill et al., 1999; Kendall-Tackett et al., 1993). For example, a 4-year-old girl who came to our clinic with a terrifying history of sexual abuse was extremely withdrawn and fearful in social situations and required six months of intensive intervention to attend preschool on a regular

Severe physical punishment and abuse have been shown to be related to aggressive behavior in victims—both concurrently and over time.

basis. However, as soon as she became familiar with the preschool environment, she began to engage her peers in openly sexual activities—for instance, by lying on top of them, kissing them on the lips, or touching their genital area. Similarly, when she was tired or not engaged in any organized activity, she would often suck her thumb while openly masturbating.

Poor Emotional Regulation, Opposition, and Aggression.   Maltreated, especially physically abused, children have difficulty regulating their emotions. They may switch unpredictably from extreme talkativeness to withdrawal, or from hyperactive agitation to passivity, probably because they live in environments where their caregivers are themselves unpredictable and have given them few, if any, opportunities to learn to control their emotions and to express them appropriately (Herman, 1992).

Abused children tend also to be more oppositional and aggressive than their nonabused counterparts, directing their aggressiveness not only at peers but also at caregivers and at inanimate objects. In addition, many of them view the world as a dangerous place. They are easily aroused by anger and hostility, and quick to attribute hostile intentions to other people (Ornduff, 2000). These children tend to respond to such emotions by becoming agitated or aggressive rather than distressed, as non-abused children do—probably because they have learned that anger and hostility in others often signal that their own safety is in danger, and that they may have to fight in order to defend themselves (Smetana et al., 1999).

More generally, poor emotional functioning is reflected in these children's low self-esteem and negative views of their own abilities (Cicchetti & Toth, 1995). Such negative views are commonly associated with feelings of guilt or shame, since many victims of abuse blame themselves—often for years—for their victimization in their repeated attempts to make sense of it (Briere, 1992; Brown & Kolko, 1999).

Compulsive Compliance. Although they can be very oppositional and aggressive, and easily "lose it" in temper tantrums or angry outbursts, young victims of abuse often engage in what has been called **compulsive compliance,** especially toward parents or caregivers who have abused them in the past. They tend to comply *more* quickly and readily with adult demands, probably because they have learned to be hypervigilant in situations in which any noncompliance on their part may provoke extreme adult anger and aggression (Herman, 1992). Compulsive compliance, unlike more adaptive forms of compliance, tends to be accompanied by little or no emotional expression; by discrepancies between words and actions (e.g., a young boy says that he is hurrying to obey but is walking slowly); and by seemingly automatized, fearful verbal responses (e.g., "I'm sorry. I'm sorry. I'm sorry."). Similarly, many young abuse victims have learned to calm or distract adults who are angry for reasons that have nothing to do with them, in order

to avoid becoming scapegoats for that anger (Wolfe & McEachran, 1997).

Middle Childhood

Physically Abused Children. As relationships with peers and adults beyond the family gain in importance in the early school years, the challenges faced by children who have been physically abused—particularly those who showed high levels of oppositional and aggressive problems in preschool—often increase considerably (Dodge et al., 1997). Their tendency to attribute hostile intentions to others and to be hypervigilant in the face of potential danger or threat often leads them into conflicts with peers—either as aggressors, who initiate fights or respond to real or perceived provocations, or as victims of peer attacks (Dodge, Pettit, & Bates, 1994; Feldman et al., 1995).

As we noted in Chapter 8, children who begin grade school with high levels of aggression tend to be quickly labeled as disruptive and to be rejected by teachers and peers and quickly fall behind academically (Rowe & Eckenrode, 1999). Early peer rejection and academic failure are major risk factors for conduct disorder, school dropout, and substance abuse in late childhood and adolescence. Abused children who follow this disruptive developmental trajectory from an early age rarely, if ever, "catch up" to their peers. Rather, their multiple problems tend to worsen over time, often making their day-to-day behavior indistinguishable from that of youth with conduct disorder (Cahill et al., 1999; Wolfe & McEachran, 1997).

In keeping with their tendency to be overaggressive, physically abused children often have poorly developed **moral reasoning** skills. Their ability to judge the moral implications of their own and other people's decisions and choices lags behind that of children without a history of abuse. For example, abused children generally consider aggression an acceptable "solution" to interpersonal problems and express little sympathy or remorse when others are hurt as a result (Cahill et al., 1999).

Many physically abused children continue to display depressive symptoms and signs of low self-esteem and self-worth in middle childhood, often to a greater extent than neglected children do (Cicchetti & Toth,

1995). In many cases, depressive and angry feelings may lead to aggressive outbursts and to self-harm as well (e.g., suicide attempts). However, some children in similar circumstances are able to develop and maintain a positive view of themselves, and to make significant developmental strides in spite of their victimization (Cicchetti & Rogosch, 1997). The circumstances that account for these children's ability to "beat the odds" remain poorly understood, but are likely to be related to the presence of one or more positive relationships in their lives with a trusted adult, sibling, or friend.

Sexually Abused Children.   The anxiety symptoms displayed by victims of sexual abuse in early childhood tend to persist in the school years, but are now often accompanied by specific fears and worries that were less prominent in earlier years (Kendall-Tackett et al., 1993). These fears are not always specific to the abuse and may include such things as the fears of dark, being alone, animals, and new places. In addition, many sexually abused children now qualify for a diagnosis of PTSD (Dubner & Motta, 1999). Many of them also begin to engage in increasingly disruptive behaviors, such as opposition and aggression, that were, until now, seen almost exclusively in their physically abused peers. However, sexualized behaviors, which were often prominent earlier, decrease considerably during this period (Kendall-Tackett et al., 1993). Sexually abused girls also appear to have poorer emotional management skills than nonabused peers (Shipman, Zeman, Penza, & Champion, 2000).

Neglected Children.   In general, victims of neglect remain less aggressive than other maltreated children in middle childhood, preferring social isolation and passivity to other forms of engagement in their interactions with adults and peers (Dodge et al., 1994). However, their symptoms of depression and anxiety often continue throughout this developmental period, putting them at risk for the negative outcomes associated with these conditions (Trickett & McBride-Chang, 1995).

Neglected children also show significant cognitive deficits, scoring lower on standardized measures of ability than nonvictimized peers or other maltreated children. These deficits lead many neglected children to fall rapidly behind in school, so much so that, on average, these children show more severe academic delays than other maltreated children (Cahill et al., 1999).

Physical Changes Related to Abuse.   Middle childhood brings about physical changes in many abused children that may be related to the maltreatment they suffered. For example, sexually victimized children often reach puberty earlier than average children (Al-Mateen, Hall, Brookman, Best, & Signh, 1999). The causes of early puberty are largely unknown, but premature sexual activity may be one of them. In addition, sexual abuse victims show higher levels of certain stress hormones, presumably as a result of relatively chronic anxiety associated with their molestation (Putnam & Trickett, 1993). Similarly, physically abused children exhibit more **neurological soft signs** than nonabused children (Wekerle & Wolfe, 1996). Soft signs are slight physical indicators of abnormal neurological functioning that may stem from earlier abuse.

Adolescence

In general, behavior patterns established in early and middle childhood tend to continue into adolescence, and many victims of abuse or neglect now meet diagnostic criteria for one or more of the disorders discussed in earlier chapters. For example, maltreated youth have a greater likelihood of being arrested for delinquent conduct than their nonvictimized peers, and many of them meet diagnostic criteria for conduct disorder (Kaufman & Widom, 1999).

Similarly, teenagers who have been sexually abused continue to exhibit symptoms of anxiety and depression in adolescence, or develop disorders such as PTSD (Wolfe, Sas, & Wekerle, 1994).

> ***Daddy***
> *Daddy said:*
> *I was a pretty girl,*
> *Daddy said:*
> *a princess.*
> *Daddy told:*
> *me he'd never hurt me*
> *and make everything alright.*

Daddy said:
that what we were doing, happens to every little girl.
Daddy said:
he'd never hurt me, boy did he lie.
All I want to do now is cry.

—Jen, 13

Depressive symptoms can be severe, and are accompanied by marked increases in suicidal ideation and in suicide attempts (Brown, Cohen, Johnson, & Smailes, 1999). Research shows that sexually and/or physically abused adolescents are more likely to think about and to attempt suicide than either youth with drug or alcohol problems or average youth (Cavaiola & Schiff, 1988).

Abuse victims—especially if they have a history of sexual maltreatment—often engage in other detrimental behaviors in adolescence, such as self-mutilation, substance abuse, and running away (Cavaiola & Schiff, 1988; Kaufman & Widom, 1999). Sexual promiscuity and victimization are also frequent (Eisenman, 2000). Specifically, teenage girls report high levels of promiscuity (McClellan et al., 1996), and as many as 60% of teenage boys arrested for sexual offenses have a history of sexual abuse (Bourke & Donohue, 1996). Such behaviors may represent a resurgence, in other forms, of the sexualized behaviors that many victims of sexual abuse display in early childhood.

Adult Adjustment

The effects of childhood maltreatment can persist beyond adolescence (see Figure 12.3, p. 358). Some physically abused children grow up to become aggressive adults who are violent toward those around them, such as dating partners, spouses, and children (Appel & Holden, 1998). However, only a relatively few child victims become adult victimizers (Box 12.5, p. 359). Adults who were physically abused in childhood are also more likely than average adults to have a criminal record and to be arrested for offenses such as theft, substance abuse, sexual misconduct, and traffic violations (Malinosky-Rummell & Hansen, 1993).

Not surprisingly, many adults who were sexually abused as children face significant emotional chal-

lenges and are at high risk for a variety of psychological disorders or for the continuation of disorders such as PTSD and depression that began in childhood or adolescence (Brown et al., 1999; Widom, 1999). In addition, many of these adults report interpersonal difficulties in close relationships (Putnam & Trickett, 1993). Evidence suggests that men and women develop different patterns of psychopathology even if they have similar abuse histories (Gold, Lucenko, Elhai, Swingle, & Sellers, 1999). For example, in a community sample, Gold and associates (1999) found that women with sexual abuse histories had more psychological disorders than men with comparable life experiences.

Etiology

There are multiple pathways to child and adolescent maltreatment, and explanations for abuse and neglect have to be sought *at the same time* within and beyond the family. Several overlapping etiological models have been proposed (e.g., Belsky, 1993; Wolfe, 1999), although none can account fully for the multiple facets of abuse and neglect, because the phenomena they address are varied and call for multiple explanatory theories. We will focus here on some of the factors associated with child and adolescent maltreatment.

Biological Factors

With the exception of gender—girls are significantly more likely to be sexually victimized than boys—there is no evidence to implicate biological factors in the etiology of any form of child maltreatment. A detailed review of the literature conducted by the National Research Council (1993) shows that, when sociodemographic and family factors are controlled for, victims of abuse or neglect do not differ in their biological characteristics from same-age average children.

Similarly, there is no evidence that certain individuals may be genetically predisposed to be abusive or neglectful toward children. However, since violent criminal behavior may be partly inherited, there may be an indirect biological cause for violent maltreatment (DiLalla & Gottesman, 1991). Although approximately

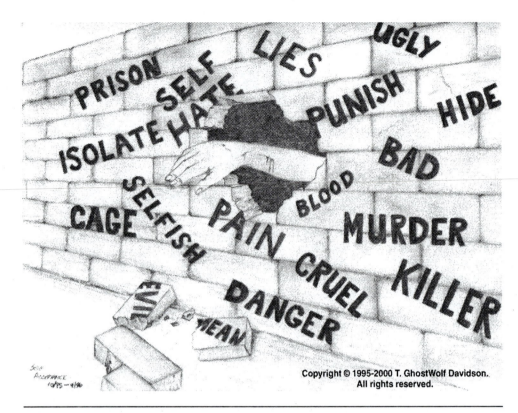

FIGURE 12.3 *Drawing by an Adult Survivor of Child Abuse.* This drawing highlights the conflicting feelings and pain associated with a history of severe abuse. For many abuse survivors, life is a continuing struggle to make sense of the events of their childhood.

From: Drawing from GhostWolf (2002) (www.nemasys.com/ghostwolf/Reflections/Art/acceptance.jpg). Copyright 1995–2000. T. GhostWolf Davidson. Reprinted by permission.

30% of abused children will become abusive parents (Oliver, 1993), this transgenerational effect can be accounted for by numerous nonbiological variables—such as the transmission of poverty from one generation to the next or modeling. In other words, maltreatment puts victims at risk for becoming abusive but does not invariably lead them to treat their children as they were treated themselves (see Box 12.5).

Family Factors

Parental Psychopathology. Early etiological theories assumed that most acts of abuse or neglect were committed by severely disturbed adults or, to put it more bluntly, that only "damaged parents" could mistreat innocent children. In most cases, these parents were assumed to have a history of criminal conduct or a major psychological disorder. This appealingly simple assumption was easily testable and led a number of researchers to focus closely on the personality characteristics of abusive and neglectful parents. In a careful review of studies spanning approximately two decades, Wolfe (1985) found little support for this etiological perspective. Evidence shows that only a minority of maltreating parents (fewer than 10%) have a psychological disorder that might explain their abusive or neglectful behavior. Similarly, there are no personality profiles or traits that reliably distinguish

BOX 12.5 • *Exploring the Cycle of Violence and Abuse*

The intergenerational transmission of violence and abuse has always been an important hypothesis in child abuse research. This hypothesis states that children who are exposed to violence during their youth—in the form of abuse or exposure to domestic violence—are likely to become aggressive and abusive adolescents and adults (Wahler & Dumas, 1986). Although countless retrospective accounts support this claim, empirical evidence shows that the cycle of violence and abuse is not as complete as the intergenerational transmission hypothesis would suggest. In a detailed study of this issue, Cathy Widom (1989) found that many children who had suffered from abuse indeed went on to abuse their own children. However, her research also showed that (1) the majority of child abusers had no history of abuse, and (2) the majority of abuse victims did not grow up to become abusive parents.

More precisely, Widom reported that about 30% of abused children in the literature she reviewed grew up to become abusive parents and that approximately 16% of those who witnessed domestic violence went on to engage in spousal aggression as adults. These figures should not lead anyone to dismiss the issue of the transmission of

violence and abuse from one generation to the next, but they show that the intergenerational cycle is, fortunately, far from complete.

This conclusion is fairly positive. However, a 25-year follow-up of 908 child victims of abuse and neglect, and of 667 nonmaltreated children matched on sex, age, ethnicity, and socioeconomic status, indicates that maltreatment predisposes to violence *in general* (Widom & Maxfield, 2001). The researchers found that children who had been abused or neglected were more likely than control children to be arrested as juveniles (27% vs. 17%) and as adults (42% vs. 33%). In addition, when they were arrested, those who had been abused or neglected were more often charged with a violent crime than the control group (18% vs. 14%). A comparison of these figures shows that "being abused or neglected as a child increased the likelihood of arrest as a juvenile by 59%, as an adult by 28%, and for a violent crime by 30%" (p. 1). In other words, data on the "cycle of violence" hypothesis do not show that most maltreated children grow up to abuse or neglect their own children; but they show clearly that maltreatment is a significant risk factor for later criminal conduct and violence.

---

between parents who victimize their children and parents who do not. In other words, these two groups of parents resemble each other much more than they differ.

Nonetheless, abusive parents often have long-standing psychological problems, including learning disabilities, intellectual deficits (or mild mental retardation), and anxiety, mood, or personality disorders (Belsky, 1993). In many cases, these parents were themselves exposed to harsh parenting or were maltreated as they grew up (Daggett, O'Brien, Zanolli, & Peyton, 2000). In addition, because of feeding problems, poor health, or temperamental difficulties, some infants and children can be very challenging, further complicating the parenting task. These problems do not play a distinct etiological role in child abuse or neglect because they are also found in families of children with several of the psychological disorders already covered in this book. For example, as shown in

Chapter 8, many parents of children with conduct disorder are likely to face similar problems.

Parent-Child Interactions. Mistreating parents are often confronted by overwhelming stressors—such as poverty, inadequate housing, marital violence, social isolation, unemployment, and neighborhood violence—and lack adequate personal and environmental resources to cope with them (Cerezo, 1997). These parents are often young and have little knowledge of how to care for children. When crises happen, many of them have no reliable friend or relative to call on for help. In addition, some mistreating parents suffer from chronic illnesses or from addictions that interfere with their ability to parent. Most tragedies of physical abuse and neglect occur in an interactional context in which a parent who is under stress or ill is unable to cope with the demands of childrearing. We can personally recall working with young parents who, in exasperation, did terrible things to their children. For example, one mother sat her 4-year-old boy on a hot electric stove for wetting his pants several times in the same day, and another deliberately broke a wooden kitchen spoon on her son's arm "for whining all the time." In both cases, these mothers were single and had no family or friends to support them in their parenting task.

Although child maltreatment cannot be attributed simply to dysfunctional parental characteristics, differences in parent-child interactions and in parents' ways of coping with stress may partly explain why some children are physically abused whereas others are neglected (Hillson & Kuiper, 1994). Physically abusive parents tend to have unrealistic expectations about how their children should behave and to be prone to anger. In situations of conflict, they react strongly and often excessively, they provide little in the form of positive guidance or praise, and they fail to consider their children's ability to comply. For example, a mother might yell at a tired and hungry 3-year-old: "Quit whining right now! I don't want to hear you! I don't want to see you until dinner. If I do, I'll beat your butt!" As abusive parents tend to ignore their children when they behave well, the children may learn early on to misbehave in order to obtain adult attention: they may whine, refuse to obey, or fight with their siblings to elicit negative but predictable reactions from their parents, in many cases preferring negative attention to no attention at all (Wahler & Dumas, 1986).

Abusive parents also may interpret their children's behavior negatively and rely on their misattributions or misperceptions to explain their angry and at times violent outbursts (Milner, 1993). The mother who broke the kitchen spoon on her child's arm said: "He does it just to bait me. You have to know him to know his whine. When he whines like that, I know he'll go on for hours just to drive me crazy. And he does!" This type of explanation obviously encourages the parent's verbal and physical aggression, probably contributing in many cases to actual acts of abuse.

Neglectful parents, in contrast, tend to limit their interactions with their children, often deliberately avoiding them and withdrawing from both harmonious and conflictual situations. Their children then are left with the impossible task of attempting to meet their basic needs in the absence of reliable adult help and guidance, thereby severely compromising their physical, emotional, and social development, as well as their safety. The father of neglected twins we worked with regularly left them to fend for themselves when he was intoxicated. He explained calmly and without much apology that he did not know how to raise children and that he was often too tired to prepare meals or to maintain a minimal routine of care for his boys. Once a week or more, his problems with alcohol—he had a long history of binge drinking—made him totally unavailable for hours to his children.

Alcoholism and other forms of drug abuse are common among maltreating parents who regularly attempt to cope with stress by isolating themselves from the overwhelming demands of their children and their lives (Harrington, Dubowitz, Black, & Binder, 1995). However, substance abuse cannot alone explain the etiology of maltreatment, since many children who are not maltreated also have parents who attempt to cope with stress through various forms of escape or avoidance.

Family Violence. Child maltreatment—especially physical abuse—often occurs in violent family contexts, especially when spousal violence is present. In approximately half of the families in which one form of violence occurs—either child abuse or spousal violence—the other form of violence is likely to be present also (Appel & Holden, 1998; Edleson, 1999). For example, in a study conducted in a public hospital setting, 59% of mothers of abused children were themselves victims of battering, compared to 13% of mothers of matched, nonabused children (McKibben, DeVos, & Newberger, 1989). This overlap, which is most likely to occur in families in which adult males are extremely violent, seriously compromises the development of affected children—both because witnessing domestic violence is traumatic and because children can become caught between their fighting parents and be injured.

Social and Cultural Factors

In 1981, David Gill, a pioneer in the study of child maltreatment, called into question the largely prevailing view then that abuse and neglect were caused by pathological family functioning, especially parental psychopathology. He wrote: "Whenever problems which are actually rooted in societal dynamics are defined as individual pathology or shortcomings, their real sources are disguised, interventions are focused on individuals . . . and the social order is absolved by implication from guilt and responsibility and may continue to function unchallenged in accordance with established patterns" (p. 312).

It would be simplistic and mistaken to claim that social and cultural factors alone can account for the etiology of child maltreatment. However, Gill's early critique and many others published since then are important because they point to the broad sociocultural context in which abusive and neglectful acts *always* occur. Many of the risk factors for child maltreatment are similar to the social and cultural variables associated with the development and maintenance of several of the disorders covered in previous chapters (especially oppositional defiant and conduct disorders; see Chapter 8). A major risk factor is poverty, which we discussed earlier (see Epidemiology); another is the American culture's high level of tolerance for violence in the family and beyond (Bennett, 1994).

In addition to these important factors, researchers and social critics often point to the role that socially and culturally sanctioned inequalities among members of society may play as risk factors, and possibly as causes, in abuse and neglect (Dobash & Dobash, 1992). These inequalities—between men and women, parents and children, majority and minority groups, etc.—can encourage and serve to justify violent conduct on the part of powerful members of society against weaker ones, thus setting the stage for abuse at least, if not neglect. This hypothesis is difficult to test empirically. However, it is indirectly supported by countless descriptions of abusive situations, as well as by studies linking differences in power within families to differences in level of family violence (Coleman & Straus, 1990). A religiously fanatic father who stormed out of our clinic proclaiming his right to discipline his son by beating him was convinced that divine authority had put him in a position of power over his family. A battered mother who attended our clinic with her young, oppositional child reflected the same reality when she said, referring to her violent husband: "You don't mess up with him. I learned that long ago. Or if you do, he'll make sure you know it."

Treatment and Prevention

In their efforts to treat or to prevent maltreatment, psychologists, psychiatrists, and other mental health professionals must answer a number of daunting questions: Should treatment for victims of sexual abuse focus on protecting them from their abusers, on helping them deal with the trauma they have suffered, on addressing their feelings of anxiety, guilt, and shame, or—as is often attempted—on all of these things at the same time? In cases of physical abuse, should the focus be on the child's emotional turmoil and educational delays, on the parents' inappropriate discipline practices, on the neglectful home conditions, or again on all of these things at the same time? Among a wide range of symptoms that differ in severity and impact, which symptoms are most susceptible to treatment? Some maltreated children and adolescents may display no apparent problem and be functioning remarkably well. Others may suffer from mental retardation because of head injury during infancy. Still others may be anxious and withdrawn, or severely depressed and suicidal. These factors combine to make treatment and prevention programs for child abuse and neglect difficult to develop and test empirically. Therefore, no single program or approach has emerged as most effective (Stevenson, 1999).

The challenges just discussed do not mean that adequate services for maltreated youth and their families are rare. Although the percentage of abused or neglected children receiving services is unknown, estimates are available. For example, a study of over six hundred youth in foster care found that 56% had received mental health services (Garland, Landsverk, Hough, & Ellis-Macleod, 1996). Interestingly, the likelihood of receiving services was not the same for all forms of maltreatment. Specifically, 77% of children with a history of sexual abuse had received mental health services, whereas the same was true for only 45% of those who were in foster care because of neglect or death or absence of a parent.

Child-Focused Treatment Approaches

Carefully evaluated treatment programs for maltreated youth are rare. Although most studies are marred by methodological issues, recent research is promising.

For example, one group of researchers tested the effectiveness of a cognitive-behavioral program for treating posttraumatic stress symptoms in sexually abused youth (see Chapter 10 for the treatment of PTSD) (King et al., 2000). This study compared outcomes in three groups: control (no treatment), child only, and child and nonoffending parent together. Results showed that children in the two active treatment conditions made significant improvements when compared to control children, but that parental involvement did not significantly improve the program's effectiveness. Improvements in social, emotional, and sexualized behaviors have also been obtained in a cognitive-behavioral program for sexually abused preschoolers. However, children from families in which the mother had limited social support did not fare as well in treatment as those whose mothers felt supported (Cohen & Mannarino, 1997, 1998). Another study, of withdrawn maltreated preschoolers, found that participants made significant progress when treatment relied on peers to stimulate their social behavior, rather than on adult-initiated stimulation or **play therapy** sessions (Fantuzzo et al., 1988). Play therapy is based on the assumption that unstructured play in a safe, therapeutic setting gives young children with psychological problems an opportunity to work through and resolve their difficulties. Although play therapy is commonly used to treat a variety of psychological problems, no controlled study has demonstrated its effectiveness. The work of Fantuzzo and associates suggests that, when play therapy is compared to another form of intervention, it may not be beneficial to young victims of maltreatment.

As the studies just summarized illustrate, child-focused treatment approaches vary considerably, both in the techniques on which they rely and in the youth they attempt to serve. Consequently, it is not currently possible to determine which approaches are most effective for which type of maltreatment at what age. Wekerle and Wolfe (1993) suggest that any child-focused treatment should ideally be designed to meet needs in at least four areas:

1. *Emotional development*—to deal with the interpersonal difficulties of most maltreated children in areas such as attachment, affect regulation, and moral understanding.

2. *Cognitive development*—to target problems in intellectual functioning and school performance.
3. *Anger and aggression management*—to teach children to manage their anger and aggression by developing and practicing self-control and social problem-solving skills.
4. *Avoidance of revictimization*—to help children learn to be safe in future relationships.

Family-Focused Treatment Approaches

A major issue facing service providers in the abuse and neglect area is the question of who should receive services. Maltreated children are victims and in need of protection and care, but what about their families? More specifically, when and under what conditions should victims of abuse or neglect be allowed to stay at home? When should they be placed temporarily in foster or other care? And when should they be removed permanently from their parents and placed for adoption or given other living arrangements? These are difficult questions that bear on child and parental rights, and on the availability of alternatives when families fail their children. These questions are beyond the scope of psychology and other helping professions, but mental health researchers and providers can make important contributions in this area, especially by identifying treatment programs that are effective in helping parents fulfill their childrearing responsibilities.

Family-focused approaches to helping maltreated children and adolescents have long sought to prevent further maltreatment by equipping parents with effective childrearing and problem-solving skills. Progress has been slow, however, in large part because work with maltreating parents is fraught with difficulties. Specifically, some parents come to treatment to avoid legal proceedings or because they have been court-ordered to do so, rather than to develop new skills or to change the manner in which family members interact. Other parents come to treatment to get their children back or to avoid having their children removed from their care. Thus, lack of motivation to change and denial are common in maltreating parents, and can make engaging and retaining them in treatment very challenging.

Despite these difficulties, family-focused parent-training approaches may be relatively effective. Ideally, Wekerle and Wolfe (1993) believe, any family-focused treatment should help participants acquire the following skills:

1. Parents need to learn to *identify their own emotions* before they become excessive or dangerous.
2. Parents must learn to *manage their anger*—to understand what triggers it and develop plans to identify and cope productively with angry feelings. This is especially true for anger toward their children.
3. Parents must learn *how to be good parents*. Parent-training programs similar to those used to treat the disruptive behavior disorders discussed in Chapters 7 and 8 are helpful in teaching parents alternatives to harsh or abusive punishment.
4. Parents need to learn *what to expect of their children as they develop*. For example, the "terrible twos" are a normal and healthy part of child development. However, parents without this developmental understanding may make negative attributions about their child's disruptive behavior and become abusive when it persists.
5. Parent must learn to *change problematic lifestyles*. Many parents of maltreated youth have personal problems such as drug and alcohol abuse that limit their ability to parent effectively. In order for abuse or neglect to stop, such problematic lifestyles must be altered.

No controlled study has assessed the importance of these components or evaluated the impact of addressing all of them at the same time. But it seems reasonable to expect that positive changes in any of these areas would be beneficial to victims of maltreatment.

Treatment Foster Care

Children and adolescents who are removed from home because of abuse or neglect are often placed in foster care, where substitute parents look after their needs until they can be returned home or permanently placed. Until recently, foster care was considered mainly as a place to keep maltreated youth safe. However, researchers have begun to intervene in this setting in an attempt to help victims of abuse or neglect. The rationale for this relatively new approach comes from findings that parent training for foster parents, together with individual treatment for youth with behavioral and emotional problems, results in significantly less jail time, runaway behavior, and hospitalization in youth who are placed in foster care (Chamberlain, 1996). Although this line of research is in its infancy, preliminary results show that preschool foster children make significant progress when their foster parents are involved in a structured parent-training program (Fisher, Gunnar, Chamberlain, & Reid, 2000).

Pharmacological Interventions

Many abused and neglected youth are medicated, usually to alleviate symptoms of inattention and hyperactivity or of anxiety and depression, rather than because they have a history of maltreatment. However, the effectiveness of pharmacological interventions in this area is largely unknown (Zima, Bussing, Crecelius, Kaufman, & Belin, 1999).

Prevention

A dreamer I am and a dreamer I'll be . . . for the hope of possibility.

—Carol McClure

Studies show that child maltreatment can be effectively prevented at a cost to society that is much smaller than the cost of treating victims of abuse or neglect. Unfortunately, however, of all the money spent every year on child maltreatment in the United States—approximately $14 billion in 1999—less than 10% is spent on prevention (APA Monitor, 1999).

An important example of an effective prevention program is the visiting-nurse program developed by David Olds and associates (Olds, 1997). This program sent trained nurses into the homes of young, unmarried mothers or mothers of low socioeconomic status during the prenatal and infancy period to provide information about child development and support. Results show that program participants were half as likely to be reported for maltreatment as nonparticipants were. However, when participants were themselves victims

Head Start, an educational program for economically disadvantaged preschoolers. Many researchers and clinicians believe that an effective way of preventing child maltreatment is to offer quality educational programs to preschoolers, and to work closely with their families through such programs.

of severe domestic violence, the program did not decrease the rate of maltreatment reports (Eckenrode et al., 2000).

Although the visiting-nurse program targets a particularly vulnerable group of mothers and their infants, a review of the prevention literature suggests that programs that work best may be those that aim to serve the whole population rather than a subgroup of families at risk. Specifically, Guterman (1999) argues that prevention approaches that target only specific groups are likely to miss a majority of families who may benefit most from an effective program; and that, for such a program to be widely accepted by parents, it must be part of the general standard of care rather than something that singles them out as different. Many quality daycare and preschool programs are designed and run in that perspective. For example, Head Start is an educational program that seeks to prepare economically disadvantaged preschoolers for school, and to help them develop physically and emotionally. The program

attempts to work closely with families also, to reduce the risk of psychological disorders and to prevent maltreatment.

Finally, in line with Head Start and other preschool programs, many researchers and clinicians believe that the most effective way to prevent child abuse and neglect is not to design and conduct particular prevention programs but to provide "general services, such as good housing, adequate financial support, available and affordable quality day care, drug counseling, family planning services, early intervention programs for children with disabilities, family resource centers and so on . . . [in order to] help parents provide better care to their children, which, in turn, is likely to decrease the rates of maltreatment" (Leventhal, 1996, pp. 647–648).

> *. . . pick on someone your own damn size*
> *stop all this sickness stop all the lies*
> *a man ain't a man when he beats his own kid*

it might take a man to admit that he did
get some help whatever it takes
get some help for children's sake
there's just no excuse for child abuse

there's just no excuse for child abuse
there's just no excuse for child abuse
                                    —anonymous

Web Links

www.calib.com/nccanch (National Clearinghouse on Child Abuse and Neglect Information. Offers a wide range of resources, including summaries of U.S. government statistics on abuse and neglect)

www.cdc.gov/ncipc (Centers for Disease Control and Prevention, National Center for Injury Prevention and Control)

www.apsac.org (American Professional Society on the Abuse of Children)

child-abuse.com (Child Abuse Prevention Network; for professionals in the field of child maltreatment)

www.ispcan.org (International Society for Prevention of Child Abuse and Neglect)

www.vaw.umn.edu (Violence Against Women Online Resources)

13

Health-Related Disorders

Children are likely to live up to what you believe in them.
—Lady Bird Johnson

This chapter focuses on health-related issues that, at first, may not seem to have a place in a psychology textbook. However, the distinction often made between physical and psychological health is artificial, since these two forms of well-being are closely related. The field of health is very broad, and the choice of which condition to highlight is difficult. Among the conditions covered here, the somatoform and elimination disorders have primarily a psychological etiology; and the chronic illnesses—cancer, asthma, and diabetes—have a biological etiology but often affect psychological functioning in major ways. We believe that these conditions are representative of the importance of psychological concerns in this vast area.

Somatoform Disorders

Pain is real when you get other people to believe in it. If no one believes in it but you, your pain is madness or hysteria.

—Naomi Wolf

Stomachaches, headaches, sore muscles, and fatigue are all part of the aches and pains associated with growing

up. Like their adult counterparts, children and adolescents frequently complain of physical symptoms that have no identifiable medical cause. For example, in a survey of parents of over 21,000 youth aged 4 to 15, two-thirds of them reported that their child had occasional aches and pains, and 11% said that their child's symptoms had warranted at least one doctor's visit. However, in most cases, medical examination did not reveal anything (Campo, Jansen-McWilliams, Comer, & Kelleher, 1999).

Somatoform disorders are a group of conditions characterized by unexplained physical symptoms that are, or are assumed to be, of psychological origin. Children and adolescents with these disorders have chronic physical complaints that disrupt their development and adaptive functioning. In some cases, these complaints have no identifiable medical cause. In others, they have such a cause, but their severity does not match the medical problem. For example, a child diagnosed with bronchial infection may complain of headaches and sore muscles far in excess of what would be expected, or continue to report symptoms long after he or she has recovered. "My head hurts so bad; I need to go to the hospital" and "I will never get better; I can hardly breathe" are examples of complaints from children with somatoform disorders. Other children with these disorders have sensory or motor symptoms, such as paralysis or seizures, that have no detectable neurological basis. Thus, an otherwise healthy girl may repeatedly fall at home or school as if she were having seizures, but doctors cannot find any abnormal brain activity that would explain her dramatic symptoms.

The DSM-IV-TR classifies several somatoform disorders. Only two of them, **somatization disorder** and **conversion disorder,** have received enough empirical attention in children and adolescents to be described in any detail. Briefly stated, somatization disorder is diagnosed in youth who exhibit a large number of medically unexplained physical problems affecting several major organ systems. Conversion disorder is diagnosed in youth who suffer from neurological symptoms that do not have an organic origin but are triggered by stress.

Historical Overview

Historically, somatoform disorders were regarded almost exclusively as adult conditions. In 1856, the French physician Paul Briquet catalogued the cases of over four hundred women with medically unexplained physical symptoms. Their condition, which was later called Briquet's syndrome, is what we know today as somatization disorder. At approximately the same time, another French physician, Jean Martin Charcot, also began classifying the physical complaints of some of his female patients but focused on the more dramatic neurological symptoms that are characteristic of conversion disorder. Charcot and his student Pierre Janet believed that conversion symptoms represented a special state of consciousness, in which awareness of specific sensory or motor functions was lost because of psychological problems.

Following in Charcot and Janet's footsteps, Sigmund Freud brought somatoform disorders to the forefront of modern psychiatry. Freud conceptualized conversion symptoms as the somatic, or bodily, expression of strong negative emotions often associated with trauma, such as physical or sexual abuse. Specifically, he believed that patients who were unable to express such emotions openly, because they were socially unacceptable or too painful, *converted* these emotions into physical symptoms that were symbolic of the original trauma. Because this conversion was unconscious, patients became emotionally cut off from their symptoms and experienced amazingly little distress as a result of their impaired physical functioning. This lack of affect, which is relatively common in adults with conversion disorder, is called *la belle indifférence,* which in French means "total indifference."

Briquet and Freud emphasized the importance of childhood experiences in somatoform disorders. Briquet noted that almost all of his patients' symptoms began before the age of 20, whereas Freud attributed these symptoms mainly to traumatic childhood experiences. Nevertheless, it took until the middle of the twentieth century for unexplained physical symptoms in children to become the focus of empirical study (e.g., Apley & Naish, 1958). However, even today this area of research remains relatively underdeveloped. In particular, we still lack the essential information to distinguish clearly between normative aches and pains in childhood and adolescence and physical symptoms that are pathological because of their nature or intensity.

Definitions, Diagnostic Criteria, and Major Characteristics

Somatization Disorder. Lipowski (1988) defines somatization as "the tendency to experience and communicate somatic distress and symptoms unaccounted for by pathological findings, to attribute them to physical illness, and to seek medical help for them" (p. 1358). Children and adolescents with somatization disorder have a variety of medically unexplained physical symptoms that persist for extended periods of time. These symptoms can occur in the context of a medical illness or an injury, but their extent or severity cannot be explained by the physical condition. For example, a boy who has been in a minor car accident may, months later, continue to complain of physical problems that cannot be explained by the accident or that clearly exceed any injury he may have suffered.

Table 13.1 (p. 368) presents the DSM-IV-TR diagnostic criteria for somatization disorder. As this table shows, the fundamental characteristic of the disorder is the presence of multiple unexplained physical

TABLE 13.1   *Somatization Disorder: DSM-IV-TR Diagnostic Criteria*

A. A history of many physical complaints beginning before age 30 years that occur over a period of several years and result in treatment being sought or significant impairment in social, occupational, or other important areas of functioning.

B. Each of the following criteria must have been met, with individual symptoms occurring at any time during the course of the disturbance.

   (1) *four pain symptoms:* a history of pain related to at least four different sites or functions (e.g., head, abdomen, back, joints, extremities, chest, rectum, during menstruation, during sexual intercourse, or during urination)

   (2) *two gastrointestinal symptoms:* a history of at least two gastrointestinal symptoms other than pain (e.g., nausea, bloating, vomiting other than during pregnancy, diarrhea, or intolerance of several different foods)

   (3) *one sexual symptom:* a history of at least one sexual or reproductive symptom other than pain (e.g., sexual indifference, erectile or ejaculatory dysfunction, irregular menses, excessive menstrual bleeding, vomiting through pregnancy)

   (4) *one pseudoneurological symptom:* a history of at least one symptom or deficit suggesting a neurological condition not limited to pain (conversion symptoms such as impaired coordination or balance, paralysis or localized weakness, difficulty swallowing or lump in throat, aphonia, urinary retention, hallucinations, loss of touch or pain sensation, double vision, blindness, deafness, seizures; dissociative symptoms such as amnesia; or loss of consciousness other than fainting).

C. Either (1) or (2):

   (1) after appropriate investigation, each of the symptoms in Criterion B cannot be fully explained by a known general medical condition or the direct effects of a substance (e.g., a drug of abuse, a medication)

   (2) when there is a related general medical condition, the physical complaints or resulting social or occupational impairment are in excess of what would be expected from the history, physical examination, or laboratory findings

D. The symptoms are not intentionally produced or feigned (as in Factitious Disorder or Malingering).

Source: American Psychiatric Association, *Diagnostic and Statistical Manual of Mental Disorders, Fourth Edition, Text Revision* (Washington, DC: American Psychiatric Association, 2000a). Copyright 2000 American Psychiatric Association. Reprinted with permission.

symptoms affecting several organ systems (e.g., gastrointestinal, respiratory, cardiovascular, etc.). These symptoms must persist for long periods of time and cannot be intentionally produced or faked. By definition, the physical symptoms associated with somatization disorder interfere with adaptive functioning. Typically, children and adolescents with the disorder miss a considerable amount of school or fail to join in age-appropriate activities because of their perceived physical limitations. The case of Suzie shows how pervasive and debilitating the disorder can be.

Suzie is almost 13. Her mother called our clinic at the encouragement of Suzie's pediatrician after she had been released from a three-day hospital stay for medically unexplained stomach pains and vomiting. According to mother and child, Suzie has always been "unhealthy." Suzie reports that her back hurts almost constantly and that she always has headaches. She has also had difficulty digesting foods such as meat and milk products for more than two years, and frequently finds urination to be painful. Suzie also describes significant coordination difficulties, which at times result in loss of balance and unexplained falls.

Suzie's mother confirms her daughter's many symptoms and explains that most of them began shortly after the death of her grandmother almost three years ago. Since that time, Suzie has seen her pediatrician almost weekly and, on occasions, as often as four times per week. Extensive tests conducted on an outpatient basis and during her past two hospital stays have consistently failed to reveal anything but minor ailments, such as colds or constipation. Numerous specialists have tried to convince Suzie that her symptoms are the result of stress, not illness, but she refuses to believe them, claiming forcefully, "I'm sick. I'm not crazy!"

Her mother is also convinced that Suzie is ill. As she explains, "I mean, you can't be so sick like she is and have nothing wrong with you. She probably has some illness that the doctors just haven't found out. That's what's so scary." Not surprisingly, Suzie has missed a large number of school days over the past two years and, when she attends school, she regularly misses class because she is resting in the nurse's office or is sent home early.

A comprehensive evaluation reveals that Suzie has a very poor self-concept, that she is depressed and often thinks about suicide, and that she is highly anxious about her school performance. She is diagnosed with major depressive disorder, generalized anxiety disorder, and somatization disorder. Although Suzie states without hesitation that she wants to go to college, she is presently failing five out of her seven classes, largely because of uncompleted assignments. She acknowledges that her school performance is unsatisfactory but explains that "this is as well as I can do when I'm sick." She refuses to accept help from the school to bring up her grades and, when faced with homework, usually becomes very upset, develops a severe headache or stomachache, and at times vomits. Her mother hesitates to set firm limits or to make her daughter do her homework, noting that "it is unfair to push someone who is feeling sick."

The DSM-IV-TR groups the disorder's symptoms into four categories: *pain, gastrointestinal, sexual,* and *pseudoneurological.* (This last category consists of symptoms that appear to be the result of neurological problems, such as seizures, but that have no known physical cause.) These four categories do not match empirically derived symptom clusters found in youth. For example, a study of a community sample of children and adolescents found that the physical symptoms they commonly reported clustered into the following four categories: *cardiovascular, gastrointestinal, pain/weakness,* and *pseudoneurological* (Garber, Walker, & Zeman, 1991). This discrepancy may limit the validity of current diagnostic practices, and will have to be addressed in future research.

Conversion Disorder. Children and adolescents with conversion disorder have unexplained sensory or motor deficits or dysfunctions. They have problems seeing, hearing, feeling, smelling, or moving that cannot be explained by a physical illness or disability. Initially, these symptoms seem to be the result of a neurological problem. However, on closer examination, they do not correspond to any known neurological disorder. A common example is glove anesthesia—an absence of sensation in the entire hand and wrist. This lack of sensation is inconsistent with the sensory organization of the hand. That is, if symptoms were due to a neurological problem, such as nerve damage, one would expect a loss of sensation on the top and on one side of the hand or on the inside of the hand, but not in the entire hand. Another example of conversion is pseudo-blindness, in which affected youth complain that they cannot see but are able to walk around obstacles without tripping or injuring themselves.

Table 13.2 (p. 370) presents the DSM-IV-TR diagnostic criteria for conversion disorder. Onset is generally acute and, in 10–60% of affected youth, is associated with a medically identifiable illness or injury. In these cases, the illness or injury goes through a process of **symptom magnification,** in which the original symptoms outlast the medical recovery or are much more severe than would be expected under typical circumstances. Symptoms of conversion usually remit without intervention within three months. In a minority of cases, however, symptoms return after a period of remission and typically signal the start of somatization disorder (Fritz, Fritsch, & Hagino, 1997). Seizures are among the most common conversion symptoms affecting children and adolescents, followed in frequency by motor disturbances, such as difficulties walking and sensory dysfunctions. Quite frequently, youth with conversion disorder also report other physical symptoms such as pain or gastrointestinal difficulties (Campo & Fritsch, 1994). *La belle indifférence* (apparent indifference about the seriousness of one's symptoms) is relatively rare in children and adolescents with conversion disorder (Spierings, Poels, Sijben, Gabreels, & Renier, 1990).

When considering a diagnosis of conversion disorder, clinicians seek not only to identify a sensory or motor problem that cannot be explained by an illness or injury, but also to link the onset or worsening of the problem to some stressor in the child's life. In some

TABLE 13.2   *Conversion Disorder: DSM-IV-TR Diagnostic Criteria*

A. One or more symptoms or deficits affecting voluntary motor or sensory function that suggest a neurological or other general medical condition.

B. Psychological factors are judged to be associated with the symptom or deficit because the initiation or exacerbation of the symptom or deficit is preceded by conflicts or other stressors.

C. The symptom or deficit is not intentionally produced or feigned (as in Factitious Disorder or Malingering).

D. The symptom or deficit cannot, after appropriate investigation, be fully explained by a general medical condition, or by the direct effects of a substance, or as a culturally sanctioned behavior or experience.

E. The symptom or deficit causes clinically significant distress or impairment in social, occupational, or other important areas of functioning or warrants medical evaluation.

F. The symptom or deficit is not limited to pain or sexual dysfunction, does not occur exclusively during the course of Somatization Disorder, and is not better accounted for by another mental disorder.

Specify type of symptom or deficit:

With Motor Symptom or Deficit

With Sensory Symptom or Deficit

With Seizures or Convulsions

With Mixed Presentation

Source: American Psychiatric Association, *Diagnostic and Statistical Manual of Mental Disorders, Fourth Edition, Text Revision* (Washington, DC: American Psychiatric Association, 2000a). Copyright 2000 American Psychiatric Association. Reprinted with permission.

cases, such as Alexia's, this stressor may be obvious, but in others it is much more difficult to determine.

Alexia is 8 and in foster care. She has lived with her current foster parents for more than four years. Her family moved to the United States as political refugees when she was 2. At age 4 Alexia was removed from her parents' care because of severe physical abuse and domestic violence.

Despite a traumatic infancy and early childhood, Alexia has done well. Her last assessment, conducted six months prior to her referral, showed her social, emotional, motor, and academic development to be age-appropriate. Her teacher describes her as somewhat "whiney" but says that she is a good student who has many friends.

Alexia became "blind" approximately one week before her referral to our clinic. Her foster parents report that one morning she woke up screaming that she could not see. They rushed her to hospital, where a full battery of tests uncovered no physical problem. Follow-up appointments with a neurologist and an ophthalmologist also revealed no organic basis for her inability to see. Questioned about stressors in Alexia's life, her foster parents report that she has recently begun to have short, unattended visits with her biolog-

ical parents and brothers. By all accounts—Alexia's, her biological parents', and her social worker's—these visits have gone very poorly, primarily because Alexia's brothers are aggressive and disruptive and are not properly disciplined by their parents. Interestingly, Alexia's blind grandmother was present at each visit.

Alexia is diagnosed with conversion disorder, although she continues to be monitored by a neurologist for any sign of neurological abnormality. All professionals involved agree that her visits with her biological parents are not only stressful but also very anxiety-provoking. This opinion is confirmed by Alexia herself, who says that she is scared of her brothers, that she does not like her biological parents, and that she does not want to return to live with her family of origin. When foster care officials assure Alexia that she will not be returned (and begin a petition to terminate parental rights), her inability to see clears up rapidly. She will continue to be monitored for some time to ensure that her symptoms do not recur.

As Alexia's story illustrates, a child may develop unexplained neurological symptoms after one or more stressful events. Her case also highlights the fact that these symptoms are often not unique to the child: Alexia shared her inability to see with her grandmother.

Exposure to her grandmother's blindness probably played a major role in the development of her disorder. Many researchers in this field believe that having an illness model is an important factor in the development of conversion symptoms (Campo & Fritsch, 1994).

Diagnostic and Developmental Considerations

Distinguishing between Medical and Psychological Conditions. Somatoform disorders are especially difficult to diagnose, primarily because the child's major symptoms are physical and a diagnosis cannot be made until all medical explanations have been ruled out. Practically, this is an almost impossible task or, at best, a very time-consuming and costly one (see Box 13.1). It is often made because none of the professionals involved can find a medical explanation for the youth's complaints, rather than because there is clear evidence of somatization or conversion. This point is important because follow-up studies of adults diagnosed with a somatoform disorder show that their symptoms often did have a medical explanation (Iezzi & Adams, 1993), something that may be also true of children and adolescents.

Lack of Normative Data. As mentioned earlier, essential normative data in this area are still unavailable. We do not know the prevalence rates of medically un-explained symptoms and have no reliable methods of distinguishing between aches and pains that are normal in childhood and adolescence, and physical symptoms that are not. The most commonly occurring physical complaints in children and adolescents in the general population include headaches (25%), fatigue (23%), sore muscles (21%), and abdominal pain (17%) (Campo & Fritsch, 1994). Such data are useful, but they do not indicate when such complaints are normal and when they are not, or which of these complaints are most likely to have a medical, and which a psychological, explanation.

Use of Adult Diagnostic Criteria. Somatoform disorders in children and adolescents are diagnosed by means of adult criteria. As a result, developmental differences in symptom patterns are largely ignored and, for the most part, difficult to take into account because of the lack of normative data just mentioned. In addition, some of the criteria used to diagnose these disorders in adults are not applicable to children. For example, to diagnose somatization disorder, the DSM-IV-TR requires the presence of eight symptoms. One of them must be sexual indifference, irregular menstruation, erectile dysfunction, or other symptoms of a sexual nature. This means, in effect, that somatization disorder cannot be diagnosed in prepubertal children unless the adult criteria are modified. More important, absence of diagnosis or use of modified diagnostic pro-

---

BOX 13.1 • *Estimating the Cost of Somatoform Disorders*

Somatic symptoms that do not have an obvious organic explanation are common in children and adults. Although no data are available on what these symptoms cost the health-care system in childhood and adolescence, figures highlight the immense financial output associated with these problems in adulthood. In fact, by some estimates, approximately half of all outpatient health care costs in the United States come from unexplained somatic complaints (Kellner, 1985).

To estimate how much more people with somatization disorder spend on health care than healthy individuals do, Smith, Monson, and Ray (1986) followed forty-one adults with the disorder for thirty months. Their outpatient visits, hospitalizations, and absences from work were recorded. Results showed that participants spent an average of seven days a month in bed because of their symptoms, in comparison to half a day a month for healthy adults. The study also found that the participants' yearly health-care costs were over eight times higher than those of average health-care consumers. Some participants actually managed to generate over $13,000 dollars in health-care costs over a three-month period without being critically ill—quite a feat when you consider that the study was conducted some twenty years ago.

cedures can make it difficult for clinicians and researchers to communicate, and probably less likely that children with somatization problems will receive adequate treatment.

Empirical Validity

There is no doubt that some children and adolescents have unexplained physical symptoms that can become chronic and interfere with their adaptive functioning. However, much more knowledge will need to be gathered before somatoform disorders are clearly understood in children and adolescents.

Associated Characteristics; Comorbidity

Somatoform disorders are associated by their very nature with a variety of medical conditions or with symptoms that appear initially to have an organic basis. Not surprisingly, these disorders are also associated with different psychological conditions.

Mood and Anxiety Disorders.
Although scientific evidence is sparse, there appears to be a relationship between somatoform disorders and both depression and anxiety. For example, Campo and associates (1999) found that as the frequency of unexplained medical symptoms increased in youth, so did their depressive and anxious symptomatology. However, these results must be interpreted with caution, given that these multiple difficulties are not defined by unique and specific sets of symptoms. Rather, physical symptoms such as fatigue and muscle tension are characteristic of somatoform disorders and of mood and anxiety disorders, thus inflating the degree of comorbidity among them.

Other Psychological Disorders.
Somatoform disorders are often thought of as separate entities that are not associated with disruptive behavior disorders. However, Egger and associates (Egger, Link, Costello, Erkanli, & Amgold, 1999) found that boys—but not girls—with ADHD or ODD presented a high number of unexplained physical complaints. This finding suggests that the reverse may also be true, and that the comorbidity of the somatoform disorders may extend beyond internalizing symptoms of depression and anxiety.

General Adaptation.
As Alexia and Suzie's cases illustrate, somatoform disorders can greatly interfere with adaptive functioning. The pain and discomfort of affected youth are real, even though they do not have a physical basis; for example, stress-induced stomach cramps and vomiting are just as unpleasant and distressing as virus-induced cramps and vomiting. Moreover, when parents share their children's conviction that they are seriously ill, children are rarely encouraged to participate in age-appropriate activities. They are regularly excused from school and are too ill to enjoy a number of social events that are an important part of growing up. This virtual isolation leads to further impairment, both social and academic, and tends to intensify the child's symptoms, thus contributing to the chronic nature of somatoform disorders. For example, every time Suzie's mother said to herself that it was unfair to push her daughter when she was feeling sick, she reinforced her daughter's passive role as a helpless patient, unable to cope with the challenges that most 13-year-olds face daily.

Epidemiology, Developmental Trajectories, and Prognosis

Somatization Disorder

Prevalence; Age and Gender Characteristics.   In the most comprehensive community study to date, Garber and associates (1991) found that 1% of the young people they assessed met DSM-III-R criteria for somatization disorder. To our knowledge, no published study has used the less restrictive DSM-IV-TR criteria. There is considerable agreement among researchers and clinicians that, because current diagnostic criteria are not developmentally sensitive, this rate underestimates the extent of the problem in children and adolescents (Fritz et al., 1997).

As we mentioned earlier, somatization symptoms appear to increase with age—probably because younger children tend to report a single symptom at a time, whereas older children and adolescents usually mention a number of symptoms. Before puberty, the most common symptom is recurrent abdominal pain. In adolescence, headaches and abdominal pain are frequently reported, as are pseudoneurological symptoms (Campo & Fritsch, 1994).

Somatization disorder affects boys and girls equally before puberty, but is more frequent in girls after puberty. Campo and Fritsch (1994) suggest that teenage boys may decrease their reporting of physical symptoms, whereas girls may not. These researchers note also that adolescent girls appear to be more willing than boys to seek medical help for physical complaints. These gender differences are consistent with what is found in adulthood (Iezzi & Adams, 1993).

Developmental Trajectory and Prognosis. The symptoms indicative of somatization disorder usually do not appear until adolescence. Traditionally it was believed that, once this pattern was established, affected adolescents were unlikely to improve. In his pioneering work on the topic, Briquet actually noted that women who had developed the disorder in their teens had a chronic condition from which they rarely made a significant and lasting recovery. However, empirical evidence challenges this pessimistic outlook. For example, in a study of the natural history of somatization disorder in adults, over 50% of participants identified because of a large number of unexplained physical symptoms had recovered after one year (Gureje & Simon, 1999). The extent to which similar results would be found in longitudinal studies of children and adolescents with the disorder is unknown. But these results are more encouraging than earlier ones and should foster new research in this area.

Conversion Disorder

Prevalence; Age and Gender Characteristics. There is no adequate epidemiological work on conversion disorder to establish its prevalence in the general population. Available data come almost exclusively from studies conducted in outpatient or hospital settings. In her review of such studies, Garralda (1992) notes that conversion disorder makes up only 1–2% of all psychiatric referrals.

Conversion disorder is rare before the age of 6. Reported cases tend to increase with age through adolescence, both in number and in severity. The disorder is more frequent in girls than boys, with a sex ratio of approximately 2 to 1 (Campo & Fritsch, 1994).

Developmental Trajectory and Prognosis. Little is known about the developmental trajectory of youth with conversion disorder, except that onset is usually sudden and that most symptoms remit in a relatively short period of time. For example, Spierings and associates (1990) noted that 72% of their sample improved over time, even though many of the children in this study did not receive treatment. When symptoms persist or return after a period of remission, they usually signal the start of somatization disorder (Fritz et al., 1997).

Social and Cultural Differences. In adults, somatoform disorders occur more frequently in lower-income individuals. Findings are less consistent with children and adolescents: some research confirms this association (Campo et al., 1999), but other research does not (Walker & Greene, 1991).

Evidence suggests that somatoform disorders may be more common in non-Western cultures. For example, in their review of the available data, Campo and Fritsch (1994) found that pseudoneurological symptoms may be one of the most common psychiatric complaints of children and adolescents in countries such as India and Turkey. Further work is required in this area.

Etiology

Biological Factors

Genetic Studies. Genetic research on somatoform disorders is in its infancy. Unexplained physical symptoms probably run in families, with as many as 20% of first-degree relatives having similar complaints (Guze, Cloninger, Martin, & Clayton, 1986). However, there is little evidence for a genetic transmission of somatoform disorders. For example, Torgensen (1986) found that none of the twin brothers or sisters of twelve identical twins with somatization disorder also had the disorder. This finding suggests that individuals do not inherit the disorder directly but rather have a genetic predisposition to personality traits that make them susceptible to the disorder. Specifically, Guze and associates (1986) hypothesize that women who inherit mild antisocial traits from their parents may later express them as unexplained physical symptoms. The researchers support their argument by showing that first-degree relatives of women with somatoform disorders often have similar disorders and also exhibit elevated levels of disruptive behavior, as measured by variables such as adolescent delinquency, teenage pregnancy, drug and alcohol abuse, and marital and social problems.

Neurobiological Studies. Neurobiological research has yielded a large body of literature on **somatosensory amplification** in individuals with somatoform disorders (Barsky, Goodson, Lane, & Cleary, 1988). Somatosensory amplification is a negative overreaction to normal bodily sensations. This overreaction develops in a three-step process. First, the child—possibly because of temperamental characteristics and/or because of exposure to people who are ill or who complain of physical discomfort—becomes hypervigilant to physical symptoms and sensations. Second, the child tends to focus on mild physical sensations that have a relatively low rate of occurrence, such as sudden stomach cramps or tightness of the chest. Finally, the child reacts to these sensations by attributing danger to them. For example, in the middle of class, a teenage girl feels an unexpected twinge in her stomach. She interprets this sensation as a sign of danger and is now on the lookout for any other discomfort in her stomach or elsewhere in her body. Attention and anxiety cause her to contract her muscles, to feel unwell, and to have a stomachache. If this cycle continues for any length of time, she may feel that she requires medical care. This three-step process is consistent with a long line of research that shows that people with somatoform disorders are much more likely to attend to minor physical symptoms and to receive treatment for these symptoms than average individuals are (see Figure 13.1).

Psychological Factors

Psychoanalytic Perspective. In line with traditional Freudian theory, modern psychoanalytic accounts of somatoform disorders emphasize the role of physical symptoms as psychological defenses against negative emotions or memories (Simon, 1991). In this perspective, some children and adolescents are unable or not allowed by parents or other persons in positions of power to express negative emotions or memories, and to deal with the feelings they provoke. They must keep their negative experiences hidden, even from themselves. This leaves them with no alternative but to man-

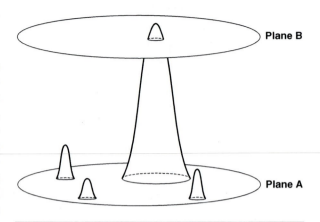

FIGURE 13.1 *Schematic Representation of Symptom Awareness in Persons with Somatoform Disorders.* In this illustration, Plane A represents a state of bodily comfort. This state is rare, because most people experience frequent minor physical aches and pains, which are represented as bumps on Plane A. The height of these bumps represents the intensity of the discomfort caused by these minor aches and pains. Plane B represents the conscious awareness people have of this discomfort. Robinson and Granfield (1986) proposed that, because youth with a somatoform disorder pay close attention to even minor aches and pains, Plane B is much closer to Plane A in these young people than in their average peers.

Source: J. O. Robinson and A. J. Granfield, "The Frequent Consulter in Primary Medical Care," *Journal of Clinical Child Psychology* 27 (1998), fig. 1. Copyright 1998 by Elsevier Science. Reprinted by permission.

ifest how they feel in more acceptable ways—namely, through unexplained physical symptoms. This perspective is intuitively appealing. However, since it has not been empirically evaluated, its etiological role remains untested.

Family Factors. Family theories feature prominently in the etiological literature on somatoform disorders. We will consider three areas of research and theoretical speculation here. First, some evidence suggests that somatoform disorders may develop in families in which children and adolescents are regularly exposed to a family member who is chronically ill and who serves as a model for illness behavior (Wasserman, Whitington, & Rivara, 1988). With conversion disorder in particular, a youth's symptoms frequently mimic those of a close relative (Spierings et al., 1990). Specifically, children like Alexia may observe or believe that people who are ill receive considerable positive attention from others and are excused from daily chores and responsibilities. We present a striking example of such family factors at work in Box 13.2.

A second area of research on family factors stems from the belief that some children use unexplained physical symptoms as a form of communica-

---

BOX 13.2 • *Family Models and Rewards for Illness*

While writing this text, the partner of one of the authors (WN) severely injured his back, so that he was thoroughly incapacitated for an extended period of time. His injury brought him a considerable amount of attention from family and friends, as well as co-workers, and excused him from most of his usual vocational and familial responsibilities. During this period, WN's 7-year-old son, Christopher, developed a mysterious backache, as well as numerous headaches and leg pains. He complained of these aches and pains day and night, and often asked for ice packs and massages to help him feel better. On occasions, his pain was so severe that he cried to be allowed to stay home from school. His discomfort was obviously met by parental sympathy and care, and he received more attention than he might otherwise have received during this time of considerable family stress.

Interestingly, while his father's pain became more manageable, Christopher's did not. Instead, his backache and many of his other symptoms intensified. After a physical examination to rule out an unknown medical cause for his discomfort, he was taught how to relax when he was feeling tense. In addition, both parents worked hard not to reward his illness behavior by attending to him when he complained or wanted to avoid responsibilities, such as going to school. This approach worked, and Christopher's multiple physical symptoms subsided fairly quickly. If children with similar complaints are not handled firmly after it has been clearly shown that their symptoms have no physical basis, they may develop somatization disorder, at least in part because of the family models they have observed and the rewards they have received for being ill.

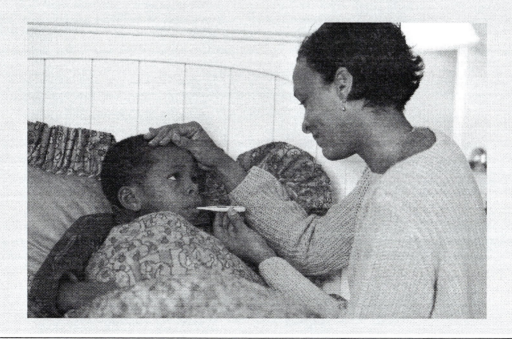

tion, as body language. This approach, which shares important features of the psychoanalytic perspective, assumes that some children rely on physical symptoms to plead for help in stressful situations, such as the loss of a loved one or sexual or physical abuse. Indirect support comes from the finding that somatoform disorders in general, and conversion disorder in particular, are linked to stressful life events (Stuart & Noyes, 1999).

Family system theorists have long speculated that unexplained physical symptoms serve to maintain balance, or homeostasis, among family members in dysfunctional families (Minuchin et al., 1975). More specifically, according to this perspective, families in which parents and children are overinvolved emotionally, or in which conflict is regularly avoided, tend to foster the development and maintenance of somatoform disorders. In times of crisis, the child or adolescent's physical symptoms divert attention from family problems by focusing it instead on the child's health. For example, in Suzie's family, marital problems were never acknowledged because of her parents' constant attention to their "sick" daughter's health.

Family theories are as intuitively appealing as psychoanalytic ones but suffer from the same shortcoming. Because they have not been rigorously tested, they remain highly speculative. In other words, although family factors probably contribute to the development of somatoform disorders, the precise nature of that role remains to be established.

Treatment and Prevention

The majority of children and adolescents with somatoform disorders are treated by medical specialists, rather than by mental health professionals (Garralda, 1999). Since somatoform symptoms are, by definition, physical, most youth who suffer from them are brought to the attention of physicians. A few doctors request a psychological consultation (Rief & Hiller, 1998); but even when such a consultation is requested, affected youth and their families are usually reluctant to consider the possibility that the symptoms might have a psychological origin. Like Suzie, whom we described earlier, most children and adolescents with somatoform disorders are convinced that they are "sick but not

crazy"—a conviction shared by family members, who worry about their health and often take them to numerous specialists for repeated physical evaluations.

A Multidisciplinary, Rehabilitation Perspective. Researchers and clinicians who specialize in the treatment of somatoform disorders believe that affected youth and their families need to receive services from a multidisciplinary team of medical and mental health professionals. In an effort to provide such services, a growing number of hospitals are setting up consultation services in which these professionals work in close collaboration to evaluate children and adolescents with unexplained physical symptoms. Garralda (1999) suggests that all multidisciplinary team members ought to follow six basic principles to facilitate a shift from a purely medical view of somatoform symptoms and to deal with the common resistance of affected youth and their families to psychological intervention.

1. Show interest in the child or adolescent's physical *and* emotional functioning from the start of treatment. If a discussion of psychosocial issues takes place long after the initial consultation, the family may see it as an attempt to dismiss the seriousness of the child's symptoms. For example, in Suzie's case, stress as a factor in her chronic abdominal pains and vomiting was not discussed until her second hospitalization. Before then, doctors had considered only medical factors, such as appendicitis and ulcers, as possible causes for her illness.

2. Assess the possible physical causes of the child or adolescent's symptoms thoroughly but quickly. Doctors should take particular care to avoid prolonged testing and to explain the absence of known physical disease as soon as possible to the youth and the family.

3. Encourage the family to explore emotional issues surrounding the child or adolescent's health, as well as other pertinent issues that may affect family functioning.

4. Offer friendly and "tactful" advice to the family about reducing stressful factors in the child or adolescent's environment. In Suzie's case, her pediatrician suggested that until her symptoms

improved her parents might want to decrease the emphasis they put on her academic success.

5. Help the child or adolescent remain in or return to school as soon as possible. Consultation with teachers and other school officials can be useful to facilitate the youth's integration in school and to promote academic success.

6. Make the psychologist or psychiatrist part of the treatment team from the outset, to help the family see that psychological concerns are relevant to a careful, comprehensive treatment approach.

When psychologists become involved in treatment, they often describe their work as rehabilitation, rather than psychological intervention or psychotherapy (Garralda, 1999). A rehabilitation perspective validates the youth's physical symptoms—"yes, the pain is real"—but shifts the focus from being ill to becoming well again. It also shifts the responsibility for getting well from one or more professionals to the child and family. Most important, a rehabilitation perspective presents wellness as a process of achieving normal functioning over time, rather than of simply getting rid of troublesome symptoms. Thus, children with severe abdominal pain should not wait until they are symptom-free to return to school. They should return immediately and increase the time they spend at school as they get better and their symptoms decrease. Although the precise components of rehabilitation vary with the symptoms the child presents, work with adults has shown that a variety of techniques may be useful to increase adaptive functioning and decrease physical complaints. They include reassurance and psychoeducation, behavior therapy, and relaxation training and biofeedback.

Reassurance and Psychoeducation. Providing families and youth with somatoform disorders with accurate information and reassurance about their condition is beneficial (Campo, 1995). In particular, explaining the results of negative medical findings can help reduce the family's concerns about the child's health. For example, clinicians often observe that the unexplained seizures of children and adolescents with conversion disorder stop after the family learns that tests indicate that everything is fine. Information and reassurance probably act to decrease anxiety in affected youth, which in turn reduces the number or severity of their physical complaints. In all likelihood, information and reassurance have similar beneficial effects on other family members, who can then focus on rewarding the child's healthy behavior instead of worrying about an unknown illness.

Behavior Therapy. Behavioral methods are a central component of most treatment approaches also (Campo, 1995). As with other disorders, these methods focus on reinforcing healthy behaviors and ignoring (and occasionally punishing) symptomatic behaviors. In Suzie's case, behavioral methods were used to reward progressively healthier ways of coping with situations she found stressful. For example, Suzie was initially given a special time with her mother whenever she attended school, even briefly. Shortly afterward, this privilege was given only when she attended a full day of school and did not go to the nurse's office. Finally, when she was attending school regularly, this and other social rewards focused on homework completion and other school-related activities.

Relaxation Training and Biofeedback. Relaxation training is also useful to alleviate the many physical symptoms of youth with somatoform disorders. Relaxation skills help them reduce the anxiety that triggers and maintains their symptoms, and gives them an active way of coping with these symptoms when they become overwhelming (see Box 10.4). The same is true of **biofeedback.** This treatment technique enables affected youth to monitor specific physiological responses that are associated with their subjective feelings of discomfort. Learning is made possible through a computerized device that provides immediate feedback—in the form of a visual or an auditory signal—as changes in blood pressure, skin temperature, or other physiological measures take place. Over time, this feedback enables youth to exercise increasing control over their physiological reactivity, and thus to learn to reduce their anxiety and its negative impact on their physical well-being.

Pharmacological Interventions. Because of the high rate of comorbidity between anxiety, mood, and somatoform disorders, anti-anxiety and antidepressant medications (especially SSRIs) are often prescribed to affected youth. These medications can be useful to control comorbid symptoms, but they have little or no direct effect on somatization or conversion symptoms. Given the multiple medical treatments young people with somatoform disorders often receive, many professionals recommend that medications targeting their emotional functioning be used with caution and discontinued as soon as possible (Campo, 1995).

Prevention.   There is no research on the prevention of somatoform disorders. Garralda (1999) suggests that providing parents with accurate information about their child's physical complaints can help prevent the development of these disorders. This very reasonable suggestion remains to be tested empirically.

Elimination Disorders

During the first years of life, learning to control the elimination of bodily waste represents a major step on the road to personal autonomy. Toilet training is as crucial to a child's successful development as learning to walk, to eat without help, and to speak. Consequently, issues surrounding toilet training are an important source of concern for many parents of young children and a frequent reason for visits to pediatricians and family doctors (Mesibov, Schroeder, & Wesson, 1977). Although most children learn to control their bladder and bowel functions without undue difficulties, significant problems can arise in this area, at times to the point of psychological dysfunction.

The DSM-IV-TR describes two elimination disorders: **enuresis** (urination in clothes or other inappropriate places) and **encopresis** (passing of feces into clothes or other inappropriate places). These disorders are not disorders of the biological functions of elimination, but rather of the *control* of these functions. In other words, children with enuresis or encopresis have failed to master age-appropriate control of these biological processes for nonmedical reasons.

Historical Overview

Elimination disorders in general and enuresis in particular have long been recognized as important child-

hood and adolescence disorders. In a historical review, Glicklich (1951) notes that enuresis was mentioned as early as 1550 B.C. in a medical text known as Papyrus Ebers. In the Middle Ages and the Renaissance, the disorder was thought to result from a physiological imbalance in the body's humors. Treatments relied primarily on foul medications to rectify this imbalance. These included herbal teas, potions, and "remedies" such as ground hedgehog testicles and burned rooster comb. By the nineteenth century, enuresis was deemed to be primarily an anatomical problem resulting from weakened sphincter muscles. Physicians therefore relied on what we would now see as abusive procedures to strengthen the sphincter muscles of children with enuresis. Treatments often amounting to torture included daily electrical stimulation of the genitals, as well as the application of medication that irritated or burned the genital or anal area.

Not surprisingly, none of the traditional "treatments" for enuresis or encopresis worked. However, their extreme nature illustrates the significance of elimination problems and the abusive measures that some parents are willing to take to stop them. A mother we worked with a few years ago had deliberately placed her 5-year-old son on top of a hot electric range because he kept wetting his pants. She explained her dramatic action, which burned the child's entire buttocks, as a desperate attempt to teach him not to wet himself during the day.

Definitions, Diagnostic Criteria, and Major Characteristics

Enuresis.   Enuresis is the repeated passage of urine in inappropriate places at an age when most children can control their bladder functions and toilet appropriately. The DSM-IV-TR diagnostic criteria, which are listed in Table 13.3, require the child to have attained a chronological *and* a mental age of 5 before a diagnosis can be made. This means that children with intellectual delays are not evaluated in the same way as their average peers. The DSM-IV-TR specifies also that urination must occur into clothes or in bed at least twice a week for a minimum of three consecutive months, or that the problem must cause obvious suffering or limit the child's adaptive functioning (APA, 2000a).

TABLE 13.3   *Enuresis: DSM-IV-TR Diagnostic Criteria*

A. Repeated voiding of urine into bed or clothes (whether involuntary or intentional).

B. The behavior is clinically significant as manifested by either a frequency of twice a week for at least 3 consecutive months or the presence of clinically significant distress or impairment in social, academic (occupational), or other important areas of functioning.

C. Chronological age is at least 5 years (or equivalent developmental level).

D. The behavior is not due exclusively to the direct physiological effect of a substance (e.g., a diuretic) or a general medical condition (e.g., diabetes, spina bifida, a seizure disorder).

Specify type:

Nocturnal Only

Diurnal Only

Nocturnal and Diurnal

Source: American Psychiatric Association, *Diagnostic and Statistical Manual of Mental Disorders, Fourth Edition, Text Revision* (Washington, DC: American Psychiatric Association, 2000a). Copyright 2000 American Psychiatric Association. Reprinted with permission.

The frequency of inappropriate urination that is characteristic of enuresis varies from one child to another. It can range from a few incidents per month to three or four per day or night (Butler, 1998). For example, in an American sample, 40–50% of children with the disorder had one or more incidents per week, but only 15% had daily incidents (Foreman & Thambirajah, 1996).

Subtypes.   The DSM-IV-TR distinguishes between *nocturnal only, diurnal only,* and combined *nocturnal and diurnal enuresis.* Nocturnal incontinence is by far the most frequent subtype, affecting 80% or more of children with the disorder (Butler, 1998). Children who are incontinent during the day often have more medical problems, such as urinary infections, and are more likely to have mental retardation than children with nocturnal enuresis only (Järvelin et al., 1991).

Primary and Secondary Enuresis.   Although no longer part of the DSM-IV-TR criteria, clinicians have

traditionally distinguished between **primary and secondary enuresis.** Children with primary enuresis have never acquired full bladder control, whereas children with secondary enuresis became incontinent only after a significant period during which they were dry. Approximately 80% of affected children have primary enuresis, and the remaining 20% have secondary enuresis (Liebert & Fischel, 1990).

Encopresis.   Encopresis is defined in the same manner as enuresis but pertains to the inappropriate passage of feces rather than urine. Table 13.4 presents the DSM-IV-TR diagnostic criteria for encopresis. This table shows that the child must have at least one incident per month for a minimum of four months, and a chronological *and* mental age of 4, before a diagnosis can be made (APA, 2000a).

    Research shows that children with encopresis have, on average, ten to fifteen incidents per week (Friman, Matthews, Finney, Christophersen, & Leibowitz, 1988). Thus, the frequency of soiling incidents is probably often higher than the diagnostic criteria would suggest.

Subtypes.   There are two subtypes of the disorder in the DSM-IV-TR. *Encopresis with constipation and*

TABLE 13.4   *Encopresis: DSM-IV-TR Diagnostic Criteria*

A. Repeated passage of feces into inappropriate places (e.g., clothing or floor) whether involuntary or intentional.

B. At least one such event a month for at least 3 months.

C. Chronological age is at least 4 years (or equivalent developmental level).

D. The behavior is not due exclusively to the direct physiological effect of a substance (e.g., laxatives) or a general medical condition except through a mechanism involving constipation.

Code as follows:

With Constipation and Overflow Incontinence

Without Constipation and Overflow Incontinence

Source: American Psychiatric Association, *Diagnostic and Statistical Manual of Mental Disorders, Fourth Edition, Text Revision* (Washington, DC: American Psychiatric Association, 2000a). Copyright 2000 American Psychiatric Association. Reprinted with permission.

overflow incontinence is the most frequent subtype, affecting between 80% and 95% of children with the disorder (Christopherson & Rapoff, 1983). This subtype usually results from chronic constipation. Typically, the child avoids defecation, resulting in an accumulation of feces in the colon and, in many cases, to an enlargement of the colon, or **megacolon.** To complicate the situation, feces become hard and painful to pass, so that the child becomes even more reluctant to use the toilet. With time, the overloaded colon overflows, and liquid feces leak out. The child has little or no control over this overflow, which can occur during the day and during sleep, although night encopresis is relatively rare. Encopresis with constipation and overflow incontinence can have serious medical consequences if left untreated or if treatment proves ineffective, mainly because accumulated waste can become toxic.

Encopresis without constipation and overflow incontinence is much less frequent, and knowledge about this subtype is limited. Some researchers speculate that it is associated with chronic diarrhea, which may be of organic origin; with toilet-training difficulties; or with behaviors such as anal masturbation (MacLean & Brayden, 1992).

Primary and Secondary Encopresis.   As in the case of enuresis, researchers often distinguish between **primary and secondary encopresis.** Though estimates vary, 40–60% of children with encopresis have never been successfully toilet-trained and can be characterized as having primary encopresis. The other 40–60% can be classified as having secondary encopresis, because their disorder developed after a period of normal fecal continence (Friman et al., 1988). Children with these two kinds of encopresis differ in important ways. For example, a clinical study of sixty-three boys with the disorder found that developmental delays, disruptive behavior disorders, and negative life events were more frequent in boys with primary than with secondary encopresis (68% vs. 10%; 45% vs. 21%; and 69% vs. 18%, respectively) (Foreman & Thambirajah, 1996).

Not surprisingly, encopresis is a source of great shame, as the following case illustrates.

Michael is 8. His mother reports that her son has a long-standing history of encopresis and that she needs help because she fears that "otherwise the school will get involved." Her fear appears to be well founded. On two recent occasions, Michael was sent home after having soiled himself in class. A complete medical examination indicates that Michael is in good health, in spite of chronic constipation. His colon is not enlarged. The doctor recommends a balanced diet rich in fruits and fiber for treatment of the boy's constipation.

Michael's problems go back to early childhood. His mother reports that he has never been fully toilet-trained, although he has had periods of varying length in which he has been without symptoms. Of greatest concern to her is that Michael's disorder has become "very sneaky." He has developed multiple ways of hiding his accidents, which take place on average four to five times a week. "You can't imagine the places where I have discovered dirty underwear. . . . If you have something to hide and you really want it well hidden, ask him! It kills me. The manipulations, the lies! The never-ending laundry, the smells, I'll spare you the details. But when I get off from work, drive home in a rush, start a load of laundry before fixing some dinner, and then, like the other day, I find a dirty pair of underwear wedged behind the refrigerator, you know, in the tubes in the back that makes it cold, that's it, I lose it. And I start shouting at him. He starts crying or shouting back, all the while lying to make me believe that he doesn't know how his underwear got behind the refrigerator. . . . It's a constant battle."

Michael lives with his mother and younger sister, who was toilet-trained without difficulty and is developing normally. His mother is separated from the children's father, but still wants her ex-husband to play an active role in the children's life. Therefore, Michael sees his father regularly. Michael's mother describes her ex-husband by saying: "We never got along, really. We never fought or even shouted at each other, but he was just impossible to live with. . . ."

Michael's mother adequately cares for her children's daily needs, but the life of the family is chaotic. This is due to Michael's problem, as well as to his mother's regular periods of depression and to her many responsibilities as a single parent. For example, despite his long history of encopresis, Michael has no apparent toileting routine and eats a very limited diet that undoubtedly contributes to his chronic constipation.

Therapy focuses on maternal support, on regular meal-times and a balanced diet for the entire family, and on a behavioral intervention targeting Michael's toileting. Unfortunately, mother and child only attend a limited number of therapy sessions and show little interest in establishing any household or toileting routine.

Diagnostic and Developmental Considerations

Medical Examination. In approximately 90% of cases, elimination disorders do not have a clear organic etiology. However, a diagnosis should not be made before the child has had a thorough medical examination, because elimination problems that have a physical origin often disappear with treatment. For example, enuresis can be the result of diseases such as diabetes or epilepsy, and encopresis can stem from physical abnormalities of the bowel or from inadequate diet (Butler, 1998). Unfortunately, as in the case of the somatoform disorders, medical examination can only indicate that the child's symptoms do not have an *identified* organic origin. It cannot conclusively rule out such an origin.

Developmental Context. Given that all infants wet and soil themselves before they acquire bladder and bowel control, diagnosis of an elimination disorder is always made in an evolving developmental context. As is true of other disorders we cover in this text, normative behavior becomes pathological here only when it persists beyond a certain period of development (MacLean & Brayden, 1992). But decisions about when a lack of bowel or bladder control amounts to a disorder are not easy to make—largely because control of these functions is acquired over an extended period of time and does not have clear-cut boundaries; moreover, there are important individual differences in normal development. For example, some children with mental retardation or developmental delays take much longer to attain full bladder and bowel control than their average peers.

Social and Cultural Determinants. The distinction between what is normal in this area and what is not depends also on the child's social and cultural background. In most societies and cultures, children are expected to attain bladder and bowel control between the ages of 3 and 5. However, this wide range hides considerable differences within and between groups (Liebert & Fischel, 1990). For example, in China more than 90% of children attain control over nocturnal urination by age 3, considerably earlier on average than in the United States (Liu, Sun, Uchiyama, Li, & Okawa, 2000). More fundamentally, enuresis and encopresis become issues of concern only when the child's family deems them to be, or when the child's elimination problems put the child in conflict with widely shared social expectations. The following case study illustrates the weight of social considerations in this area.

Tim is 11. He is referred to our clinic by his school counselor. In her referral letter, the counselor mentions numerous aggressive incidents during the past year, including violent fights, unprovoked attacks against peers, and explosive outbursts of anger. The report also indicates that Tim has significant learning problems and is two years behind academically.

A detailed assessment—based on information provided by Tim, his mother and grandmother (with whom he lives on alternate days), and his teacher—shows that Tim meets diagnostic criteria for conduct disorder and has numerous symptoms of learning disabilities. The assessment also shows that Tim has been wetting himself for years—on average two to three times per week at night, and twice a week during the day, often at school. However, Tim and his family initially dismiss the problem by refusing to talk about it. In fact, when the psychologist raises the issue with the family, Tim's mother and grandmother both laugh and say that they each had the same problem when they were children. In his grandmother's words, "Don't worry about that. He'll grow out of it like we all did."

When pushed to talk about his enuresis, Tim shows little concern about the fact that he still wets his bed but is extremely embarrassed by his "accidents" at school. "At night, I don't know, it doesn't really matter, but at school it does because the guys make fun of me." When asked what he does when his friends tease him, Tim quickly replies, "I beat them up!" He also notes proudly that this strategy can be very effective in quieting his tormenters. "The other day, this guy wouldn't stop annoying me in class all day, saying things like 'Pissy baby' and I should have diapers and things like that. . . . At lunch, when the teacher was not there, I went after him and I put my fist in his fat belly a few times, real good." Demonstrating the blows with his clenched fist and smiling, Tim adds, "He doesn't annoy me anymore." Despite his bravado, when the therapist asks him how he feels about being teased, Tim can only look away and cry.

A treatment plan is put in place to help Tim address his enuresis problem; but it fails, most likely because the family is only concerned about his aggressiveness at school and refuses to cooperate with any attempt to help him become dry.

Empirical Validity

There is no doubt that a significant number of children have elimination problems that seriously affect their adaptive functioning and cause major difficulties for their families. Consequently, the issue of primary importance in the empirical validity of the elimination disorders is not whether these disorders exist but how best to classify them. Specifically, what is at stake is the validity of the subtypes described in the DSM-IV-TR, and of the distinctions between nocturnal and diurnal enuresis, and between primary and secondary enuresis or encopresis.

We are not aware of any studies that assess the validity of the DSM-IV-TR subtypes. However, there is some evidence for the validity of the distinction between nocturnal and diurnal enuresis. For example, when they are compared to children who wet only at night, children with combined nocturnal and diurnal enuresis are more likely to have had a difficult birth or low birth weight; to have minor developmental delays and neurological abnormalities, especially in motor functioning; and to have psychosocial difficulties (Järvelin, 1989). Some research also suggests that neurophysiological variables are of paramount importance in primary enuresis and encopresis, whereas developmental and psychosocial variables are more likely to play a crucial role in secondary enuresis and encopresis (Harbeck-Weber & Peterson, 1996). Although much remains to be learned, these studies provide some support for the empirical validity of the manner in which elimination disorders are described today.

Associated Characteristics; Comorbidity

Medical Conditions.   As we noted earlier, in some 90% of cases elimination disorders cannot be attributed to an identifiable medical condition. However, children with elimination disorders often face significant medical problems. For example, children with enuresis have a very high rate of urinary tract infections (von Gontard, 1998), and many children with encopresis suffer from a chronically enlarged colon, or megacolon (Ondersma & Walker, 1998).

Psychological Disorders

Elimination Disorders.   Approximately one-third of children with encopresis also have enuresis (Liebert & Fischel, 1990). The reverse is much rarer, probably because the prevalence of encopresis is much lower than that of enuresis. Children with primary encopresis are more likely than their counterparts with secondary encopresis to also suffer from enuresis (47% versus 24%; Foreman & Thambirajah, 1996).

Other Disorders.   Although clinical reports often indicate that children with elimination disorders have other psychological problems, studies of community samples suggest that in a majority of cases this is not true (Abrahamian & Lloyd-Still, 1984; Friman et al., 1988). Butler (1998) notes that the commonly held view that most bedwetters are emotionally disturbed youngsters comes from clinical studies that are not representative of the population at large.

In clinical samples, the comorbid disorders most often associated with enuresis and encopresis are the disruptive behavior disorders. Precise figures are difficult to find, but it is estimated that 20–35% of children with enuresis and/or encopresis have clinically significant levels of hyperactive, impulsive, or aggressive symptoms (Foreman & Thambirajah, 1996; Johnston & Wright, 1993). Similarly, elimination disorders are more frequent among children with ADHD than in the general population (Biederman et al., 1995).

General Adaptation.   As Tim and Michael's case studies illustrate, elimination disorders are often accompanied by significant problems in adaptive functioning at home and school (Liebert & Fischel, 1990).

Children and adolescents with enuresis or encopresis are often teased by family and friends, and their difficulties create numerous disturbances in age-appropriate activities. For example, children with nocturnal enuresis cannot spend the night with a friend, invite a friend to their house, or go to camp, for fear that their "accidents" may embarrass them. Similarly, parents often report having to organize activities such as family visits and vacations to minimize the risk of "accidents," something that can be very humiliating for both parents and child. The mother of a 7-year-old boy we treated described this situation well:

Every time we have to go on a trip that will take a few hours, I put him in diapers because I can bet he will have an accident. . . . And when we go to his grandmother's, he spends the entire time in diapers because she just can't accept his problem. If he has an accident when we are at her place, she criticizes him, she criticizes me, well it's hell for everybody. . . . To tell you the truth, we avoid traveling as much as possible. . . . Last Thanksgiving, Jim [the boy's father] signed up to work all the time so we wouldn't have to visit his family or mine. It's sad, but what else can we do?

Epidemiology, Developmental Trajectories, and Prognosis

Urination and defecation occur more frequently during the first months of life than they do later in development. They also occur reflexively, since infants do not have control over their bladder and bowel functions. It is only between 12 and 24 months that children become conscious of these functions and able to exercise some control over them. At that time, they gradually learn to control the muscles associated with elimination and thus the timing of urination and defecation. For most children, this training takes several months, or even a year or two. In some cases, however, this training is never achieved completely or is disturbed after a period of normal development.

Enuresis.   Approximately 20% of children are unable to control their bladder function by age 4. They cannot be considered to have enuresis according to DSM-IV-TR criteria, however, because the minimum

age for a diagnosis is 5. Epidemiological data indicate also that about 15% of 5- to 7-year-olds, and 7–9% of 9- to 11-year olds have enuresis (see Figure 13.2, p. 384). As this figure shows, the prevalence of the disorder decreases rapidly with age, affecting only 2–3% of adolescents and fewer than 2% of young adults (Oppel, Harper, & Rider, 1968). The rate of spontaneous remission is approximately 15% per year. In other words, 15% of affected youth, on average, can be expected to get better without professional intervention when they become a year older (Liebert & Fischel, 1990).

The prevalence of primary enuresis decreases more rapidly as children get older than that of secondary enuresis. Some research actually indicates that the rate of secondary enuresis increases with age during childhood. For example, in a longitudinal study, Fergusson, Horwood, and Shannon (1990) found an increase in the prevalence rates of secondary enuresis from 3% at age 5, to 6% at 7 years, and 8% at age 10.

Epidemiological data hide important gender differences. Enuresis is more frequent in boys than girls during childhood (1.5 to 2 boys for each girl) (von Gontard, 1998)—probably because toilet training is generally slower in boys than girls. A Dutch epidemiological study found that it was only around age 8 that the proportion of boys who remained dry at night matched the proportion of girls already dry at age 5 (Verhulst et al., 1985).

Encopresis.   Encopresis is not as prevalent as enuresis, affecting approximately 3% of 4-year-olds and 1.5% of 7-year-olds in the general population (Liebert & Fischel, 1990). The disorder is also more frequent in boys than girls (sex ratio 3:1) and has a relatively high rate of spontaneous remission (28% per year according to Schaefer, 1979). Although the prevalence of the disorder decreases with age, symptoms can become chronic and persist throughout adolescence and even into adulthood.

Social and Cultural Differences.   Some studies report that enuresis and encopresis—usually of the secondary type—occur more frequently in children who are exposed to high levels of stressful life events or come from underprivileged backgrounds (e.g., Lunsing, Hadders-Algra, Touwen, & Huisjes, 1991; Rona,

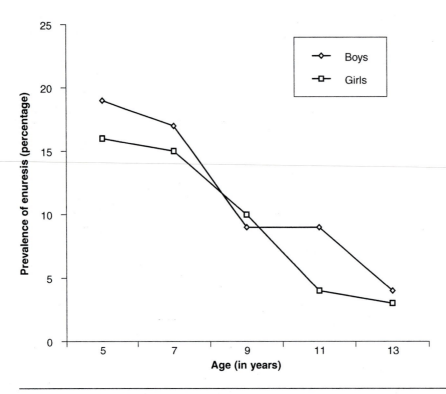

FIGURE 13.2 *Prevalence of Enuresis by Age.* This figure illustrates the rapid decrease in prevalence of enuresis (primary and secondary combined) with age. This decrease applies to both genders.

Source: M. Freeham, R. McGee, and P. Silva, "A 6-Year Follow-Up of Childhood Enuresis," *Journal of Pediatrics and Child Health 26* (1990), fig. 1. Copyright 1990 by Blackwell Science Asia. Reprinted by permission.

Li, & Chinn, 1997). However, this relationship is weak and often disappears when researchers take into account other variables, such as marital discord or maternal tolerance for incontinence.

Elimination disorders have been described in similar ways in different countries and are probably a universal phenomenon. However, cross-cultural comparisons are difficult to make. For example, a French study reported prevalence rates for enuresis that were much lower than those typically found in the United States (Lagrue & Milliez, 1970). In contrast, a study conducted in Nigeria found much higher rates of the disorder than those found in American studies (Peltzer & Taiwo, 1993). There are no straightforward ways of interpreting these findings. They may represent actual differences in prevalence rates or, more simply, methodological differences in the manner in which enuresis was defined and assessed in various studies.

Etiology

Biological Factors: Genetic Studies. A number of twin and family studies suggest that genetic factors play a role in the etiology of elimination disorders. For example, monozygotic twins have a concordance rate for enuresis that is almost twice as high as that of dizygotic twins (68% vs. 36%). Similarly, children with two parents who have a history of enuresis have a much higher probability of developing the disorder than children with one or no parent with such a history (77%, 44%, and 15%, respectively) (Bakwin, 1973). Comparable findings have been reported in research on encopresis (Abrahamian & Lloyd-Still, 1984). However, the genetic processes involved remain to be discovered and are very unlikely to be the same in all cases (von Gontard et al., 1996). In addition, genetic factors are probably influential only in the presence of other risk factors. Thus, a boy with encopresis may have inherited a predisposition to constipation, but would not necessarily have developed the disorder if his family had instituted a regular toileting routine early in his development and had not been initially tolerant of his soiling.

Biological Factors: Neurophysiological and Neuropsychological Studies.
Neurophysiological and neuropsychological studies have focused on a number of factors that may play a role in the etiology of elimination disorders. These include neurological defects and developmental delays, hormonal regulation, bladder capacity, and sleep and arousability.

Neurological Defects and Developmental Delays. Elimination disorders are associated with mild neurological defects, such as abnormal reflexes or fine motor coordination problems, as well as with developmental delays in language and other skills. For example, children with enuresis walk, talk, and achieve sexual maturity later, on average, than their nonaffected peers. Similarly, many of these children have a history of special education or grade repetition (Lunsing et al., 1991). Encopresis has also been associated with delays in motor skills, language, and/or reading acquisition (Foreman & Thambirajah, 1996).

Hormonal Regulation. Enuresis has also been linked to disturbances in the hormonal regulation of the urinary system. Studies have specifically focused on **antidiuretic hormone** (ADH) as a possible etiological factor. This hormone allows the body to retain water and concentrate urine. Researchers have hypothesized that children with nocturnal enuresis secrete less ADH during the night than their nonaffected peers and that, therefore, they produce more urine than youth who remain dry at night. However, evidence does not support this etiological factor, since there are no clear differences in ADH secretion between children with and without nocturnal enuresis (Butler, 1998).

Bladder Capacity. One of the oldest medical theories of enuresis, especially nocturnal, is that affected children have a smaller **functional bladder capacity** (FBC) than their average peers. Put simply, their bladder does not hold as much urine as that of average children. To test this theory, researchers give affected children a specific amount of liquid to drink and ask the children to wait to urinate for as long as possible. After the children urinate, researchers estimate the capacity of their bladder by measuring how much urine they void. Evidence shows that some children with enuresis have small FBCs. However, there is a considerable amount of overlap between the bladder capacity of continent and incontinent youth, raising doubt about the etiological role that this factor plays in the disorder. It is just as likely that the reduced FBC found in some children is a result of the disorder; that is, because they do not retain urine at night, affected youth may fail to stretch their bladders adequately (Ondersma & Walker, 1998).

Sleep and Arousability. Parents often report that children with nocturnal enuresis sleep so soundly that they are unaware that their bladder is full and, consequently, wet their bed regularly (Butler, 1998). However, there does not appear to be a relationship between sleep patterns and nocturnal enuresis. Bedwetting is actually found in all stages of sleep, not only in stages of deep sleep (Ondersma & Walker, 1998).

Investigators have also examined arousability as a possible etiological factor in nocturnal enuresis. Jenkins, Lambert, Nielsen, McPherson, and Wells (1996) conducted an elegantly designed study in which children had to turn off a computer-controlled buzzer at different times during the night. This system allowed the researchers to determine how loud the buzzer had to be to awaken the children. As many parents of children with enuresis report, bedwetters were harder to awaken than their nonaffected peers. This promising line of research may, in time, lead to important etiological findings in this area.

Psychological, Family, and Social Factors

Pyschoanalytic Approach. A number of psychological theories have been proposed to account for the etiology of elimination disorders. Psychoanalytic theorists have traditionally considered elimination disorders as expressions of anxiety about sexual conflicts between children and their mothers (e.g., Fenichel, 1945). In more recent formulations of this perspective, these disorders are still assumed to arise in situations of conflict between children and their parents (mostly mothers), but these conflicts are not necessarily sexual in nature. They can be directly related to toilet training or develop because of other family problems. In a clinical description of several cases of encopresis, Bemporad, Pfeifer, Gibbs, Cortner, and Bloom (1971) wrote: "There is little doubt that once established, the fecal soiling [is] directed at the mother. The symptom serve[s] both to repay her for her own demands and to get her attention. In terms of eliciting a response from the mother, these children certainly seem . . . to have discovered her Achilles heel" (p. 291).

This and similar claims are extreme and have little or no empirical basis. In the absence of clear evidence for their validity, they lay a burden of guilt on parents and probably do more harm than good. This is not to say that conflicts around elimination, which almost invariably arise in families of children with enuresis or encopresis, are of little importance. However, these conflicts are probably as much a consequence as a cause of these disorders.

Behavioral Approach. Behavioral theorists hypothesize that elimination disorders result from inadequate or incomplete toilet training. In this perspective, elimination problems can be brought about or aggravated by a number of different factors. For example, some parents may fail to implement a toileting routine or may accompany such a routine with repeated criticism or punitive discipline. Limited parenting skills may not directly cause elimination disorders but may put children who are particularly anxious or who have a tendency to be constipated at risk of developing problems that could develop into enuresis or encopresis over time (Houts, 1991).

There is extensive empirical evidence that elimination disorders can be successfully treated through the use of behavioral techniques (Ondersma & Walker, 1998). However, in the absence of longitudinal studies—research showing clearly that inadequate or incomplete toilet training is at the origin of enuresis or encopresis—causality has not been established.

Family Stress and Negative Life Events. Stressful family events—such as a divorce, the birth of a sibling, or the hospitalization or death of a relative—are associated with elimination disorders, nocturnal and secondary enuresis in particular. For example, a longitudinal study of a community sample of youth found that children who had been exposed to four stressful life events or more over a one-year period ran a risk of developing secondary enuresis 2.6 times higher than their peers who had not been exposed to so much stress (Fergusson et al., 1990). Likewise, in a longitudinal follow-up of more than 2,600 Bangladeshi children aged 2 to 9 years, Durkin, Khan, Davidson, Zaman, and Stein (1993) reported that the area in which the children lived was struck by severe floods in the course of the study. A detailed assessment of 134 children who were continent before this natural disaster showed that 45 (34%) developed secondary enuresis after the disaster. (None developed encopresis.) As the authors emphasize, this large percentage is striking because the second assessment took place when the children were almost a year older and, presumably, better able to control their bladder functions then. Although this study is unique, it supports the conclusion that children who are exposed to stressful life events that are beyond their control run an increased risk of developing secondary enuresis and have symptoms persist well beyond the event.

Treatment and Prevention

Enuresis

Psychological Interventions. Psychological interventions for enuresis focus primarily on nocturnal enuresis. As we noted earlier, children and adolescents with diurnal or combined nocturnal and diurnal enuresis often have comorbid medical conditions, and are usually treated by urologists or other medical specialists. Behavioral methods have consistently been found to be the most effective techniques for treating nocturnal enuresis (Mellon & McGrath, 2000). Specifically, research has shown that a **urine alarm** is the treatment of choice for this disorder.

The urine alarm is based on the principles of classical conditioning (see Box 1.2). It is designed to teach youth with enuresis to associate the sensation of a full bladder with awakening. A moisture-sensitive monitor is placed under the child's bed sheet or fitted to the child's underwear. As soon as the child begins to urinate, the monitor triggers the alarm and a bell goes off, awakening the child. The child is instructed to get up immediately, turn off the alarm, and go to the bathroom to finish urinating. Over time, the child learns to associate the sensations of a full bladder with awakening and to awaken and get up before the alarm goes off. A review of the treatment outcome literature shows that 66% of youth with enuresis stop wetting themselves with this system and that 51% remain consistently dry in long-term follow-ups (Houts, Berman, & Abramson, 1994). The urine alarm is probably most successful when used in conjunction with other behavioral techniques. For example, many researchers and clinicians advocate setting up a reward system to reinforce the child or adolescent after every dry night, and making the child or adolescent responsible for cleaning after an accident (with help, if necessary).

Pharmacological Interventions. In spite of the effectiveness of the urine alarm, the majority of affected youth are treated with medication—probably because children and adolescents with enuresis are usually treated by their primary-care physicians, who overwhelmingly prescribe pharmacological rather than behavioral interventions (Foxman, Valdez, & Brook, 1986).

Until relatively recently, **tricyclic antidepressants** (TCAs) were commonly prescribed to treat enuresis. TCAs are believed to prevent accidental urination by relaxing the muscles surrounding the bladder, thereby reducing the frequency with which the child urinates. A review of the literature indicates that as many as 85% of youth treated with TCAs show an immediate improvement in incontinence, but that only half of them show a complete (or near complete) cessation of bedwetting. Although these results are positive, the usefulness of TCAs has been questioned, because the majority of youth relapse as soon as they stop taking TCAs (Butler, 1998; Ondersma & Walker, 1998), and also because TCAs have serious side effects (see Chapter 9). Therefore, they are no longer considered as the pharmacological intervention of choice in this area.

DDAVP is a synthetic form of ADH, the antidiuretic hormone mentioned earlier (see Etiology). DDAVP is often prescribed to treat enuresis because it helps the body retain water, thus allowing the child to urinate less frequently. As many as 91% of affected youth improve with DDAVP. However, it results in complete dryness in only 25% of cases. And, as with TCAs, the majority of youth who are dry thanks to DDVAP relapse when they stop taking it (Ondersma & Walker, 1998).

Encopresis

Psychological Interventions. To quote leaders in the field, "treatment outcome research [on encopresis] is decades behind that of enuresis" (Ondersma & Walker, 1998, p. 369). With this limitation in mind, most researchers and clinicians agree that, to be effective, treatment necessitates close collaboration between physicians and mental health practitioners (McGrath, Mellon, & Murphy, 2000), because treatment requires a combination of medical and psychological interventions to eliminate chronic constipation, teach basic toileting, and train and reinforce the child for regular bowel movements on the toilet.

As mentioned earlier, most children and adolescents with encopresis are chronically constipated. A treatment program aimed at reducing and eventually eliminating chronic constipation includes the following steps: the child's colon is initially emptied with enemas, suppositories, or laxatives. The child is then put on a high-fiber diet that naturally facilitates the passage of feces. Mineral oils or over-the-counter laxatives may also be prescribed for some time. The goal of this aspect of treatment is to cleanse the child's colon and to make sure that he or she does not become constipated again. In parallel with or shortly after this initial step, the child is given instruction on proper toileting behavior. Specifically, affected youth are taught to sit correctly on the toilet and are often given exercises to learn which muscles to move when they feel the urge to defecate (Mellon & Houts, 1995).

Behavioral methods also play a major role in most treatment programs for encopresis. Different procedures can be used, but most researchers and clinicians suggest that the child be given a structured toileting schedule and set rewards for bowel movements on the toilet. For example, the child may have to sit on the toilet three times a day for a specified period of time. A psychologist may also help the family design a chart on which the child earns a silver star for each proper bowel movement and a gold star for each "clean pants" day. These stars can then be exchanged for rewards, such as a special time with a parent or a special dessert, until the child learns to control his or her biological functions without help.

Treatment programs with components similar to those just described have been successful in reducing or eliminating encopresis. For example, Young, Brennen, Baker, and Baker (1995) found that such a program resulted in reductions in soiling in 42% of participants and in the elimination of encopresis in 37% of them. Interestingly, many children who participated in this program also made progress in other developmental areas, suggesting that the successful treatment of elimination disorders often allows children to "grow up" in other important ways.

Pharmacological Interventions.   Apart from enemas, suppositories, and laxatives, there are no pharmacological interventions for encopresis.

Prevention.   We are not aware of any research designed to prevent elimination disorders. Proper toilet training for all children obviously offers the best way of preventing enuresis and encopresis. Although an apparently straightforward goal, it is one that many families find difficult to attain.

Chronic Illness

Chronic illness is not a psychological disorder. It is not listed as a diagnostic category in the DSM-IV-TR. However, children and adolescents who have illnesses such as cancer, asthma, or diabetes are at increased risk for social and emotional problems when compared to healthy peers, although their adjustment is usually much better than that of most youth receiving treatment for psychological disorders. In other words, chronically ill children and adolescents are more vulnerable to a variety of psychological difficulties, such as feeling anxious and depressed, because of the added stress that comes from being ill (see Box 13.3). Andrea's case study illustrates the complex and often subtle relationship between chronic illness and psychological well-being.

Andrea is 6. Her parents referred her to a pediatric psychology clinic to find out if she was ready to begin first grade. Andrea's parents note that she has difficulty attending and retaining material covered in kindergarten and worry that she may be less socially mature than her peers.

BOX 13.3 • *Depressive Symptoms in Chronically Ill Youth*

A number of factors have been found to predict depressive symptoms in chronically ill youth. A review of the pediatric psychology literature found that between 4% and 14% of children and adolescents with a chronic illness suffered at least one episode of major depression in the first three months after diagnosis (Burke & Elliot, 1999). Those most likely to report feelings of depression were adolescent girls, children from families with a history of depression, and young people with a negative attributional style. These risk factors are the same as those we discussed in Chapter 9 with respect to the etiology of mood disorders. In keeping with a diathesis-stress model of depression, Burke and Elliot's review suggests that chronic illness acts as a stressor that is most likely to produce depressive symptoms in children and adolescents who are already vulnerable to such symptoms. Importantly, this review also shows that depressive symptoms tend to increase in response to some specifics of chronic illness—namely severe restrictions on activities or perceived decreases in attractiveness. Interestingly, they did not find that the fatality of the disease predicted depression, contrary to the commonly held belief that children and adolescents who are fatally ill feel depressed at the thought of their impending death.

Andrea's mother reports that her daughter was born prematurely (at 28 weeks). She spent a lengthy stay in neonatal intensive care but made good progress and, according to her latest developmental assessment, has no significant language or motor delays. Andrea was also diagnosed with diabetes at age 4. Andrea's mother reports that she monitors her daughter's diet and gives her daily injections of insulin. Although Andrea has adjusted fairly well to her chronic illness, the family has been having some difficulty managing her blood glucose levels.

A complete intellectual assessment shows that Andrea has low-average verbal skills and average non-verbal reasoning and motor skills. Although she makes obvious efforts to do well during testing and often seeks reassurance from the interviewer, her ability to attend to the test fluctuates greatly. At one point during testing she puts her head on the table and says in a slow, slurred voice, "So low, too low." Asked about Andrea's blood glucose level, her mother explains that this is her way of communicating that her blood glucose is low. However, her mother shrugs off the incident as normal and gives Andrea a snack. This allows her to perk up and complete the assessment.

When asked about their daughter's social and emotional behavior, Andrea's parents report that she is very demanding and gets frustrated easily. They laugh and say: "She can't wait for anything. She always has to have it now!" They mention that they generally give her whatever she asks for, no matter how unreasonable the demand, "except for things that are not on her diet." They also note that her teacher reports similar behaviors at school, stating that Andrea is both "demanding and pushy" with peers, and "whiny when she doesn't get her way."

Andrea's parents see their daughter's premature birth as a "miracle" and her later diagnosis of diabetes as somehow their fault. Her mother wonders aloud if things would have turned out differently had she "given her much more healthy foods and no sugar before we found out she has diabetes." And her father feels helpless and "bad because life has already put so much on her little shoulders." Both parents acknowledge that her illness makes it difficult for them to set appropriate limits for Andrea. They give in to her easily, not only in what they allow her to do, but also at times in what they allow her to eat. Treatment focuses on helping Andrea's parents see that limit-setting offers the best way of showing their daughter that they care, and that such limits must be imposed consistently.

Diabetes management is made an integral part of the program, with particular care to teach Andrea to take on increasing responsibilities for what and when she eats. Treatment progresses well. Reports from home and school after a six-month follow-up period indicate that Andrea's behavior has improved considerably and that she is able to learn as well as her peers.

This case study highlights the interaction between chronic health problems, such as diabetes, and psychological functioning. Andrea's parents' feelings about her prematurity and diabetes made it difficult for them to set the limits that children need if they are to develop harmoniously and to learn. In addition, their feelings interfered with the strict dietary control that children like Andrea need in order to minimize the impact of diabetes on their physiological and psychological well-being.

Pediatric psychology is a relatively new field that has rapidly gained in importance because of the large number of children who suffer from chronic illnesses. Roberts, LaGreca, and Harper (1988) describe its purpose and scope as follows:

> Pediatric psychology is an interdisciplinary field addressing the full range of physical and mental development, health, and illness issues affecting children, adolescents, and families. [It encompasses] . . . a wide variety of topics exploring the relationship between psychological and physical well-being of children and adolescents, including: understanding, assessment, and intervention with developmental disorders; evaluation and treatment of behavioral and emotional problems and concomitants of disease and illness; the role of psychology in pediatric medicine; the promotion of health and development; and the prevention of illness and injury among children and youth (p. 2).

In the United States, some 30% of children have a chronic health condition, most commonly allergies, ear infections, or asthma. In a majority of cases, these conditions are mild and cause few significant problems.

In others, however, they are a major source of stress and interfere not only with the child's functioning but also with the life and well-being of the entire family. In the last topic to be covered in this chapter, we discuss the adjustment problems of children and adolescents with cancer, asthma, and diabetes.

Cancer

The treatment and prognosis for pediatric cancer have changed dramatically in the past fifty years (Eiser, 1998). As you can see in Figure 13.3, young people diagnosed with cancer today have a much greater chance of surviving than they had a few decades earlier. In Western societies, almost one out of every thousand young people alive today is a survivor of childhood cancer. Thus, a disease that was usually terminal forty years ago is now something that a large number of children survive.

Until fairly recently, low survival rates from most cancers meant that the few psychologists and psychiatrists who worked in this area focused their efforts primarily on helping families come to terms with their child's impending death. Significant improvements in treatment now mean not only that children live longer after diagnosis, but also that they may live through multiple occurrences and remissions of their cancer. These changes are positive but bring new problems of their own. First, affected children now face prolonged uncertainty about their own survival; they and their families often live as if they were under a stay of execution. Second, children who recover from their initial cancer are six times more likely to have cancer again than children in the general population (Hawkins, Draper, & Kingston, 1987). Not surprisingly, uncertainty about the future plays a major role in psychological adjustment (Eiser, 1998). To understand the impact of cancer on adjustment, it is helpful to focus on the typical stages children and adolescents go through as they are diagnosed, undergo cancer treatment, and (in many instances) recover.

Diagnosis and Treatment. Unlike youth with other illnesses, children and adolescents with cancer often

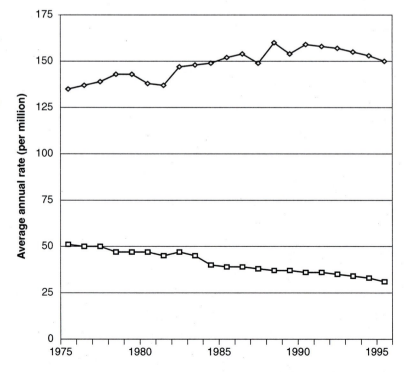

FIGURE 13.3   *Epidemiological Trends in Childhood and Adolescent Cancer in the United States from 1975 to 1995.* This figure shows that the incidence of juvenile cancer has increased steadily in recent decades but that mortality from cancer has followed an opposite trend. The figure is based on data for youth up to age 19, averaged across gender and race/ethnicity.

Source: Ries (2001, p. 165).

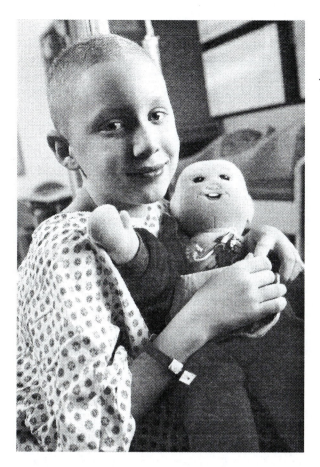

Child undergoing medical treatment for cancer. Cancer treatment can be very painful and often involves numerous debilitating side effects, which add to the many adjustment problems brought about by the disease.

feel relatively fine at the time of their diagnosis. In fact, for many of them, the side effects of cancer treatment seem worse than the disease (Katz, 1980). The physical discomfort brought about by treatment can be so great that many youth who complete cancer therapy say that they would not undergo additional treatment if the cancer were to reappear (Van Dongen-Melman & Sanders-Woudstra, 1996). John's struggle with bone cancer illustrates this issue.

John D. was 12 years old when his illness was diagnosed as osteosarcoma [i.e., a malignant bone tumor] *of the left proximal tibia [i.e., lower leg]. Approximately 2 to 3 months prior to the diagnosis, he reported pain in his leg and was seen by a physician who referred him to the cancer center for evaluation and treatment. After confirmation of the diagnosis, a series of treatments was planned. . . . After four treatments, however, John developed hypertension and renal [kidney] problems. . . . Because he was too young for a limb salvage procedure . . . the physician suggested that the family consider an amputation. They agreed, and amputation was performed (Copeland & Davidson, 1989, p. 322).*

Cancer treatment often also has multiple side effects. The following are among the most common and debilitating (Eiser, 1998):

- *Changes in appearance.* **Alopecia** (loss of body hair associated with chemotherapy) is one of the most distressing aspects of cancer treatment for children and adolescents. Some of them may also experience other physical changes, such as weight gain because of steroid usage; skin changes from chemotherapy; surgical scars; or, like John, even amputations.
- *Pain.* Many of the procedures used to treat cancer are painful. Intravenous needles, lumbar punctures, bone marrow transplants, and surgical procedures are all associated with significant pain and discomfort.
- *Nausea and vomiting.* Chemotherapy often results in nausea and vomiting, which can be severe. In addition, these sensations may become associated with certain foods the child ate immediately prior to chemotherapy and lead to the appearance of conditioned taste aversions that remain resistant to change long after the end of treatment.
- *Disruption of activities.* Because of multiple hospital visits and serious side effects, cancer treatment often means frequent school absences and disruptions of typical childhood after-school activities. In particular, when a child must have a bone marrow transplant, he or she is required to remain in protective isolation for periods ranging from three to ten weeks (Harbeck-Weber &

Peterson, 1996). During these extended periods, the child is usually allowed only a few visitors, who must wear hospital gowns and keep their hair, face, and hands covered during visits.

- *Anxiety.* During treatment, children often report being anxious about their own survival, as well as about the treatment procedures themselves. In the past, most physicians did not discuss prognosis with children, assuming that they had a limited understanding of death and that they needed to be shielded from the truth of their condition (Van Dongen-Melman & Sanders-Woudstra, 1996). Many health professionals today prefer a more open and developmentally appropriate approach to explaining cancer treatment and prognosis to affected children, in large part because this approach can help reduce anxiety.

Recovery and Long-Term Consequences. After successful treatment, children and adolescents with cancer enter a period of remission. This period may last weeks or months, or a lifetime. Most childhood cancer survivors show few adjustment problems, if any. For example, the incidence of psychological problems in a sample of pediatric cancer patients and survivors was similar to that found in the general population (Butler, Rizzi, & Bandilla, 1999). Overall, affected youth were more likely to complain of multiple physical symptoms and to be withdrawn than their healthy peers, but most ill children did not score in the clinical range on these variables. Not surprisingly, the study found that children who faced the greatest psychological difficulties were younger at the time they were first diagnosed, spent a longer time in treatment, and/or had to undergo particularly stressful procedures, such as cranial radiation therapy. Similar findings have been reported in a study of the incidence of posttraumatic stress disorder (PTSD) in cancer survivors (Kazak, Barakat, Meeske, & Christakis, 1997). These survivors did not have an increased rate of PTSD when compared to healthy controls, although nightmares and other symptoms of the disorder were more frequent in survivors.

Surviving childhood cancer may actually have positive long-term effects. For example, survivors generally achieve the same educational and marital status as healthy controls, and frequently report that cancer had a positive impact on their lives, often remarking that they no longer take life for granted (Gray et al., 1992). Likewise, survivors are less likely to report illegal drug experimentation or usage, and may be less aggressive and antisocial than healthy peers (Verrill, Schafer, Vannatta, & Noll, 2000).

Asthma

Asthma is a chronic lung disease in which the muscles surrounding the bronchia contract and the airways become inflamed and swollen. Asthma attacks can be triggered by allergies, exercise, weather, and emotional stress. During an attack, breathing takes on a raspy, wheezing sound as the child has difficulty getting enough air. In most cases, the condition is mild, and treatment involves only the use of anti-inflammatory inhalers. Nevertheless, asthma is one of the most common chronic illnesses of childhood and one of the leading causes of school absences and even death among children in the United States (Fitzgerald, 1992). About 5% of girls and 8% of boys are thought to suffer from asthma.

Asthma and Emotions. Unlike most other chronic illnesses, asthma attacks can be triggered by emotions. For example, anxiety can cause muscle tension, shallow and rapid breathing, and hyperventilation, which in turn can trigger an asthma attack. Unfortunately, the attack itself is usually anxiety-provoking and contributes further to a link between anxiety and asthma. The case of Anastasia illustrates this close link.

Anastasia was diagnosed with asthma when she was 5 years old. She was successfully treated with an anti-inflammatory inhaler until she was 10. At that time, her parents divorced and she moved with her mother and brother into a small apartment. The move entailed a change of school, and Anastasia complained that she now had little contact with most of her old friends. In addition, the separation and move resulted in considerable conflict between her parents.

An assessment for Anastasia was requested by her physician after she had visited the emergency room four times in a three-month period. According to her mother, Anastasia had been having frequent asthma at-

tacks that could not be controlled by medication. Her mother said that each time they had gone to emergency it was because she felt that her daughter might die of asphyxiation.

In reviewing Anastasia's current asthma attacks, the clinic staff noted that her most severe episodes—especially those that resulted in hospital visits—occurred after altercations between her parents. Anastasia said that when she heard her parents fighting she became very scared. She explained that she would then notice herself breathing hard and become afraid that she would have an asthma attack. With her attention split between her fighting parents and her rapid breathing, Anastasia often had an attack. She said that as soon as the wheezing began she had a feeling of terror and impending death. She also mentioned that these feelings made it difficult for her to work on reducing her asthma symptoms. Her mother stated that once these attacks began there seemed to be nothing that she or her daughter could do to stop them. Interestingly, her attacks also resulted in fewer parental arguments because both adults had then to care for Anastasia.

Treatment for Anastasia focused on having her learn to recognize the link between her emotions and her symptoms. In addition, she learned techniques to slow her breathing and relax her muscles to reverse the tension associated with asthma and anxiety. Unfortunately, Anastasia and her mother had difficulty understanding the emotional component of her condition and did little to follow the treatment recommendations. She was eventually placed on anti-anxiety medication, after which the severity of her asthma attacks decreased considerably.

Adaptive Functioning.   On average, children with asthma have a poorer psychological adjustment than their healthy peers. For example, Vila and colleagues completed detailed psychological assessments of almost one hundred children and adolescents with asthma and found that the asthmatic subjects had more DSM-IV-TR diagnoses (mostly of anxiety disorders) than either healthy controls or youth with diabetes (Vila, Nollet-Clemencon, de Blic, Mouren-Simoeoni, & Scheinmann, 2000).

Research conducted within a dimensional approach also indicates that children with severe asthma tend to function more poorly than healthy peers or peers with a mild form of the illness. Specifically, illness severity is a significant predictor of internalizing symptoms such as depression, anxiety, and withdrawal; somatic complaints; and behavior problems (Bussing, Halfon, Benjamin, & Wells, 1995; Wamboldt, Fritz, Mansell, McQuaid, & Klein, 1998).

Given that asthma is a major cause of school absences and that youth with asthma often have to abstain from a variety of age-appropriate activities, research has also looked at the relationship between this illness and social competence and self-esteem. Interestingly, there are few differences in social competence between children with and without asthma (Nassau & Drotar, 1995; Vila et al., 2000). Similarly, young people with asthma report comparable feelings of self-esteem and self-confidence to those reported by children with diabetes or healthy controls (Holden, Chmielewski, Nelson, & Kager, 1997).

Family Relationships.   As Anastasia's case shows, the family plays an important role in the prognosis and treatment of asthma. There is actually evidence that, in extreme cases, conflict with family members predicts death from asthma (Strunk, Fukuhara, LaBrecque, & Mrazek, 1989). Investigators in this area have especially focused on the concept of expressed emotion. You will recall from Chapter 5 that expressed emotion (EE) is a measure of emotional quality or tone used to describe family communication. Theoretically, high EE—that is, emotionally charged, critical comments from family members—could provoke a negative emotional state that might trigger an attack in children with asthma. To test this hypothesis, researchers have looked at speech samples from parents of children and adolescents with the illness. They have found that families of youth with asthma often express more critical comments and emotions than families of healthy youth (Wamboldt, O'Connor, Wamboldt, Gavin, & Klinnert, 2000). More work is needed in this area, however, to determine the role that EE may play in the course of the illness. Specifically, it is not clear whether children with asthma who live in families with high levels of EE have more severe or chronic symptoms, or a poorer prognosis, than children who live in families with low levels of EE.

Diabetes

Insulin-dependent diabetes mellitus (IDDM) is a chronic illness characterized by an inability to metabolize carbohydrates. This metabolic problem is caused by the insufficient release of insulin from the pancreas. Without enough insulin, the body cannot convert carbohydrates into glucose—an essential source of energy. IDDM is a relatively common pediatric illness, affecting approximately two children in every thousand (Rovet, Ehrlich, Czuchta & Akler, 1993). IDDM is generally diagnosed in childhood or early adolescence, typically between the ages of 5 and 6 or 11 and 13. Unlike cancer or asthma, IDDM has few or no visible signs. However, it is an invasive illness because its management depends on a complex balance of insulin injections, diet, and exercise. At a minimum, affected youth require daily injections, close monitoring of their glucose levels, and adherence to fairly strict dietary restrictions. If these minimum requirements are not met, children with the illness have either too much or too little insulin. Hypoglycemia, or a low level of blood sugar resulting from too much insulin, causes irritability and shakiness and, in extreme cases, leads to coma. Hyperglycemia, which is the opposite, can result in coma also. In addition to these immediate consequences, long-term failure to maintain adequate insulin levels can provoke blindness, kidney failure, and blood circulation problems that can lead to gangrene. In short, IDDM is a chronic illness with a variable prognosis and for which there is unfortunately no cure.

Adaptive Functioning.

In general, youth with IDDM do not show as many adjustment difficulties as children and adolescents with asthma (Hoare & Mann, 1994). However, like children with cancer, they tend to have more psychosocial problems than their healthy peers, but do not usually present a comorbid psychological disorder (Holmes, Respess, Greer, & Frentz, 1998). Interestingly, in a study by Northam and associates (Northam, Anderson, Adler, Werther, & Warne, 1996), the researchers found a relative increase in psychosocial difficulties when children were first diagnosed with IDDM, but this increase was absent at a one-year follow-up. Furthermore, the increase was indicative of mild problems that remained within the average range of functioning, rather than of problems of clinical intensity.

Psychological adjustment is most likely to be compromised in children whose diabetes begins early (by age 5) and is severe (Rovet at al., 1993). The severity of IDDM is usually gauged by a measure of metabolic control. Metabolic control is determined by measuring glucohemoglobin (i.e., average blood sugar levels). Overall, youth with good metabolic control are as well adjusted as healthy peers (Daviss et al., 1995). However, youth with poor metabolic control often have significant adjustment problems. For example, Liss and associates (1998) found that youth with very poor control, who were studied after they had received emergency care because of their illness, had a very high rate of psychological disorders (88%). These youth also reported lower self-competence and self-esteem than peers with adequate metabolic control.

Family Relationships.

Like other chronic illnesses, IDDM invariably affects family relationships—but not necessarily in a negative way. This is how Bryan, the older brother of a child with IDDM, sees the impact of the illness on his life:

*Hi! My name is Bryan, and I'm 7.5 years old. When I found out Michael had diabetes, I was real scared. Being only 5 [then], I didn't understand why everyone was so upset, and why he had to live at the hospital for so long. It was just before Christmas, and I kept asking my Mom when Michael was coming home and when we could be a family again. When he did come home, I was a little put out at all the attention he was getting. Because he couldn't eat all the "good stuff," I couldn't either—and that wasn't fair to me. Also, my Mom was pregnant and it seemed all she talked about was Michael and the new baby. Then on top of everything, I thought he was going to die (**DI**abetes), and now because the baby was coming, we had to share a room—and for sure I'd catch it, and die too!!*

Well, thanks to lots of help from [people at the hospital], lots of patience from Mom and Dad, and the fact that I'm a lot older, I know none of those things are true. Michael just started kindergarten, and I help look after him. My friends think it's real cool that he gives himself needles and blood tests, and we all look out for him on the playground. Once in a while, he needs help at night and I'm always there for him. My parents are really happy about that!

It still bugs me that I can't eat all the stuff that I want to when I want to, but I guess that's OK. Sometimes Mom and Dad put special things in my lunch, or take me out for a special meal by myself. At Halloween, I trade Michael some of my candy that he can have when he has a low, and he gives me the stuff that isn't really good for him. And when he has a "bad" needle, or gets kind of sad, I hold his hand and give him a big hug!

Family factors play an important role in the management of IDDM, at least in Western societies. (See Box 13.4 for evidence that family factors might not be as important in non-Western countries, such as Hong Kong.) It is generally agreed that, for diabetes to be well controlled, the family must be involved in the planning and monitoring of the child's daily activities, especially as they relate to diabetic management, and must learn to set effective limits (Ievers, Drotar, Dahms, Doershuk, & Stern, 1994). In other words, children who have more control in the day-to-day monitoring of their illness tend to have *poorer* metabolic control than children who are given less of a say in what they must do to manage their illness (Weissberg-Benchell & Glasgow, 1997). Although youth should be involved in the management of their diabetes, they will be successful only if caregivers also are involved. Obviously, less is expected of caregivers in the management of an older teenager's disease than in that of an elementary school child.

Treatment Issues

Although the treatment of chronic illness is largely the province of medicine, psychology plays an important role in this area. This role, which has been growing in recent years, centers on key issues such as improving adherence to prescribed medical treatment, helping caregivers appropriately parent a child or adolescent who is chronically ill, and easing family distress.

Adherence.   Adherence or, more precisely, nonadherence to prescribed medical treatment is a major issue in all chronic illnesses. As Bauman (2000) notes: "It is puzzling and frustrating to have successful medical treatments available for a patient's serious health condition only to have them ignored. In the provider's

---

BOX 13.4 • *Family Factors and Diabetes in Hong Kong Youth*

As we note in the text, studies conducted in Western countries have shown that parental involvement in the management of diabetes is essential for good metabolic control in affected children and adolescents. Specifically, like youth in general, youth with diabetes do best when raised by *authoritative* parents—parents who set clear and firm limits but also emphasize negotiating and compromise between adult and child.

Little is known about the importance of family factors in metabolic control in youth from other cultures. Stewart and associates (2000) therefore studied seventy adolescents with insulin-dependent diabetes from Hong Kong. Contrary to what Western data suggest, these researchers found that metabolic control in Chinese adolescents was not related to authoritative parenting. In fact, neither parenting style nor parent-child conflict predicted metabolic control. Rather, adolescents with strong feelings of self-efficacy were most likely to follow the diabetic treatment they had been prescribed and, consequently, to have good metabolic control. This study also found that gender and age were significant predictors of treatment adherence and metabolic control, with girls and older adolescents managing their illness better than boys and younger adolescents.

These results suggest that the factors that predict treatment adherence and metabolic control in diabetes may vary depending on cultural background. Greater knowledge in this important area should not only contribute to a better understanding of the link between cultural factors and chronic illness, but also facilitate the development of interventions that are best suited to the needs of youth from different backgrounds.

mind, the patient came in for care and sought his or her advice, and therefore should comply with the prescribed medical regimen" (p. 71). Unfortunately, this is not always or even often the case. For example, youth with asthma take their medication on approximately half of the days they are supposed to take them (Bender, Milgrom, Rand, & Ackerson, 1998; Celano, Geller, Phillips, & Ziman, 1998). Furthermore, on days when they do take their medication, they often do not take it as prescribed. In fact, Bender and associates found that children and adolescents took their medication exactly as prescribed on only 3% of the days they were studied.

Researchers distinguish between two types of nonadherence: volitional and inadvertent (Bauman, 2000). Volitional nonadherence occurs whenever youth and/or their families deliberately go against treatment recommendations. Some families refuse to have their children treated for cancer for religious reasons. Some adolescents decide not to take a prescribed medication because they do not trust their doctor, are convinced that the medication does not help, or deny that they are ill.

Inadvertent nonadherence, which is probably much more common, occurs whenever youth and/or their families believe that they are complying with treatment recommendations when they are not. There can be several reasons for this: (1) They may not be following a prescribed treatment because they do not understand or remember the instructions they received. (2) They may be following these instructions haphazardly but "well enough" in their eyes to make the treatment work. (3) They may regularly forget to attend appointments, take medication, or renew an important prescription on time.

These two types of nonadherence were illustrated in a study by Buston and Wood (2000). Among the adolescents in this study who admitted that they had not taken their asthma medication as prescribed, most of them explained that they simply "forgot." Others said that they chose not to take it because they thought the medication was ineffective, because they feared unpleasant side effects, or because they did not have a chronic illness.

Efforts to improve adherence can occur at many levels. They can take the form of better doctor-patient communication, with medical practitioners taking the time to make sure that patients and their families understand not only the treatment recommendations but also the need and rationale for the prescribed treatment. Adherence can also be improved through interventions designed specifically to provide affected youth and their families with treatment information. For example, Gebert and associates (1998) developed a family-training program that resulted in better self-management of asthma symptoms. Similar programs are being developed to facilitate the management of other chronic illnesses, such as diabetes (Anderson et al., 2000).

Parenting. Parents of youth with chronic illnesses face unusual challenges. In addition to their day-to-day parenting responsibilities, they must care for a sick child, help the child manage the distress associated with the illness, and learn to manage their own distress. To help parents cope with these multiple challenges, researchers and clinicians are developing specialized parenting classes that teach the skills necessary to manage chronically ill children or adolescents, and offer support and guidance to parents as they struggle to sort through their own feelings about the illness (Hoesktra-Weebers, Heuvel, Japers, Kamps, & Klip, 1998). Although research in this area has only begun, these specialized classes are likely to be beneficial not only to successful treatment but also to the child's long-term adjustment, especially when parents find it difficult to set appropriate limits because of their emotional turmoil about their child's condition.

Managing Distress. Doctors who are concerned about a patient or family's ability to cope with the distress associated with chronic illness may request a psychological consultation or refer the family for parenting or other specialized services. At that time, the needs of the family are assessed and a treatment plan is developed. This plan may include counseling to help members of the family cope with the disruptions that the illness has brought into their lives. Or it may focus more directly on the child or adolescent, to decrease symptoms of anxiety or depression that can occur in the context of the illness, or to reduce distress and pain associated with necessary medical procedures. For example, Kazak and associates (1997) developed a treatment program to reduce symptoms of PTSD in youth recovering from cancer. This family-oriented, cognitive-behavioral program involved affected children or adolescents and their parents, and combined both individual and family work. It was found to be effective in reducing anxiety symptoms at the end of treatment and at a later follow-up.

Mental health professionals are also often called upon to prepare chronically ill youth to undergo painful medical procedures in ways that are likely to produce cooperation and minimize distress (Powers, 1999). Venipuncture (drawing blood), surgery, chemotherapy, and many other medical interventions can be painful, especially when patients are anxious or refuse to cooperate. For example, a behavioral program for children with cancer and their families significantly reduced distress during venipuncture. This decrease in distress was accompanied by an increase in the child's compliance with the procedure, as evidenced by less use of physical restraint (Manne et al., 1990). As research and practice develop in this rapidly growing area, programs designed to manage different aspects of distress are becoming part of the standard care for chronically ill youth. These programs for chronically ill youth highlight the importance of psychological factors in well-being and the need to employ a truly biopsychosocial model for treatment and prevention.

Web Links

www.athealth.com/Practitioner/newsletter/FPN_4_21.html (At Health Information Center; a Website with information for professionals on a variety of psychological disorders, including somatoform disorders)

www.peds.umn.edu/Centers/NES/ (National Enuresis Society)

hsc.virginia.edu/cmc/tutorials/constipation/constip.htm (University of Virginia Children's Medical Center; information on chronic constipation and encopresis in children)

www.r-place.freeserve.co.uk (UK Encopresis Information Exchange; a Website for parents of children with encopresis)

www.cancer.org (American Cancer Society)

www.lungusa.org (American Lung Association; for information on asthma)

www.diabetes.org (American Diabetes Association; for information on juvenile diabetes)

www.childrenwithdiabetes.com (Children with Diabetes; Website for children, families, and adults with diabetes)

Glossary

acetylcholine (Ach) Neurotransmitter involved in the control of many body systems and functions, as well as in learning, attention, and memory.

active phase Phase of schizophrenia during which the symptoms required for diagnosis are present. Positive symptoms are usually most obvious during this phase.

ADHD, combined type Subtype of ADHD (attention deficit hyperactivity disorder) in which the child has six or more symptoms of inattention and six or more symptoms of hyperactivity and impulsivity.

ADHD, predominantly hyperactive-impulsive type Subtype of ADHD described by the DSM-IV-TR, in which the child has six or more symptoms of hyperactivity and impulsivity, but fewer than six symptoms of inattention.

ADHD, predominantly inattentive type Subtype of ADHD in which the child has six or more symptoms of inattention, but fewer than six symptoms of hyperactivity and impulsivity.

affective flattening Nonexistent or inappropriate display of emotions typical of persons with schizophrenia. Also described as blunted emotions or affect.

age of onset Age at which a disorder or its major symptoms appear for the first time.

aggression-related happiness Emotion displayed by highly aggressive children who appear happy and gleeful as they taunt or fight with adults or peers.

agoraphobia Pathological anxiety about being outside of a safe place and helpless.

alogia Poverty of speech. A negative symptom of schizophrenia consisting of minimal speech and lack of fluency.

alopecia Loss of body hair associated with chemotherapy for cancer treatment.

amenorrhea Absence of at least three consecutive menstrual cycles. Common in females with anorexia nervosa.

American Association on Mental Retardation (AAMR) Public association that disseminates information and advocates on behalf of persons with mental retardation.

amniocentesis Prenatal test of amniotic fluid to determine the presence of diseases or genetic defects in the developing fetus.

anhedonia Lack of interest or pleasure in normally enjoyable activities; common in mood disorders.

anomie Pervasive feelings of alienation and hopelessness found in many high-crime, disadvantaged neighborhoods; a disregard for social rules can accompany such feelings.

anorexia, binge-eating/purging type Subtype of anorexia in which the individual resorts regularly to binge eating and/or purging behaviors.

anorexia nervosa Eating disorder in which the individual's weight falls below 85 percent of expected weight because of chronic failure to eat for fear of gaining weight and becoming fat.

anorexia, restricting type Subtype of anorexia in which the individual loses weight by restricting food intake, as well as by fasting and excessive exercise, but not by binge eating and/or purging behaviors.

antecedents Environmental conditions that precede a desirable or undesirable behavior. Antecedents are central in a behavioral approach to the etiology and treatment of psychological disorders.

antidiuretic hormone (ADH) A hormone that allows the body to retain water and concentrate urine. Some researchers believe that this hormone plays an etiological role in enuresis.

anxiety disorders A group of disorders characterized by intense and persistent feelings of fear or anxiety.

anxiety sensitivity Fear of the negative feelings and sensations that children and adolescents with anxiety disorders associate with what they actually fear. Also known as the fear of fear.

applied behavior analysis Set of methods used to assess antecedents and consequences of a child's problem behavior in order to develop testable hypotheses about the most effective ways of changing it.

Asperger's disorder (or Asperger syndrome) A pervasive developmental disorder similar to autism, but without severe impairments in communication and social behavior. Called high-functioning autism by some researchers and clinicians.

398

attachment   Close relationship or bond between infants or children and their caregivers.

attachment theory   Developmental theory proposed by John Bowlby. This theory assumes that the attachment that very young children develop with their caregivers, primarily their mothers, plays a central role in later psychological adjustment.

attention deficit hyperactivity disorder (ADHD)   Disorder characterized by developmentally inappropriate levels of inattention, hyperactivity, and impulsivity.

attributions   Cognitive processes used by individuals to explain events in causal terms.

attrition   Tendency for participants in longitudinal studies to drop out as time passes.

autism (or autistic disorder)   A pervasive developmental disorder characterized by severe social and communication impairments; a limited behavioral repertoire; and repetitive, stereotypical movements. Begins in early childhood, before the age of 3.

avolition   Lack of will, interest, or drive. A negative symptom of schizophrenia.

battered child syndrome   Term coined by Kempe and colleagues in 1962 to describe child victims of nonaccidental injuries.

behavioral activation system   The behavioral approach or activation system is a reward system that plays a major role in purposeful activity. It controls the individual's tendency to approach and engage in interaction with the environment, especially to seek and respond to positive stimuli and situations.

behavioral approach   Theoretical approach that assumes that much of human behavior is learned and, therefore, that the proper subject matter for psychology is directly observable and measurable behavior and the environment in which it occurs.

behavioral approach or activation system   Neurobiological system enabling individuals to engage in goal-directed activity. This system controls an individual's tendency to approach and interact with the environment, especially to seek and respond to positive stimuli and situations.

behavioral contract   Plan of action negotiated and agreed upon by a child or adolescent and concerned others. This plan is designed to help change unwanted behavior by specifying clearly what is expected of the youth and the consequences to follow as behavior changes.

behavioral inhibition   Temperamental style of children who are irritable as infants and later become shy, fearful, and cautious. This style predisposes some children to develop anxiety disorders.

behavioral inhibition system   Neurobiological system enabling individuals to stop their ongoing activity and increase their level of nonspecific arousal, thus leading them to pay attention to their surroundings and to plan their behavior accordingly.

binge eating   Consumption of an unusually large amount of food in a short time period (usually within two hours). Binge eating is accompanied by a subjective sense of loss of control, which is probably more important than the actual quantity of food consumed.

binge-eating disorder   Eating disorder in which the adolescent engages in regular binge eating but does not resort to the compensatory behaviors that are characteristic of bulimia.

bioecological model   Descriptive model that puts children at the center of a set of nested transactional systems that shape normal and dysfunctional development.

biofeedback   Treatment technique that enables individuals to learn to monitor and exercise control over specific physiological responses.

biological perspective   Theoretical perspective that focuses on the biological aspects of normal and abnormal functioning.

biopsychosocial model   Broad theoretical perspective that emphasizes the multiple—biological, psychological, and social—determinants of behavior.

bipolar disorder   Mood disorder characterized by the presence of manic episodes. Young people with bipolar disorder may cycle between periods of mania, depression, and normal mood.

bulimia nervosa   Eating disorder in which individuals regularly engage in binge eating and in compensatory behaviors (such as purging, excessive exercise, or fasting) designed to help them lose weight or at least avoid gaining weight.

bulimia, nonpurging type   Subtype of bulimia in which individuals regularly engage in compensatory behaviors (such as fasting or excessive exercise) to counter excessive eating, but not in self-induced vomiting or the misuse of laxatives, diuretics, or enemas.

bulimia, purging type   Subtype of bulimia in which individuals regularly engage in self-induced vomiting or misuse laxatives, diuretics, or enemas to counter excessive eating.

catatonia   Extreme lack of reactivity to the environment observed in some persons with schizophrenia. Can include complete unresponsiveness; physical rigidity; posturing; resistance to instruction; or excessive, excited motor behavior.

categorical approach   Approach to abnormal behavior that seeks to classify persons with psychological disorders into qualitatively distinct groups on the basis of sets of explicitly stated diagnostic criteria.

child abuse   Avoidable and nonaccidental acts that endanger the physical and/or mental health of a child. Abusive acts are performed by the child's primary caregiver or by a person in a position of power over the child, either because of age, physical size, or position in the community. These acts can be acts of commission (e.g., hitting, burning, sexual exploitation) or omission (failure to provide adequate care or supervision).

Child Protective Services (CPS)   Governmental agency charged with the investigation of alleged cases of child abuse and neglect.

childhood disintegrative disorder (CDD)   A pervasive developmental disorder that begins after the age of 2, following an apparently normal period of development. The disorder is characterized by severe deterioration in all previously acquired skills (e.g., communication, social, and intellectual deficits comparable to autism), and by severe or profound mental retardation.

childhood psychoses   Group of disorders characterized by major disturbances in cognitive, social, emotional, and motor functioning.

classical conditioning   A behavioral theory of learning that hypothesizes that a response can be elicited (i.e., conditioned) by repeatedly pairing an unconditioned stimulus with a conditioned stimulus. Over time, the organism learns that the conditioned stimulus is a reliable predictor. Classical conditioning principles have long played an important role in abnormal psychology, especially in our understanding of disorders in which strong negative emotions, such as fear and anxiety, are prominent.

clitoradectomy   Surgical procedure common in parts of Africa involving the removal of a young girl's clitoris, a part of the sexual organs extremely sensitive to stimulation. Considered as a fundamental rite of passage into womanhood by its proponents, it is seen as culturally sanctioned sexual abuse by its opponents.

coercion theory   A theory created by Gerald Patterson to explain the interactional style of families with aggressive and oppositional children. In this model, parents and children learn to influence each other, not through dialogue, but mainly through the use of negative and coercive behaviors—such as provocation, disobedience, yelling, and criticism. Over time, coercive exchanges teach children to become increasingly defiant and aggressive and teach parents to be easily angered and to rely on more and more forceful but ineffective attempts at discipline (in extreme cases, to the point of physical abuse).

cognitive-behavioral approach   Psychological approach that focuses on how people process information about themselves, others, and their environment, and on how the beliefs that result from this processing affect their behavior.

cognitive-behavioral therapy   Treatment approach designed to change inappropriate behavior by modifying the thoughts or cognitions that are believed to control it.

cognitive errors   Mistaken beliefs that promote continued psychological problems because they are based on false, but unchallenged, negative predictions about potential threats and about one's ability to cope with them. Commonly observed in youth with anxiety and mood disorders.

cognitive triad   Cycle of negative automatic thoughts about the self, the world, and the future. Assumed by Aaron Beck to play a major role in the development and maintenance of mood disorders.

cohort effects   Effects that depend less on the nature of the disorder being studied than on the historical period in which a particular sample was recruited to study it.

communication disorders   Group of conditions characterized by major difficulties in producing age-appropriate speech sounds, or combining and manipulating the various components of language (i.e., phonemes, syllables, and words) for fluent, effective communication.

comorbid, comorbidity   The presence of two or more psychological disorders existing at the same time.

compensatory behaviors   Behaviors such as excessive exercise, self-induced vomiting, and misuse of laxatives, diuretics, or enemas commonly found in children and adolescents with anorexia or bulimia.

compulsions   Repetitive, ritualistic behaviors performed to reduce anxiety associated with obsessions. A diagnostic feature of obsessive-compulsive disorder, compulsions often focus on washing, checking, sorting, or arranging.

compulsive compliance   Tendency of some abused children to comply more quickly and readily to the demands of significant adults than other children do. This tendency, which probably stems from a hypervigilance to social cues, may serve to protect these children from abuse by caregivers.

concordance rate   Rate at which a particular disorder is found to co-occur in relatives such as parents or siblings.

conduct disorder (CD)   Psychological disorder characterized by a pervasive pattern of aggressive and/or antisocial behaviors that violate the basic rights of others or major social rules or norms. These behaviors must significantly impair a child or adolescent's functioning for diagnosis to be possible.

consequences   Environmental conditions that follow a desirable or undesirable behavior. Consequences are central in a behavioral approach to the etiology and treatment of psychological disorders.

constitutional factors   Physical and psychological characteristics that are inherited or develop very early, often in the course of pregnancy.

contingency management programs   Intensive behavior modification plans that are individually tailored to enable children or adolescents to earn points for appropriate target behaviors (and usually to lose points for inappropriate behaviors). Points can later be exchanged for group activities, such as field trips, as well as for privileges and other rewards.

conversion disorder   Somatoform disorder characterized by unexplained deficits or dysfunctions in sensory or motor functioning that are triggered by stress.

correlation   Statistical estimate of the extent to which two variables are related or associated. Correlations can range from −1.0 to +1.0.

cortisol   Hormone secreted by the body during times of stress.

covert behavior problems   Problems that stem from behaviors that are typically difficult to observe directly, such as lying, stealing, skipping school, and fraud.

cross-sectional studies   Studies that compare two or more groups of individuals who share similar characteristics but who are not of the same age.

daily report card   Form used to track a child's progress on a limited number of treatment goals, and to facilitate communication between school and home.

defense mechanisms   Psychological processes that distort reality in order to protect the ego from overwhelming anxiety.

delinquency   Legal concept used to describe an array of antisocial behaviors that generally begin and end during adolescence.

delusions   Persistent beliefs that others (in one's family or culture) do not share and consider odd, exaggerated, irrational, or false.

dementia praecox   Term coined by Morel to describe major deterioration in mental functioning in physically healthy young people.

depersonalization   Loss of one's sense of personal identity or the detachment of physical sensations.

depressive attributional style   Belief system in which people attribute negative outcomes to stable, internal, and global characteristics in themselves. Plays a major role in the cognitive perspective on depression.

depressive equivalents   See masked depression.

descriptive studies   Studies designed to provide careful, detailed descriptions of the characteristics of a phenomenon. Common forms of descriptive studies are surveys, case studies, and comparative studies.

developmental perspective (in mental retardation)   Theoretical perspective that assumes that children with mental retardation have the same abilities as average children, but that these abilities develop more slowly or at a different pace.

developmental psychopathology   Approach to research and intervention that emphasizes the importance of normal development to a comprehensive understanding of child and adolescent disorders.

developmental trajectory   Description and study of the manner in which psychological disorders typically evolve over time and of the factors associated with this evolution.

dexamethasone suppression test (DST)   Test for detecting depression. Dexamethasone is a cortisol-like chemical that suppresses cortisol secretion for twenty-four hours or more in average individuals. Many depressed adults fail to show this pattern of suppression, as do some children and adolescents, especially when their symptoms are severe.

diathesis-stress model   Etiological model that assumes that psychological disorders occur in the presence of a vulnerability (or diathesis) and of stressful life circumstances. Neither vulnerability nor stress is sufficient alone to produce a disorder.

differential perspective (in mental retardation)   Theoretical perspective that assumes that children with mental retardation have abilities that are different from those of average children and that often reflect the specific nature of their retardation.

dimensional approach   Approach to abnormal behavior that seeks to quantify the particular strengths and vulnerabilities of persons with psychological disorders.

direct aggression   Form of aggression in which the child or adolescent directly attacks another person. "Getting in someone's face" and fistfighting are examples of direct aggression.

direct instruction   Treatment approach for learning disabilities that focuses mainly on the content of the material that students find difficult to master, exposing them regularly to this material in highly structured lessons, and giving them feedback about the accuracy of their performance.

disorder of written expression   Disorder in which a child or adolescent has major difficulties with handwriting, vocabulary, spelling, and organizing written compositions.

disorganized symptoms   Patterns of speech and motor activity that appear illogical and have no apparent purpose or goal. Common in schizophrenia.

disruptive behavior disorders   Loosely defined group of "behavior problems" or disorders that include attention deficit hyperactivity disorder, oppositional defiant disorder, and conduct disorder. Children and adolescents with these disorders disturb, provoke, defy, or victimize those around them.

dopamine   Neurotransmitter that inhibits the transmission of nerve impulses in several regions of the brain and plays an important function in reward and reward-seeking behaviors; implicated in the etiology of several disorders (e.g., schizophrenia, attention deficit hyperactivity disorder).

double-bind theory   Bateson and colleagues' theory that schizophrenia is the result of a contradictory pattern of communication within the family.

double depression   Simultaneous presence of major depressive disorder and dysthymic disorder in the same person.

Down syndrome   Genetic condition associated with mental retardation (also called Trisomy 21 because it involves partial duplication of chromosome 21).

dyscalculia   Term generally used as a synonym for mathematics disorder, although some researchers and clinicians use the term to refer to a subtype of that disorder.

dysgraphia   Term generally used as a synonym for disorder of written expression, although some researchers and clinicians use the term to refer to a subtype of that disorder.

dyslexia   Term generally used as a synonym for reading disorder, although some researchers and clinicians use the term to refer to a subtype of that disorder, or to the tendency to reverse or transpose letters observed in some children.

dysthymic disorder (or dysthymia)   Mood disorder in which symptoms are less severe but more chronic than they are in major depressive disorder, and in which fluctuations between depressive periods and periods of remission are less marked.

eating disorders   Group of disorders characterized by major dysfunctions in several behaviors associated with eating. See anorexia nervosa, bulimia, and binge-eating disorder.

echolalia   Repetition of words or phrases out of context. This repetition may be immediate or delayed.

Education of the Handicapped Act   Public Law 94-142 (passed in 1975), which legally defines learning disabilities and mandates school interventions.

educational neglect   Most commonly reported form of neglect. Includes any behavior by a caregiver that significantly limits a child's educational opportunities or allows the child to remain out of school for extended periods.

ego   Personality structure that Freud believed mediates between the instinctual urges of the id and the limits imposed by reality.

emotional abuse   Maladaptive parenting behaviors, outside of physical and sexual abuse and neglect, that may adversely affect a child's emotional development (e.g., persistent verbal threats and demeaning comments, open rejection).

emotional neglect   Persistent disregard of a child's emotional needs, to the point of putting the child's emotional development in jeopardy.

empirical validity   Degree to which empirical research supports the manner in which psychological disorders are currently described and classified.

encopresis   Elimination disorder characterized by the passing of feces into clothes or other inappropriate places.

endogenous symptoms   Symptoms of depression that cannot be explained by observable changes in the environment and that are assumed to result from internal, presumably biological, factors.

enuresis   Elimination disorder characterized by urination in clothes or other inappropriate places.

epidemiology   Study of the frequency, distribution, and co-morbidity of disorders within the population.

equifinality   Principle according to which different causes can have the same consequence for development.

etiology   Study of the origins or causes of disorders.

eugenics   Claim that the human race can be improved through selective breeding. Just as cows and other animals are bred for specific features, eugenicists believe that humans with valued characteristics (e.g., high intelligence) must be encouraged to mate with "suitable" individuals to produce children endowed with similar characteristics. Conversely, eugenicists believe that humans with traits they consider less desirable should be discouraged or prevented from having children (e.g., through forced sterilization).

evoked potentials   Brain electrical activity occurring in response to a task or other stimulation.

executive functions   Neuropsychological processes that underlie self-regulation. These processes are essential to behavioral planning, monitoring, and self-regulation.

exposure   Critical component of treatment of anxiety disorders. Consists of exposing anxious youth to the situations or stimuli they fear most.

expressed emotion   Measure of emotional quality or tone used to describe communication in families of persons with schizophrenia or other psychological disorders.

expressive language disorder   Disorder in which children or adolescents have major difficulties expressing themselves.

extinction   Behavioral treatment method that consists of ignoring an undesirable behavior to make it disappear.

extrapyramidal symptoms   Potentially extreme muscle and motor disturbances, such as acute spasms of the tongue, neck, and head, brought about by use of certain psychotropic medications.

factitious disorder by proxy   Disorder in which a caregiver fakes a mental or physical illness in a child in order to get the attention of medical or mental health professionals. In this disorder, the caregiver deliberately induces symptoms in the child and then takes the child in for treatment. Also known as Munchausen by proxy.

fear hierarchy   List of the situations or stimuli of which a youth is afraid in order of increasing severity. Used in cognitive-behavioral treatment of anxiety disorders.

feeding disorders   Psychological disturbances in the food intake process most often observed in young children or in persons with severe or profound mental retardation (e.g., the child eats nonedible substances or eats but fails to put on weight as expected).

fetal alcohol syndrome Syndrome affecting some children who were exposed to maternal alcohol abuse before birth (*in utero*). This syndrome includes mental retardation, facial abnormalities, and learning difficulties.

flashbacks Brief periods in which a child or adolescent relives a traumatic event, often in a near-panic state; symptomatic of posttraumatic stress disorder.

flight of ideas Symptom of mania in which racing thoughts interfere with a person's ability to talk coherently.

fragile X syndrome Genetic condition associated with mental retardation (so-called because affected individuals have a weak or "pinched" X chromosome).

functional bladder capacity The amount of urine a child's bladder can contain. It has been hypothesized that youth with enuresis have a smaller functional bladder capacity than their average peers, although research provides little support for this hypothesis.

functional communication training A therapy developed for youth with autism and designed to teach socially appropriate responses that serve the same function as self-injurious, aggressive, or self-stimulating behaviors.

gamma-amino-butyric acid (GABA) Neurotransmitter that inhibits the transmission of nerve impulses; involved in the control of fear and other emotions, and implicated in the etiology of anxiety disorders.

generalized anxiety disorder (GAD) Anxiety disorder characterized by severe, uncontrollable anxiety or worry about a range of activities, events, or skills, and accompanied by one or more physiological symptoms (typically, physical tension, agitation, restlessness, or physical pains such as stomachaches or headaches).

genes Units of hereditary information composed of DNA (deoxyribonucleic acid) and located at a fixed position on a chromosome.

habituation Reduction in a child or adolescent's fearfulness brought about by exposure.

hallucinations Perceptual experiences that others do not share.

heritability Quantitative measure of the extent to which observed differences between people—in intelligence, aggressiveness, fearfulness, and other such characteristics—can be attributed to genetic influences.

hippocampus Brain structure that plays a central role in learning, memory, and emotion regulation.

hormones Chemicals produced by the endocrine glands; they travel in the bloodstream, from where they influence the functioning of the entire organism.

hostile aggression Form of aggression in which the child or adolescent attacks another person in order to inflict harm, rather than to achieve an instrumental goal.

hostile attributional bias Tendency of children and adolescents with oppositional defiant disorder or conduct disorder to interpret the intentions of another child or adult as hostile, when these intentions are actually ambiguous or unclear.

hypomanic episodes Manic-like episodes in which full diagnostic criteria for mania are not met, but enough manic symptoms are present to disturb functioning.

hypothalamic-pituitary-adrenal axis (HPA) Hormonal system consisting of the hypothalamus, pituitary gland, and adrenal glands. Implicated in the regulation of emotions.

hypotheses Tentative explanations designed to account for some observations.

id Personality structure that Freud believed provides psychological energy or drive. Totally unconscious and driven by instincts, the id seeks only its own selfish satisfaction.

ideas of reference Delusional thinking that credits trivial or unimportant events with great personal significance.

incest Sexual relations between a child and a close relative. The term is most often used to describe sexual relations between a female child and her father or stepfather.

incidence Estimate of the number of new cases of a disorder that develop in the population over a specified period of time (typically one year).

indirect (or relational) aggression Form of aggression in which the child or adolescent harms another person through indirect means—for instance, by spreading false rumors or using a third person to attack one's victim.

instrumental aggression Form of aggression in which the child or adolescent attacks another person in order to achieve a specific goal (e.g., a young child may hit a peer to obtain a desired toy).

intelligence quotient (IQ) The most common measure of intellectual abilities used in industrial countries (although the nature of human intelligence is still debated).

interpersonal therapy Psychological treatment approach designed to help distressed and withdrawn youth gain access to positive sources of reinforcement in order to combat their depression.

intrusive symptoms Recurrent memories, flashbacks, and nightmares through which the child or adolescent reexperiences a traumatic event. Characteristic of posttraumatic stress disorder.

la belle indifférence Lack of affect and apparent indifference about the seriousness of their symptoms shown by some adults with somatoform disorders, especially conversion disorder. Rare in children and adolescents with conversion disorder.

learned helplessness   Term coined by Martin Seligman, who hypothesized that depression arises from repeated experiences with uncontrollable, noncontingent events. Individuals who have been exposed to such experiences are assumed to give up quickly when faced with challenges because they have learned that outcomes are not contingent on their behavior.

learning disorders or disabilities   Group of conditions characterized by major difficulties in reading, writing, or mathematics that cannot be attributed to mental retardation, emotional problems, or physical conditions. These difficulties are unexpected given the child or adolescent's intellectual ability and schooling experience.

Lesch-Nyhan syndrome   Genetic condition associated with mental retardation. The syndrome, which affects boys only, is characterized by moderate mental retardation, marked cerebral palsy, digestive difficulties, and self-injurious behaviors that often cause extreme distress to child and family.

lithium   Naturally occurring alkali metal used in the treatment of bipolar disorder.

longitudinal studies   Research studies in which the same individuals are studied on multiple occasions over an extended period of time.

loose (illogical) associations   Associations without logical or experiential connections between events or ideas. Eugen Bleuler believed that a loosening of associations was at the core of schizophrenia.

lunago   Fine, downy hair on the face and body. Common in youth with anorexia.

magnetic resonance imaging (MRI)   An imaging technique that allows researchers to take three-dimensional pictures of the brain while the child is awake and completing a cognitive task.

major depressive disorder (MDD)   Mood disorder characterized by the occurrence of one or more depressive episodes, each lasting at least two weeks.

mania (and manic episodes)   Mania is the core feature of bipolar disorder. Manic episodes are periods of extreme elation or irritability, and increased activity level and reduced need for sleep. An inflated sense of self-worth and an overestimation of one's own abilities or importance are also common during manic episodes.

masked depression   Theoretical perspective that historically played an important role in understanding mood disorders in children. According to this perspective, these disorders are manifested mainly through depressive equivalents—that is, symptoms that reflect but mask depression. Depressive equivalents include but are not limited to aggressive, hyperactive, and anxious symptoms.

mathematics disorder   Disorder in which a child or adolescent has major difficulties carrying out basic arithmetic operations (addition, subtraction, multiplication, and division) and solving mathematical problems.

megacolon   Enlargement of the colon resulting from chronic constipation and affecting some children with encopresis.

mental retardation   Group of psychological disorders with different etiologies but sharing as their main features the fact that the person has a below-average IQ and impaired adaptive behavior that began before the age of 18.

meta-analysis   Method of statistical analysis that combines data from multiple studies. The findings of a meta-analysis tend to be more robust than the results of a single study.

minimal brain damage   A theory of learning disorders that hypothesizes that learning difficulties are the result of minimal, often undetectable, brain damage.

mixed episodes   Periods in which a child or adolescent meets full diagnostic criteria for both manic and depressive episodes, and rapidly cycles between mania, major depression, and normal mood.

mixed receptive-expressive language disorder   Disorder in which a child or adolescent has major difficulties in self-expression and in understanding spoken language.

modeling   A behavioral theory of learning that hypothesizes that behavior is learned by observing the actions of others.

monoamines   Class of brain chemicals that includes neurotransmitters such as serotonin, norepinephrine, and dopamine.

mood disorders   Class of disorders characterized by significant disturbances in mood. This class includes major depressive disorder, dysthymic disorder, and bipolar disorder.

mood stabilizers   Anticonvulsant medications used in the treatment of bipolar disorder.

moral reasoning   Ability to judge the moral implications of one's behavior. Moral reasoning may be hampered in some children and adolescents (e.g., in victims of physical abuse).

multiaxial system   System of classification in which a person's functioning is described on multiple dimensions or domains called axes.

multifinality   Principle according to which the same cause can have different consequences for development.

multisystemic therapy   Treatment approach designed to address the many problems that disruptive youth present across multiple social systems, such as family, school, and community.

Munchausen's syndrome by proxy   See factitious disorder by proxy.

negative affectivity   Subjective feelings of tension, fear, hostility, sadness, and distress that accompany mood and anxiety disorders, and that may account in part for their comorbidity.

negative automatic thoughts Tendency of individuals to think negatively about themselves and others, and to let that negativity color their judgment.

negative symptoms Symptoms of schizophrenia that are marked by behavior deficits, such as affective flattening, alogia, and avolition.

neglect Caregiver's failure to provide a child or adolescent with a minimal, safe environment in which to develop normally.

neural plasticity Process by which experience brings about changes in brain structures or functions and, in turn, such brain changes influence and shape experience.

neuroleptics Psychotropic drugs that are part of a class of compounds that specifically target dopamine receptors and lead to an overall decrease in available dopamine in the brain. Used to treat positive symptoms in schizophrenia.

neurological soft signs Slight physical indicators that may be indicative of neurological damage.

neuropeptides Hormone-like substances that act as neurotransmitters in the central nervous system.

neurotransmitters Naturally occurring chemicals that are responsible for the transmission of neural impulses along the nerve axon and across the synapse to the next neuron.

nonverbal learning disabilities (NLD) A group of deficits theorized to occur in children and adolescents with significant impairments in the ability to identify, understand, and use nonverbal cues. Some researchers hypothesize that Asperger's disorder may be related to NLD.

norepinephrine Hormone and neurotransmitter involved in the processing of environmental information, especially by alerting the organism to danger and focusing attention; prepares the organism for "fight or flight."

obsessions Unwelcome thoughts, impulses, or irresistible urges that reflect an irrational fear or an emotionally charged topic, often of a sexual, aggressive, or religious nature. Characteristic of obsessive-compulsive disorder.

obsessive-compulsive disorder (OCD) Anxiety disorder characterized by intrusive obsessions and compulsions.

operant conditioning A behavioral theory of learning that hypothesizes that behavior is largely determined by its antecedents and consequences—that is, by the environmental conditions that precede and follow the behavior.

oppositional defiant disorder (ODD) Psychological disorder characterized by a pattern of age-inappropriate negativistic, defiant, oppositional, or disobedient behaviors. These behaviors must significantly impair a child or adolescent's functioning for diagnosis to be possible.

overanxious disorder Anxiety disorder of childhood described in the DSM-II, DSM-III, and DSM-III-R. Overanxious disorder, which is similar to generalized anxiety disorder, involves significant worry about past and future behavior, as well as social, academic, and physical competency.

overt behavior problems Problems that stem from generally observable behaviors, such as defiance, opposition, and verbal and physical aggression.

panic attack Unexpected and uncontrollable, but time-limited, attack of anxiety that is not brought about by life-threatening events, medical conditions, or other disorders (e.g., drug addiction). Characteristic of panic and other anxiety disorders.

panic disorder Anxiety disorder characterized by sudden, unexpected panic attacks and by the impending fear that is associated with them.

parent training Psychosocial intervention designed to teach caregivers to modify the antecedents and consequences they provide for their children's desirable and undesirable behavior. Often used to treat a variety of psychological disorders of childhood and adolescence.

parenting Broad concept used to refer to the attitudes, beliefs, and skills that parents bring to the childrearing task.

pediatric psychology Interdisciplinary area of research and intervention concerned with physical and mental development, health, and illness issues affecting children, adolescents, and their families.

pedophilia Disorder in which adults—mostly men—are sexually attracted to and aroused by children. Generally, this attraction is limited to children and does not extend to adolescents.

perseveration Term used to describe the tendency of some children to keep making the same mistakes, even in the face of failure, or to dwell on a question, topic, or behavior much longer than is productive.

phenylketonuria (PKU) Genetic condition associated with mental retardation. Children with this syndrome cannot process a protein called phenylalanine. This protein accumulates in the body and creates toxins that cause brain damage and, if left untreated, lead to mental retardation.

phoneme Smallest unit of speech.

phonological disorder Disorder in which a child or adolescent has major difficulties producing age-appropriate speech sounds.

phonological rules Rules for selecting and combining the speech sounds of a language.

physical abuse Avoidable, nonaccidental actions on the part of a caregiver that lead to the physical harm of a child or adolescent. Physical abuse includes, but is not limited to, slapping, punching, beating with an object, burning or scalding, as well as deliberate exposure of the child or adolescent to elements in the environment that may cause physical harm.

physical neglect   Failure to provide a child or adolescent with adequate food, clothing, medical care, or hygiene. Includes also inadequate supervision and abandonment.

pivotal areas   Areas of functioning that are central to a child's adaptation because they control multiple skills and behaviors.

play therapy   Treatment technique based on the assumption that unstructured play in a safe, therapeutic setting gives young children with psychological problems an opportunity to work through and resolve their difficulties.

polygenic   Common form of genetic influence resulting from multiple genes acting in concert.

positive symptoms   Symptoms of schizophrenia that are marked by behavior excesses, such as delusions and hallucinations.

posttraumatic stress disorder (PTSD)   Anxiety disorder that develops after exposure to a traumatic event, such as child abuse, a natural disaster or war, an accident, or the serious injury or violent death of a loved one.

Prader-Willi syndrome   Genetic condition associated with mental retardation. The syndrome is characterized by an obsession with food, a failure to grow normally, and difficulties with muscle tone.

prevalence   Estimate of the number of persons with a particular disorder in the population at a specific point or period of time, irrespective of the length of time the disorder has been present in each case (i.e., prevalence rates do not distinguish between newly diagnosed and chronic cases).

prevention   Interventions designed to keep psychological disorders from happening, usually in individuals who are at risk for such disorders because of adverse personal or environmental circumstances.

primary and secondary encopresis   Children with primary encopresis have never acquired bowel control, whereas children with secondary encopresis become incontinent only after a significant period during which they were able to control their bowel functions.

primary and secondary enuresis   Children with primary enuresis have never acquired full bladder control, whereas children with secondary enuresis become incontinent only after a significant period during which they were dry.

proactive aggression   Form of aggression in which the child or adolescent takes the offensive and attacks someone with little or no provocation. Proactive aggression usually has a goal (instrumental or hostile) and is not associated with a high level of emotional or central nervous system activity.

progressive muscle relaxation   Treatment procedure designed to teach a person to tense and relax different muscles sys-

tematically. Commonly used in the treatment of anxiety disorders.

pronoun reversal   Confusion of the personal pronouns I/me with you/she. A child with pronoun reversal might say, "He wants to play now" instead of "I want to play now."

protective factors   Variables that lower the probability or risk that a psychological disorder will develop in the presence of other adverse variables (or risk factors).

pseudoneurological symptoms   Symptoms that appear to be the result of neurological problems, such as seizures, but that have no known physical cause.

psychoanalytic approach   Theoretical approach that assumes that human behavior is largely determined by unconscious emotional processes.

psycholinguistics   Study of the psychological factors associated with speech and communication.

psychological autopsy   Examination of a child or adolescent's psychological functioning after the youth has committed suicide. Psychological autopsy typically relies on in-depth review of clinical records and on interviews with family, friends, and teachers.

psychological perspective   Theoretical perspective that focuses (1) on the influences of behavioral, emotional, and cognitive factors on normal and abnormal functioning, and (2) on the influences of psychological processes within the family and the peer group.

psychostimulants   Class of drugs that increase central nervous system activity. Commonly used in the treatment of ADHD.

psychotropic drugs   Drugs prescribed to alleviate symptoms of psychological disorders.

punishment   Environmental condition that tends to decrease the likelihood of a particular behavior.

purging   Set of behaviors common in eating disorders. These behaviors include self-induced vomiting and excessive use of laxatives, diuretics, or enemas to avoid weight gain.

random assignment   Process of assigning participants in scientific studies at random to groups that will be compared on some critical variable.

reactive aggression   Form of aggression in which the child or adolescent responds to someone's behavior in a hurtful or harmful manner. Reactive aggression often reflects a hostile interpretation of the behavior of others and is typically accompanied by high levels of negative emotions (especially anger) and of central nervous system activation (e.g., increased heart rate and respiration).

reading disorder   Disorder in which a child or adolescent has major difficulties decoding and recognizing words, reading fluently, and understanding what is read.

rebound effect   Side effect of stimulant medications, in which some children and adolescents show high levels of activity, irritability, insomnia, and other behavioral difficulties a few hours after taking the drug.

reciprocal social interactions Social interactions in which two or more people are mutually involved and play active roles. Include the reciprocal exchange of ideas, feelings, and experiences.

reinforcement Environmental condition that tends to increase the likelihood of a particular behavior.

relationship stress Concept that highlights the fact that many psychological disorders result from stressful relationships between affected children and adolescents and the important persons in their lives.

reliability Extent to which a scientific instrument yields the same results when it is used by different people or administered on different occasions.

representative sample Sample whose characteristics match those of the population to which the results of a scientific study are meant to apply.

response prevention Treatment technique that consists of prohibiting youth with obsessive-compulsive disorder from engaging in the compulsions they have developed to relieve their anxiety.

retention control training Technique used in the treatment of enuresis that consists of rewarding the ability to postpone urination for increasingly longer periods of time (up to forty-five minutes). This postponement allows affected youth to enhance the muscles used to retain urine, as well as to increase their functional bladder capacity.

Rett's disorder (or **Rett syndrome**) A pervasive developmental disorder that begins after five to forty-eight months of normal development. The disorder, which is usually found only in girls, is characterized by severe deterioration in all previously acquired skills (e.g., communication, social, and intellectual), and accompanied by stereotypical hand movements and severe or profound mental retardation.

risk factors Variables that increase the probability or risk that a psychological disorder will develop. Risk factors can be but are not necessarily etiological (i.e., causal) factors.

schizoid (or shizotypal) personality disorder A personality style that is emotionally aloof and indifferent to others. Individuals with the disorder are usually described as loners. Considered to be part of the schizophrenia spectrum of disorders.

schizophrenia Psychological disorder characterized by major disturbances in thought, emotion, and behavior.

schizophrenogenic Term used to describe a parenting style that is emotionally aloof, indifferent, and rejecting. Believed at one time to be a causal factor in the development of schizophrenia.

schizotypal personality disorder A personality style characterized by odd thoughts (e.g., magical thinking) and unusual sensory perceptions. Individuals with the disorder are socially isolated and described as eccentric. Considered to be part of the schizophrenia spectrum of disorders.

school refusal Extreme reluctance or outright refusal to attend school on the part of a child who has no objective reason to fear school.

selective serotonin reuptake inhibitors (SSRIs) Psychotropic medications used in the treatment of mood disorders.

self-fulfilling prophecies Negative thought patterns in which a person's predictions about a future event will affect how the person behaves. Commonly observed in youth with mood disorders.

self-injurious behaviors Repetitive behaviors, such as rocking, scratching, and head banging, that can cause serious self-inflicted injury.

separation anxiety disorder (SAD) Anxiety disorder in which children or adolescents have an excessive fear of being separated from their loved ones.

serotonin Neurotransmitter involved in the control of behavioral and emotional expression; implicated in the etiology of several disorders (e.g., mood, anxiety, and eating disorders).

sexual abuse Sexual contact between a child and a person who is in a position of power because of age, physical size, or position of authority; or sexual exploitation of a child by such a person (e.g., for prostitution).

shaken baby syndrome Syndrome in which infants who are shaken violently sustain serious brain injuries that may result in mental retardation and other disorders.

social awareness Awareness of the rules governing social behavior, and of their role in guiding social interactions.

social phobia Anxiety disorder characterized by a marked and persistent fear of one or more social situations in which negative evaluation or embarrassment could occur. These fears lead to the avoidance of the feared situations.

social reciprocity Reciprocal sharing of feelings, ideas, and experiences in the course of social interactions.

social skills training Set of intervention methods designed to teach appropriate and effective social behaviors in order to improve essential interpersonal skills.

somatization disorder Somatoform disorder characterized by medically unexplained physical symptoms that persist for extended periods of time. These symptoms can occur in the context of a medical illness or injury, but their extent or their severity cannot be explained by the physical condition.

somatoform disorders Group of disorders characterized by unexplained physical symptoms that are, or are assumed to be, of psychological origin. Somatization disorder and conversion disorder are examples of somatoform disorders.

somatosensory amplification   Negative overreaction to normal bodily sensations that is characteristic of individuals with somatoform disorders.

specific phobia   Anxiety disorder characterized by a marked and persistent fear of a particular object or situation. It is the specific focus of fear that distinguishes specific phobia from the other anxiety disorders.

spina bifida   Syndrome associated with a malformation of the spinal cord. It causes hydrocephalus (an accumulation of cerebrospinal fluid in the brain ventricles) and leads to mental retardation in 20% to 25% of child sufferers.

startle response   Exaggerated reaction to sudden noises or surprises. Characteristic of posttraumatic stress disorder.

strategy instruction   Treatment approach for learning disabilities that focuses less on the acquisition of specific skills than on teaching students to deal effectively with the many aspects of learning, such as how to organize material and ask relevant questions.

stuttering   Disorder in which a child or adolescent's speech flow is disrupted because of repetitions, lengthening of words or sounds, and hesitations between sounds or words.

suicidal ideation   Thoughts about death or dying, or plans to commit suicide. Commonly observed in youth with mood disorders.

superego   Personality structure that Freud believed reflects the values and rules that children acquire in the course of development.

supportive psychotherapy   Psychological treatment approach in which the therapist listens and provides support but does not challenge erroneous beliefs or directly teach youth to behave differently.

symptom magnification   Process whereby the original symptoms of an illness or injury outlast the medical recovery or are much more severe than would be expected under typical circumstances. This process plays a role in the onset of some cases of somatization and conversion disorders.

syndrome   Distinct cluster of symptoms that tend to be characteristic of a specific disorder.

target behaviors   Behaviors that are of primary concern in treatment or prevention.

TEACCH program   A statewide, comprehensive intervention program for individuals with autism in North Carolina.

temperament   Individual differences in reactivity and self-regulation that are constitutionally based.

testosterone   Hormone that controls the development of male sex organs, and of facial hair, deepening of the voice, and other masculine characteristics.

theory of mind   Ability to infer mental states (e.g., thoughts, feelings) in others and awareness that these states may be different from one's own.

thin-ideal internalization   Extent to which individuals accept socially defined ideals of attractiveness and take steps to reach those ideals. Believed to be a causal factor in the development of eating disorders.

tic disorders   Group of disorders in which tics feature prominently. Tics are rapid, repeated, nonrhythmical motor movements or vocalizations that have no apparent purpose.

time-out   Effective punishment for inappropriate behavior that consists of removing the child from pleasurable activities and from the company of others for a brief period of time.

token economy   Behavior modification technique that allows individuals to earn points for positive behavior and to lose them for inappropriate behavior.

transactional approach   Approach to the study of human development that assumes that a proper understanding of normal and abnormal behavior requires a focus not on people per se but on what happens when people come in contact with others and their environment.

treatment foster care   Placement of a child with special needs in a family that has been specially trained to receive children with emotional or behavioral problems, and/or medical conditions.

tricyclic antidepressants (TCAs)   Psychotropic medications used in the treatment of mood disorders.

urine alarm   Behavioral method for treating nocturnal enuresis based on the hypothesis that affected youth have not learned the relationship between the sensation of a full bladder and awakening. In this procedure, a bell goes off every time they begin to urinate in their sleep. Over time, they learn to associate the sensations of a full bladder with awakening.

validity   Extent to which a research instrument adequately measures what it is designed to measure.

vasovagal response   Abnormal physiological response often observed in the blood-injection-injury type of specific phobia. This response is characterized by a brief increase in heart rate, followed by a significant drop in heart rate and blood pressure. Behaviorally, this response often results in fainting at the sight of the phobic stimulus (e.g., blood).

vegetative symptoms   Somatic symptoms that include hypersomnia (i.e., sleeping too much) or insomnia (i.e., sleeping too little), weight gain or loss, changes in appetite, and fatigue. Commonly observed in youth with mood disorders.

"whole language" approach   Method of teaching reading in which the meaning of a word is inferred through its context, rather than decoded by relying on phonetics.

References

Aaron, F., Joshi, R., Ayotollah, M., Ellsberry, A., Henderson, J., & Lindsey, K. (1999). Decoding and sight-word naming: Are they independent components of word recognition skill? *Reading and Writing, 11,* 89–127.

Abrahamian, F. P., & Lloyd-Still, J. D. (1984). Chronic constipation in childhood: A longitudinal study of 186 patients. *Journal of Pediatric Gastroenterology and Nutrition, 3,* 460–467.

Abramowicz, H. K., & Richardson, S. (1975). Epidemiology of severe mental retardation in children: Community studies. *American Journal of Mental Deficiency, 80,* 18–39.

Abramson, L. Y., Seligman, M. E. P., & Teasdale, J. D. (1978). Learned helplessness in humans: Critique and reformulation. *Journal of Abnormal Psychology, 37,* 49–74.

Achenbach, T. M. (1990). Conceptualization of developmental psychopathology. In M. Lewis & S. M. Miller (Eds.), *Handbook of developmental psychopathology* (pp. 3–14). New York: Plenum.

Achenbach, T. M. (1991). The derivation of taxonomic constructs: A necessary stage in the development of developmental psychopathology. In D. Cicchetti & S. Toth (Eds.), *Rochester symposium on developmental psychopathology: Models and integrations* (Vol. 3, pp. 43–74). Hillsdale, NJ: Erlbaum.

Achenbach, T. M. (1993). Taxonomy and comorbidity of conduct problems: Evidence from empirically-based approaches. *Development and Psychopathology, 5,* 51–64.

Achenbach, T. M., Conners, C. K., Quay, H. C., Verhulst, F. C., & Howell, C. T. (1989). Replication of empirically derived syndromes as a basis for taxonomy of child/adolescent psychopathology. *Journal of Abnormal Child Psychology, 17,* 299–323.

Achenbach, T. M., & Edelbrock, C. (1991). *Manual for the Child Behavior Checklist and Revised Child Behavior Profile.* Burlington, VT: Department of Psychiatry, University of Vermont.

Achenbach, T. M., McConaughy, S. H., & Howell, C. T. (1987). Child/adolescent behavioral and emotional problems: Implications of cross-informant for situational stability. *Psychological Bulletin, 101,* 213–232.

Ackerman, B. P., Kogos, J., Youngstrom, E., Schoff, K., & Izard, C. (1999). Family instability and the problem behaviors of children from economically disadvantaged families. *Developmental Psychology, 35,* 258–268.

Agras, W. S. (1987). *Eating disorders: Management of obesity, bulimia, and anorexia nervosa.* Elmsford, NY: Pergamon.

Aguilar, B., O'Brien, K. M., August, G. J., Aoun, S. L., & Hektner, J. M. (2001). Relationship quality of aggressive children and their siblings: A multiinformant, multimeasure investigation. *Journal of Abnormal Child Psychology, 29,* 479–489.

Ainsworth, M. D. S. (1982). Attachment: Retrospect and perspective. In C. M. Parkes & J. Stevenson-Hinde (Eds.), *The place of attachment in human behavior* (pp. 3–29). New York: Basic Books.

Ainsworth, M. D. S., Blehar, M. C., Waters, E., & Wall, S. (1978). *Patterns of attachment: A psychological study of the strange situation.* Hillsdale, NJ: Erlbaum.

Alaghband-Rad, J., Hamburger, S. D., Giedd, J. N., Frazier, J. A., & Rapoport, J. L. (1997). Childhood-onset schizophrenia: Biological markers in relation to clinical characteristics. *American Journal of Psychiatry, 154,* 64–68.

Albano, A. M., Chorpita, B. R., & Barlow, D. H. (1996). Childhood anxiety disorders. In E. J. Mash & R. A. Barkley (Eds.), *Child psychopathology* (pp. 196–241). New York: Guilford.

Alessi, N. E., & Magen, J. (1988). Panic disorder in psychiatrically hospitalized children. *American Journal of Psychiatry, 145,* 1450–1452.

Alessi, N., Naylor, M. W., Ghaziuddin, M., & Zubieta, J. K. (1994). Update on lithium carbonate therapy in children and adolescents. *Journal of the American Academy of Child and Adolescent Psychiatry, 33,* 291–304.

Al-Mateen, C., Hall, P. D., Brookman, R. R., Best, A. L., & Signh, N. N. (1999). Sexual abuse and perimenstrual symptoms in adolescent girls. *Journal of Interpersonal Violence, 14,* 1211–1224.

Alpert, M., Clark, A., & Pouget, E. R. (1994). The syntactic role of pauses in the speech of schizophrenic patients with alogia. *Journal of Abnormal Psychology, 103,* 750–757.

Aman, M. G., Van Bourgondien, M. E., Wolford, P. L., & Sarphare, G. (1995). Psychotropic and anticonvulsant drugs in subjects with autism: Prevalence and patterns of use. *Journal of the American Academy of Child and Adolescent Psychiatry, 34,* 1672–1681.

Amato, P. R., & Keith, B. (1991). Parental divorce and the well-being of children: A meta-analysis. *Psychological Bulletin, 110*, 26–46.

American Academy of Child and Adolescent Psychiatry (AACAP). (1997a). Practice parameters for the assessment and treatment of children, adolescents, and adults with attention-deficit/hyperactivity disorder. *Journal of the American Academy of Child and Adolescent Psychiatry, 36,* 85S–121S.

American Academy of Child and Adolescent Psychiatry (AACAP). (1997b). Practice parameters for the assessment and treatment of children and adolescents with anxiety disorders. *Journal of the American Academy of Child and Adolescent Psychiatry, 36,* 69S–84S.

American Academy of Child and Adolescent Psychiatry (AACAP). (1997c). Practice parameters for the assessment and treatment of children and adolescents with bipolar disorder. *Journal of the American Academy of Child and Adolescent Psychiatry, 36,* 138–157.

American Academy of Child and Adolescent Psychiatry (AACAP). (1997d). Practice parameters for the assessment and treatment of children and adolescents with conduct disorder. *Journal of the American Academy of Child and Adolescent Psychiatry, 36,* 122S–139S.

American Academy of Child and Adolescent Psychiatry (AACAP). (1998a). Practice parameters for the assessment and treatment of children and adolescents with depressive disorders. *Journal of the American Academy of Child and Adolescent Psychiatry, 37,* 63S–83S.

American Academy of Child and Adolescent Psychiatry (AACAP). (1998b). Practice parameters for the assessment and treatment of children and adolescents with language and learning disorders. *Journal of the American Academy of Child and Adolescent Psychiatry, 37,* 42S–62S.

American Academy of Child and Adolescent Psychiatry (AACAP). (1998c). Practice parameters for the assessment and treatment of children and adolescents with obsessive-compulsive disorder. *Journal of the American Academy of Child and Adolescent Psychiatry, 37,* 27S–45S.

American Academy of Child and Adolescent Psychiatry (AACAP). (1998d). Practice parameters for the assessment and treatment of children and adolescents with posttraumatic stress disorder. *Journal of the American Academy of Child and Adolescent Psychiatry, 37,* 4S–26S.

American Academy of Child and Adolescent Psychiatry (AACAP). (1999a). Practice parameters for the assessment and treatment of children, adolescents, and adults with autism, and other pervasive developmental disorders. *Journal of the American Academy of Child and Adolescent Psychiatry, 38,* 32S–54S.

American Academy of Child and Adolescent Psychiatry (AACAP). (1999b). Practice parameters for the assessment and treatment of children, adolescents, and adults with mental retardation and comorbid mental disorders. *Journal of the American Academy of Child and Adolescent Psychiatry, 38,* 5S–31S.

American Association on Mental Retardation. (1992). *Mental retardation: Definition, classification, and systems of support.* Washington, DC: Author.

American Psychiatric Association (APA). (1952). *Diagnostic and statistical manual of mental disorders.* Washington, DC: Author.

American Psychiatric Association (APA). (1968). *Diagnostic and statistical manual of mental disorders* (2nd ed.). Washington, DC: Author.

American Psychiatric Association (APA). (1980). *Diagnostic and statistical manual of mental disorders* (3rd ed.; DSM-III). Washington, DC: Author.

American Psychiatric Association (APA). (1987). *Diagnostic and statistical manual of mental disorders* (3rd ed., revised; DSM-III-R). Washington, DC: Author.

American Psychiatric Association (APA). (1994). *Diagnostic and statistical manual of mental disorders* (4th ed.; DSM-IV). Washington, DC: Author.

American Psychiatric Association (APA). (2000a). *Diagnostic and statistical manual of mental disorders* (4th ed., text revision; DSM-IV-TR). Washington, DC: Author.

American Psychiatric Association (APA). (2000b). Practice guidelines for the treatment of patients with eating disorders (revised). *American Journal of Psychiatry, 157,* 1–39.

American Psychological Association. (1997). *Protecting our children from abuse and neglect.* Washington, DC: Author.

Anderson, B. J., Laffel, L., Goebel-Fabbri, A. E., Mansfield, A., Fisher, A., Connell, A., & Vangsness, L. (2000). *Optimizing adherence and glycemia in youth with newly diagnosed Type 1 diabetes.* Paper presented at the Wynne Center for Family Research Conference, Canandaigua, NY.

Anderson, C. A., Benjamin, A. J., & Bartholow, B. D. (1998). Does the gun pull the trigger? Automatic priming effects of weapon pictures and weapon names. *Psychological Science, 9,* 308–314.

Anderson, J. C. (1994). Epidemiological issues. In T. H. Ollendick, N. J. King, & W. Yule (Eds.), *International handbook of phobic and anxiety disorders in children and adolescents* (pp. 43–65). New York: Plenum.

Anderson, J. C., & McGee, R. (1994). Comorbidity of depression in children and adolescents. In W. M. Reynolds & H. F. Johnston (Eds.), *Handbook of depression in children and adolescents* (pp. 581–601). New York: Plenum.

Anderson, J. C., Williams, S., McGee, R., & Silva, P. A. (1987). DSM-III disorders in preadolescent children: Prevalence in a large sample from the general population. *Archives of General Psychiatry, 44,* 69–76.

Andreasen, N. C., Arndt, S., Alliger, R., Miller, D., & Flaum, M. (1995). Symptoms of schizophrenia: Methods, meanings, and mechanisms. *Archives of General Psychiatry, 52,* 341–351.

Angold, A., & Costello, E. J. (1995). The epidemiology of depression in children and adolescents. In I. M. Goodyer

(Ed.), *The depressed child and adolescent: Developmental and clinical perspectives* (pp. 127–147). Cambridge, UK: Cambridge University Press.

Angold, A., Costello, E. J., Erkanli, A., & Worthman, C. M. (1999). Pubertal changes in hormone levels and depression in girls. *Psychological Medicine, 29,* 1043–1053.

Angold, A., Costello, E. J., & Worthman, C. M. (1998). Puberty and depression: The roles of age, pubertal status, and pubertal timing. *Psychological Medicine, 28,* 51–61.

Anonymous (1994). First-person account: Schizophrenia with childhood onset. (1994). *Schizophrenia Bulletin, 20,* 587–590.

Apley, J., & Naish, N. (1958). Recurrent abdominal pains: A field survey of 1,000 school children. *Archives of Disease in Children, 33,* 165–170.

Appel, A. E., & Holden, G. W. (1998). The co-occurrence of spouse and physical child abuse: A review and appraisal. *Journal of Family Psychology, 12,* 578–599.

Applegate, B., Lahey, B., Hart, E. L., Waldman, L., Biederman, J., Hynd, G., Barkley, R., Ollendick, T., Frick, P., Greenhill, L., McBurnett, K., Newcorn, J., Kerdyk, L., Garfinkel, B., & Schaffer, D. (1997). The age of onset for DSM-IV attention-deficit hyperactivity disorder: A report of the DSM-IV field trials. *Journal of the American Academy of Child and Adolescent Psychiatry, 36,* 1211–1221.

Ards, S., Chung, C., & Myers, S. (1998). The effects of sample selection bias on racial differences in child abuse reporting. *Child Abuse and Neglect, 22,* 103–115.

Arsenio, W. F., Cooperman, S., & Lover, A. (2000). Affective predictors of preschoolers' aggression and peer acceptance: Direct and indirect effects. *Developmental Psychology, 36,* 438–448.

Artiles, A. J., & Trent, S. C. (1994). Overrepresentation of minority students in special education: A continuing debate. *Journal of Special Education, 27,* 410–437.

Asarnow, J. R. (1994). Annotation: Childhood-onset schizophrenia. *Journal of Child Psychology and Psychiatry, 35,* 1345–1371.

Asarnow, J. R., & Asarnow, R. F. (1996). Childhood-onset schizophrenia. In E. J. Mash & R. A. Barkley (Eds.), *Child psychopathology* (pp. 340–361). New York: Guilford.

Asarnow, J. R., Jaycox, L. H., & Tompson, M. C. (2001). Depression in youth: Psychosocial interventions. *Journal of Clinical Child Psychology, 30,* 33–47.

Asarnow, J. R., & Tompson, M. (1999). Childhood-onset schizophrenia: A follow-up study. *European Child and Adolescent Psychiatry, 8,* 9–12.

Asarnow, J. R., Tompson, M., & Goldstein, M. J. (1994). Childhood-onset schizophrenia: A follow-up study. *Schizophrenia Bulletin, 20,* 599–618.

Asarnow, J. R., Tompson, M., Woo, S., & Cantwell, D. P. (2001). Is expressed emotion a specific risk factor for depression or a nonspecific correlate of psychopathology? *Journal of Abnormal Child Psychology, 29,* 573–583.

Asarnow, R. F., Asamen, J., Granhol, E., Sherman, T., Watkins, J. M., & Williams, M. E. (1994). Cognitive/neuropsychological studies of children with a schizophrenic disorder. *Schizophrenia Bulletin, 20,* 647–669.

Asarnow, R. F., Asarnow, J. R., & Strandburg, R. (1989). Schizophrenia: A developmental perspective. In D. Cicchetti (Ed.), *Rochester Symposium on Developmental Psychopathology: The emergence of a discipline* (pp. 189–219). Hillsdale, NJ: Erlbaum.

Asperger, H. (1944). Die "Autistischen Psychopathen" im Kindesalter. *Archive für Psychiatrie und Nervenkrankheiten, 117,* 76–136. (A translation of this text can be found in Frith, 1991.)

Atkins, M. S., & Stoff, D. M. (1993). Instrumental and hostile aggression in childhood disruptive behavior disorders. *Journal of Abnormal Child Psychology, 21,* 165–178.

Atkinson, S. D. (1994). Grieving and loss in parents with a schizophrenic child. *American Journal of Psychiatry, 151,* 1137–1139.

Attia, E., Haiman, C., Walsh, B. T., & Flater, S. (1998). Does fluoxetine augment the inpatient treatment of anorexia nervosa? *American Journal of Psychiatry, 155,* 548–551.

Attwood, A., Frith, U., & Hermelin, B. (1988). The understanding and use of interpersonal gestures by autistic and Down's syndrome children. *Journal of Autism and Developmental Disorders, 18,* 241–257.

August, G. J., Realmuto, G. M., MacDonald, A. W., Nugent, S. M., & Crosby, R. (1996). Prevalence of ADHD and comorbid disorders among elementary school children screened for disruptive behavior. *Journal of Abnormal Child Psychology, 24,* 571–595.

Aussilloux, C., & Misès, R. (1997). Évolution de l'enfance à l'âge adulte. In R. Misès & P. Grand (Eds.), *Parents et professionnels devant l'autisme* (pp. 109–123). Paris: CT-NERHI.

Autism Society (1999). *David: A different kind of miracle.* [On line]. Available at http://www.autism-society.org.

Autti-Raemoe, I. (2000). Twelve-year follow-up of children exposed to alcohol in utero. *Developmental Medicine and Child Neurology, 42,* 406–411.

Ayres, A. J. (1978). Learning disabilities and the vestibular system. *Journal of Learning Disabilities, 11,* 30–41.

Bachevalier, J. (1994). Medial temporal lobe structures and autism: A review of clinical and experimental findings. *Neuropsychologia, 32,* 627–648.

Baker, L., & Cantwell, D. P. (1991). Disorders of language, speech, and communication. In M. Lewis (Ed.), *Child and adolescent psychiatry: A comprehensive textbook* (pp. 516–521). Baltimore: Williams and Wilkins.

Bakwin, H. (1973). The genetics of enuresis. In I. Kolvin, R. C. MacKeith, & S. R. Meadow (Eds.), *Bladder control and enuresis* (pp. 73–77). London: Heinemann.

Ballenger, J. C., Davidson, J. R. T., Lecrubier, Y., Nutt, D. J., Bobes, J., Beidel, D. C., Ono, Y., & Westenberg, H. G. M. (1998). Consensus statement on social anxiety disorder from the International Consensus Group on Depression and Anxiety. *Journal of Clinical Psychiatry, 59,* 54–60.

Baranek, G. T. (1999). Autism during infancy: A retrospective video analysis of sensory-motor and social behaviors at 9–12 months of age. *Journal of Autism and Developmental Disorders, 29,* 213–224.

Barkley, R. A. (1996). Attention-deficit/hyperactivity disorder. In E. J. Mash & R. A. Barkley (Eds.), *Child psychopathology* (pp. 63–112). New York: Guilford.

Barkley, R. A. (1997). Behavioral inhibition, sustained attention, and executive functions: Constructing a unifying theory of ADHD. *Psychological Bulletin, 121,* 65–94.

Barkley, R. A. (1998). Attention-deficit/hyperactivity disorder. In E. J. Mash & R. A. Barkley (Eds.), *Treatment of childhood disorders* (2nd ed., pp. 55–110).

Barkley, R. A. (2000). Genetics of childhood disorders: XVII. ADHD, Part 1: The executive functions and ADHD. *Journal of the American Academy of Child and Adolescent Psychiatry, 39,* 1064–1068.

Barkley, R. A., Fischer, M., Edelbrock, C. S., & Smallish, L. (1990). The adolescent outcome of hyperactive children diagnosed by research criteria: I. An 8 year prospective follow-up study. *Journal of the American Academy of Child and Adolescent Psychiatry, 29,* 546–557.

Barkley, R. A., Fischer, M., Edelbrock, C. S., & Smallish, L. (1991). The adolescent outcome of hyperactive children diagnosed by research criteria: III. Mother-child interactions, family conflicts, and maternal psychopathology. *Journal of Child Psychology and Psychiatry, 32,* 233–255.

Barkley, R. A., Shelton, T. L., Crosswait, C., Moorehouse, M., Fletcher, K., Barrett, S., Jenkins, L., & Metevia, L. (2000). Multi-method psycho-educational intervention for preschool children with disruptive behavior: Preliminary results at post-treatment. *Journal of Child Psychology and Psychiatry, 41,* 319–332.

Barlow, D. H. (1988). *Anxiety and its disorders: The nature and treatment of anxiety and panic.* New York: Guilford.

Barnett, D., Ganiban, J., and Cicchetti, D. (1999). Maltreatment, negative expressivity, and the development of type D attachments from 12 to 24 months of age. *Monographs of the Society for Research in Child Development, 64,* 97–118.

Baron-Cohen, S., Cross, P., Crowson, M., & Robertson, M. (1994). Can children with Gilles de la Tourette syndrome edit their intentions? *Psychological Medicine, 24,* 29–40.

Baron-Cohen, S., Leslie, A. M., & Frith, U. (1985). Does the autistic child have a 'theory of the mind'? *Cognition, 21,* 37–46.

Baron-Cohen, S., & Wheelwright, S. (1999). 'Obsessions' in children with autism or Asperger syndrome: Content analysis in terms of core domains of cognition. *British Journal of Psychiatry, 175,* 484–490.

Barrett, P. M. (1998). Evaluation of cognitive-behavioral group treatments for childhood anxiety disorders. *Journal of Clinical Child Psychology, 27,* 459–468.

Barrett, P. M., Dadds, M. R., & Rapee, R. M. (1996). Family treatment of childhood anxiety: A controlled trial. *Journal of Consulting and Clinical Psychology, 64,* 333–342.

Barrett, P. M., Rapee, R. M., Dadds, M. M., & Ryan, S. M. (1996). Family enhancement of cognitive style in anxious and aggressive children. *Journal of Abnormal Child Psychology, 24,* 187–203.

Barsky, A. J., Goodson, J. D., Lane, R. S., & Cleary, P. D. (1988). The amplification of somatic symptoms. *Psychosomatic Medicine, 50,* 510–519.

Barton, M., & Volkmar, F. (1998). How commonly are known medical conditions associated with autism? *Journal of Autism and Developmental Disorders, 28,* 273–278.

Bates, J. E., Pettit, G. S., Dodge, K. A., & Ridge, B. (1998). The interaction of temperamental resistance to control and restrictive parenting in the development of externalizing behavior. *Developmental Psychology, 34,* 982–995.

Bateson, G., Jackson, D. D., Haley, J., & Weakland, J. (1956). Toward a theory of schizophrenia. *Behavioral Science, 1,* 251–264.

Battle, Y. L., Martin, B. C., Dorfman, J. H., & Miller, L. S. (1999). Seasonality and infectious disease in schizophrenia: The birth hypothesis revisited. *Journal of Psychiatric Research, 33,* 501–509.

Bauman, L. J. (2000). A patient-centered approach to adherence: Risks for nonadherence. In D. Drotar (Ed.), *Promoting adherence to medical treatment in chronic childhood illness: Concepts, methods, and interventions* (pp. 71–93). Mahwah, NJ: Erlbaum.

Baumeister, R. F., Bushman, B. J., & Campbell, W. K. (2000). Self-esteem, narcissism, and aggression: Does violence result from low self-esteem or from threatened egotism? *Current Directions in Psychological Sciences, 9,* 26–29.

Baumrind, D. (1967). Child care practices anteceding three patterns of preschool behavior. *Genetic Psychology Monographs, 75,* 43–88.

Baving, L., Laucht, M., & Schmidt, M. H. (2000). Oppositional children differ from healthy children in frontal brain activation. *Journal of Abnormal Child Psychology, 28,* 267–275.

Beardslee, W. R., Hoke, L., Wheelock, I., Rothberg, P. C., van de Velde, P., & Swatling, S. (1992). Initial findings on preventive interventions for families with parental affective disorder. *American Journal of Psychiatry, 149,* 1335–1340.

Beardslee, W. R., Versage, E. M., & Gladstone, T. R. G. (1998). Children of affectively ill parents: A review of the past 10 years. *Journal of the American Academy of Child and Adolescent Psychiatry, 37,* 1134–1141.

Beck, A. T. (1967). *Depression: Clinical, experimental, and theoretical aspects.* New York: Harper & Row.

Beck, A. T. (1999). *Prisoners of hate: The cognitive basis of anger, hostility, and violence.* New York: HarperCollins.

Bedwell, J., Keller, S., Keller, B., Smith, A., Hamburger, S., Kumra, S., & Rapoport, J. (1999). Why does postpsychotic

IQ decline in childhood-onset schizophrenia? *American Journal of Psychiatry, 156,* 1996–1997.

Beeman, M. J., & Chiarello, C. (1998). Complementary right- and left-hemisphere language comprehension. *Current Directions in Psychological Sciences, 7,* 2–8.

Beiser, M., Dion, R., & Gotowiec, A. (2000). The structure of attention-deficit and hyperactivity symptoms among native and non-native elementary school children. *Journal of Abnormal Child Psychology, 28,* 425–437.

Beitchman, J. H., & Brownlie, E. B. (1996). Childhood speech and language disorders. In L. Hechtman (Ed.), *Do they grow out of it? Long-term outcomes of childhood disorders* (pp. 225–253). Washington, DC: American Psychiatric Press.

Beitchman, J. H., & Young, A. R. (1997). Learning disorders with a special emphasis on reading disorders: A review of the past 10 years. *Journal of the American Academy of Child and Adolescent Psychiatry, 36,* 1020–1032.

Beitchman, J. H., Zucker, K. J., Hood, J. E., DaCosta, G. A., Akman, D., & Cassavia, E. (1992). A review of the long-term effects of child sexual abuse. *Child Abuse & Neglect, 16,* 101–118.

Belfer, M. L., & Munir, K. (1997). Acquired immune deficiency syndrome. In J. M. Weiner (Ed.), *Textbook of child and adolescent psychiatry* (pp. 711–725). Washington, DC: American Psychiatric Press.

Belsky, J. (1993). Etiology of child maltreatment: A developmental-ecological analysis. *Psychological Bulletin, 114,* 413–434.

Bemporad, J. R., Pfeifer, C. M., Gibbs, L., Cortner, R. H., & Bloom, W. (1971). Characteristics of encopretic patients and their families. *Journal of the American Academy of Child Psychiatry, 10,* 272–292.

Bender, B., Milgrom, H., Rand, C., & Ackerson, L. (1998). Psychological factors associated with medication nonadherence in asthmatic children. *Journal of Asthma, 35,* 347–353.

Bender, L., & Blau, A. (1937). The reactions of children to sexual relationships with adults. *American Journal of Orthopsychiatry, 7,* 500–518.

Benjamin, R. S., Costello, E. J., & Warren, M. (1990). Anxiety disorders in a pediatric sample. *Journal of Anxiety Disorders, 4,* 293–316.

Bennett, W. J. (1994). *The index of leading cultural indicators.* New York: Simon & Schuster.

Bennington, B., Filipek, P., Lefly, D., Churchwell, J., Kennedy, D., Simon, J., Filley, C., Galaburda, A., Alarcon, M., & DeFries, J. (1999). Brain morphometry in reading-disabled twins. *Neurology, 53,* 732–729.

Berk, L. E., & Potts, M. K. (1991). Development and functional significance of private speech among attention-deficit hyperactivity disorder and normal boys. *Journal of Abnormal Child Psychology, 19,* 357–377.

Berman, S. L., Weems, C. F., Silverman, W. K., & Kurtines, W. M. (2000). Predictors of outcome in exposure-based cognitive and behavioral treatments for phobic and anxiety disorders in children. *Behavior Therapy, 31,* 713–731.

Berndt, T. J. (1999). Friends' influence on children's adjustment to school. In W. A. Collins & B. Laursen (Eds.), *Relationships as developmental contexts: The Minnesota Symposia on Child Psychology* (Vol. 30, pp. 85–108). Mahwah, NJ: Erlbaum.

Bernhardt, P. C. (1997). Influences of serotonin and testosterone in aggression and dominance: Convergence with social psychology. *Current Directions in Psychological Sciences, 6,* 44–48.

Bernheimer, C., & Keogh, B. (1988). Stability of cognitive performance of children with developmental delays. *American Journal on Mental Deficiency, 92,* 539–542.

Berninger, V. W. (1994). Future directions for research on writing disabilities. In G. R. Lyon (Ed.), *Frames of reference for the assessment of learning disabilities* (pp. 419–439). Baltimore: Brookes Publishing Co.

Bertelsen, A., Harvald, B., & Hauge, M. (1977). A Danish twin study of manic-depressive disorders. *British Journal of Psychiatry, 130,* 330–351.

Bettelheim, B. (1967). *The empty fortress.* New York: Free Press.

Beumont, P. J. V., Russell, J., & Touyz, S. (1995). Psychological concerns in the maintenance of dieting disorders. In G. I. Szmukler, C. Dare, & J. Treasure (Eds.), *Handbook of eating disorders: Theory, treatment and research* (pp. 221–241). Chichester, UK: Wiley.

Biederman, J., Faraone, S. V., Hirshfeld-Becker, D. R., Friedman, D., Robin, J. A., & Rosenbaum, J. F. (2001). Patterns of psychopathology and dysfunction in high-risk children of parents with panic disorder and major depression. *American Journal of Psychiatry, 158,* 49–57.

Biederman, J., Faraone, S. V., Keenan, K., Knee, D., & Tsuang, M. T. (1990). Family-genetic and psychosocial risk factors in DSM-III attention deficit disorder. *Journal of the American Academy of Child and Adolescent Psychiatry, 29,* 526–533.

Biederman, J., Faraone, S. V., & Lapey, K. (1992). Comorbidity of diagnosis in attention-deficit hyperactivity disorder. *Child and Adolescent Psychiatric Clinics of North America, 1,* 335–360.

Biederman, J., Faraone, S. V., Marrs, A., Moore, P., Garcia, J., Ablon, S., Mick, E., Gershon, J., & Kearns, M. E. (1997). Panic disorder and agoraphobia in consecutively referred children and adolescents. *Journal of the American Academy of Child and Adolescent Psychiatry, 36,* 214–223.

Biederman, J., Faraone, S. V., Mick, E., Wozniak, J., Chen, L., & Ouellette, C. (1996). Attention-deficit hyperactivity disorder and juvenile mania: An overlooked comorbidity? *Journal of the American Academy of Child and Adolescent Psychiatry, 35,* 997–1008.

Biederman, J., Mick, E., Faraone, S. V., Braaten, E., Doyle, A., Spencer, T., Wilens, T., Frazier, E., & Johnson, M. A. (2002). Influence of gender on attention deficit hyperactivity disorder in children referred to a psychiatric clinic. *American Journal of Psychiatry, 159,* 36–42.

Biederman, J., Mick, E., Faraone, S. V., Spencer, T., Wilens, T. E., & Wozniak, J. (2000). Pediatric mania: A developmental subtype of bipolar disorder? *Biological Psychiatry, 48,* 458–466.

Biederman, J., Milberger, S., Faraone, S. V., Guite, J., & Warburton, R. (1994). Associations between childhood asthma and ADHD: Issues of psychiatric comorbidity and familiality. *Journal of the American Academy of Child and Adolescent Psychiatry, 33,* 842–848.

Biederman, J., Rosenbaum, J. F., Chaloff, J., & Kagan, J. (1995). Behavioral inhibition as a risk factor for anxiety disorders. In J. S. March (Ed.), *Anxiety disorders in children and adolescents* (pp. 61–81). New York: Guilford.

Biederman, J., Santangelo, S. L., Faraone, S. V., Kiely, K., Guite, J., Mick, E., Reed, E. D., Kraus, I., Jellinek, M., & Perrin, J. (1995). Clinical correlates of enuresis in ADHD and non-ADHD children. *Journal of Child Psychology and Psychiatry, 36,* 865–877.

Biederman, J., Wozniak, J., Kiely, K., & Ablon, S. (1995). CBCL clinical scales discriminate prepubertal children with structured interview–derived diagnosis of mania from those with ADHD. *Journal of the American Academy of Child and Adolescent Psychiatry, 34,* 464–471.

Bienvenu, T., Carrie, A., de Roux, N., Vinet, M. C., Jonveaux, P., Couvert, P., Villard, L., Arzimanoglou, A., Beldjord, C., Fontes, M., Tardieu, M., & Chelly, J. (2000). MeCP2 mutations account for most cases of typical forms of Rett syndrome. *Human Molecular Genetics, 9,* 1377–1384.

Birchwood, M., McGorry, P., & Jackson, H. (1997). Early intervention in schizophrenia. *British Journal of Psychiatry, 170,* 2–5.

Bird, H. R., Canino, G. J., Davies, M., Zhang, H., Ramirez, R., & Lahey, B. B. (2001). Prevalence and correlates of antisocial behaviors among three ethnic groups. *Journal of Abnormal Child Psychology, 29,* 465–478.

Bird, H. R., Canino, G., Rubio-Stipec, M., Gould, M. S., Ribera, J., Sesman, M., Woodbury, M., Huertas-Goldman, S., Pagan, A., Sanchez-Lacay, A., & Moscoso, H. (1988). Estimates of the prevalence of childhood maladjustment in a community survey in Puerto Rico. *Archives of General Psychiatry, 45,* 1120–1126.

Birmaher, B., Kaufman, J., Brent, D. A., Dahl, R. E., Perel, J. M., Al-Shabbout, M., Nelson, B., Stull, S., Rao, U., Waterman, G. S., Williamson, D. E., & Ryan, N. D. (1997). Neuroendocrine response to 5-hydroxy-L-tryptophan in prepubertal children at high risk of major depressive disorder. *Archives of General Psychiatry, 54,* 1113–1119.

Birmaher, B., Ryan, N. D., Williamson, D. E., Brent, D. A., Kaufman, J., Dahl, R. E., Perel, J., & Nelson, B. (1996). Childhood and adolescent depression: A review of the past 10 years. *Journal of the American Academy of Child and Adolescent Psychiatry, 35,* 1427–1439.

Black, M., & Dubowitz, H. (1991). Failure to thrive: Lessons from animal models and developing countries. *Developmental and Behavioral Pediatrics, 12,* 259–267.

Blair, R. J. R., Colledge, E., Murray, L., & Mitchell, D. G. V. (2001). A selective impairment in the processing of sad and fearful expressions in children with psychopathic tendencies. *Journal of Abnormal Child Psychology, 29,* 491–498.

Bleuler, E. (1950). *Dementia praecox and the group of schizophrenias* (J. Zinkin, trans.). New York: International University Press. (Original work published 1911)

Block, J. H., Block, J., & Gjerde, P. F. (1986). The personality of children prior to divorce: A prospective study. *Child Development, 57,* 827–840.

Boddy, J. M., & Skuse, D. H. (1994). Annotation: The process of parenting in failure to thrive. *Journal of Child Psychology and Psychiatry, 35,* 401–424.

Boergers, J., Spirito, A., & Donaldson, D. (1998). Reasons for adolescent suicide attempts: Associations with psychological functioning. *Journal of the American Academy of Child and Adolescent Psychiatry, 37,* 1287–1293.

Bögels, S. M., & Zigterman, D. (2000). Dysfunctional cognitions in children with social phobia, separation anxiety disorder, and generalized anxiety disorder. *Journal of Abnormal Child Psychology, 28,* 205–211.

Bolger, K. E., Patterson, C. J., Thompson, W. W., & Kupersmidt, J. B. (1995). Psychosocial adjustment among children experiencing persistent and intermittent family economic hardship. *Child Development, 66,* 1107–1129.

Bolton, P. F., Murphy, M., MacDonald, H., Whitlock, B., Pickles, A., & Rutter, M. (1997). Obstetric complications in autism: Consequences or causes of the condition? *Journal of the American Academy of Child and Adolescent Psychiatry, 36,* 272–281.

Bosch, X. (2000). Please don't pass the paella: Eating disorders upset Spain. *Journal of the American Medical Association, 283,* 1405–1410.

Bourgeois, P., & Clark, B. (1986). *Franklin in the dark.* New York: Scholastic Books.

Bourke, M., & Donohue, B. (1996). Assessment and treatment of juvenile sex offenders: An empirical review. *Journal of Child Sexual Abuse, 5,* 47–70.

Bowlby, J. (1973). *Attachment and loss: Vol. 2. Separation: Anxiety and anger.* New York: Basic Books.

Boyle, M. H., Offord, D. R., Racine, Y. A., Szatmari, P., Fleming, J. E., & Link S. P. S. (1992). Predicting substance use in late adolescence: Results from the Ontario Child Health Study follow-up. *American Journal of Psychiatry, 149,* 761–767.

Bradley, S. A., & Shankweiler, D. P. (1991). *Phonological processes in literacy.* Hillsdale, NJ: Erlbaum.

Brame, B., Nagin, D. S., & Tremblay, R. E. (2001). Developmental trajectories of physical aggression from school entry to late adolescence. *Journal of Child Psychology and Psychiatry, 42,* 503–512.

Breiner, S. (1990). *Slaughter of the innocents.* New York: Plenum.

Bremner, D. J., Randall, P., Vermetten, E., Staib, L., Bronen, R. A., Mazure, C., Capelli, S., McCarthy, G., Innis, R. B., & Charney, D. S. (1997). Magnetic resonance imaging–based measurements of hippocampal volume in posttraumatic stress disorder related to childhood physical and sexual abuse: A preliminary report. *Biological Psychiatry, 41,* 23–32.

Brenner, S., Fisher, H., & Mann-Gray, S. (1989). Race and the shaken baby syndrome: Experience at one hospital. *Journal of the National Medical Association, 81,* 183–184.

Brent, D. A., Kolko, D. J., Birhamer, B., Baugher, M., Bridge, J., Roth, C., & Holder, D. (1998). Predictors of treatment efficacy in a clinical trial of three psychosocial treatments for adolescent depression. *Journal of the American Academy of Child and Adolescent Psychiatry, 37,* 906–914.

Brent, D. A., Perper, J. A., Moritz, G., Allman, C., Friend, A., Roth, C., Schweers, J., Balach, L., & Baugher, M. (1993). Psychiatric risk factors for adolescent suicide: A case control study. *Journal of the American Academy of Child and Adolescent Psychiatry, 32,* 521–529.

Breunlin, D. C., Desai, V. J., Stone, M. F., & Swilley, J. A. (1983). Failure to thrive with no organic etiology: A critical review of the literature. *International Journal of Eating Disorders, 2,* 25–49.

Briere, J. (1992). *Child abuse trauma: Theory and treatment of the lasting effects.* Newbury Park, CA: Sage.

Broman, S., Nichols, P. L., Shaughnessy, P., & Kennedy, W. (1987). *Retardation in young children: A developmental study of cognitive deficit.* Hillsdale, NJ: Erlbaum.

Bronfenbrenner, U. (1979). *The ecology of human development: Experiments by nature and design.* Cambridge, MA: Harvard University Press.

Bronfenbrenner, U. (1999). Environments in developmental perspective: Theoretical and operational models. In S. L. Friedman & T. D. Wachs (Eds.), *Measuring environment across the life span* (pp. 3–28). Washington, DC: American Psychological Association.

Brown, E., & Kolko, D. (1999). Child victims' attributions about being physically abused: An examination of factors associated with symptom severity. *Journal of Abnormal Child Psychology, 27,* 311–322.

Brown, J., Cohen, P., Johnson, J. G., & Smailes, E. (1999). Childhood abuse and neglect: Specificity and effects on adolescents and young adult depression and suicidality. *Journal of the American Academy of Child and Adolescent Psychiatry, 38,* 1490–1496.

Brownell, K. D. (1991). Dieting and the search for the perfect body: Where physiology and culture collide. *Behavior Therapy, 22,* 1–12.

Brumberg, J. J. (1997). *The body project: An intimate history of American girls.* New York: Random House.

Bruun, R. D., & Budman, C. L. (1993). The natural history of Gilles de la Tourette syndrome. In R. Kurlan (Ed.), *Handbook of Tourette syndrome and related tic and behavioral disorders* (pp. 27–42). New York: Marcel Dekker.

Bryson, S. E., Clark, B. S., & Smith, I. M. (1988). First report of a Canadian epidemiological study of autistic syndromes. *Journal of Child Psychology and Psychiatry, 29,* 433–445.

Buchsbaum, M. S. (1990). Frontal lobes, basal ganglia, temporal lobes: Three sites for schizophrenia? *Schizophrenia Bulletin, 16,* 379–839.

Buhrmester, D., Camparo, L., Christensen, A., Gonzalez, L. S., & Hinshaw, S. P. (1992). Mothers and fathers interacting in dyads and triads with normal and hyperactive sons. *Developmental Psychology, 28,* 500–509.

Buitelaar, J. K., & Willemsen-Swinkels, S. H. N. (2000). Autism: Current theories regarding its pathogenesis and implications for rational pharmacotherapy. *Pediatric Drugs, 2,* 67–81.

Bulik, C. M., Sullivan, P. F., & Kendler, K. S. (2000). An empirical study of the classification of eating disorders. *American Journal of Psychiatry, 157,* 886–895.

Bullinger, A. (1996). Approche instrumentale de l'autisme infantile. In R. Pry (Ed.), *Autisme et régulation de l'action* (pp. 147–164). Les Cahiers du CERFEE, no. 13. Montpellier: Université de Montpellier III.

Burge, D., & Hammen, C. (1991). Maternal communication: Predictors of outcome at follow-up in a sample of children at high and low risk for depression. *Journal of Abnormal Psychology, 100,* 174–180.

Burke, P., & Elliott, M. (1999). Depression in pediatric chronic illness: A diathesis-stress model. *Psychosomatics, 40,* 5–17.

Burns, D. D. (1989). *The feeling good handbook: Using the new mood therapy in everyday life.* New York: William Morrow.

Bussing, R., Halfon, N., Benjamin, B., & Wells, K. B. (1995). Prevalence of behavior problems in US children with asthma. *Archives of Pediatrics and Adolescent Medicine, 149,* 565–572.

Buston, K. M., & Wood, S. F. (2000). Non-compliance amongst adolescents with asthma: Listening to what they tell us about self-management. *Family Practice, 17,* 134–138.

Butler, R. J. (1998). Night wetting in children: Psychological aspects. *Journal of Child Psychology and Psychiatry, 39,* 453–463.

Butler, R. W., Rizzi, L. P., & Bandilla, E. B. (1999). The effects of childhood cancer and its treatment on two objective measures of psychological functioning. *Children's Health Care, 28,* 311–327.

Byely, L., Archibald, A. B., Graber, J., & Brooks-Gunn, J. (2000). A prospective study of familial and social influences on girls' body image and dieting. *International Journal of Eating Disorders, 28,* 155–164.

Cadoret, R. J., & Stewart, M. A. (1991). An adoption study of attention deficit/hyperactivity/aggression and their relationship to adult antisocial personality. *Comprehensive Psychiatry, 32,* 73–82.

Cahill, L., Kaminer, R., & Johnson, P. (1999). Developmental, cognitive, and behavioral sequelae of child abuse. *Child and Adolescent Psychiatric Clinics of North America, 8,* 827–841.

Cairns, R. B. (1991). Multiple metaphors for a single idea. *Developmental Psychology, 27,* 23–26.

Cairns, R. B., & Cairns, B. D. (1994). *Lifelines and risks: Pathways of youth in our time.* New York: Cambridge University Press.

Campo, J. V. (1995). Somatization disorder. In R. T. Ammerman & M. Hersen (Eds.*), Handbook of child behavior therapy in the psychiatric setting* (pp. 427–452). New York: Wiley.

Campo, J. V., & Fritsch, S. L. (1994). Somatization in children and adolescents. *Journal of the American Academy of Child and Adolescent Psychiatry, 33,* 1223–1235.

Campo, J. V., Jansen-McWilliams, L., Comer, D. M., & Kelleher, K. J. (1999). Somatization in pediatric primary care: Association with psychopathology, functional impairment, and use of services. *Journal of the American Academy of Child and Adolescent Psychiatry, 38,* 1093–1101.

Cantwell, D. P., & Baker, L. (1991). *Psychiatrics and developmental disorders in children with communication disorder.* Washington, DC: American Psychiatric Press.

Cantwell, D. P., & Baker, L. (1992). Association between attention deficit–hyperactivity disorder and learning disorders. In S. E. Shaywitz & B. A. Shaywitz (Eds.), *Attention deficit disorder comes of age: Toward the twenty-first century* (pp. 145–164). Austin, TX: Pro-ed.

Caplan, R. (1994a). Communication deficits in childhood schizophrenia spectrum disorders. *Schizophrenia Bulletin, 20,* 671–684.

Caplan, R. (1994b). Thought disorder in childhood. *Journal of the American Academy of Child and Adolescent Psychiatry, 33,* 605–615.

Capps, L., Losh, M., & Thurber, C. (2000). "The frog ate the bug and made his mouth sad": Narrative competence in children with autism. *Journal of Abnormal Child Psychology, 28,* 193–204.

Carlson, E. A. (1998). A prospective longitudinal study of disorganized/disoriented attachment. *Child Development, 69,* 1107–1128.

Carlson, E. A., Jacobvitz, D., & Sroufe, L. A. (1995). A developmental investigation of inattentiveness and hyperactivity. *Child Development, 66,* 37–54.

Carlson, G. A. (1990). Child and adolescent mania: Diagnostic considerations. *Journal of Child Clinical Psychology, 31,* 331–342.

Carlson, G. A. (1994). Adolescent bipolar disorder: Phenomenology and treatment implications. In W. M. Reynolds & H. F. Johnston (Eds.), *Handbook of depression in children and adolescents: Issues in clinical child psychology* (pp. 41–60). New York: Plenum.

Carlson, G. A., & Abbott, S. F. (1995). Mood disorders and suicide. In H. I Kaplan & B. J. Sadock, *Comprehensive textbook of psychiatry* (6th ed., pp. 2367–2391). Baltimore: Williams and Wilkins.

Carlson, G. A., & Kashani, J. H. (1988). Phenomenology of major depression from childhood through adulthood: Analysis of three studies. *American Journal of Psychiatry, 145,* 1222–1225.

Carlson, G. A. & Strober, M. (1979). Manic-depressive illness in early adolescence. A study of clinical and diagnostic characteristics in six cases. *Journal of the American Academy of Child Psychiatry, 17,* 138–153.

Carlsson, A. (1995). The dopamine theory revisited. In S. R. Hirsch & D. R. Weinberger (Eds.), *Schizophrenia* (pp. 379–400). Oxford, UK: Blackwell Empirical Publications.

Carnine, D. (1991). Reforming mathematics instruction: The role of curriculum materials. *Journal of Behavioral Education, 1,* 37–57.

Carr, J. (1990). Down syndrome. In J. Hogg, J. Sebba, & L. Lambe (Eds.), *Profound retardation and multiple impairment* (pp. 40–53). London: Chapman & Hall.

Caspi, A., Lynam, D., Moffitt, T. E., & Silva, P. A. (1993). Unraveling girls' delinquency: Biological, dispositional, and contextual contributions to adolescent misbehavior. *Developmental Psychology, 23,* 308–313.

Castelloe, P., & Dawson, G. (1993). Subclassification of children with autism and pervasive developmental disorder: A questionnaire based on Wing's subgrouping scheme. *Journal of Autism and Developmental Disorders, 23,* 229–241.

Catalano, R. A. (Ed.). (1998). *When autism strikes: Families cope with childhood disintegrative disorder.* New York: Plenum.

Cavaiola, A. A., & Schiff, M. (1988). Behavioral sequelae of physical and/or sexual abuse in adolescents. *Child Abuse & Neglect, 12,* 181–188.

Celano, M., Geller, R. J., Phillips, K. M., & Ziman, R. (1998). Treatment adherence among low-income children with asthma. *Journal of Pediatric Psychology, 23,* 345–349.

Cepeda, N. J., Cepeda, M. L., & Kramer, A. F. (2000). Task switching and attention deficit hyperactivity disorder. *Journal of Abnormal Child Psychology, 28,* 213–226.

Cerezo, M. A. (1997). Abusive family interaction: A review. *Aggression and Violent Behavior: A Review Journal, 2,* 215–240.

Chadwick, O., Taylor, E., Taylor, A., Heptinstall, E., & Danckaerts, M. (1999). Hyperactivity and reading disability: A longitudinal study of the nature of the association. *Journal of Child Psychology and Psychiatry, 40,* 1039–1050.

Chamberlain, P. (1996). Intensified foster care: Multi-level treatment for adolescents with conduct disorders in out-of-home care. In E. D. Hibbs & P. S. Jensen (Eds.), *Psychosocial treatments for child and adolescent disorders: Empirically based strategies for clinical practice* (pp. 475–495). Washington, DC: American Psychological Association.

Chang, K. K. D., Steiner, H., & Ketter, T. A. (2000). Psychiatric phenomenology of child and adolescent bipolar offspring. *Journal of the American Academy of Child and Adolescent Psychiatry, 39,* 453–460.

Channon, S., deSilva, P., Hemsley, D., & Perkins, R. (1989). A controlled trial of cognitive-behavioural and behavioural treatment of anorexia nervosa. *Behaviour Research and Therapy, 27,* 529–535.

Chess, S. (1960). Diagnosis and treatment of the hyperactive child. *New York State Journal of Medicine, 60,* 2379–2385.

Chorpita, B. F., Albano, A. M., & Barlow, D. H. (1998). The structure of negative emotions in a clinical sample of children and adolescents. *Journal of Abnormal Psychology, 107,* 74–85.

Chorpita, B. F., & Barlow, D. H. (1998). The development of anxiety: The role of control in the early environment. *Psychological Bulletin, 124,* 3–21.

Christophersen, E. M., & Rapoff, M. A. (1983). Toileting problems in children. In C. E. Walker & M. C. Roberts (Eds.), *Handbook of clinical child psychology* (pp. 593–615). New York: Wiley.

Cicchetti, D., & Rogosch, F. A. (1997). The role of self-organization in the promotion of resilience in maltreated children. *Development and Psychopathology, 9,* 797–815.

Cicchetti, D., & Toth, S. L. (1995). A developmental psychopathology perspective on child abuse and neglect. *Journal of the American Academy of Child and Adolescent Psychiatry, 34,* 541–565.

Clark, A. F., & Lewis, S. W. (1998). Practitioner review: Treatment of schizophrenia in childhood and adolescence. *Journal of Child Psychology and Psychiatry, 39,* 1071–1081.

Clark, C., Prior, M., & Kinsella, G. J. (2000). Do executive function deficits differentiate between adolescents with ADHD and oppositional defiant/conduct disorder? A neuropsychological study using the six elements test and Hayling sentence completion test. *Journal of Abnormal Child Psychology, 28,* 403–414.

Clark, L. A., & Watson, D. (1991). Tripartite model of anxiety and depression: Psychometric evidence and taxonomic implications. *Journal of Abnormal Psychology, 100,* 316–336.

Clarke, G. N., Hawkins, W., Murphy, M., & Sheeber, L. (1993). School-based primary prevention of depressive symptomatology in adolescents: Findings from two studies. *Journal of Adolescent Research, 8,* 183–204.

Clarke, G. N., Hawkins, W., Murphy, M., Sheeber, L. B., Lewinsohn, P. M., & Seeley, J. R. (1995). Targeted prevention for unipolar depressive disorder in an at-risk sample of high school adolescents: A randomized trial of a cognitive intervention. *Journal of the American Academy of Child and Adolescent Psychiatry, 33,* 312–321.

Clarke, G. N., Rhode, P., Lewinsohn, P. M., Hops, H., & Seeley, J. R. (1999). Cognitive-behavioral treatment of adolescent depression: Efficacy of acute group treatment and booster sessions. *Journal of the American Academy of Child and Adolescent Psychiatry, 38,* 272–279.

Cohen, J. A., & Mannarino, A. P. (1997). A treatment study for sexually abused preschool children: Outcome during a one-year follow-up. *Journal of the American Academy of Child and Adolescent Psychiatry, 36,* 1228–1235.

Cohen, J. A., & Mannarino, A. P. (1998). Factors that mediate treatment outcome of sexually abused preschool children: Six- and 12-month follow-up. *Journal of the American Academy of Child and Adolescent Psychiatry, 37,* 44–51.

Cohen, J. A., Mannarino, A. P., Berliner, L., & Deblinger, E. (2000). Trauma-focused cognitive behavioral therapy for children and adolescents: An empirical update. *Journal of Interpersonal Violence, 15,* 1202–1222.

Coie, J. D., & Dodge, K. A. (1997). Aggression and antisocial behavior. In W. Damon & N. Eisenberg (Eds.), *Handbook of child psychology: Vol. 3. Social, emotional, and personality development* (5th ed., pp. 779–862). New York: Wiley.

Coie, J. D., & Lenox, K. F. (1994). The development of antisocial individuals. In D. Fowles, P. Sutker, & S. Goodman (Eds.), *Psychopathy and antisocial personality: A developmental perspective* (pp. 45–72). New York: Springer.

Cole, P. M., Zahn-Waxler, C., & Smith, D. (1994). Expressive control during a disappointment: Variations related to preschoolers' behavior problems. *Developmental Psychology, 30,* 835–846.

Coleman, D. H., & Straus, M. A. (1990). Marital power, conflict, and violence in a nationally representative sample of American couples. In M. A. Straus & R. J. Gelles (Eds.), *Physical violence in American families* (pp. 287–304). New Brunswick, NJ: Transaction Publishers.

Comfort, R. L. (1992). *Teaching the unconventional child.* Englewood, CO: Teacher Ideas Press.

Condry, J. C., & Ross, D. F. (1985). Sex and aggression: The influence of gender label on the perception of aggression in children. *Child Development, 56,* 225–233.

Conduct Problems Prevention Research Group. (1999). Initial impact of the Fast Track prevention trial for conduct problems: I. The high-risk sample. *Journal of Consulting and Clinical Psychology, 67,* 631–647.

Conger, R. D., Elder, G. H., Lorenz, F. O., Simons, R. L., & Whitbeck, L. B. (Eds.). (1994). *Families in troubled times: Adapting to change in rural America.* New York: Aldine de Gruyter.

Conner, K. R., & Nilsen, W. J. (2001). The relationship between child abuse, trauma, and current suicidal ideation. Submitted for publication.

Connor, D. F., Barkley, R. A., & Davis, H. T. (2000). A pilot study of methylphenidate, clonidine, or the combination in ADHD comorbid with aggressive oppositional defiant or conduct disorder. *Clinical Pediatrics, 39,* 15–25.

Copeland, D. R., & Davidson, E. R. (1989). Comprehensive treatment of the child with cancer. In M. C. Roberts & C. E. Walker (Eds.), *Casebook of child and pediatric psychology* (pp. 319–345). New York: Guilford.

Costello, E. J., & Angold, A. (1995a). Developmental epidemiology. In D. Cicchetti & D. J. Cohen (Eds.), *Developmental psychopathology: Vol. 1. Theory and methods* (pp. 23–56). New York: Wiley.

Costello, E.J., & Angold, A. (1995b). Epidemiology. In J. S. March (Ed.), *Anxiety disorders in children and adolescents* (pp. 109–124). New York: Guilford.

Costello, E. J., Burns, B. J., Angold, A., & Leaf, P. J. (1993). How can epidemiology improve mental health services for children and adolescents? *Journal of the Academy of Child and Adolescent Psychiatry, 32,* 1106–1113.

Costello, E. J., Costello, A. M., Edelbrock, C., Burns, B. J., Dulcan, M. K., Brent, D., & Janiszewski, S. (1988). Psychiatric disorders in pediatric primary care. *Archives of General Psychiatry, 45,* 1107–1116.

Costello, E., Loeber, R., & Stouthamer-Loeber, M. (1991). Pervasive and situational hyperactivity–Confounding effect of informant: A research note. *Journal of Child Psychology and Psychiatry, 32,* 367–376.

Costin, L. B., Karger, H. J., & Stoesz, D. (1996). *The politics of child abuse in America.* New York: Oxford University Press.

Côté, S., Zoccolillo, M., Tremblay, R. E., Nagin, D., & Vitaro, F. (2001). Predicting girls' conduct disorder in adolescence from childhood trajectories of disruptive behaviors. *Journal of the American Academy of Child and Adolescent Psychiatry, 40,* 678–684.

Crick, N. R., & Bigbee, M. A. (1998). Relational and overt forms of peer victimization: A multi-informant approach. *Journal of Consulting and Clinical Psychology, 66,* 337–347.

Crisp, A. H. (1997). Anorexia nervosa as flight from growth: Assessment and treatment based on the model. In D. Garner & P. E. Garfinkel (Eds.), *Handbook of treatment for eating disorders* (2nd ed., pp. 248–277). New York: Guilford.

Cunningham, C. E., & Siegel, L. S. (1987). Peer interactions of normal and attention-deficit disordered boys during free-play, cooperative task, and simulated classroom situations. *Journal of Abnormal Child Psychology, 15,* 247–268.

Cunningham, P. B., & Henggeler, S. W. (1999). Engaging multi-problem families in treatment: Lessons learned throughout the development of multisystemic therapy. *Family Process, 38,* 265–286.

Curry, J. F., & Murphy, L. B. (1995). Comorbidity of anxiety disorders. In J. S. March (Ed.), *Anxiety disorders in children and adolescents* (pp. 301–307). New York: Guilford.

Dadds, M. R., Barrett, P. M., Rapee, R. M., & Ryan, S. (1996). Family process and child anxiety and aggression: An observational analysis. *Journal of Abnormal Child Psychology, 24,* 715–734.

Dadds, M. R., Sanders, M. R., Morrison, M., & Regbetz, M. (1992). Childhood depression and conduct disorder: II. An analysis of family interaction patterns in the home. *Journal of Abnormal Psychology, 101,* 505–513.

Dadds, M. R., Spence, S. H., Holland, D. E., Barrett, P. M., & Laurens, K. R. (1997). Prevention and early intervention for anxiety disorders: A controlled trial. *Journal of Consulting and Clinical Psychology, 65,* 627–635.

Daggett, J., O'Brien, M., Zanolli, K., & Peyton, V. (2000). Parents' attitudes about children: Associations with parental life histories and child-rearing quality. *Journal of Family Psychology, 14,* 187–199.

Daly, M., & Wilson, M. I. (1996). Violence against stepchildren. *Current Directions in Psychological Sciences, 5,* 77–81.

Daniels, D., & Moos, R. H. (1990). Assessing life stressors and social resources among adolescents: Applications to depressed youth. *Journal of Adolescent Research, 5,* 268–289.

Daugherty, T. K., & Quay, H. C. (1991). Response perseveration and delayed responding in childhood behavior disorders. *Journal of Child Psychology and Psychiatry, 32,* 453–461.

Davies, S. P. (1959). *The mentally retarded in society.* New York: Columbia University Press.

Davis, L., & Siegel, L. J. (2000). Posttraumatic stress disorder in children and adolescents: A review and analysis. *Clinical Child and Family Psychology Review, 3,* 135–154.

Daviss, W. B., Coon, H., Whitehead, P., Ryan, K., Burkley, M., & McMahon, W. (1995). Predicting diabetic control from competence, adherence, adjustment, and psychopathology. *Journal of the American Academy of Child and Adolescent Psychiatry, 34,* 1629–1636.

Dawson, G., & Adams, A. (1984). Imitation and social responsiveness in autistic children. *Journal of Abnormal Child Psychology, 12,* 209–225.

Dawson, G., Hill, D., Spencer, A., Galpert, L., & Watson, L. (1990). Affective exchanges between young autistic children and their mothers. *Journal of Abnormal Child Psychology, 18,* 335–345.

Day, M. (1998). Coming home. In R. A. Catalano (Ed.), *When autism strikes: Families cope with childhood disintegrative disorder* (pp. 69–90). New York: Plenum.

Deater-Deckard, K., Dodge, K. A., Bates, J. E., & Pettit, G. S. (1996). Physical discipline among African-American and European-American mothers: Links to children's externalizing behaviors. *Developmental Psychology, 32,* 1065–1072.

DeFries, J. C., Olson, R. K., Pennington, B. F., & Smith, S. D. (1991). Colorado Reading Project: An update. In D. Duane & D. Gray (Eds.), *The reading brain: The biological basis of dyslexia* (pp. 53–87). Parkton, MD: York Press.

DeKlyen, M., Speltz, M. L., & Greenberg, M. T. (1998). Fathering and early onset conduct problems: Positive and negative parenting, father-son attachment, and the marital context. *Clinical Child and Family Psychology Review, 1,* 3–21.

DeLong, G. R., & Dwyer, J. T. (1988). Correlation of family history with specific autistic subgroups: Asperger's syndrome and bipolar affective disease. *Journal of Autism and Developmental Disorders, 18,* 593–600.

DeLong, R. (1995). Medical and pharmacologic treatment of learning disabilities. *Journal of Child Neurology, 10,* S92–S95.

Devlin, M. J., Walsh, B. T., Spitzer, R. L., & Hasin, D. (1992). Is there another binge eating disorder? A review of the literature on overeating in the absence of bulimia nervosa. *International Journal of Eating Disorders, 11,* 333–340.

Dewey, J., & Bentley, A. F. (1949). *Knowing and the known.* Boston: Beacon Press.

Dewey, M. (1991). Living with Asperger's syndrome. In U. Frith (Ed.), *Autism and Asperger syndrome* (pp.184–206). Cambridge, UK: Cambridge University Press.

Dickens, C. (1949). *The adventures of Oliver Twist.* New York: Oxford University Press. (Original work published 1837–1838)

Diener, M. B., & Milich, R. (1997). Effects of positive feedback on the social interactions of boys with attention deficit hyperactivity disorder: A test of the self-protective hypothesis. *Journal of Clinical Child Psychology, 26,* 256–265.

DiFilippo, J. M., & Overholser, J. C. (2000). Suicidal ideation in adolescent psychiatric inpatients as associated with depression and attachment relationships. *Journal of Clinical Child Psychology, 29,* 155–166.

DiLalla, L. F., & Gottesman, I. I. (1991). Biological and genetic contributors to violence: Widom's untold tale. *Psychological Bulletin, 109,* 125–129.

Dishion, T. J., & Patterson, G. R. (1992). Age effects in parent training outcome. *Behavior Therapy, 23,* 719–729.

Dissanayake, C., & Crossley, S. A. (1996). Proximity and sociable behaviours in autism: Evidence for attachment. *Journal of Child Psychology and Psychiatry, 37,* 149–156.

Dobash, R. E., & Dobash, R. P. (1992). *Women, violence, and social change.* New York: Routledge.

Dodge, K. A. (1993). Social-cognitive mechanisms in the development of conduct disorder and depression. *Annual Review of Psychology, 44,* 559–584.

Dodge, K. A. (1997, June). *The development of conduct disorder.* Paper presented at the meeting of the International Society for Research in Child and Adolescent Psychopathology, Paris.

Dodge, K. A., Bates, J. E., & Pettit, G. S. (1990). Mechanisms in the cycle of violence. *Science, 250,* 1678–1683.

Dodge, K. A., Coie, J. D., Pettit, G. S., & Price, J. M. (1990). Peer status and aggression in boys' groups: Developmental and contextual analyses. *Child Development, 61,* 1289–1309.

Dodge, K. A., Pettit, G. S., & Bates, J. E. (1994). Effects of physical maltreatment on the development of peer relations. *Development and Psychopathology, 6,* 43–55.

Dodge, K. A., Pettit, G. S., & Bates, J. E. (1997). How the experience of early physical abuse leads children to become chronically aggressive. In D. Cicchetti & S. L. Toth (Eds.), *Developmental perspectives on trauma: Vol. 9. Theory, research, and intervention* (pp. 263–288). Rochester, NY: University of Rochester Press.

Donnelly, C. L., Amaya-Jackson, L., & March, J. S. (1999). Psychopharmacology of pediatric posttraumatic stress disorder. *Journal of Child and Adolescent Psychopharmacology, 9,* 203–220.

Donnerstein, E., Slaby, R. G., & Eron, L. D. (1994). The mass media and youth aggression. In L. D. Eron & J. H. Gentry (Eds.), *Reason to hope: A psychological perspective on violence and youth* (pp. 219–250). Washington, DC: American Psychological Association.

Donovan, C. L., & Spence, S. H. (2000). Prevention of childhood anxiety disorders. *Clinical Psychology Review, 20,* 509–531.

Dubner, A. E., & Motta, R. W. (1999). Sexually and physically abused foster care children and posttraumatic stress disorder. *Journal of Consulting and Clinical Psychology, 67,* 367–373.

Dulcan, M. K., & Popper, C. W. (1991). *Concise guide to child and adolescent psychiatry.* Washington, DC: American Psychiatric Press.

Dulmus, C. N., & Smyth, N. J. (2000). Early-onset schizophrenia: A literature review of empirically based interventions. *Child and Adolescent Social Work Journal, 17,* 55–69.

Dumas, J. E. (1979). Modification of constant facial manipulations in a moderately subnormal man. *British Journal of Mental Subnormality, 25,* 19–26.

Dumas, J. E. (1986). Indirect influence of maternal social contacts on mother-child interactions in distressed families. *Journal of Abnormal Child Psychology, 14,* 205–216.

Dumas, J. E. (1994). Conduct disorder. In R. J. Corsini (Ed.), *Encyclopedia of psychology* (2nd ed., pp. 289–293). New York: Wiley Interscience.

Dumas, J. E. (1997). Home and school correlates of early at-risk status: A transactional perspective. In R. F. Kronick (Ed.), *At-risk youth: Theory, practice, reform* (pp. 97–117). New York: Garland Publishing.

Dumas, J. E. (2001). *PACE—Parenting Our Children to Excellence. A program to promote parenting effectiveness and child coping-competence in the preschool years.* Unpublished manual.

Dumas, J. E., & LaFreniere, P. J. (1993). Mother-child relationships as sources of support or stress: A comparison of competent, normative, aggressive, and anxious dyads. *Child Development, 64,* 1732–1754.

Dumas, J. E., LaFreniere, P. J., & Serketich, W. J. (1995). "Balance of power": A transactional analysis of control in mother-child dyads involving socially competent, aggressive, and anxious children. *Journal of Abnormal Psychology, 104,* 104–113.

Dumas, J. E., & Lechowicz, J. G. (1989). When do noncompliant children comply? Implications for family behavior therapy. *Child and Family Behavior Therapy, 11,* 21–38.

Dumas, J. E., Prinz, R. J., Smith, E. P., & Laughlin, J. (1999). The EARLY ALLIANCE prevention trial: An integrated set of interventions to promote competence and reduce risk for conduct disorder, substance abuse, and school failure. *Clinical Child and Family Psychology Review, 2,* 37–53.

Dumas, J. E., Rollock, D., Prinz, R. J., Hops, H., & Blechman, E. A. (1999). Cultural sensitivity: Problems and solutions in applied and preventive intervention. *Applied and Preventive Psychology, 8,* 175–196.

Dumas, J. E., & Wahler, R. G. (1983). Predictors of treatment outcome in parent training: Mother insularity and socioeconomic disadvantage. *Behavioral Assessment, 5,* 301–313.

Dumas, J. E., & Wahler, R. G. (1985). Indiscriminate mothering as a contextual factor in aggressive-oppositional child behavior: "Damned if you do, damned if you don't." *Journal of Abnormal Child Psychology, 13,* 1–17.

Dumas, J. E., & Wekerle, C. (1995). Maternal reports of child behavior problems and personal distress as predictors of dysfunctional parenting. *Development and Psychopathology, 7,* 465–479.

Dumas, J. E., Wolf, L. C., Fisman, S. N., & Culligan, A. (1991). Parenting stress, child behavior problems, and dysphoria in parents of children with autism, Down syndrome, behavior disorders and normal development. *Exceptionality, 2,* 97–110.

Dupree, D., Beale-Spencer, M., & Bell, S. (1997). African American children. In G. Johnson-Powell & J. Yamamoto (Eds.), *Transcultural child development: Psychological assessment and treatment* (pp. 237–268). New York: Wiley.

Durkin, M. S., Khan, N., Davidson, L. L., Zaman, S. S., & Stein, Z. A. (1993). The effects of a natural disaster on child behavior: Evidence for posttraumatic stress. *American Journal of Public Health, 83,* 1549–1553.

Durning, P. (1995). *Éducation familiale: acteurs, processus et enjeux.* Paris: PUF.

Dykens, E. M., Leckman, J. F., Riddle, M. A., Hardin, M. T., Schwartz, S., & Cohen, D. J. (1990). Intellectual, academic, and adaptive functioning of Tourette syndrome children with and without attention deficit disorder. *Journal of Abnormal Child Psychology, 18,* 607–614.

Dyslexia: The gift. (2002). *Famous people with the gift of dyslexia.* [On line]. Available at www.dyslexia.com/qafame.htm.

Eckenrode, J., Ganzel, B., Henderson, C. R., Smith, E., Olds, D. L., Powers, J., Cole, R., Kitzman, H., & Sidora, K. (2000). Preventing child abuse and neglect with a program of nurse home visitation: The limiting effects of domestic violence. *Journal of the American Medical Association, 284,* 1385–1391.

Edleson, J. L. (1999). The overlap between child maltreatment and woman battering. *Violence Against Women, 5,* 134–154.

Edwards, G., Barkley, R. A., Laneri, M., Fletcher, K., & Metevia, L. (2001). Parent-adolescent conflict in teenagers with ADHD and ODD. *Journal of Abnormal Child Psychology, 29,* 557–572.

Egger, H., Link, Costello, E. J., Erkanli, A., & Angold, A. (1999). Somatic complaints and psychopathology in children and adolescents: Stomach aches, musculoskeletal pains, and headaches. *Journal of the American Academy of Child and Adolescent Psychiatry, 38,* 852–860.

Eggers, C., & Bunk D. (1997). The long-term course of childhood-onset schizophrenia: A 42-year follow up. *Schizophrenia Bulletin, 23,* 105–117.

Eggers, C., Bunk, D., Volberg, G., & Roepcke, B. (1999). The ESSEN study of childhood-onset schizophrenia: Selected results. *European Child and Adolescent Psychiatry, 8,* 21–28.

Eisen, A. R., Engler, L. B., & Geyer, B. (1998). Parent training for separation anxiety disorder. In J. M. Briesmeister & C. E. Schaefer (Eds.), *Handbook of parent training: Parents as co-therapists for children's behavior problems* (2nd ed., pp. 205–224). New York: Wiley.

Eisenman, R. (2000). Explaining sex offenders: The concept of imprinting. *International Journal of Adolescence and Youth, 8,* 1–9.

Eiser, C. (1998). Practitioner review: Long-term consequences of childhood cancer. *Journal of Child Psychology and Psychiatry, 39,* 621–633.

Eisler, I. (1995). Family models of eating disorders. In G. I. Szmukler, C. Dare, & J. Treasure (Eds.), *Handbook of eating disorders: Theory, treatment and research* (pp. 155–176). Chichester, UK: Wiley.

Elder, G. H., Eccles, J. S., Ardelt, M., & Lord, S. (1995). Inner-city parents under economic pressure: Perspectives on the strategies of parenting. *Journal of Marriage and the Family, 57,* 771–784.

Eley, T. C., & Stevenson, J. (2000). Specific life events and chronic experiences differentially associated with depression and anxiety in young twins. *Journal of Abnormal Child Psychology, 28,* 383–394.

Ellis, C. R., Singh, N. N., & Ruane, A. L. (1999). Nutritional, dietary, and hormonal treatments for individuals with mental retardation and developmental disabilities. *Mental Retardation and Developmental Disabilities Research Reviews, 5,* 335–341.

Emde, R. (1994). Individuality, context, and the search for meaning. *Child Development, 65,* 719–737.

Emslie, G. J., Rush, J., Weinberg, W. A., Kowatch, R. A., Hughes, C. W., Carmody, T., & Rintelmann, J. (1997). A double-blind, randomized, placebo-controlled trial of fluoxetine in children and adolescents with depression. *Archives of General Psychiatry, 54,* 1031–1037.

Emslie, G., Weinberg, W., Kennard, B., & Kowatch, R. (1994). Neurobiological aspects of depression in children and adolescents. In W. M. Reynolds & H. F. Johnston (Eds.), *Handbook of depression in children and adolescents: Issues in clinical child psychology* (pp. 143–165). New York: Plenum.

Epstein, J. N., Conners, C. K., Erhardt, D., Arnold, L. E., Hechtman, L., Hinshaw, S. P., Hoza, B., Newcorn, J. H., Swanson, J. M., & Vitiello, B. (2000). Familial aggregation of ADHD characteristics. *Journal of Abnormal Child Psychology, 28,* 585–594.

Epstein, L. H., Valoski, A., Wing, R. R., & McCurley, J. (1994). Ten-year outcomes of behavioral family-based treatment for childhood obesity. *Health Psychology, 13,* 373–383.

Erhardt, D., & Hinshaw, S. P. (1994). Initial sociometric impressions of attention-deficit-hyperactivity disorder and comparison boys: Predictions from social behaviors and from nonsocial variables. *Journal of Consulting and Clinical Psychology, 62,* 833–842.

Essau, C. A., Conradt, J., & Petermann, F. (2000). Frequency, comorbidity, and psychosocial impairment of specific phobia in adolescents. *Journal of Clinical Child Psychology, 29,* 221–231.

Eyberg, S. M., & Boggs, S. R. (1998). Parent-child interaction therapy: A psychosocial intervention for the treatment of young conduct-disordered children. In J. M. Briesmeister & C. E. Schaefer (Eds.), *Handbook of parent training: Parents as co-therapists for children's behavior problems* (2nd ed., pp. 61–97). New York: Wiley.

Fairburn, C. G. (1994). Interpersonal psychotherapy for bulimia. In G. Klerman & M. M. Weissman (Eds.), *New application of interpersonal therapy* (pp. 353–378). New York: Guilford.

Fairburn, C. G., & Beglin, S. J. (1990). Studies of the epidemiology of bulimia nervosa. *American Journal of Psychiatry, 147,* 401–408.

Fairburn, C.G., & Cooper, P. J. (1984). The clinical features of bulimia nervosa. *British Journal of Psychiatry, 144,* 238–246.

Fairburn, C. G., Cooper, Z., Doll, H. A., Norman, P., & O'Connor, M. (2000). The natural course of bulimia nervosa and binge eating disorder in young women. *Archives of General Psychiatry, 57,* 659–665.

Fairburn, C. G., Cowen, P. J., & Harrison, P. J. (1999). Twin studies and the etiology of eating disorders. *International Journal of Eating Disorders, 26,* 349–358.

Fairburn, C. G., Jones, R., Peveler, R. C., Hope, R. A., & O'Conner, M. F. (1991). Three psychological treatments for bulimia nervosa: A comparative trial. *Archives of General Psychiatry, 48,* 463–469.

Fantuzzo, J. W., Jurecic, L., Stovall, A., Hightower, A. D., Goins, C., & Schactel, D. (1988). Effects of adult and peer social initiations on the social behavior of withdrawn, maltreated preschool children. *Journal of Consulting and Clinical Psychology, 56,* 34–39.

Faraone, S. V., Biederman, J., Mennin, D., Wozniak, J., & Spencer, T. (1997). Attention-deficit hyperactivity disorder with bipolar disorder: A familial subtype? *Journal of the American Academy of Child and Adolescent Psychiatry, 36,* 1378–1387.

Faraone, S. V., Biederman, J., Mick, E., Williamson, S., Wilens, T., Spencer, T., Weber, W., Jetton, J., Kraus, I., Pert, J., & Zallen, B. (2000). Family study of girls with attention deficit hyperactivity disorder. *American Journal of Psychiatry, 157,* 1077–1083.

Faraone, S. V., Biederman, J., Weiffenbach, B., Keith, T., Chu, M. P., Weaver, A., Spencer, T. J., Wilens, T. E., Frazier, J., Cleves, M., & Sakai, J. (1999). Dopamine D-sub-4 gene 7-repeat allele and attention deficit hyperactivity disorder. *American Journal of Psychiatry, 156,* 768–770.

Farrington, D. P., Lambert, S., & West, D. J. (1998). Criminal careers of two generations of family members in the Cambridge Study in Delinquent Development. *Studies on Crime and Crime Prevention, 7,* 85–106.

Farrington, D. P., & Loeber, R. (1998). Transatlantic replicability of risk factors in the development of delinquency. In P. Cohen, C. Slomkowski, & L. N. Robins (Eds.), *Where and when: Geographic and generational influences on psychopathology* (pp. 299–329). Mahwah, NJ: Erlbaum.

Farver, J. A. M., & Frosch, D. L. (1996). L. A. stories: Aggression in preschoolers after the riots of 1992. *Child Development, 67,* 19–32.

Feehan, M., McGee, R., Stanton, W., & Silva, P. (1990). A 6-year follow-up of childhood enuresis: Prevalence in adolescence and consequences for mental health. *Journal of Pediatric and Child Health, 26,* 75–79.

Feingold, B. F. (1975). *Why your child is hyperactive.* New York: Random House.

Feldman, R. S., Salzinger, S., Rosario, M., Alvarado, L., Caraballo, L., & Hammer, M. (1995). Parent, teacher, and peer ratings of psychically abused and non-maltreated children's behavior. *Journal of Abnormal Child Psychology, 23,* 317–334.

Fenichel, O. (1945). *The psychoanalytical theory of the neuroses.* New York: Norton.

Ferguson, C. P., & Pigott, T. A. (2000). Anorexia and bulimia nervosa: Neurobiology and pharmacotherapy. *Behavior Therapy, 31,* 237–263.

Fergusson, D. M., Fergusson, J. E., Horwood, L. J., & Kinzett, N. G. (1988). A longitudinal study of dentine lead levels, intelligence, school performance and behaviour: Part III. *Journal of Child Psychology and Psychiatry, 29,* 811–824.

Fergusson, D. M., & Horwood, L. J. (1995). Early disruptive behavior, IQ, and later school achievement and delinquent behavior. *Journal of Abnormal Child Psychology, 23,* 183–199.

Fergusson, D. M., Horwood, L. J., & Beautrais, A. L. (1999). Is sexual orientation related to mental health problems and suicidality in young people? *Archives of General Psychiatry, 56,* 876–880.

Fergusson, D. M., Horwood, L. J., & Lynskey, M. T. (1993). Prevalence and comorbidity of DSM-III-R diagnoses in a birth cohort of 5 year olds. *Journal of the American Academy of Child and Adolescent Psychiatry, 32,* 1127–1134.

Fergusson, D. M., Horwood, L. J., & Shannon, F. T. (1990). Secondary enuresis in a birth cohort of New Zealand children. *Pediatric and Perinatal Epidemiology, 4,* 53–63.

Fergusson, D. M., Woodward, L., & Horwood, L. J. (1999). Childhood peer relationship problems and young people's involvement with deviant peers in adolescence. *Journal of Abnormal Child Psychology, 27,* 357–369.

Field, A. E., Camargo, C. A., Taylor, C. B., Berkey, C. S., Frazier, L., Gillman, M. W., & Colditz, G. A. (1999). Overweight, weight concerns, and bulimic behaviors among girls and boys. *Journal of the American Academy of Child and Adolescent Psychiatry, 38,* 754–760.

Finkelhor, D., & Browne, A. (1985). The traumatic impact of sexual abuse: A conceptualization. *American Journal of Orthopsychiatry, 55:4,* 530–541.

Fisher, M., Golden, N., Katzman, D., Kreipe, R., Rees, J., Schebendach, J., Sigman, G., Ammerman, S., & Hoberman, H. (1995). Eating disorders in adolescents: A background paper. *Journal of Adolescent Health, 16,* 420–437.

Fisher, P. A., Gunnar, M. R., Chamberlain, P., & Reid, J. B. (2000). Preventive intervention for maltreated preschool children: Impact on children's behavior, neuroendocrine activity, and foster parent functioning. *Journal of the American Academy of Child and Adolescent Psychiatry, 39,* 1356–1364.

Fitzgerald, S. T. (1992). National Asthma Education Program Expert Panel report: Guidelines for the diagnosis and management of asthma. *AAOHN Journal, 40,* 376–382.

Flament, M. F., Koby, E., Rapoport, J. L., Berg, C.J., Zahn, T., Cox, C., Denckla, M., & Lenane, M. (1990). Childhood obsessive-compulsive disorder: A prospective follow-up study. *Journal of Child Psychology and Psychiatry, 31,* 363–380.

Fleishner, J. E. (1994). Diagnosis and assessment of mathematics learning disabilities. In G. R. Lyon (Ed.), *Frames of reference for the assessment of learning disabilities: New views on measurement issues* (pp. 441–458). Baltimore, MD: Brookes.

Fleming, J. E., & Offord, D. R. (1990). Epidemiology of childhood depressive disorders: A critical review. *Journal of the American Academy of Child and Adolescent Psychiatry, 29,* 571–580.

Fleming, J. E., Offord, D. R., & Boyle, M. H. (1989). Prevalence of childhood and adolescent depression in the community. *British Journal of Psychiatry, 155,* 647–654.

Fletcher, E. F. (1996). Childhood posttraumatic stress disorder. In E. J. Mash & R. A. Barkley (Eds.), *Child psychopathology* (pp. 242–276). New York: Guilford.

Fletcher, J. M., Shaywitz, S. E., Shankweiler, D. P., Katz, L., Liberman, I. Y., Stuebing, K. K., Francis, D. J., Fowler, A. E., & Shaywitz, B. A. (1994). Cognitive profiles of reading disability: Comparisons of discrepancy and low achievement definitions. *Journal of Educational Psychology, 86,* 6–23.

Flischer, A. J., Kramer, R. A., Hoven, C. W., Greenwald, S., Alegria, M., Bird, H. R., Canino, R., & Moore, R. E. (1997). Psychosocial characteristics of physically abused children and adolescents. *Journal of the American Academy of Child and Adolescent Psychiatry, 36,* 123–131.

Foa, E., Rothbaum, D., Riggs, B., & Murdock, T. (1991). Treatment of PTSD in rape victims: A comparison between cognitive-behavioral procedures and counseling. *Journal of Consulting and Clinical Psychology, 59,* 715–723.

Folstein, S., & Rutter, M. (1977). Infantile autism: A genetic study of 21 twin pairs. *Journal of Autism and Developmental Disorders, 18,* 3–30.

Fombonne, E. (1995). Études épidémiologiques de l'autisme infantile. In S. Lebovici, R. Diatkine, & M. Soulé, *Nouveau traité de psychiatrie de l'enfant et de l'adolescent* (Vol. 2, pp. 1171–1185). Paris: PUF.

Fombonne, E. (1998). L'épidémiologie de l'autisme en France. *Psychologie Française, 43,* 119–125.

Ford, J., Racusin, R., Daviss, W., Ellis, C., Thomas, J., Rogers, K., Reiser, J., Schiffmann, J., & Sengupta, A. (1999). Trauma exposure among children with oppositional defiant disorder and attention deficit–hyperactivity disorder. *Journal of Consulting and Clinical Psychology, 67,* 786–789.

Foreman, D. M., & Thambirajah, M. S. (1996). Conduct disorder, enuresis and specific developmental delays in two types of encopresis: A case-note study of 63 boys. *European Child and Adolescent Psychiatry, 5,* 33–37.

Foxman, B., Valdez, R. B., & Brook, R. H. (1986). Childhood enuresis: Prevalence, perceived impact, and prescribed treatments. *Pediatrics, 77,* 482–487.

Frame, C. L., & Matson, J. L. (1987). *Handbook of assessment in childhood psychopathology: Applied issues in differential diagnosis and treatment evaluation.* New York: Plenum Press.

Francis, D. J., Shaywitz, S. E., Stuebing, K. K., Shaywitz, B. A., & Fletcher, J. M. (1994). The measurement of change: Assessing behavior over time and within a developmental context. In G. R. Lyon (Ed.), *Frames of reference for the assessment of learning disabilities* (pp. 29–58). Baltimore: Brookes Publishing Co.

Frazier, J. A., Alaghband-Rad, J., Jacobsen, L., Lenane, M. C., Hamburger, S., Albus, K., Smith, A., McKenna, K., & Rapoport, J. L. (1997). Pubertal development and onset of psychosis in childhood onset schizophrenia. *Psychiatry Research, 70,* 1–7.

Frazier, J. A., Giedd, J. N., Hamburger, S. D., Albus, K. E., Kaysen, D., Vaituzis, A. C., Rajapakse, J. C., Lenane, M. C., McKenna, K., Jacobsen, L. K., Gordon, C. T., Breier, A., & Rapoport, J. L. (1996). Brain anatomic magnetic resonance imaging. I. Childhood-onset schizophrenia. *Archives of General Psychiatry, 53,* 617–624.

Freud, S. (1961a). Analysis of a phobia in a five-year-old boy. In J. Strachey (Ed. and Trans.), *The standard edition of the complete psychological works of Sigmund Freud* (Vol. 10, pp. 3–149). London: Hogarth Press. (Original work published 1909)

Freud, S. (1961b). Mourning and melancholia. In J. Strachey (Ed. and Trans.), *The standard edition of the complete psychological works of Sigmund Freud* (Vol. 14, pp. 38–51). London: Hogarth Press. (Original work published 1917)

Frick, P. J., & Ellis, M. (1999). Callous-unemotional traits and subtypes of conduct disorder. *Clinical Child and Family Psychology Review, 2,* 149–168.

Frick, P. J., Kamphaus, R. W., Lahey, B. B., Loeber, R., Christ, M. A. G., Hart, E. L., & Tannenbaum, T. E. (1991). Academic underachievement and the disruptive behavior disorders. *Journal of Consulting and Clinical Psychology, 59,* 289–294.

Friman, P. C., Mathews, J. R., Finney, J. W., Christophersen, E. R., & Leibowitz, J. M. (1988). Do encopretic children have clinically significant behavior problems? *Pediatrics, 82,* 407–409.

Frith, U. (1989). *Autism: Explaining the enigma.* Oxford, UK: Basil Blackwell.

Frith, U. (1991). Asperger and his syndrome. In U. Frith (Ed.), *Autism and Asperger syndrome* (pp. 1–36). Cambridge, UK: Cambridge University Press.

Fritz, G. K., Fritsch, S., & Hagino, O. (1997). Somatoform disorders in children and adolescents: A review of the past 10 years. *Journal of the American Academy of Child and Adolescent Psychiatry, 36,* 1329–1338.

Fromm-Reichman, F. (1948). Notes on the development of treatment of schizophrenics by psychoanalytic psychotherapy. *Psychiatry, 11,* 263–273.

Gadnow, K. D., Sverd, J., Sprafkin, J., Nolan, E. E., & Grossman, S. (1999). Long-term methylphenidate therapy in children with comorbid attention-deficit hyperactivity disorder and chronic multiple tic disorder. *Archives of General Psychiatry, 56,* 330–336.

Gagnon, C., Craig, W. M., Tremblay, R. E., Zhou, R. M., & Vitaro, F. (1995). Kindergarten predictors of boys' stable behavior problems at the end of elementary school. *Journal of Abnormal Child Psychology, 23,* 751–766.

Gaillard, F. (1997). Comprendre pour apprendre à lire. *Revue Suisse de Psychologie, 56,* 165–174.

Gaillard, F., & Converso, G. (1988). Lecture et latéralisation: Le retour de l'homme calleux. *Bulletin d'Audiophonologie, Annales Scientifiques de l'Université de Franche-Comté, 4,* 497–508.

Garber, J., Kriss, M. R., Koch, M., & Lindholm, L. (1988). Recurrent depression in adolescents: A follow-up study. *Journal of the American Academy of Child and Adolescent Psychiatry, 27,* 49–54.

Garber, J., Walker, L. S., & Zeman, J. (1991). Somatization symptoms in a community sample of children and adolescents: Further validation of the Children's Somatization Inventory. *Psychological Assessment, 3,* 588–595.

Garland, A. F., Landsverk, J. L., Hough, R. L., & Ellis-Macleod, E. (1996). Type of maltreatment as a predictor of mental health service use for children in foster care. *Child Abuse & Neglect, 20,* 675–688.

Garner, D. M. (1997). Psychoeducational principles in treatment. In D. M. Garner & P. E. Garfinkel (Eds.), *Handbook of treatment for eating disorders* (2nd ed., pp. 144–177). New York: Guilford.

Garner, D. M., & Bemis, K. M. (1985). Cognitive therapy for anorexia nervosa. In D. M. Garner & P. E. Garfinkel (Eds.), *Handbook of psychotherapy for anorexia nervosa and bulimia* (pp. 107–146). New York: Guilford.

Garner, D. M., & Fairburn, C. G. (1988). Relationship between anorexia nervosa and bulimia nervosa: Diagnostic implications. In D. M. Garner & P. E. Garfinkel (Eds.), *Diagnostic issues in anorexia nervosa and bulimia nervosa* (pp. 56–79). New York: Brunner/Mazel.

Garner, D. M., Garfinkel, P. E., & Olmsted, M. (1983). An overview of sociological factors in the development of anorexia nervosa. In P. L. Darby, P. E. Garfinkel, D. M. Garner, & D. V. Coscina (Eds.), *Anorexia nervosa: Recent developments in research* (pp. 65–82). New York: Alan R. Liss Publishers.

Garner, D. M., Rockert, W., Olmstead, M. P., Johnson, C. L., & Coscina, D. V. (1985). Psychoeducational principles in the treatment of bulimia and anorexia nervosa. In D. M. Garner & P. E. Garfinkel (Eds.), *Handbook of treatment for eating disorders* (pp. 513–572). New York: Guilford.

Garner, D. M., Vitousek, K. M., & Pike, K. M. (1997). Cognitive-behavioral therapy for anorexia nervosa. In D. M. Garner & P. E. Garfinkel (Eds.), *Handbook of treatment for eating disorders* (2nd ed., pp. 94–144). New York: Guilford.

Garralda, M. E. (1992). A selective review of child psychiatric syndromes with a somatic presentation. *British Journal of Psychiatry, 161,* 759–773.

Garralda, M. E. (1996). Somatisation in children. *Journal of Child Psychology and Psychiatry, 37,* 13–33.

Garralda, M. E. (1999). Assessment and management of somatization in childhood and adolescence: A practical perspective. *Journal of Child Psychology and Psychiatry, 40,* 1159–1167.

Geary, D. C., Bow-Thomas, C. C., Liu, F., & Siegler, R. S. (1996). Development of arithmetical competencies in Chinese and American children: Influence of age, language, and schooling. *Child Development, 67,* 2022–2044.

Geary, D. C., Hamson, C. O., Chen, G., Liu, F., Hoard, M. K., & Salthouse, T. A. (1997). Computational and reasoning abilities in arithmetic: Cross-generational changes in China and the United States. *Psychonomic Bulletin and Review, 4,* 425–430.

Gebert, N., Hummelink, R., Konning, J., Staab, D., Schmidt, S., Szczepanski, R., Runde, B., & Wahn, U. (1998). Efficacy of a self-management program for childhood asthma—A prospective controlled study. *Patient Education and Counseling, 35,* 213–220.

Gehring, W. J., Himle, J., & Nisenson, L. G. (2000). Action-monitoring dysfunction in obsessive-compulsive disorder. *Psychological Science, 11,* 1–6.

Geller, B., Craney, J. L., Bolhofner, K., DelBello, M. P., Williams, M., & Zimerman, B. (2001). One-year recovery and relapse rates of children with a prepubertal and early adolescent bipolar disorder phenotype. *American Journal of Psychiatry, 158,* 303–305.

Geller, B., Fox, L., & Clark, K. (1994). Rate and predictors of prepubertal bipolarity during follow-up of 6- to 12-year-old depressed children. *Journal of the American Academy of Child and Adolescent Psychiatry, 33,* 461–468.

Geller, B., & Luby, J. (1997). Child and adolescent bipolar disorder: A review of the past 10 years. *Journal of the American Academy of Child and Adolescent Psychiatry, 36,* 1668–1176.

Gerlsma, C., Emmelkamp, P. M. G., & Arrindell, W. A. (1990). Anxiety, depression, and perception of early parenting: A meta-analysis. *Clinical Psychology Review, 10,* 251–277.

Gerull, F. C., & Rapee, R. M. (2002). Mother knows best: Effects of maternal modelling on the acquisition of fear and avoidance behaviour in toddlers. *Behaviour Research and Therapy, 40,* 279–287.

Ghaziuddin, M., Shakal, J., & Tsai, L. (1995). Obstetric factors in Asperger syndrome: Comparison with high-functioning autism. *Journal of Intellectual Disability Research, 39,* 538–543.

Ghaziuddin, M., Zaccagnini, J., Tsai, L., & Elardo, S. (1999). Is megalencephaly specific to autism? *Journal of Intellectual Disability Research, 43,* 279–282.

Giles, D. E., Kupfer, D. J., Rush, A. J., & Roffwarg, H. P. (1998). Controlled comparison of electrophysiological sleep in families of probands with unipolar depression. *American Journal of Psychiatry, 155,* 192–199.

Gilger, J. W., Pennington, B. F., & DeFries, J. C. (1992). A twin study of the etiology of comorbidity: Attention-deficit hyperactivity disorder and dyslexia. *Journal of the American Academy of Child and Adolescent Psychiatry, 31,* 343–348.

Gill, D. (1981). The United States vs. child abuse. In L. Pelton (Ed.), *The social context of child abuse and neglect* (pp. 291–324). New York: Human Sciences Press.

Gillberg, C. (1989). Asperger syndrome in 23 Swedish children. *Developmental Medicine and Child Neurology, 31,* 520–531.

Gillberg, C. (1991a). Clinical and neurobiological aspects of Asperger syndrome in six family studies. In U. Frith (Ed.), *Autism and Asperger syndrome* (pp. 122–146). Cambridge, UK: Cambridge University Press.

Gillberg, C. (1991b). Outcome in autism and autistic-like conditions. *Journal of the American Academy of Child and Adolescent Psychiatry, 30,* 375–382.

Gillberg, I. C., Hellgren, L., & Gillberg, C. (1993). Psychotic disorders diagnosed in adolescence: Outcome at age 30 years. *Journal of Child Psychology and Psychiatry, 34,* 1173–1185.

Gillberg, C., & Wing, L. (1999). Autism: Not an extremely rare disorder. *Acta Psychiatrica Scandinavica, 99,* 399–406.

Gillham, J. E., & Reivich, K. J. (1999). Prevention of depressive symptoms in school children: A research update. *Psychological Science, 10,* 461–462.

Glaser, K. (1967). Masked depression in children and adolescents. *American Journal of Psychotherapy, 21,* 565–574.

Glassberg, L. A., Hooper, S. R., & Mattison, R. E. (1999). Prevalence of learning disabilities at enrollment in special education students with behavioral disorders. *Behavioral Disorders, 25,* 9–21.

Gleaves, D. H., Lowe, M. R., Greene, B. A., Cororve, M. B., & Williams, T. L. (2000). Do anorexia and bulimia nervosa occur on a continuum? A taxometric analysis. *Behavior Therapy, 31,* 195–219.

Gleaves, D. H., Lowe, M. R., Snow, A. C., Green, B. A., & Murphy-Eberenz, K. P. (2000). Continuity and discontinuity models of bulimia nervosa: A taxometric investigation. *Journal of Abnormal Psychology, 109,* 56–68.

Glicklich, L. B. (1951). An historical account of enuresis. *Pediatrics, 8,* 859–876.

Gold, S., Lucenko, B., Elhai, J., Swingle, J., & Sellers, A. (1999). A comparison of psychological/psychiatric symptomatology of women and men sexually abused as children. *Child Abuse & Neglect, 23,* 683–692.

Goldbloom, D. S., Olmstead, M., Davis, R., Clewes, J., Heinmaa, M., Rockert, W., & Shaw, B. (1997). A randomized controlled trial of fluoxetine and cognitive behavioral therapy in bulimia nervosa: Short-term outcome. *Behaviour Research and Therapy, 35,* 308–311.

Goldstein, M. J. (1987). The UCLA High Risk Project. *Schizophrenia Bulletin, 13,* 505–514.

Gomes-Schwartz, B., Horowitz, J. M., & Cardarelli, A. P. (1990). *Child sexual abuse: The initial effect.* Newbury Park, CA: Sage.

Gorski, B. (1979). *Beyond limitations: The creative art of the mentally retarded.* Springfield, IL: Charles C. Thomas.

Gotlib, I. H., & Hammen, C. L. (1992). *Psychological aspects of depression: Toward a cognitive-interpersonal integration.* London: Wiley.

Gottesman, I. I. (1991). *Schizophrenia genesis: The origins of madness.* New York: W. H. Freeman.

Gottesman, I. I. (1996). Blind men and elephants: Genetic and other perspectives on schizophrenia. In L. L. Hall (Ed.), *Genetics and mental illness: Evolving issues from research and society* (pp. 51–77). New York: Plenum.

Gottlieb, L. (2000). *Stick figure: A diary of my former self.* New York: Simon and Schuster.

Grados, M. A., & Riddle, M. A. (2001). Psychopharmacological treatment of childhood obsessive-compulsive disorders: From theory to practice. *Journal of Clinical Child Psychology, 30,* 67–79.

Gray, J. A. (1987). *The psychology of fear and stress* (2nd ed.). New York: Cambridge University Press.

Gray, J. A. (1994). Three fundamental emotion systems. In P. Eckman & R. J. Davidson (Eds.), *The nature of emotion: Fundamental questions.* New York: Oxford University Press.

Gray, R. E., Doan, B. D., Shermer, P., Vatter-Fitzgerald, A., Berry, M. P., Jenkins, D., & Collins, W. P. (1992). Surviving childhood cancer: A descriptive approach to understanding the impact of life-threatening illness. *Psycho-Oncology, 1,* 235–246.

Green, S. M., Russo, M. F., Navatril, J. L., & Loeber, R. (1999). Sexual and physical abuse among adolescent girls with disruptive behavior problems. *Journal of Child and Family Studies, 8,* 151–168.

Green, W., Campbell, M., Hardesty, A., Grega, D., Padron-Gayol, M., Shell, J., & Erlenmeyer-Kimling, L. (1984). A comparison of schizophrenic and autistic children. *Journal of the American Academy of Child Psychiatry, 23,* 399–409.

Green, W. H., Padron-Gayol, M., Hardesty, A. S., & Bassiri, M. (1992). Schizophrenia with childhood onset: A phenomenological study of 38 cases. *Journal of the American Academy of Child and Adolescent Psychiatry, 31,* 968–976.

Greenberg, M. T., Cicchetti, D., & Cummings, M. (1990). *Attachment in the preschool years: Theory, research, and intervention.* Chicago: University of Chicago Press.

Gresham, F. M., Beebe-Frankenberger, M. E., & MacMillan, D. L. (1999). A selective review of treatments for children with autism: Description and methodological considerations. *School Psychology Review, 28,* 559–575.

Gresham, F. M., MacMillan, D. L., Bocian, K. M., Ward, S. L., & Forness, S. R. (1998). Comorbidity of hyperactivity-impulsivity-inattention and conduct problems: Risk factors in social, affective, and academic domains. *Journal of Abnormal Child Psychology, 26,* 393–406.

Grossman, D., & Kloske, G. (Eds.). (1996). *On killing: The psychological cost of learning to kill in war and society.* Boston: Little, Brown.

Gross-Tsur, V., Shalev, R. S., & Amir, N. (1991). Attention deficit disorder: association with familial-genetic factors. *Pediatric Neurology, 7,* 258–261.

Grusec, J. E., Goodnow, J. J., & Kuczynski, L. (2000). New directions in analyses of parenting contributions to children's acquisition of values. *Child Development, 71,* 205–211.

Gull, W. W. (1874). Anorexia nervosa (apepsia hysterica, anorexia hysterica). *Transactions of the Clinical Society of London, 7,* 22–28.

Gunewardene, A., Huon, G. F., & Zheng, R. (2001). Exposure to westernization and dieting: A cross-cultural study. *International Journal of Eating Disorders, 29,* 289–293.

Günther-Genta, F., Bovet, P., & Hohlfeld, P. (1994). Obstetric complications and schizophrenia: A case-controlled study. *British Journal of Psychiatry, 164,* 165–170.

Gureje, O., & Simon, G. E. (1999). The natural history of somatization in primary care. *Psychological Medicine, 29,* 669–676.

Guterman, N. B. (1999). Enrollment strategies in early home visitation to prevent physical child abuse and neglect and the "universal versus targeted" debate: A meta-analysis of population-based and screening-based programs. *Child Abuse & Neglect, 23,* 863–890.

Guze, S. B., Cloninger, C. R., Martin, R. L., & Clayton, P. J. (1986). A follow-up and family study of Briquet's syndrome. *British Journal of Psychiatry, 149,* 17–23.

Hagberg, B. (1985). Rett syndrome: Swedish approach to analysis of prevalence and cause. *Brain and Development, 7,* 277–280.

Hagopian, L. P., & Ollendick, T. H. (1997). Anxiety disorders. In R. T. Ammerman & M. Hersen (Eds.), *Handbook of prevention and treatment with children and adolescents* (pp. 431–454). New York: Wiley.

Hall, G. S. (1904). *Adolescence: Its psychology and its relations to physiology, anthropology, sociology, sex, crime, religion, and education* (Vol. 1). Englewood Cliffs, NJ: Prentice-Hall.

Halmi, K. A. (1995). Current concepts and definitions. In G. I. Szmukler, C. Dare, & J. Treasure (Eds.), *Handbook of eating disorders: Theory, treatment and research* (pp. 29–42). Chichester, UK: Wiley.

Halmi, K. A., Goldberg, S. C., Casper, R. C., Eckert, E. D., & Davis, J. M. (1979). Pretreatment predictors of outcome in anorexia nervosa. *British Journal of Psychiatry, 134,* 71–78.

Halperin, J. M. (1996). Conceptualizing, describing, and measuring components of attention: A summary. In G. R. Lyon, N. A. Krasnegor, et al. (Eds.), *Attention, memory, and executive function* (p. 119–136). Baltimore: Brookes Publishing Co.

Halperin, J. M., Matier, K., Bedi, G., & Sharma, V. (1992). Specificity of inattention, impulsivity, and hyperactivity to the diagnosis of attention-deficit hyperactivity disorder. *Journal of the American Academy of Child and Adolescent Psychiatry, 31,* 190–196.

Hammen, C. (1991). *Depression runs in families: The social context of risk and resilience in children of depressed mothers.* New York: Springer-Verlag.

Hammen, C., Burge, D., & Stansbury, K. (1990). Relationship of mother and child variables to child outcomes in a high risk sample: A causal modeling analysis. *Developmental Psychology, 26,* 24–30.

Hammen, C., & Rudolph, K. D. (1996). Childhood depression. In E. J. Mash & R. A. Barkley (Eds.), *Child psychopathology* (pp. 153–195). New York: Guilford.

Hanna, G. L. (1995). Demographic and clinical features of obsessive-compulsive disorder in children and adolescents. *Journal of the American Academy of Child and Adolescent Psychiatry, 34,* 19–27.

Harbeck-Weber, C., & Peterson, L. (1996). Health-related disorders. In E. J. Mash & R. A. Barkley (Eds.), *Child psychopathology* (pp. 572–601). New York: Guilford.

Harrington, R. C., Dubowitz, H., Black, M. M., & Binder, A. (1995). Maternal substance use and neglectful parenting: Relations with children's development. *Journal of Clinical Child Psychology, 24,* 258–263.

Harrington, R., Fudge, H., Rutter, M., Pickles, A., & Hill, J. (1991). Adult outcomes of childhood and adolescent depression: II. Links with antisocial disorder. *Journal of the American Academy of Child and Adolescent Psychiatry, 30,* 434–439.

Harris, S. L., & Handelman, J. S. (2000). Age and IQ at intake as predictors of placement for young children with autism: A four- to six- year follow-up. *Journal of Autism and Developmental Disorders, 30,* 137–142.

Hawkins, J. D., Herrenkohl, T., Farrington, D. P., Brewer, D., Catalano, R. F., & Harachi, T. W. (1998). A review of predictors of youth violence. In R. Loeber & D. P. Farrington (Eds.), *Serious and violent juvenile offenders: Risk factors and successful interventions* (pp. 106–146). Thousand Oaks, CA: Sage.

Hawkins, M. M., Draper, G. J., & Kingston, J. E. (1987). Incidence of second primary tumors among childhood cancer survivors. *British Journal of Cancer, 56,* 339–347.

Hay, P. J., Fairburn, C. G., & Doll, H. A. (1996). The classification of bulimic eating disorders: A community-based cluster analysis study. *Psychological Medicine, 26,* 801–812.

Hecht, S. A., Burgess, S. R., Torgesen, J. K., Wagner, R. K., & Rashotte, C. A. (2000). Explaining social class differences in growth of reading skills from beginning kindergarten through fourth-grade: The role of phonological awareness, rate of access, and print knowledge. *Reading and Writing, 12,* 99–127.

Hendry, C. N. (2000). Childhood disintegrative disorder: Should it be considered a distinct diagnosis? *Child Psychology Review, 20,* 77–90.

Henggeler, S. W., Schoenwald, S., Borduin, C., Rowland, M., & Cunningham, P. (1998). *Multisystemic treatment of antisocial behavior in children and adolescents.* New York: Guilford.

Henin, A., & Kendall, P. C. (1997). Obsessive-compulsive disorder in childhood and adolescence. In T. H. Ollendick & R. J. Prinz (Eds.), *Advances in Clinical Child Psychology* (Vol. 19, pp. 75–131). New York: Plenum.

Herbert, M. (1989). *Discipline: A positive guide for parents.* Oxford, UK: Basil Blackwell.

Herman, J. L. (1992). *Trauma and recovery: The aftermath of violence—from domestic abuse to political terror.* New York: Basic Books.

Herrnstein, R. J., & Murray, C. A. (1994). *The bell curve: Intelligence and class structure in American life.* New York: Free Press.

Herzog, D. B. (1988). Eating disorders. In A. M. Nicoli (Ed.), *The new Harvard guide to psychiatry* (pp. 434–445). Boston: Harvard University Press.

Herzog, D. B. (1995). Psychodynamic therapy for anorexia nervosa. In C. G. Fairburn & G. T. Wilson (Eds.), *Binge eating: Nature, assessment, and treatment* (pp. 330–335). New York: Guilford.

Herzog, D. B., Dorer, D. J., Keel, P. K., Selwyn, S. E., Ekeblad, E. R., Flores, A. T., Greenwood, D. N., Burwell, R. A., & Keller, M. B. (2000). Recovery and relapse in anorexia and bulimia nervosa: A 7.5-year follow-up study. *Journal of the American Academy of Child and Adolescent Psychiatry, 39,* 829–837.

Hibbs, E. D., Hamburger, S. D., Lenane, M., Rapoport, J. L., Kreusi, M. J. P., Keysor, C. S., & Goldstein, M. J. (1991). Determinants of expressed emotion in families of disturbed and normal children. *Journal of Child Psychology and Psychiatry, 32,* 757–770.

Hillson, J. M. C., & Kuiper, N. A. (1994). A stress and coping model of child maltreatment. *Clinical Psychology Review, 14,* 261–285.

Hinshaw, S. P. (1992). Externalizing behavior problems and academic underachievement in childhood and adolescence: Causal relationships and underlying mechanisms. *Psychological Bulletin, 111,* 127–155.

Hinshaw, S. P., Heller, T., & McHale, J. P. (1992). Covert antisocial behavior in boys with attention-deficit hyperactivity disorder: External validation and effects of methylphenidate. *Journal of Consulting and Clinical Psychology, 60,* 274–281.

Hinshaw, S. P., Lahey, B. B., & Hart, E. L. (1993). Issues of taxonomy and comorbidity in the development of conduct disorder. *Development and Psychopathology, 5,* 31–49.

Hoare, P., & Mann, H. (1994). Self-esteem and behavioural adjustment in children with epilepsy and children with diabetes. *Journal of Psychosomatic Research, 38,* 859–869.

Hodapp, R. M., & Dykens, E. M. (1996). Mental retardation. In E. J. Mash & R. A. Barkley (Eds.), *Child psychopathology* (pp. 362–389). New York: Guilford.

Hodapp, R. M., Dykens, E., Ort, S., Zelinsky, D., & Leckman, J. (1991). Changing profiles of intellectual strengths and weaknesses in males with fragile X syndrome. *Journal of Autism and Developmental Disorders, 21,* 503–516.

Hodapp, R. M., & Zigler, E. (1990). Applying the developmental perspective to individuals with Down syndrome. In D. Cicchetti & M. Beeghly (Eds.), *Children with Down syndrome: A developmental approach* (pp. 1–28). New York: Cambridge University Press.

Hodapp, R. M., & Zigler, E. (1995). Past, present, and future issues in the developmental approach to mental retardation. In D. Cicchetti & D. Cohen (Eds.), *Manual of developmental psychopathology* (pp. 299–331). New York: Wiley.

Hoekstra-Weebers, J. E., Heuvel, F., Jaspers, J. P., Kamps, W. A., & Klip, E. C. (1998). Brief report: An intervention program for parents of pediatric cancer patients: A randomized controlled trial. *Journal of Pediatric Psychology, 23,* 207–214.

Hoffmann, H. (1995). *Struwwelpeter in English translation.* New York: Dover Publications. (Originally published 1845)

Holcomb, H. H., Cascella, N. G., Thaker, G. K., Medoff, D. R., Dannals, R. F., & Tamminga, C. A. (1996). Functional sites of neuroleptic drug action in the human brain: PET/FDG studies with and without haloperidol. *American Journal of Psychiatry, 153,* 41–49.

Holden, E. W., Chmielewski, D., Nelson, C. C., & Kager, V. A. (1997). Controlling for general and disease-specific effects in child and family adjustment to chronic childhood illness. *Journal of Pediatric Psychology, 22,* 15–27.

Hollis, C. (1995). Child and adolescent (juvenile onset) schizophrenia: A case control study of premorbid developmental impairments. *British Journal of Psychiatry, 166,* 489–495.

Hollis, C. (2000). Adult outcomes of child- and adolescent-onset schizophrenia: Diagnostic stability and predictive validity. *American Journal of Psychiatry, 157,* 1652–1659.

Holmes, C. S., Respess, D., Greer, T., & Frentz, J. (1998). Behavior problems in children with diabetes: Disentangling possible scoring confounds on the Child Behavior Checklist. *Journal of Pediatric Psychology, 23,* 179–185.

Hook, E. B. (1982). Epidemiology of Down syndrome. In S. M. Pueschel & J. E. Rynders (Eds.), *Down syndrome: Advances in biomedicine and the behavioural sciences* (pp. 11–88). Cambridge, UK: Ware Press.

Hooley, J. M. (1985). Expressed emotion: A review of the clinical literature. *Clinical Psychology Review, 5,* 119–139.

Hooper, S. R., Montgomery, J., Swartz, C., Reed, M. S., Sandler, A. D., Levine, M. D., Watson, T. E., & Wasileski, T. (1994). Measurement of written language expression. In G. R. Lyon (Ed.), *Frames of reference for the assessment of learning disabilities* (pp. 375–417). Baltimore: Brookes Publishing Co.

Houts, A. C. (1991). Nocturnal enuresis as a biobehavioral problem. *Behavior Therapy, 22,* 133–151.

Houts, A. C., Berman, J. S., & Abramson, H. (1994). The effectiveness of psychological and psychopharmacological treatments for nocturnal enuresis. *Journal of Consulting and Clinical Psychology, 62,* 737–745.

Howlin, P., & Yule, W. (1990). Taxonomy of major disorders in childhood. In M. Lewis & S. M. Miller, (Eds.), *Handbook of developmental psychopathology* (pp. 371–383). New York: Plenum.

Hoza, B., Pelham, W. E., Milich, R., Pillow, D., & McBride, K. (1993). The self-perceptions and attributions of attention deficit hyperactivity disordered and nonreferred boys. *Journal of Abnormal Child Psychology, 21,* 271–286.

Hoza, B., Waschbusch, D. A., Pelham, W. E., Molina, B. S. G., & Milich, R. (2000). Attention-deficit/hyperactivity disordered and control boys' responses to social success and failure. *Child Development, 71,* 432–446.

Hsu, L. K. G. (1996). Epidemiology of the eating disorders. *Psychiatric Clinics of North America, 19,* 681–700.

Hsu, L. K. G., Kaye, W. H., & Weltzin, T. (1993). Are the eating disorders related to obsessive-compulsive disorder? *International Journal of Eating Disorders, 14,* 305–318.

Hudziak, J. J., Heath, A. C., Madden, P. F., Reich, W., Bucholz, K. K., Slutske, W., Bierut, L. J., Neuman, R. J., & Todd, R. D. (1998). Latent class and factor analysis of DSM-IV ADHD: A twin study of female adolescents. *Journal of the American Academy of Child and Adolescent Psychiatry, 37,* 848–857.

Hudziak, J. J., Rudiger, L. P., Neale, M. C., Heath, A. C., & Todd, R. D. (2000). A twin study of inattentive, aggressive, and anxious/depressed behaviors. *Journal of the American Academy of Child and Adolescent Psychiatry, 39,* 469–476.

Huesman, L. R., Eron, L. D., Lefkowitz, M. M., & Walder, L. O. (1992). The effects of television violence on aggression: A reply to a skeptic. In P. Suedfeld & P. E. Tetlock (Eds.), *Psychology and social policy* (pp. 191–200). New York: Hemisphere Publishing.

Hughes, C. W., Emslie, G. J., Crisom, M. L., Wagner, K. D., Birhamer, B., & Geller, B. (1999). The Texas children's medication algorithm project: Report of the Texas Consensus Conference Panel on Medication Treatment of Childhood Major Depressive Disorder. *Journal of the American Academy of Child and Adolescent Psychiatry, 38,* 1442–1454.

Hughes, C., White, A., Sharpen, J., & Dunn, J. (2000). Antisocial, angry, and unsympathetic: "Hard-to-manage" preschoolers' peer problems and possible cognitive influences. *Journal of Child Psychology and Psychiatry, 41,* 169–179.

Hunter, K. (1999). *The Rett syndrome handbook.* Clinton, MD: International Rett Syndrome Association.

Hyde, M. (1986). *Cry softly! The story of child abuse.* Philadelphia: Westminster Press.

Hynd, G. W., Hern, K. L., Novey, E. S., Eliopulos, D., Marshall, R., Gonzalez, J. J., & Voeller, K. K. (1993). Attention-deficit hyperactivity disorder and asymmetry of the caudate nucleus. *Journal of Child Neurology, 8,* 339–347.

Hynd, G. W., Semrud-Clikeman, M., Lorys, A. R., Novey, E. S., & Eliopulos, D. (1990). Brain morphology in developmental dyslexia and attention deficit disorder/hyperactivity. *Archives of Neurology, 47,* 919–926.

Hynd, G. W., Semrud-Clikeman, M., Lorys, A. R., & Novey, E. S. (1991). Corpus callosum morphology in attention deficit–hyperactivity disorder: Morphometric analysis of MRI. *Journal of Learning Disabilities, 24,* 141–146.

Ievers, C. E., Drotar, D., Dahms, W. T., Doershuk, C. F., & Stern, R. C. (1994). Maternal child-rearing behavior in three groups: Cystic fibrosis, insulin-dependent diabetes mellitus, and healthy children. *Journal of Pediatric Psychology, 19,* 681–687.

Iezzi, A., & Adams, H. E. (1993). Somatoform and factitious disorders. In P. B. Sutker & H. E. Adams (Eds.), *Comprehensive handbook of psychopathology* (2nd ed., pp. 167–201). New York: Plenum.

International Consensus Statement on ADHD (2002). [On line]. Available at: http://home.regent.edu/willhat/adhd.htm

Irving, L. M. (2000). Promoting size acceptance in elementary school children: The EDAP puppet program. *Eating Disorders: The Journal of Treatment and Prevention, 8,* 221–232.

Irving, L. M., DuPen, J., & Berel, S. (1998). A media literacy program for high school females. *Eating Disorders: The Journal of Treatment and Prevention, 6,* 119–132.

Jacob, T. (1975). Family interactions in disturbed and normal families: A methodological and substantive review. *Psychological Bulletin, 82,* 33–65.

Jacobsen, L. K., & Rapoport, J. L. (1998). Research update: Childhood-onset schizophrenia: Implications of clinical and neurobiological research. *Journal of Child Psychology and Psychiatry, 39,* 101–113.

Jacobson, J. W. (1990). Do some mental disorders occur less frequently among persons with mental retardation? *American Journal on Mental Retardation, 94,* 596–602.

Järvelin, M. R. (1989). Developmental history and neurological findings in enuretic children. *Developmental Medicine and Child Neurology, 31,* 728–736.

Järvelin, M. R., Moilanen, I., Kangas, P., Moring, K., Vikevainen-Tervonen, L., Huttenen, N. P., & Seppanen, J. (1991). Aetiological and precipitating factors for childhood enuresis. *Acta Paediatrica Scandinavica, 80,* 363–369.

Jay, M., Gorwood, P., & Feingold, J. (1997). Les schizophrénies familiales à l'Île de la Réunion. *L'Information Psychiatrique, 73,* 1021–1027.

Jenkins, J. H., & Karno, M. (1992). The meaning of expressed emotion: Theoretical issues raised by cross-cultural research. *American Journal of Psychiatry, 149,* 9–21.

Jenkins, P. H., Lambert, M. J., Nielsen, S. L., McPherson, D. L., & Wells, M. G. (1996). Nocturnal task responsiveness of primary nocturnal enuretic boys: A behavioral approach to enuresis. *Children's Health Care, 25,* 143–156.

Jensen, P. S., & Hoagwood, K. Y. (1997). The book of names: DSM-IV in context. *Development and Psychopathology, 9,* 231–249.

Jersild, A. T., & Holmes, F. B. (1935). *Children's fears* (Child Development Monograph, No. 20). New York: Columbia University.

Johnson-Sabine, E., Wood, K., Patton, G., Mann, A., & Wakeling, A. (1988). Abnormal eating attitudes in London schoolgirls—a prospective epidemiological study: Factors associated with abnormal response on screening questionnaires. *Psychological Medicine, 18,* 615–622.

Johnston, B. D., & Wright, J. A. (1993). Attentional dysfunction in children with encopresis. *Developmental and Behavioral Pediatrics, 14,* 381–385.

Johnston, C., & Mash, E. J. (2001). Families of children with attention-deficit/hyperactivity disorder: Review and recommendations for future research. *Clinical Child and Family Psychology Review, 4,* 183–207.

Joiner, T. E., Vohs, K. D., & Heatherton, T. F. (2000). Three studies on the factorial distinctiveness of binge eating and bulimic symptoms among nonclinical men and women. *International Journal of Eating Disorders, 27,* 198–205.

Jones, D. H., Forehand, R., & Neary, E. M. (2001). Family transmission of depressive symptoms: Replication across Caucasian and African American mother-child dyads. *Behavior Therapy, 32,* 123–138.

Jones, L. M., & Finkelhor, D. (2001). The decline in child sexual abuse cases. *Juvenile Justice Bulletin.* Washington, DC: U.S. Department of Justice, Office of Justice Programs, Office of Juvenile Justice and Delinquency Prevention.

Jones, M. C. (1924). A laboratory study of fear: The case of Peter. *Pedagogical Seminars, 31,* 308–315.

Kagan, J. (1989). Temperamental contributions to social behavior. *American Psychologist, 44,* 668–674.

Kanbayashi, Y., Nakata, Y., Fujji, K., Kita, M., & Wada, K. (1994). ADHD-related behavior among non-referred children: Parents' ratings of DSM-III-R symptoms. *Child Psychiatry and Human Development, 25,* 13–29.

Kandel, D. B., & Davies, M. (1986). Adult sequelae of adolescent depressive symptoms. *Archives of General Psychiatry, 43,* 255–262.

Kanner, L. (1943). Autistic disturbances of affective contact. *Nervous Child, 2,* 217–250.

Kanner, L. (1949). Problems of nosology and psychodynamics of early infantile autism. *American Journal of Orthopsychiatry, 19,* 416–426.

Kanner, L. (1964). *A history of the care and study of the mentally retarded.* Springfield, IL: Charles C. Thomas.

Kanner, L. (1971). Follow-up study of eleven autistic children originally reported in 1943. *Journal of Autism and Childhood Schizophrenia, 1,* 119–145.

Kantor, J. R., & Smith, N. W. (1975). *The science of psychology: An interbehavioral survey.* Chicago: Principia Press.

Kaplan, S., Pelcovitz, D., & Labruna, V. (1999). Child and adolescent abuse and neglect research: A view of the past 10 years. Part 1: Physical and emotional abuse and neglect. *Journal of the American Academy of Child and Adolescent Psychiatry, 38,* 1214–1222.

Kaplan, S., Pelcovitz, D., & Weiner, M. (1994). Adolescent physical abuse. *Child and Adolescent Psychiatric Clinics of North America, 3,* 695–711.

Kashani, J. H., & Carlson, G. A. (1987). Seriously depressed preschoolers. *American Journal of Psychiatry, 144,* 348–350.

Kashani, J. H., Carlson, G. A., Beck, N. C., Hoeper, E. W., Corcoran, C. M., McAllister, J. A., Fallahi, C., Rosenberg, T. K., & Reid, J. C. (1987). Depression, depressive symptoms, and depressed mood among a community sample of adolescents. *American Journal of Psychiatry, 144,* 931–934.

Kashani, J. H., & Orvaschel, H. (1988). Anxiety disorders in mid-adolescence: A community sample. *American Journal of Psychiatry, 145,* 960–964.

Kashdan, T. B., & Herbert, J. D. (2001). Social anxiety disorder in childhood and adolescence: Current status and future directions. *Clinical Child and Family Psychology Review, 4,* 37–61.

Katz, E. R. (1980). Illness impact and social reintegration. In J. Kellerman (Ed.), *Psychological aspects of childhood cancer* (pp. 14–16). Springfield, IL: Charles C. Thomas.

Katz, L. F., & Gottman, J. M. (1993). Patterns of marital conflict predict children's internalizing and externalizing behaviors. *Developmental Psychology, 29,* 940–950.

Kaufman, A. S., & Kaufman, N. L. (1983). *Administration and scoring manual for the Kaufman Assessment Battery for Children.* Circle Pines, MN: American Guidance Service.

Kaufman, J., Plotsky, P. M., Nemeroff, C. B., & Charney, D. S. (2000). Effects of early adverse experiences on brain structure and function: Clinical implications. *Biological Psychiatry, 48,* 778–790.

Kaufman, J. G., & Widom, C. S. (1999). Childhood victimization, running away, and delinquency. *Journal of Research in Crime and Delinquency, 36,* 347–370.

Kavale, K. A. (1988). The long-term consequences of learning disabilities. In M. C. Wang, M. C. Reynolds, & H. J. Walberg (Eds.), *Handbook of special education: Research and practice* (Vol. 2, pp. 303–344). Oxford, UK: Pergamon.

Kaye, W. H., & Weltzin, T. (1991). Serotonin activity in anorexia and bulimia nervosa: Relationship to the modulation of feeding and mood. *Journal of Clinical Psychiatry, 52,* 41–48.

Kaye, W. H., Weltzin, T., & Hsu, L. K. G. (1993). Relationship between anorexia nervosa and obsessive-compulsive behaviors. *Psychiatric Annals, 23,* 365–373.

Kaye, W. H., Weltzin, T., Hsu, L. K. G., McConaha, C. W., & Bolton, B. (1993). Amount of calories retained after binge eating and vomiting. *American Journal of Psychiatry, 150,* 969–971.

Kazak, A. E., Barakat, L. P., Meeske, K., & Christakis, D. (1997). Posttraumatic stress, family functioning, and social support in survivors of childhood leukemia and their mothers and fathers. *Journal of Consulting and Clinical Psychology, 65,* 120–129.

Kazdin, A. E. (1990). Childhood depression. *Journal of Child Psychology and Psychiatry, 31,* 121–160.

Kazdin, A. E. (1996). Problem solving and parent management in treating aggressive and antisocial behavior. In E. D. Hibbs & P. S. Jensen (Eds.), *Psychosocial treatments for child and adolescent disorders: Empirically based strategies for clinical practice* (pp. 377–408). Washington, DC: American Psychological Association.

Kazdin, A. E. (1997). Practitioner review: Psychosocial treatments for conduct disorder in children. *Journal of Child Psychiatry and Psychology, 38,* 161–178.

Kazdin, A. E., & Wassell, G. (2000). Therapeutic changes in children, parents, and families resulting from treatment of children with conduct problems. *Journal of the American Academy of Child and Adolescent Psychiatry, 39,* 414–420.

Kearney, C. A. (2001). *School refusal behavior in youth: A functional approach to assessment and treatment.* Washington, DC: American Psychological Association.

Keel, P. K., Mitchell, J. E., Miller, K. B., David, T. L., & Crow, S. J. (2000). Predictive validity of bulimia nervosa as a diagnostic category. *American Journal of Psychiatry, 157,* 136–138.

Keenan, K., Loeber, R., & Green, S. (1999). Conduct disorder in girls: A review of the literature. *Clinical Child and Family Psychology Review, 2,* 3–19.

Keenan, K., Loeber, R., Zhang, Q., Stouthamer-Loeber, M., & Van Kammen, W. B. (1995). The influence of deviant peers on the development of boys' disruptive and delinquent behavior: A temporal analysis. *Development and Psychopathology, 7,* 715–726.

Keenan, K., & Wakschlag, L. S. (2000). More than the terrible twos: The nature and severity of behavior problems in clinic-referred preschool children. *Journal of Abnormal Child Psychology, 28,* 33–46.

Kellner, R. (1985). Functional somatic symptoms and hypochondriasis: A survey of empirical studies. *Archives of General Psychiatry, 42,* 821–833.

Kempe, C. H., Silverman, F. N., Steele, B. F., Droegenmueller, W., & Silver, H. K. (1962). The battered child syndrome. *Journal of the American Medical Association, 181,* 17–24.

Kendall, P. C. (1994). Treating anxiety disorders in children: Results of a randomized clinical trial. *Journal of Consulting and Clinical Psychology, 62,* 100–110.

Kendall, P. C., Flannery-Schroeder, E., Panichelli-Mindel, S. M., Southam-Gerow, M., Henin, A., & Warman, M. (1997). Treatment of anxiety disorders in youth: A second randomized trial. *Journal of Consulting and Clinical Psychology, 65,* 366–380.

Kendall, P. C., & Treadwell, K. (1996). Cognitive-behavioral treatment for childhood anxiety disorders. In E. D. Hibbs & P. S. Jensen (Eds.), *Psychosocial treatments for child and adolescent disorders: Empirically based strategies for clinical practice* (pp. 23–41). Washington, DC: American Psychological Association.

Kendall-Tackett, K. A., Williams, L. M., & Finkelhor, D. (1993). Impact of sexual abuse on children: A review and synthesis of recent empirical studies. *Psychological Bulletin, 113,* 164–180.

Kendler, K. S. (1998). Adversity, stress, and psychopathology: A psychiatric genetic perspective. In B. P. Dohrenwend (Ed.), *Adversity, stress, and psychopathology* (pp. 477–485). New York: Oxford University Press.

Kendler, K. S., Davis, C. G., & Kessler, R. C. (1997). The familial aggregation of common psychiatric and substance use disorders in the National Comorbidity Survey: A family history study. *British Journal of Psychiatry, 170,* 541–548.

Kendler, K. S., & Diehl, S. R. (1993). The genetics of schizophrenia: A current, genetic-epidemiological perspective. *Schizophrenia Bulletin, 19,* 261–285.

Kendler, K. S., MacLean, C., Neale, M., Kessler, R., Heath, A., & Eaves, L. (1991). The genetic epidemiology of bulimia nervosa. *American Journal of Psychiatry, 148,* 1627–1637.

Kendler, K. S., McGuire, M., Gruenberg, A. M., O'Hare, A., Spellman, M., & Walsh, D. (1993). The Roscommon Family Study: I. Methods, diagnosis of probands, and risk of schizophrenia in relatives. *Archives of General Psychiatry, 50,* 527–540.

Kendler, K. S., Myers, J. M., O'Neill, F. A., Martin, R., Murphy, B., MacLean, C. J., Walsh, D., & Straub, R. E. (2000). Clinical features of schizophrenia and linkage to chromosomes 5q, 6p, 8p, and 10p in the Irish Study of High Density Schizophrenia Families. *American Journal of Psychiatry, 157,* 402–408.

Kendler, K. S., Neale, M. C., Kessler, R. C., & Heath, A. C. (1992). Major depression and generalized anxiety disorder: Same genes, (partly) different environments? *Archives of General Psychiatry, 49,* 716–722.

Kennedy, R. (1997). An African American female and school. In R. F. Kronick (Ed.), *At-risk youth: Theory, practice, reform* (pp. 191–201). New York: Garland Publishing.

Kenny, M. C., & McEachern, A. G. (2000). Racial, ethnic, and cultural factors of childhood sexual abuse: A selected review of the literature. *Clinical Psychology Review, 20,* 905–922.

Kent, A., & Waller, G. (2000). Childhood emotional abuse and eating psychopathology. *Clinical Psychology Review, 20,* 887–903.

Keogh, B. K., & Sears, S. (1991). Learning disabilities from a developmental perspective: Early identification and prediction. In B. Y. L. Wong (Ed.), *Learning about learning disabilities* (pp. 485–503). San Diego: Academic Press.

Kerr, A., & Stephenson, J. B. P. (1986). A study of the natural history of Rett syndrome in 23 girls. *American Journal of Medical Genetics, 24,* 77–83.

Kerr, M. A., Black, M. M., & Krishnakumar, A. (2000). Failure-to-thrive, maltreatment and the behavior and development of 6-year-old children from low-income, urban families: A cumulative risk model. *Child Abuse & Neglect, 24,* 587–598.

Kety, S. S. (1988). Schizophrenic illness in the families of schizophrenic adoptees: Findings from the Danish national sample. *Schizophrenia Bulletin, 14,* 217–222.

Kety, S. S., Wender, P. H., Jacobsen, B., Ingraham, L. J., Jansson, L., Faber, B., & Kinney, D. K. (1994). Mental illness in the biological and adoptive relatives of schizophrenic adoptees: Replication of the Copenhagen Study in the rest of Denmark. *Archives of General Psychiatry, 51,* 442–455.

Keys, A., Brozek, J., Henschel, A., Mickelsen, O., & Taylor, H. L. (1950). *The biology of human starvation.* Minneapolis: University of Minnesota Press.

Kiely, M., & Lubin, R. A. (1991). Epidemiological methods. In J. L. Matson & J. A. Mulick (Eds.), *Handbook of mental retardation* (2nd ed., pp. 586–602). New York: Pergamon.

Killen, J. D., Taylor, C. B., Hammer, L. D., Litt, I., Wilson, D. M., Rich, T., Hayward, C., Simmonds, B., Kraemer, H., & Varady, A. (1993). An attempt to modify unhealthy eating attitudes and weight regulation practices of young adolescent girls. *International Journal of Eating Disorders, 13,* 368–384.

Killias, M., & Rabasa, J. (1997). Weapons and athletic constitution as factors linked to violence among male juveniles. *British Journal of Criminology, 37,* 446–457.

King, N. J., Gullone, E., Tonge, B. J., & Ollendick, T. H. (1993). Self-reports of panic attacks and manifest anxiety in adolescents. *Behaviour Research and Therapy, 31,* 111–116.

King, N. J., Tonge, B. J., Mullen, P., Myerson, N., Heyne, D., Rollings, S., Martin, R., & Ollendick, T. H. (2000). Treating sexually abused children with posttraumatic stress symptoms: A randomized clinical trial. *Journal of the American Academy of Child and Adolescent Psychiatry, 39,* 1347–1355.

Kingsley, J., & Levitz, M. (1994). *Count us in: Growing up with Down syndrome.* San Diego: Harcourt Brace.

Kirk, S. A. (1963). Behavioral diagnosis and remediation of learning disabilities. *Conference Exploring Problems of the Perceptually Handicapped Child, 1,* 1–23.

Klein, M. (1932). *The psychoanalysis of children.* London: Hogarth Press.

Klein, R. G., & Last, C. G. (1989). *Anxiety disorders in children.* Newbury Park, CA: Sage.

Klein, R. G., & Mannuzza, S. (1991). Long-term outcome of hyperactive children: A review. *Journal of the American Academy of Child and Adolescent Psychiatry, 30,* 383–387.

Klein, R. G., Pine, D. S., & Klein, D. F. (1998). Resolved: Mania is mistaken for ADHD in prepubertal children. *Journal of the American Academy of Child and Adolescent Psychiatry, 37,* 1093–1096.

Kleitman, N. (1963). *Sleep and wakefulness.* Chicago: University of Illinois Press.

Kliewer, W., Lepore, S. J., Oskin, D., & Johnson, P. D. (1998). The role of social and cognitive processes in children's adjustment to community violence. *Journal of Consulting and Clinical Psychology, 66,* 199–209.

Klin, A., Sparrow, S. S., de Bildt, A., Cicchetti, D. V., Cohen, D. J., & Volkmar, F. R. (1999). A normed study of face recognition in autism and related disorders. *Journal of Autism and Developmental Disorders, 29,* 499–508.

Klin, A., Volkmar, F. R., Sparrow, S. S., Cicchetti, D. V., & Rourke, B. P. (1995). Validity and neuropsychological characterization of Asperger syndrome: Convergence with nonverbal learning disabilities syndrome. *Journal of Child Psychology and Psychiatry, 36,* 1127–1140.

Klinger, L. G., & Dawson, G. (1996). Autistic disorder. In E. J. Mash & R. A. Barkley (Eds.), *Child psychopathology* (pp. 311–339). New York: Guilford.

Knutson, J. F., & Selner, M. B. (1994). Punitive childhood experiences reported by young adults over a 10-year period. *Child Abuse & Neglect, 18,* 155–166.

Kobayashi, R., Murata, T., & Yoshinaga, K. (1992). A follow-up study of 201 children with autism in Kyushu and Yamaguchi areas. *Japanese Journal of Autism and Developmental Disorders, 22,* 395–411.

Koegel, L. K. (1995). Communication and language intervention. In R. L. Koegel & L. K. Koegel (Eds.), *Teaching children with autism* (pp. 17–32). Baltimore: Brookes Publishing Co.

Koegel, L. K., & Koegel, R. L. (1996). The child with autism as an active communicative partner: Child-initiated strategies for improving communication and reducing behavior problems. In E. D. Hibbs & P. S. Jensen (Eds.), *Psychological treatments for child and adolescent disorders: Empirically based strategies for clinical practice* (pp. 553–572). Washington, DC: American Psychological Association.

Koegel, R. L., Koegel, L. K., & McNerney, E. K. (2001). Pivotal areas in intervention for autism. *Journal of Clinical Child Psychology, 30,* 19–32.

Koegel, R. L., Schreibman, L., O'Neill, R. E., & Burke, J. C. (1983). The personality and family-interaction characteristics of parents of autistic children. *Journal of Consulting and Clinical Psychology, 51,* 683–692.

Koeppen, A. S. (1974). Relaxation training for children. *Elementary School Guidance & Counseling, 9,* 14–21.

Kohler, F. W., Strain, P. S., & Shearer, D. D. (1996). Examining levels of social inclusion within an integrated preschool for children with autism. In L. K. Koegel & R. L. Koegel (Eds.), *Positive behavioral support: Including people with difficult behavior in the community* (pp. 305–332). Baltimore: Brookes Publishing Co.

Kolko, D. J. (1992). Characteristics of child victims of physical violence: Research findings and clinical implications. *Journal of Interpersonal Violence, 7,* 244–276.

Kolko, D. J., Bukstein, O. G., & Barron, J. (1999). Methylphenidate and behavior modification in children with ADHD and comorbid ODD or CD: Main and incremental effects across settings. *Journal of the American Academy of Child and Adolescent Psychiatry, 38,* 578–586.

Kolvin, I. (1971). Psychoses in childhood—A comparative study. In M. Rutter (Ed.), *Childhood-onset autism: Concepts, characteristics and treatment* (pp. 7–26). Edinburgh: Churchill Livingstone.

Kolvin, I., Barrett, M. L., Bhate, S. R., Berney, T. P., Famnuiwa, O. O., Fundudis, T., & Tyrer, S. (1991). The Newcastle Child Depression Project: Diagnosis and classification of depression. *British Journal of Psychiatry, 159* (Supp. 11), 9–21.

Konstantareas, M. M. (1991). Autistic, learning disabled, and delayed children's impact on their parents. *Canadian Journal of Behavioral Science, 23,* 358–375.

Konstantareas, M. M., & Homatidis, S. (1999). Chromosomal abnormalities in a series of children with autistic disorder. *Journal of Autism and Developmental Disorders, 29,* 275–285.

Kovacs, M., (1990). Comorbid anxiety disorders in childhood-onset depressions. In J. D. Maser & C. R. Cloninger (Eds.), *Comorbidity of mood and anxiety disorders* (pp. 272–281). Washington, DC: American Psychiatric Press.

Kovacs, M., Akiskal, H. S., Gatsonis, C., & Parrone, P. L. (1994). Childhood-onset dysthymic disorder: Clinical features and prospective naturalistic outcome. *Archives of General Psychiatry, 51,* 365–374.

Kovacs, M., Gatsonis, C., Paulauskas, S., & Richards, C. (1989). Depressive disorders in childhood: A longitudinal study of comorbidity with and risk for anxiety disorders. *Archives of General Psychiatry, 46,* 776–782.

Kovacs, M., Obrosky, D. S., Gatsonis, C., & Richards, C. (1997). First-episode major depressive and dysthymic disorder in childhood: Clinical and sociodemographic factors in recovery. *Journal of the American Academy of Child and Adolescent Psychiatry, 36,* 777–784.

Kovacs, M., & Pollock, M. (1995). Bipolar disorder and comorbid conduct disorder in childhood and adolescence. *Journal of the American Academy of Child and Adolescent Psychiatry, 34,* 715–723.

Kozlowski, B. W. (1992). Megavitamin treatment of mental retardation in children: A review of effects on behavior and cognition. *Journal of Child and Adolescent Psychopharmacology, 2,* 307–320.

Kraepelin, E. (1883). *Kompendium der Psychiatrie.* Leipzig, Germany: Abel.

Kratzer, L., & Hodgins, S. (1997). Adult outcomes of child conduct problems: A cohort study. *Journal of Abnormal Child Psychology, 25,* 65–81.

Kring, A. M., & Neale, J. M. (1996). Do schizophrenic patients show a disjunctive relationship among expressive, experiential, and psychophysiological components of emotion? *Journal of Abnormal Psychology, 105,* 249–257.

Krystal, J. H., Deutsch, D. N., & Charney, D. S. (1996). The biological basis of panic disorder. *Journal of Clinical Psychiatry, 57,* 23–33.

Kumpfer, K. L., Moolgaard, V., & Spoth, R. (1996). The Strengthening Families Program for the prevention of delinquency and drug use. In R. D. Peters & R. D. McMahon (Eds.), *Preventing childhood disorders, substance abuse, and delinquency* (pp. 241–267). Thousand Oaks, CA: Sage.

Kumra, S. (2000). The diagnosis and treatment of children and adolescents with schizophrenia. *Child and Adolescent Psychiatric Clinics of North America, 9,* 183–199.

Kumra, S., Frazier, J. A., Jacobsen, L. K., McKenna, K., Gordon, C. T., Lenane, M. C., Hamburger, S. D., Smith, A. K., Albus, K. E., Alaghband-Rad, J., & Rapoport, J. L. (1996). Childhood-onset schizophrenia: A double-blind clozapine-haloperidol comparison. *Archives of General Psychiatry, 53,* 1090–1097.

Kumra, S., Wiggs, E., Krasnewich, D., Meck, J., Smith, A. C. M., Bedwell, J., Fernandez, T., Jacobsen, L. K., Lenane, M., & Rapoport, J. L. (1998). Association of sex chromosome anomalies with childhood-onset psychotic disorders. *Journal of the American Academy of Child and Adolescent Psychiatry, 37,* 292–296.

Kuntsi, J., & Stevenson, J. (2000). Hyperactivity in children: A focus on genetic research and psychological theories. *Clinical Child and Family Psychology Review, 3,* 1–24.

Kupersmidt, J. B., Griesler, P. C., DeRosier, M. E., Patterson, C. J., & Davis, P. W. (1995). Childhood aggression and peer relations in the context of family and neighborhood factors. *Child Development, 66,* 360–375.

Kurita, H., Kita, M., & Miyake, Y. (1992). A comparative study of development and symptoms among disintegrative psychosis and infantile autism with and without speech loss. *Journal of Autism and Developmental Disorders, 22,* 175–188.

LaFreniere, P. J., & Capuano, F. (1997). Preventive intervention as means of clarifying direction of effects in socialization: Anxious-withdrawn preschoolers case. *Development and Psychopathology, 9,* 551–564.

LaFreniere, P. J., & Dumas, J. E. (1995). *Social Competence and Behavior Evaluation—Preschool edition (SCBE).* Los Angeles: Western Psychological Services.

La Greca, A. M., & Lopez, N. (1998). Social anxiety among adolescents: Linkages with peer relations and friendships. *Journal of Abnormal Child Psychology, 26,* 83–94.

Lagrue, G., & Milliez, P. (1970). La signification de l'énurésie, sa valeur sémiologique en uronéphrologie. *Médecine et Hygiène, 28,* 350–352.

Lahey, B. B., Goodman, S. H., Waldman, I. D., Bird, H., Canino, G., Jensen, P., Regier, D., Leaf, P. J., Gordon, R., & Applegate, B. (1999). Relation of age of onset to the type and severity of child and adolescent conduct problems. *Journal of Abnormal Child Psychology, 27,* 247–260.

Lahey, B. B., Hart, E. L., Pliszka, S., Applegate, B., & McBurnett, K. (1993). Neurophysiological correlates of conduct disorder: A rationale and a review of research. *Journal of Clinical Child Psychology, 22,* 141–153.

Lahey, B. B., Loeber, R., Hart, E. L., Frick, P. J., Applegate, B., Zhang, Q., Green, S. M., & Russo, M. F. (1995). Four-year longitudinal study of conduct disorder in boys: Patterns and predictors of persistence. *Journal of Abnormal Psychology, 104,* 83–93.

Lahey, B. B., Loeber, R., Quay, H. C., Frick, P. J., & Grimm, S. (1992). Oppositional defiant and conduct disorders: Issues to be resolved for DSM-IV. *Journal of the American Academy of Child and Adolescent Psychiatry, 31,* 539–546.

Lahey, B. B., Loeber, R., Stouthamer-Loeber, M., Christ, M. A. G., Green, S., Russo, M. F., Frick, P. J., & Dulcan, M. (1990). Comparison of DSM-III and DSM-III-R diagnoses for prepubertal children: Changes in prevalence and validity. *Journal of the American Academy of Child and Adolescent Psychiatry, 29,* 620–626.

Lainhart, J. E., & Folstein, S. E. (1994). Affective disorders in people with autism: A review of published cases. *Journal of Autism and Developmental Disorders, 24,* 587–601.

Lambert, E. W., Wahler, R. G., Andrade, A. R., & Bickman, L. (2001). Looking for disorder in conduct disorder. *Journal of Abnormal Psychology, 110,* 110–123.

Lambert, J. L. (1997). *Trisomie 21 et âge adulte.* Lausanne: Éditions des Sentiers.

Lambert, N. M. (1981). Psychological evidence in Larry P. vs. Wilson Riles: An evaluation by a witness for the defense. *American Psychologist, 36,* 937–952.

Lane, H. (1977). *The wild boy of Averyron.* Cambridge, MA: Harvard University Press.

Lasègue, E. C. (1964). On hysterical anorexia. In M. R. Kaufman & M. Heiman (Eds.), *Evolution of psychosomatic concepts* (pp. 141–155). New York: International Universities Press. (Original work published 1873)

Lask, B., & Bryant-Waugh, R. (1997). Prepubertal eating disorders. In D. M. Garner & P. E. Garfinkel (Eds.), *Handbook of treatment for eating disorders* (2nd ed., pp. 476–483). New York: Guilford.

Last, C. G., Hersen, M., Kazdin, A. E., Francis, G., & Grubb, H. J. (1987). Psychiatric illness in the mothers of anxious children. *American Journal of Psychiatry, 144,* 1580–1583.

Last, C. G., Perrin, S., Hersen, M., & Kazdin, A. E. (1992). DSM-III-R anxiety disorders in children: Sociodemographic and clinical characteristics. *Journal of the American Academy of Child and Adolescent Psychiatry, 31,* 1070–1076.

Last, C. G., & Strauss, C. C. (1990). School refusal in anxiety-disordered children and adolescents. *Journal of the American Academy of Child and Adolescent Psychiatry, 29,* 31–35.

Lecocq, P. (1986). Sensibilité à la similarité phonétique chez les enfants dyslexiques et les bons lecteurs. *L'Année Psychologique, 86,* 201–221.

Lee, B., & Goerge, R. (1999). Poverty, early childbearing, and child maltreatment: A multinomial method. *Children and Youth Services Review, 21,* 755–780.

Lee, S., Hsu, L. K. G., & Wing, Y. K. (1992). Bulimia nervosa in Hong Kong Chinese patients. *British Journal of Psychiatry, 161,* 545–551.

Lee, S., Leung, C. M., Wing, Y. K., Chiu, H. F., & Chen, C. (1991). Acne as a risk factor for anorexia nervosa in Chinese. *Australian and New Zealand Journal of Psychiatry, 25,* 134–137.

Leff, J. P. (1991). The relevance of psychosocial risk factors for treatment and prevention. In P. E. Bebbington (Ed.), *Social psychiatry: Theory, methodology, and practice* (pp. 247–264). New Brunswick, NJ: Transaction Publishers.

Leff, J., Sartorius, N., Jablensky, A., Korten, A., & Ernberg, G. (1992). The International Pilot Study of Schizophrenia: Five-year follow-up findings. *Psychological Medicine, 22,* 131–145.

Leff, J., & Vaughn, C. (1985). *Expressed emotion in families: Its significance for mental illness.* New York: Guilford.

Leventhal, J. M. (1996). Twenty years later: We do know how to prevent child abuse and neglect. *Child Abuse & Neglect, 20,* 647–655.

Levine, M. D. (1983). Encopresis. In M. D. Levine, W. B. Carey, A. C. Crocker, & R. T. Gross (Eds.), *Developmental behavioral pediatrics* (pp. 586–595). Philadelphia: Saunders.

Lewinsohn, P. M. (1974). A behavioral approach to depression. In R. Friedman & M. Katz (Eds.), *The psychology of depression: Contemporary theory and research* (pp. 157–185). Washington, DC: Winston-Wiley.

Lewinsohn, P. M., Gotlib, I. H., Lewinsohn, M., Seeley, J. R., & Allen, N. B. (1998). Gender differences in anxiety disorders and anxiety symptoms in adolescents. *Journal of Abnormal Psychology, 107,* 109–117.

Lewinsohn, P. M., Hops, H., Roberts, R. E., Seeley, J. R., & Andrews, J. A. (1993). Adolescent psychopathology: I. Prevalence and incidence of depression and other DSM-III-R disorders in high school students. *Journal of Abnormal Psychology, 102,* 133–144.

Lewinsohn, P. M., Roberts, R. E., Seeley, J. R., Rohde, P., Gotlib, I. H., & Hops, H. (1994). Adolescent psychopathology: II. Psychosocial risk factors for depression. *Journal of Abnormal Psychology, 103,* 302–315.

Lewis, B. A. (1990). Familial phonological disorders: Four pedigrees. *Journal of Speech and Hearing Disorders, 55,* 160–170.

Lewis, C. C. (1981). The effects of parental firm control: A reinterpretation of the findings. *Psychological Bulletin, 90,* 547–563.

Lewis, C., Hitch, G. J., & Walker, P. (1994). The prevalence of specific arithmetic difficulties and specific reading difficulties in 9- to 10-year-old boys and girls. *Journal of Child Psychology and Psychiatry, 35,* 283–292.

Lewis, G., Croft-Jeffreys, C., & Anthony, D. (1990). Are British psychiatrists racist? *British Journal of Psychiatry, 157,* 410–415.

Lezak, M. D. (1995). *Neuropsychological assessment* (3rd ed.). New York: Oxford University Press.

Liberman, I. Y., & Shankweiler, D. (1991). Phonology and beginning reading: A tutorial. In L. Rieben & C. A. Perfetti (Eds.), *Learning to read: Basic research and its implications* (pp. 46–73). Hillsdale, NJ: Erlbaum.

Liebert, R. M., & Fischel, J. E. (1990). The elimination disorders: Enuresis and encopresis. In M. Lewis & S. M. Miller (Eds.), *Handbook of developmental psychopathology* (pp. 421–429). New York: Plenum.

Lipowski, Z. J. (1988). Somatization: The concept and its clinical application. *American Journal of Psychiatry, 145,* 1358–1368.

Liss, D. S., Waller, D. A., Kennard, B. D., McIntire, D., Capra, P., & Stephens, J. (1998). Psychiatric illness and family support in children and adolescents with diabetic ketoacidosis: A controlled study. *Journal of the American Academy of Child and Adolescent Psychiatry, 37,* 536–544.

Liu, X., Sun, Z., Uchiyama, M., Li, Y., & Okawa, M. (2000). Attaining nocturnal urinary control, nocturnal enuresis, and behavioral problems in Chinese children aged 6 through 16 years. *Journal of the American Academy of Child and Adolescent Psychiatry, 39,* 1557–1564.

Loeber, R., & Farrington, D. P. (Eds.). (1998). *Serious and violent juvenile offenders: Risk factors and successful interventions.* Thousand Oaks, CA: Sage.

Loeber, R., & Farrington, D. P. (2000). Young children who commit crime: Epidemiology, developmental origins, risk factors, early interventions, and policy implications. *Development and Psychopathology, 12,* 737–762.

Loeber, R., Green, S. M., Keenan, K., & Lahey, B. B. (1995). Which boys will fare worse? Early predictors of the onset of conduct disorder in a six-year longitudinal study. *Journal of the American Academy of Child and Adolescent Psychiatry, 34,* 499–509.

Loeber, R. Green, S. M., Lahey, B. B., Frick, P. J., & McBurnett, K. (2000). Findings on disruptive behavior disorders from the first decade of the Developmental Trends Study. *Clinical Child and Family Psychology Review, 3,* 37–60.

Loeber, R., Green, S. M., Lahey, B. B., & Kalb, L. (2000). Physical fighting in childhood as a risk factor for later mental health problems. *Journal of the American Academy of Child and Adolescent Psychiatry, 39,* 421–428.

Lombroso, P., Pauls, D., & Leckman, J. (1994). Genetic mechanisms in childhood psychiatric disorders. *Journal of the American Academy of Child and Adolescent Psychiatry, 33,* 921–938.

Loney, J., Paternite, C. E., Schwartz, J. E., & Roberts, M. A. (1997). Associations between clinic-referred boys and their fathers on childhood inattention-overactivity and aggression dimensions. *Journal of Abnormal Child Psychology, 25,* 499–509.

Lotter, V. (1966). Epidemiology of autistic conditions in young children. *Social Psychiatry, 1,* 124–137.

Lou, H. C., Henriksen, L., & Bruhn, P. (1984). Focal cerebral hypoperfusion in children with dysphasia and/or attention deficit disorder. *Archives of Neurology, 41,* 825–829.

Lovaas, I. (1987). Behavioral treatment and normal educational and intellectual functioning in young autistic children. *Journal of Consulting and Clinical Psychology, 55,* 3–9.

Lowry-Webster, H. M., Barrett, P. M., & Dadds, M. R. (2001). A universal prevention trial of anxiety and depressive symptomatology in childhood: Preliminary data from an Australian study. *Behaviour Change, 18,* 36–50.

Lucas, A. R., Beard, C. M., O'Fallon, W. M., & Kurlan, L. T. (1991). 50-year trends in the incidence of anorexia nervosa in Rochester, Minn.: A population-based study. *American Journal of Psychiatry, 148,* 917–922.

Lucero, L. D., Hill, F. A., & Ferraro, F. R. (1999). Body dissatisfaction in young children. *Psychology—A Quarterly Journal of Human Behavior, 36,* 36–42.

Luckasson, R., Coulter, D. L., Polloway, E. A., Reiss, S., Schalock, R. L., Snell, M. E., Spitalnik, D. M., & Stark, J. A. (1992). *Mental retardation: Definition, classification, and systems of support.* Washington, DC: American Association on Mental Retardation.

Lunsing, R. J., Hadders-Algra, M., Touwen, B. C. L., & Huisjes, H. J. (1991). Nocturnal enuresis and minor neurological dysfunction at 12 years: A follow-up study. *Developmental Medicine and Child Neurology, 33,* 439–445.

Lyman, D. E. (1986). *Making the words stand still: A master teacher tells how to overcome specific learning disability, dyslexia, and old-fashioned word blindness.* Boston: Houghton Mifflin.

Lynam, D. R. (1996). Early identification of chronic offenders: Who is the fledgling psychopath? *Psychological Bulletin, 120,* 209–234.

Lynam, D., Moffitt, T., & Stouthamer-Loeber, M. (1993). Explaining the relation between IQ and delinquency: Class, race, test motivation, school failure, or self-control? *Journal of Abnormal Psychology, 102,* 187–196.

Lyon, G. R. (1994). Critical issues in the measurement of learning disabilities. In G. R. Lyon (Ed.), *Frames of reference for the assessment of learning disabilities* (pp. 3–13). Baltimore: Brookes Publishing Co.

Lyon, G. R. (1996). Learning disabilities. In E. J. Mash & R. A. Barkley (Eds.), *Child psychopathology* (pp. 390–435). New York: Guilford.

Macaulay, J. L., & Kleinknecht, R. A. (1989). Panic and panic attacks in adolescents. *Journal of Anxiety Disorders, 3,* 221–241.

MacLean, W. E., & Brayden, R M. (1992). Elimination disorders. In S. R. Hooper, G. W. Hynd, & R. E. Mattison (Eds.), *Child psychopathology: Diagnostic criteria and clinical assessment* (pp. 379–407). Hillsdale, NJ: Erlbaum.

Madrid, A. L., State, M. W., & King, B. H. (2000). Pharmacologic management of psychiatric and behavioral symptoms in mental retardation. *Psychopharmacology, 9,* 225–243.

Maedgen, J. W., & Carlson, C. L. (2000). Social functioning and emotional regulation in the attention deficit hyperactivity disorder subtypes. *Journal of Clinical Child Psychology, 29,* 30–42.

Mahoney, A., Donnelly, W. O., Lewis, T., & Maynard, C. (2000). Mother and father self-reports of corporal punishment and severe physical aggression toward clinic-referred youth. *Journal of Clinical Child Psychology, 29,* 266–281.

Malinowsky-Rummell, R., & Hansen, D. J. (1993). Long-term consequences of childhood physical abuse. *Psychological Bulletin, 114,* 68–79.

Mancini, C., van Ameringen, M., Szatmari, P., Fugere, C., & Boyle, M. H. (1996). A high-risk pilot study of the children of adults with social phobia. *Journal of the American Academy of Child and Adolescent Psychiatry, 35,* 1511–1517.

Manne, S. L., Redd, W. H., Jacobsen, P. B., Gorfinkle, K., Schorr, O., & Rapkin, B. (1990). Behavioral intervention to reduce child and parent distress during venipuncture. *Journal of Consulting and Clinical Psychology, 58,* 565–572.

Mannuzza, S., & Klein, R. G. (1992). Predictors of outcome of children with attention deficit hyperactivity disorder. *Child and Adolescent Psychiatric Clinics of North America, 1,* 567–578.

Mannuzza, S., & Klein, R. G. (2000). Long-term prognosis in attention-deficit/hyperactivity disorder. *Child and Adolescent Psychiatric Clinics of North America, 9,* 711–726.

Mannuzza, S., Klein, R. G., Bessler, A., Malloy, P., & LaPadula, M. (1998). Adult psychiatric status of hyperactive boys grown up. *American Journal of Psychiatry, 155,* 493–498.

Mannuzza, S., Klein, R. G., Konig, P. H., & Giampino, T. L. (1989). Hyperactive boys almost grown up: IV. Criminality and its relationship to psychiatric status. *Archives of General Psychiatry, 46,* 1073–1079.

March, J. S., Franklin, M., Nelson, A., & Foa, E. (2001). Cognitive-behavioral psychotherapy for pediatric obsessive-compulsive disorder. *Journal of Clinical Child Psychology, 30,* 8–18.

March, J. S., & Mulle, K. (1996). Banishing OCD: Cognitive-behavioral psychotherapy for obsessive-compulsive disorders. In E. D. Hibbs & P. S. Jensen (Eds.), *Psychosocial treatments for child and adolescent disorders: Empirically based strategies for clinical practice* (pp. 83–102). Washington, DC: American Psychological Association.

Marchi, M., & Cohen, P. (1990). Early childhood eating behaviors and adolescent eating disorders. *Journal of the American Academy of Child and Adolescent Psychiatry, 29,* 112–117.

Marcus, M. D. (1997). Adapting treatment for patients with binge-eating disorder. In D. M. Garner & P. E. Garfinkel (Eds.), *Handbook of treatment for eating disorders* (2nd ed., pp. 484–493). New York: Guilford.

Martin, C., Cabrol, S., Bouvard, M. P., Lepine, J. P., & Mouren-Simeoni, M. C. (1999). Anxiety and depressive disorders in fathers and mothers of anxious school-refusing children. *Journal of the American Academy of Child and Adolescent Psychiatry, 38,* 916–922.

Mash, E. J., & Dozois, D. J. A. (1996). Child psychopathology. A developmental-systems perspective. In E. J. Mash & R. A. Barkley (Eds.), *Child psychopathology* (pp. 3–60). New York: Guilford.

Mash, E. J., & Johnston, C. (1990). Determinants of parenting stress: Illustrations from families of hyperactive children and families of physically abused children. *Journal of Clinical Child Psychology, 19,* 313–328.

Mason, D. A., & Frick, P. J. (1994). The heritability of antisocial behavior: A meta-analysis of twin and adoption studies. *Journal of Psychopathology and Behavioral Assessment, 16,* 301–323.

Matson, J. L., Bamburg, J. W., Mayville, E. A., Pinkston, J., Bielecki, J., Kuhn, D., Smalls, Y., & Logan, J. R. (2000). Psychopharmacology and mental retardation: A 10-year review (1990–1999). *Research in Developmental Disabilities, 21,* 263–296.

Matson, J. L., Benavidez, D. A., Compton, L. S., Paclawskyj, T., & Baglio, C. (1996). Behavioral treatment of autistic persons: A review of the research from 1980 to the present. *Research in Developmental Disabilities, 17,* 433–465.

Matsuura, M., Okubo, Y., Kojima, T., Takahashi, R., Wang, Y. F., Shen, Y. C., & Lee, C. K. (1993). A cross-national prevalence study of children with emotional and behavioral problems—A WHO collaborative study in the Western Pacific region. *Journal of Child Psychology and Psychiatry, 34,* 307–315.

Mattis, S. G., & Ollendick, T. H. (1997). Children's cognitive responses to the somatic symptoms of panic. *Journal of Abnormal Child Psychology, 25,* 47–57.

Maudsley, H. (1867). *The physiology and pathology of the mind.* London: Macmillan.

Maughan, B., Pickles, A., Rowe, R., Costello, E. J., & Angold, A. (2000). Developmental trajectories of aggressive and non-aggressive conduct problems. *Journal of Quantitative Criminology, 16,* 199–221.

Mayes, S. D., Calhoun, S. L., & Crites, D. L. (2001). Does DSM-IV Asperger's disorder exist? *Journal of Abnormal Child Psychology, 29,* 263–271.

McBurnett, K., Lahey, B. B., Rathouz, P. J., & Loeber, R. (2000). Low salivary cortisol and persistent aggression in boys referred for disruptive behavior. *Archives of General Psychiatry, 57,* 38–43.

McCauley, E., Mitchell, J. R., Burke, P., & Moss, S. (1988). Cognitive attributes of depression in children and adolescents. *Journal of Consulting and Clinical Psychology, 56,* 903–908.

McCauley, E., Myers, K., Mitchell, J. R., Calderon, R., Schloredt, K., & Treder, R. (1993). Depression in young people: Initial presentation and clinical course. *Journal of the American Academy of Child and Adolescent Psychiatry, 32,* 714–722.

McClellan, J., McCurry, C., Ronnei, M., Adams, J., Eisner, A., & Storck, M. (1996) Age of onset of sexual abuse: Relationship to sexually inappropriate behaviors. *Journal of the American Academy of Child and Adolescent Psychiatry, 34,* 1375–1383.

McClellan, J. M., & Werry, J. S. (1992). Schizophrenia. *Psychiatric Clinics of North America, 15,* 131–148.

McCellan, J., & Werry, J. (1994). Practice parameters for the assessment and treatment of children and adolescents with schizophrenia. *Journal of the American Academy of Child and Adolescent Psychiarty, 33,* 616–635.

McClure, E. B., Brennan, P. A., Hammen, C., & Le Brocque, R. M. (2001). Parental anxiety disorders, child anxiety disorders, and the perceived parent-child relationship in an Australian high-risk sample. *Journal of Abnormal Child Psychology, 29,* 1–10.

McCord, W., & McCord, J. (1959). *Origins of crime.* New York: Columbia University Press.

McDermott, P. A., & Schaefer, B. A. (1996). A demographic survey of rare and common problem behaviors among American students. *Journal of Clinical Child Psychology, 25,* 352–362.

McEachin, J. J., Smith, T., & Lovaas, O. I. (1993). Long-term outcome for children with autism who received early intensive behavioral treatment. *American Journal on Mental Retardation, 97,* 359–372.

McGee, R., Feehan, M., Williams, S., Partridge, F., Silva, P. A., & Kelly, J. (1990). DSM-III disorders in a large sample of adolescents. *Journal of the American Academy of Child and Adolescent Psychiatry, 29,* 611–619.

McGrath, M. L., Mellon, M. W., & Murphy, L. (2000). Empirically supported treatments in pediatric psychology: Constipation and encopresis. *Journal of Pediatric Psychology, 25,* 225–254.

McGuire, S., & Clifford, J. (2000). Genetic and environmental contributions to loneliness in children. *Psychological Science, 11,* 487–491.

McKenna, K., Gordon, C. T., Lenane, M., Kaysen, D., Fahey, K., & Rapoport, J. L. (1994). Looking for childhood-onset schizophrenia: The first 71 cases screened. *Journal of the American Academy of Child and Adolescent Psychiatry, 33,* 636–644.

McKibben, L., DeVos, E., & Newberger, E. (1989). Victimization of mothers of abused children: A controlled study. *Pediatrics, 84,* 531–535.

Mellon, M. W., & Houts, R. C. (1995). Elimination disorders. In R. T. Ammerman & M. Hersen (Eds.), *Handbook of child behavior therapy in the psychiatric setting* (pp. 341–366). New York: Wiley.

Mellon, M. W., & McGrath, M. L. (2000). Empirically supported treatments in pediatric psychology: Nocturnal enuresis. *Journal of Pediatric Psychology, 25,* 193–214.

Melnick, S. M., & Hinshaw, S. P. (2000). Emotion regulation and parenting in AD/HD and comparison boys: Linkages with social behaviors and peer preference. *Journal of Abnormal Child Psychology, 28,* 73–86.

Melville, H. (1948). *Billy Budd.* Cambridge, MA: Harvard University Press. (Original work written 1891, published 1924)

Mesibov, G. B., Schroeder, C. S., & Wesson, L. (1977). Parental concerns about their children. *Journal of Pediatric Psychology, 2,* 13–17.

Messerschmitt, P. (1990). Actualités cliniques de l'autisme et des psychoses infantiles. In P. Messerschmitt (Ed.), *Clinique des syndromes autistiques* (pp. 18–33). Paris: Maloine.

Michael, K. D., & Crowley, S. L. (2002). How effective are treatments for child and adolescent depression? A meta-analytic review. *Clinical Psychology Review, 22,* 247–269.

Milich, R., Wolraich, M. L., & Lindgren, S. (1986). Sugar and hyperactivity: Critical review of empirical findings. *Clinical Psychology Review, 6,* 493–513.

Miller, J. N., & Ozonoff, S. (1997). Did Asperger's cases have Asperger disorder? A research note. *Journal of Child Psychology and Psychiatry and Allied Disciplines, 38,* 247–251.

Miller, T. R., Cohen, M. A., & Rossman, S. B. (1993). Victim costs of violent crime and resulting injuries. *Health Affairs, 12,* 186–197.

Miller-Johnson, S., Lochman, J. E., Coie, J. D., Perry, R., & Hyman, C. (1998). Comorbidity of conduct and depressive problems at sixth grade: Substance use outcomes across adolescence. *Journal of Abnormal Child Psychology, 26,* 221–232.

Milner, J. S. (1993). Social information processing and physical child abuse. *Clinical Psychology Review, 13,* 275–294.

Mink, I. T., Nihira, K., & Meyers, C. (1983). Taxonomy of family life styles: I. Homes with TMR children. *American Journal of Mental Deficiency, 87,* 484–497.

Minuchin, S., Baker, L., Rosman, B. L., Liebman, R., Milman, L., & Todd, T. C. (1975). A conceptual model of psychosomatic illness in children: Family organization and family therapy. *Archives of General Psychiatry, 32,* 1031–1038.

Misès, R., Perron, R., & Salbreux, R. (1994). *Retards et troubles de l'intelligence de l'enfant.* Paris: ESF.

Mitchell, J., McCauley, E., Burke, P. M., & Moss, S. J. (1988). Phenomenology of depression in children and adolescents. *Journal of the American Academy of Child and Adolescent Psychiatry, 27,* 12–20.

Mitchell, J., McCauley, E., Burke, P. M., & Moss, S. J. (1989). Psychopathology in parents of depressed children and adolescents. *Journal of the American Academy of Child and Adolescent Psychiatry, 28,* 352–357.

Mitchell, J. E., & Mussell, M. P. (1995). Comorbidity and binge eating disorder. *Addictive Behaviors, 20,* 725–732.

Mitchell, J. E., Pomeroy, C., & Adson, D. E. (1997). Managing medical complications. In D. M. Garner & P. E. Garfinkel (Eds.), *Handbook of treatment for eating disorders* (2nd ed., pp. 383–393). New York: Guilford.

Mitchell, J. E., & Pyle, R. L. (1988). The diagnosis and clinical characteristics of bulimia. In B. J. Blinder, B. F. Chaitin, & R. S. Goldstein (Eds.), *The eating disorders: Medical and physiological bases of diagnosis and treatment* (pp. 315–329). New York: PMA Publishing.

Mitsis, E. M., McKay, K. E., Schulz, K. P., Newcorn, J. H., & Halperin, J. M. (2000). Parent-teacher concordance for DSM-IV attention-deficit/hyperactivity disorder in a clinic-referred sample. *Journal of the American Academy of Child and Adolescent Psychiatry, 39,* 308–313.

Moffitt, T. E. (1993). Adolescence-limited and life-course-persistent antisocial behavior: A developmental taxonomy. *Psychological Review, 100,* 674–701.

Moreau de Tours, P. (1888). *La folie chez les enfants.* Paris: Librairie J.-B. Baillière.

Morgan, A. B., & Lilienfeld, S. O. (2000). A meta-analytic review of the relation between antisocial behavior and neuropsychological measures of executive function. *Clinical Psychology Review, 20,* 113–136.

Morgan, W. P. (1896). A case of congenital word blindness. *The British Medical Journal, 2,* 1378.

Mowrer, O. H. (1960). *Learning theory and behavior.* New York: Wiley.

Mraovich, L., & Wilson, F. (1999). Patterns of child abuse and neglect associated with the chronological age of children living in a midwestern county. *Child Abuse & Neglect, 23,* 899–903.

MTA Cooperative Group (1999). A 14-month randomized clinical trial of treatment strategies for attention-deficit/hyperactivity disorder. *Archives of General Psychiatry, 56,* 1073–1086.

Mufson, L., Moreau, D., Weissman, M. M., & Klerman, G. L. (1993). *Interpersonal psychotherapy for depressed adolescents.* New York: Guilford.

Mufson, L., Weissman, M. M., Moreau, D., & Garfinkel, R. (1999). Efficacy of interpersonal psychotherapy for depressed adolescents. *Archives of General Psychiatry, 56,* 573–579.

Mundy, P., Robertson, M., Robertson, J., & Greenblatt, M. (1990). The prevalence of psychotic symptoms in homeless adolescents. *Journal of the American Academy of Child and Adolescent Psychiatry, 29,* 724–731.

Muris, P., & Merckelbach, H. (2000). How serious are common childhood fears? II. The parent's point of view. *Behaviour Research and Therapy, 38,* 813–818.

Muris, P., Merckelbach, H., & Damsma, E. (2000). Threat perception bias in nonreferred, socially anxious children. *Journal of Clinical Child Psychology, 29,* 348–359.

Muris, P., Merckelbach, H., Gadet, B., & Moulaert, V. (2000). Fears, worries, and scary dreams in 4- to 12-year-old children: Their content, developmental pattern, and origins. *Journal of Clinical Child Psychology, 29,* 43–52.

Murphy, D. A., Marelich, W. D., & Hoffman, D. (2000). Assessment of anxiety and depression in young children: Support for two separate constructs. *Journal of Clinical Child Psychology, 29,* 383–391.

Myers, H. F., Alvy, K. T., Arrington, A., Richardson, M. A., Marigna, M., Huff, R., Main, M., & Newcomb, M. D. (1992). The impact of a parent training program on inner-city African American families. *Journal of Community Psychology, 20,* 132–147.

Nadel, J., & Pezé, A. (1993). What makes immediate imitation communicative in toddlers and autistic children? In J. Nadel & L. Camaioni (Eds.), *New perspectives in early communicative development* (pp. 139–156). London: Routledge.

Nandu, S., Murphy, M., Moser, H. W., & Rett, A. (1986). Rett syndrome: Natural history in 70 cases. *American Journal of Medical Genetics, 24,* S61–S72.

Nassau, J. H., & Drotar, D. (1995). Social competence in children with IDDM and asthma: Child, teacher, and parent reports of children's social adjustment, social performance, and social skills. *Journal of Pediatric Psychology, 20,* 187–204.

Nasser, M. (1986). Comparative study of the prevalence of abnormal eating attitudes among Arab female students of both London and Cairo universities. *Psychological Medicine, 16,* 621–625.

National Institute of Mental Health, DISC Editorial Board. (1998). *NIMH Diagnostic Interview Schedule for Children.* New York: Author.

National Institutes of Health (NIH) Consensus Development Conference (2000). National Institutes of Health Consensus Development Conference statement: Diagnosis and treatment of attention-deficit/hyperactivity disorder

(ADHD). *Journal of the American Academy of Child and Adolescent Psychiatry, 39,* 182–193.

National Research Council (1993). *Understanding child abuse and neglect.* Washington, DC: National Academy Press.

Naumberg, M. (1950). *Schizophrenic art: Its meaning in psychotherapy.* New York: Grune & Stratton.

Neisser, U., Boodoo, G., Bouchard, T. J., Boykin, A. W., Brody, N., Ceci, S. J., Halpern, D. F., Loehlin, J. C., Perloff, R., Sternberg, R. J., & Urbina, S. (1996). Intelligence: Knowns and unknowns. *American Psychologist, 51,* 77–101.

Nelson, C. A. (1999). Neural plasticity and human development. *Current Directions in Psychological Sciences, 8,* 42–45.

Nelson, J. C., & Davis, J. M. (1997). DST studies in psychotic depression: A meta-analysis. *American Journal of Psychiatry, 154,* 1497–1503.

Nemeroff, C. B. (1998). The neurobiology of depression. *Scientific American, 282,* 42–49.

Nettles, S. M., & Pleck, J. H. (1994). Risk, resilience, and development: The multiple ecologies of black adolescents in the United States. In R. J. Haggerty, L. R. Sherrod, N. Garmezy, & M. Rutter (Eds.), *Stress, risk, and resilience in children and adolescents: Processes, mechanisms, and interventions* (pp. 147–181). New York: Cambridge University Press.

Neuman, R. J., Todd, R. D., Heath, A. C., Reich, W., Hudziak, J. J., Bucholz, K. K., Madden, P. A. F., Begleiter, H., Porjesz, B., Kuperman, S., Hesselbrock, V., & Reich, T. (1999). Evaluation of ADHD typology in three contrasting samples: A latent class approach. *Journal of the American Academy of Child and Adolescent Psychiatry, 38,* 25–33.

Nilsen, W. J. (2001). *Retrospective accounts of childhood sexual abuse and current psychological functioning: A cross-cultural comparison.* Unpublished manuscript.

Nirje, B. (1969). The normalization principle and its human management implications. In R. Kugel & W. Woltensberger (Eds.), *Changing patterns in residential services for the mentally retarded.* Washington, DC: President's Committee on Mental Retardation.

Noethen, M., Schulte-Koerne, G., Grimm, T., Cichon, S., & Vogt, I. (1999). Genetic linkage analysis with dyslexia: Evidence for linkage of spelling disability to chromosome 15. *European Child and Adolescent Psychiatry, 8,* 56–59.

Noh, S., Dumas, J. E., Wolf, L. C., & Fisman, S. N. (1989). Delineating sources of stress in parents of exceptional children. *Family Relations, 38,* 456–461.

Nolen-Hoeksema, S., Girgus, J. S., & Seligman, M. E. P. (1992). Predictors and consequences of childhood depressive symptoms: A 5-year longitudinal study. *Journal of Abnormal Psychology, 101,* 405–422.

Nordentoft, M., Kou, H. C., Hansen, D., Nim, J., Pryds, O., Rubin, P., & Hemmingsen, R. (1996). Intrauterine growth retardation and premature delivery: The influence of maternal smoking and psychosocial factors. *American Journal of Public Health, 86,* 347–354.

Northam, E., Anderson, P., Adler, R., Werther, G., & Warne, G. (1996). Psychosocial and family functioning in children with insulin-dependent diabetes at diagnosis and one year later. *Journal of Pediatric Psychology, 21,* 699–717.

Obese? Renegade gene seems to tip the scales. (1994, Dec. 2). *International Herald Tribune,* p. 1.

Oates, R. K., & Bross, D. C. (1995). What have we learned about treating child physical abuse? A literature review of the last decade. *Child Abuse & Neglect, 19,* 463–473.

O'Dea, J. A., & Abraham, S. (2000). Improving the body image, eating attitudes, and behaviors of young male and female adolescents: A new educational approach that focuses on self-esteem. *International Journal of Eating Disorders, 28,* 43–57.

O'Donnell, C. R. (1995). Firearm deaths among children and youth. *American Psychologist, 50,* 771–776.

Offord, D. R., Alder, R. J., & Boyle, M. H. (1986). Prevalence and sociodemographic correlates of conduct disorder. *American Journal of Social Psychiatry, 6,* 272–278.

Ohara, K., Suzuki, Y., Ochiai, M., Yoshida, K., & Ohara, K. (1999). Age of onset anticipation in anxiety disorders. *Psychiatry Research, 89,* 215–221.

Olafson, E., Corwin, D. L., & Summit, R. C. (1993). Modern history of child sexual abuse awareness: Cycles of discovery and suppression. *Child Abuse & Neglect, 17,* 7–24.

Olds, D. (1997).The prenatal early infancy project: Preventing child abuse and neglect in the context of promoting maternal and child health. In D. A. Wolfe & R. J. McMahon (Eds.), *Child abuse: New directions in prevention and treatment across the lifespan* (pp. 130–154). Thousand Oaks, CA: Sage.

Olin, S. S., & Mednick, S. A. (1996). Risk factors of psychosis: Identifying vulnerable populations premorbidly. *Schizophrenia Bulletin, 22,* 223–240.

Oliver, J. E. (1993). Intergenerational transmission of child abuse: Rates, research, and clinical implications. *American Journal of Psychiatry, 150,* 1315–1324.

Ollendick, T. H. (1995). Cognitive behavioral treatment of panic disorder with agoraphobia in adolescents: A multiple baseline design analysis. *Behavior Therapy, 26,* 517–531.

Ollendick, T. H., Hagopian, L. P., & King, N. J. (1997). Specific phobias in children. In G. C. L. Davey (Ed.), *Phobias: A handbook of theory, research, and treatment* (pp. 201–224). New York: Wiley.

Ollendick, T. H., Yang, B., King, N. J., Dong, Q., & Akande, A. (1996). Fears in American, Australian, Chinese, and Nigerian children and adolescents: A cross-cultural study. *Journal of Child Psychology and Psychiatry, 37,* 213–220.

Olson, S. L., Bates, J. E., Sandy, J. M., & Lanthier, R. (2000). Early developmental precursors of externalizing behavior in middle childhood and adolescence. *Journal of Abnormal Child Psychology, 28,* 119–133.

Ondersma, S. J., & Walker, C. E. (1998). Elimination disorders. In T. Ollendick & M. Hersen (Eds.), *Handbook of child psychopathology* (pp. 355–378). New York: Plenum.

Oppel, W. C., Harper, P. A., & Rider, R. V. (1968). Social psychological and neurological factors associated with nocturnal enuresis. *Pediatrics, 42,* 627–641.

Ornduff, S. R. (2000). Childhood maltreatment and malevolence: Quantitative research findings. *Clinical Psychology Review, 20,* 997–1018.

Orton, S. (1937). *Reading, writing, and speech problems in children: A presentation of some types of disorders in the development of the language faculty.* New York: Norton.

Ozols, E. J., & Rourke, B. P. (1988). Characteristics of young learning-disabled children classified according to patterns of academic achievement: Auditory-perceptual and visual-perceptual abilities. *Journal of Clinical Child Psychology, 17,* 44–52.

Ozonoff, S., Rogers, S. J., & Pennington, B. F. (1991). Asperger's syndrome: Evidence of an empirical distinction from high-functioning autism. *Journal of Child Psychology and Psychiatry, 32,* 1107–1122.

Pain, J., Barrier, E., & Robin, D. (1997). *Violences à l'école: Allemagne, Angleterre, France.* Paris: Matrice.

Parks, G. (2000). The High/Scope Perry Preschool Project. *Juvenile Justice Bulletin* (NCJ 181725). Washington, DC: U.S. Department of Justice, Office of Juvenile Justice and Delinquency Prevention.

Parry-Jones, W. L. (1995). Historical aspects of mood and its disorders in young people. In I. M. Goodyer (Ed.), *The depressed child and adolescent: Developmental and clinical perspectives* (pp. 1–25). Cambridge, UK: Cambridge University Press.

Patterson, G. R. (1982). *Coercive Family Process.* Eugene, OR: Castalia.

Patterson, G. R., Reid, J. B., & Dishion, T. J. (1992). *Antisocial Boys.* Eugene, OR: Castalia.

Patton, G. C., Johnson-Sabine, E., Wood, K., Mann, A. H., & Wakeling, A. (1990). Abnormal eating attitudes in London school girls—A prospective epidemiological study: Outcome at twelve-month follow-up. *Psychological Medicine, 20,* 383–394.

Pelham, W. E., Gnagy, E. M., Greenslade, K., & Milich, R. (1992). Teacher ratings of DSM-III-R symptoms for the disruptive behavior disorders. *Journal of the American Academy of Child and Adolescent Psychiatry, 31,* 210–218.

Pelham, W. E., Greiner, A. R., Gnagy, E. M., Hoza, B., Martin, L., Sams, S. E., & Wilson, T. (1996). A summer treatment program for children with ADHD. In M. Roberts & A. La Greca (Eds.), *Model programs for service delivery for child and family mental health* (pp. 193–212). Hillsdale, NJ: Erlbaum.

Pelham, W. E., Lang, A. R., Atkeson, B., Murphy, D. A., Gnagy, E. M., Greiner, A. R., Vodde-Hamilton, M., & Greenslade, K. E. (1997). Effects of deviant child behavior on parental distress and alcohol consumption in laboratory interactions. *Journal of Abnormal Child Psychology, 25,* 413–424.

Pelham, W. E., & Waschbusch, D. A. (1999). Behavioral intervention in attention-deficit/hyperactivity disorder. In H. E. Quay & A. E. Hogan (Eds.), *Handbook of disruptive behavior disorders* (pp. 255–278). New York: Kluwer Academic.

Peltzer, K., & Taiwo, O. (1993). Enuresis in a population of Nigerian children. *Journal of Psychology in Africa, 1,* 136–150.

Pennington, B. F. (1999). Toward an integrated understanding of dyslexia: Genetic, neurological, and cognitive mechanisms. *Development and Psychopathology, 11,* 629–654.

Pennington, B. F., Groisser, D., & Welsh, M. C. (1993). Contrasting cognitive deficits in attention deficit hyperactivity disorder versus reading disability. *Developmental Psychology, 29,* 511–523.

Pennington, B. F., & Ozonoff, S. (1996). Executive functions and developmental psychopathology. *Journal of Child Psychology and Psychiatry, 37,* 51–87.

Pereira-Laird, J., Deane, F., & Bunnell, J. (1999). Defining reading disability using a multifaceted approach. *Learning Disability Quarterly, 22,* 59–71.

Petersen, A. C., Compas, B. E., Brooks Gunn, J., Stemmler, M., Ey, S., & Grant, K. E. (1993). Depression in adolescence. *American Psychologist, 48,* 155–168.

Peterson, C., & Mitchell, J. (1999). Psychosocial and pharmacological treatment of eating disorders: A review of research findings. *Journal of Clinical Psychology, 55,* 685–697.

Pfeffer, C. R., Lipkins, R., Plutchik, R., & Mizruchi, M. S. (1988). Normal children at risk for suicidal behavior: A two-year follow-up study. *Journal of the American Academy of Child and Adolescent Psychiatry, 27,* 34–41.

Piaget, J., & Inhelder, B. (1969). *The psychology of the child.* New York: Basic Books.

Pierce, W. D., & Epling, W. F. (1999). *Behavior analysis and learning* (2nd ed.). Upper Saddle River, NJ: Prentice Hall.

Pinderhughes, E. E., Dodge, K. A., Bates, J. E., Pettit, G. S., & Zelli, A. (2000). Discipline responses: Influences of parents' socioeconomic status, ethnicity, beliefs about parenting, stress, and cognitive-emotional processes. *Journal of Family Psychology, 14,* 380–400.

Pine, D. S., Cohen, P., Gurley, D., Brook, J., & Ma, Y. (1998). The risk for early-adulthood anxiety and depressive disorders in adolescents with anxiety and depressive disorders. *Archives of General Psychiatry, 55,* 56–64.

Pineda, D., Ardila, A., Rosselli, M., Arias, B. E., Henao, G. C., Gomez, L. F., Mejia, S. E., & Miranda, M. L. (1999). Prevalence of attention-deficit/hyperactivity disorder symptoms in 4- to 17-year-old children in the general population. *Journal of Abnormal Child Psychology, 27,* 455–462.

Pliszka, S. R. (2000). Patterns of psychiatric comorbidity with attention-deficit/hyperactivity disorder. *Child and Adolescent Psychiatric Clinics of North America, 9,* 525–540.

Pliszka, S. R., Liotti, M., & Woldorff, M. G. (2000). Inhibitory control in children with attention-deficit/hyperactivity disorder: Event-related potentials identify the processing component and timing of an impaired right-frontal response-inhibition mechanism. *Biological Psychiatry, 48,* 238–246.

Pliszka, S., Sherman, J., Barrow, M., & Irick, S. (2000). Affective disorder in juvenile offenders: A preliminary study. *American Journal of Psychiatry, 157,* 130–132.

Plomin, R., Fulker, D. W., Corley, R., & DeFries, J. C. (1997). Nature, nurture, and cognitive development from 1 to 16 years: A parent offspring adoption study. *Psychological Science, 8,* 442–447.

Polloway, E. A., Schewel, R., & Patton, J. R. (1992). Learning disabilities in adulthood: Personal perspectives. *Journal of Learning Disabilities, 25,* 520–522.

Pope, H. G., Mangweth, B., Negrao, A. B., Hudson, J. I., & Cordas, T. A. (1994). Childhood sexual abuse and bulimia nervosa: A comparison of American, Austrian, and Brazilian women. *American Journal of Psychiatry, 147,* 871–875.

Powers, P. S. (1997). Management of patients with comorbid medical conditions. In D. Garner & P. E. Garfinkel (Eds.), *Handbook of treatment for eating disorders* (2nd ed., pp. 424–436). New York: Guilford.

Powers, S. W. (1999). Empirically supported treatments in pediatric psychology: Procedure-related pain. *Journal of Pediatric Psychology, 24,* 131–145.

Prendergast, M., Taylor, E., Rapoport, J. L., Bartko, J., Donnelly, M., Zametkin, A., Ahearn, M. B., Dunn, G., & Wieselberg, H. M. (1988). The diagnosis of childhood hyperactivity: A U.S.–U.K. cross-national study of DSM-III and ICD-9. *Journal of Child Psychology and Psychiatry, 29,* 289–300.

Prior, M., Smart, D., Sanson, A., & Oberklaid, F. (2000). Does shy-inhibited temperament in childhood lead to anxiety problems in adolescence? *Journal of the American Academy of Child and Adolescent Psychiatry, 39,* 461–468.

Pry, P. (1998). Composantes cognitive et comportementale dans le trouble "Déficit attentionnel/hyperactivité" chez l'enfant de 7 ans. *Neuropsychiatrie de l'enfance et de l'adolescence, 46,* 94–101.

Pugh, K. R., Mencl, W. E., Shaywitz, B. A., Shaywitz, S. E., Fulbright, R. K., Constable, R. T., Skudlarski, P., Marchione, K. E., Jenner, A. R., Fletcher, J. M., Liberman, A. M., Shankweiler, D. P., Katz, L., Lacadie, C., & Gore, J. C. (2000). The angular gyrus in developmental dyslexia: Task-specific differences in functional connectivity within posterior cortex. *Psychological Science, 11,* 51–56.

Putnam, F. W., & Trickett, P. K. (1993). *Cortisol abnormalities in sexually abused girls.* Paper presented at annual meeting of the American Psychological Society, Washington, DC.

Puzzanchera, C. M. (2000). Self-reported delinquency by 12-year-olds, 1997. *Office of Juvenile Justice and Delinquency Prevention Fact Sheet* (FS 200003). Washington, DC: U.S. Department of Justice, Office of Justice Programs.

Quay, H. C. (1987). Patterns of delinquent behavior. In H. C. Quay (Ed.), *Handbook of juvenile delinquency* (pp. 118–138). New York: Wiley.

Quay, H. C. (1993). The psychobiology of undersocialized aggressive conduct disorder: A theoretical perspective. *Development and Psychopathology, 5,* 165–180.

Quay, H. C. (1997). Inhibition and attention deficit hyperactivity disorder. *Journal of Abnormal Child Psychology, 25,* 7–13.

Raffi, A. R., Rondini, M., Grandi, S., & Fava, G. A. (2000). Life events and prodromal symptoms in bulimia nervosa. *Psychological Medicine, 30,* 727–731.

Raim, J. (1982). *Case reports in reading and learning disabilities.* Springfield, IL: Charles C. Thomas.

Ramey, C. T., Campbell, F. A., Burchinal, M., Skinner, M. L., Gardner, D. M., & Ramey, S. L. (2000). Persistent effects of early childhood education on high-risk children and their mothers. *Applied Developmental Science, 4,* 2–14.

Ramey, C. T., & Ramey, S. L. (1998). Prevention of intellectual disabilities: Early interventions to improve cognitive development. *Preventive Medicine, 27,* 224–232.

Ramey, S. L., & Ramey, C. T. (1992). Early educational intervention with disadvantaged children: To what effect? *Applied and Preventive Psychology, 1,* 131–140.

Rao, U., Hammen, C., & Daley, S. E. (1999). Continuity of depression during the transition to adulthood: A 5-year longitudinal study of young women. *Journal of the American Academy of Child and Adolescent Psychiatry, 38,* 908–915.

Rao, U., Weissman, M. M., Martin, J. A., & Hammond, R. W. (1993). Childhood depression and risk of suicide: A preliminary report of a longitudinal study. *Journal of the American Academy of Child and Adolescent Psychiatry, 32,* 21–27.

Reinherz, H. Z., Stewart-Berghauer, G., Pakiz, B., Frost, A. K., Moeykens, B. A., & Holmes, W. M. (1989). The relationship of early risk and current mediators to depressive symptomatology in adolescence. *Journal of the American Academy of Child and Adolescent Psychiatry, 28,* 942–947.

Remschmidt, H. E., Schulz, E., Martin, M., Warnke, A., & Trott, G.-E. (1994). Childhood-onset schizophrenia: History of the concept and recent studies. *Schizophrenia Bulletin, 20,* 727–745.

Rende, R., & Plomin, R. (1995). Nature, nurture, and the development of psychopathology. In D. Cicchetti & D. J. Cohen (Eds.), *Developmental psychopathology: Vol. 1. Theory and methods* (pp. 291–314). New York: Wiley.

Research Unit on Pediatric Psychopharmacology Anxiety Study Group (2001). Fluvoxamine for the treatment of anxiety disorders in children and adolescents. *New UK Journal of Medicine, 344,* 1279–1285.

Rey, J. M. (1993). Oppositional defiant disorder. *American Journal of Psychiatry, 150,* 1769–1778.

Richters, J. E., & Martinez, P. (1993). The NIMH Community Violence Project: I. Children as victims of and witnesses to violence. *Psychiatry, 56,* 7–21.

Rief, W., & Hiller, W. (1998). Somatization—Future perspectives on a common phenomenon. *Journal of Psychosomatic Research, 44,* 529–536.

440   *References*

Ries, L. A. G. (2001). *Childhood cancer mortality.* (Seer Pediatric Monograph, No. 14.) Washington, DC: National Cancer Institute.

Rimland, B. (1964). *Infantile autism: The syndrome and its implications for a neural theory of behavior.* New York: Appleton-Century-Crofts.

Roberts, M., LaGreca, A., & Harper, D. (1988). Journal of pediatric psychology: Another stage of development. *Journal of Pediatric Psychology, 13,* 1–5.

Roberts, R. E., Lewinsohn, P. M., & Seeley, J. R. (1995). Symptoms of DSM-III-R major depression in adolescence: Evidence from an epidemiologic survey. *Journal of the American Academy of Child and Adolescent Psychiatry, 34,* 1608–1617.

Robin, A. L., Gilroy, M., & Dennis, A. B. (1998). Treatment of eating disorders in children and adolescents. *Clinical Psychology Review, 18,* 421–446.

Robin, A. L., Siegel, P. T., Moye, A. W., Gilroy, M., Dennis, A. B., & Sikund, A. (1999). A controlled comparison of family versus individual therapy for adolescents with anorexia nervosa. *Journal of the American Academy of Child and Adolescent Psychiatry, 38,* 1482–1489.

Robins, L. N. (1966). *Deviant children grown up: A sociological and psychiatric study of sociopathic personality.* Baltimore: Williams and Wilkins.

Robinson, J. O., & Granfield, A. J. (1986). The frequent consulter in primary medical care. *Journal of Psychosomatic Research, 30,* 589–600.

Rodier, P. M. (2000). The early origins of autism. *Scientific American, 282,* 56–63.

Rogers, S. J. (1998). Empirically supported comprehensive treatments for young children with autism. *Journal of Clinical Child Psychology, 27,* 168–179.

Rona, R. J., Li, L., & Chinn, S. (1997). Determinants of nocturnal enuresis in UK and Scotland in the '90s. *Developmental Medicine and Child Neurology, 39,* 677–681.

Rosen, J. C., Leitenberg, H., Fisher, C., & Khazam, C. (1986). Binge-eating episodes in bulimia nervosa: The amount and type of food consumed. *International Journal of Eating Disorders, 5,* 255–267.

Rosenbaum, J. F., Biederman, J., Bolduc, E. A., Hirshfield, D. R., Faraone, S. V., & Kagan, J. (1992). Comorbidity of parental anxiety disorders as risk for childhood-onset anxiety in inhibited children. *American Journal of Psychiatry, 149,* 475–481.

Rosenbaum, J. F., Biederman, J., Hirshfield, D. R., Bolduc, E. A., Faraone, S. V., Kagan, J., Snidman, N., & Reznick, J. S. (1991). Further evidence of an association between behavioral inhibition and anxiety disorders: Results from a family study of children from a non-clinical sample. *Journal of Psychiatric Research, 25,* 49–65.

Ross, R. T., Begab, M. J., Dondis, E. H., Giampiccolo, J., & Meyers, C. E. (1985). *Lives of the retarded: A forty-year follow-up study.* Stanford, CA: Stanford University Press.

Rothbart, M. K., & Bates, J. E. (1998). Temperament. In W. Damon & N. Eisenberg (Eds.), *Handbook of child psychology: Social, emotional, and personality development* (Vol. 3, pp. 105–176). New York: Wiley.

Rothbart, M. K., & Mauro, J. A. (1990). Questionnaire approaches to the study of infant temperament. In J. W. Fagen & J. Colombo (Eds.), *Individual differences in infancy: Reliability, stability, and prediction* (pp. 411–429). Hillsdale, NJ: Erlbaum.

Rothstein, A. (1981). Hallucinatory phenomena in childhood. *Journal of the American Academy of Child Psychiatry, 20,* 623–635.

Rourke, B. P. (Ed.) (1995). *Syndrome of nonverbal learning disabilities: Neurodevelopmental expressions.* New York: Guilford.

Rovet, J. F., Ehrlich, R. M., Czuchta, D., & Akler, M. (1993). Psychoeducational characteristics of children and adolescents with insulin-dependent diabetes mellitus. *Journal of Learning Disabilities, 26,* 7–22.

Rowe, E., & Eckenrode, J. (1999). The timing and academic difficulties among maltreated and nonmaltreated children. *Child Abuse & Neglect, 23,* 813–832.

Rowland, A. S., Umbach, D. M., Stallone, L., Naftel, J., Bohlig, E. M., & Sandler, D. P. (2001). Prevalence of medication treatment for attention deficit/hyperactivity disorder among elementary school children in Johnston County, North Carolina. *American Journal of Public Health, 92,* 231–234.

Rudolph, K. D., Hammen, C., & Burge, D. (1994). Interpersonal functioning and depressive symptoms in childhood: Addressing the issues of specificity and comorbidity. *Journal of Abnormal Child Psychology, 22,* 355–371.

Russell, A. T. (1994). The clinical presentation of childhood-onset schizophrenia. *Schizophrenia Bulletin, 20,* 631–646.

Russell, A. T., Bott, L., & Sammons, C. (1989). The phenomenology of schizophrenia occurring in childhood. *Journal of the American Academy of Child and Adolescent Psychiatry, 28,* 399–407.

Russell, G. (1979). Bulimia nervosa: An ominous variant of anorexia nervosa. *Psychological Medicine, 9,* 429–448.

Russell, G. F. M. (1995). Anorexia nervosa through time. In G. I. Szmukler, C. Dare, and J. Treasure (Eds.), *Handbook of eating disorders: Theory, treatment and research* (pp. 5–17). Chichester, UK: Wiley.

Russo, M. F., & Beidel, D. C. (1994). Comorbidity of childhood anxiety and externalizing disorders: Prevalence, associated characteristics, and validation issues. *Clinical Psychology Review, 14,* 199–221.

Rutter, M. (1972). Childhood schizophrenia reconsidered. *Journal of Autism and Childhood Schizophrenia, 2,* 315–337.

Rutter, M. (1978). Diagnosis and definition. In M. Rutter & E. Schopler (Eds.), *Autism: A reappraisal of concepts and treatment* (pp. 1–25). New York: Plenum.

Rutter, M. (2000). Genetic studies of autism: From the 1970s into the millennium. *Journal of Abnormal Child Psychology, 28,* 3–14.

Rutter, M., & Bartak, L. (1973). Special educational treatment of autistic children: A comparative study: II. Follow-up findings and implications for services. *Journal of Child Psychology and Psychiatry, 14,* 241–270.

Rutter, M., Greenfeld, D., & Lockyer, L. (1967). A five to fifteen year follow-up study of childhood-onset psychosis: II. Social and behavioral outcome. *British Journal of Psychiatry, 113,* 1183–1199.

Rutter, M., Macdonald, H., Le Couteur, A., Harrington, R., Bolton, P., & Bailey, A. (1990). Genetic factors in child psychiatric disorders: II. Empirical findings. *Journal of Child Psychology and Psychiatry, 31,* 39–83.

Rutter, M., & Schopler, E. (1992). Classification of pervasive developmental disorders: Some concepts and practical considerations. *Journal of Autism and Developmental Disorders, 22,* 459–482.

Ryan, N. D., Puig-Antich, J., Ambrosini, P., Rabinovich, H., Robinson, D., Nelson, B., Iyengar, S., & Twomey, J. (1987). The clinical picture of major depression in children and adolescents. *Archives of General Psychiatry, 44,* 854–861.

Ryan, N. D., Williamson, D. E., Iyengar, S., Orvaschel, H., Reich, T., Dahl, R. E., & Puig-Antich, J. (1992). A secular increase in child and adolescent onset affective disorder. *Journal of the American Academy of Child and Adolescent Psychiatry, 31,* 600–605.

Sabbagh, M. A., & Taylor, M. (2000). Neural correlates of theory-of-mind reasoning: An event-related potential study. *Psychological Science, 11,* 46–50.

Safer, D. J. (1997). Changing patterns of psychotropic medications by child psychiatrists in the 1990s. *Journal of Child and Adolescent Psychopharmacology, 7,* 267–274.

Salbreux, R., & d'Anthenaise, M. (1982). Prévalence de la déficience mentale suivant les pays et les époques: Revue de la littérature. In M. Manciaux (Ed.), *Child health and development: Vol. 1. Handicaps in childhood* (pp. 53–72). Basel: Karger.

Sandler, A. D., Sutton, K. A., DeWeese, J., Girardi, M. A., Sheppard, V., & Bodfish, J. W. (1999). Lack of benefit of a single dose of synthetic human secretin in the treatment of autism and pervasive developmental disorder. *New UK Journal of Medicine, 341,* 1801–1806.

Sanson, A., Smart, D., Prior, M., & Oberklaid, F. (1993). Precursors of hyperactivity and aggression. *Journal of the American Academy of Child and Adolescent Psychiatry, 32,* 1207–1216.

Sapolsky, R. M. (1994). Contemplating navels as a moral failing. *ADVANCES: The Journal of Mind-Body Health, 10,* 35–39.

Sartorius, N., Jablensky, A., Ernberg, G., Leff, J., & Gulbinat, W. (1987). Course of schizophrenia in different countries: Some results of a WHO international comparative 5-year follow-up study. In H. Hafner, W. F. Gattaz, & W. Janzarik (Eds.), *Search for the causes of schizophrenia* (Vol. 1, pp. 107–113). Berlin: Springer-Verlag.

Sattler, J. M. (1992). *Assessment of children. Revised and updated third edition.* San Diego, CA: Jerome M. Sattler, Publishers.

Schachar, R. J., Mota, V. L., Logan, G. D., Tannock, R., & Klim, P. (2000). Confirmation of an inhibitory control deficit in attention-deficit/hyperactivity disorder. *Journal of Abnormal Child Psychology, 28,* 227–235.

Schachar, R. J., Tannock, R., & Logan, G. D. (1993). Inhibitory control in normal development and childhood psychopathology. *Developmental Psychology, 26,* 710–720.

Schaefer, C. E. (1979). *Childhood encopresis and enuresis.* New York: Van Nostrand Reinhold.

Scheerenberger, R. C. (1983). *A history of mental retardation.* Baltimore: Brookes Publishing Co.

Schlundt, D. G., & Johnson, W. G. (1990). *Eating disorders: Assessment and treatment.* Boston: Allyn & Bacon.

Schopler, E. (1998). Prevention and management of behavior problems: The TEACCH approach. In E. Sanavio (Ed.), *Behavior and cognitive therapy today: Essays in honor of Hans J. Eysenck* (pp. 249–259). New York: Elsevier Science.

Schore, A. N. (1996). The experience-dependent maturation of a regulatory system in the orbital prefrontal cortex and the origin of developmental psychopathology. *Developmental Psychopathology, 8,* 59–87.

Schreibman, L., & Charlop, M. H. (1989). Infantile autism. In T. H. Ollendick & M. Hersen (Eds.), *Handbook of child psychopathology* (2nd ed., pp. 105–129). New York: Plenum.

Schulterbrand, J. G., &. Raskin, A. (1977). *Depression in childhood: Diagnosis, treatment and conceptual models.* New York: Raven Press.

Schwartz, D., & Proctor, L. J. (2000). Community violence exposure and children's social adjustment in the school peer group: The mediating roles of emotion regulation and social cognition. *Journal of Consulting and Clinical Psychology, 68,* 670–683.

Schwarz, J. (1992). *Another door to learning: True stories of learning disabled children and adults, and the keys to their success.* New York: Crossroad.

Schweinhart, L. J., & Weikart, D. P. (1997). *Lasting differences: The High/Scope preschool curriculum comparison study through age 23.* (Monograph of the High/Scope Educational Research Foundation, No. 12.) Ypsilanti, MI: High/Scope Press.

Seeley, J. R., Lewinsohn, P. M., & Rohde, P. (1997, June). *Comorbidity between conduct disorder and major depression during adolescence: Impact on phenomenology, associated clinical characteristics, and continuity into young adulthood.* Paper presented at the meeting of the International Society for Research in Child and Adolescent Psychopathology, Paris.

Seligman, L. M., & Ollendick, T. H. (1998). Comorbidity of anxiety and depression in children and adolescents: An integrative review. *Clinical Child and Family Psychology Review, 1,* 125–144.

Seligman, M. E. P. (1975). *Helplessness: On depression, development, and death.* San Francisco: W. H. Freeman.

Serketich, W. J., & Dumas, J. E. (1996). The effectiveness of behavioral parent training to modify antisocial behavior in children: A meta-analysis. *Behavior Therapy, 27,* 171–186.

Serpell, R. (2000). Intelligence and culture. In R. J. Sternberg (Ed.), *Handbook of intelligence* (pp. 549–577). New York: Cambridge University Press.

Shannon, M. P., Lonigan, C. J., Finch, A. J., & Taylor, C. M. (1994). Children exposed to disaster: I. Epidemiology of posttraumatic symptoms and symptom profiles. *Journal of the American Academy of Child and Adolescent Psychiatry, 33,* 80–93.

Shapiro, E. S., & Lentz, F. E. (1991). Vocational-technical programs: Follow-up of students with learning disabilities. *Exceptional Children, 58,* 47–59.

Shaw, C. R. (1931). *The natural history of a delinquent career.* Chicago: University of Chicago Press.

Shaw, D. S., Vondra, J. I., Hommerding, K. D., Keenan, K., & Dunn, M. (1994). Chronic family adversity and early child behavior problems: A longitudinal study of low income families. *Journal of Child Psychology and Psychiatry, 35,* 1109–1122.

Shaywitz, B. A., Fletcher, J. M., Holahan, J. M., & Shaywitz, S. E. (1992). Discrepancy compared to low achievement definitions of reading disability: Results of the Connecticut longitudinal study. *Journal of Learning Disabilities, 25,* 639–648.

Shaywitz, S. E., Escobar, M. D., Shaywitz, B. A., & Fletcher, J. M. (1990). Prevalence of reading disabilities in boys and girls: Results of the Connecticut longitudinal study. *Journal of the American Medical Association, 264,* 998–1002.

Shaywitz, S. E., Escobar, M. D., Shaywitz, B. A., Fletcher, J. M., & Makuch, R. (1992). Evidence that dyslexia may represent the lower tail of a normal distribution of reading ability. *New England Journal of Medicine, 326,* 145–150.

Sheeber, L., Allen, N., Davis, B., & Sorensen, E. (2000). Regulation of negative affect during mother-child problem-solving interactions: Adolescent depressive status and family processes. *Journal of Abnormal Child Psychology, 28,* 467–479.

Sheeber, L., Hops, H., Andrews, J., Alpert, T., & Davis, B. (1998). Interactional processes in families with depressed and nondepressed adolescents: Reinforcement of depressive behavior. *Behaviour Research and Therapy, 36,* 417–427.

Sheeber, L., Hops, H., & Davis, B. (2001). Family processes in adolescent depression. *Clinical Child and Family Psychology Review, 4,* 19–35.

Shen, Y. C., Wang, Y. F., & Yang, X. L. (1985). An epidemiological investigation of minimal brain dysfunction in six elementary schools in Beijing. *Journal of Child Psychology and Psychiatry, 26,* 777–787.

Sherman, M., & Hertzig, M. E. (1991). Prescribing practices of Ritalin: The Suffolk County, New York study. In L. L. Greenhill & B. B. Osman (Eds.), *Ritalin: Theory and patient management* (pp. 187–193). New York: Liebet.

Shipman, K., Zeman, J., Penza, S., & Champion, K. (2000). Emotion management skills in sexually maltreated and nonmaltreated girls: A developmental psychopathology perspective. *Development and Psychopathology, 12,* 47–62.

Shochet, I. M., Dadds, M. R., Holland, D., Whitefield, K., Harnett, P. H., & Osgarby, S. M. (2001). The efficacy of a universal school-based program to prevent adolescent depression. *Journal of Clinical Child Psychology, 30,* 303–315.

Shortt, A. L., Barrett, P. M., & Fox, T. L. (2001). Evaluating the FRIENDS program: A cognitive-behavioral group treatment for anxious children and their parents. *Journal of Clinical Child Psychology, 30,* 525–535.

Shue, K. L., & Douglas, V. I. (1992). Attention-deficit hyperactivity disorder and the frontal lobe syndrome. *Brain and Cognition, 20,* 104–124.

Siegel, B., Pilner, C., Eschler, J., & Elliot, G. R. (1988). How children with autism are diagnosed: Difficulties in identification of children with multiple developmental delays. *Development and Behavioral Pediatrics, 9,* 199–204.

Siegel, L. S. (1989). IQ is irrelevant to the definition of learning disabilities. *Journal of Learning Disabilities, 22,* 469–486.

Siegel, P. T., & Howard, F. (2001). Munchausen by proxy syndrome: Barriers to detection, confirmation, and intervention. *Children's Services: Social Policy, Research, and Practice, 4,* 31–50.

Sigman, M., & Mundy, P. (1989). Social attachments in autistic children. *Journal of the American Academy of Child and Adolescent Psychiatry, 28,* 74–81.

Silva, R. R., Matzner, F., Diaz, J., Singh, S., & Dummit, E. S. (1999). Bipolar disorder in children and adolescents: A guide to diagnosis and treatment. *CNS Drugs, 12,* 437–450.

Silverman, W. K., Kurtines, W. M., Ginsburg, G. S., Weems, C. G., Lumpkin, P. W., & Carmichael, D. H. (1999). Treating anxiety disorders in children with group cognitive behavioral therapy: A randomized clinical trial. *Journal of Consulting and Clinical Psychology, 67,* 995–1003.

Silverman, W. K., & Rabian, B. (1993). Simple phobias. *Child and Adolescent Psychiatric Clinics of North America, 2,* 603–622.

Silverman, W. K., & Weems, C. F. (1999). Anxiety sensitivity in children. In S. Taylor (Ed.), *Anxiety sensitivity: Theory, research, and treatment of the fear of anxiety* (pp. 239–268). Mahwah, NJ: Erlbaum.

Silverstein, B., Perdue, L., Peterson, B., & Kelly, E. (1986). The role of mass media in promoting a thin standard of bodily attractiveness for women. *Sex Roles, 14,* 519–532.

Simner, L. M (1991). Estimating a child's learning potential from form errors in a child's printing. In J. Wann, A. M. Wing, & N. Sõvik (Eds.), *Development of graphic skills:*

Research perspectives and educational implications (pp. 205–222). London: Academic Press.

Simner, L. M. (1996). The use of handwriting legibility scales in grade one to help identify children at risk of early school failure. In M. L. Simner, C. G. Leedham, & A. J. W. M. Thomassen (Eds.), *Handwriting and drawing research: Basic and applied issues* (pp. 197–202). Toronto: IOS Press.

Simner, L. M., & Barnes, M. J. (1991). Relationship between first-grade marks and the high school dropout problem. *Journal of School Psychology, 29,* 331–335.

Simon, G. E. (1991). Somatization and psychiatric disorders. In L. J. Kirmayer & J. Robbins (Eds.), *Current concepts of somatization: Research and clinical perspectives. Progress in psychiatry* (pp. 37–62). Washington, DC: American Psychiatric Press.

Smalley, S. L. (1991). Genetic influences in autism. *Psychiatric Clinics of North America, 14,* 125–139.

Smeets, M., Ingleby, J., Hoek, H., & Panhuysen, G. (1999). Body size perception in anorexia nervosa: A signal detection approach. *Journal of Psychosomatic Research, 46,* 465–477.

Smetana, J. G., Daddis, C., Toth, S. L., Cicchetti, D., Bruce, J., & Kane, P. (1999). Effects of provocation on maltreated and nonmaltreated preschoolers' understanding of moral transgression. *Social Development, 8,* 335–348.

Smith, B. H., Waschbusch, D. A., Willoughby, M. T., & Evans, S. (2000). The efficacy, safety, and practicality of treatments for adolescents with attention-deficit/hyperactivity disorder (ADHD). *Clinical Child and Family Psychology Review, 3,* 243–267.

Smith, G. R., Monson, R. A., & Ray, D. C. (1986). Psychiatric consultation in somatization disorder: A randomized controlled study. *New England Journal of Medicine, 314,* 1407–1413.

Smith, J. E., & Krejci, J. (1991). Minorities join the majority: Eating disturbances among Hispanic and Native American youth. *International Journal of Eating Disorders, 10,* 179–186.

Smith, T., Buch, G. A., & Gamby, T. E. (2000). Parent-directed intensive early intervention with pervasive developmental disorder. *Research in Developmental Disabilities, 21,* 297–309.

Smithmyer, C. M., Hubbard, J. A., & Simons, R. F. (2000). Proactive and reactive aggression in delinquent adolescents: Relations to aggression outcome expectancies. *Journal of Clinical Child Psychology, 29,* 86–93.

Snodgrass, S. R. (1994). Cocaine babies: A result of multiple teratogenic influences. *Journal of Child Neurology, 9,* 227–233.

Sonnander, K., Emanuelsson, I., & Kebbon, L. (1993). Pupils with mild mental retardation in regular Swedish schools: Prevalence, objective characteristics, and subjective evaluations. *American Journal on Mental Retardation, 97,* 692–701.

Sparrow, S. S., Balla, D. A., & Cicchetti, D. V. (1984). *Vineland Adaptive Behavior Scales.* Circle Pines, MN: American Guidance Service.

Spence, S. H., Donovan, C., & Brechman-Toussaint, M. (1999). Social skills, social outcomes, and cognitive features of childhood social phobia. *Journal of Abnormal Psychology, 108,* 211–221.

Spencer, E. K., & Campbell, M. (1994). Schizophrenic children: Diagnosis, phenomenology, and pharmacotherapy. *Schizophrenia Bulletin, 20,* 713–726.

Spierings, C., Poels, P. J., Sijben, N., Gabreels, F. J., & Reiner, W. O. (1990). Conversion disorders in childhood: A retrospective follow-up study of 84 inpatients. *Developmental Medicine and Child Neurology, 32,* 865–871.

Spitzer, R. L., Davies, M., & Barkley, R. A. (1990). The DSM-III-R field trial of disruptive behavior disorders. *Journal of the American Academy of Child and Adolescent Psychiatry, 29,* 690–697.

Spreen, O. (2001). Learning disabilities and their neurological foundations, theories, and subtypes. In A. S. Kaufman & N. L. Kaufman (Eds.), *Specific learning disabilities and difficulties in children and adolescents: Psychological assessment and evaluation* (pp. 283–308). New York: Cambridge University Press.

Sprich-Buckminster, S., Biederman, J., Milberger, S., Faraone, S. V., & Lehman, B. K. (1993). Are perinatal complications relevant to the manifestation of ADD? Issues of comorbidity and familiality. *Journal of the American Academy of Child and Adolescent Psychiatry, 32,* 1032–1037.

Sroufe, L. A. (1997). Psychopathology as an outcome of development. *Development and Psychopathology, 9,* 251–268.

Stark, K., Napolitano, S., Sweater, S., Schmidt, K., Jaramillo, D., & Hoyle, J. (1996). Issues in the treatment of depressed children. *Applied and Preventative Psychology, 5,* 59–83.

Steele, R. G., Armistead, L., & Forehand, R. (2000). Concurrent and longitudinal correlates of depressive symptoms among low-income, urban, African American children. *Journal of Clinical Child Psychology, 29,* 76–85.

Steffenburg, S., Gillberg, C., Hellgren, L., Andersson, L., Gillberg, I. C., Jakobsson, G., & Bohman, M. (1989). A twin study of autism in Denmark, Finland, Iceland, Norway, and Sweden. *Journal of Child Psychology and Psychiatry, 30,* 405–416.

Stein, A., Murray, L., Cooper, P., & Fairburn, C. G. (1996). Infant growth in the context of maternal eating disorders and maternal depression: A comparative study. *Psychological Medicine, 26,* 569–574.

Stein, A., Woolley, H., Cooper, S. D., & Fairburn, C. G. (1994). An observational study of mothers with eating disorders and their infants. *Journal of Child Psychology and Psychiatry, 35,* 733–748.

Stein, D. M., & Laakso, W. (1988). Bulimia: A historical perspective. *International Journal of Eating Disorders, 7,* 201–210.

Steinberg, L., & Darling, N. (1994). The broader context of social influence in adolescence. In R. K. Silbereisen & E. Todt (Eds.), *Adolescence in context: The interplay of family, school, peers, and work in adjustment* (pp. 25–45). New York: Springer Verlag.

Steiner, H., & Lock, J. (1998). Anorexia nervosa and bulimia nervosa in children and adolescents: A review of the past 10 years. *Journal of the American Academy of Child and Adolescent Psychiatry, 37,* 352–359.

Steinhausen, H. C., Seidel, R., & Metzke, C. W. (2000). Evaluation of treatment and intermediate and long-term outcome of adolescent eating disorders. *Psychological Medicine, 30,* 1089–1098.

Stevenson, J. (1992). Evidence for a genetic etiology in hyperactivity in children. *Behavior Genetics, 22,* 337–343.

Stevenson, J. (1999). The treatment of the long-term sequelae of child abuse. *Journal of Child Psychology and Psychiatry, 40,* 89–111.

Stewart, S. M., Lee, P. W. H., Low, L. C. K., Cheng, A., Yeung, W., Huen, K., & O'Donnell, D. (2000). Pathways from emotional adjustment to glycemic control in youth with diabetes in Hong Kong. *Journal of Pediatric Psychology, 25,* 393–402.

Stice, E. (2001). Risk factors for eating pathology: Recent advances and future directions. In R. H. Striegel-Moore & L. Smolak (Eds.), *Eating disorders: Innovative directions for research and practice* (pp. 51–73). Washington, DC: American Psychological Association.

Stice, E., & Bearman, S. K. (2001). Body-image and eating disturbances prospectively predict increases in depressive symptoms in adolescent girls: A growth curve analysis. *Developmental Psychology, 37,* 597–607.

Stormshak, E. A., Bierman, K. L., McMahon, R. J., Lengua, L. J., & Conduct Problems Prevention Research Group. (2000). Parenting practices and child disruptive behavior problems in early elementary school. *Journal of Clinical Child Psychology, 29,* 17–29.

Strain, P. S., Kohler, F. W., & Goldstein, H. (1996). Peer-mediated interventions for young children with autism. In E. D. Hibbs & P. S. Jensen (Eds.), *Psychological treatments for child and adolescent disorders: Empirically based strategies for clinical practice* (pp. 573–587). Washington, DC: American Psychological Association.

Strandburg, R. J., Marsh, J. T., Brown, W. S., Asarnow, R. F., & Guthrie, D. (1994). Information-processing deficits across childhood- and adult-onset schizophrenia. *Schizophrenia Bulletin, 20,* 685–695.

Strauss, A. A., & Lehtinen, L. E. (1947). *Psychopathology and education of the brain-injured child.* New York: Grune & Stratton.

Striegel-Moore, R. H., Schreiber, G. B., Lo, A., Crawford, P., Obarzanek, E., & Rodin, J. (2000). Eating disorder symptoms in a cohort of 11- to 16-year-old black and white girls: The NHLBI Growth and Health Study. *International Journal of Eating Disorders, 27,* 49–66.

Striegel-Moore, R. H., Silberstein, L. R., & Rodin, J. (1986). Toward an understanding of risk factors for bulimia. *American Psychologist, 41,* 246–263.

Strober, M. (1995). Family-genetic perspectives on anorexia nervosa and bulimia nervosa. In K. D. Brownell & C. G. Fairburn (Eds.), *Eating disorders and obesity: A comprehensive handbook* (pp. 212–218). New York: Guilford.

Strober, M., Freeman, R., Lampert, C., Diamond, J., & Kaye, W. (2000). Controlled family study of anorexia nervosa and bulimia nervosa: Evidence of shared liability and transmission of partial syndromes. *American Journal of Psychiatry, 157,* 393–401.

Strober, M., Freeman, R., & Morrell, W. (1997). The long-term course of severe anorexia nervosa in adolescents: Survival analysis of recovery, relapse, and outcome predictors over 10–15 years in a prospective study. *International Journal of Eating Disorders, 22,* 339–360.

Strober, M., Lampert, C., Schmidt, S., & Morrell, W. (1993). The course of major depressive disorder in adolescents: Recovery and risk of manic switching in a 24-month prospective, naturalistic follow-up of psychotic and nonpsychotic subtypes. *Journal of the American Academy of Child and Adolescent Psychiatry, 32,* 34–42.

Strunk, R. C., Fukuhara, J. T., LaBrecque, J. F., & Mrazek, D. A. (1989). Outcome of long-term hospitalization for asthma in children. *Journal of Allergy and Clinical Immunology, 83,* 17–25.

Stuart, S., & Noyes, R. (1999). Attachment and interpersonal communication in somatization. *Psychosomatics, 40,* 34–43.

Stubbe, D. E., Zahner, G., Goldstein, M. J., & Leckman, J. F. (1993). Diagnostic specificity of a brief measure of expressed emotion: A community study of children. *Journal of Child Psychology and Psychiatry, 34,* 139–154.

Stunkard, A. J. (1959). The results of treatment for obesity. *Archives of Internal Medicine, 103,* 79–85.

Suarez, L., & Bell-Dolan, D. (2001). The relationship of child worry to cognitive biases: Threat interpretation and likelihood of event occurrence. *Behavior Therapy, 32,* 425–442.

Swanson, H. L., Carson, C., & Sachse-Lee, C. (2000). A selective synthesis of intervention research for students with learning disabilities. *School Psychology Review, 25,* 370–391.

Swanson, H. L., & Sachse-Lee, C. (2000). A meta-analysis of single-subject-design intervention research for students with LD. *Journal of Learning Disabilities, 33,* 114–136.

Szapocznik, J., & Williams, R. A. (2000). Brief strategic family therapy: Twenty-five years of interplay among theory, research and practice in adolescent behavior problems and drug abuse. *Clinical Child and Family Psychology Review, 3,* 117–134.

Szatmari, P. (1992). The epidemiology of attention-deficit hyperactivity disorders. *Child and Adolescent Psychiatric Clinics of North America, 1,* 361–371.

Szatmari, P., Offord, D. R., & Boyle, M. H. (1989a). Correlates, associated impairments and patterns of service utilization of children with attention deficit disorder: Findings from the Ontario Child Health Study. *Journal of Child Psychology and Psychiatry, 30*, 205–217.

Szatmari, P., Offord, D. R., & Boyle, M. H. (1989b). Ontario Child Health Study: Prevalence of attention deficit disorder with hyperactivity. *Journal of Child Psychology and Psychiatry, 30*, 219–230.

Szatmari, P., Tuff, L., Finlayson, M. A., & Bartolucci, G. (1989). Asperger's syndrome and autism: Neurocognitive aspects. *Journal of the American Academy of Child and Adolescent Psychiatry, 28*, 130–136.

Szmukler, G. I., & Tantam, D. (1984). Anorexia nervosa: Starvation dependence. *British Journal of Medical Psychology, 57*, 303–310.

Tam, W. C., & Sewell, K. W. (1995). Seasonality of birth in schizophrenia in Taiwan. *Schizophrenia Bulletin, 21*, 117–127.

Tanguay, P. E. (2000). Pervasive developmental disorders: A 10-year review. *Journal of the American Academy of Child and Adolescent Psychiatry, 39*, 1079–1095.

Tanoue, Y., Oda, S., Asano, F., & Kawashima, K. (1988). Epidemiology of infantile autism in Southern Ibaraki, Japan: Differences in prevalence in birth cohorts. *Journal of Autism and Developmental Disorders, 2*, 155–166.

Tantam, D. (1991). Asperger syndrome in adulthood. In U. Frith (Ed.), *Autism and Asperger syndrome* (pp. 147–183). Cambridge, UK: Cambridge University Press.

Terman, L. (1916). *The measurement of intelligence.* Cambridge, MA: Riverside Press.

Thapar, A., Holmes, J., Poulton, K., & Harrington, R. (1999). Genetic basis of attention deficit and hyperactivity. *British Journal of Psychiatry, 174*, 105–111.

Theander, S. (1970). Anorexia nervosa: A psychiatric investigation of 94 female patients. *Acta Psychiatrica Scandinavica, 214S*, 1–194.

Thomas, A., & Chess, S. (1977). *Temperament and development.* New York: Brunner/Mazel.

Thompson, J. K., & Stice, E. (2001). Thin-ideal internalization: Mounting evidence for a new risk factor for body-image disturbance and eating pathology. *Current Directions in Psychological Sciences, 5*, 181–183.

Thomsen, P. H. (1996). Schizophrenia with childhood and adolescent onset—A nationwide register-based study. *Acta Psychiatrica Scandinavica, 94*, 187–193.

Thorndike, R. L., Hagen, E. P., & Sattler, J. M. (1986). *Technical manual for the Sanford-Binet Intelligence Scale: Fourth edition.* Chicago: Riverside.

Toren, P., Laor, N., & Weizman, A. (1998). Use of atypical neuroleptics in child and adolescent psychiatry. *Journal of Clinical Psychiatry, 59*, 644–656.

Torgensen, S. (1986). Genetics of somatoform disorders. *Archives of General Psychiatry, 43*, 502–505.

Torgesen, J. K. (1982). The learning disabled child as an inactive learner: Educational implications. *Topics in Learning and Learning Disabilities, 2*, 45–52.

Torgesen, J. K. (1991). Learning disabilities: Historical and conceptual issues. In B. Y. L. Wong (Ed.), *Learning about learning disabilities* (pp. 3–37). San Diego: Academic Press.

Torgesen, J. K. (1993). Variations on theory in learning disabilities. In G. R. Lyon, D. B. Gray, J. F. Kavanagh, & N. A. Krasnegor (Eds.), *Better understanding learning disabilities* (pp. 153–170). Baltimore: Brookes Publishing Co.

Torgesen, J. K. (2000). Individual differences in response to early interventions in reading: The lingering problem of treatment resisters. *Learning Disabilities Research and Practice, 15*, 55–64.

Torrey, E. F., Bowler, A. E., Rawlings, R., & Terrazas, A. (1993). Seasonality of schizophrenia and stillbirths. *Schizophrenia Bulletin, 19*, 557–562.

Tousignant, M., Habimana, E., Biron, C., Malo, C., Sidoli-LeBlanc, E., & Bendris, N. (1999). The Quebec adolescent refugee project: Psychopathology and family variables in a sample from 35 nations. *Journal of the American Academy of Child and Adolescent Psychiatry, 38*, 1426–1432.

Towbin, K. E., & Riddle, M. A. (1993). Attention-deficit/hyperactivity disorder. In R. Kurlan (Ed.), *Handbook of Tourette syndrome and related tic and behavioral disorders* (pp. 89–109). New York: Marcel Dekker.

Tremblay, R. E., LeMarquand, D., & Vitaro, F. (1999). The prevention of oppositional defiant disorder and conduct disorder. In H. E. Quay & A. E. Hogan (Eds.), *Handbook of disruptive behavior disorders* (pp. 255–278). New York: Kluwer Academic.

Tremblay, R. E., Phil, R. O., Vitaro, F., & Dobkin, P. L. (1994). Predicting early onset of male antisocial behavior from preschool behavior. *Archives of General Psychiatry, 51*, 732–738.

Treuting, J. J., & Hinshaw, S. P. (2001). Depression and self-esteem in boys with attention-deficit/hyperactivity disorder: Associations with comorbid aggression and explanatory attributional mechanisms. *Journal of Abnormal Child Psychology, 29*, 23–39.

Trickett, P. K., & McBride-Chang, C. (1995). The developmental impact of different forms of child abuse and neglect. *Developmental Review, 15*, 311–337.

Tsuang, M. T., Stone, W. S., & Faraone, S. V. (2000). Towards the prevention of schizophrenia. *Biological Psychiatry, 48*, 349–356.

Twain, M. (1959). *Tom Sawyer and Huckleberry Finn.* London: Dent. (Original work—Hukleberry Finn—published 1884)

Ulloa, R. E., Birmaher, B., Axelson, D., Williamson, D. E., Brent, D. A., Ryan, N. D., Bridge, J., & Baugher, M. (2000). Psychosis in a pediatric mood and anxiety disorders clinic: Phenomenology and correlates. *Journal of the American Academy of Child and Adolescent Psychiatry, 39*, 337–345.

Ungerer, J. (1989). The early development of autistic children: Implications for defining primary deficits. In G. Dawson (Ed.), *Autism: Nature, diagnosis, and treatment* (pp. 75–91). New York: Guilford.

U.S. Advisory Board on Child Abuse and Neglect. (1990). *Child abuse and neglect: Critical first steps in response to a national emergency.* Washington, DC: Government Printing Office.

U.S. Department of Education (1998). *Early warning, timely response: A guide to safe schools.* Washington, DC: Author.

U.S. Department of Health and Human Services (USDHHS). (1980). *Study findings: Study of National Incidence and Prevalence of Child Abuse and Neglect* (NIS-1). Washington, DC: Author.

U.S. Department of Health and Human Services (USDHHS). (1988). *Study findings: Study of National Incidence and Prevalence of Child Abuse and Neglect* (NIS-2). Washington, DC: Author.

U.S. Department of Health and Human Services (USDHHS). (1996). *Third national incidence study of child abuse and neglect: Final report* (NIS-3). Washington, DC: Government Printing Office.

U.S. Department of Health and Human Services (USDHHS). (1999). *Child maltreatment 1997: Report from the States to the National Child Abuse and Neglect Data System.* Washington, DC: Government Printing Office.

U.S. Department of Justice (1999). *Juvenile offenders and victims: 1999 National Report.* Rockville, MD: Juvenile Justice Clearinghouse.

U.S. Drug Enforcement Agency (2000). *DEA congressional testimony* [On line]. Available at: www.usdoj.gov/dea/pubs/cngrtest/ct051600.htm.

Upham, D. A., & Trumbull, V. H. (1997). *Making the grade: Reflections on being learning disabled.* Portsmouth, NH: Heinemann.

Usiskin, S. I., Nicolson, R., Krasnewich, D. M., Yah, W., Lenane, M., Wudarsky, M., Hamburger, S., & Rapoport, J. (1999). Velocardiofacial syndrome in childhood-onset schizophrenia. *Journal of the American Academy of Child and Adolescent Psychiatry, 38,* 1536–1543.

Valla, J. P., Bergeron, L., & Smolla, N. (2000). The Dominic-R: A pictorial interview for 6- to 11-year-old children. *Journal of the American Academy of Child and Adolescent Psychiatry, 39,* 85–93.

van Acker, R. (1991). Rett syndrome: A review of current knowledge. *Journal of Autism and Developmental Disorders, 21,* 381–406.

van Deth, R., & Vandereycken, W. (2000). Food refusal and insanity: Sitophobia and anorexia nervosa in Victorian asylums. *International Journal of Eating Disorders, 27,* 390–404.

Van Dongen-Melman, J. E., & Sanders-Woudstra, J. A. (1986). Psychosocial aspects of childhood cancer: A review of the literature. *Journal of Child Psychology and Psychiatry, 27,* 145–180.

Van Goozen, S. H. M., Matthys, W., Cohen-Kettenis, P. T., Buitelaar, J. K., & van Engeland, H. (2000). Hypothalamic-pituitary-adrenal axis and autonomic nervous system activity in disruptive children and matched controls. *Journal of the American Academy of Child and Adolescent Psychiatry, 39,* 1438–1445.

Van Kammen, W., Loeber, R., & Stouthamer-Loeber, M. (1991). Substance use and its relationship to conduct problems and delinquency in young boys. *Journal of Youth and Adolescence, 20,* 399–413.

Vehmanen, L., Kaprio, J., & Loennqvist, J. (1995). Twin studies on concordance for bipolar disorder. *Psychiatria Fennica, 26,* 107–116.

Venter, A., Lord, C., & Schopler, E. (1992). A follow-up study of high-functioning autistic children. *Journal of Child Psychology and Psychiatry, 33,* 489–507.

Verhulst, F. C., van der Lee, J. H., Akkerhuis, G. W., Sanders-Woudstra, J. A. R., Timmer, F. C., & Donkhorst, I. D. (1985). The prevalence of nocturnal enuresis: Do DSM-III criteria need to be changed? A brief research report. *Journal of Child Psychology and Psychiatry, 26,* 989–993.

Vernon, P. (1979). *Intelligence: Heredity and environment.* San Francisco: W.H. Freeman.

Verrill, J. R., Schafer, J., Vannatta, K., & Noll, R. B. (2000). Aggression, antisocial behavior, and substance abuse in survivors of pediatric cancer: Possible protective effects of cancer and its treatment. *Journal of Pediatric Psychology, 25,* 493–502.

Vila, G., Nollet-Clemencon, C., de Blic, J., Mouren-Simeoni, M. C., & Scheinmann, P. (2000). Prevalence of DSM-IV anxiety and affective disorders in a pediatric population of asthmatic children and adolescents. *Journal of Affective Disorders, 58,* 223–231.

Vitaro, F., Gendreau, P. L., Tremblay, R. E., & Oligny, P. (1998). Reactive and proactive aggression differentially predict later conduct problems. *Journal of Child Psychology and Psychiatry, 39,* 1–9.

Volkmar, F. R. (1992). Childhood disintegrative disorder: Issues for DSM-IV. *Journal of Autism and Developmental Disorders, 22,* 625–642.

Volkmar, F. R. (1996). Childhood and adolescent psychosis: A review of the past 10 years. *Journal of the American Academy of Child and Adolescent Psychiatry, 35,* 843–851.

Volkmar, F. R. (2001). Pharmacological interventions in autism: Theoretical and practical issues. *Journal of Clinical Child Psychology, 30,* 80–87.

Volkmar, F. R., Klin, A., Schulta, R., Bronen, R., Marans, W. D., Sparrow, S., & Cohen, D. J. (1996). Asperger's syndrome. *Journal of the American Academy of Child and Adolescent Psychiatry, 35,* 118–123.

Volkmar, F. R., Szatmari, P., & Sparrow, S. S. (1993). Sex differences in pervasive developmental disorders. *Journal of Autism and Developmental Disorders, 23,* 579–591.

von Gontard, A. (1998). Day and night wetting in children: A paediatric and child psychiatric perspective. *Journal of Child Psychology and Psychiatry, 39,* 439–451.

von Gontard, A., Hollmann, E., Eiberg, H., Benden, B., Rittig, S., & Lehmkuhl, G. (1996). Clinical enuresis phenotypes in familial nocturnal enuresis. *Scandinavian Journal of Urology and Nephrology, 183,* 11–16.

von Ranson, K. M., Walter, H., Weltzin, T. E., Rao, R., & Matsunaga, H. (1999). Obsessive-compulsive disorder symptoms before and after recovery from bulimia nervosa. *American Journal of Psychiatry, 156,* 1703–1708.

Vygotsky, L. S. (1931). Compensatory processes in the development of the retarded child. In J. E. Knox & C. B. Stevens (Eds.), *The collected works of L. S. Vygotsky: Vol. 2. The fundamentals of defectology* (pp. 123–138). New York: Plenum, 1993.

Vygotsky, L. S. (1935). The problem of mental retardation. In J. E. Knox & C. B. Stevens (Eds.), *The collected works of L. S. Vygotsky: Vol. 2. The fundamentals of defectology* (pp. 220–240). New York: Plenum.

Wagner, K. D., & Ambrosini, P. J. (2001). Childhood depression: Pharmacological therapy/treatment. *Journal of Clinical Child Psychology, 30,* 88–97.

Wahlberg, K. E., Wynne, L. C., Oja, H., Keskitalo, P., Pykalainen, L., Lahti, I., Moring, J., Naarala, M., Sorri, A., Seitamaa, M., Laksy, K., Kolassa, J., & Tienari, P. (1997). Gene-environment interaction in vulnerability to schizophrenia: Findings from the Finnish Adoptive Family Study of Schizophrenia. *American Journal of Psychiatry, 154,* 355–362.

Wahler, R. G., & Dumas, J. E. (1986). "A chip off the old block": Some interpersonal characteristics of coercive children across generations. In P. Strain, M. Guralnick, & H. Walker (Eds.), *Children's social behavior: Development, assessment, and modification* (pp. 49–91). New York: Academic Press.

Walker, E., & Lewine, R. J. (1990). Prediction of adult-onset schizophrenia from childhood home movies of the patients. *American Journal of Psychiatry, 147,* 1052–1056.

Walker, J. L., Lahey, B. B., Russo, M. F., Christ, M. A. G., McBurnett, K., Loeber, R., Stouthamer-Loeber, M., & Green, S. M. (1991). Anxiety, inhibition, and conduct disorder in children: I. Relation to social impairment. *Journal of the American Academy of Child and Adolescent Psychiatry, 30,* 187–191.

Walker, L. S., & Greene, J. W. (1991). Negative life events and symptom resolution in pediatric abdominal pain patients. *Journal of Pediatric Psychology, 16,* 341–360.

Walsh, B. T., & Garner, D. M. (1997). Diagnostic issues. In D. M. Garner & P. E. Garfinkel (Eds.), *Handbook of treatment for eating disorders* (2nd ed., pp. 25–33). New York: Guilford.

Walsh, B. T., & Kahn, C. B. (1997). Diagnostic criteria for eating disorders: Current concerns and future directions. *Psychopharmacology Bulletin, 33(3),* 369–372.

Walters, E. E., Neale, M. C., Eaves, L. J., Health, A. C., Kessler, R. C., & Kendler, K. S. (1992). Bulimia nervosa and major depression: A study of common genetic and environmental factors. *Psychological Medicine, 22,* 617–622.

Wamboldt, F. S., O'Connor, S. L., Wamboldt, M. Z., Gavin, L. A., & Klinnert, M. D. (2000). The Five Minute Speech Sample in children with asthma: Deconstructing the construct of expressed emotion. *Journal of Child Psychology and Psychiatry, 41,* 887–898.

Wamboldt, M. Z., Fritz, G., Mansell, A., McQuaid, E. L., & Klein, R. B. (1998). Relationship of asthma severity and psychological problems in children. *Journal of the American Academy of Child and Adolescent Psychiatry, 37,* 943–950.

Warner, V., Weissman, M. M., Mufson, L., & Wickramaratne, P. J. (1999). Grandparents, parents, and grandchildren at high risk for depression: A three-generation study. *Journal of the American Academy of Child and Adolescent Psychiatry, 38,* 289–296.

Waschbusch, D. A., & Hill, G. P. (2001). Alternative treatments for children with attention-deficit/hyperactivity disorder: What does the research say? *The Behavior Therapist, 24,* 161–171.

Wasserman, A. L., Whitington, P. F., & Rivara, F. P. (1988). Psychogenic basis for abdominal pain in children and adolescents. *Journal of the American Academy of Child and Adolescent Psychiatry, 27,* 179–184.

Waters, T. L., & Barrett, P. M. (2000). The role of the family in childhood obsessive-compulsive disorder. *Clinical Child and Family Psychology Review, 3,* 173–184.

Watkins, J. M., Asarnow, R. F., & Tanguay, P. E. (1988). Symptom development in childhood onset schizophrenia. *Journal of Child Psychology and Psychiatry, 29,* 865–878.

Watson, J. B., & Rayner, R. (1920). Conditioned affective reactions. *Journal of Experimental Psychology, 3,* 1–14.

Webster, J. J., & Palmer, R. L. (2000). The childhood and family background of women with clinical eating disorders: A comparison with women with major depression and women without psychiatric disorder. *Psychological Medicine, 30,* 53–60.

Wechsler, D. (1991). *Wechsler Intelligence Scale for Children, third edition: Manual.* New York: Psychological Corporation.

Weckowicz, T. E., & Liebel-Weckowicz, H. P. (1990). *A history of great ideas in abnormal psychology.* Amsterdam: North Holland.

Weeks, S. J., & Hobson, R. P. (1987). The salience of facial expression for autistic children. *Journal of Child Psychology and Psychiatry, 28,* 137–152.

Weinberger, D. R. (1995). Schizophrenia as a neurodevelopmental disorder. In S. R. Hirsch & D. R. Weinberger (Eds.), *Schizophrenia* (pp. 293–323). Oxford, UK: Blackwell Empirical Publications.

Weine, S. M., Becker, D. E., Levy, K. N., Edell, W. S., & McGlashen, T. H. (1997). Childhood trauma histories in adolescent inpatients. *Journal of Traumatic Stress, 10,* 291–298.

Weiss, E. (1989). *Mothers talk about learning disabilities: Personal feelings, practical advice.* New York: Prentice Hall Press.

Weiss, G., & Hechtman, L. T. (1993). *Hyperactive children grown up* (2nd ed.). New York: Guilford.

Weissberg-Benchell, J., & Glasgow, A. (1997). The role of temperament in children with insulin-dependent diabetes mellitus. *Journal of Pediatric Psychology, 22,* 795–809.

Weisz, J. R., Rudolph, K. D., Granger, D. A., & Sweeney, L. (1992). Cognition, competence, and coping in child and adolescent depression: Research findings, developmental concerns, therapeutic implications. *Development and Psychopathology, 4,* 627–653.

Wekerle, C., & Wolfe, D. A. (1993). Prevention of child physical abuse and neglect: Promising new directions. *Clinical Psychology Review, 13,* 501–540.

Wekerle, C., & Wolfe, D. A. (1996). Child maltreatment. In E. J. Marsh & R. A. Barkley (Eds.), *Child psychopathology* (pp. 492–537). New York: Guilford.

Weller, E. B., Weller, R. A., & Fristad, M. A. (1995). Bipolar disorder in children: Misdiagnosis, underdiagnosis, and future directions. *Journal of the American Academy of Child and Adolescent Psychiatry, 34,* 709–714.

Werry, J. S. (1991). Overanxiety disorder: A review of its taxonomic properties. *Journal of the American Academy of Child and Adolescent Psychiatry, 30,* 533–544.

Werry, J. S. (1992). Child and adolescent (early onset) schizophrenia: A review in light of DSM-III-R. *Journal of Autism and Developmental Disorders, 22,* 601–624.

Werry, J. S., & McClellan, J. M. (1992). Predicting outcome in child and adolescent (early onset) schizophrenia and bipolar disorder. *Journal of the American Academy of Child and Adolescent Psychiatry, 31,* 147–150.

Werry, J. S., McClellan, J. M., Andrews, L. K., & Ham, M. (1994). Clinical features and outcome of child and adolescent schizophrenia. *Schizophrenia Bulletin, 20,* 619–630.

Werry, J. S., McClellan, J. M., & Chard, L. (1991). Childhood and adolescent schizophrenia, bipolar, and schizoaffective disorders: A clinical and outcome study. *Journal of the American Academy of Child and Adolescent Psychiatry, 30,* 457–465.

Westenberg, P. M., Siebelink, B. M., Warmenhoven, N. J., & Treffers, P. D. (1999). Separation anxiety and overanxious disorders. Relations to age and level of psychosocial maturity. *Journal of the American Academy of Child and Adolescent Psychiatry, 38,* 1000–1007.

Whaley, S. E., Pinto, A., & Sigman, M. (1999). Characterizing interactions between anxious mothers and their children. *Journal of Consulting and Clinical Psychology, 67,* 826–836.

Whipple, E., & Richey, C. (1997). Crossing the line from physical discipline to child abuse: How much is too much? *Child Abuse & Neglect, 21,* 431–444.

Widom, C. S. (1989). Does violence beget violence? A critical examination of the literature. *Psychological Bulletin, 106,* 3–28.

Widom, C. S. (1999). Posttraumatic stress disorder in abused and neglected children grown up. *American Journal of Psychiatry, 156,* 1223–1229.

Widom, C. S., & Maxfield, M. G. (2001). An update on the "cycle of violence." *National Institute of Justice Research in Brief* (NCJ 184894). Washington, DC: U.S. Department of Justice, National Institute of Justice.

Willcutt, E., Pennington, B., Chabildas, N., Friedman, M., & Alexander, J. (1999). Psychiatric comorbidity associated with DSM-IV ADHD in a nonreferred sample of twins. *Journal of the American Academy of Child and Adolescent Psychiatry, 38,* 1355–1362.

Willi, J., Giacometti, G., & Limacher, B. (1990). Update on the epidemiology of anorexia nervosa in a defined region of Switzerland. *American Journal of Psychiatry, 147,* 1514–1517.

Willi, J., & Grossmann, S. (1983). Epidemiology of anorexia in a defined region of Switzerland. *American Journal of Psychiatry, 140,* 564–567.

Williamson, D. A., Bentz, B. G., & Rabalais, J. Y. (1998). Eating disorders. In T. H. Ollendick & M. Hersen (Eds.), *Handbook of child psychopathology* (pp. 291–305). New York: Plenum.

Willoughby, M. T., Curran, P. J., Costello, E. J., & Angold, A. (2000). Implications of early versus late onset of attention-deficit/hyperactivity disorder symptoms. *Journal of the American Academy of Child and Adolescent Psychiatry, 39,* 1512–1519.

Willoughby, M., Kupersmidt, J., & Bryant, D. (2001). Overt and covert dimensions of antisocial behavior in early childhood. *Journal of Abnormal Child Psychology, 29,* 177–187.

Wills, T. A., Vaccaro, D., McNamara, G., & Hirky, A. E. (1996). Escalated substance use: A longitudinal grouping analysis from early to middle adolescence. *Journal of Abnormal Psychology, 105,* 166–180.

Wilson, G. T. (1991). The addiction model of eating disorders: A critical analysis. *Advances in Behaviour Research and Therapy, 13,* 27–72.

Wilson, G. T., Fairburn, C. G., & Agras, W. S. (1997). Cognitive-behavioral therapy for bulimia nervosa. In D. M. Garner & P. E. Garfinkel (Eds.), *Handbook of treatment for eating disorders* (pp. 67–93). New York: Guilford.

Wilson, G. T., Heffernan, K., & Black, C. (1996). Eating disorders. In E. J. Mash & R. A. Barkley (Eds.), *Child psychopathology* (pp. 541–571). New York: Guilford.

Wing, L. (1988). The continuum of autistic characteristics. In E. Schopler & G. Mesibov (Eds.), *Diagnosis and assessment in autism* (pp. 91–110). New York: Plenum.

Wing, L. (1991). The relationship between Asperger's syndrome and Kanner's autism. In U. Frith (Ed.), *Autism and Asperger syndrome* (pp. 93–121). Cambridge, UK: Cambridge University Press.

Wing, L., & Gould, J. (1979). Severe impairments of social interaction and associated abnormalities in children: Epidemiology and classification. *Journal of Autism and Developmental Disorders, 9,* 11–29.

Wing, L., Yeates, S. R., Brierley, L. M., & Gould, J. (1976). The prevalence of early childhood autism: Comparison of administrative and epidemiological studies. *Psychological Medicine, 6,* 89–100.

Wiseman, C. G., Gray, J. J., Mosimann, J. E., & Ahrens, A. J. (1992). Cultural expectations of thinness in women: An update. *International Journal of Eating Disorders, 11,* 85–89.

Wolfe, D. A. (1985). Child-abusive parents: An empirical review and analysis. *Psychological Bulletin, 97,* 462–482.

Wolfe, D. A. (1999). *Child abuse: Implications for child development and psychopathology.* Thousand Oaks, CA: Sage.

Wolfe, D. A., & Jaffe, P. (1991). Child abuse and family violence as determinants of child psychopathology. *Canadian Journal of Behavioural Science, 23,* 282–299.

Wolfe, D. A., & McEachran, A. (1997). Child abuse and neglect. In E. J. Mash & L. G. Terdal (Eds.), *Behavioral assessment of childhood disorders* (3rd ed.). New York: Guilford.

Wolfe, D. A., Sas, L., & Wekerle, C. (1994). Factors associated with the development of posttraumatic stress disorder among child victims of sexual abuse. *Child Abuse & Neglect, 18,* 37–50.

Wolfe, D. A., & Wekerle, C. (1993). Treatment strategies for child physical abuse and neglect: A critical progress report. *Clinical Psychology Review, 13,* 473–500.

Wonderlich, S., Crosby, R., Mitchell, J., Thompson, K., Redlin, J., Demuth, G., & Smyth, J. (2001). Pathways mediating sexual abuse and eating disturbance in children. *International Journal of Eating Disorders, 29,* 270–279.

Wood, D., Flower, P., & Black, D. (1998). Should parents take charge of their child's eating disorder? Some preliminary findings and suggestions for future research. *International Journal of Psychiatry in Clinical Practice, 2,* 295–301.

Wood, F. B., Felton, R. H., Flowers, L., & Naylor, C. (1991). Neurobehavioral definition of dyslexia. In D. D. Duane & D. B. Gray (Eds.), *The reading brain: The biological basis of dyslexia* (pp. 1–25). Parkton, MD: York Press.

Woolley, J. D. (1997). Thinking about fantasy: Are children fundamentally different thinkers and believers from adults? *Child Development, 68,* 991–1011.

Wootton, J. M., Frick, P. J., Shelton, K. K., & Silverthorn, P. (1997). Ineffective parenting and childhood conduct problems: The moderating role of callous-unemotional traits. *Journal of Consulting and Clinical Psychology, 65,* 301–308.

Wright, S., Takei, N., Murray, R. M., & Sham, P. C. (1999). Seasonality, prenatal influenza exposure, and schizophrenia. In E. Susser & A. S. Brown (Eds.), *Prenatal exposures in schizophrenia: Progress in psychiatry* (pp. 89–112). Washington, DC: American Psychiatric Press.

Wright, P., Takei, N., Rifkin, L., & Murray, R. M. (1995). Maternal influenza, obstetric complications, and schizophrenia. *American Journal of Psychiatry, 152,* 1714–1720.

Wyatt, G. E., Loeb, T. B., Solis, B., Carmona, J. V., & Romero, G. (1999). The prevalence and circumstances of child sexual abuse: Changes across a decade. *Child Abuse & Neglect, 23,* 45–60.

Young, M. H., Brennen, L. C., Baker, R. D., & Baker, S. (1995). Functional encopresis: Symptom reduction and behavioral improvement. *Developmental and Behavioral Pediatrics, 16,* 226–232.

Ysseldyke, J. E., Algozzine, B., Shinn, M., & McGue, M. (1982). Similarities and differences between underachievers and students labeled learning disabled. *Journal of Special Education, 16,* 73–85.

Yung, A. R., Phillips, L. J., McGorry, P. D., McFarlane, C. A., Francey, S., Harrigan, S., Patton, G. C., & Jackson, H. J. (1998). Prediction of psychosis: A step towards indicated prevention of schizophrenia. *British Journal of Psychiatry, 172,* 14–20.

Zahn, T. P., Jacobsen, L. K., Gordon, C. T., McKenna, K., Frazier, J. A., & Rapoport, J. L. (1998). Attention deficits in childhood-onset schizophrenia: Reaction time studies. *Journal of Abnormal Psychology, 107,* 97–108.

Zahn, T. P., Kruesi, M. J. P., & Rapoport, J. L. (1991). Reaction time indices of attention deficits in boys with disruptive behavior disorders. *Journal of Abnormal Child Psychology, 19,* 233–252.

Zaider, T. I., Johnson, J. G., & Cockell, S. J. (2000). Psychiatric comorbidity associated with eating disorder symptomatology among adolescents in the community. *International Journal of Eating Disorders, 28,* 58–67.

Zentall, S. S. (1988). Production deficiencies in elicited language but not in the spontaneous verbalizations of hyperactive children. *Journal of Abnormal Child Psychology, 16,* 657–673.

Zigler, E., & Hodapp, R. M. (1986). *Understanding mental retardation.* New York: Cambridge University Press.

Zima, B. T., Bussing, R., Crecelius, G. M., Kaufman, A., & Belin, T. R. (1999). Psychotropic medication treatment patterns among school-aged children in foster care. *Journal of Child and Adolescent Psychopharmacology, 9,* 135–147.

Zito, J. M., Safer, D. J., dosReis, S., Gardner, J. F., Boles, M., & Lynch, F. (2000). Trends in prescribing of psychotropic medications to preschoolers. *Journal of the American Medical Association, 283,* 1025–1030.

Zoccolillo, M. (1992). Co-occurrence of conduct disorder and its adult outcomes with depressive and anxiety disorders: A review. *Journal of the American Academy of Child and Adolescent Psychiatry, 31,* 547–556.

Zoccolillo, M. (1993). Gender and the development of conduct disorder. *Development and Psychopathology, 5,* 65–78.

Zoccolillo, M., Pickles, A., Quinton, D., & Rutter, M. (1992). The outcome of conduct disorder: Implications for defining adult personality disorder and conduct disorder. *Psychological Medicine, 22,* 971–986.

Name Index

Subject Index